Hobbes's Leviathan : reprinted from the edition of 1651

Thomas Hobbes, W G. Pogson Smith

HOBBES'S LEVIATHAN

REPRINTED FROM THE EDITION OF 1651

WITH AN ESSAY BY THE LATE

W. G. POGSON SMITH

OXFORD

AT THE CLARENDON PRESS

OXFORD UNIVERSITY PRESS
AMEN HOUSE, E C 4
LONDON EDINBURGH GLASGOW
LEIPZIG NEW YORK TORONTO
MELBOURNE CAPETOWN BOMBAY
CALCUTTA MADRAS SHANGHAI
HUMPHREY MILFORD
PUBLISHER TO THE
UNIVERSITY

Impression of 1929
First edition, 1909

Printed in Great Britain

PREFACE

It was well known to all students of philosophy and history in Oxford, and to many others, that W. G. Pogson Smith had been for many years engaged in preparing for an exhaustive treatment of the place of Hobbes in the history of European thought, and that he had accumulated a great mass of materials towards this. These materials fill many notebooks, and are so carefully arranged and indexed that it is clear that with a few more months he would have been able to produce a work worthy of a very high place in philosophical literature. Unhappily the work that he could have done himself cannot be done by any one else unless he has given something like the same time and brings to the collection something like the same extensive and intimate knowledge of the philosophy of the period as Pogson Smith possessed. It is hoped indeed that, by the permission of his representatives, this great mass of material will be deposited in the Bodleian Library and made available for scholars, and that thus the task which he had undertaken may some time be carried out.

Among his papers has been found an essay which presents a very interesting and suggestive treatment of the position of Hobbes. The essay is undated, and it is quite uncertain for what audience it was prepared. It is this essay which is here published as an introduction to the *Leviathan*. It is printed with only the necessary verification of references, and one or two corrections of detail. It is always difficult to judge how far it is right to print work which the author himself has not revised, but we feel that, while something must inevitably be lost, the essay has so much real value that, even as it stands, it should be published. Something may even be gained for the reader in the fresh and unconstrained character of the paper. The pursuit of the ideal of a perfect and rounded criticism, which all serious scholars aim at, has sometimes the unfortunate result of depriving a man's work of some spontaneity. In Oxford at any rate, and it is probably the case everywhere, many a scholar says his best things and expresses his most penetrating judgements in the least formal manner. Those who were Mr. Pogson Smith's friends or pupils will find here much of the man himself—something of his quick insight, of his unconventional directness, of his broad but solid learning; something also of his profound feeling for truth, of his scorn of the pretentious, of his keen but kindly humour.

THE PHILOSOPHY OF HOBBES

AN ESSAY

WHEREIN does the greatness of Hobbes consist? It is a question I often put to myself, as I lay him down. It was a question which exercised his contemporaries—friends or foes—and drove them to their wits' end to answer. If I were asked to name the highest and purest philosopher of the seventeenth century I should single out Spinoza without a moment's hesitation. But Spinoza was not of the world; and if a man will be perverse enough to bind the Spirit of Christ in the fetters of Euclid, how shall he find readers? If I were asked to select the true founders of modern science I should bracket Galileo, Descartes, and Newton, and resolutely oppose Hobbes's claim to be of the company. If his studies in Vesalius prepared him to extend his approbation to Harvey's demonstration of the circulation of the blood, his animosity to Oxford and her professors would never allow him seriously to consider the claims of a science advanced by Dr. Wallis; the sight of a page of algebraic symbols never elicited any feeling but one of sturdy contempt, and the remark that it looked 'as if a hen had been scratching there'. To the end of his days he dwelt among points of two dimensions, and superficies of three; he squared the circle and he doubled the cube. ''Twas pity,' said Sir Jonas Moore, and many more, 'that he had not began the study of mathematics sooner, for such a working head would have made great advancement in it.'[1]

Of inductive science he is very incredulous. Bacon, contemplating 'in his delicious walkes at Gorhambury', might indeed better like Mr. Hobbes taking down his thoughts than any other, because he understood what he wrote; he probably learnt to understand my Lord, who dictated his alphabet of simple natures, his receipts for the discovery of forms, his peddling experiments and his laborious conceits. I mention this because most German critics, with perhaps more than their usual careless audacity of assumption, find a niche for Hobbes as the spiritual fosterling of the great empiricist Bacon. Now if there was one thing for which Hobbes had neither sympathy nor even patience, it was experimental science. The possession of a great telescope was no doubt a curious and useful delight; but 'not every one that brings from beyond seas a new gin, or other jaunty device, is therefore a philosopher'.[2] Let the gentlemen of Gresham College, whose energy it must be granted shames the sloth of our ancient universities,—let them apply themselves to Mr. Hobbes's doctrine of motion, and then he will deign

[1] Aubrey's *Brief Lives*, in 2 vols, edited by A. Clark, 1898. i. 332.
[2] Aubrey, i. 335–6.

to cast an eye on their experiments. He did not think their gropings would carry them very far. 'Experience concludeth nothing universally.'[1] If he despaired of wringing her secret from Nature, he never doubted that he held the key to every corner of the human heart. He offers us a theory of man's nature which is at once consistent, fascinating, and outrageously false. Only the greatest of realists could have revealed so much and blinded himself to so much more. You cry angrily—It is false, false to the core; and yet the still small voice will suggest, But how much of it is really true? It is poor, immoral stuff! so you might say in the pulpit, but you know that it probes very deep. It is only the exploded Benthamite philosophy with its hedonistic calculus tricked out in antique piquancy of phrase! If you really hold this, if you think that Hobbes's man is nothing more than a utilitarian automaton led by the nose by suburban pleasures and pains, you have no sense of power, of pathos, or of irony. It is only the trick of the cheap cynic, you retort in fine. Yes, it is cynicism; but it is not cheap. Nature has made man a passionate creature, desirous not of pleasure but of power; the passions themselves are not simple emotions, but charged with and mastered by the appetite for power; honour consisteth only in the opinion of power; the *worth* of a man is, as of all other things, his price; that is to say, so much as would be given for the use of his power; the

[1] Hobbes's *English Works*, iv. 18, ed Molesworth, 1839.

public worth of a man, which is the value set on him by the commonwealth, is that which men commonly call dignity. Leave men to themselves, they struggle for power; competition, diffidence, vainglory driving them. Sober half-hours hush with their lucid intervals the tumult of the passions; even so on earth they bring no beatitude. Care for the future is never banished from thought; felicity is a continual progress of the desire from one object to another.

'So that in the first place, I put for a general inclination of all mankind, a perpetual and restless desire of power after power, that ceaseth only in death.'[1]

'For as Prometheus, which interpreted is, *the prudent man*, was bound to the hill Caucasus, a place of large prospect, where an eagle, feeding on his liver, devoured in the day as much as was repaired in the night: so that man, which looks too far before him, in the care of future time, hath his heart all the day long, gnawed on by fear of death, poverty, or other calamity; and has no repose nor pause of his anxiety, but in sleep.'[2]

Such, then, is the lust and the burden of man. What is the deliverance? Spinoza found it in philosophy; the truth shall make you free: but Hobbes was a philosopher who had no faith in truth. Pascal found it in the following of Christ; but I doubt whether religion ever meant much more

[1] p. 75. [2] p. 82

than an engine of political order to Hobbes. Rousseau, whose survey of human nature often strangely and suspiciously resembles that of Hobbes, advocated—in some moods at least—a return to nature. Rousseau's 'nature' was a pig-sty, but Hobbes's state of nature was something far worse than that.

Hobbes was never disloyal to intellect, grievously as he affronted its paramount claims; he was not of those who see virtue in the renunciation of mathematics, logic, and clothes. Passion-ridden intellect had mastered man in a state of nature; a passion-wearied intellect might deliver man from it. If man cannot fulfil his desire, he can seek peace and ensue it by the invention of fictions. It is not prudence, but curiosity, that distinguisheth man from beast He wonders; he is possessed; a passionate thought leaps to the utterance; the word is born; the idea is fixed; from henceforth he will boldly conclude universally; science has come in the train of language. This most noble and profitable invention of speech, 'without which there had been amongst men neither commonwealth nor society, nor contract nor peace, no more than amongst lions, bears, and wolves,'[1] is man's proudest triumph over nature. By his own art he fetters himself with his own fictions—the fictions of the tongue You shall no longer hold that men acquired speech because man was a reasoning animal; in truth man became capable of science, i.e. reason, because he invented speech. It was not

[1] p. 24.

nature which in secular travail brought reason to the birth; but man saw nature's poverty of invention, and boldly substituted his own. He created reason in the interests of peace. Voltaire profanely said that if there were no God it would be necessary to invent one; convictions of similar cogency drove the Hobbean man to bow his neck to the dictatorship of the neologist. 'The Greeks have but one word, λόγος, for both speech and reason; not that they thought there was no speech without reason, but no reasoning without speech.'[1] Truth is a necessity; but necessary truth is a will-o'-the-wisp. Seekers after truth—how Hobbes despised them, all that deluded race who dreamt of a law whose seat is the bosom of God, her voice the harmony of the world: all things in heaven and earth doing her homage! Rather, boldly conclude that truth is not to be sought, but *made*. Let men agree what is to be truth, and truth it shall be There is truth and truth abounding when once it is recognized that truth is only of universals, that there is nothing in the world universal but names, and that names are imposed *arbitrio hominum*. Fiction is not, as people hold, the image or the distortion of the real which it counterfeits; it is the very and only foundation of that reality which is rational. Here is Hobbes's answer to that question which, in its varied phrasing, has never ceased to trouble philosophy Are there innate ideas? What is the ultimate criterion of truth?

[1] p. 29.

Is there a transcendent reason? What is common sense? Are there any undemonstrable and indubitable axioms fundamental to all thought? How is a synthetic *a priori* judgement possible?

The same temper which leads him to stifle thought with language carries him on to substitute definitions for first principles. *Prima philosophia*—metaphysics in Aristotle's sense—is first a body of definitions. These definitions are our points of departure: we must start by agreeing upon them. For 'the light of human minds is perspicuous words, by exact definitions first snuffed and purged from ambiguity'.[1] A definition must be held to be satisfactory if it be clear. The master claims a free and absolute right of arbitrary definition. The scholar queries: Is the definition true? is it adequate? does it assort with reality? To whom the master testily replies: You are irrelevant; your only right is to ask, Is it clear? Unless my definitions are accepted as first principles, science, i.e. a deductive system of consequences, is impossible, and inference foreclosed. Let me remind you again that agreement on definitions is the *sine qua non* of intelligible reasoning; and then for the sake of peace and lucidity let me beg—nay insist—that you accept my ruling on the use of names. Are they not arbitrary? Is not one man's imposition as good as another's? Mine therefore—at least for purposes of argument—rather better than yours? Hobbes knew what he was about;

[1] p. 37.

he was 'rare at definitions', said the admiring John Aubrey.[1] It was because he very clearly saw that in the prerogative of definition lay the sovereignty in philosophy.

But, you say, he must recognize some real, unconventional, transcendent standard of truth somewhere: for otherwise by what right does he distinguish between truth and error? And what is the meaning of the charges 'absurd' and 'insignificant' so freely lavished on opinions with which he disagrees? I can only reply that his distinctions between truth and falsehood, sense and absurdity, are perfectly consistent with the doctrine I have been expounding. Man's privilege of reason 'is allayed by another: and that is, by the privilege of absurdity; to which no living creature is subject, but man only. . . . For it is most true that Cicero saith of them somewhere: that there can be nothing so absurd but may be found in the books of philosophers.'[2] 'As men abound in copiousness of language, so they become more wise, or more mad than ordinary. . . For words are wise men's counters, they do but reckon by them; but they are the money of fools, that value them by the authority of an Aristotle, a Cicero, or a Thomas, or any other doctor whatsoever.'[3] The causes of this endowment of absurdity are but want of definition, want of adherence to definitions, want of the power of syllogizing. A glance at Hobbes's relentless application of this fundamental principle

[1] Aubrey, i. 394 [2] p 35. [3] p. 29.

will be sufficient. Good and evil are terms of individual imposition; by tacit agreement one may say they are left to a personal interpretation; there is no common rule of good and evil to be taken from the nature of the objects themselves. But the moral virtues and vices are universal names: they take their definition *ex arbitrio hominum*, i.e. from the will of the State. 'The fool hath said in his heart, there is no such thing as justice; and sometimes also with his tongue.'[1] The fool might arrive at his conclusion by an easy deduction from the principles of Hobbes. For if he had studied Hobbes's code of nature with ordinary care he would have discovered that the justice of which *Leviathan* is begotten is carefully emptied of all ethical content. There is indeed a justice, an obligation arising out of contract, which naturally refuses to discuss its own title; and there is another justice, the parody of equity, which explains itself with a humorous grin as the fiction of equality playing the peace-maker. You, X, say you're as good as any one else: Y says he's quite your match, and he'll take you on: permit me to assume them for purposes of codification a hypothesis of universal equality, and to refer you to the golden rule for your future behaviour!

At length man's pride and passions compel him to submit himself to government. Leviathan is set on his feet; he is the king of the proud; but his feet are of clay; he too is a fiction This time

[1] p III.

Hobbes resorts to the lawyers, borrows from them their mystico-legal fiction of the *persona moralis*, the corporation, and sends the mystical elements in it to the right about. 'It is the *unity* of the representer, not the *unity* of the represented, that maketh the person *one*: . . and *unity* cannot otherwise be understood in multitude.'[1] The sovereign is the soul, the person, the representative, the will, the conscience of the commonwealth; i.e. the sovereign *is* the commonwealth in that fictional sense which alone is truth in science and in practice. Once again there is no such thing as objective right: therefore we must invent a substitute for it by establishing a sovereign who shall declare what shall be right for us. On this point Hobbes is unmistakably emphatic.

'The law is all the right reason we have, and (though he, as often as it disagreeth with his own reason, deny it) is the infallible rule of moral goodness. The reason whereof is this, that because neither mine nor the Bishop's reason is right reason fit to be a rule of our moral actions, we have therefore set up over ourselves a sovereign governor, and agreed that his laws shall be unto us, whatsoever they be, in the place of right reason, to dictate to us what is really good. In the same manner as men in playing turn up trump, and as in playing their game their morality consisteth in not renouncing, so

[1] p. 126.

in our civil conversation our morality is all contained in not disobeying of the laws.' [1]—*Hobbes's debate with Dr. Bramhall, Bishop of Derry.*

'For, but give the authority of defining punishments to any man whatsoever, and let that man define them, and right reason has defined them, suppose the definition be both made, and made known before the offence committed. For such authority is to trump in card-playing, save that in matter of government, when nothing else is turned up, clubs are trumps.' [2]—*A Dialogue of the Common Laws.*

It is idle to qualify or defend such a political philosophy: it is rotten at the core. It is valueless save in so far as it stimulates to refutation. We may be content to leave it as a precious privilege to the lawyers, who need definitions and have no concern with morality. And yet no thinker on politics has ever probed its fundamental conceptions more thoroughly; and I say it advisedly, if you would think clearly of rights and duties, sovereignty and law, you must begin with the criticism of Hobbes. For any philosophy which is worth the name must spring out of scepticism; and every system of philosophy which is worth serious attention must achieve the conquest of scepticism. It is only a very botcher in philosophy or a very genial personage who can really rest content with a merely sceptical attitude. Hobbes was no Carneades of riotous

[1] Molesworth, v. 194. [2] Ibid., vi. 122.

dialectic, no Montaigne of cheerful and humorous resignation. His logic plunged him into the abyss of scepticism; but the fierce dogmatism of his nature revolted against it. David Hume imagined that it was left for him to send philosophy to its euthanasia; but in truth Hobbes had seen it all, the whole sceptic's progress—seen it, and travelled it, and loathed it long ago.

Hobbes clutched at mathematics as the dogmatist's last straw. Spite of the wreck of objective ideals, what might not be effected with matter and motion! Here, if anywhere, certainty might be found; here reason, baffled and disillusioned, might find a *punctum stans;* a fulcrum to explain the universe.

Hobbes and Descartes.

Hobbes thought in an atmosphere of dualism—yet Hobbes was a resolute opponent of dualism. From 1637, the date of the *Discours*, the relation between matter and mind, body and soul, was a cardinal—*the* cardinal problem Descartes had awarded to each substance co-ordinate, independent, absolute rights. The future business of Cartesianism was to find a *trait d'union*—an explanation for a relation in fact which had been demonstrated in theory inconceivable.

At first blush one might be inclined to say Hobbes remained untouched by the new method. Starting on a basis of empiricism he developed a materialistic philosophy in perfect independence of the current of idealistic thought which was flowing so strongly on the Continent. It would be a mistaken view. Hobbes is powerfully influenced by Descartes. Descartes prescribes for him his method—not Gassendi or Bacon. But with Descartes' dualism he will not away. He suspected Descartes of paltering with philosophy to appease the Jesuits—his philosophy must find a corner for the mysteries of the Catholic faith, e.g. transubstantiation, *pro salute animae*; and was a system to be received which fell hopelessly apart in the middle, and which demanded a miracle to restore a unity which a philosophy worthy of the name was bound to demonstrate impossible?

A system—or philosophy—must be coherent at any price; a philosopher, whose business it was to define, should see to that: words are wise men's counters, and the philosopher must play to win; coherence, not comprehension, is with Hobbes the touchstone of philosophy, the test of truth. To Hobbes, rationalism is the fundamental postulate; and a rational universe must be deduced from a single and simple principle. Dualism was the consecration of the irrational.

But Hobbes deals in back blows—he does not meet the dualist face to face; he refuses to see eye to eye with him; the problem shall be eluded, the position turned, in an emergency the question at issue begged. Sensation need offer no difficulties: sensation is only motion; it can only be caused by motion, it is only a form, a manifestation of motion. Fancy, memory, comparison, judgement, are really carried with sense—'sense hath necessarily some memory adhering to it.'[1]

And reason—pure intellection—the faculty of science—surely here we must appeal to another source (cf. Descartes and Gassendi), surely we have passed into another realm. Hobbes emphatically assures us that it is this reason, this capacity for general hypothetical reason, this science or sapience, which marks man off from the brutes The distinction between science and experience, sapience and prudence, is fundamental in his philosophy. And yet if we look more narrowly we shall find this marvellous endowment of man is really the child of language—that most noble and profitable invention. This bald paradox is a masterpiece of tactics. Speech is ushered in with the fanfaronade, and lo! reason is discovered clinging to her train. Instinct says, reason begets speech; paradox inverts, speech begets reason. Man acquires speech because he is reasonable)(man becomes capable of science because he has *invented* speech. A wonderful *hysteron proteron.*

Hobbes derives some account from his audacity.

1. We easily understand how error is possible—no need of tedious discussion—error dogs the heels of language.

2. Seeing that thought (science) depends on language, it is evident that to clarify thought we must

[1] Molesworth, i. 393.

purge language—re-definition the true task of philosophy.

In my necessarily harsh review I may have seemed to have found no answer to my opening question. Does it not involve a *petitio principii*? *Is* he great after all? I am content to rest the issue on one test alone—the test of style. I am adopting no superficial test, when I boldly affirm that every great thinker reveals his greatness in his style. It is quite possible—unhappily common—to cultivate style without thought; it is absolutely impossible to think really, deeply, passionately, without forging a style. Now Hobbes's style is something quite unique in our literature. Of course I don't mean it stands out of the seventeenth century; to read a paragraph is to fix its date. But no other seventeenth-century writer has a style like it: it is inimitable. It would be childish to measure it with the incommensurable; to pit it against the fluent magnificence of Milton or the quaint and unexpected beauties of Sir Thomas Browne. But it is fair to try Hobbes's English by the touchstone of Bacon's. Those critics who deny Bacon's title to a primacy in philosophy are generally ready enough to acknowledge his high position as a writer. And Bacon and Hobbes are writers of the same order. They are both sententious; they are both grave and didactic; they both wield the weapons of imagery, apophthegm, and epigram, they are both—let us admit it—laboured stylists. It is, I think, highly probable that Hobbes learnt something of literary craftsmanship from Bacon in those Gorhambury contemplations. But Hobbes's writing is just as decisively superior to Bacon's, as his philosophy. Bacon aimed at concealing the poverty of his thought by the adornment of his style. he wrote for ostentation. When that solemn humbug, that bourgeois Machiavel, took up his pen to edify mankind, he first opened his commonplace books, stuffed with assorted anecdotes, quotations, conceits, and *mucrones verborum*, and then with an eye to the anthology, proceeded to set down 'what oft was thought, but ne'er so well expressed'.

It must be admitted it reads remarkably well. The sentences are brave and brief at first inspection: you mistake terseness of language for condensation of thought. But read again. Many examples of this can be found in such an essay as 'Of Study'. Now turn to Hobbes; but before you do so, open Aubrey and learn the open secret of his style.

'He was never idle; his thoughts were always working.'[1]

'He sayd that he sometimes would sett his thoughts upon researching and contemplating, always with this rule, that he very much and deeply considered one thing at a time (scilicet a weeke or sometimes a fortnight).'[2]

'He walked much and contemplated, and he had in the head of his staffe a pen and inke-horne, carried

[1] Aubrey, i. 351.

[2] Ibid., i. 339

always a note booke in his pocket, and as soon as a thought darted, he presently entred it into his booke, or otherwise he might perhaps have lost it. . . . Thus that book (the *Leviathan*) was made.'[1]

In Hobbes the clauses are clean, the sentences jolt, the argument is inevitable. Bacon wrote to display his wit. Hobbes to convince and confute. Bacon invented epigram to coax the public ear; Hobbes found his epigram after he had crystallized his thought. In sum, the difference between the styles of Bacon and Hobbes is to be measured by the difference between ostentation and passionate thought. We can compare Hobbes's own defence of his style and method.

'There is nothing I distrust more than my elocution, which nevertheless I am confident, excepting the mischances of the press, is not obscure. That I have neglected the ornament of quoting ancient poets, orators, and philosophers, contrary to the custom of late time, (whether I have done well or ill in it,) proceedeth from my judgement, grounded on many reasons. For first, all truth of doctrine dependeth either upon *reason*, or upon *Scripture*; both which give credit to many, but never receive it from any writer. Secondly, the matters in question are not of *fact*, but of *right*, wherein there is no place for *witnesses*. There is scarce any of those old writers that contradicteth not sometimes both him-

[1] Aubrey, i. 334

self and others; which makes their testimonies insufficient. Fourthly, such opinions as are taken only upon credit of antiquity, are not intrinsically the judgement of those that cite them, but words that pass, like gaping, from mouth to mouth. Fifthly, it is many times with a fraudulent design that men stick their corrupt doctrine with the cloves of other men's wit. Sixthly, I find not that the ancients they cite, took it for an ornament, to do the like with those that wrote before them. Seventhly, it is an argument of indigestion, when Greek and Latin sentences unchewed come up again, as they use to do, unchanged. Lastly, though I reverence those men of ancient time, that either have written truth perspicuously, or set us in a better way to find it out ourselves; yet to the antiquity itself I think nothing due. For if we will reverence the age, the present is the oldest. If the antiquity of the writer, I am not sure, that generally they to whom such honour is given, were more ancient when they wrote, than I am that am writing. But if it be well considered, the praise of ancient authors proceeds not from the reverence of the dead, but from the competition, and mutual envy of the living.'[1]

Aubrey has more to tell us. For instance, about his reading:

'He had read much, if one considers his long life; but his contemplation was much more than his

[1] pp 555–6.

reading. He was wont to say that if he had read as much as other men, he should have knowne no more than other men.'[1]

About his love of 'ingeniose conversation':

'I have heard him say, that at his lord's house in the country there was a good library, and bookes enough for him, and that his lordship stored the library with what bookes he thought fitt to be bought, but he sayd, the want of learned conversation was a very great inconvenience, and that though he conceived he could order his thinking as well perhaps as another man, yet he found a great defect.'[2]

Studying Hobbes as we do in historical manuals of philosophy, with their extracted systems, we usually fail to recognize how strongly the blood of the controversialist ran in his veins. Yet the *Leviathan* is first and foremost a controversial episode—a fighting work. Hobbes himself professed regret that his thoughts for those ten years of civil war were so unhinged from the mathematics, but he certainly entered into the quarrel with alacrity. His interests were pre-eminently occupied with ecclesiastical problems. Born in 1588, an Oxford student at the time of the Gunpowder Plot, an indignant witness of the struggle of that age between religion and science, like every honest Englishman he pursued Pope and Jesuit with an undying hate. For the aversion to Rome and the Roman claims there

[1] Aubrey, i. 349 [2] Ibid., i. 337-8.

was ample justification. By his Bull of Deposition in 1570 Pope Pius V had challenged the struggle, and rendered the position of English Catholics untenable From a respected if prohibited faith they became recusants: from recusants, traitors. It was the Papal policy and its indefatigable agents the Jesuits which were to blame. What peace was possible with men who repudiated moral obligations, who hesitated at no crime *ad maiorem Dei gloriam*? The same dishonesty which covered their actions and their name with infamy for succeeding generations, rendered their apologetic literature the poorest trash and the most immoral stuff that was ever justly consigned to oblivion. Bellarmine and Baronius once were names to conjure with: does any one respect them now? Their only merit is that they called for answer—and some of the answers are among the most precious treasures of English Theology. Hobbes too must break a lance with Bellarmine in the *Leviathan*. And Hobbes was not the least vigorous or the worst equipped of the English champions.

For indeed Hobbes deserves a place among the Masters in English Theology. Strange company, it may seem. But if Hobbes be read in connexion with the line of great English apologists—apologists for Protestantism and apologists for Anglicanism, it will at once be evident to any unprejudiced mind that the lines of defence and attack on which the Fathers of Anglicanism—Jewel, Hooker, Andrewes,

Laud, Chillingworth, Jeremy Taylor—conducted the debate were adopted with a thoroughness all his own by Hobbes. He dotted the i's and crossed the t's of the divines; sharpened their logic, sounded their inferences, and appended a few corollaries from which they themselves might have shrunk. The theory of a national and autonomous Church outlined by Jewel and compendiously stated by Hooker ('the prince has power to change the public face of religion'), hardly allowed of clearer definition in Hobbes's brief chapter[1] on the identity of Church and Commonwealth and the consequences flowing therefrom.

Again, the distinction between the necessary and the variable, fundamentals and non-fundamentals, articles of faith and matters of opinion, was the real principle of the Reformation. For the constant effort of the Roman Church was to extend the list of matters which were *de fide*, and to minimize the variable element as far as possible So that, when he asserts and proves that the *unum necessarium*, the only article of faith, which the Scripture maketh necessary to salvation, is this, that Jesus is the Christ, Hobbes is taking the Anglican position occupied for instance by Chillingworth and Jeremy Taylor. Not that he ever dreamt, as they did, of allowing the antithesis to become the premiss of religious freedom. With him—as with Laud—it drove to an opposite conclusion. If a practice, an

[1] Chapter xxxix, pp 361-3

opinion, is non-essential, then it is indifferent; if indifferent, then the commonwealth, i.e. the sovereign, must decide. What the rule was did not matter, all that mattered was that a rule there should be.

Once again, Anglican polemics had been constrained to welcome the aid of philology against controversialists who—let us charitably assume in ignorance of Greek—employed texts which were forgeries, and emended those which were not. Jeremy Taylor was more than doubtful as to the value of patristic testimony, and could not away with the Athanasian Creed.

Hobbes goes so far as to subject the whole canon of Scripture to a critical examination, which in its boldness anticipates the *Tractatus Theologico-Politicus* of Spinoza.

And yet the Church of England always viewed this self-constituted ally with something more than suspicion. His Erastianism was of a type which only Selden and a few lawyers could appreciate. Honest Baillie spoke of him as Hobbes the Atheist; there were those who hinted darkly that he was no other than Antichrist. It is true his views on the Trinity were of a Sabellian complexion; and in one famous passage he was incautious enough to make Moses one of the three persons thereof. In Hobbes's time Legate and Wightman had been burnt for less. He himself would have made an unwilling martyr. 'There was a report (and surely true),' says Aubrey, 'that in Parliament, not long after the king was settled, (in fact it was 1668), some of the bishops made a motion to have the good old gentleman burnt for a heretique.'[1] I don't know that they actually went as far as that, whatever they thought; but certain it is they inquired into his books, that the University of Cambridge in 1669 compelled one Daniel Scargill, Fellow of Corpus Christi, to recant his Hobbism,[2] and that Hobbes himself was grievously alarmed. And with some justice: for despite his eloquent legal defence, I doubt whether the common lawyers would have been deterred from issuing the writ *de haeretico comburendo*.

Happily the only result was to send up the price of his books—this from the good Pepys, who tried to buy them. What did Pepys think of them?

Hobbes may well have been uncomfortable: he knew, better probably than even the bishops, how thoroughly he deserved to be burnt. With sophistry and sense, with satire and suggestion, he had been fighting, single-handed, in the cause of the lay intellect. 'When Mr. T. Hobbes was sick in France the divines came to him and tormented him (both Roman Catholic, Church of England, and Geneva). Sayd he to them, "Let me alone or else I will detect all your cheates from Aaron to yourselves."'[3] The

[1] Aubrey, i. 339

[2] Somers Tracts, ed. 1809-12, vol. vii, p 371.

[3] Aubrey, i. 357.

threatened attack—vivacious, detailed, and precise—was delivered in the last two books of the *Leviathan*. How thorough the assault was you may judge for yourselves if you will read them ; the tone you may estimate from a few illustrations, which may perhaps encourage you to read further.[1]

A good-natured critic will refuse to see in Hobbes anything more than the sturdy Protestant, the stalwart champion of national religion, denouncing with equal emphasis the frauds of priestcraft and the irresponsibility of private judgement. His friends certainly believed that 'the good old gentleman' was a sound Christian at heart. He may have been : it is more evident that he was an Erastian. Many of us—most of us in fact—are Erastians with certain limitations. Hobbes was an Erastian without limitations. It is customary to count him among the pioneers of Natural Religion and Rational Theology. For such a view I can find no evidence. Natural Law is indeed the law of reason—found out by reason : but National Religion is not the religion of reason Nature indeed plants the seeds of religion—fear and ignorance ; kingcraft and priestcraft water and tend it. The religion of reason is the religion of the State—and the State bids us captivate our reason. 'It is with the mysteries of our religion as with wholesome pills for the sick :

[1] Cf on Inspiration, pp. 312–14, on Hell, p 351 ; on the Soul, p 526; on the Hot-houses of Vain Philosophy, p 518, on Aristotelity and Theology, pp. 523–4, on the Universities, p. 523. Cf. his sketch of the origin and history of Universities, p. 523.

which swallowed whole have the virtue to cure; but chewed are for the most part cast up again without effect.'[1]

Hobbes had his bitter jest with his contemporaries, and the whirligig of time has had its revenges. He has suffered much from his opponents, more from his defenders, most from his plagiarists. Oxford once burnt the *Leviathan*: she now prescribes it to her students; but the prescribed portion is very limited, and there is no reason to suppose that she has ever understood him. It was, after all, a nemesis well deserved. A great partisan by nature, Hobbes became by the sheer force of his fierce, concentrated intellect a master builder in philosophy. The stimulus of opposition roused him to think. He hated error, and therefore, to confute it, he shouldered his way into the very sanctuary of truth. But his hands were not clean, nor his spirit pure; patient research and absolute devotion were not in his nature to give; he never felt the 'bright shoots of everlastingness', and resolutely closed his eyes to the high vision. With all his intellectual power he is of the earth earthy; at best the Lydian stone of philosophy, and 'rare at definitions'.[2]

[1] p 287.

[2] Aubrey, i. 394.

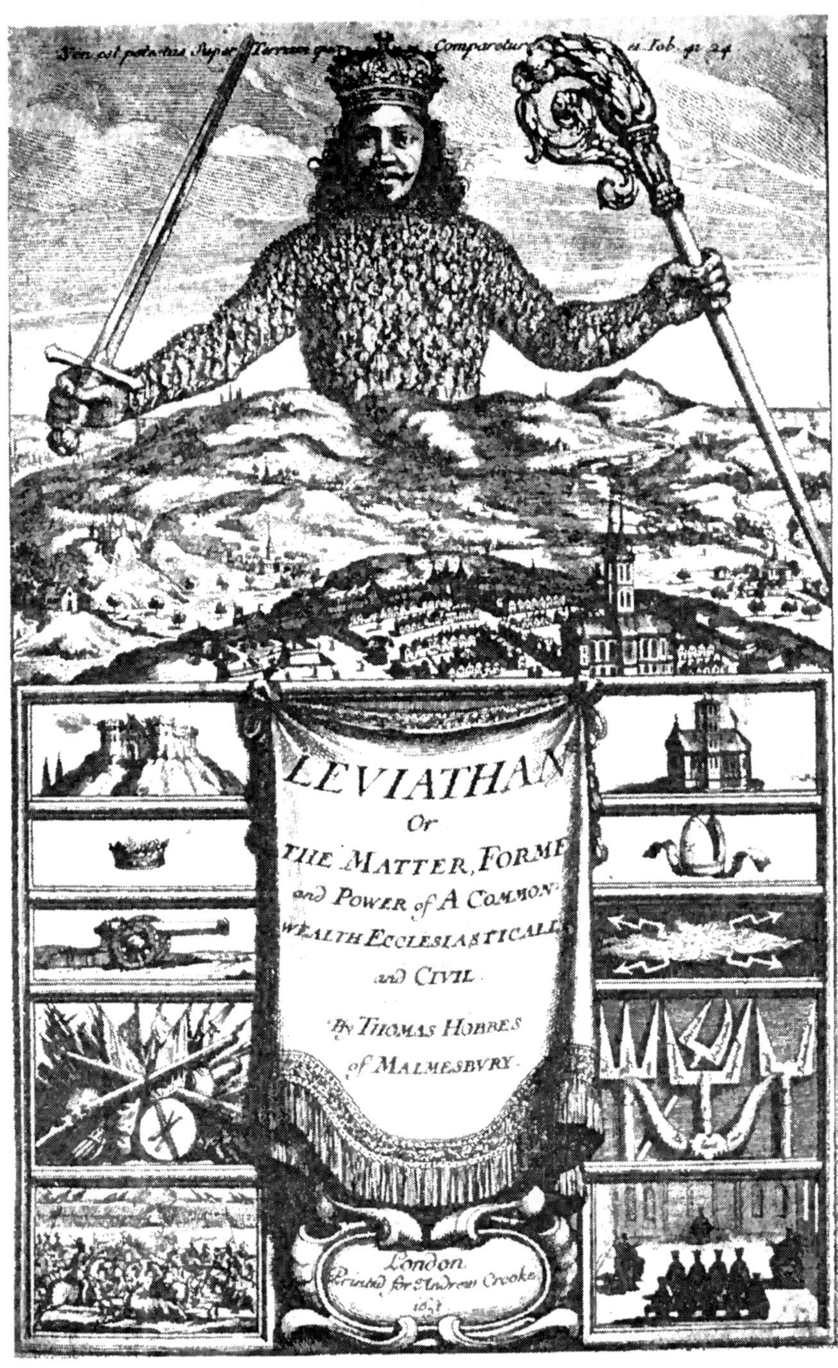
Non est potestas Super Terram
Comparetur
Iob. 41. 24
LEVIATHAN
Or
THE MATTER, FORME
and POWER of A COMMON-
WEALTH ECCLESIASTICALL
and CIVIL
By THOMAS HOBBES
of MALMESBURY
London
Printed for Andrew Crooke

LEVIATHAN,

OR

The Matter, Forme, & Power

OF A

COMMON-WEALTH

ECCLESIASTICALL

AND

CIVILL.

By THOMAS HOBBES *of* Malmesbury.

LONDON,

Printed for ANDREW CROOKE, at the Green Dragon in St. *Pauls* Church-yard, 1651.

TO

MY MOST HONOR'D FRIEND
Mr *FRANCIS GODOLPHIN*
of *Godolphin.*

Honor'd Sir,

YOUR most worthy Brother Mr *Sidney Godolphin*, when he lived, was pleas'd to think my studies something, and otherwise to oblige me, as you know, with reall testimonies of his good opinion, great in themselves, and the greater for the worthinesse of his person. For there is not any vertue that disposeth a man, either to the service of God, or to the service of his Country, to Civill Society, or private Friendship, that did not manifestly appear in his conversation, not as acquired by necessity, or affected upon occasion, but inhærent, and shining in a generous constitution of his nature. Therefore in honour and gratitude to him, and with devotion to your selfe, I humbly Dedicate unto you this my discourse of Common-wealth. I know not how the world will receive it, nor how it may reflect on those that shall seem to favour it. For in a way beset with those that contend, on one side for too great Liberty, and on the other side for too much Authority, 'tis hard to passe between the points of both unwounded. But yet, me thinks, the endeavour to advance the Civill Power, should not be by the Civill Power condemned, nor private men, by reprehending it, declare they think that Power too great. Besides, I speak not of the men, but (in the Abstract) of the Seat of Power, (like to those simple and unpartiall creatures in the Roman Capitol, that with their noyse defended those within it, not because they were they, but there,) offending none, I think, but those without, or such within (if there be any such) as favour them. That which perhaps may most offend, are certain Texts of Holy Scripture, alledged by me to other purpose than ordinarily they use to be by others. But I have done it with due submission, and also (in order to my Subject) necessarily, for they are the Outworks of the [illegible], from whence they impugne the Civill Power. If notwithstanding this, you find my labour generally decryed, you may be pleased to excuse your selfe, and say I am a man that love my own opinions, and think all true I say, that I honoured your Brother, and honour you, and have presum'd on that, to assume the Title (without your knowledge) of being, as I am,

SIR,

Your most humble, and most

obedient servant,

Paris. *Aprill* $\frac{15}{25}$. 1651. THO. HOBBES.

The Contents of the Chapters

The first Part,

Of MAN.

The second Part,

Of COMMON-WEALTH.

THE CONTENTS.

The third Part.

Of A Christian Common-wealth.

THE CONTENTS.

The fourth Part.

Of The Kingdome Of Darknesse

Errata.

PAGE 48. In the Margin, for *love Praise*, read *love of Praise*. p 75 l 5 for *signied*, r. *signified* p 88 l 1 for *performe*, r. *forme*. l. 35. for *Soveraign*, r. *the Soveraign* p 94. l 14. for *lands*, r. *hands*. p. 100. l. 28 for *in*, r. *in his* p 102. l 46. for *in*, r. *is*, p. 105. in the margin, for *ver.* 10. r. *ver.* 19. &c. p. 116. l. 46 for *are involved*, r *are not involved* p. 120. l. 42. for *Those Bodies*, r. *These Bodies*. p 137. l. 2 for *in generall*. r, *in generall*, p. 139. l 36 for *were*, r. *where* p 166. l. 18 for *benefit*, r. *benefits*. p. 200. l. 48. dele *also*. l. 49. for *delivered*, r. *deliver*. p. 203 l 35. for *other*, r. *higher*. p 204 l 15 for *and left*, r. *if left* l. 39. for *write*, r *writt* p. 206. l. 19. for *of the*, r. *over the*. p 234. l. 1. for *but of*, r *but by mediation of* l. 15. dele *and*. l 38. for *putting*, r. *pulling*. p. 262. l. 19 for *tisme*, r. *Baptisme*. p. 268. l 48 for *that the*, r *that*. p. 271. l. 1. for *observe*, r. *obey*. l. 4. for *contrary the*, r. *contrary to the*. p. 272. l. 36. for *our Saviours of life*, r. *of our Saviours life*. p. 275 l. 18 for *if shall*, r. *if he shall* l. 30. for *haven*, r. *heaven*. l 45 for *of Church*, r *of the Church*. p. 276. l. 38. dele *inter*. l 46. dele *are*. p 285 l 11 for *he had*, r. *he hath*. p 287 l 10 dele *of*. p 298. l. 36. for *to ay*, r *to Lay*. p. 361. l. 36. for *him*, r *them*.

[These errata have been corrected in the text of this reprint]

[1]

THE INTRODUCTION.

NATURE (the Art whereby God hath made and governes the World) is by the *Art* of man, as in many other things, so in this also imitated, that it can make an Artificial Animal. For seeing life is but a motion of Limbs, the begining whereof is in some principall part within; why may we not say, that all *Automata* (Engines that move themselves by springs and wheeles as doth a watch) have an artificiall life? For what is the *Heart*, but a *Spring*; and the *Nerves*, but so many *Strings*; and the *Joynts*, but so many *Wheeles*, giving motion to the whole Body, such as was intended by the Artificer? *Art* goes yet further, imitating that Rationall and most excellent worke of Nature, *Man*. For by Art is created that great LEVIATHAN called a COMMON-WEALTH, or STATE, (in latine CIVITAS) which is but an Artificiall Man; though of greater stature and strength than the Naturall, for whose protection and defence it was intended; and in which, the *Soveraignty* is an Artificiall *Soul*, as giving life and motion to the whole body; The *Magistrates*, and other *Officers* of Judicature and Execution, artificiall *Joynts*; *Reward* and *Punishment* (by which fastned to the seate of the Soveraignty, every joynt and member is moved to performe his duty) are the *Nerves*, that do the same in the Body Naturall; The *Wealth* and *Riches* of all the particular members, are the *Strength*, *Salus Populi* (the *peoples safety*) its *Businesse*; *Counsellors*, by whom all things needfull for it to know, are suggested unto it, are the *Memory*, *Equity* and *Lawes*, an artificiall *Reason* and *Will*; *Concord*, *Health*; *Sedition*, *Sicknesse*; and *Civill war*, *Death*. Lastly, the *Pacts* and *Covenants*, by which the parts of this Body Politique were at first made, set together, and united, resemble that *Fiat*, or the *Let us make man*, pronounced by God in the Creation.

To describe the Nature of this Artificiall man, I will consider [2]

First, the *Matter* thereof, and the *Artificer*; both which is *Man*.

Secondly, *How*, and by what *Covenants* it is made; what are the *Rights* and just *Power* or *Authority* of a *Soveraigne*, and what it is that *preserveth* and *dissolveth* it.

Thirdly, what is a *Christian Common-wealth*.

Lastly, what is the *Kingdome of Darkness*.

Concerning the first, there is a saying much usurped of late, That *Wisedome* is acquired, not by reading of *Books*, but of *Men*. Consequently whereunto, those persons, that for the most part can give no other proof of being wise, take great delight to shew what they think they have read in men, by uncharitable censures of one another behind their backs. But there is another saying not of late understood, by which they might learn truly to read one another, if they would take the pains; and that is, *Nosce teipsum, Read thy self*: which was not meant, as it is now used, to countenance, either the barbarous state of men in power, towards their inferiors; or to encourage men of low degree, to a sawcie behaviour towards their betters; But to teach us, that for the similitude of the thoughts, and Passions of one man, to the thoughts, and Passions of another, whosoever looketh into himself, and considereth what he doth, when he does *think, opine, reason, hope, feare*, &c, and upon what grounds; he shall thereby read and know, what are the thoughts, and Passions of all other men, upon the like occasions I say the similitude of *Passions*, which are the same in all men, *desire, feare, hope*, &c; not the similitude of the *objects* of the Passions, which are the things *desired, feared, hoped*, &c. for these the constitution individuall, and particular education do so vary, and they are so easie to be kept from our knowledge, that the characters of mans heart, blotted and confounded as they are, with dissembling, lying, counterfeiting, and erroneous doctrines, are legible onely to him that searcheth hearts. And though by mens actions wee do discover their designe sometimes; yet to do it without comparing them with our own, and distinguishing all circumstances, by which the case may come to be altered, is to decypher without a key, and be for the most part deceived, by too much trust, or by too much diffidence; as he that reads, is himself a good or evil man.

But let one man read another by his actions never so perfectly, it serves him onely with his acquaintance, which are but few. He that is to govern a whole Nation, must read in himself, not this, or that particular man; but Man-kind: which though it be hard to do, harder than to learn any Language, or Science; yet, when I shall have set down my own reading orderly, and perspicuously, the pains left another, will be onely to consider, if he also find not the same in himself For this kind of Doctrine, admitteth no other Demonstration.

OF MAN. [3]

CHAP. I.

Of SENSE.

CONCERNING the Thoughts of man, I will consider them first *Singly*, and afterwards in *Trayne*, or dependance upon one another. *Singly*, they are every one a *Representation* or *Apparence*, of some quality, or other Accident of a body without us; which is commonly called an *Object*. Which Object worketh on the Eyes, Eares, and other parts of mans body; and by diversity of working, produceth diversity of Apparences.

The Originall of them all, is that which we call SENSE; (For there is no conception in a mans mind, which hath not at first, totally, or by parts, been begotten upon the organs of *Sense*.) The rest are derived from that originall.

To know the naturall cause of Sense, is not very necessary to the business now in hand; and I have elsewhere written of the same at large. Nevertheless, to fill each part of my present method, I will briefly deliver the same in this place.

The cause of Sense, is the Externall Body, or Object, which presseth the organ proper to each Sense, either immediatly, as in the Tast and Touch; or mediately, as in Seeing, Hearing, and Smelling: which pressure, by the mediation of Nerves, and other strings, and membranes of the body, continued inwards to the Brain, and Heart, causeth there a resistance, or counter-pressure, or endeavour of the heart, to deliver it self: which endeavour because *Outward*, seemeth to be some matter without. And this *seeming*, or *fancy*, is that which men call *Sense*, and consisteth, as to the Eye, in a *Light*, or *Colour figured*, To the Eare, in a *Sound*, To the Nostrill, in an *Odour*; To the Tongue and Palat, in a *Savour*; And to the rest of the body, in *Heat*, *Cold*, *Hardnesse*, *Softnesse*, and such other qualities, as we discern by *Feeling*. All which qualities called *Sensible*, are in the

object that causeth them, but so many several motions of the matter, by which it presseth our organs diversly. Neither in us that are pressed, are they any thing else, but divers motions; (for motion, produceth nothing but motion.) But their apparence to us is Fancy, the same waking, that dreaming. And as pressing, rubbing, or striking the Eye, makes us fancy a light; and pressing the Eare, produceth a dinne, so do the bodies also we see, or hear, produce the same by their strong, though unobserved action. For if those Colours, and Sounds, were in the Bodies, or Objects that cause them, they
[4] could not bee severed from them, as by glasses, and in Ecchoes by reflection, wee see they are; where we know the thing we see, is in one place; the apparence, in another. And though at some certain distance, the reall, and very object seem invested with the fancy it begets in us; Yet still the object is one thing, the image or fancy is another. So that Sense in all cases, is nothing els but originall fancy, caused (as I have said) by the pressure, that is, by the motion, of externall things upon our Eyes, Eares, and other organs thereunto ordained.

But the Philosophy-schooles, through all the Universities of Christendome, grounded upon certain Texts of *Aristotle*, teach another doctrine; and say, For the cause of *Vision*, that the thing seen, sendeth forth on every side a *visible species* (in English) a *visible shew, apparition*, or *aspect*, or *a being seen*; the receiving whereof into the Eye, is *Seeing*. And for the cause of *Hearing*, that the thing heard, sendeth forth an *Audible species*, that is, an *Audible aspect*, or *Audible being seen*; which entring at the Eare, maketh *Hearing*. Nay for the cause of *Understanding* also, they say the thing Understood sendeth forth *intelligible species*, that is, an *intelligible being seen*; which comming into the Understanding, makes us Understand. I say not this, as disapproving the use of Universities: but because I am to speak hereafter of their office in a Common-wealth, I must let you see on all occasions by the way, what things would be amended in them: amongst which the frequency of insignificant Speech is one.

CHAP. II.

Of IMAGINATION.

THAT when a thing lies still, unlesse somewhat els stirre it, it will lye still for ever, is a truth that no man doubts of. But that when a thing is in motion, it will eternally be in motion, unless somewhat els stay it, though the reason be the same, (namely, that nothing can change it selfe,) is not so easily assented to. For men measure, not onely other men, but all other things, by themselves: and because they find themselves subject after motion to pain, and lassitude, think every thing els growes weary of motion, and seeks repose of its own accord; little considering, whether it be not some other motion, wherein that desire of rest they find in themselves, consisteth. From hence it is, that the Schooles say, Heavy bodies fall downwards, out of an appetite to rest, and to conserve their nature in that place which is most proper for them, ascribing appetite and Knowledge of what is good for their conservation, (which is more than man has) to things inanimate, absurdly.

When a Body is once in motion, it moveth (unless something els hinder it) eternally, and whatsoever hindreth it, cannot in an instant, but in time, and by degrees quite extinguish it: And as wee see in the water, though the wind cease, the waves give not over rowling
for a long time after; so also it happeneth in that [5]
motion, which is made in the internall parts of a man, then, when he Sees, Dreams, &c. For after the object is removed, or the eye shut, wee still retain an image of the thing seen, though more obscure than when we see it. And this is it, the Latines call *Imagination*, from the image made in seeing, and apply the same, though improperly, to all the other senses. But the Greeks call it *Fancy*, which signifies *apparence*, and is as proper to one sense, as to another. IMAGINATION therefore is nothing but *decaying sense*; and is found in men, and many other living Creatures, aswell sleeping, as waking.

The decay of Sense in men waking, is not the decay of the motion made in sense; but an obscuring of it, in

such manner, as the light of the Sun obscureth the light of the Starres; which starrs do no less exercise their vertue by which they are visible, in the day, than in the night. But because amongst many stroaks, which our eyes, eares, and other organs receive from externall bodies, the predominant onely is sensible; therefore the light of the Sun being predominant, we are not affected with the action of the starrs. And any object being removed from our eyes, though the impression it made in us remain; yet other objects more present succeeding, and working on us, the Imagination of the past is obscured, and made weak; as the voyce of a man is in the noyse of the day. From whence it followeth, that the longer the time is, after the sight, or Sense of any object, the weaker is the Imagination. For the continuall change of mans body, destroyes in time the parts which in sense were moved: So that distance of time, and of place, hath one and the same effect in us. For as at a great distance of place, that which wee look at, appears dimme, and without distinction of the smaller parts; and as Voyces grow weak, and inarticulate: so also after great distance of time, our imagination of the Past is weak; and wee lose (for example) of Cities wee have seen, many particular Streets; and of Actions, many particular Circumstances. This *decaying sense*, when wee would express the thing it self, (I mean *fancy* it selfe,) wee call *Imagination*, as I said before: But when we would express the *decay*, and signifie that the Sense is fading, old, and past, it is called *Memory*.
Memory. So that *Imagination* and *Memory*, are but one thing, which for divers considerations hath divers names.

Much memory, or memory of many things, is called *Experience*. Againe, Imagination being only of those things which have been formerly perceived by Sense, either all at once, or by parts at severall times; The former, (which is the imagining the whole object, as it was presented to the sense) is *simple Imagination*; as when one imagineth a man, or horse, which he hath seen before. The other is *Compounded*; as when from the sight of a man at one time, and of a horse at another, we conceive in our mind a Centaure. So when a man compoundeth the image of his own person, with the image of the actions of an other man; as when a man imagins himselfe a *Hercules*, or an *Alexander*, (which happeneth often to them that are much taken with reading of Romants) it is a compound imagination, and properly but a Fiction of the mind. There be also other Imagina- [6] tions that rise in men, (though waking) from the great impression made in sense: As from gazing upon the Sun, the impression leaves an image of the Sun before our eyes a long time after, and from being long and vehemently attent upon Geometricall Figures, a man shall in the dark, (though awake) have the Images of Lines, and Angles before his eyes: which kind of Fancy hath no particular name; as being a thing that doth not commonly fall into mens discourse.

Dreams. The imaginations of them that sleep, are those we call *Dreams*. And these also (as all other Imaginations) have been before, either totally, or by parcells in the Sense. And because in sense, the Brain, and Nerves, which are the necessary Organs of sense, are so benummed in sleep, as not easily to be moved by the action of Externall Objects, there can happen in sleep, no Imagination; and therefore no Dreame, but what proceeds from the agitation of the inward parts of mans body; which inward parts, for the connexion they have with the Brayn, and other Organs, when they be distempered, do keep the same in motion; whereby the Imaginations there formerly made, appeare as if a man were waking; saving that the Organs of Sense being now benummed, so as there is no new object, which can master and obscure them with a more vigorous impression, a Dreame must needs be more cleare, in this silence of sense, than are our waking thoughts. And hence it cometh to passe, that it is a hard matter, and by many thought impossible to distinguish exactly between Sense and Dreaming. For my part, when I consider, that in Dreames, I do not often, nor constantly think of the same Persons, Places, Objects, and Actions that I do waking; nor remember so long a trayne of coherent thoughts, Dreaming, as at other times, And because waking I often observe the absurdity of Dreames, but never dream of the absurdities of my waking Thoughts ; I am well satisfied, that being awake, I know I dreame not ; though when I dreame, I think my selfe awake.

And seeing dreames are caused by the distemper of some of the inward parts of the Body ; divers distempers must needs cause different Dreams. And hence it is, that lying cold breedeth Dreams of Feare, and raiseth the thought and Image of some fearfull object (the motion from the brain to the inner parts, and from the inner parts to the Brain being reciprocall:) And that as Anger causeth heat in some parts of the Body, when we are awake ; so when we sleep, the over heating of the same parts causeth Anger, and raiseth up in the brain the Imagination of an Enemy. In the same manner ; as naturall kindness, when we are awake causeth desire ; and desire makes heat in certain other parts of the body; so also, too much heat in those parts, while wee sleep, raiseth in the brain an imagination of some kindness shewn. In summe, our Dreams are the reverse of our waking Imaginations ; The motion when we are awake, beginning at one end ; and when we Dream, at another.

The most difficult discerning of a mans Dream, from his
[7] waking thoughts, is then, when by some accident we observe not that we have slept : which is easie to happen to a man full of fearfull thoughts ; and whose conscience is much troubled ; and that sleepeth, without the circumstances, of going to bed, or putting off his clothes, as one that noddeth in a chayre For he that taketh pains, and industriously layes himself to sleep, in case any uncouth and exorbitant fancy come unto him, cannot easily think it other than a Dream. We read of *Marcus Brutus*, (one that had his life given him by *Julius Cæsar*, and was also his favorite, and notwithstanding murthered him,) how at *Philippi*, the night before he gave battell to *Augustus Cæsar*, hee saw a fearfull apparition, which is commonly related by Historians as a Vision · but considering the circumstances, one may easily judge to have been but a short Dream. For sitting in his tent, pensive and troubled with the horrour of his rash act, it was not hard for him, slumbering in the cold, to dream of that which

Apparitions or Visions

most affrighted him ; which feare, as by degrees it made him wake ; so also it must needs make the Apparition by degrees to vanish : And having no assurance that he slept, he could have no cause to think it a Dream, or any thing but a Vision. And this is no very rare Accident : for even they that be perfectly awake, if they be timorous, and supperstitious, possessed with fearfull tales, and alone in the dark, are subject to the like fancies ; and believe they see spirits and dead mens Ghosts walking in Church-yards ; whereas it is either their Fancy onely, or els the knavery of such persons, as make use of such superstitious feare, to passe disguised in the night, to places they would not be known to haunt.

From this ignorance of how to distinguish Dreams, and other strong Fancies, from Vision and Sense, did arise the greatest part of the Religion of the Gentiles in time past, that worshipped Satyres, Fawnes, Nymphs, and the like ; and now adayes the opinion that rude people have of Fayries, Ghosts, and Goblins ; and of the power of Witches. For as for Witches, I think not that their witchcraft is any reall power ; but yet that they are justly punished, for the false beliefe they have, that they can do such mischiefe, joyned with their purpose to do it if they can · their trade being neerer to a new Religion, than to a Craft or Science. And for Fayries, and walking Ghosts, the opinion of them has I think been on purpose, either taught, or not confuted, to keep in credit the use of Exorcisme, of Crosses, of holy Water, and other such inventions of Ghostly men. Neverthelesse, there is no doubt, but God can make unnaturall Apparitions : But that he does it so often, as men need to feare such things, more than they feare the stay, or change, of the course of Nature, which he also can stay, and change, is no point of Christian faith. But evill men under pretext that God can do any thing, are so bold as to say any thing when it serves their turn, though they think it untrue ; It is the part of a wise man, to believe them no further, than right reason makes that which they say, appear credible. If this superstitious fear of Spirits were taken away, and with it, Prognostiques from Dreams, false Prophecies, and many other things depending

[8] thereon, by which, crafty ambitious persons abuse the simple people, men would be much more fitted than they are for civill Obedience.

And this ought to be the work of the Schooles: but they rather nourish such doctrine. For (not knowing what Imagination, or the Senses are), what they receive, they teach: some saying, that Imaginations rise of themselves, and have no cause: Others that they rise most commonly from the Will; and that Good thoughts are blown (inspired) into a man, by God; and Evill thoughts by the Divell: or that Good thoughts are powred (infused) into a man, by God, and Evill ones by the Divell. Some say the Senses receive the Species of things, and deliver them to the Common-sense; and the Common Sense delivers them over to the Fancy, and the Fancy to the Memory, and the Memory to the Judgement, like handing of things from one to another, with many words making nothing understood.

Understanding. The Imagination that is raysed in man (or any other creature indued with the faculty of imagining) by words, or other voluntary signes, is that we generally call *Understanding*; and is common to Man and Beast. For a dogge by custome will understand the call, or the rating of his Master; and so will many other Beasts. That Understanding which is peculiar to man, is the Understanding not onely his will; but his conceptions and thoughts, by the sequell and contexture of the names of things into Affirmations, Negations, and other formes of Speech: And of this kinde of Understanding I shall speak hereafter.

CHAP. III.

Of the Consequence or TRAYNE *of Imaginations.*

BY *Consequence*, or TRAYNE of Thoughts, I understand that succession of one Thought to another, which is called (to distinguish it from Discourse in words) *Mentall Discourse.*

When a man thinketh on any thing whatsoever, His next Thought after, is not altogether so casuall as it seems to be. Not every Thought to every Thought suc-

ceeds indifferently. But as wee have no Imagination, whereof we have not formerly had Sense, in whole, or in parts; so we have no Transition from one Imagination to another, whereof we never had the like before in our Senses. The reason whereof is this. All Fancies are Motions within us, reliques of those made in the Sense: And those motions that immediately succeeded one another in the sense, continue also together after Sense: In so much as the former comming again to take place, and be prædominant, the later followeth, by coherence of the matter moved, in such manner, as water upon a plain Table is drawn which way any one part of it is guided by the finger. But because in sense, to one and the same thing perceived, sometimes one thing, sometimes another succeedeth, it comes to passe in time, that in the Imagining of any thing, there is no certainty [9]
what we shall Imagine next; Onely this is certain, it shall be something that succeeded the same before, at one time or another.

Trayne of Thoughts unguided

This Trayne of Thoughts, or Mentall Discourse, is of two sorts. The first is *Unguided, without Designe*, and inconstant; Wherein there is no Passionate Thought, to govern and direct those that follow, to it self, as the end and scope of some desire, or other passion: In which case the thoughts are said to wander, and seem impertinent one to another, as in a Dream. Such are Commonly the thoughts of men, that are not onely without company, but also without care of any thing; though even then their Thoughts are as busie as at other times, but without harmony; as the sound which a Lute out of tune would yeeld to any man; or in tune, to one that could not play. And yet in this wild ranging of the mind, a man may oft-times perceive the way of it, and the dependance of one thought upon another. For in a Discourse of our present civill warre, what could seem more impertinent, than to ask (as one did) what was the value of a Roman Penny? Yet the Cohærence to me was manifest enough. For the Thought of the warre, introduced the Thought of the delivering up the King to his Enemies; The Thought of that, brought in the Thought of the delivering up of Christ; and that again the Thought of the 30 pence, which was the price of that treason . and thence easily followed that malicious question; and all this in a moment of time, for Thought is quick.

Trayne of Thoughts regulated. The second is more constant; as being *regulated* by some desire, and designe. For the impression made by such things as wee desire, or feare, is strong, and permanent, or, (if it cease for a time,) of quick return: so strong it is sometimes, as to hinder and break our sleep. From Desire, ariseth the Thought of some means we have seen produce the like of that which we ayme at; and from the thought of that, the thought of means to that mean; and so continually, till we come to some beginning within our own power. And because the End, by the greatnesse of the impression, comes often to mind, in case our thoughts begin to wander, they are quickly again reduced into the way: which observed by one of the seven wise men, made him give men this præcept, which is now worne out, *Respice finem*; this is to say, in all your actions, look often upon what you would have, as the thing that directs all your thoughts in the way to attain it

The Trayn of regulated Thoughts is of two kinds; One, when of an effect imagined, wee seek the causes, or means that produce it: and this is common to Man and Beast. The other is, when imagining any thing whatsoever, wee seek all the possible effects, that can by it be produced; that is to say, we imagine what we can do with it, when wee have it Of which I have not at any time seen any signe, but in man onely; for this is a curiosity hardly incident to the nature of any living creature that has no other Passion but sensuall, such as are hunger, thirst, lust, and anger. In summe, the Discourse of the Mind, when it is governed by designe, is nothing but *Seeking*, or the faculty of Inven-
[10] tion. which the Latines call *Sagacitas*, and *Solertia*, a hunting out of the causes, of some effect, present or past; or of the effects, of some present or past cause. Sometimes a man seeks what he hath lost; and from that place, and time, wherein hee misses it, his mind runs back, from place to place, and time to time, to find

where, and when he had it; that is to say, to find some certain, and limited time and place, in which to begin a method of seeking. Again, from thence, his thoughts run over the same places and times, to find what action, or other occasion might make him lose it. This we call *Remembrance*, or Calling to mind: the Latines call it *Reminiscentia*, as it were a *Re-conning* of our former actions. *Remembrance.*

Sometimes a man knows a place determinate, within the compasse whereof he is to seek; and then his thoughts run over all the parts thereof, in the same manner, as one would sweep a room, to find a jewell; or as a Spaniel ranges the field, till he find a sent; or as a man should run over the Alphabet, to start a rime.

Prudence

Sometime a man desires to know the event of an action; and then he thinketh of some like action past, and the events thereof one after another; supposing like events will follow like actions. As he that foresees what wil become of a Criminal, re-cons what he has seen follow on the like Crime before; having this order of thoughts, The Crime, the Officer, the Prison, the Judge, and the Gallowes. Which kind of thoughts is called *Foresight*, and *Prudence*, or *Providence*, and sometimes *Wisdome*; though such conjecture, through the difficulty of observing all circumstances, be very fallacious. But this is certain; by how much one man has more experience of things past, than another; by so much also he is more Prudent, and his expectations the seldomer faile him. The *Present* onely has a being in Nature, things *Past* have a being in the Memory onely, but things *to come* have no being at all, the *Future* being but a fiction of the mind, applying the sequels of actions Past, to the actions that are Present; which with most certainty is done by him that has most Experience; but not with certainty enough. And though it be called Prudence, when the Event answereth our Expectation; yet in its own nature, it is but Presumption For the foresight of things to come, which is Providence, belongs onely to him by whose will they are to come. From him onely, and supernaturally, proceeds Prophecy. The best Prophet naturally is the best guesser; and the best guesser, he that is most versed and studied in the matters he guesses at: for he hath most *Signes* to guesse by.

Signes. A *Signe*, is the Event Antecedent, of the Consequent; and contrarily, the Consequent of the Antecedent, when the like Consequences have been observed, before: And the oftner they have been observed, the lesse uncertain is the Signe. And therefore he that has most experience in any kind of businesse, has most Signes, whereby to guesse at the Future time; and consequently is the most prudent: And so much more prudent than he that is new in that kind of business, as not to be equalled by any advantage of naturall and extemporary wit: though perhaps many young men think the contrary.

Neverthelesse it is not Prudence that distinguisheth
[11] man from beast. There be beasts, that at a year old observe more, and pursue that which is for their good, more prudently, than a child can do at ten.

Conjecture of the time past. As Prudence is a *Præsumtion* of the *Future*, contracted from the *Experience* of time *Past*: So there is a Præsumtion of things Past taken from other things (not future but) past also. For he that hath seen by what courses and degrees, a flourishing State hath first come into civil warre, and then to ruine; upon the sight of the ruines of any other State, will guesse, the like warre, and the like courses have been there also. But this conjecture, has the same incertainty almost with the conjecture of the Future; both being grounded onely upon Experience.

There is no other act of mans mind, that I can remember, naturally planted in him, so, as to need no other thing, to the exercise of it, but to be born a man, and live with the use of his five Senses. Those other Faculties, of which I shall speak by and by, and which seem proper to man onely, are acquired, and encreased by study and industry; and of most men learned by instruction, and discipline; and proceed all from the invention of Words, and Speech. For besides Sense, and Thoughts, and the Trayne of thoughts, the mind of man has no other motion; though by the help of Speech, and Method, the same Facultyes may be improved to such a height, as to distinguish men from all other living Creatures.

Whatsoever we imagine, is *Finite*. Therefore there is no Idea, or conception of any thing we call *Infinite*. No man can have in his mind an Image of infinite magnitude; nor conceive infinite swiftness, infinite time, or infinite force, or infinite power. When we say any thing is infinite, we signifie onely, that we are not able to conceive the ends, and bounds of the thing named; having no Conception of the thing, but of our own inability. And therefore the Name of *God* is used, not to make us conceive him; (for he is *Incomprehensible*; and his greatnesse, and power are unconceivable;) but that we may honour him. Also because whatsoever (as I said before,) we conceive, has been perceived first by sense, either all at once, or by parts; a man can have no thought, representing any thing, not subject to sense. No man therefore can conceive any thing, but he must conceive it in some place; and indued with some determinate magnitude, and which may be divided into parts; nor that any thing is all in this place, and all in another place at the same time; nor that two, or more things can be in one, and the same place at once: For none of these things ever have, or can be incident to Sense; but are absurd speeches, taken upon credit (without any signification at all,) from deceived Philosophers, and deceived, or deceiving Schoolemen.

CHAP. IV. [12]

Of Speech.

Originall of Speech.

THE Invention of *Printing*, though ingenious, compared with the invention of *Letters*, is no great matter. But who was the first that found the use of Letters, is not known. He that first brought them into *Greece*, men say was *Cadmus*, the sonne of *Agenor*, King of Phænicia. A profitable Invention for continuing the memory of time past, and the conjunction of mankind, dispersed into so many, and distant regions of the Earth; and with all difficult, as proceeding from a watchfull observation of the divers motions of the Tongue, Palat, Lips, and other organs of Speech; whereby to make as many differences of characters, to remember them. But the most noble and profitable invention of all other, was that of SPEECH, consisting of *Names* or *Appellations*, and their Connexion; whereby men register their Thoughts; recall them when they are past; and also declare them one to another for mutuall utility and conversation; without which, there had been amongst men, neither Common-wealth, nor Society, nor Contract, nor Peace, no more than amongst Lyons, Bears, and Wolves. The first author of Speech was *God* himself, that instructed *Adam* how to name such creatures as he presented to his sight; For the Scripture goeth no further in this matter. But this was sufficient to direct him to adde more names, as the experience and use of the creatures should give him occasion; and to joyn them in such manner by degrees, as to make himself understood; and so by succession of time, so much language might be gotten, as he had found use for; though not so copious, as an Orator or Philosopher has need of. For I do not find any thing in the Scripture, out of which, directly or by consequence can be gathered, that *Adam* was taught the names of all Figures, Numbers, Measures, Colours, Sounds, Fancies, Relations; much less the names of Words and Speech, as *Generall, Speciall, Affirmative, Negative, Interrogative, Optative, Infinitive,* all which are usefull; and least of all, of *Entity, Intentionality, Quiddity,* and other insignificant words of the School

But all this language gotten, and augmented by *Adam* and his posterity, was again lost at the tower of *Babel*, when by the hand of God, every man was stricken for his rebellion, with an oblivion of his former language. And being hereby forced to disperse themselves into severall parts of the world, it must needs be, that the diversity of Tongues that now is, proceeded by degrees from them, in such manner, as need (the mother of all inventions) taught them; and in tract of time grew every where more copious.

The use of Speech. The generall use of Speech, is to transferre our Mentall Discourse, into Verbal, or the Trayne of our Thoughts, into a Trayne of Words; and that for two commodities, whereof one is, the Registring of the Consequences of [13] our Thoughts; which being apt to slip out of our memory, and put us to a new labour, may again be recalled, by such words as they were marked by. So that the first use of names, is to serve for *Markes*, or *Notes* of remembrance. Another is, when many use the same words, to signifie (by their connexion and order,) one to another, what they conceive, or think of each matter; and also what they desire, feare, or have any other passion for. And for this use they are called *Signes*. Speciall uses of Speech are these; First, to Register, what by cogitation, wee find to be the cause of any thing, present or past; and what we find things present or past may produce, or effect: which in summe, is acquiring of Arts. Secondly, to shew to others that knowledge which we have attained; which is, to Counsell, and Teach one another. Thirdly, to make known to others our wills, and purposes, that we may have the mutuall help of one another. Fourthly, to please and delight our selves, and others, by playing with our words, for pleasure or ornament, innocently.

Abuses of Speech

To these Uses, there are also foure correspondent Abuses. First, when men register their thoughts wrong, by the inconstancy of the signification of their words; by which they register for their conceptions, that which they never conceived; and so deceive themselves. Secondly, when they use words metaphorically; that is, in other sense than that they are ordained for; and thereby deceive others Thirdly, when by words they declare that to be their will, which is not. Fourthly, when they use them to grieve one another: for seeing nature hath armed living creatures, some with teeth, some with horns, and some with hands, to grieve an enemy, it is but an abuse of Speech, to grieve him with the tongue, unlesse it be one whom wee are obliged to govern; and then it is not to grieve, but to correct and amend.

The manner how Speech serveth to the remembrance of the consequence of causes and effects, consisteth in the imposing of *Names*, and the *Connexion* of them.

Names Proper & Common.

Of Names, some are *Proper*, and singular to one onely thing; as *Peter*, *John*, *This man*, *this Tree*: and some are *Common* to many things; as *Man, Horse, Tree*; every of which though but one Name, is nevertheless the name of divers particular things; in respect of all which together, it is called an *Universall*; there being nothing in the world Universall but Names; for the things named, are every one of them Individuall and Singular.

Universall

One Universall name is imposed on many things, for their similitude in some quality, or other accident: And wheras a Proper Name bringeth to mind one thing onely; Universals recall any one of those many.

And of Names Universall, some are of more, and some of lesse extent; the larger comprehending the less large: and some again of equall extent, comprehending each other reciprocally. As for example, the Name *Body* is of larger signification than the word *Man*, and comprehendeth it; and the names *Man* and *Rationall*, are of equall extent, comprehending mutually one another

[14] But here wee must take notice, that by a Name is not alwayes understood, as in Grammar, one onely Word; but sometimes by circumlocution many words together For all these words, *Hee that in his actions observeth the Lawes of his Country*, make but one Name, equivalent to this one word, *Just*.

By this imposition of Names, some of larger, some of stricter signification, we turn the reckoning of the consequences of things imagined in the mind, into a reckoning of the consequences of Appellations. For example, a man that hath no use of Speech at all, (such, as is born and remains perfectly deafe and dumb,) if he set before his eyes a triangle, and by it two right angles, (such as are the corners of a square figure,) he may by meditation compare and find, that the three angles of that triangle, are equall to those two right angles that stand by it. But if another triangle be shewn him different in shape from the former, he cannot know without a new labour, whether the three angles of that also be equall to the same. But he that hath the use of words, when he observes, that such equality was consequent, not to the length of the sides, nor to any other particular thing in his triangle, but onely to this, that the sides were straight, and the angles three; and that that was all, for which he named it a Triangle; will boldly conclude Universally, that such equality of angles is in all triangles whatsoever; and register his invention in these generall termes, *Every triangle hath its three angles equall to two right angles.* And thus the consequence found in one particular, comes to be registred and remembred, as an Universall rule; and discharges our mentall reckoning, of time and place; and delivers us from all labour of the mind, saving the first; and makes that which was found true *here*, and *now*, to be true in *all times* and *places*.

But the use of words in registring our thoughts, is in nothing so evident as in Numbring. A naturall foole that could never learn by heart the order of numerall words, as *one*, *two*, and *three*, may observe every stroak of the Clock, and nod to it, or say one, one, one; but can never know what houre it strikes. And it seems, there was a time when those names of number were not in use; and men were fayn to apply their fingers of one or both hands, to those things they desired to keep account of; and that thence it proceeded, that now our numerall words are but ten, in any Nation, and in some but five, and then they begin again. And he that can tell ten, if he recite them out of order, will lose himselfe, and not know when he has done: Much lesse will he be able to adde, and substract, and performe all other operations of Arithmetique. So that without words, there is no possibility of reckoning of Numbers; much lesse of Magnitudes, of Swiftnesse, of Force, and other things, the reckonings whereof are necessary to the being, or well-being of man-kind.

When two Names are joyned together into a Consequence, or Affirmation; as thus, *A man is a living creature*; or thus, *if he be a man, he is a living creature*, If the later name *Living creature*, signifie all that the former name *Man* signifieth, then the affirmation, or consequence is *true*; otherwise *false*. For *True* and *False* [15]
are attributes of Speech, not of Things. And where Speech is not, there is neither *Truth* nor *Falshood*. *Errour* there may be, as when wee expect that which

shall not be; or suspect what has not been: but in neither case can a man be charged with Untruth.

Necessity of Definitions. Seeing then that *truth* consisteth in the right ordering of names in our affirmations, a man that seeketh precise *truth*, had need to remember what every name he uses stands for; and to place it accordingly; or else he will find himselfe entangled in words, as a bird in lime-twiggs; the more he struggles, the more belimed. And therefore in Geometry, (which is the onely Science that it hath pleased God hitherto to bestow on mankind,) men begin at settling the significations of their words; which settling of significations, they call *Definitions*; and place them in the beginning of their reckoning.

By this it appears how necessary it is for any man that aspires to true Knowledge, to examine the Definitions of former Authors; and either to correct them, where they are negligently set down; or to make them himselfe. For the errours of Definitions multiply themselves, according as the reckoning proceeds; and lead men into absurdities, which at last they see, but cannot avoyd, without reckoning anew from the beginning; in which lyes the foundation of their errours. From whence it happens, that they which trust to books, do as they that cast up many little summs into a greater, without considering whether those little summes were rightly cast up or not; and at last finding the errour visible, and not mistrusting their first grounds, know not which way to cleere themselves, but spend time in fluttering over their bookes; as birds that entring by the chimney, and finding themselves inclosed in a chamber, flutter at the false light of a glasse window, for want of wit to consider which way they came in. So that in the right Definition of Names, lyes the first use of Speech; which is the Acquisition of Science: And in wrong, or no Definitions, lyes the first abuse; from which proceed all false and senslesse Tenets, which make those men that take their instruction from the authority of books, and not from their own meditation, to be as much below the condition of ignorant men, as men endued with true Science are above it. For between true Science, and erroneous Doctrines, Ignorance is in the middle. Naturall sense and imagination, are not subject to absurdity Nature it selfe cannot erre · and as men abound in copiousnesse of language; so they become more wise, or more mad than ordinary. Nor is it possible without Letters for any man to become either excellently wise, or (unless his memory be hurt by disease, or ill constitution of organs) excellently foolish. For words are wise mens counters, they do but reckon by them: but they are the mony of fooles, that value them by the authority of an *Aristotle*, a *Cicero*, or a *Thomas*, or any other Doctor whatsoever, if but a man.

Subject to Names

Subject to Names, is whatsoever can enter into, or be considered in an account; and be added one to another to make a summe; or substracted one from another, and leave a remainder The Latines called Accounts [16] of mony *Rationes*, and accounting, *Ratiocinatio*: and that which we in bills or books of account call *Items*, they called *Nomina*; that is, *Names*: and thence it seems to proceed, that they extended the word *Ratio*, to the faculty of Reckoning in all other things The Greeks have but one word λόγος, for both *Speech* and *Reason*; not that they thought there was no Speech without Reason; but no Reasoning without Speech. And the act of reasoning they called *Syllogisme*; which signifieth summing up of the consequences of one saying to another. And because the same things may enter into account for divers accidents; their names are (to shew that diversity) diversly wrested, and diversified. This diversity of names may be reduced to foure generall heads.

First, a thing may enter into account for *Matter*, or *Body*; as *living*, *sensible*, *rationall*, *hot*, *cold*, *moved*, *quiet*; with all which names the word *Matter*, or *Body* is understood; all such, being names of Matter.

Secondly, it may enter into account, or be considered, for some accident or quality, which we conceive to be in it; as for *being moved*, for *being so long*, for *being hot*, &c; and then, of the name of the thing it selfe, by a little change or wresting, wee make a name for that accident, which we consider, and for *living* put into the account *life*; for *moved*, *motion*; for *hot*, *heat*; for *long*, *length*, and the like: And all such Names, are the names of the accidents and properties, by which one Matter, and Body is distinguished from another These are called *names Abstract*; because severed (not from Matter, but) from the account of Matter.

Thirdly, we bring into account, the Properties of our own bodies, whereby we make such distinction: as when any thing is *Seen* by us, we reckon not the thing it selfe; but the *sight*, the *Colour*, the *Idea* of it in the fancy· and when any thing is *heard*, wee reckon it not; but the *hearing*, or *sound* onely, which is our fancy or conception of it by the Eare: and such are names of fancies.

Fourthly, we bring into account, consider, and give names, to *Names* themselves, and to *Speeches*: For, *generall, universall, speciall, æquivocall,* are names of Names. And *Affirmation, Interrogation, Commandement, Narration, Syllogisme, Sermon, Oration,* and many other such, are names of Speeches. And this is all the variety of Names *Positive*; which are put to mark somewhat which is in Nature, or may be feigned by the mind of man, as Bodies that are, or may be conceived to be; or of bodies, the Properties that are, or may be feigned to be; or Words and Speech.

Use of Names Positive

Negative Names with their Uses.

There be also other Names, called *Negative*; which are notes to signifie that a word is not the name of the thing in question; as these words *Nothing, no man, infinite, indocible, three want foure,* and the like; which are nevertheless of use in reckoning, or in correcting of reckoning; and call to mind our past cogitations, though they be not names of any thing; because they make us refuse to admit of Names not rightly used.

Words insig-[17]nificant.

All other Names, are but insignificant sounds; and those of two sorts. One, when they are new, and yet their meaning not explained by Definition; whereof there have been aboundance coyned by Schoole-men, and pusled Philosophers.

Another, when men make a name of two Names, whose significations are contradictory and inconsistent, as this name, an *incorporeall body,* or (which is all one) an *incorporeall substance,* and a great number more. For whensoever any affirmation is false, the two names of which it is composed, put together and made one, signifie nothing at all. For example, if it be a false affirmation to say *a quadrangle is round*, the word *round quadrangle* signifies nothing; but is a meere sound. So likewise if it be false, to say that vertue can be powred, or blown up and down; the words *In-powred vertue*, *In-blown vertue*, are as absurd and insignificant, as a *round quadrangle*. And therefore you shall hardly meet with a senslesse and insignificant word, that is not made up of some Latin or Greek names. A Frenchman seldome hears our Saviour called by the name of *Parole*, but by the name of *Verbe* often; yet *Verbe* and *Parole* differ no more, but that one is Latin, the other French.

Understanding

When a man upon the hearing of any Speech, hath those thoughts which the words of that Speech, and their connexion, were ordained and constituted to signifie; Then he is said to understand it: *Understanding* being nothing else, but conception caused by Speech. And therefore if Speech be peculiar to man (as for ought I know it is,) then is Understanding peculiar to him also. And therefore of absurd and false affirmations, in case they be universall, there can be no Understanding; though many think they understand, then, when they do but repeat the words softly, or con them in their mind.

What kinds of Speeches signifie the Appetites, Aversions, and Passions of mans mind; and of their use and abuse, I shall speak when I have spoken of the Passions.

Inconstant names.

The names of such things as affect us, that is, which please, and displease us, because all men be not alike affected with the same thing, nor the same man at all times, are in the common discourses of men, of *inconstant* signification For seeing all names are imposed to signifie our conceptions; and all our affections are but conceptions; when we conceive the same things differently, we can harldy avoyd different naming of them For though the nature of that we conceive, be the same; yet the diversity of our reception of it, in respect of different constitutions of body, and prejudices of opinion, gives every thing a tincture of our different passions And therefore in reasoning, a man must take heed of words; which besides the signification of what we imagine of their nature, have a signification also of the nature, disposition, and interest of the speaker; such as are the names of Vertues, and Vices; For one man calleth *Wisdome*, what another calleth *feare*; and one *cruelty*, what another *justice*; one *prodigality*, what another *magnanimity*; and one *gravity*, what another *stupidity*, &c. And therefore such names can never be true grounds of any ratiocination. No more can Metaphors, and Tropes of speech: but these are less dangerous, because they profess their inconstancy; which the other do not.

[18]

CHAP. V.

Of REASON, and SCIENCE.

Reason what it is. WHEN a man *Reasoneth*, hee does nothing else but conceive a summe totall, from *Addition* of parcels; or conceive a Remainder, from *Substraction* of one summe from another: which (if it be done by Words,) is conceiving of the consequence of the names of all the parts, to the name of the whole; or from the names of the whole and one part, to the name of the other part. And though in some things, (as in numbers,) besides *Adding* and *Substracting*, men name other operations, as *Multiplying* and *Dividing*; yet they are the same; for Multiplication, is but Adding together of things equall; and Division, but Substracting of one thing, as often as we can. These operations are not incident to Numbers onely, but to all manner of things that can be added together, and taken one out of another. For as Arithmeticians teach to adde and substract in *numbers*; so the Geometricians teach the same in *lines*, *figures* (solid and superficiall,) *angles*, *proportions*, *times*, degrees of *swiftnesse*, *force*, *power*, and the like; The Logicians teach the same in *Consequences of words*; adding together *two Names*, to make an *Affirmation*; and *two Affirmations*, to make a *Syllogisme*; and *many Syllogismes* to make a *Demonstration*, and from the *summe*, or *Conclusion* of a *Syllogisme*, they substract one *Proposition*, to finde the other. Writers of Politiques, adde together *Pactions*, to find mens *duties*, and Lawyers, *Lawes*, and *facts*, to find what is *right* and *wrong* in the actions of private men.

In summe, in what matter soever there is place for *addition* and *substraction,* there also is place for *Reason* ; and where these have no place, there *Reason* has nothing at all to do.

Reason defined.

Out of all which we may define, (that is to say determine,) what that is, which is meant by this word *Reason,* when wee reckon it amongst the Faculties of the mind. For REASON, in this sense, is nothing but *Reckoning* (that is, Adding and Substracting) of the Consequences of generall names agreed upon, for the *marking* and *signifying* of our thoughts ; I say *marking* them, when we reckon by our selves ; and *signifying,* when we demonstrate, or approve our reckonings to other men

Right Reason where.

And as in Arithmetique, unpractised men must, and Professors themselves may often erre, and cast up false ; so also in any other subject of Reasoning, the ablest, most attentive, and most practised men, may deceive themselves, and inferre false Conclusions ; Not but that Reason it selfe is alwayes Right Reason, as well as Arithmetique is a certain and infallible Art : But no one mans Reason, nor the Reason of any one number of men, makes the certaintie ; no more than an account is therefore well cast up, because a great many men have unanimously approved it. And therfore, as when there is a controversy in an account, the parties must by their [19] own accord, set up for right Reason, the Reason of some Arbitrator, or Judge, to whose sentence they will both stand, or their controversie must either come to blowes, or be undecided, for want of a right Reason constituted by Nature ; so is it also in all debates of what kind soever : And when men that think themselves wiser than all others, clamor and demand right Reason for judge ; yet seek no more, but that things should be determined, by no other mens reason but their own, it is as intolerable in the society of men, as it is in play after trump is turned, to use for trump on every occasion, that suite whereof they have most in their hand. For they do nothing els, that will have every of their passions, as it comes to bear sway in them, to be taken for right Reason, and that in their own controversies bewraying their want of right Reason, by the claym they lay to it.

The use of Reason.

The Use and End of Reason, is not the finding of the summe, and truth of one, or a few consequences, remote from the first definitions, and settled significations of names; but to begin at these; and proceed from one consequence to another. For there can be no certainty of the last Conclusion, without a certainty of all those Affirmations and Negations, on which it was grounded, and inferred. As when a master of a family, in taking an account, casteth up the summs of all the bills of expence, into one sum; and not regarding how each bill is summed up, by those that give them in account; nor what it is he payes for; he advantages himself no more, than if he allowed the account in grosse, trusting to every of the accountants skill and honesty: so also in Reasoning of all other things, he that takes up conclusions on the trust of Authors, and doth not fetch them from the first Items in every Reckoning, (which are the significations of names settled by definitions), loses his labour; and does not know any thing; but onely beleeveth.

Of Error and Absurdity

When a man reckons without the use of words, which may be done in particular things, (as when upon the sight of any one thing, wee conjecture what was likely to have preceded, or is likely to follow upon it;) if that which he thought likely to follow, followes not; or that which he thought likely to have preceded it, hath not preceded it, this is called ERROR; to which even the most prudent men are subject. But when we Reason in Words of generall signification, and fall upon a generall inference which is false; though it be commonly called *Error*, it is indeed an ABSURDITY, or senslesse Speech For Error is but a deception, in presuming that somewhat is past, or to come; of which, though it were not past, or not to come; yet there was no impossibility discoverable. But when we make a generall assertion, unlesse it be a true one, the possibility of it is unconceivable. And words whereby we conceive nothing but the sound, are those we call *Absurd*, *Insignificant*, and *Non-sense*. And therefore if a man should talk to me of a *round Quadrangle*; or *accidents of Bread in Cheese*, or *Immateriall Substances*; or of *A free Subject*; *A free-Will*; or any

Free, but free from being hindred by opposition, I should not say he were in an Errour; but that his words were without meaning; that is to say, Absurd.

I have said before, (in the second chapter,) that a Man [20] did excell all other Animals in this faculty, that when he conceived any thing whatsoever, he was apt to enquire the consequences of it, and what effects he could do with it. And now I adde this other degree of the same excellence, that he can by words reduce the consequences he findes to generall Rules, called *Theoremes*, or *Aphorismes*; that is, he can Reason, or reckon, not onely in number; but in all other things, whereof one may be added unto, or substracted from another.

But this priviledge, is allayed by another; and that is, by the priviledge of Absurdity; to which no living creature is subject, but man onely. And of men, those are of all most subject to it, that professe Philosophy. For it is most true that *Cicero* sayth of them somewhere; that there can be nothing so absurd, but may be found in the books of Philosophers And the reason is manifest. For there is not one of them that begins his ratiocination from the Definitions, or Explications of the names they are to use, which is a method that hath been used onely in Geometry; whose Conclusions have thereby been made indisputable.

Causes of absurditie I.

The first cause of Absurd conclusions I ascribe to the want of Method. in that they begin not their Ratiocination from Definitions; that is, from settled significations of their words: as if they could cast account, without knowing the value of the numerall words, *one*, *two*, and *three*

And whereas all bodies enter into account upon divers considerations, (which I have mentioned in the precedent chapter,) these considerations being diversly named, divers absurdities proceed from the confusion, and unfit connexion of their names into assertions. And therefore

The second cause of Absurd assertions, I ascribe to the giving of names of *bodies*, to *accidents*; or of *accidents*, to *bodies*, As they do, that say, *Faith is infused*, or *inspired*, when nothing can be *powred*, or *breathed* into any thing, but body; and that, *extension* is *body*; that *phantasmes* are *spirits*, &c.

3. The third I ascribe to the giving of the names of the *accidents* of *bodies without us*, to the *accidents* of our *own bodies*; as they do that say, the *colour is in the body*; *the sound is in the ayre*, &c.

4. The fourth, to the giving of the names of *bodies*, to *names*, or *speeches*; as they do that say, that *there be things universall*; that *a living creature is Genus*, or *a generall thing*, &c.

5. The fifth, to the giving of the names of *accidents*, to *names* and *speeches*; as they do that say, *the nature of a thing is its definition*; *a mans command is his will*; and the like.

6. The sixth, to the use of Metaphors, Tropes, and other Rhetoricall figures, in stead of words proper. For though it be lawfull to say; (for example) in common speech, *the way goeth, or leadeth hither, or thither, The Proverb sayes this or that* (whereas wayes cannot go, nor Proverbs speak:) yet in reckoning, and seeking of truth, such speeches are not to be admitted.

7. The seventh, to names that signifie nothing; but are
[21] taken up, and learned by rote from the Schooles, as *hypostatical, transubstantiate, consubstantiate, eternal-Now* and the like canting of Schoolemen.

To him that can avoyd these things, it is not easie to fall into any absurdity, unlesse it be by the length of an account; wherein he may perhaps forget what went before. For all men by nature reason alike, and well, when they have good principles. For who is so stupid, as both to mistake in Geometry, and also to persist in it, when another detects his error to him?

Science. By this it appears that Reason is not as Sense, and Memory, borne with us; nor gotten by Experience onely, as Prudence is; but attayned by Industry; first in apt imposing of Names; and secondly by getting a good and orderly Method in proceeding from the Elements, which are Names, to Assertions made by Connexion of one of them to another; and so to Syllogismes, which are the Connexions of one Assertion to another, till we come to a knowledge of all the Consequences of names appertaining to the subject in hand; and that is it, men call SCIENCE. And whereas Sense and Memory are but knowledge of Fact, which is a thing past, and irrevocable, *Science* is the knowledge of Consequences, and dependance of one fact upon another. by which, out of that we can presently do, we know how to do something else when we will, or the like, another time: Because when we see how any thing comes about, upon what causes, and by what manner; when the like causes come into our power, wee see how to make it produce the like effects.

Children therefore are not endued with Reason at all, till they have attained the use of Speech: but are called Reasonable Creatures, for the possibility apparent of having the use of Reason in time to come. And the most part of men, though they have the use of Reasoning a little way, as in numbring to some degree; yet it serves them to little use in common life; in which they govern themselves, some better, some worse, according to their differences of experience, quicknesse of memory, and inclinations to severall ends; but specially according to good or evill fortune, and the errors of one another. For as for *Science*, or certain rules of their actions, they are so farre from it, that they know not what it is. Geometry they have thought Conjuring: But for other Sciences, they who have not been taught the beginnings, and some progresse in them, that they may see how they be acquired and generated, are in this point like children, that having no thought of generation, are made believe by the women, that their brothers and sisters are not born, but found in the garden.

But yet they that have no *Science*, are in better, and nobler condition with their naturall Prudence, than men, that by mis-reasoning, or by trusting them that reason wrong, fall upon false and absurd generall rules. For ignorance of causes, and of rules, does not set men so farre out of their way, as relying on false rules, and taking for causes of what they aspire to, those that are not so, but rather causes of the contrary.

To conclude, The Light of humane minds is Perspicuous
Words, but by exact definitions first snuffed, and purged [22]
from ambiguity; *Reason* is the *pace*; Encrease of *Science*, the *way*, and the Benefit of man-kind, the *end*. And on the contrary, Metaphors, and senslesse and

ambiguous words, are like *ignes fatui*; and reasoning upon them, is wandering amongst innumerable absurdities; and their end, contention, and sedition, or contempt.

Prudence & Sapience, with their difference.

As, much Experience, is *Prudence*; so, is much Science, *Sapience*. For though wee usually have one name of Wisedome for them both; yet the Latines did alwayes distinguish between *Prudentia* and *Sapientia*; ascribing the former to Experience, the later to Science. But to make their difference appeare more cleerly, let us suppose one man endued with an excellent naturall use, and dexterity in handling his armes; and another to have added to that dexterity, an acquired Science, of where he can offend, or be offended by his adversarie, in every possible posture, or guard: The ability of the former, would be to the ability of the later, as Prudence to Sapience; both usefull; but the later infallible. But they that trusting onely to the authority of books, follow the blind blindly, are like him that trusting to the false rules of a master of Fence, ventures præsumptuously upon an adversary, that either kills, or disgraces him.

Signes of Science

The signes of Science, are some, certain and infallible; some, uncertain. Certain, when he that pretendeth the Science of any thing, can teach the same; that is to say, demonstrate the truth thereof perspicuously to another: Uncertain, when onely some particular events answer to his pretence, and upon many occasions prove so as he sayes they must. Signes of prudence are all uncertain; because to observe by experience, and remember all circumstances that may alter the successe, is impossible. But in any businesse, whereof a man has not infallible Science to proceed by; to forsake his own naturall judgement, and be guided by generall sentences read in Authors, and subject to many exceptions, is a signe of folly, and generally scorned by the name of Pedantry. And even of those men themselves, that in Councells of the Common-wealth, love to shew their reading of Politiques and History, very few do it in their domestique affaires, where their particular interest is concerned: having Prudence enough for their private affaires: but in publique they study more the reputation of their owne wit, than the successe of anothers businesse.

CHAP. VI. [23]

Of the Interiour Beginnings of Voluntary Motions; commonly called the PASSIONS. *And the Speeches by which they are expressed.*

Motion Vitall and Animal.

THERE be in Animals, two sorts of *Motions* peculiar to them: One called *Vitall*; begun in generation, and continued without interruption through their whole life; such as are the *course* of the *Bloud*, the *Pulse*, the *Breathing*, the *Concoction, Nutrition, Excretion*, &c; to which Motions there needs no help of Imagination: The other is *Animall motion*, otherwise called *Voluntary motion*; as to *go*, to *speak*, to *move* any of our limbes, in such manner as is first fancied in our minds. That Sense, is Motion in the organs and interiour parts of mans body, caused by the action of the things we See, Heare, &c; And that Fancy is but the Reliques of the same Motion, remaining after Sense, has been already sayd in the first and second Chapters. And because *going*, *speaking*, and the like Voluntary motions, depend alwayes upon a precedent thought of *whither, which way*, and *what*; it is evident, that the Imagination is the first internall beginning of all Voluntary Motion. And although unstudied men, doe not conceive any motion at all to be there, where the thing moved is invisible; or the space it is moved in, is (for the shortnesse of it) insensible; yet that doth not hinder, but that such Motions are. For let a space be never so little, that which is moved over a greater space, whereof that little one is part, must first be moved over that. These small beginnings of Motion, within the body of Man, before they appear in walking, speaking, striking, and other visible actions, are commonly called ENDEAVOUR.

Endeavour.

Appetite. Desire. Hunger. Thirst. Aversion.

This Endeavour, when it is toward something which causes it, is called APPETITE, or DESIRE; the later, being the generall name; and the other, often-times restrayned to signifie the Desire of Food, namely *Hunger* and *Thirst*. And when the Endeavour is fromward something, it is generally called AVERSION. These words *Appetite*, and *Aversion* we have from the *Latines*; and they both of them signifie the motions, one of approaching, the other of retiring. So also do the Greek words for the same, which are ὁρμὴ, and ἀφορμὴ. For Nature it selfe does often presse upon men those truths, which afterwards, when they look for somewhat beyond Nature, they stumble at. For the Schooles find in meere Appetite to go, or move, no actuall Motion at all: but because some Motion they must acknowledge, they call it Metaphoricall Motion; which is but an absurd speech: for though Words may be called metaphoricall; Bodies, and Motions cannot

Love. *Hate.* That which men Desire, they are also sayd to LOVE: and to HATE those things, for which they have Aversion.
[24] So that Desire, and Love, are the same thing; save that by Desire, we alwayes signifie the Absence of the Object; by Love, most commonly the Presence of the same. So also by Aversion, we signifie the Absence, and by Hate, the Presence of the Object.

Of Appetites, and Aversions, some are born with men; as Appetite of food, Appetite of excretion, and exoneration, (which may also and more properly be called Aversions, from somewhat they feele in their Bodies;) and some other Appetites, not many. The rest, which are Appetites of particular things, proceed from Experience, and triall of their effects upon themselves, or other men. For of things wee know not at all, or believe not to be, we can have no further Desire, than to tast and try. But Aversion wee have for things, not onely which we know have hurt us; but also that we do not know whether they will hurt us, or not.

Contempt. Those things which we neither Desire, nor Hate, we are said to *Contemne*: CONTEMPT being nothing else but an immobility, or contumacy of the Heart, in resisting the action of certain things; and proceeding from that the Heart is already moved otherwise, by other more potent objects; or from want of experience of them.

And because the constitution of a mans Body, is in continuall mutation; it is impossible that all the same things should alwayes cause in him the same Appetites, and Aversions. much lesse can all men consent, in the Desire of almost any one and the same Object.

But whatsoever is the object of any mans Appetite or Desire; that is it, which he for his part calleth *Good* *Good.* And the object of his Hate, and Aversion, *Evill*; And of *Evill.* his Contempt, *Vile* and *Inconsiderable.* For these words of Good, Evill, and Contemptible, are ever used with relation to the person that useth them: There being nothing simply and absolutely so; nor any common Rule of Good and Evill, to be taken from the nature of the objects themselves; but from the Person of the man (where there is no Common-wealth;) or, (in a Common-wealth,) from the Person that representeth it; or from an Arbitrator or Judge, whom men disagreeing shall by consent set up, and make his sentence the Rule thereof.

The Latine Tongue has two words, whose significations approach to those of Good and Evill; but are not precisely the same; And those are *Pulchrum* and *Turpe.* *Pulchrum.* *Turpe.* Whereof the former signifies that, which by some apparent signes promiseth Good; and the later, that, which promiseth Evil. But in our Tongue we have not so generall names to expresse them by. But for *Pulchrum,* we say in some things, *Fayre*; in others, *Beautifull,* or *Handsome*; or *Gallant,* or *Honourable,* or *Comely,* or *Amiable*, and for *Turpe, Foule, Deformed, Ugly, Base, Nauseous,* and the like, as the subject shall require; All which words, in their proper places signifie nothing els, but the *Mine,* or Countenance, that promiseth Good and Evil. So that of Good there be three kinds; Good in the Promise, that is *Pulchrum*, Good in Effect, as the end desired, which is called *Jucundum, Delightfull*; and *Delightfull.* Good as the Means, which is called *Utile, Profitable*; and *Profitable.* as many of Evil: For *Evill,* in Promise, is that they call *Turpe*, Evil in Effect, and End, is *Molestum, Unpleasant,* [25] *Troublesome*: and Evill in the Means, *Inutile, Unprofitable, Hurtfull.* *Unpleasant.* *Unprofitable.*

As, in Sense, that which is really within us, is (as I have sayd before) onely Motion, caused by the action of externall objects, but in apparence; to the Sight, Light and Colour; to the Eare, Sound; to the Nostrill, Odour, *&c*: so, when the action of the same object is continued from the Eyes, Eares, and other organs to the Heart; the reall effect there is nothing but Motion, or Endeavour; which consisteth in Appetite, or Aversion, to, or from the object moving. But the apparence, or sense of that motion, is that wee either call DELIGHT, or TROUBLE OF MIND.

Delight Displeasure.

Pleasure

This Motion, which is called Appetite, and for the apparence of it *Delight*, and *Pleasure*, seemeth to be, a corroboration of Vitall motion, and a help thereunto; and therefore such things as caused Delight, were not improperly called *Jucunda*, (*à Juvando*,) from helping or fortifying; and the contrary, *Molesta*, *Offensive*, from hindering, and troubling the motion vitall.

Offence

Pleasure therefore, (or *Delight*,) is the apparence, or sense of Good; and *Molestation* or *Displeasure*, the apparence, or sense of Evill. And consequently all Appetite, Desire, and Love, is accompanied with some Delight more or lesse; and all Hatred, and Aversion, with more or lesse Displeasure and Offence.

Pleasures of sense

Of Pleasures, or Delights, some arise from the sense of an object Present; And those may be called *Pleasures of Sense*, (The word *sensuall*, as it is used by those onely that condemn them, having no place till there be Lawes.) Of this kind are all Onerations and Exonerations of the body; as also all that is pleasant, in the *Sight*, *Hearing*, *Smell*, *Tast*, *or Touch*; Others arise from the Expectation, that proceeds from foresight of the End, or Consequence of things; whether those things in the Sense Please or Displease. And these are *Pleasures of the Mind* of him that draweth those consequences; and are generally called JOY In the like manner, Displeasures, are some in the Sense, and called PAYNE, others, in the Expectation of consequences, and are called GRIEFE.

Pleasures of the Mind.
Joy.
Paine.
Griefe.

These simple Passions called *Appetite*, *Desire*, *Love*, *Aversion*, *Hate*, *Joy*, and *Griefe*, have their names for divers considerations diversified. As first, when they one succeed another, they are diversly called from the opinion men have of the likelihood of attaining what they desire. Secondly, from the object loved or hated Thirdly, from the consideration of many of them together. Fourthly, from the Alteration or succession it selfe.

For *Appetite* with an opinion of attaining, is called HOPE. *Hope.*

The same, without such opinion, DESPAIRE. *Despaire.*

Aversion, with opinion of *Hurt* from the object, FEARE. *Feare.*

The same, with hope of avoyding that Hurt by resistence, COURAGE. *Courage.*

Sudden *Courage,* ANGER. *Anger.*

Constant *Hope,* CONFIDENCE of our selves. *Confidence.*

Constant *Despayre,* DIFFIDENCE of our selves. *Diffidence.*

Anger for great hurt done to another, when we conceive [26]
the same to be done by Injury, INDIGNATION. *Indignation.*

Desire of good to another, BENEVOLENCE, GOOD WILL, CHARITY. If to man generally, GOOD NATURE. *Benevolence.* *Good Nature.*

Desire of Riches, COVETOUSNESSE: a name used alwayes in signification of blame; because men contending for them, are displeased with one anothers attaining them; though the desire in it selfe, be to be blamed, or allowed, according to the means by which those Riches are sought. *Covetousnesse.*

Desire of Office, or precedence, AMBITION: a name used also in the worse sense, for the reason before mentioned. *Ambition.*

Desire of things that conduce but a little to our ends; And fear of things that are but of little hindrance, PUSILLANIMITY. *Pusillanimity.*

Contempt of little helps, and hindrances, MAGNANIMITY. *Magnanimity.*

Magnanimity, in danger of Death, or Wounds, VALOUR, FORTITUDE. *Valour.*

Magnanimity, in the use of Riches, LIBERALITY. *Liberality.*

Pusillanimity, in the same WRETCHEDNESSE, MISERABLENESSE; or PARSIMONY; as it is liked, or disliked. *Miserablenesse.*

Love of Persons for society, KINDNESSE. *Kindnesse.*

Love of Persons for Pleasing the sense onely, NATURALL LUST. *Naturall Lust.*

Love of the same, acquired from Rumination, that is, Imagination of Pleasure past, LUXURY. *Luxury.*

Love of one singularly, with desire to be singularly beloved, THE PASSION OF LOVE. The same, with fear that the love is not mutuall, JEALOUSIE. *The Passion of Love.* *Jealousie.*

Desire, by doing hurt to another, to make him condemn some fact of his own, REVENGEFULNESSE. *Revengefulnesse.*

Curiosity. *Desire*, to know why, and how, CURIOSITY ; such as is in no living creature but *Man* : so that Man is distinguished, not onely by his Reason ; but also by this singular Passion from other *Animals* ; in whom the appetite of food, and other pleasures of Sense, by prædominance, take away the care of knowing causes ; which is a Lust of the mind, that by a perseverance of delight in the continuall and indefatigable generation of Knowledge, exceedeth the short vehemence of any carnall Pleasure.

Religion. Superstition. True Religion. *Feare* of power invisible, feigned by the mind, or imagined from tales publiquely allowed, RELIGION ; not allowed, SUPERSTITION. And when the power imagined, is truly such as we imagine, TRUE RELIGION

Panique Terrour. *Feare*, without the apprehension of why, or what, PANIQUE TERROR ; called so from the Fables, that make *Pan* the author of them , whereas in truth, there is alwayes in him that so feareth, first, some apprehension of the cause, though the rest run away by Example ; every one supposing his fellow to know why And therefore this Passion happens to none but in a throng, or multitude of people.

Admiration. *Joy*, from apprehension of novelty, ADMIRATION ; proper to Man, because it excites the appetite of knowing the cause.

Joy, arising from imagination of a mans own power
[27] and ability, is that exultation of the mind which is called
Glory. GLORYING : which if grounded upon the experience of his own former actions, is the same with *Confidence* : but if grounded on the flattery of others ; or onely supposed by himself, for delight in the consequences of it, is called *Vain-glory.* VAINE-GLORY · which name is properly given ; because a well grounded *Confidence* begetteth Attempt ; whereas the supposing of power does not, and is therefore rightly called *Vaine*.

Dejection. *Griefe*, from opinion of want of power, is called DEJECTION of mind.

The *vain-glory* which consisteth in the feigning or supposing of abilities in our selves, which we know are not, is most incident to young men, and nourished by the Histories, or Fictions of Gallant Persons ; and is corrected oftentimes by Age, and Employment.

Sudden Glory, is the passion which maketh those *Grimaces* called LAUGHTER; and is caused either by some sudden act of their own, that pleaseth them; or by the apprehension of some deformed thing in another, by comparison whereof they suddenly applaud themselves. And it is incident most to them, that are conscious of the fewest abilities in themselves; who are forced to keep themselves in their own favour, by observing the imperfections of other men. And therefore much Laughter at the defects of others, is a signe of Pusillanimity. For of great minds, one of the proper workes is, to help and free others from scorn; and compare themselves onely with the most able. *Sudden Glory. Laughter.*

On the contrary, *Sudden Dejection*, is the passion that causeth WEEPING; and is caused by such accidents, as suddenly take away some vehement hope, or some prop of their power: And they are most subject to it, that rely principally on helps externall, such as are Women, and Children. Therefore some Weep for the losse of Friends; Others for their unkindnesse; others for the sudden stop made to their thoughts of revenge, by Reconciliation. But in all cases, both Laughter, and Weeping, are sudden motions; Custome taking them both away. For no man Laughs at old jests; or Weeps for an old calamity. *Sudden Dejection. Weeping.*

Griefe, for the discovery of some defect of ability, is SHAME, or the passion that discovereth it selfe in BLUSHING; and consisteth in the apprehension of some thing dishonourable; and in young men, is a signe of the love of good reputation; and commendable: In old men it is a signe of the same; but because it comes too late, not commendable. *Shame. Blushing.*

The *Contempt* of good Reputation is called IMPUDENCE. *Impudence.*

Griefe, for the Calamity of another, is PITTY; and ariseth from the imagination that the like calamity may befall himselfe; and therefore is called also COMPASSION, and in the phrase of this present time a FELLOW-FEELING: And therefore for Calamity arriving from great wickedness, the best men have the least Pitty; and for the same Calamity, those have least Pitty, that think themselves least obnoxious to the same. *Pitty.*

Cruelty. *Contempt*, or little sense of the calamity of others, is [28] that which men call CRUELTY ; proceeding from Security of their own fortune. For, that any man should take pleasure in other mens great harmes, without other end of his own, I do not conceive it possible.

Griefe, for the successe of a Competitor in wealth, honour, or other good, if it be joyned with Endeavour to enforce our own abilities to equall or exceed him, is called EMULATION : But joyned with Endeavour to supplant, or hinder a Competitor, ENVIE.

Emulation.

Envy.

When in the mind of man, Appetites, and Aversions, Hopes, and Feares, concerning one and the same thing, arise alternately ; and divers good and evill consequences of the doing, or omitting the thing propounded, come successively into our thoughts ; so that sometimes we have an Appetite to it ; sometimes an Aversion from it ; sometimes Hope to be able to do it ; sometimes Despaire, or Feare to attempt it ; the whole summe of Desires, Aversions, Hopes and Fears, continued till the thing be either done, or thought impossible, is that we call DELIBERATION.

Deliberation.

Therefore of things past, there is no *Deliberation* ; because manifestly impossible to be changed : nor of things known to be impossible, or thought so ; because men know, or think such Deliberation vain. But of things impossible, which we think possible, we may Deliberate ; not knowing it is in vain. And it is called *Deliberation* ; because it is a putting an end to the *Liberty* we had of doing, or omitting, according to our own Appetite, or Aversion.

This alternate Succession of Appetites, Aversions, Hopes and Fears, is no lesse in other living Creatures then in Man : and therefore Beasts also Deliberate.

Every *Deliberation* is then sayd to *End*, when that whereof they Deliberate, is either done, or thought impossible ; because till then wee retain the liberty of doing, or omitting, according to our Appetite, or Aversion.

In *Deliberation*, the last Appetite, or Aversion, immediately adhæring to the action, or to the omission thereof, is that wee call the WILL ; the Act, (not the faculty,) of *Willing*. And Beasts that have *Deliberation*, must

The Will

necessarily also have *Will*. The Definition of the *Will*, given commonly by the Schooles, that it is a *Rationall Appetite*, is not good. For if it were, then could there be no Voluntary Act against Reason. For a *Voluntary Act* is that, which proceedeth from the *Will*, and no other. But if in stead of a Rationall Appetite, we shall say an Appetite resulting from a precedent Deliberation, then the Definition is the same that I have given here. *Will* therefore *is the last Appetite in Deliberating*. And though we say in common Discourse, a man had a Will once to do a thing, that neverthelesse he forbore to do; yet that is properly but an Inclination, which makes no Action Voluntary, because the action depends not of it, but of the last Inclination, or Appetite. For if the intervenient Appetites, make any action Voluntary, then by the same Reason all intervenient Aversions, should make the same action Involuntary; and so one and the same action, should be both Voluntary & Involuntary.

By this it is manifest, that not onely actions that have [29]
their beginning from Covetousnesse, Ambition, Lust, or other Appetites to the thing propounded; but also those that have their beginning from Aversion, or Feare of those consequences that follow the omission, are *voluntary actions*.

Formes of Speech, in Passion

The formes of Speech by which the Passions are expressed, are partly the same, and partly different from those, by which wee expresse our Thoughts. And first, generally all Passions may be expressed *Indicatively*; as *I love, I feare, I joy, I deliberate, I will, I command*: but some of them have particular expressions by themselves, which neverthelesse are not affirmations, unlesse it be when they serve to make other inferences, besides that of the Passion they proceed from. Deliberation is expressed *Subjunctively*; which is a speech proper to signifie suppositions, with their consequences; as, *If this be done, then this will follow*; and differs not from the language of Reasoning, save that Reasoning is in generall words, but Deliberation for the most part is of Particulars. The language of Desire, and Aversion, is *Imperative*; as *Do this, forbeare that*; which when the party is obliged to do, or forbeare, is *Command*, otherwise *Prayer*; or els *Counsell* The language of Vain-Glory, of Indignation, Pitty and Revengefulness, *Optative*: But of the Desire to know, there is a peculiar expression, called *Interrogative*; as, *What is it, when shall it, how is it done,* and *why so?* other language of the Passions I find none. For Cursing, Swearing, Reviling, and the like, do not signifie as Speech; but as the actions of a tongue accustomed.

These formes of Speech, I say, are expressions, or voluntary significations of our Passions: but certain signes they be not; because they may be used arbitrarily, whether they that use them, have such Passions or not The best signes of Passions present, are either in the countenance, motions of the body, actions, and ends, or aimes, which we otherwise know the man to have.

And because in Deliberation, the Appetites, and Aversions are raised by foresight of the good and evill consequences, and sequels of the action whereof we Deliberate; the good or evill effect thereof dependeth on the foresight of a long chain of consequences, of which very seldome any man is able to see to the end. But for so farre as a man seeth, if the Good in those consequences, be greater than the Evill, the whole chaine is that which Writers call *Apparent*, or *Seeming Good*. And contrarily, when the Evill exceedeth the Good, the whole is *Apparent* or *Seeming Evill*. so that he who hath by Experience, or Reason, the greatest and surest prospect of Consequences, Deliberates best himselfe; and is able when he will, to give the best counsell unto others.

Good and Evill apparent.

Continuall successe in obtaining those things which a man from time to time desireth, that is to say, continuall prospering, is that men call FELICITY; I mean the Felicity of this life. For there is no such thing as perpetuall Tranquillity of mind, while we live here; because Life it selfe is but Motion, and can never be [30] without Desire, nor without Feare, no more than without Sense. What kind of Felicity God hath ordained to them that devoutly honour him, a man shall no sooner know, than enjoy; being joyes, that now are as incomprehensible, as the word of Schoole-men *Beatificall Vision* is unintelligible.

Felicity

The forme of Speech whereby men signifie their opinion of the Goodnesse of any thing, is PRAISE. That whereby they signifie the power and greatnesse of any thing, is MAGNIFYING. And that whereby they signifie the opinion they have of a mans Felicity, is by the Greeks called μακαρισμός, for which wee have no name in our tongue. And thus much is sufficient for the present purpose, to have been said of the PASSIONS.

Praise.

Magnification.

μακαρισμός

CHAP. VII.

Of the Ends, *or* Resolutions *of* DISCOURSE.

OF all *Discourse*, governed by desire of Knowledge, there is at last an *End*, either by attaining, or by giving over. And in the chain of Discourse, wheresoever it be interrupted, there is an End for that time.

If the Discourse be meerly Mentall, it consisteth of thoughts that the thing will be, and will not be, or that it has been, and has not been, alternately. So that wheresoever you break off the chayn of a mans Discourse, you leave him in a Præsumption of *it will be*, or, *it will not be*; or *it has been*, or, *has not been*. All which is *Opinion* And that which is alternate Appetite, in Deliberating concerning Good and Evil; the same is alternate Opinion, in the Enquiry of the truth of *Past*, and *Future*. And as the last Appetite in Deliberation, is called the *Will*; so the last Opinion in search of the truth of Past, and Future, is called the JUDGEMENT, or *Resolute* and *Finall Sentence* of him that *discourseth*. And as the whole chain of Appetites alternate, in the question of Good, or Bad, is called *Deliberation*, so the whole chain of Opinions alternate, in the question of True, or False, is called DOUBT.

Judgement, or Sentence final.

Doubt.

No Discourse whatsoever, can End in absolute knowledge of Fact, past, or to come. For, as for the knowledge of Fact, it is originally, Sense; and ever after, Memory. And for the knowledge of Consequence, which I have said before is called Science, it is not Absolute, but

Conditionall. No man can know by Discourse, that this, or that, is, has been, or will be, which is to know absolutely: but onely, that if This be, That is; if This has been, That has been; if This shall be, That shall be which is to know conditionally; and that not the consequence of one thing to another; but of one name of a thing, to another name of the same thing.

And therefore, when the Discourse is put into Speech, and begins with the Definitions of Words, and proceeds by Connexion of the same into generall Affirmations,
[31] and of these again into Syllogismes; the End or last summe is called the Conclusion; and the thought of the mind by it signified, is that conditionall Knowledge, or Knowledge of the consequence of words, which is commonly called SCIENCE. But if the first ground of such Discourse, be not Definitions; or if the Definitions be not rightly joyned together into Syllogismes, then the End or Conclusion, is again OPINION, namely of the truth of somewhat said, though sometimes in absurd and senslesse words, without possibility of being understood. When two, or more men, know of one and the same fact, they are said to be CONSCIOUS of it one to another; which is as much as to know it together. And because such are fittest witnesses of the facts of one another, or of a third; it was, and ever will be reputed a very Evill act, for any man to speak against his *Conscience*; or to corrupt or force another so to do. Insomuch that the plea of Conscience, has been alwayes hearkened unto very diligently in all times. Afterwards, men made use of the same word metaphorically, for the knowledge of their own secret facts, and secret thoughts, and therefore it is Rhetorically said, that the Conscience is a thousand witnesses. And last of all, men, vehemently in love with their own new opinions, (though never so absurd,) and obstinately bent to maintain them, gave those their opinions also that reverenced name of Conscience, as if they would have it seem unlawfull, to change or speak against them; and so pretend to know they are true, when they know at most, but that they think so.

Science. *Opinion.* *Conscience.*

When a mans Discourse beginneth not at Definitions, it beginneth either at some other contemplation of his own, and then it is still called Opinion ; Or it beginneth at some saying of another, of whose ability to know the truth, and of whose honesty in not deceiving, he doubteth not ; and then the Discourse is not so much concerning the Thing, as the Person , And the Resolution is called BELEEFE, and FAITH : *Faith, in* the man ; *Beleefe*, both *Beleefe.*
of the man, and *of* the truth of what he sayes. So that *Faith.*
in Beleefe are two opinions ; one of the saying of the man ; the other of his vertue. To *have faith in*, or *trust to*, or *beleeve a man*, signifie the same thing , namely, an opinion of the veracity of the man: But to *beleeve what is said*, signifieth onely an opinion of the truth of the saying. But wee are to observe that this Phrase, *I beleeve in* ; as also the Latine, *Credo in* ; and the Greek, πιστεύω ἐις, are never used but in the writings of Divines. In stead of them, in other writings are put, *I beleeve him* ; *I trust him* . *I have faith in him* ; *I rely on him* ; and in Latin, *Credo illi* ; *fido illi* : and in Greek, πιστεύω ἀυτῷ. and that this singularity of the Ecclesiastique use of the word hath raised many disputes about the right object of the Christian Faith.

But by *Beleeving in*, as it is in the Creed, is meant, not trust in the Person . but Confession and acknowledgement of the Doctrine. For not onely Christians, but all manner of men do so believe in God, as to hold all for truth they heare him say, whether they understand it, or not ; which is all the Faith and trust can possibly be had in any person whatsoever · But they do not all believe the Doctrine of the Creed.

From whence we may inferre, that when wee believe [32]
any saying whatsoever it be, to be true, from arguments taken, not from the thing it selfe, or from the principles of naturall Reason, but from the Authority, and good opinion wee have, of him that hath sayd it , then is the speaker, or person we believe in, or trust in, and whose word we take, the object of our Faith ; and the Honour done in Believing, is done to him onely. And consequently, when wee Believe that the Scriptures are the

word of God, having no immediate revelation from God himselfe, our Beleefe, Faith, and Trust is in the Church; whose word we take, and acquiesce therein. And they that believe that which a Prophet relates unto them in the name of God, take the word of the Prophet, do honour to him, and in him trust, and believe, touching the truth of what he relateth, whether he be a true, or a false Prophet. And so it is also with all other History. For if I should not believe all that is written by Historians, of the glorious acts of *Alexander*, or *Cæsar*, I do not think the Ghost of *Alexander*, or *Cæsar*, had any just cause to be offended; or any body else, but the Historian. If *Livy* say the Gods made once a Cow speak, and we believe it not, wee distrust not God therein, but *Livy*. So that it is evident, that whatsoever we believe, upon no other reason, then what is drawn from authority of men onely, and their writings; whether they be sent from God or not, is Faith in men onely.

CHAP. VIII.

Of the VERTUES *commonly called* INTELLECTUALL; *and their contrary* DEFECTS.

Intellectuall Vertue defined.

VERTUE generally, in all sorts of subjects, is somewhat that is valued for eminence; and consisteth in comparison. For if all things were equally in all men, nothing would be prized. And by *Vertues* INTELLECTUALL, are alwayes understood such abilityes of the mind, as men praise, value, and desire should be in themselves; and go commonly under the name of a *good wit*; though the same word WIT, be used also, to distinguish one certain ability from the rest

Wit, Naturall, or Acquired.

These *Vertues* are of two sorts; *Naturall*, and *Acquired*. By Naturall, I mean not, that which a man hath from his Birth: for that is nothing else but Sense: wherein men differ so little one from another, and from brute Beasts, as it is not to be reckoned amongst Vertues. But I mean, that *Wit*, which is gotten by Use onely, and

Experience; without Method, Culture, or Instruction. This NATURALL WIT, consisteth principally in two things, *Celerity of Imagining,* (that is, swift succession of one thought to another;) and *steddy direction* to some approved end. On the Contrary a slow Imagination, maketh that Defect, or fault of the mind, which is commonly called DULNESSE, *Stupidity,* and sometimes by other names that signifie slownesse of motion, or difficulty to be moved.

Naturall Wit.

And this difference of quicknesse, is caused by the [33] difference of mens passions; that love and dislike, some one thing, some another: and therefore some mens thoughts run one way, some another; and are held to, and observe differently the things that passe through their imagination. And whereas in this succession of mens thoughts, there is nothing to observe in the things they think on, but either in what they be *like one another,* or in what they be *unlike,* or *what they serve for,* or *how they serve to such a purpose;* Those that observe their similitudes, in case they be such as are but rarely observed by others, are sayd to have a *Good Wit,* by which, in this occasion, is meant a *Good Fancy.* But they that observe their differences, and dissimilitudes; which is called *Distinguishing,* and *Discerning,* and *Judging* between thing and thing; in case, such discerning be not easie, are said to have a *good Judgement:* and particularly in matter of conversation and businesse; wherein, times, places, and persons are to be discerned, this Vertue is called DISCRETION. The former, that is, Fancy, without the help of Judgement, is not commended as a Vertue: but the later which is Judgement, and Discretion, is commended for it selfe, without the help of Fancy. Besides the Discretion of times, places, and persons, necessary to a good Fancy, there is required also an often application of his thoughts to their End; that is to say, to some use to be made of them. This done; he that hath this Vertue, will be easily fitted with similitudes, that will please, not onely by illustration of his discourse, and adorning it with new and apt metaphors; but also, by the rarity of their invention. But without Steddinesse, and Direction to some End, a great Fancy is one kind of

Good Wit, or Fancy.

Good Judgement.

Discretion.

Madnesse; such as they have, that entring into any discourse, are snatched from their purpose, by every thing that comes in their thought, into so many, and so long digressions, and Parentheses, that they utterly lose themselves Which kind of folly, I know no particular name for: but the cause of it is, sometimes want of experience; whereby that seemeth to a man new and rare, which doth not so to others: sometimes Pusillanimity; by which that seems great to him, which other men think a trifle· and whatsoever is new, or great, and therefore thought fit to be told, withdrawes a man by degrees from the intended way of his discourse

In a good Poem, whether it be *Epique*, or *Dramatique*; as also in *Sonnets*, *Epigrams*, and other Pieces, both Judgement and Fancy are required· But the Fancy must be more eminent; because they please for the Extravagancy; but ought not to displease by Indiscretion.

In a good History, the Judgement must be eminent; because the goodnesse consisteth, in the Method, in the Truth, and in the Choyse of the actions that are most profitable to be known. Fancy has no place, but onely in adorning the stile.

In Orations of Prayse, and in Invectives, the Fancy is prædominant; because the designe is not truth, but to Honour or Dishonour; which is done by noble, or by vile comparisons The Judgement does but suggest what circumstances make an action laudable, or culpable

[34] In Hortatives, and Pleadings, as Truth, or Disguise serveth best to the Designe in hand; so is the Judgement, or the Fancy most required.

In Demonstration, in Councell, and all rigourous search of Truth, Judgement does all, except sometimes the understanding have need to be opened by some apt similitude, and then there is so much use of Fancy. But for Metaphors, they are in this case utterly excluded. For seeing they openly professe deceipt; to admit them into Councell, or Reasoning, were manifest folly.

And in any Discourse whatsoever, if the defect of Discretion be apparent, how extravagant soever the Fancy be, the whole discourse will be taken for a signe of want of wit; and so will it never when the Discretion is manifest, though the Fancy be never so ordinary.

The secret thoughts of a man run over all things, holy, prophane, clean, obscene, grave, and light, without shame, or blame; which verball discourse cannot do, farther than the Judgement shall approve of the Time, Place, and Persons. An Anatomist, or a Physitian may speak, or write his judgement of unclean things; because it is not to please, but profit: but for another man to write his extravagant, and pleasant fancies of the same, is as if a man, from being tumbled into the dirt, should come and present himselfe before good company. And 'tis the want of Discretion that makes the difference. Again, in profest remissnesse of mind, and familiar company, a man may play with the sounds, and æquivocall significations of words; and that many times with encounters of extraordinary Fancy: but in a Sermon, or in publique, or before persons unknown, or whom we ought to reverence, there is no Gingling of words that will not be accounted folly. and the difference is onely in the want of Discretion. So that where Wit is wanting, it is not Fancy that is wanting, but Discretion. Judgement therefore without Fancy is Wit, but Fancy without Judgement not.

When the thoughts of a man, that has a designe in hand, running over a multitude of things, observes how they conduce to that designe; or what designe they may conduce unto; if his observations be such as are not easie, or usuall, This wit of his is called PRUDENCE; *Prudence.* and dependeth on much Experience, and Memory of the like things, and their consequences heretofore. In which there is not so much difference of Men, as there is in their Fancies and Judgements; Because the Experience of men equall in age, is not much unequall, as to the quantity, but lyes in different occasions; every one having his private designes. To govern well a family, and a kingdome, are not different degrees of Prudence; but different sorts of businesse, no more then to draw a picture in little, or as great, or greater then the life, are different degrees of Art. A plain husband-man is more Prudent in affaires of his own house, then a Privy Counseller in the affaires of another man.

To Prudence, if you adde the use of unjust, or dishonest means, such as usually are prompted to men by Feare, or Want; you have that Crooked Wisdome, which is

Craft. [35] called CRAFT, which is a signe of Pusillanimity. For Magnanimity is contempt of unjust, or dishonest helps. And that which the Latines call *Versutia,* (translated into English, *Shifting,*) and is a putting off of a present danger or incommodity, by engaging into a greater, as when a man robbs one to pay another, is but a shorter sighted Craft, called *Versutia,* from *Versura,* which signifies taking mony at usurie, for the present payment of interest.

Acquired Wit. As for *acquired Wit,* (I mean acquired by method and instruction,) there is none but Reason, which is grounded on the right use of Speech; and produceth the Sciences. But of Reason and Science, I have already spoken in the fifth and sixth Chapters.

The causes of this difference of Witts, are in the Passions: and the difference of Passions, proceedeth partly from the different Constitution of the body, and partly from different Education. For if the difference proceeded from the temper of the brain, and the organs of Sense, either exterior or interior, there would be no lesse difference of men in their Sight, Hearing, or other Senses, than in their Fancies, and Discretions It proceeds therefore from the Passions; which are different, not onely from the difference of mens complexions; but also from their difference of customes, and education.

The Passions that most of all cause the differences of Wit, are principally, the more or lesse Desire of Power, of Riches, of Knowledge, and of Honour. All which may be reduced to the first, that is Desire of Power. For Riches, Knowledge and Honour are but severall sorts of Power.

And therefore, a man who has no great Passion for any of these things; but is as men terme it indifferent;

though he may be so farre a good man, as to be free from giving offence, yet he cannot possibly have either a great Fancy, or much Judgement For the Thoughts, are to the Desires, as Scouts, and Spies, to range abroad, and find the way to the things Desired: All Stedinesse of the minds motion, and all quicknesse of the same, proceeding from thence. For as to have no Desire, is to be Dead: so to have weak Passions, is Dulnesse; and to have Passions indifferently for every thing, GIDDINESSE, and *Distraction*, and to have stronger, and more vehement Passions for any thing, than is ordinarily seen in others, is that which men call MADNESSE.

Giddinesse

Madnesse.

Whereof there be almost as many kinds, as of the Passions themselves. Sometimes the extraordinary and extravagant Passion, proceedeth from the evill constitution of the organs of the Body, or harme done them; and sometimes the hurt, and indisposition of the Organs, is caused by the vehemence, or long continuance of the Passion. But in both cases the Madnesse is of one and the same nature.

The Passion, whose violence, or continuance maketh Madnesse, is either great *vaine-Glory*; which is commonly called *Pride*, and *selfe-conceipt*; or great *Dejection* of mind.

Pride, subjecteth a man to Anger, the excesse whereof, is the Madnesse called RAGE, and FURY. And thus it comes to passe that excessive desire of Revenge, [36] when it becomes habituall, hurteth the organs, and becomes Rage: That excessive love, with jealousie, becomes also Rage Excessive opinion of a mans own selfe, for divine inspiration, for wisdome, learning, forme, and the like, becomes Distraction, and Giddinesse: The same, joyned with Envy, Rage. Vehement opinion of the truth of any thing, contradicted by others, Rage.

Rage.

Dejection, subjects a man to causelesse fears; which is a Madnesse commonly called MELANCHOLY, apparent also in divers manners; as in haunting of solitudes, and graves; in superstitious behaviour; and in fearing some one, some another particular thing. In summe, all Passions that produce strange and unusuall behaviour,

Melancholy.

are called by the generall name of Madnesse. But of the severall kinds of Madnesse, he that would take the paines, might enrowle a legion. And if the Excesses be madnesse, there is no doubt but the Passions themselves, when they tend to Evill, are degrees of the same.

(For example,) Though the effect of folly, in them that are possessed of an opinion of being inspired, be not visible alwayes in one man, by any very extravagant action, that proceedeth from such Passion; yet when many of them conspire together, the Rage of the whole multitude is visible enough. For what argument of Madnesse can there be greater, than to clamour, strike, and throw stones at our best friends? Yet this is somewhat lesse than such a multitude will do. For they will clamour, fight against, and destroy those, by whom all their life-time before, they have been protected, and secured from injury. And if this be Madnesse in the multitude, it is the same in every particular man. For as in the middest of the sea, though a man perceive no sound of that part of the water next him; yet he is well assured, that part contributes as much, to the Roaring of the Sea, as any other part, of the same quantity: so also, though wee perceive no great unquietnesse, in one, or two men; yet we may be well assured, that their singular Passions, are parts of the Seditious roaring of a troubled Nation. And if there were nothing else that bewrayed their madnesse; yet that very arrogating such inspiration to themselves, is argument enough. If some man in Bedlam should entertaine you with sober discourse; and you desire in taking leave, to know what he were, that you might another time requite his civility; and he should tell you, he were God the Father; I think you need expect no extravagant action for argument of his Madnesse.

This opinion of Inspiration, called commonly, Private Spirit, begins very often, from some lucky finding of an Errour generally held by others; and not knowing, or not remembring, by what conduct of reason, they came to so singular a truth, (as they think it, though it be many times an untruth they light on,) they presently admire themselves; as being in the speciall grace of God Almighty, who hath revealed the same to them supernaturally, by his Spirit.

Again, that Madnesse is nothing else, but too much appearing Passion, may be gathered out of the effects of Wine, which are the same with those of the evill disposition of the organs. For the variety of behaviour [37]
in men that have drunk too much, is the same with that of Mad-men: some of them Raging, others Loving, others Laughing, all extravagantly, but according to their severall domineering Passions: For the effect of the wine, does but remove Dissimulation; and take from them the sight of the deformity of their Passions. For, (I believe) the most sober men, when they walk alone without care and employment of the mind, would be unwilling the vanity and Extravagance of their thoughts at that time should be publiquely seen: which is a confession, that Passions unguided, are for the most part meere Madnesse.

The opinions of the world, both in antient and later ages, concerning the cause of madnesse, have been two. Some, deriving them from the Passions; some, from Dæmons, or Spirits, either good, or bad, which they thought might enter into a man, possesse him, and move his organs in such strange, and uncouth manner, as mad-men use to do. The former sort therefore, called such men, Mad-men: but the Later, called them sometimes *Dæmoniacks,* (that is, possessed with spirits;) sometimes *Energumeni,* (that is, agitated, or moved with spirits;) and now in *Italy* they are called not onely *Pazzi,* Mad-men; but also *Spiritati,* men possest.

There was once a great conflux of people in *Abdera,* a City of the Greeks, at the acting of the Tragedy of *Andromeda,* upon an extream hot day: whereupon, a great many of the spectators falling into Fevers, had this accident from the heat, and from the Tragedy together, that they did nothing but pronounce Iambiques, with the names of *Perseus* and *Andromeda*; which together with the Fever, was cured, by the comming on of Winter: And this madnesse was thought to proceed from the Passion imprinted by the Tragedy. Likewise

there raigned a fit of madnesse in another Græcian City, which seized onely the young Maidens; and caused many of them to hang themselves. This was by most then thought an act of the Divel. But one that suspected, that contempt of life in them, might proceed from some Passion of the mind, and supposing they did not contemne also their honour, gave counsell to the Magistrates, to strip such as so hang'd themselves, and let them hang out naked. This the story sayes cured that madnesse. But on the other side, the same Græcians, did often ascribe madnesse, to the operation of the Eumenides, or Furyes; and sometimes of *Ceres*, *Phœbus*, and other Gods so much did men attribute to Phantasmes, as to think them aëreal living bodies; and generally to call them Spirits. And as the Romans in this, held the same opinion with the Greeks. so also did the Jewes; For they called mad-men Prophets, or (according as they thought the spirits good or bad) Dæmoniacks; and some of them called both Prophets, and Dæmoniacks mad-men; and some called the same man both Dæmoniack, and mad-man. But for the Gentiles, 'tis no wonder; because Diseases, and Health; Vices, and Vertues; and many naturall accidents, were with them termed, and worshipped as Dæmons. So that a man was to understand by Dæmon, as well (sometimes) an Ague, as a Divell
[38] But for the Jewes to have such opinion, is somewhat strange. For neither *Moses*, nor *Abraham* pretended to Prophecy by possession of a Spirit, but from the voyce of God, or by a Vision or Dream. Nor is there any thing in his Law, Morall, or Ceremoniall, by which they were taught, there was any such Enthusiasme; or any Possession. When God is sayd, *Numb.* 11. 25. to take from the Spirit that was in *Moses*, and give to the 70. Elders, the Spirit of God (taking it for the substance of God) is not divided. The Scriptures by the Spirit of God in man, mean a mans spirit, enclined to Godlinesse And where it is said *Exod.* 28. 3. *Whom I have filled with the spirit of wisdome to make garments for Aaron*, is not meant a spirit put into them, that can make garments; but the wisdome of their own spirits in that kind of work. In the like sense, the spirit of man, when it produceth

unclean actions, is ordinarily called an unclean spirit; and so other spirits, though not alwayes, yet as often as the vertue or vice so stiled, is extraordinary, and Eminent. Neither did the other Prophets of the old Testament pretend Enthusiasme; or, that God spake in them; but to them by Voyce, Vision, or Dream; and the *Burthen of the Lord* was not Possession, but Command. How then could the Jewes fall into this opinion of possession? I can imagine no reason, but that which is common to all men; namely, the want of curiosity to search naturall causes; and their placing Felicity, in the acquisition of the grosse pleasures of the Senses, and the things that most immediately conduce thereto. For they that see any strange, and unusuall ability, or defect in a mans mind; unlesse they see withall, from what cause it may probably proceed, can hardly think it naturall; and if not naturall, they must needs thinke it supernaturall; and then what can it be, but that either God, or the Divell is in him? And hence it came to passe, when our Saviour (*Mark* 3. 21.) was compassed about with the multitude, those of the house doubted he was mad, and went out to hold him: but the Scribes said he had *Belzebub*, and that was it, by which he cast out divels; as if the greater mad-man had awed the lesser. And that (*John* 10. 20.) some said, *He hath a Divell, and is mad*; whereas others holding him for a Prophet, sayd, *These are not the words of one that hath a Divell.* So in the old Testament he that came to anoynt *Jehu*, 2 *Kings* 9. 11. was a Prophet; but some of the company asked *Jehu, What came that mad-man for?* So that in summe, it is manifest, that whosoever behaved himselfe in extraordinory manner, was thought by the Jewes to be possessed either with a good, or evill spirit; except by the Sadduces, who erred so farre on the other hand, as not to believe there were at all any spirits, (which is very neere to direct Atheisme;) and thereby perhaps the more provoked others, to terme such men Dæmoniacks, rather than mad-men.

But why then does our Saviour proceed in the curing of them, as if they were possest; and not as if they were mad? To which I can give no other kind of answer, but

that which is given to those that urge the Scripture in like manner against the opinion of the motion of the Earth. The Scripture was written to shew unto men the kingdome of God, and to prepare their mindes to become
[39] his obedient subjects; leaving the world, and the Philosophy thereof, to the disputation of men, for the exercising of their naturall Reason Whether the Earths, or Suns motion make the day, and night; or whether the Exorbitant actions of men, proceed from Passion, or from the Divell, (so we worship him not) it is all one, as to our obedience, and subjection to God Almighty; which is the thing for which the Scripture was written. As for that our Saviour speaketh to the disease, as to a person; it is the usuall phrase of all that cure by words onely, as Christ did, (and Inchanters pretend to do, whether they speak to a Divel or not) For is not Christ also said (*Math.* 8. 26.) to have rebuked the winds? Is not he said also (*Luk.* 4. 39.) to rebuke a Fever? Yet this does not argue that a Fever is a Divel. And whereas many of those Divels are said to confesse Christ; it is not necessary to interpret those places otherwise, than that those mad-men confessed him. And whereas our Saviour (*Math.* 12. 43.) speaketh of an unclean Spirit, that having gone out of a man, wandreth through dry places, seeking rest, and finding none; and returning into the same man, with seven other spirits worse than himselfe; It is manifestly a Parable, alluding to a man, that after a little endeavour to quit his lusts, is vanquished by the strength of them, and becomes seven times worse than he was. So that I see nothing at all in the Scripture, that requireth a beliefe, that Dæmoniacks were any other thing but Mad-men.

Insignificant Speech.

There is yet another fault in the Discourses of some men; which may also be numbred amongst the sorts of Madnesse; namely, that abuse of words, whereof I have spoken before in the fifth chapter, by the Name of Absurdity. And that is, when men speak such words, as put together, have in them no signification at all; but are fallen upon by some, through misunderstanding of the words they have received, and repeat by rote; by others, from intention to deceive by obscurity. And this

is incident to none but those, that converse in questions of matters incomprehensible, as the Schoole-men; or in questions of abstruse Philosophy. The common sort of men seldome speak Insignificantly, and are therefore, by those other Egregious persons counted Idiots. But to be assured their words are without any thing correspondent to them in the mind, there would need some Examples; which if any man require, let him take a Schoole-man into his hands, and see if he can translate any one chapter concerning any difficult point; as the Trinity; the Deity; the nature of Christ; Transubstantiation; Free-will, *&c.* into any of the moderne tongues, so as to make the same intelligible; or into any tolerable Latine, such as they were acquainted withall, that lived when the Latine tongue was Vulgar. What is the meaning of these words. *The first cause does not necessarily inflow any thing into the second, by force of the Essentiall subordination of the second causes, by Which it may help it to worke?* They are the Translation of the Title of the sixth chapter of *Suarez* first Booke, *Of the Concourse, Motion, and Help of God.* When men write whole volumes of such stuffe, are they not Mad, or intend to make others so? And particularly, in the question of [40]
Transubstantiation; where after certain words spoken, they that say, the White*nesse*, Round*nesse*, Magni*tude*, Quali*ty*, Corruptibili*ty*, all which are incorporeall, *&c.* go out of the Wafer, into the Body of our blessed Saviour, do they not make those *Nesses*, *Tudes*, and *Ties*, to be so many spirits possessing his body? For by Spirits, they mean alwayes things, that being incorporeall, are neverthelesse moveable from one place to another. So that this kind of Absurdity, may rightly be numbred amongst the many sorts of Madnesse; and all the time that guided by clear Thoughts of their worldly lust, they forbear disputing, or writing thus, but Lucide Intervals. And thus much of the Vertues and Defects Intellectuall.

CHAP. IX.

Of the Severall SUBJECTS *of* KNOWLEDGE.

THERE are of KNOWLEDGE two kinds; whereof one is *Knowledge of Fact*: the other *Knowledge of the Consequence of one Affirmation to another.* The former is nothing else, but Sense and Memory, and is *Absolute Knowledge*; as when we see a Fact doing, or remember it done: And this is the Knowledge required in a Witnesse. The later is called *Science*; and is *Conditionall*; as when we know, that, *If the figure showne be a Circle, then any straight line through the Center shall divide it into two equall parts* And this is the Knowledge required in a Philosopher, that is to say, of him that pretends to Reasoning.

The Register of *Knowledge of Fact* is called *History.* Whereof there be two sorts. one called *Naturall History*; which is the History of such Facts, or Effects of Nature, as have no Dependance on Mans *Will*; Such as are the Histories of *Metalls, Plants. Animals, Regions,* and the like. The other, is *Civill History*; which is the History of the Voluntary Actions of men in Commonwealths

The Registers of Science, are such *Books* as contain the *Demonstrations* of Consequences of one Affirmation, to another; and are commonly called *Books of Philosophy*, whereof the sorts are many, according to the diversity of the Matter; And may be divided in such manner as I have divided them in the following Table.

E, is, w. e of se- nces; ch is d also o- y.

- Consequences from the Accidents of Bodies Naturall; which is called NATURALL PHILOSOPHY.
  - Consequences from the Accidents common to all Bodies Naturall; which are *Quantity*, and *Motion*.
    - Consequences from Quantity, and Motion *indeterminate*; which being the Principles, or first foundation of Philosophy, is called *Philosophia Prima*. — PHILOSOPHIA PRIMA.
    - Consequences from Motion, and Quantity *determined*.
      - Consequences from Quantity, and Motion determined.
        - By Figure, . . . — *Mathematiques*, — GEOMETRY.
        - By Number, . . — *Mathematiques*, — ARITHMETIQUE.
      - Consequences from the Motion, and Quantity of Bodies in *speciall*.
        - Consequences from the Motion, and Quantity of the great parts of the World, as the *Earth* and *Starres*, — *Cosmography*,
          - ASTRONOMY.
          - GEOGRAPHY.
        - Consequences from the Motion of Special kinds, and Figures of Body, — *Mechaniques*, Doctrine of *Weight*,
          - *Science* of ENGINEERS.
          - ARCHITECTURE.
          - NAVIGATION.
  - PHYSIQUES, or Consequences from *Qualities*.
    - Consequences from the Qualities of Bodyes *Transient*, such as sometimes appear, sometimes vanish, — METEOROLOGY.
    - Consequences from the Qualities of Bodies *Permanent*.
      - Consequences from the Qualities of the *Starres*.
        - Consequences from the *Light* of the Starres. Out of this, and the Motion of the Sunne, is made the Science of . . . . . — SCIOGRAPHY.
        - Consequences from the *Influence* of the Starres, ... — ASTROLOGY.
      - Consequences of the Qualities from *Liquid* Bodies that fill the space between the Starres; such as are the *Ayre*, or substance ætheriall.
      - Consequences from the Qualities of Bodies *Terrestriall*.
        - Consequences from the parts of the Earth, that are *without Sense*,
          - Consequences from the Qualities of *Minerals*, as *Stones*, *Metalls*, &c.
          - Consequences from the Qualities of *Vegetables*.
        - Consequences from the Qualities of *Animals*.
          - Consequences from the Qualities of *Animals in generall*
            - Consequences from *Vision*, . . — OPTIQUES.
            - Consequences from *Sounds*, . . — MUSIQUE.
            - Consequences from the rest of the *Senses*.
          - Consequences from the Qualities of *Men in speciall*
            - Consequences from the *Passions* of Men, ... — ETHIQUES.
            - Consequences from *Speech*,
              - In *Magnifying*, *Vilifying*, &c. — POETRY.
              - In *Perswading*, — RHETHORIQUE.
              - In *Reasoning*, — LOGIQUE.
              - In *Contracting*, — The *Science* of JUST and UNJUST.
- Consequences from the Accidents of *Politique* Bodies; which is called POLITIQUES, and CIVILL PHILOSOPHY.
  1. Of Consequences from the *Institution* of COMMON-WEALTHS, to the *Rights*, and *Duties* of the *Body Politique*, or *Soveraign*.
  2. Of Consequences from the same, to the *Duty*, and *Right* of the *Subjects*.

[41]

CHAP. X.

Of POWER, WORTH, DIGNITY, HONOUR, *and* WORTHINESSE.

Power. THE POWER *of a Man*, (to take it Universally,) is his present means, to obtain some future apparent Good. And is either *Originall*, or *Instrumentall*.

Naturall Power, is the eminence of the Faculties of Body, or Mind: as extraordinary Strength, Forme, Prudence, Arts, Eloquence, Liberality, Nobility. *Instrumentall* are those Powers, which acquired by these, or by fortune, are means and Instruments to acquire more: as Riches, Reputation, Friends, and the secret working of God, which men call Good Luck. For the nature of Power, is in this point, like to Fame, increasing as it proceeds; or like the motion of heavy bodies, which the further they go, make still the more hast.

The Greatest of humane Powers, is that which is compounded of the Powers of most men, united by consent, in one person, Naturall, or Civill, that has the use of all their Powers depending on his will; such as is the Power of a Common-wealth: Or depending on the wills of each particular; such as is the Power of a Faction, or of divers factions leagued. Therefore to have servants, is Power; To have friends, is Power: for they are strengths united.

Also Riches joyned with liberality, is Power; because it procureth friends, and servants. Without liberality, not so; because in this case they defend not; but expose men to Envy, as a Prey.

Reputation of power, is Power, because it draweth with it the adhærence of those that need protection.

So is Reputation of love of a mans Country, (called Popularity,) for the same Reason

Also, what quality soever maketh a man beloved, or feared of many; or the reputation of such quality, is Power; because it is a means to have the assistance, and service of many.

Good successe is Power; because it maketh reputation of Wisdome, or good fortune; which makes men either feare him, or rely on him.

Affability of men already in power, is encrease of Power; because it gaineth love.

Reputation of Prudence in the conduct of Peace or War, is Power; because to prudent men, we commit the government of our selves, more willingly than to others.

Nobility is Power, not in all places, but onely in those Common-wealths, where it has Priviledges: for in such priviledges consisteth their Power.

Eloquence is power; because it is seeming Prudence.

Forme is Power; because being a promise of Good, it recommendeth men to the favour of women and [42] strangers.

The Sciences, are small Power; because not eminent; and therefore, not acknowledged in any man; nor are at all, but in a few; and in them, but of a few things. For Science is of that nature, as none can understand it to be, but such as in a good measure have attayned it.

Arts of publique use, as Fortification, making of Engines, and other Instruments of War; because they conferre to Defence, and Victory, are Power: And though the true Mother of them, be Science, namely the Mathematiques; yet, because they are brought into the Light, by the hand of the Artificer, they be esteemed (the Midwife passing with the vulgar for the Mother,) as his issue.

The *Value*, or WORTH of a man, is as of all other things, *Worth.** his Price; that is to say, so much as would be given for the use of his Power: and therefore is not absolute; but a thing dependant on the need and judgement of another. An able conductor of Souldiers, is of great Price in time of War present, or imminent; but in Peace not so. A learned and uncorrupt Judge, is much Worth in time of Peace; but not so much in War. And as in other things, so in men, not the seller, but the buyer determines the Price. For let a man (as most men do,) rate themselves at the highest Value they can; yet their true Value is no more than it is esteemed by others.

The manifestation of the Value we set on one another, is that which is commonly called Honouring, and Dishonouring. To Value a man at a high rate, is to *Honour* him; at a low rate, is to *Dishonour* him. But high, and low, in this case, is to be understood by comparison to the rate that each man setteth on himselfe.

Dignity. The publique worth of a man, which is the Value set on him by the Common-wealth, is that which men commonly call DIGNITY. And this Value of him by the Common-wealth, is understood, by offices of Command, Judicature, publike Employment; or by Names and Titles, introduced for distinction of such Value.

To Honour and Dishonour. To pray to another, for ayde of any kind, is *to* HONOUR, because a signe we have an opinion he has power to help; and the more difficult the ayde is, the more is the Honour.

To obey, is to Honour, because no man obeyes them, whom they think have no power to help, or hurt them. And consequently to disobey, is to *Dishonour*.

To give great gifts to a man, is to Honour him; because 'tis buying of Protection, and acknowledging of Power. To give little gifts, is to Dishonour; because it is but Almes, and signifies an opinion of the need of small helps.

To be sedulous in promoting anothers good; also to flatter, is to Honour; as a signe we seek his protection or ayde. To neglect, is to Dishonour.

To give way, or place to another, in any Commodity, is to Honour; being a confession of greater power. To arrogate, is to Dishonour.

To shew any signe of love, or feare of another, is to
[43] Honour; for both to love, and to feare, is to value. To contemne, or lesse to love or feare, then he expects, is to Dishonour; for 'tis undervaluing.

To praise, magnifie, or call happy, is to Honour; because nothing but goodnesse, power, and felicity is valued. To revile, mock, or pitty, is to Dishonour.

To speak to another with consideration, to appear before him with decency, and humility, is to Honour him; as signes of fear to offend. To speak to him rashly, to do any thing before him obscenely, slovenly, impudently, is to Dishonour.

To believe, to trust, to rely on another, is to Honour him; signe of opinion of his vertue and power. To distrust, or not believe, is to Dishonour.

To hearken to a mans counsell, or discourse of what kind soever, is to Honour; as a signe we think him wise, or eloquent, or witty. To sleep, or go forth, or talk the while, is to Dishonour.

To do those things to another, which he takes for signes of Honour, or which the Law or Custome makes so, is to Honour; because in approving the Honour done by others, he acknowledgeth the power which others acknowledge. To refuse to do them, is to Dishonour.

To agree with in opinion, is to Honour; as being a signe of approving his judgement, and wisdome. To dissent, is Dishonour; and an upbraiding of errour; and (if the dissent be in many things) of folly.

To imitate, is to Honour; for it is vehemently to approve. To imitate ones Enemy, is to Dishonour.

To honour those another honours, is to Honour him; as a signe of approbation of his judgement. To honour his Enemies, is to Dishonour him.

To employ in counsell, or in actions of difficulty, is to Honour; as a signe of opinion of his wisdome, or other power. To deny employment in the same cases, to those that seek it, is to Dishonour.

All these wayes of Honouring, are naturall; and as well within, as without Common-wealths. But in Common-wealths, where he, or they that have the supreme Authority, can make whatsoever they please, to stand for signes of Honour, there be other Honours.

A Soveraigne doth Honour a Subject, with whatsoever Title, or Office, or Employment, or Action, that he himselfe will have taken for a signe of his will to Honour him.

The King of *Persia*, Honoured *Mordecay*, when he appointed he should be conducted through the streets in the Kings Garment, upon one of the Kings Horses, with a Crown on his head, and a Prince before him, proclayming, *Thus shall it be done to him that the King will honour.* And yet another King of *Persia*, or the same another time, to one that demanded for some great service, to weare one of the Kings robes, gave him leave

so to do; but with this addition, that he should weare it as the Kings foole; and then it was Dishonour. So that of Civill Honour, the Fountain is in the person of the Common-wealth, and dependeth on the Will of the Soveraigne; and is therefore temporary, and called
[44] *Civill Honour*; such as are Magistracy, Offices, Titles; and in some places Coats, and Scutchions painted: and men Honour such as have them, as having so many signes of favour in the Common-wealth; which favour is Power.

Honourable. *Honourable* is whatsoever possession, action, or quality, is an argument and signe of Power.

And therefore To be Honoured, loved, or feared of many, is Honourable; as arguments of Power. To be Honoured of few or none, *Dishonourable.*

Dishonourable. Dominion, and Victory is Honourable; because acquired by Power; and Servitude, for need, or feare, is Dishonourable.

Good fortune (if lasting,) Honourable; as a signe of the favour of God. Ill fortune, and losses, Dishonourable. Riches, are Honourable; for they are Power. Poverty, Dishonourable. Magnanimity, Liberality, Hope, Courage, Confidence, are Honourable; for they proceed from the conscience of Power. Pusillanimity, Parsimony, Fear, Diffidence, are Dishonourable.

Timely Resolution, or determination of what a man is to do, is Honourable; as being the contempt of small difficulties, and dangers. And Irresolution, Dishonourable; as a signe of too much valuing of little impediments, and little advantages: For when a man has weighed things as long as the time permits, and resolves not, the difference of weight is but little; and therefore if he resolve not, he overvalues little things, which is Pusillanimity.

All Actions, and Speeches, that proceed, or seem to proceed from much Experience, Science, Discretion, or Wit, are Honourable; For all these are Powers. Actions, or Words that proceed from Errour, Ignorance, or Folly, Dishonourable.

Gravity, as farre forth as it seems to proceed from a mind employed on some thing else, is Honourable;

because employment is a signe of Power. But if it seem to proceed from a purpose to appear grave, it is Dishonourable. For the gravity of the former, is like the steddinesse of a Ship laden with Merchandise; but of the later, like the steddinesse of a Ship ballasted with Sand, and other trash.

To be Conspicuous, that is to say, to be known, for Wealth, Office, great Actions, or any eminent Good, is Honourable; as a signe of the power for which he is conspicuous. On the contrary, Obscurity, is Dishonourable.

To be descended from conspicuous Parents, is Honourable; because they the more easily attain the aydes, and friends of their Ancestors. On the contrary, to be descended from obscure Parentage, is Dishonourable.

Actions proceeding from Equity, joyned with losse, are Honourable; as signes of Magnanimity: for Magnanimity is a signe of Power. On the contrary, Craft, Shifting, neglect of Equity, is Dishonourable.

Covetousnesse of great Riches, and ambition of great Honours, are Honourable; as signes of power to obtain them. Covetousnesse, and ambition, of little gaines, or preferments, is Dishonourable.

Nor does it alter the case of Honour, whether an action (so it be great and difficult, and consequently a signe of [45] much power,) be just or unjust: for Honour consisteth onely in the opinion of Power. Therefore the ancient Heathen did not thinke they Dishonoured, but greatly Honoured the Gods, when they introduced them in their Poems, committing Rapes, Thefts, and other great, but unjust, or unclean acts: In so much as nothing is so much celebrated in *Jupiter*, as his Adulteries; nor in *Mercury*, as his Frauds, and Thefts: of whose praises, in a hymne of *Homer*, the greatest is this, that being born in the morning, he had invented Musique at noon, and before night, stolne away the Cattell of *Apollo*, from his Herdsmen.

Also amongst men, till there were constituted great Common-wealths, it was thought no dishonour to be a Pyrate, or a High-way Theefe; but rather a lawfull Trade, not onely amongst the Greeks, but also amongst all other Nations; as is manifest by the Histories of antient time. And at this day, in this part of the world, private Duels are, and alwayes will be Honourable, though unlawfull, till such time as there shall be Honour ordained for them that refuse, and Ignominy for them that make the Challenge. For Duels also are many times effects of Courage; and the ground of Courage is alwayes Strength or Skill, which are Power; though for the most part they be effects of rash speaking, and of the fear of Dishonour, in one, or both the Combatants; who engaged by rashnesse, are driven into the Lists to avoyd disgrace.

Coats of Armes. Scutchions, and Coats of Armes hæreditary, where they have any eminent Priviledges, are Honourable; otherwise not. for their Power consisteth either in such Priviledges, or in Riches, or some such thing as is equally honoured in other men. This kind of Honour, commonly called Gentry, has been derived from the Antient Germans. For there never was any such thing known, where the German Customes were unknown. Nor is it now any where in use, where the Germans have not inhabited. The antient Greek Commanders, when they went to war, had their Shields painted with such Devises as they pleased, insomuch as an unpainted Buckler was a signe of Poverty, and of a common Souldier: but they transmitted not the Inheritance of them. The Romans transmitted the Marks of their Families: but they were the Images, not the Devises of their Ancestors. Amongst the people of *Asia*, *Afrique*, and *America*, there is not, nor was ever, any such thing. The Germans onely had that custome; from whom it has been derived into *England*, *France*, *Spain* and *Italy*, when in great numbers they either ayded the Romans, or made their own Conquests in these Westerne parts of the world.

For *Germany*, being antiently, as all other Countries, in their beginnings, divided amongst an infinite number of little Lords, or Masters of Families, that continually had wars one with another; those Masters, or Lords, principally to the end they might, when they were Covered with Arms, be known by their followers; and partly for ornament, both painted their Armor, or their Scutchion, or Coat, with the picture of some Beast, or other thing; and also put some eminent and visible [46] mark upon the Crest of their Helmets. And this ornament both of the Armes, and Crest, descended by inheritance to their Children; to the eldest pure, and to the rest with some note of diversity, such as the Old master, that is to say in Dutch, the *Here-alt* thought fit. But when many such Families, joyned together, made a greater Monarchy, this duty of the Herealt, to distinguish Scutchions, was made a private Office a part. And the issue of these Lords, is the great and antient Gentry; which for the most part bear living creatures, noted for courage, and rapine: or Castles, Battlements, Belts, Weapons, Bars, Palisadoes, and other notes of War; nothing being then in honour, but vertue military. Afterwards, not onely Kings, but popular Commonwealths, gave divers manners of Scutchions, to such as went forth to the War, or returned from it, for encouragement, or recompence to their service. All which, by an observing Reader, may be found in such antient Histories, Greek and Latine, as make mention of the German Nation, and Manners, in their times.

Titles of Honour.

Titles of *Honour*, such as are Duke, Count, Marquis, and Baron, are Honourable; as signifying the value set upon them by the Soveraigne Power of the Commonwealth: Which Titles, were in old time titles of Office, and Command, derived some from the Romans, some from the Germans, and French. Dukes, in Latine *Duces*, being Generalls in War: Counts, *Comites*, such as bare the Generall company out of friendship; and were left to govern and defend places conquered, and pacified: Marquises, *Marchiones*, were Counts that governed the Marches, or bounds of the Empire. Which titles of Duke, Count, and Marquis, came into the Empire, about the time of *Constantine* the Great, from the customes of the German *Militia*. But Baron, seems to have been a Title of the Gaules, and signifies a Great man; such as were the Kings, or Princes men, whom they employed in war about their persons; and seems to be derived from *Vir*, to *Ber*, and *Bar*, that signified the same in the Language of the Gaules, that *Vir* in Latine; and thence to *Bero*, and *Baro*: so that such men were called *Berones*, and after *Barones*; and (in Spanish) *Varones*. But he that would know more particularly the originall of Titles of Honour, may find it, as I have done this, in Mr. *Seldens* most excellent Treatise of that subject. In processe of time these offices of Honour, by occasion of trouble, and for reasons of good and peaceable government, were turned into meer Titles; serving for the most part, to distinguish the precedence, place, and order of subjects in the Common-wealth: and men were made Dukes, Counts, Marquises, and Barons of Places, wherein they had neither possession, nor command: and other Titles also, were devised to the same end.

Worthinesse Fitnesse

WORTHINESSE, is a thing different from the worth, or value of a man; and also from his merit, or desert; and consisteth in a particular power, or ability for that, whereof he is said to be worthy: which particular ability, is usually named FITNESSE, or *Aptitude*.

For he is Worthiest to be a Commander, to be a Judge, or to have any other charge, that is best fitted, with the
[47] qualities required to the well discharging of it; and Worthiest of Riches, that has the qualities most requisite for the well using of them: any of which qualities being absent, one may neverthelesse be a Worthy man, and valuable for some thing else. Again, a man may be Worthy of Riches, Office, and Employment, that neverthelesse, can plead no right to have it before another; and therefore cannot be said to merit or deserve it. For Merit, præsupposeth a right, and that the thing deserved is due by promise: Of which I shall say more hereafter, when I shall speak of Contracts.

CHAP. XI.

Of the difference of MANNERS.

What is here meant by Manners.

BY MANNERS, I mean not here, Decency of behaviour; as how one man should salute another, or how a man should wash his mouth, or pick his teeth before company, and such other points of the *Small Moralls*; But those qualities of man-kind, that concern their living together in Peace, and Unity. To which end we are to consider, that the Felicity of this life, consisteth not in the repose of a mind satisfied. For there is no such *Finis ultimus*, (utmost ayme,) nor *Summum Bonum*, (greatest Good,) as is spoken of in the Books of the old Morall Philosophers. Nor can a man any more live, whose Desires are at an end, than he, whose Senses and Imaginations are at a stand. Felicity is a continuall progresse of the desire, from one object to another ; the attaining of the former, being still but the way to the later. The cause whereof is, That the object of mans desire, is not to enjoy once onely, and for one instant of time ; but to assure for ever, the way of his future desire. And therefore the voluntary actions, and inclinations of all men, tend, not onely to the procuring, but also to the assuring of a contented life ; and differ onely in the way : which ariseth partly from the diversity of passions, in divers men ; and partly from the difference of the knowledge, or opinion each one has of the causes, which produce the effect desired.

A restlesse desire of Power, in all men.

So that in the first place, I put for a generall inclination of all mankind, a perpetuall and restlesse desire of Power after power, that ceaseth onely in Death. And the cause of this, is not alwayes that a man hopes for a more intensive delight, than he has already attained to ; or that he cannot [illegible] content with a moderate power : but because he [illegible] assure the power and means to live well, which [illegible]th present, without the acquisition of more. And [illegible] hence it is, that Kings, whose power is greatest, turn their endeavours to the assuring it at home by Lawes, or abroad by Wars : and when that is done, there succeedeth a new desire ; in some, of Fame from new Conquest ; in others, of ease and sensuall pleasure ; in others, of admiration, or being flattered for excellence in some art, or other ability of the mind.

Love of Contention from Competition.

Competition of Riches, Honour, Command, or other power, enclineth to Contention, Enmity, and War : [48] Because the way of one Competitor, to the attaining of his desire, is to kill, subdue, supplant, or repell the other. Particularly, competition of praise, enclineth to a reverence of Antiquity. For men contend with one living, not with the dead; to these ascribing more than due, that they may obscure the glory of the other.

Obedience from love of Ease. Desire of Ease, and sensuall Delight, disposeth men to obey a common Power: Because by such Desires, a man doth abandon the protection might be hoped for from his own Industry, and labour. *From feare of Death, or Wounds.* Fear of Death, and Wounds, disposeth to the same; and for the same reason. On the contrary, needy men, and hardy, not contented with their present condition; as also, all men that are ambitious of Military command. are enclined to continue the causes of warre; and to stirre up trouble and sedition. for there is no honour Military but by warre; nor any such hope to mend an ill game, as by causing a new shuffle

And from love of Arts. Desire of Knowledge, and Arts of Peace, enclineth men to obey a common Power: For such Desire, containeth a desire of leasure; and consequently protection from some other Power than their own.

Love of Vertue, from love of Praise. Desire of Praise, disposeth to laudable actions, such as please them whose judgement they value; for of those men whom we contemn, we contemn also the Praises. Desire of Fame after death does the same. And though after death, there be no sense of the praise given us on Earth, as being joyes, that are either swallowed up in the unspeakable joyes of Heaven, or extinguished in the extreme torments of Hell. yet is not such Fame vain; because men have a present delight therein, from the foresight of it, and of the benefit that may redound thereby to their posterity: which though they now see not, yet they imagine; and any thing that is pleasure in the sense, the same also is pleasure in the imagination.

Hate, from difficulty of Requiting great Benefits. To have received from one, to whom we think our selves equall, greater benefits than there is hope to Requite, disposeth to counterfeit love, but really secret hatred; and puts a man into the estate of a desperate debtor, that in declining the sight of his creditor, tacitely wishes him there, where he might never see him more. For benefits oblige; and obligation is thraldome, and unrequitable obligation, perpetuall thraldome; which is to ones equall, hatefull. But to have received benefits from one, whom we acknowledge for superiour, enclines to love; because the obligation is no new depression: and cheerfull acceptation, (which men call *Gratitude*,) is such an honour done to the obliger, as is taken generally for retribution. Also to receive benefits, though from an equall, or inferiour, as long as there is hope of requitall, disposeth to love: for in the intention of the receiver, the obligation is of ayd, and service mutuall; from whence proceedeth an Emulation of who shall exceed in benefiting; the most noble and profitable contention possible; wherein the victor is pleased with his victory, and the other revenged by confessing it.

And from Conscience of deserving to be hated.

To have done more hurt to a man, than he can, or is willing to expiate, enclineth the doer to hate the sufferer. For he must expect re|venge, or forgivenesse; both which are hatefull.

[49]

Promptnesse to hurt, from Fear.

Feare of oppression, disposeth a man to anticipate, or to seek ayd by society: for there is no other way by which a man can secure his life and liberty.

And from distrust of their own wit.

Men that distrust their own subtilty, are in tumult, and sedition, better disposed for victory, than they that suppose themselves wise, or crafty. For these love to consult, the other (fearing to be circumvented,) to strike first. And in sedition, men being alwayes in the procincts of battell, to hold together, and use all advantages of force, is a better stratagem, than any that can proceed from subtilty of Wit.

Vain undertaking from Vain-glory.

Vain-glorious men, such as without being conscious to themselves of great sufficiency, delight in supposing themselves gallant men, are enclined onely to ostentation; but not to attempt: Because when danger or difficulty appears, they look for nothing but to have their insufficiency discovered.

Vain-glorious men, such as estimate their sufficiency by the flattery of other men, or the fortune of some precedent action, without assured ground of hope from the true knowledge of themselves, are enclined to rash engaging: and in the approach of danger, or difficulty, to retire if they can: because not seeing the way of safety, they will rather hazard their honour, which may be salved with an excuse; than their lives, for which no salve is sufficient.

Ambition, from opinion of sufficiency. Men that have a strong opinion of their own wisdome in matter of government, are disposed to Ambition. Because without publique Employment in counsell or magistracy, the honour of their wisdome is lost. And therefore Eloquent speakers are enclined to Ambition; for Eloquence seemeth wisedome, both to themselves and others

Irresolution, from too great valuing of small matters. Pusillanimity disposeth men to Irresolution, and consequently to lose the occasions, and fittest opportunities of action. For after men have been in deliberation till the time of action approach, if it be not then manifest what is best to be done, 'tis a signe, the difference of Motives, the one way and the other, are not great: Therefore not to resolve then, is to lose the occasion by weighing of trifles; which is Pusillanimity.

Frugality, (though in poor men a Vertue,) maketh a man unapt to atchieve such actions, as require the strength of many men at once: For it weakeneth their Endeavour, which is to be nourished and kept in vigor by Reward.

Confidence in others from Ignorance of the marks of Wisdome and Kindnesse. Eloquence, with flattery, disposeth men to confide in them that have it, because the former is seeming Wisdome, the later seeming Kindnesse. Adde to them Military reputation, and it disposeth men to adhære, and subject themselves to those men that have them. The two former, having given them caution against danger from him; the later gives them caution against danger from others.

And from Ignorance of naturall causes Want of Science, that is, Ignorance of causes, disposeth, or rather constraineth a man to rely on the advise, and authority of others. For all men whom the truth concernes, if they rely not on their own, must rely on the opinion of some other, whom they think wiser than themselves, and see not why he should deceive them.

[50] *And from want of Understanding.* Ignorance of the signification of words; which is, want of understanding, disposeth men to take on trust, not onely the truth they know not; but also the errors, and which is more, the non-sense of them they trust:

For neither Error, nor non-sense, can without a perfect understanding of words, be detected.

From the same it proceedeth, that men give different names, to one and the same thing, from the difference of their own passions: As they that approve a private opinion, call it Opinion; but they that mislike it, Hæresie: and yet hæresie signifies no more than private opinion; but has onely a greater tincture of choler.

From the same also it proceedeth, that men cannot distinguish, without study and great understanding, between one action of many men, and many actions of one multitude; as for example, between the one action of all the Senators of *Rome* in killing *Catiline*, and the many actions of a number of Senators in killing *Cæsar*; and therefore are disposed to take for the action of the people, that which is a multitude of actions done by a multitude of men, led perhaps by the perswasion of one.

Adhærence to Custome from Ignorance of the nature of Right and Wrong.

Ignorance of the causes, and originall constitution of Right, Equity, Law, and Justice, disposeth a man to make Custome and Example the rule of his actions; in such manner, as to think that Unjust which it hath been the custome to punish; and that Just, of the impunity and approbation whereof they can produce an Example, or (as the Lawyers which onely use this false measure of Justice barbarously call it) a Precedent; like little children, that have no other rule of good and evill manners, but the correction they receive from their Parents, and Masters; save that children are constant to their rule, whereas men are not so; because grown strong, and stubborn, they appeale from custome to reason, and from reason to custome, as it serves their turn; receding from custome when their interest requires it, and setting themselves against reason, as oft as reason is against them: Which is the cause, that the doctrine of Right and Wrong, is perpetually disputed, both by the Pen and the Sword: Whereas the doctrine of Lines, and Figures, is not so; because men care not, in that subject what be truth, as a thing that crosses no mans ambition, profit, or lust. For I doubt not, but if it had been a thing contrary to any mans right of dominion, or to the interest of men that have dominion, *That the three Angles of a Triangle, should be equall to two Angles of a Square*; that doctrine should have been, if not disputed, yet by the burning of all books of Geometry, suppressed, as farre as he whom it concerned was able.

Adhærence to private men, From Ignorance of the Causes of Peace.

Ignorance of remote causes, disposeth men to attribute all events, to the causes immediate, and Instrumentall: For these are all the causes they perceive. And hence it comes to passe, that in all places, men that are grieved with payments to the Publique, discharge their anger upon the Publicans, that is to say, Farmers, Collectors, and other Officers of the publique Revenue; and adhære to such as find fault with the publike Government; and thereby, when they have engaged themselves beyond hope
[51] of justification, fall also upon the Supreme Authority, for feare of punishment, or shame of receiving pardon.

Credulity from Ignorance of nature.

Ignorance of naturall causes disposeth a man to Credulity, so as to believe many times impossibilities: For such know nothing to the contrary, but that they may be true; being unable to detect the Impossibility. And Credulity, because men love to be hearkened unto in company, disposeth them to lying: so that Ignorance it selfe without Malice, is able to make a man both to believe lyes, and tell them; and sometimes also to invent them.

Curiosity to know, from Care of future time.

Anxiety for the future time, disposeth men to enquire into the causes of things: because the knowledge of them, maketh men the better able to order the present to their best advantage.

Naturall Religion, from the same.

Curiosity, or love of the knowledge of causes, draws a man from consideration of the effect, to seek the cause; and again, the cause of that cause; till of necessity he must come to this thought at last, that there is some cause, whereof there is no former cause, but is eternall; which is it men call God. So that it is impossible to make any profound enquiry into naturall causes, without being enclined thereby to believe there is one God Eternall; though they cannot have any Idea of him in their mind, answerable to his nature. For as a man that is born blind, hearing men talk of warming themselves by the fire, and being brought to warm himself by the same, may easily conceive, and assure himselfe, there is somewhat there, which men call *Fire,* and is the cause of the heat he feeles; but cannot imagine what it is like; nor have an Idea of it in his mind, such as they have that see it: so also, by the visible things of this world, and their admirable order, a man may conceive there is a cause of them, which men call God; and yet not have an Idea, or Image of him in his mind.

And they that make little, or no enquiry into the naturall causes of things, yet from the feare that proceeds from the ignorance it selfe, of what it is that hath the power to do them much good or harm, are enclined to suppose, and feign unto themselves, severall kinds of Powers Invisible; and to stand in awe of their own imaginations; and in time of distresse to invoke them; as also in the time of an expected good successe, to give them thanks; making the creatures of their own fancy, their Gods. By which means it hath come to passe, that from the innumerable variety of Fancy, men have created in the world innumerable sorts of Gods. And this Feare of things invisible, is the naturall Seed of that, which every one in himself calleth Religion; and in them that worship, or feare that Power otherwise than they do, Superstition.

And this seed of Religion, having been observed by many; some of those that have observed it, have been enclined thereby to nourish, dresse, and forme it into Lawes; and to adde to it of their own invention, any opinion of the causes of future events, by which they thought they should best be able to govern others, and make unto themselves the greatest use of their Powers.

CHAP. XII. [52]

Of Religion.

Religion, in Man onely.

SEEING there are no signes, nor fruit of *Religion*, but in Man onely; there is no cause to doubt, but that the seed of *Religion*, is also onely in Man; and consisteth in some peculiar quality, or at least in some eminent degree therof, not to be found in other Living creatures.

First, from his desire of knowing Causes.

And first, it is peculiar to the nature of Man, to be inquisitive into the Causes of the Events they see, some more, some lesse; but all men so much, as to be curious in the search of the causes of their own good and evill fortune.

From the consideration of the Beginning of things.

Secondly, upon the sight of any thing that hath a Beginning, to think also it had a cause, which determined the same to begin, then when it did, rather than sooner or later.

From his observation of the Sequell of things

Thirdly, whereas there is no other Felicity of Beasts, but the enjoying of their quotidian Food, Ease, and Lusts; as having little, or no foresight of the time to come, for want of observation, and memory of the order, consequence, and dependance of the things they see, Man observeth how one Event hath been produced by another; and remembreth in them Antecedence and Consequence; And when he cannot assure himselfe of the true causes of things, (for the causes of good and evill fortune for the most part are invisible,) he supposes causes of them, either such as his own fancy suggesteth; or trusteth to the Authority of other men, such as he thinks to be his friends, and wiser than himselfe.

The naturall Cause of Religion, the Anxiety of the time to come.

The two first, make Anxiety. For being assured that there be causes of all things that have arrived hitherto, or shall arrive hereafter; it is impossible for a man, who continually endeavoureth to secure himselfe against the evill he feares, and procure the good he desireth, not to be in a perpetuall solicitude of the time to come; So that every man, especially those that are over provident, are in an estate like to that of *Prometheus*. For as *Prometheus*, (which interpreted, is, *The prudent man*,) was bound to the hill *Caucasus*, a place of large prospect, where, an Eagle feeding on his liver, devoured in the day, as much as was repayred in the night: So that man, which looks too far before him, in the care of future time, hath his heart all the day long, gnawed on by feare of death, poverty, or other calamity; and has no repose, nor pause of his anxiety, but in sleep.

Which makes them fear the Power

This perpetuall feare, alwayes accompanying mankind in the ignorance of causes, as it were in the Dark, must needs have for object something. And therefore when *of Invisible things.*

there is nothing to be seen, there is nothing to accuse, either of their good, or evill fortune, but some *Power*, or Agent *Invisible*: In which sense perhaps it was, that some of the old Poets said, that the Gods were at first created by humane Feare: which spoken of the Gods, [53]
(that is to say, of the many Gods of the Gentiles) is very true. But the acknowledging of one God Eternall, Infinite, and Omnipotent, may more easily be derived, from the desire men have to know the causes of naturall bodies, and their severall vertues, and operations; than from the feare of what was to befall them in time to come. For he that from any effect hee seeth come to passe, should reason to the next and immediate cause thereof, and from thence to the cause of that cause, and plonge himselfe profoundly in the pursuit of causes; shall at last come to this, that there must be (as even the Heathen Philosophers confessed) one First Mover; that is, a First, and an Eternall cause of all things; which is that which men mean by the name of God: And all this without thought of their fortune; the solicitude whereof, both enclines to fear, and hinders them from the search of the causes of other things; and thereby gives occasion of feigning of as many Gods, as there be men that feigne them.

And suppose them Incorporeall.

And for the matter, or substance of the Invisible Agents, so fancyed; they could not by naturall cogitation, fall upon any other conceipt, but that it was the same with that of the Soule of man; and that the Soule of man, was of the same substance, with that which appeareth in a Dream, to one that sleepeth; or in a Looking-glasse, to one that is awake; which, men not knowing that such apparitions are nothing else but creatures of the Fancy, think to be reall, and externall Substances; and therefore call them Ghosts; as the Latines called them *Imagines*, and *Umbræ*; and thought them Spirits, that is, thin aëreall bodies; and those Invisible Agents, which they feared, to bee like them; save that they appear, and vanish when they please. But the opinion that such Spirits were Incorporeall, or Immateriall, could never enter into the mind of any man by nature; because, though men may put together words of contradictory signification, as *Spirit*, and *Incorporeall*; yet they can never have the imagination of any thing answering to them: And therefore, men that by their own meditation, arrive to the acknowledgement of one Infinite, Omnipotent, and Eternall God, choose rather to confesse he is Incomprehensible, and above their understanding; than to define his Nature by *Spirit Incorporeall*, and then confesse their definition to be unintelligible: or if they give him such a title, it is not *Dogmatically*, with intention to make the Divine Nature understood; but *Piously*, to honour him with attributes, of significations, as remote as they can from the grossenesse of Bodies Visible.

But know not the way how they effect any thing.

Then, for the way by which they think these Invisible Agents wrought their effects; that is to say, what immediate causes they used, in bringing things to passe, men that know not what it is that we call *causing*, (that is, almost all men) have no other rule to guesse by, but by observing, and remembring what they have seen to precede the like effect at some other time, or times before, without seeing between the antecedent and subsequent Event, any dependance or connexion at all: And therefore from the like things past, they expect the like things to come; and hope for good or evill luck, superstitiously, from things that have no part at all in the
[54] causing of it: As the Athenians did for their war at *Lepanto*, demand another *Phormio*; The Pompeian faction for their warre in *Afrique*, another *Scipio*; and others have done in divers other occasions since. In like manner they attribute their fortune to a stander by, to a lucky or unlucky place, to words spoken, especially if the name of God be amongst them; as Charming, and Conjuring (the Leiturgy of Witches,) insomuch as to believe, they have power to turn a stone into bread, bread into a man, or any thing, into any thing.

But honour them as they honour men.

Thirdly, for the worship which naturally men exhibite to Powers invisible, it can be no other, but such expressions of their reverence, as they would use towards men; Gifts, Petitions, Thanks, Submission of Body, Considerate Addresses, sober Behaviour, premeditated Words, Swearing (that is, assuring one another of their promises,) by invoking them. Beyond that reason suggesteth nothing; but leaves them either to rest there; or for further ceremonies, to rely on those they believe to be wiser than themselves.

And attribute to them all extraordinary events.

Lastly, concerning how these Invisible Powers declare to men the things which shall hereafter come to passe, especially concerning their good or evill fortune in generall, or good or ill successe in any particular undertaking, men are naturally at a stand; save that using to conjecture of the time to come, by the time past, they are very apt, not onely to take casuall things, after one or two encounters, for Prognostiques of the like encounter ever after, but also to believe the like Prognostiques from other men, of whom they have once conceived a good opinion.

Foure things, Naturall seeds of Religion.

And in these foure things, Opinion of Ghosts, Ignorance of second causes, Devotion towards what men fear, and Taking of things Casuall for Prognostiques, consisteth the Naturall seed of *Religion*; which by reason of the different Fancies, Judgements, and Passions of severall men, hath grown up into ceremonies so different, that those which are used by one man, are for the most part ridiculous to another

Made different by Culture.

For these seeds have received culture from two sorts of men. One sort have been they, that have nourished, and ordered them, according to their own invention. The other, have done it, by Gods commandement, and direction: but both sorts have done it, with a purpose to make those men that relyed on them, the more apt to Obedience, Lawes, Peace, Charity, and civill Society. So that the Religion of the former sort, is a part of humane Politiques; and teacheth part of the duty which Earthly Kings require of their Subjects. And the Religion of the later sort is Divine Politiques; and containeth Precepts to those that have yeelded themselves subjects in the Kingdome of God. Of the former sort, were all the founders of Common-wealths, and the Law-givers of the Gentiles. Of the later sort, were *Abraham*, *Moses*, and our *Blessed Saviour*; by whom have been derived unto us the Lawes of the Kingdome of God.

The absurd opinion of Gentilisme. [55] And for that part of Religion, which consisteth in opinions concerning the nature of Powers Invisible, there is almost nothing that has a name, that has not been esteemed amongst the Gentiles, in one place or another, a God, or Divell, or by their Poets feigned to be inanimated, inhabited, or possessed by some Spirit or other.

The unformed matter of the World, was a God, by the name of *Chaos*.

The Heaven, the Ocean, the Planets, the Fire, the Earth, the Winds, were so many Gods.

Men, Women, a Bird, a Crocodile, a Calf, a Dogge, a Snake, an Onion, a Leeke, Deified. Besides, that they filled almost all places, with spirits called *Dæmons*: the plains, with *Pan*, and *Panises*, or Satyres; the Woods, with Fawnes, and Nymphs; the Sea, with Tritons, and other Nymphs; every River, and Fountayn, with a Ghost of his name, and with Nymphs; every house, with its *Lares*, or Familiars; every man, with his *Genius*; Hell, with Ghosts, and spirituall Officers, as *Charon*, *Cerberus*, and the *Furies*; and in the night time, all places with *Larvæ*, *Lemures*, Ghosts of men deceased, and a whole kingdome of Fayries, and Bugbears. They have also ascribed Divinity, and built Temples to meer Accidents, and Qualities; such as are Time, Night, Day, Peace, Concord, Love, Contention, Vertue, Honour, Health, Rust, Fever, and the like; which when they prayed for, or against, they prayed to, as if there were Ghosts of those names hanging over their heads, and letting fall, or withholding that Good, or Evill, for, or against which they prayed. They invoked also their own Wit, by the name of *Muses*; their own Ignorance, by the name of *Fortune*; their own Lust, by the name of *Cupid*; their own Rage, by the name *Furies*; their own privy members by the name of *Priapus*; and attributed their pollutions, to *Incubi*, and *Succubæ*: insomuch as there was nothing, which a Poet could introduce as a person in his Poem, which they did not make either a *God*, or a *Divel*.

The same authors of the Religion of the Gentiles, observing the second ground for Religion, which is mens Ignorance of causes; and thereby their aptnesse to attribute their fortune to causes, on which there was no dependance at all apparent, took occasion to obtrude on their ignorance, in stead of second causes, a kind of second and ministeriall Gods; ascribing the cause of Fœcundity, to *Venus*; the cause of Arts, to *Apollo*; of Subtilty and Craft, to *Mercury*; of Tempests and stormes, to *Æolus*; and of other effects, to other Gods: insomuch as there was amongst the Heathen almost as great variety of Gods, as of businesse.

And to the Worship, which naturally men conceived fit to bee used towards their Gods, namely Oblations, Prayers, Thanks, and the rest formerly named; the same Legislators of the Gentiles have added their Images, both in Picture, and Sculpture; that the more ignorant sort, (that is to say, the most part, or generality of the people,) thinking the Gods for whose representation they were made, were really included, and as it were housed within them, might so much the more stand in feare of them: And endowed them with lands, and houses, and officers, and revenues, set apart from all other humane uses; that is, consecrated, and made holy to those their Idols; as Caverns, Groves, Woods, Mountains, and whole Ilands; and have attributed to [56]
them, not onely the shapes, some of Men, some of Beasts, some of Monsters; but also the Faculties, and Passions of men and beasts; as Sense, Speech, Sex, Lust, Generation, (and this not onely by mixing one with another, to propagate the kind of Gods; but also by mixing with men, and women, to beget mongrill Gods, and but inmates of Heaven, as *Bacchus*, *Hercules*, and others;) besides, Anger, Revenge, and other passions of living creatures, and the actions proceeding from them, as Fraud, Theft, Adultery, Sodomie, and any vice that may be taken for an effect of Power, or a cause of Pleasure; and all such Vices, as amongst men are taken to be against Law, rather than against Honour.

Lastly, to the Prognostiques of time to come; which are naturally, but Conjectures upon the Experience of time past; and supernaturally, divine Revelation; the same authors of the Religion of the Gentiles, partly upon pretended Experience, partly upon pretended

Revelation, have added innumerable other superstitious wayes of Divination; and made men believe they should find their fortunes, sometimes in the ambiguous or senslesse answers of the Priests at *Delphi*, *Delos*, *Ammon*, and other famous Oracles; which answers, were made ambiguous by designe, to own the event both wayes; or absurd, by the intoxicating vapour of the place, which is very frequent in sulphurous Cavernes: Sometimes in the leaves of the Sibills; of whose Prophecyes (like those perhaps of *Nostradamus*; for the fragments now extant seem to be the invention of later times) there were some books in reputation in the time of the Roman Republique: Sometimes in the insignificant Speeches of Mad-men, supposed to be possessed with a divine Spirit; which Possession they called Enthusiasme; and these kinds of foretelling events, were accounted Theomancy, or Prophecy Sometimes in the aspect of the Starres at their Nativity, which was called Horoscopy, and esteemed a part of judiciary Astrology: Sometimes in their own hopes and feares, called Thumomancy, or Presage: Sometimes in the Prediction of Witches, that pretended conference with the dead; which is called Necromancy, Conjuring, and Witchcraft, and is but juggling and confederate knavery: Sometimes in the Casuall flight, or feeding of birds; called Augury: Sometimes in the Entrayles of a sacrificed beast; which was *Aruspicina*: Sometimes in Dreams: Sometimes in Croaking of Ravens, or chattering of Birds: Sometimes in the Lineaments of the face; which was called Metoposcopy; or by Palmistry in the lines of the hand; in casuall words, called *Omina*. Sometimes in Monsters, or unusuall accidents; as Ecclipses, Comets, rare Meteors, Earthquakes, Inundations, uncouth Births, and the like, which they called *Portenta*, and *Ostenta*, because they thought them to portend, or foreshew some great Calamity to come: Somtimes, in meer Lottery, as Crosse and Pile; counting holes in a sive; dipping of Verses in *Homer*, and *Virgil*; and innumerable other such vaine conceipts. So easie are men to be drawn to believe any thing, from such men as have gotten credit with them; and can with gentlenesse, and dexterity, take hold of their fear, and ignorance.

[57] *The designes of the Authors of the Religion of the Heathen.*

And therefore the first Founders, and Legislators of Common-wealths amongst the Gentiles, whose ends were only to keep the people in obedience, and peace, have in all places taken care; First, to imprint in their minds a beliefe, that those precepts which they gave concerning Religion, might not be thought to proceed from their own device, but from the dictates of some God, or other Spirit; or else that they themselves were of a higher nature than mere mortalls, that their Lawes might the more easily be received: So *Numa Pompilius* pretended to receive the Ceremonies he instituted amongst the Romans, from the Nymph *Egeria*: and the first King and founder of the Kingdome of *Peru*, pretended himselfe and his wife to be the children of the Sunne: and *Mahomet*, to set up his new Religion, pretended to have conferences with the Holy Ghost, in forme of a Dove. Secondly, they have had a care, to make it believed, that the same things were displeasing to the Gods, which were forbidden by the Lawes. Thirdly, to prescribe Ceremonies, Supplications, Sacrifices, and Festivalls, by which they were to believe, the anger of the Gods might be appeased; and that ill success in War, great contagions of Sicknesse, Earthquakes, and each mans private Misery, came from the Anger of the Gods; and their Anger from the Neglect of their Worship, or the forgetting, or mistaking some point of the Ceremonies required. And though amongst the antient Romans, men were not forbidden to deny, that which in the Poets is written of the paines, and pleasures after this life; which divers of great authority, and gravity in that state have in their *Harangues* openly derided; yet that beliefe was alwaies more cherished, than the contrary.

And by these, and such other Institutions, they obtayned in order to their end, (which was the peace of the Commonwealth,) that the common people in their misfortunes, laying the fault on neglect, or errour in their Ceremonies, or on their own disobedience to the lawes, were the lesse apt to mutiny against their

Governors And being entertained with the pomp, and pastime of Festivalls, and publike Games, made in honour of the Gods, needed nothing else but bread, to keep them from discontent, murmuring, and commotion against the State. And therefore the Romans, that had conquered the greatest part of the then known World, made no scruple of tollerating any Religion whatsoever in the City of *Rome* it selfe; unlesse it had something in it, that could not consist with their Civill Government; nor do we read, that any Religion was there forbidden, but that of the Jewes; who (being the peculiar Kingdome of God) thought it unlawfull to acknowledge subjection to any mortall King or State whatsoever. And thus you see how the Religion of the Gentiles was a part of their Policy.

The true Religion, and the lawes of Gods kingdome the same

But where God himselfe, by supernaturall Revelation, planted Religion; there he also made to himselfe a peculiar Kingdome; and gave Lawes, not only of behaviour towards himselfe; but also towards one another; and thereby in the Kingdome of God, the Policy, and lawes Civill, are a part of Religion; and
[58] therefore the distinction of Temporall, and Spirituall Domination, hath there no place. It is true, that God is King of all the Earth. Yet may he be King of a peculiar, and chosen Nation. For there is no more incongruity there in, than that he that hath the generall command of the whole Army, should have withall a peculiar Regiment, or Company of his own God is King of all the Earth by his Power: but of his chosen people, he is King by Covenant. But to speake more largly of the Kingdome of God, both by Nature, and Covenant, I have in the following discourse assigned an other place

Chap. 35

The causes of Change in Religion

From the propagation of Religion, it is not hard to understand the causes of the resolution of the same into its first seeds, or principles; which are only an opinion of a Deity, and Powers invisible, and supernaturall; that can never be so abolished out of humane nature, but that new Religions may againe be made to spring out of them, by the culture of such men, as for such purpose are in reputation

For seeing all formed Religion, is founded at first, upon the faith which a multitude hath in some one person, whom they believe not only to be a wise man, and to labour to procure their happiness, but also to be a holy man, to whom God himselfe vouchsafeth to declare his will supernaturally; It followeth necessarily, when they that have the Goverment of Religion, shall come to have either the wisedome of those men, their sincerity, or their love suspected; or that they shall be unable to shew any probable token of Divine Revelation; that the Religion which they desire to uphold, must be suspected likewise; and (without the feare of the Civill Sword) contradicted and rejected.

Injoyning beleefe of Impossibilities.

That which taketh away the reputation of Wisedome, in him that formeth a Religion, or addeth to it when it is allready formed, is the enjoyning of a beliefe of contradictories: For both parts of a contradiction cannot possibly be true: and therefore to enjoyne the beleife of them, is an argument of ignorance; which detects the Author in that; and discredits him in all things else he shall propound as from revelation supernaturall: which revelation a man may indeed have of many things above, but of nothing against naturall reason.

Doing contrary to the Religion they establish.

That which taketh away the reputation of Sincerity, is the doing, or saying of such things, as appeare to be signes, that what they require other men to believe, is not believed by themselves; all which doings, or sayings are therefore called Scandalous, because they be stumbling blocks, that make men to fall in the way of Religion: as Injustice, Cruelty, Prophanesse, Avarice, and Luxury. For who can believe, that he that doth ordinarily such actions, as proceed from any of these rootes, believeth there is any such Invisible Power to be feared, as he affrighteth other men withall, for lesser faults?

That which taketh away the reputation of Love, is the being detected of private ends: as when the beliefe they require of others, conduceth or seemeth to conduce to the acquiring of Dominion, Riches, Dignity, or secure [59]
Pleasure, to themselves onely, or specially. For that which men reap benefit by to themselves, they are thought to do for their own sakes, and not for love of others.

Want of the testimony of Miracles. Lastly, the testimony that men can render of divine Calling, can be no other, than the operation of Miracles; or true Prophecy, (which also is a Miracle;) or extraordinary Felicity. And therefore, to those points of Religion, which have been received from them that did such Miracles; those that are added by such, as approve not their Calling by some Miracle, obtain no greater beliefe, than what the Custome, and Lawes of the places, in which they be educated, have wrought into them. For as in naturall things, men of judgement require naturall signes, and arguments; so in supernaturall things, they require signes supernaturall, (which are Miracles,) before they consent inwardly, and from their hearts

All which causes of the weakening of mens faith, do manifestly appear in the Examples following. First, we have the Example of the children of Israel; who when *Moses*, that had approved his Calling to them by Miracles, and by the happy conduct of them out of *Egypt*, was absent but 40 dayes, revolted from the worship of the true God, recommended to them by him; and
*Exod 32. 1, 2. setting up * a Golden Calfe for their God, relapsed into the Idolatry of the Egyptians; from whom they had been so lately delivered. And again, after *Moses*, *Aaron*, *Joshua*, and that generation which had seen the great
*Judges 2. 11 works of God in Israel, * were dead; another generation arose, and served *Baal*. So that Miracles fayling, Faith also failed

*1 Sam. 8 3. Again, when the sons of *Samuel*, * being constituted by their father Judges in *Bersabee*, received bribes, and judged unjustly, the people of Israel refused any more to have God to be their King, in other manner than he was King of other people; and therefore cryed out to *Samuel*, to choose them a King after the manner of the Nations. So that Justice fayling, Faith also fayled: Insomuch, as they deposed their God, from reigning over them.

And whereas in the planting of Christian Religion, the Oracles ceased in all parts of the Roman Empire, and the number of Christians encreased wonderfully every day, and in every place, by the preaching of the Apostles, and Evangelists; a great part of that successe, may reasonably be attributed, to the contempt, into which the Priests of the Gentiles of that time, had brought themselves, by their uncleannesse, avarice, and jugling between Princes. Also the Religion of the Church of *Rome*, was partly, for the same cause abolished in *England*, and many other parts of Christendome; insomuch, as the fayling of Vertue in the Pastors, maketh Faith faile in the People: and partly from bringing of the Philosophy, and doctrine of *Aristotle* into Religion, by the Schoole-men; from whence there arose so many contradictions, and absurdities, as brought the Clergy into a reputation both of Ignorance, and of Fraudulent intention; and enclined people to revolt from them, either against the will of their own Princes, as in *France*, and *Holland*; or with their will, as in *England*.

Lastly, amongst the points by the Church of *Rome* declared necessary for Salvation, there be so many, manifestly to the advantage of the Pope, and of his spirituall subjects, residing in the territories of other Christian Princes, that were it not for the mutuall emulation of those Princes, they might without warre, or trouble, exclude all forraign Authority, as easily as it has been excluded in *England*. For who is there that does not see, to whose benefit it conduceth, to have it believed, that a King hath not his Authority from Christ, unlesse a Bishop crown him? That a King, if he be a Priest, cannot Marry? That whether a Prince be born in lawfull Marriage, or not, must be judged by Authority from *Rome*? That Subjects may be freed from their Alleageance, if by the Court of *Rome*, the King be judged an Heretique? That a King (as *Chilperique* of *France*) may be deposed by a Pope (as Pope *Zachary*,) for no cause; and his Kingdome given to one of his Subjects? That the Clergy, and Regulars, in what Country soever, shall be exempt from the Jurisdiction of their King, in cases criminall? Or who does not see, to whose profit redound the Fees of private Masses, and Vales of Purgatory; with other signes of private interest, enough to mortifie the most lively Faith, if (as I sayd) the civill Magistrate, and Custome did not more sustain it, than any opinion they have of the Sanctity, Wisdome, or Probity of their Teachers? So that I may attribute all the changes of Religion in the world, to one and the same cause; and that is, unpleasing Priests; and those not onely amongst Catholiques, but even in that Church that hath presumed most of Reformation.

CHAP. XIII.

Of the NATURALL CONDITION *of Mankind, as concerning their Felicity, and Misery.*

NATURE hath made men so equall, in the faculties of body, and mind; as that though there bee found one man sometimes manifestly stronger in body, or of quicker mind then another; yet when all is reckoned together, the difference between man, and man, is not so considerable, as that one man can thereupon claim to himselfe any benefit, to which another may not pretend, as well as he. For as to the strength of body, the weakest has strength enough to kill the strongest, *Exod 1, 2. either by secret machination, or by confederacy with others, that are in the same danger with himselfe.

And as to the faculties of the mind, (setting aside the arts grounded upon words, and especially that skill of *Judges 2 11. proceeding upon generall, and infallible rules, called Science; which very few have, and but in few things; as being not a native faculty, born with us; nor attained, *1 Sam. 3. (as Prudence,) while we look after somewhat els,) I find yet a greater equality amongst men, than that of strength. For Prudence, is but Experience; which equall time, [61] equally bestowes on all men, in those things they equally apply themselves unto. That which may perhaps make such equality incredible, is but a vain conceipt of ones owne wisdome, which almost all men think they have in a greater degree, than the Vulgar; that is, than all men but themselves, and a few others, whom by Fame, or for concurring with themselves, they approve. For such is the nature of men, that howsoever they may acknowledge many others to be more witty, or more eloquent, or more learned; Yet they will hardly believe maye be many so wise as themselves: For they see their own wit at hand, and other mens at a distance. But this proveth rather that men are in that point equall, than unequall. For there is not ordinarily a greater signe of the equall distribution of any thing, than that every man is contented with his share.

From Equality proceeds Diffidence.

From this equality of ability, ariseth equality of hope in the attaining of our Ends. And therefore if any two men desire the same thing, which neverthelesse they cannot both enjoy, they become enemies; and in the way to their End, (which is principally their owne conservation, and sometimes their delectation only,) endeavour to destroy, or subdue one an other. And from hence it comes to passe, that where an Invader hath no more to feare, than an other mans single power; if one plant, sow, build, or possesse a convenient Seat, others may probably be expected to come prepared with forces united, to dispossesse, and deprive him, not only of the fruit of his labour, but also of his life, or liberty. And the Invader again is in the like danger of another.

From Diffidence Warre.

And from this diffidence of one another, there is no way for any man to secure himselfe, so reasonable, as Anticipation; that is, by force, or wiles, to master the persons of all men he can, so long, till he see no other power great enough to endanger him: And this is no more than his own conservation requireth, and is generally allowed. Also because there be some, that taking pleasure in contemplating their own power in the acts of conquest, which they pursue farther than their security requires; if others, that otherwise would be glad to be at ease within modest bounds, should not by invasion increase their power, they would not be able, long time, by standing only on their defence, to subsist. And by consequence, such augmentation of dominion over men, being necessary to a mans conservation, it ought to be allowed him.

Againe, men have no pleasure, (but on the contrary a great deale of griefe) in keeping company, where there is no power able to over-awe them all. For every man looketh that his companion should value him, at the same rate he sets upon himselfe: And upon all signes of contempt, or undervaluing, naturally endeavours, as far as he dares (which amongst them that have no common power to keep them in quiet, is far enough to make them destroy each other,) to extort a greater value from his contemners, by dommage; and from others, by the example.

So that in the nature of man, we find three principall causes of quarrell. First, Competition; Secondly, Diffidence; Thirdly, Glory.

[62] The first, maketh men invade for Gain; the second, for Safety; and the third, for Reputation. The first use Violence, to make themselves Masters of other mens persons, wives, children, and cattell; the second, to defend them; the third, for trifles, as a word, a smile, a different opinion, and any other signe of undervalue, either direct in their Persons, or by reflexion in their Kindred, their Friends, their Nation, their Profession, or their Name.

Out of Civil States, there is alwayes Warre *of every one against every one.*

Hereby it is manifest, that during the time men live without a common Power to keep them all in awe, they are in that condition which is called Warre; and such a warre, as is of every man, against every man. For WARRE, consisteth not in Battell onely, or the act of fighting; but in a tract of time, wherein the Will to contend by Battell is sufficiently known: and therefore the notion of *Time*, is to be considered in the nature of Warre; as it is in the nature of Weather. For as the nature of Foule weather, lyeth not in a showre or two of rain; but in an inclination thereto of many dayes together: So the nature of War, consisteth not in actuall fighting; but in the known disposition thereto, during all the time there is no assurance to the contrary. All other time is PEACE.

The Incommodities of such a War.

Whatsoever therefore is consequent to a time of Warre, where every man is Enemy to every man; the same is consequent to the time, wherein men live without other security, than what their own strength, and their own invention shall furnish them withall. In such condition, there is no place for Industry; because the fruit thereof is uncertain: and consequently no Culture of the Earth; no Navigation, nor use of the commodities that may be imported by Sea; no commodious Building; no Instruments of moving, and removing such things as require much force; no Knowledge of the face of the Earth; no account of Time; no Arts; no Letters; no Society; and which is worst of all, continuall feare, and danger of violent death; And the life of man, solitary, poore, nasty, brutish, and short.

It may seem strange to some man, that has not well weighed these things; that Nature should thus dissociate, and render men apt to invade, and destroy one another: and he may therefore, not trusting to this Inference, made from the Passions, desire perhaps to have the same confirmed by Experience. Let him therefore consider with himselfe, when taking a journey, he armes himselfe, and seeks to go well accompanied; when going to sleep, he locks his dores; when even in his house he locks his chests; and this when he knowes there bee Lawes, and publike Officers, armed, to revenge all injuries shall bee done him; what opinion he has of his fellow subjects, when he rides armed; of his fellow Citizens, when he locks his dores; and of his children, and servants, when he locks his chests. Does he not there as much accuse mankind by his actions, as I do by my words? But neither of us accuse mans nature in it. The Desires, and other Passions of man, are in themselves no Sin. No more are the Actions, that proceed from those Passions, till they know a Law that forbids them: which till Lawes be made they cannot know: nor can any Law be made, till they have agreed upon the Person that shall make it.

It may peradventure be thought, there was never [63]
such a time, nor condition of warre as this; and I believe it was never generally so, over all the world: but there are many places, where they live so now. For the savage people in many places of *America*, except the government of small Families, the concord whereof dependeth on naturall lust, have no government at all; and live at this day in that brutish manner, as I said before. Howsoever, it may be perceived what manner of life there would be, where there were no common Power to feare; by the manner of life, which men that have

formerly lived under a peacefull government, use to degenerate into, in a civill Warre.

But though there had never been any time, wherein particular men were in a condition of warre one against another; yet in all times, Kings, and Persons of Soveraigne authority, because of their Independency, are in continuall jealousies, and in the state and posture of Gladiators; having their weapons pointing, and their eyes fixed on one another; that is, their Forts, Garrisons, and Guns upon the Frontiers of their Kingdomes; and continuall Spyes upon their neighbours; which is a posture of War. But because they uphold thereby, the Industry of their Subjects; there does not follow from it, that misery, which accompanies the Liberty of particular men.

In such a Warre, nothing is Unjust.

To this warre of every man against every man, this also is consequent; that nothing can be Unjust. The notions of Right and Wrong, Justice and Injustice have there no place. Where there is no common Power, there is no Law: where no Law, no Injustice. Force, and Fraud, are in warre the two Cardinall vertues. Justice, and Injustice are none of the Faculties neither of the Body, nor Mind. If they were, they might be in a man that were alone in the world, as well as his Senses, and Passions. They are Qualities, that relate to men in Society, not in Solitude. It is consequent also to the same condition, that there be no Propriety, no Dominion, no *Mine* and *Thine* distinct; but onely that to be every mans, that he can get; and for so long, as he can keep it. And thus much for the ill condition, which man by meer Nature is actually placed in; though with a possibility to come out of it, consisting partly in the Passions, partly in his Reason.

The Passions that incline men to Peace.

The Passions that encline men to Peace, are Feare of Death; Desire of such things as are necessary to commodious living; and a Hope by their Industry to obtain them. And Reason suggesteth convenient Articles of Peace, upon which men may be drawn to agreement. These Articles, are they, which otherwise are called the Lawes of Nature: whereof I shall speak more particularly, in the two following Chapters.

CHAP. XIV. [64]

Of the first and second NATURALL LAWES, *and of* CONTRACTS.

Right of Nature what.

THE RIGHT OF NATURE, which Writers commonly call *Jus Naturale*, is the Liberty each man hath, to use his own power, as he will himselfe, for the preservation of his own Nature; that is to say, of his own Life; and consequently, of doing any thing, which in his own Judgement, and Reason, hee shall conceive to be the aptest means thereunto.

Liberty what.

By LIBERTY, is understood, according to the proper signification of the word, the absence of externall Impediments: which Impediments, may oft take away part of a mans power to do what hee would; but cannot hinder him from using the power left him, according as his judgement, and reason shall dictate to him.

A Law of Nature what.

A LAW OF NATURE, (*Lex Naturalis*,) is a Precept, or generall Rule, found out by Reason, by which a man is forbidden to do, that, which is destructive of his life, or taketh away the means of preserving the same; and to omit, that, by which he thinketh it may be best preserved. For though they that speak of this subject, use to confound *Jus*, and *Lex*, *Right* and *Law*; yet they ought to be distinguished; because RIGHT, consisteth in liberty to do, or to forbeare; Whereas LAW, determineth, and bindeth to one of them: so that Law, and Right, differ as much, as Obligation, and Liberty; which in one and the same matter are inconsistent.

Difference of Right and Law.

Naturally every man has Right to every thing.

And because the condition of Man, (as hath been declared in the precedent Chapter) is a condition of
. Whensoever a man st every one; in which case
nounceth it; it is eith his own Reason; and there
reciprocally transferred of, that may not be a help
good he hopeth for the life against his enemyes; It
and of the voluntary a ition, every man has a Right
some *Good to himselfe*. nothers body. And there-
Rights, which no man ca ght of every man to every
or other signes, to have a
first a man cannot lay dow

thing endureth, there can be no security to any man, (how strong or wise soever he be,) of living out the time, which Nature ordinarily alloweth men to live. And consequently it is a precept, or generall rule of Reason, *That every man, ought to endeavour Peace, as farre as he has hope of obtaining it; and when he cannot obtain it, that he may seek, and use, all helps, and advantages of Warre.* The first branch of which Rule, containeth the first, and Fundamentall Law of Nature; which is, *to seek Peace, and follow it.* The Second, the summe of the Right of Nature; which is, *By all means we can, to defend our selves.*

The Fundamentall Law of Nature.

The second Law of Nature.

From this Fundamentall Law of Nature, by which men are commanded to endeavour Peace, is derived the second Law; *That a man be willing, when others are so*
[65] *too, as farre-forth, as for Peace, and defence of himselfe he shall think it necessary, to lay down this right to all things; and be contented with so much liberty against other men, as he would allow other men against himselfe.* For as long as every man holdeth this Right, of doing any thing he liketh; so long are all men in the condition of Warre. But if other men will not lay down their Right, as wel as he; then there is no Reason for any one, to devest himselfe of his: For that were to expose himselfe to Prey, (which no man is bound to) rather than to dispose himselfe to Peace. This is that Law of the Gospell; *Whatsoever you require that others should do to you, that do ye to them.* And that Law of all men, *Quod tibi fieri non vis, alteri ne feceris.*

What it is to lay down a Right.

To *lay downe* a mans *Right* to any thing, is to *devest* himselfe of the *Liberty*, of hindring another of the benefit of his own Right to the same. For he that renounceth or passeth away his Right, giveth not to any other man a Right which he had not before; because
nothing to which every man l
but onely standeth out of his
his own originall Right, wit
not without hindrance from
which redoundeth to one m
of Right, is but so much d
the use of his own Right o

to Peace, are Feare of
are necessary to com-
their Industry to obtain
convenient Articles of
be drawn to agreement.
otherwise are called the
shall speak more particu-
apters.

Renouncing a Right what it is. Transferring Right what. Obligation. Duty. Injustice.

Right is layd aside, either by simply Renouncing it; or by Transferring it to another. By *Simply* RENOUNCING; when he cares not to whom the benefit thereof redoundeth. By TRANSFERRING; when he intendeth the benefit thereof to some certain person, or persons. And when a man hath in either manner abandoned, or granted away his Right; then is he said to be OBLIGED, or BOUND, not to hinder those, to whom such Right is granted, or abandoned, from the benefit of it: and that he *Ought*, and it is his DUTY, not to make voyd that voluntary act of his own: and that such hindrance is INJUSTICE, and INJURY, as being *Sine Jure*; the Right being before renounced, or transferred. So that *Injury*, or *Injustice*, in the controversies of the world, is somewhat like to that, which in the disputations of Scholers is called *Absurdity*. For as it is there called an Absurdity, to contradict what one maintained in the Beginning: so in the world, it is called Injustice, and Injury, voluntarily to undo that, which from the beginning he had voluntarily done. The way by which a man either simply Renounceth, or Transferreth his Right, is a Declaration, or Signification, by some voluntary and sufficient signe, or signes, that he doth so Renounce, or Transferre; or hath so Renounced, or Transferred the same, to him that accepteth it. And these Signes are either Words onely, or Actions onely; or (as it happeneth most often) both Words, and Actions. And the same are the BONDS, by which men are bound, and obliged: Bonds, that have their strength, not from their own Nature, (for nothing is more easily broken then a mans word,) but from Feare of some evill consequence upon the rupture.

Not all Rights are alienable. [66]

Whensoever a man Transferreth his Right, or Renounceth it; it is either in consideration of some Right reciprocally transferred to himselfe; or for some other good he hopeth for thereby. For it is a voluntary act: and of the voluntary acts of every man, the object is some *Good to himselfe*. And therefore there be some Rights, which no man can be understood by any words, or other signes, to have abandoned, or transferred. As first a man cannot lay down the right of resisting them, that assault him by force, to take away his life; because he cannot be understood to ayme thereby, at any Good to himselfe. The same may be sayd of Wounds, and Chayns, and Imprisonment; both because there is no benefit consequent to such patience; as there is to the patience of suffering another to be wounded, or imprisoned: as also because a man cannot tell, when he seeth men proceed against him by violence, whether they intend his death or not. And lastly the motive, and end for which this renouncing, and transferring of Right is introduced, is nothing else but the security of a mans person, in his life, and in the means of so preserving life, as not to be weary of it. And therefore if a man by words, or other signes, seem to despoyle himselfe of the End, for which those signes were intended; he is not to be understood as if he meant it, or that it was his will; but that he was ignorant of how such words and actions were to be interpreted.

Contract what. The mutuall transferring of Right, is that which men call CONTRACT

There is difference, between transferring of Right to the Thing; and transferring, or tradition, that is, delivery of the Thing it selfe. For the Thing may be delivered together with the Translation of the Right; as in buying and selling with ready mony; or exchange of goods, or lands: and it may be delivered some time after.

Again, one of the Contractors, may deliver the Thing contracted for on his part, and leave the other to perform his part at some determinate time after, and in the mean time be trusted: and then the Contract on his part, is called PACT, or COVENANT. Or both parts may contract now, to performe hereafter: in which cases, he that is to performe in time to come, being trusted, his performance is called *Keeping of Promise*, or Faith; and the fayling of performance (if it be voluntary) *Violation of Faith*.

Covenant what.

When the transferring of Right, is not mutuall; but one of the parties transferreth, in hope to gain thereby friendship, or service from another, or from his friends; or in hope to gain the reputation of Charity, or Magnanimity; or to deliver his mind from the pain of compassion; or in hope of reward in heaven; This is not Contract, but GIFT, FREE-GIFT, GRACE: which words signifie one and the same thing. *Free-gift.*

Signes of Contract, are either *Expresse*, or *by Inference*. Expresse, are words spoken with understanding of what they signifie: And such words are either of the time *Present*, or *Past*; as, *I Give, I Grant, I have Given, I have Granted, I will that this be yours:* Or of the future; as, *I will Give, I will Grant:* which words of the future, are called PROMISE. *Signes of Contract Expresse.*

Signes by Inference, are sometimes the consequence of Words; sometimes the consequence of Silence; sometimes the consequence of Actions; somtimes the consequence of Forbearing an Action: and generally a signe by Inference, of any Contract, is whatsoever sufficiently argues the will of the Contractor. [67] *Signes of Contract by Inference.*

Words alone, if they be of the time to come, and contain a bare promise, are an insufficient signe of a Free-gift and therefore not obligatory. For if they be of the time to Come, as, *To morrow I will Give,* they are a signe I have not given yet, and consequently that my right is not transferred, but remaineth till I transferre it by some other Act. But if the words be of the time Present, or Past, as, *I have given, or do give to be delivered to morrow*, then is my to morrows Right given away to day; and that by the vertue of the words, though there were no other argument of my will. And there is a great difference in the signification of these words, *Volo hoc tuum esse cras*, and *Cras dabo*; that is, between *I will that this be thine to morrow*, and, *I will give it thee to morrow*: For the word *I will*, in the former manner of speech, signifies an act of the will Present; but in the later, it signifies a promise of an act of the will to Come: and therefore the former words, being of the Present, transferre a future right; the later, that be of the Future, transferre nothing. But if there be other signes of the Will to transferre a Right, besides Words; then, though the gift be Free, yet may the Right be understood to passe by words of the future: as if a man propound a Prize to him that comes first to the *Free gift passeth by words of the Present or Past.*

end of a race, The gift is Free; and though the words be of the Future, yet the Right passeth: for if he would not have his words so be understood, he should not have let them runne.

Signes of Contract are words both of the Past, Present, and Future.

In Contracts, the right passeth, not onely where the words are of the time Present, or Past; but also where they are of the Future. because all Contract is mutuall translation, or change of Right; and therefore he that promiseth onely, because he hath already received the benefit for which he promiseth, is to be understood as if he intended the Right should passe: for unlesse he had been content to have his words so understood, the other would not have performed his part first. And for that cause, in buying, and selling, and other acts of Contract, a Promise is equivalent to a Covenant; and therefore obligatory.

Merit what

He that performeth first in the case of a Contract, is said to MERIT that which he is to receive by the performance of the other; and he hath it as *Due*. Also when a Prize is propounded to many, which is to be given to him onely that winneth; or mony is thrown amongst many, to be enjoyed by them that catch it; though this be a Free gift; yet so to Win, or so to Catch, is to *Merit*, and to have it as DUE. For the Right is transferred in the Propounding of the Prize, and in throwing down the mony; though it be not determined to whom, but by the Event of the contention. But there is between these two sorts of Merit, this difference, that In Contract, I Merit by vertue of my own power, and the Contractors need; but in this case of Free gift, I am enabled to Merit onely by the benignity of the Giver: In Contract, I merit at the Contractors
[68] hand that hee should depart with his right; In this case of Gift, I Merit not that the giver should part with his right; but that when he has parted with it, it should be mine, rather than anothers. And this I think to be the meaning of that distinction of the Schooles, between *Meritum congrui*, and *Meritum condigni*. For God Almighty, having promised Paradise to those men (hoodwinkt with carnall desires,) that can walk through this world according to the Precepts, and Limits pre-

scribed by him; they say, he that shall so walk, shall Merit Paradise *Ex congruo.* But because no man can demand a right to it, by his own Righteousnesse, or any other power in himselfe, but by the Free Grace of God onely; they say, no man can Merit Paradise *ex condigno.* This I say, I think is the meaning of that distinction; but because Disputers do not agree upon the signification of their own termes of Art, longer than it serves their turn; I will not affirme any thing of their meaning: onely this I say; when a gift is given indefinitely, as a prize to be contended for, he that winneth Meriteth, and may claime the Prize as Due.

Covenants of Mutuall trust, when Invalid.

If a Covenant be made, wherein neither of the parties performe presently, but trust one another; in the condition of meer Nature, (which is a condition of Warre of every man against every man,) upon any reasonable suspition, it is Voyd: But if there be a common Power set over them both, with right and force sufficient to compell performance; it is not Voyd. For he that performeth first, has no assurance the other will performe after; because the bonds of words are too weak to bridle mens ambition, avarice, anger, and other Passions, without the feare of some coerceive Power; which in the condition of meer Nature, where all men are equall, and judges of the justnesse of their own fears, cannot possibly be supposed. And therfore he which performeth first, does but betray himselfe to his enemy; contrary to the Right (he can never abandon) of defending his life, and means of living.

But in a civill estate, where there is a Power set up to constrain those that would otherwise violate their faith, that feare is no more reasonable; and for that cause, he which by the Covenant is to perform first, is obliged so to do.

The cause of feare, which maketh such a Covenant invalid, must be alwayes something arising after the Covenant made; as some new fact, or other signe of the Will not to performe: else it cannot make the Covenant voyd. For that which could not hinder a man from promising, ought not to be admitted as a hindrance of performing.

Right to the End, Containeth Right to the Means He that transferreth any Right, transferreth the Means of enjoying it, as farre as lyeth in his power. As he that selleth Land, is understood to transferre the Herbage, and whatsoever growes upon it; Nor can he that sells a Mill turn away the Stream that drives it. And they that give to a man the Right of government in Soveraignty, are understood to give him the right of levying mony to maintain Souldiers; and of appointing Magistrates for the administration of Justice.

No Covenant with Beasts. To make Covenants with bruit Beasts, is impossible; because not understanding our speech, they understand [69] not, nor accept of any translation of Right; nor can translate any Right to another: and without mutuall acceptation, there is no Covenant.

Nor with God without special Revelation. To make Covenant with God, is impossible, but by Mediation of such as God speaketh to, either by Revelation supernaturall, or by his Lieutenants that govern under him, and in his Name: For otherwise we know not whether our Covenants be accepted, or not. And therefore they that Vow any thing contrary to any law of Nature, Vow in vain; as being a thing unjust to pay such Vow. And if it be a thing commanded by the Law of Nature, it is not the Vow, but the Law that binds them.

No Covenant, but of Possible and Future. The matter, or subject of a Covenant, is alwayes something that falleth under deliberation; (For to Covenant, is an act of the Will; that is to say an act, and the last act, of deliberation;) and is therefore alwayes understood to be something to come; and which is judged Possible for him that Covenanteth, to performe.

And therefore, to promise that which is known to be Impossible, is no Covenant. But if that prove impossible afterwards, which before was thought possible, the Covenant is valid, and bindeth, (though not to the thing it selfe,) yet to the value; or, if that also be impossible, to the unfeigned endeavour of performing as much as is possible: for to more no man can be obliged.

Covenants how made voyd. Men are freed of their Covenants two wayes; by Performing; or by being Forgiven. For Performance, is the naturall end of obligation; and Forgivenesse, the restitution of liberty ; as being a re-transferring of that Right, in which the obligation consisted.

Covenants extorted by feare are valide.

Covenants entred into by fear, in the condition of meer Nature, are obligatory. For example, if I Covenant to pay a ransome, or service for my life, to an enemy ; I am bound by it. For it is a Contract, wherein one receiveth the benefit of life ; the other is to receive mony, or service for it ; and consequently, where no other Law (as in the condition, of meer Nature) forbiddeth the performance, the Covenant is valid. Therefore Prisoners of warre, if trusted with the payment of their Ransome, are obliged to pay it : And if a weaker Prince, make a disadvantageous peace with a stronger, for feare ; he is bound to keep it ; unlesse (as hath been sayd before) there ariseth some new, and just cause of feare, to renew the war. And even in Common-wealths, if I be forced to redeem my selfe from a Theefe by promising him mony, I am bound to pay it, till the Civill Law discharge me. For whatsoever I may lawfully do without Obligation, the same I may lawfully Covenant to do through feare : and what I lawfully Covenant, I cannot lawfully break.

The former Covenant to one, makes voyd the later to another.

A former Covenant, makes voyd a later. For a man that hath passed away his Right to one man to day, hath it not to passe to morrow to another : and therefore the later promise passeth no Right, but is null

A mans Covenant not to defend himselfe, is voyd.

A Covenant not to defend my selfe from force, by force, is alwayes voyd. For (as I have shewed before) no man can transferre, or lay down his Right to save himselfe from Death, Wounds, and Imprisonment, (the avoyding whereof is the onely End of laying down any Right, and [70] therefore the promise of not resisting force, in no Covenant transferreth any right ; nor is obliging. For though a man may Covenant thus, *Unlesse I do so, or so, kill me* ; he cannot Covenant thus, *Unlesse I do so, or so, I will not resist you, when you come to kill me.* For man by nature chooseth the lesser evill, which is danger of death in resisting ; rather than the greater, which is certain and present death in not resisting. And this is granted to be true by all men, in that they lead Criminals to Execution, and Prison, with armed men, notwithstanding that such Criminals have consented to the Law, by which they are condemned.

No man obliged to accuse himself. A Covenant to accuse ones selfe, without assurance of pardon, is likewise invalide. For in the condition of Nature, where every man is Judge, there is no place for Accusation: and in the Civill State, the Accusation is followed with Punishment; which being Force, a man is not obliged not to resist. The same is also true, of the Accusation of those, by whose Condemnation a man falls into misery; as of a Father, Wife, or Benefactor. For the Testimony of such an Accuser, if it be not willingly given, is præsumed to be corrupted by Nature; and therefore not to be received: and where a mans Testimony is not to be credited, he is not bound to give it. Also Accusations upon Torture, are not to be reputed as Testimonies. For Torture is to be used but as means of conjecture, and light, in the further examination, and search of truth: and what is in that case confessed, tendeth to the ease of him that is Tortured; not to the informing of the Torturers: and therefore ought not to have the credit of a sufficient Testimony: for whether he deliver himselfe by true, or false Accusation, he does it by the Right of preserving his own life.

The End of an Oath. The force of Words, being (as I have formerly noted) too weak to hold men to the performance of their Covenants, there are in mans nature, but two imaginable helps to strengthen it. And those are either a Feare of the consequence of breaking their word; or a Glory, or Pride in appearing not to need to breake it. This later is a Generosity too rarely found to be presumed on, especially in the pursuers of Wealth, Command, or sensuall Pleasure; which are the greatest part of Mankind. The Passion to be reckoned upon, is Fear; whereof there be two very generall Objects: one, The Power of Spirits Invisible; the other, The Power of those men they shall therein Offend. Of these two, though the former be the greater Power, yet the feare of the later is commonly the greater Feare. The Feare of the former is in every man, his own Religion: which hath place in the nature of man before Civill Society. The later hath not so; at least not place enough, to keep men to their promises;

because in the condition of meer Nature, the inequality of Power is not discerned, but by the event of Battell. So that before the time of Civill Society, or in the interruption thereof by Warre, there is nothing can strengthen a Covenant of Peace agreed on, against the temptations of Avarice, Ambition, Lust, or other strong desire, but the feare of that Invisible Power, which they every one Worship as God; and Feare as a Revenger of their perfidy All therefore that can be done between two [71] men not subject to Civill Power, is to put one another to swear by the God he feareth: Which *Swearing*, or OATH, is a *Forme of Speech, added to a Promise; by which he that promiseth, signifieth, that unlesse he performe, he renounceth the mercy of his God, or calleth to him for vengeance on himselfe.* Such was the Heathen Forme, *Let* Jupiter *kill me else, as I kill this Beast.* So is our Forme, *I shall do thus, and thus, so help me God.* And this, with the Rites and Ceremonies, which every one useth in his own Religion, that the feare of breaking faith might be the greater.

The forme of an Oath.

No Oath, but by God.

By this it appears, that an Oath taken according to any other Forme, or Rite, then his, that sweareth, is in vain; and no Oath: And that there is no Swearing by any thing which the Swearer thinks not God. For though men have sometimes used to swear by their Kings, for feare, or flattery; yet they would have it thereby understood, they attributed to them Divine honour. And that Swearing unnecessarily by God, is but prophaning of his name. and Swearing by other things, as men do in common discourse, is not Swearing, but an impious Custome, gotten by too much vehemence of talking.

An Oath addes nothing to the Obligation.

It appears also, that the Oath addes nothing to the Obligation. For a Covenant, if lawfull, binds in the sight of God, without the Oath, as much as with it: if unlawfull, bindeth not at all; though it be confirmed with an Oath.

CHAP. XV.

Of other Lawes of Nature.

The third Law of Nature, Justice.

FROM that law of Nature, by which we are obliged to transferre to another, such Rights, as being retained, hinder the peace of Mankind, there followeth a Third, which is this, *That men performe their Covenants made:* without which, Covenants are in vain, and but Empty words; and the Right of all men to all things remaining, wee are still in the condition of Warre.

Justice and Injustice what.

And in this law of Nature, consisteth the Fountain and Originall of JUSTICE. For where no Covenant hath preceded, there hath no Right been transferred, and every man has right to every thing; and consequently, no action can be Unjust. But when a Covenant is made, then to break it is *Unjust*: And the definition of INIUSTICE, is no other than *the not Performance of Covenant.* And whatsoever is not Unjust, is *Just.*

Justice and Propriety begin with the Constitution of Common-wealth.

But because Covenants of mutuall trust, where there is a feare of not performance on either part, (as hath been said in the former Chapter,) are invalid; though the Originall of Justice be the making of Covenants; yet Injustice actually there can be none, till the cause of such feare be taken away; which while men are in the naturall condition of Warre, cannot be done. Therefore before the names of Just, and Unjust can have place, there must be some coërcive Power, to compell men equally to the performance of their Covenants, by the terrour of some punishment, greater than the benefit
[72] they expect by the breach of their Covenant; and to make good that Propriety, which by mutuall Contract men acquire, in recompence of the universall Right they abandon: and such power there is none before the erection of a Common-wealth. And this is also to be gathered out of the ordinary definition of Justice in the Schooles: For they say, that *Justice is the constant Will of giving to every man his own.* And therefore where there is no *Own*, that is, no Propriety, there is no Injustice; and where there is no coërceive Power erected, that is, where there is no Common-wealth, there is no Propriety; all men having Right to all things: Therefore where there

is no Common-wealth, there nothing is Unjust. So that the nature of Justice, consisteth in keeping of valid Covenants: but the Validity of Covenants begins not but with the Constitution of a Civill Power, sufficient to compell men to keep them: And then it is also that Propriety begins.

Justice not Contrary to Reason.

The Foole hath sayd in his heart, there is no such thing as Justice; and sometimes also with his tongue; seriously alleaging; that every mans conservation, and contentment, being committed to his own care, there could be no reason, why every man might not do what he thought conduced thereunto: and therefore also to make, or not make; keep, or not keep Covenants, was not against Reason, when it conduced to ones benefit. He does not therein deny, that there be Covenants; and that they are sometimes broken, sometimes kept; and that such breach of them may be called Injustice, and the observance of them Justice: but he questioneth, whether Injustice, taking away the feare of God, (for the same Foole hath said in his heart there is no God,) may not sometimes stand with that Reason, which dictateth to every man his own good; and particularly then, when it conduceth to such a benefit, as shall put a man in a condition, to neglect not onely the dispraise, and revilings, but also the power of other men. The Kingdome of God is gotten by violence: but what if it could be gotten by unjust violence? were it against Reason so to get it, when it is impossible to receive hurt by it? and if it be not against Reason, it is not against Justice: or else Justice is not to be approved for good. From such reasoning as this, Succesfull wickednesse hath obtained the name of Vertue: and some that in all other things have disallowed the violation of Faith; yet have allowed it, when it is for the getting of a Kingdome. And the Heathen that believed, that *Saturn* was deposed by his son *Jupiter*, believed neverthelesse the same *Jupiter* to be the avenger of Injustice: Somewhat like to a piece of Law in *Cokes* Commentaries on *Litleton*; where he sayes, If the right Heire of the Crown be attainted of Treason; yet the Crown shall descend to him, and *eo instante* the Atteynder be voyd: From which instances a man will be very prone to inferre;

that when the Heire apparent of a Kingdome, shall kill him that is in possession, though his father; you may call it Injustice, or by what other name you will; yet it can never be against Reason, seeing all the voluntary actions of men tend to the benefit of themselves; and those actions are most Reasonable, that conduce most to
[73] their ends. This specious reasoning is neverthelesse false.

For the question is not of promises mutuall, where there is no security of performance on either side; as when there is no Civill Power erected over the parties promising; for such promises are no Covenants: But either where one of the parties has performed already; or where there is a Power to make him performe, there is the question whether it be against reason, that is, against the benefit of the other to performe, or not. And I say it is not against reason. For the manifestation whereof, we are to consider; First, that when a man doth a thing, which notwithstanding any thing can be foreseen, and reckoned on, tendeth to his own destruction, howsoever some accident which he could not expect, befalling may turne it to his benefit; yet such events do not make it reasonably or wisely done. Secondly, that in a condition of Warre, wherein every man to every man, for want of a common Power to keep them all in awe, is an Enemy, there is no man can hope by his own strength, or wit, to defend himselfe from destruction, without the help of Confederates; where every one expects the same defence by the Confederation, that any one else does: and therefore he which declares he thinks it reason to deceive those that help him, can in reason expect no other means of safety, than what can be had from his own single Power. He therefore that breaketh his Covenant, and consequently declareth that he thinks he may with reason do so, cannot be received into any Society, that unite themselves for Peace and Defence, but by the errour of them that receive him; nor when he is received, be retayned in it, without seeing the danger of their errour; which errours a man cannot reasonably reckon upon as the means of his security: and therefore if he be left, or cast out of Society, he perisheth, and if he live in Society, it is by the errours of other men, which he could not foresee, nor reckon upon; and consequently against the reason of his preservation; and so, as all men that contribute not to his destruction, forbear him onely out of ignorance of what is good for themselves.

As for the Instance of gaining the secure and perpetual felicity of Heaven, by any way; it is frivolous: there being but one way imaginable; and that is not breaking, but keeping of Covenant.

And for the other Instance of attaining Soveraignty by Rebellion; it is manifest, that though the event follow, yet because it cannot reasonably be expected, but rather the contrary; and because by gaining it so, others are taught to gain the same in like manner, the attempt thereof is against reason. Justice therefore, that is to say, Keeping of Covenant, is a Rule of Reason, by which we are forbidden to do any thing destructive to our life; and consequently a Law of Nature.

There be some that proceed further; and will not have the Law of Nature, to be those Rules which conduce to the preservation of mans life on earth; but to the attaining of an eternall felicity after death; to which they think the breach of Covenant may conduce; and consequently be just and reasonable; (such are they that think it a work of merit to kill, or depose, or rebell [74] against, the Soveraigne Power constituted over them by their own consent.) But because there is no naturall knowledge of mans estate after death; much lesse of the reward that is then to be given to breach of Faith; but onely a beliefe grounded upon other mens saying, that they know it supernaturally, or that they know those, that knew them, that knew others, that knew it supernaturally; Breach of Faith cannot be called a Precept of Reason, or Nature.

Covenants not discharged by the Vice of the Person to whom they are made.

Others, that allow for a Law of Nature, the keeping of Faith, do neverthelesse make exception of certain persons; as Heretiques, and such as use not to performe their Covenant to others: And this also is against reason. For if any fault of a man, be sufficient to discharge our Covenant made; the same ought in reason to have been sufficient to have hindred the making of it.

Justice of Men, & Justice of Actions what. The names of Just, and Injust, when they are attributed to Men, signifie one thing; and when they are attributed to Actions, another. When they are attributed to Men, they signifie Conformity, or Inconformity of Manners, to Reason. But when they are attributed to Actions, they signifie the Conformity or Inconformity to Reason, not of Manners, or manner of life, but of particular Actions. A Just man therefore, is he that taketh all the care he can, that his Actions may be all Just: and an Unjust man, is he that neglecteth it. And such men are more often in our Language stiled by the names of Righteous, and Unrighteous; then Just, and Unjust; though the meaning be the same. Therefore a Righteous man, does not lose that Title, by one, or a few unjust Actions, that proceed from sudden Passion, or mistake of Things, or Persons: nor does an Unrighteous man, lose his character, for such Actions, as he does, or forbeares to do, for feare: because his Will is not framed by the Justice, but by the apparent benefit of what he is to do. That which gives to humane Actions the relish of Justice, is a certain Noblenesse or Gallantnesse of courage, (rarely found,) by which a man scorns to be beholding for the contentment of his life, to fraud, or breach of promise. This Justice of the Manners, is that which is meant, where Justice is called a Vertue; and Injustice a Vice.

But the Justice of Actions denominates men, not Just, *Guiltlesse*: and the Injustice of the same, (which is also called Injury,) gives them but the name of *Guilty*.

Justice of Manners, and Justice of Actions. Again, the Injustice of Manners, is the disposition, or aptitude to do Injurie; and is Injustice before it proceed to Act; and without supposing any individuall person injured. But the Injustice of an Action, (that is to say Injury,) supposeth an individuall person Injured; namely him, to whom the Covenant was made: And therefore many times the injury is received by one man, when the dammage redoundeth to another. As when the Master commandeth his servant to give mony to a stranger; if it be not done, the Injury is done to the Master, whom he had before Covenanted to obey; but the dammage redoundeth to the stranger, to whom he had no Obligation ; and therefore could not Injure him. And so also in Common-wealths, private [75] men may remit to one another their debts ; but not robberies or other violences, whereby they are endammaged ; because the detaining of Debt, is an Injury to themselves ; but Robbery and Violence, are Injuries to the Person of the Common-wealth.

Nothing done to a man, by his own consent can be Injury.

Whatsoever is done to a man, conformable to his own Will signified to the doer, is no Injury to him. For if he that doeth it, hath not passed away his originall right to do what he please, by some Antecedent Covenant, there is no breach of Covenant ; and therefore no Injury done him. And if he have ; then his Will to have it done being signified, is a release of that Covenant : and so again there is no Injury done him.

Justice Commutative, and Distributive.

Justice of Actions, is by Writers divided into *Commutative*, and *Distributive :* and the former they say consisteth in proportion Arithmeticall ; the later in proportion Geometricall. Commutative therefore, they place in the equality of value of the things contracted for ; And Distributive, in the distribution of equall benefit, to men of equall merit. As if it were Injustice to sell dearer than we buy ; or to give more to a man than he merits. The value of all things contracted for, is measured by the Appetite of the Contractors : and therefore the just value, is that which they be contented to give. And Merit (besides that which is by Covenant, where the performance on one part, meriteth the performance of the other part, and falls under Justice Commutative, not Distributive,) is not due by Justice ; but is rewarded of Grace onely. And therefore this distinction, in the sense wherein it useth to be expounded, is not right. To speak properly, Commutative Justice, is the Justice of a Contractor ; that is, a Performance of Covenant, in Buying, and Selling ; Hiring, and Letting to Hire ; Lending, and Borrowing ; Exchanging, Bartering, and other acts of Contract.

And Distributive Justice, the Justice of an Arbitrator ; that is to say, the act of defining what is Just. Wherein, (being trusted by them that make him Arbitrator,) if he performe his Trust, he is said to distribute to every man his own: and this is indeed Just Distribution, and may be called (though improperly) Distributive Justice; but more properly Equity; which also is a Law of Nature, as shall be shewn in due place.

The fourth Law of Nature, Gratitude. As Justice dependeth on Antecedent Covenant, so does GRATITUDE depend on Antecedent Grace; that is to say, Antecedent Free-gift: and is the fourth Law of Nature; which may be conceived in this Forme, *That a man which receiveth Benefit from another of meer Grace, Endeavour that he which giveth it, have no reasonable cause to repent him of his good will.* For no man giveth, but with intention of Good to himselfe; because Gift is Voluntary; and of all Voluntary Acts, the Object is to every man his own Good; of which if men see they shall be frustrated, there will be no beginning of benevolence, or trust; nor consequently of mutuall help; nor of reconciliation of one man to another; and therefore they are to remain still in the condition of *War*; which is contrary to the first and Fundamentall Law of Nature, which commandeth men to *Seek Peace.* The breach of [76] this Law, is called *Ingratitude*; and hath the same relation to Grace, that Injustice hath to Obligation by Covenant.

The fifth, Mutuall accommodation, or Compleasance. A fifth Law of Nature, is COMPLEASANCE; that is to say, *That every man strive to accommodate himselfe to the rest.* For the understanding whereof, we may consider, that there is in mens aptnesse to Society, a diversity of Nature, rising from their diversity of Affections; not unlike to that we see in stones brought together for building of an Ædifice. For as that stone which by the asperity, and irregularity of Figure, takes more room from others, than it selfe fills; and for the hardnesse, cannot be easily made plain, and thereby hindereth the building, is by the builders cast away as unprofitable, and troublesome: so also, a man that by asperity of Nature, will strive to retain those things which to himselfe are superfluous, and to others necessary; and for the stubbornness of his Passions, cannot be corrected, is to be left, or cast out of Society, as combersome thereunto. For seeing every man, not onely by Right, but also by necessity of Nature, is supposed to endeavour all he can, to obtain that which is necessary for his conservation; He that shall oppose himselfe against it, for things superfluous, is guilty of the warre that thereupon is to follow; and therefore doth that, which is contrary to the fundamentall Law of Nature, which commandeth *to seek Peace.* The observers of this Law, may be called SOCIABLE, (the Latines call them *Commodi*;) The contrary, *Stubborn, Insociable, Froward, Intractable.*

The sixth, Facility to Pardon.

A sixth Law of Nature, is this, *That upon caution of the Future time, a man ought to pardon the offences past of them that repenting, desire it.* For PARDON, is nothing but granting of Peace; which though granted to them that persevere in their hostility, be not Peace, but Feare; yet not granted to them that give caution of the Future time, is signe of an aversion to Peace; and therefore contrary to the Law of Nature.

The seventh, that in Revenges, men respect onely the future good.

A seventh is, *That in Revenges,* (that is, retribution of Evil for Evil,) *Men look not at the greatnesse of the evill past, but the greatnesse of the good to follow.* Whereby we are forbidden to inflict punishment with any other designe, than for correction of the offender, or direction of others. For this Law is consequent to the next before it, that commandeth Pardon, upon security of the Future time. Besides, Revenge without respect to the Example, and profit to come, is a triumph, or glorying in the hurt of another, tending to no end; (for the End is alwayes somewhat to Come;) and glorying to no end, is vain-glory, and contrary to reason; and to hurt without reason, tendeth to the introduction of Warre; which is against the Law of Nature; and is commonly stiled by the name of *Cruelty.*

The eighth, against Contumely

And because all signes of hatred, or contempt, provoke to fight; insomuch as most men choose rather to hazard their life, than not to be revenged; we may in the eighth place, for a Law of Nature, set down this Precept, *That no man by deed, word, countenance, or gesture, declare Hatred, or Contempt of another.* The breach of which Law, is commonly called *Contumely.*

The ninth, against Pride.

The question who is the better man, has no place in the condition of meer Nature; where, (as has been shewn before,) all men are equall. The inequallity that now is, [77] has bin introduced by the Lawes civill. I know that *Aristotle* in the first booke of his Politiques, for a foundation of his doctrine, maketh men by Nature, some more worthy to Command, meaning the wiser sort (such as he thought himselfe to be for his Philosophy;) others to Serve, (meaning those that had strong bodies, but were not Philosophers as he;) as if Master and Servant were not introduced by consent of men, but by difference of Wit which is not only against reason; but also against experience. For there are very few so foolish, that had not rather governe themselves, than be governed by others: Nor when the wise in their own conceit, contend by force, with them who distrust their owne wisdome, do they alwaies, or often, or almost at any time, get the Victory. If Nature therefore have made men equall, that equalitie is to be acknowledged: or if Nature have made men unequall; yet because men that think themselves equall, will not enter into conditions of Peace, but upon Equall termes, such equalitie must be admitted. And therefore for the ninth law of Nature, I put this, *That every man acknowledge other for his Equall by Nature.* The breach of this Precept is *Pride.*

The tenth, against Arrogance.

On this law, dependeth another, *That at the entrance into conditions of Peace, no man require to reserve to himselfe any Right, which he is not content should be reserved to every one of the rest.* As it is necessary for all men that seek peace, to lay down certaine Rights of Nature; that is to say, not to have libertie to do all they list: so is it necessarie for mans life, to retaine some; as right to governe their owne bodies; enjoy aire, water, motion, waies to go from place to place; and all things else without which a man cannot live, or not live well. If in this case, at the making of Peace, men require for themselves, that which they would not have to be granted to others, they do contrary to the precedent law, that commandeth the acknowledgment of naturall equalitie, and therefore also against the law of Nature. The observers of this law, are those we call *Modest,* and the breakers *Arrogant* men. The Greeks call the violation of this law πλεονεξία; that is, a desire of more than their share.

Also if *a man be trusted to judge between man and man,* it is a precept of the Law of Nature, *that he deale Equally between them.* For without that, the Controversies of men cannot be determined but by Warre. He therefore that is partiall in judgment, doth what in him lies, to deterre men from the use of Judges, and Arbitrators; and consequently, (against the fundamentall Lawe of Nature) is the cause of Warre. *The eleventh Equity.*

The observance of this law, from the equall distribution to each man, of that which in reason belongeth to him, is called EQUITY, and (as I have sayd before) distributive Justice: the violation, *Acception of persons,* προσωποληψία.

And from this followeth another law, *That such things as cannot be divided, be enjoyed in Common, if it can be; and if the quantity of the thing permit, without Stint; otherwise Proportionably to the number of them that have Right.* For otherwise the distribution is Unequall, and contrary to Equitie. *The twelfth, Equall use of things Common.*

But some things there be, that can neither be divided, [78] nor enjoyed in common. Then, The Law of Nature, which prescribeth Equity, requireth, *That the Entire Right; or else, (making the use alternate,) the First Possession, be determined by Lot.* For equall distribution, is of the Law of Nature; and other means of equall distribution cannot be imagined. *The thirteenth, of Lot.*

Of *Lots* there be two sorts, *Arbitrary,* and *Naturall.* Arbitrary, is that which is agreed on by the Competitors: Naturall, is either *Primogeniture,* (which the Greek calls Κληρονομία, which signifies, *Given by Lot;*) or *First Seisure.* *The fourteenth, of Primogeniture, and First seising.*

And therefore those things which cannot be enjoyed in common, nor divided, ought to be adjudged to the First Possessor; and in some cases to the First-Borne, as acquired by Lot.

It is also a Law of Nature, *That all men that mediate Peace, be allowed safe Conduct.* For the Law that commandeth Peace, as the *End,* commandeth Intercession, as the *Means;* and to Intercession the Means is safe Conduct. *The fifteenth, of Mediators.*

And because, though men be never so willing to observe these Lawes, there may neverthelesse arise *The sixteenth, of*

Submission to Arbitrement.

questions concerning a mans action; First, whether it were done, or not done; Secondly (if done) whether against the Law, or not against the Law; the former whereof, is called a question *Of Fact*; the later a question *Of Right;* therefore unlesse the parties to the question, Covenant mutually to stand to the sentence of another, they are as farre from Peace as ever. This other, to whose Sentence they submit, is called an ARBITRATOR. And therefore it is of the Law of Nature, *That they that are at controversie, submit their Right to the judgement of an Arbitrator.*

The seventeenth, No man is his own Judge.

And seeing every man is presumed to do all things in order to his own benefit, no man is a fit Arbitrator in his own cause: and if he were never so fit; yet Equity allowing to each party equall benefit, if one be admitted to be Judge, the other is to be admitted also; & so the controversie, that is, the cause of War, remains, against the Law of Nature.

The eighteenth, no man to be Judge, that has in him a natural cause of Partiality.

For the same reason no man in any Cause ought to be received for Arbitrator, to whom greater profit, or honour, or pleasure apparently ariseth out of the victory of one party, than of the other: for hee hath taken (though an unavoydable bribe, yet) a bribe; and no man can be obliged to trust him. And thus also the controversie, and the condition of War remaineth, contrary to the Law of Nature.

The nineteenth, of Witnesses.

And in a controversie of *Fact*, the Judge being to give no more credit to one, than to the other, (if there be no other Arguments) must give credit to a third; or to a third and fourth; or more For else the question is undecided, and left to force, contrary to the Law of Nature.

These are the Lawes of Nature, dictating Peace, for a means of the conservation of men in multitudes; and which onely concern the doctrine of Civill Society. There be other things tending to the destruction of particular men, as Drunkenness, and all other parts of Intemperance; which may therefore also be reckoned amongst those things which the Law of Nature hath
[79] forbidden; but are not necessary to be mentioned, nor are pertinent enough to this place.

A Rule, by which the Laws of Nature may easily be examined.

And though this may seem too subtile a deduction of the Lawes of Nature, to be taken notice of by all men; whereof the most part are too busie in getting food, and the rest too negligent to understand; yet to leave all men unexcusable, they have been contracted into one easie sum, intelligible, even to the meanest capacity; and that is, *Do not that to another, which thou wouldest not have done to thy selfe*; which sheweth him, that he has no more to do in learning the Lawes of Nature, but, when weighing the actions of other men with his own, they seem too heavy, to put them into the other part of the ballance, and his own into their place, that his own passions, and selfe-love, may adde nothing to the weight; and then there is none of these Lawes of Nature that will not appear unto him very reasonable.

The Lawes of Nature oblige in Conscience alwayes, but in Effect then onely when there is Security.

The Lawes of Nature oblige *in foro interno*; that is to say, they bind to a desire they should take place: but *in foro externo*; that is, to the putting them in act, not alwayes. For he that should be modest, and tractable, and performe all he promises, in such time, and place, where no man els should do so, should but make himselfe a prey to others, and procure his own certain ruine, contrary to the ground of all Lawes of Nature, which tend to Natures preservation. And again, he that having sufficient Security, that others shall observe the same Lawes towards him, observes them not himselfe, seeketh not Peace, but War; & consequently the destruction of his Nature by Violence.

And whatsoever Lawes bind *in foro interno*, may be broken, not onely by a fact contrary to the Law, but also by a fact according to it, in case a man think it contrary. For though his Action in this case, be according to the Law; yet his Purpose was against the Law; which where the Obligation is *in foro interno*, is a breach.

The Laws of Nature are Eternal;

The Lawes of Nature are Immutable and Eternall; For Injustice, Ingratitude, Arrogance, Pride, Iniquity, Acception of persons, and the rest, can never be made lawfull. For it can never be that Warre shall preserve life, and Peace destroy it.

And yet Easie.

The [same] Lawes, because they oblige onely to a desire, and endeavour, I mean an unfeigned and constant endeavour, are easie to be observed. For in that they require nothing but endeavour; he that endeavoureth their performance, fulfilleth them; and he that fulfilleth the Law, is Just.

The Science of these Lawes, is the true Morall Philosophy.

And the Science of them, is the true and onely Moral Philosophy. For Morall Philosophy is nothing else but the Science of what is *Good*, and *Evill*, in the conversation, and Society of man-kind. *Good*, and *Evill*, are names that signifie our Appetites, and Aversions; which in different tempers, customes, and doctrines of men, are different: And divers men, differ not onely in their Judgement, on the senses of what is pleasant, and unpleasant to the tast, smell, hearing, touch, and sight; but also of what is conformable, or disagreeable to Reason, in the actions of common life. Nay, the same man, in divers times, differs from himselfe; and one time praiseth, that is, calleth Good, what another time he
[80] dispraiseth, and calleth Evil: From whence arise Disputes, Controversies, and at last War. And therefore so long a man is in the condition of meer Nature, (which is a condition of War,) as private Appetite is the measure of Good, and Evill: And consequently all men agree on this, that Peace is Good, and therefore also the way, or means of Peace, which (as I have shewed before) are *Justice, Gratitude, Modesty, Equity, Mercy*, & the rest of the Laws of Nature, are good; that is to say, *Morall Vertues*; and their contrarie *Vices*, Evill. Now the science of Vertue and Vice, is Morall Philosophie, and therfore the true Doctrine of the Lawes of Nature, is the true Morall Philosophie. But the Writers of Morall Philosophie, though they acknowledge the same Vertues and Vices; Yet not seeing wherein consisted their Goodnesse; nor that they come to be praised, as the meanes of peaceable, sociable, and comfortable living; place them in a mediocrity of passions: as if not the Cause, but the Degree of daring, made Fortitude; or not the Cause, but the Quantity of a gift, made Liberality.

These dictates of Reason, men use to call by the name of Lawes; but improperly: for they are but Conclusions, or Theoremes concerning what conduceth to the conservation and defence of themselves; wheras Law, properly is the word of him, that by right hath command over others. But yet if we consider the same Theoremes, as delivered in the word of God, that by right commandeth all things; then are they properly called Lawes.

CHAP. XVI.

Of PERSONS, AUTHORS, *and things Personated.*

A person what. A PERSON, is he, *whose words or actions are considered, either as his own, or as representing the words or actions of an other man, or of any other thing to whom they are attributed, whether Truly or by Fiction.*

Person Naturall and Artificiall. When they are considered as his owne, then is he called a *Naturall Person*. And when they are considered as representing the words and actions of an other, then is he a *Feigned* or *Artificiall person.*

The word Person, whence. The word Person is latine: insteed whereof the Greeks have πρόσωπον, which signifies the *Face*, as *Persona* in latine signifies the *disguise*, or *outward appearance* of a man, counterfeited on the Stage; and somtimes more particularly that part of it, which disguiseth the face, as a Mask or Visard: And from the Stage, hath been translated to any Representer of speech and action, as well in Tribunalls, as Theaters. So that a *Person*, is the same that an *Actor* is, both on the Stage and in common Conversation; and to *Personate*, is to *Act*, or *Represent* himselfe, or an other; and he that acteth another, is said to beare his Person, or act in his name; (in which sence *Cicero* useth it where he saies, *Unus sustineo tres Personas; Mei, Adversarii, & Judicis,* I beare three Persons; my own, my Adversaries, and the Judges;) and is called in diverse occasions, diversly; as a *Repre-* [81] *senter*, or *Representative*, a *Lieutenant*, a *Vicar*, an *Attorney*, a *Deputy*, a *Procurator*, an *Actor*, and the like.

Of Persons Artificiall, some have their words and actions *Owned* by those whom they represent. And then the Person is the *Actor*; and he that owneth his words and actions, is the AUTHOR: In which case the Actor acteth by Authority. For that which in speaking of *Actor, Author,* goods and possessions, is called an *Owner*, and in latine *Dominus*, in Greeke κύριος; speaking of Actions, is called Author. And as the Right of possession, is called Dominion; so the Right of doing any Action, is called AUTHORITY. So that by Authority, is alwayes understood a Right of doing any act: and *done by Authority*, done by Commission, or Licence from him whose right it is.

Authority.

Covenants by Authority, bind the Author.

From hence it followeth, that when the Actor maketh a Covenant by Authority, he bindeth thereby the Author, no lesse than if he had made it himselfe; and no lesse subjecteth him to all the consequences of the same. And therfore all that hath been said formerly, (*Chap.* 14.) of the nature of Covenants between man and man in their naturall capacity, is true also when they are made by their Actors, Representers, or Procurators, that have authority from them, so far-forth as is in their Commission, but no farther.

And therefore he that maketh a Covenant with the Actor, or Representer, not knowing the Authority he hath, doth it at his own perill For no man is obliged by a Covenant, whereof he is not Author, nor consequently by a Covenant made against, or beside the Authority he gave.

But not the Actor.

When the Actor doth any thing against the Law of Nature by command of the Author, if he be obliged by former Covenant to obey him, not he, but the Author breaketh the Law of Nature. for though the Action be against the Law of Nature, yet it is not his: but contrarily, to refuse to do it, is against the Law of Nature, that forbiddeth breach of Covenant.

The Authority is to be shewne.

And he that maketh a Covenant with the Author, by mediation of the Actor, not knowing what Authority he hath, but onely takes his word; in case such Authority be not made manifest unto him upon demand, is no longer obliged: For the Covenant made with the Author, is not valid, without his Counter-assurance. But if he that so Covenanteth, knew before hand he was to expect no other assurance, than the Actors word; then is the Covenant valid, because the Actor in this case maketh himselfe the Author And therefore, as when the

Authority is evident, the Covenant obligeth the Author, not the Actor; so when the Authority is feigned, it obligeth the Actor onely; there being no Author but himselfe.

Things personated, Inanimate. There are few things, that are uncapable of being represented by Fiction. Inanimate things, as a Church, an Hospital, a Bridge, may be personated by a Rector, Master, or Overseer. But things Inanimate, cannot be Authors, nor therefore give Authority to their Actors: Yet the Actors may have Authority to procure their maintenance, given them by those that are Owners, or [82] Governours of those things. And therefore, such things cannot be Personated, before there be some state of Civill Government.

Irrational; Likewise Children, Fooles, and Mad-men that have no use of Reason, may be Personated by Guardians, or Curators; but can be no Authors (during that time) of any action done by them, longer then (when they shall recover the use of Reason) they shall judge the same reasonable. Yet during the Folly, he that hath right of governing them, may give Authority to the Guardian. But this again has no place but in a State Civill, because before such estate, there is no Dominion of Persons.

False Gods; An Idol, or meer Figment of the brain, may be Personated; as were the Gods of the Heathen; which by such Officers as the State appointed, were Personated, and held Possessions, and other Goods, and Rights, which men from time to time dedicated, and consecrated unto them. But Idols cannot be Authors: for an Idol is nothing. The Authority proceeded from the State: and therefore before introduction of Civill Government, the Gods of the Heathen could not be Personated.

The true God. The true God may be Personated. As he was; first, by *Moses*; who governed the Israelites, (that were not his, but Gods people,) not in his own name, with *Hoc dicit Moses*, but in Gods Name, with *Hoc dicit Dominus*. Secondly, by the Son of man, his own Son, our Blessed Saviour *Jesus Christ*, that came to reduce the Jewes, and induce all Nations into the Kingdome of his Father; not as of himselfe, but as sent from his Father. And thirdly, by the Holy Ghost, or Comforter, speaking, and working in the Apostles: which Holy Ghost, was a Comforter that came not of himselfe; but was sent, and proceeded from them both.

A Multitude of men, how one Person.

A Multitude of men, are made *One* Person, when they are by one man, or one Person, Represented, so that it be done with the consent of every one of that Multitude in particular. For it is the *Unity* of the Representer, not the *Unity* of the Represented, that maketh the Person *One*. And it is the Representer that beareth the Person, and but one Person: And *Unity*, cannot otherwise be understood in Multitude.

Every one is Author.

And because the Multitude naturally is not *One*, but *Many*; they cannot be understood for one; but many Authors, of every thing their Representative saith, or doth in their name; Every man giving their common Representer, Authority from himselfe in particular; and owning all the actions the Representer doth, in case they give him Authority without stint: Otherwise, when they limit him in what, and how farre he shall represent them, none of them owneth more, than they gave him commission to Act.

An Actor may be Many men made One by Plurality of Voyces.

And if the Representative consist of many men, the voyce of the greater number, must be considered as the voyce of them all. For if the lesser number pronounce (for example) in the Affirmative, and the greater in the [83] Negative, there will be Negatives more than enough to destroy the Affirmatives; and thereby the excesse of Negatives, standing uncontradicted, are the onely voyce the Representative hath.

Representatives, when the number is even, unprofitable

And a Representative of even number, especially when the number is not great, whereby the contradictory voyces are oftentimes equall, is therefore oftentimes mute, and uncapable of Action Yet in some cases contradictory voyces equall in number, may determine a question; as in condemning, or absolving, equality of votes, even in that they condemne not, do absolve; but not on the contrary condemne, in that they absolve not For when a Cause is heard; not to condemne, is to absolve · but on the contrary, to say that not absolving, is condemning, is not true. The like it is in a deliberation of executing presently, or deferring till another time: For when the voyces are equall, the not decreeing Execution, is a decree of Dilation.

Negative voyce.

Or if the number be odde, as three, or more, (men, or assemblies;) whereof every one has by a Negative Voice, authority to take away the effect of all the Affirmative Voices of the rest, This number is no Representative; because by the diversity of Opinions, and Interests of men, it becomes oftentimes, and in cases of the greatest consequence, a mute Person, and unapt, as for many things else, so for the government of a Multitude, especially in time of Warre.

Of Authors there be two sorts. The first simply so called; which I have before defined to be him, that owneth the Action of another simply. The second is he, that owneth an Action, or Covenant of another conditionally; that is to say, he undertaketh to do it, if the other doth it not, at, or before a certain time. And these Authors conditionall, are generally called SURETYES, in Latine *Fidejussores*, and *Sponsores*; and particularly for Debt, *Prædes*; and for Appearance before a Judge, or Magistrate, *Vades*.

[85]

OF COMMON-WEALTH.

CHAP. XVII.

Of the Causes, Generation, and Definition of a COMMON-WEALTH

The End of Common-wealth, particular Security.

THE finall Cause, End, or Designe of men, (who naturally love Liberty, and Dominion over others,) in the introduction of that restraint upon themselves, (in which wee see them live in Common-wealths,) is the foresight of their own preservation, and of a more contented life thereby; that is to say, of getting themselves out from that miserable condition of Warre, which is necessarily consequent (as hath been shewn) to the naturall Passions of men, when there is no visible Power to keep them in awe, and tye them by feare of punishment to the performance of their Covenants, and observation of those Lawes of Nature set down in the fourteenth and fifteenth Chapters.

Chap. 13.

Which is not to be had from the Law of Nature:

For the Lawes of Nature (as *Justice, Equity, Modesty, Mercy,* and (in summe) *doing to others, as wee would be done to,*) of themselves, without the terrour of some Power, to cause them to be observed, are contrary to our naturall Passions, that carry us to Partiality, Pride, Revenge, and the like. And Covenants, without the Sword, are but Words, and of no strength to secure a man at all. Therefore notwithstanding the Lawes of Nature, (which every one hath then kept, when he has the will to keep them, when he can do it safely,) if there be no Power erected, or not great enough for our security; every man will, and may lawfully rely on his own strength and art, for caution against all other men. And in all places, where men have lived by small Families, to robbe and spoyle one another, has been a Trade, and so farre from being reputed against the Law of Nature, that the greater spoyles they gained, the greater was their honour; and men observed no other Lawes therein, but the Lawes of Honour; that is, to abstain from cruelty, leaving to men their livings and instruments of husbandry. And as small Familyes did then; so now do Cities and Kingdomes which are but greater Families (for their own security) enlarge their Dominions, upon all pretences of danger, and fear of Invasion, or assistance that may be given to Invaders, endeavour as much as they can, to subdue, or weaken their neighbours, by open force, and secret arts, for want of other Caution, justly; and are remembred for it in after ages with honour.

Nor the conjunction of a few men or familyes:

Nor is it the joyning together of a small number of men, that gives them this security, because in small numbers, small additions on the one side or the other, [86]
make the advantage of strength so great, as is sufficient to carry the Victory; and therefore gives encouragement to an Invasion. The Multitude sufficient to confide in for our Security, is not determined by any certain number, but by comparison with the Enemy we feare; and is then sufficient, when the odds of the Enemy is not of so visible and conspicuous moment, to determine the event of warre, as to move him to attempt.

Nor from a great Multitude, unlesse directed by one judgement.

And be there never so great a Multitude; yet if their actions be directed according to their particular judgements, and particular appetites, they can expect thereby no defence, nor protection, neither against a Common enemy, nor against the injuries of one another. For being distracted in opinions concerning the best use and application of their strength, they do not help, but hinder one another; and reduce their strength by mutuall opposition to nothing: whereby they are easily, not onely subdued by a very few that agree together; but also when there is no common enemy, they make warre upon each other, for their particular interests. For if we could suppose a great Multitude of men to consent in the observation of Justice, and other Lawes of Nature, without a common Power to keep them all in awe; we might as well suppose all Man-kind to do the same; and then there neither would be, nor need to be any Civill Government, or

Common-wealth at all; because there would be Peace without subjection.

And that continually.

Nor is it enough for the security, which men desire should last all the time of their life, that they be governed, and directed by one judgement, for a limited time; as in one Battell, or one Warre For though they obtain a Victory by their unanimous endeavour against a forraign enemy; yet afterwards, when either they have no common enemy, or he that by one part is held for an enemy, is by another part held for a friend, they must needs by the difference of their interests dissolve, and fall again into a Warre amongst themselves.

TheEnd Commo wealth parti. Secuin ..eatures without reason, or speech, do neverthelesse live in Society, without any coercive Power.

It is true, that certain living creatures, as Bees, and Ants, live sociably one with another, (which are therefore by *Aristotle* numbred amongst Politicall creatures;) and yet have no other direction, than their particular judgements and appetites; nor speech, whereby one of them can signifie to another, what he thinks expedient for the common benefit: and therefore some man may perhaps desire to know, why Man-kind cannot do the same. To which I answer,

First, that men are continually in competition for Honour and Dignity, which these creatures are not; and consequently amongst men there ariseth on that ground, Envy and Hatred, and finally Warre; but amongst these not so.

Secondly, that amongst these creatures, the Common good differeth not from the Private; and being by nature enclined to their private, they procure thereby the common benefit. But man, whose Joy consisteth in comparing himselfe with other men, can relish nothing but what is eminent.

Thirdly, that these creatures, having not (as man) the use of reason, do not see, nor think they see any
[87] fault, in the administration of their common businesse: whereas amongst men, there are very many, that thinke themselves wiser, and abler to govern the Publique, better than the rest; and these strive to reforme and innovate, one this way, another that way; and thereby bring it into Distraction and Civill warre.

Fourthly, that these creatures, though they have some use of voice, in making knowne to one another their desires, and other affections; yet they want that art of words, by which some men can represent to others, that which is Good, in the likenesse of Evill; and Evill, in the likenesse of Good; and augment, or diminish the apparent greatnesse of Good and Evill; discontenting men, and troubling their Peace at their pleasure.

Fiftly, irrationall creatures cannot distinguish betweene *Injury*, and *Dammage*; and therefore as long as they be at ease, they are not offended with their fellowes: whereas Man is then most troublesome, when he is most at ease: for then it is that he loves to shew his Wisdome, and controule the Actions of them that governe the Common-wealth.

Lastly, the agreement of these creatures is Naturall; that of men, is by Covenant only, which is Artificiall: and therefore it is no wonder if there be somwhat else required (besides Covenant) to make their Agreement constant and lasting; which is a Common Power, to keep them in awe, and to direct their actions to the Common Benefit.

The Generation of a Common-wealth.

The only way to erect such a Common Power, as may be able to defend them from the invasion of Forraigners, and the injuries of one another, and thereby to secure them in such sort, as that by their owne industrie, and by the fruites of the Earth, they may nourish themselves and live contentedly; is, to conferre all their power and strength upon one Man, or upon one Assembly of men, that may reduce all their Wills, by plurality of voices, unto one Will: which is as much as to say, to appoint one Man, or Assembly of men, to beare their Person; and every one to owne, and acknowledge himselfe to be Author of whatsoever he that so beareth their Person, shall Act, or cause to be Acted, in those things which concerne the Common Peace and Safetie; and therein to submit their Wills, every one to his Will, and their Judgements, to his Judgment. This is more than Consent, or Concord; it is a reall Unitie of them all, in one and the same Person, made by Covenant of every man with every man, in such manner, as if every

man should say to every man, *I Authorise and give up my Right of Governing my selfe, to this Man, or to this Assembly of men, on this condition, that thou give up thy Right to him, and Authorise all his Actions in like manner.* This done, the Multitude so united in one Person, is called a COMMON-WEALTH, in latine CIVITAS This is the Generation of that great LEVIATHAN, or rather (to speake more reverently) of that *Mortall God*, to which wee owe under the *Immortall God*, our peace and defence. For by this Authoritie, given him by every particular man in the Common-Wealth, he hath the use of so much
[88] Power and Strength conferred on him, that by terror thereof, he is inabled to forme the wills of them all, to Peace at home, and mutuall ayd against their enemies abroad. And in him consisteth the Essence of the Common-wealth; which (to define it,) is *One Person, of whose Acts a great Multitude, by mutuall Covenants one with another, have made themselves every one the Author, to the end he may use the strength and means of them all, as he shall think expedient, for their Peace and Common Defence.*

The Definition of a Common-wealth

Soveraigne, and Subject, what.

And he that carryeth this Person, is called SOVERAIGNE, and said to have *Soveraigne Power*; and every one besides, his SUBJECT.

The attaining to this Soveraigne Power, is by two wayes. One, by Naturall force; as when a man maketh his children, to submit themselves, and their children to his government, as being able to destroy them if they refuse; or by Warre subdueth his enemies to his will, giving them their lives on that condition. The other, is when men agree amongst themselves, to submit to some Man, or Assembly of men, voluntarily, on confidence to be protected by him against all others. This later, may be called a Politicall Common-wealth, or Common-wealth by *Institution*; and the former, a Common-wealth by *Acquisition*. And first, I shall speak of a Common-wealth by Institution.

CHAP. XVIII.

Of the Rights *of Soveraignes by Institution.*

The act of Instituting a Common-wealth, what.

A *Common-wealth* is said to be *Instituted,* when a *Multitude* of men do Agree, and *Covenant, every one, with every one,* that to whatsoever *Man,* or *Assembly of Men,* shall be given by the major part, the *Right* to *Present* the Person of them all, (that is to say, to be their *Representative* ;) every one, as well he that *Voted for it,* as he that *Voted against it,* shall *Authorise* all the Actions and Judgements, of that Man, or Assembly of men, in the same manner, as if they were his own, to the end, to live peaceably amongst themselves, and be protected against other men.

The Consequences to such Institution, are

From this Institution of a Common-wealth are derived all the *Rights,* and *Facultyes* of him, or them, on whom the Soveraigne Power is conferred by the consent of the People assembled.

1. The Subjects cannot change the forme of government.

First, because they Covenant, it is to be understood, they are not obliged by former Covenant to any thing repugnant hereunto. And Consequently they that have already Instituted a Common-wealth, being thereby bound by Covenant, to own the Actions, and Judgements of one, cannot lawfully make a new Covenant, amongst themselves, to be obedient to any other, in any thing whatsoever, without his permission. And therefore, they that are subjects to a Monarch, cannot without his leave cast off Monarchy, and return to the confusion of a disunited Multitude ; nor transferre their Person from him that beareth it, to another Man, or other Assembly of men : for they are bound, every man [89]
to every man, to Own, and be reputed Author of all, that he that already is their Soveraigne, shall do, and judge fit to be done : so that any one man dissenting, all the rest should break their Covenant made to that man, which is injustice : and they have also every man given the Soveraignty to him that beareth their Person ; and therefore if they depose him, they take from him that which is his own, and so again it is injustice. Besides, if he that attempteth to depose his Soveraign,

be killed, or punished by him for such attempt, he is author of his own punishment, as being by the Institution, Author of all his Soveraign shall do: And because it is injustice for a man to do any thing, for which he may be punished by his own authority, he is also upon that title, unjust. And whereas some men have pretended for their disobedience to their Soveraign, a new Covenant, made, not with men, but with God; this also is unjust: for there is no Covenant with God, but by mediation of some body that representeth Gods Person, which none doth but Gods Lieutenant, who hath the Soveraignty under God. But this pretence of Covenant with God, is so evident a lye, even in the pretenders own consciences, that it is not onely an act of an unjust, but also of a vile, and unmanly disposition.

2. Soveraigne Power cannot be forfeited.

Secondly, Because the Right of bearing the Person of them all, is given to him they make Soveraigne, by Covenant onely of one to another, and not of him to any of them; there can happen no breach of Covenant on the part of the Soveraigne, and consequently none of his Subjects, by any pretence of forfeiture, can be freed from his Subjection. That he which is made Soveraigne maketh no Covenant with his Subjects before-hand, is manifest: because either he must make it with the whole multitude, as one party to the Covenant; or he must make a severall Covenant with every man. With the whole, as one party, it is impossible; because as yet they are not one Person: and if he make so many severall Covenants as there be men, those Covenants after he hath the Soveraignty are voyd, because what act soever can be pretended by any one of them for breach thereof, is the act both of himselfe, and of all the rest, because done in the Person, and by the Right of every one of them in particular. Besides, if any one, or more of them, pretend a breach of the Covenant made by the Soveraigne at his Institution, and others, or one other of his Subjects, or himselfe alone, pretend there was no such breach, there is in this case, no Judge to decide the controversie. it returns therefore to the Sword again; and every man recovereth the right of

Protecting himselfe by his own strength, contrary to the designe they had in the Institution. It is therefore in vain to grant Soveraignty by way of precedent Covenant. The opinion that any Monarch receiveth his Power by Covenant, that is to say on Condition, proceedeth from want of understanding this easie truth, that Covenants being but words, and breath, have no force to oblige, contain, constrain, or protect any man, but what it has from the publique Sword, that is, from the untyed hands of that Man, or Assembly of men that hath the Soveraignty, and whose actions are avouched by them all, and performed by the strength [90]
of them all, in him united. But when an Assembly of men is made Soveraigne; then no man imagineth any such Covenant to have past in the Institution; for no man is so dull as to say, for example, the People of *Rome*, made a Covenant with the Romans, to hold the Soveraignty on such or such conditions; which not performed, the Romans might lawfully depose the Roman People. That men see not the reason to be alike in a Monarchy, and in a Popular Government, proceedeth from the ambition of some, that are kinder to the goverment of an Assembly, whereof they may hope to participate, than of Monarchy, which they despair to enjoy

3. No man can without injustice protest against the Institution of the Soveraigne declared by the major part.

Thirdly, because the major part hath by consenting voices declared a Soveraigne; he that dissented must now consent with the rest; that is, be contented to avow all the actions he shall do, or else justly be destroyed by the rest. For if he voluntarily entered into the Congregation of them that were assembled, he sufficiently declared thereby his will (and therefore tacitely covenanted) to stand to what the major part should ordayne: and therefore if he refuse to stand thereto, or make Protestation against any of their Decrees, he does contrary to his Covenant, and therfore unjustly. And whether he be of the Congregation, or not; and whether his consent be asked, or not, he must either submit to their decrees, or be left in the condition of warre he was in before, wherein he might without injustice be destroyed by any man whatsoever.

4. The Soveraigns Actions cannot be justly accused by the Subject.

Fourthly, because every Subject is by this Institution Author of all the Actions, and Judgments of the Soveraigne Instituted; it followes, that whatsoever he doth, it can be no injury to any of his Subjects; nor ought he to be by any of them accused of Injustice. For he that doth any thing by authority from another, doth therein no injury to him by whose authority he acteth. But by this Institution of a Common-wealth, every particular man is Author of all the Soveraigne doth; and consequently he that complaineth of injury from his Soveraigne, complaineth of that whereof he himselfe is Author; and therefore ought not to accuse any man but himselfe; no nor himselfe of injury; because to do injury to ones selfe, is impossible. It is true that they that have Soveraigne power, may commit Iniquity; but not Injustice, or Injury in the proper signification.

5. What soever the Soveraigne doth, is unpunishable by the Subject.

Fiftly, and consequently to that which was sayd last, no man that hath Soveraigne power can iustly be put to death, or otherwise in any manner by his Subjects punished. For seeing every Subject is Author of the actions of his Soveraigne; he punisheth another, for the actions committed by himselfe.

6 The Soveraigne is judge of what is necessary for the Peace and Defence of his Subjects.

And because the End of this Institution, is the Peace and Defence of them all; and whosoever has right to the End, has right to the Means, it belongeth of Right, to whatsoever Man, or Assembly that hath the Soveraignty, to be Judge both of the meanes of Peace and Defence; and also of the hindrances, and disturbances of the same, and to do whatsoever he shall think necessary to be done, both before hand, for the preserving of Peace and Security, by prevention of Discord at
[91] home, and Hostility from abroad; and, when Peace and Security are lost, for the recovery of the same. And therefore,

And Judge of what Doctrines are fit to be taught them.

Sixtly, it is annexed to the Soveraignty, to be Judge of what Opinions and Doctrines are averse, and what conducing to Peace; and consequently, on what occasions, how farre, and what, men are to be trusted withall, in speaking to Multitudes of people; and who shall examine the Doctrines of all bookes before they be published. For the Actions of men proceed from their

Opinions; and in the wel governing of Opinions, consisteth the well governing of mens Actions, in order to their Peace, and Concord. And though in matter of Doctrine, nothing ought to be regarded but the Truth; yet this is not repugnant to regulating of the same by Peace. For Doctrine repugnant to Peace, can no more be True, than Peace and Concord can be against the Law of Nature. It is true, that in a Common-wealth, where by the negligence, or unskilfullnesse of Governours, and Teachers, false Doctrines are by time generally received; the contrary Truths may be generally offensive: Yet the most sudden, and rough busling in of a new Truth, that can be, does never breake the Peace, but only somtimes awake the Warre. For those men that are so remissely governed, that they dare take up Armes, to defend, or introduce an Opinion, are still in Warre; and their condition not Peace, but only a Cessation of Armes for feare of one another; and they live as it were, in the procincts of battaile continually It belongeth therefore to him that hath the Soveraign Power, to be Judge, or constitute all Judges of Opinions and Doctrines, as a thing necessary to Peace; therby to prevent Discord and Civill Warre

7. The Right of making Rules, whereby the Subjects may every man know what is so his owne, as no other Subject can without injustice take it from him.

Seventhly, is annexed to the Soveraigntie, the whole power of prescribing the Rules, whereby every man may know, what Goods he may enjoy, and what Actions he may doe, without being molested by any of his fellow Subjects: And this is it men call *Propriety*. For before constitution of Soveraign Power (as hath already been shewn) all men had right to all things, which necessarily causeth Warre: and therefore this Proprietie, being necessary to Peace, and depending on Soveraign Power, is the Act of that Power, in order to the publique peace. These Rules of Propriety (or *Meum* and *Tuum*) and of *Good*, *Evill*, *Lawfull*, and *Unlawfull* in the actions of Subjects, are the Civill Lawes; that is to say, the Lawes of each Commonwealth in particular; though the name of Civill Law be now restrained to the antient Civill Lawes of the City of *Rome*; which being the head of a great part of the World, her Lawes at that time were in these parts the Civill Law.

8. To him also belongeth the Right of all Judicature and decision of Controversies:

Eightly, is annexed to the Soveraigntie, the Right of Judicature; that is to say, of hearing and deciding all Controversies, which may arise concerning Law, either Civill, or Naturall, or concerning Fact. For without the decision of Controversies, there is no protection of one Subject, against the injuries of another; the Lawes concerning *Meum* and *Tuum* are in vaine; and to every man remaineth, from the naturall and necessary appetite of his own conservation, the right of protecting himselfe
[92] by his private strength, which is the condition of Warre; and contrary to the end for which every Common-wealth is instituted.

9 And of making War, and Peace, as he shall think best

Ninthly, is annexed to the Soveraignty, the Right of making Warre, and Peace with other Nations, and Common-wealths; that is to say, of Judging when it is for the publique good, and how great forces are to be assembled, armed, and payd for that end, and to levy mony upon the Subjects, to defray the expences thereof. For the Power by which the people are to be defended, consisteth in their Armies; and the strength of an Army, in the union of their strength under one Command; which Command the Soveraign Instituted, therefore hath; because the command of the *Militia*, without other Institution, maketh him that hath it Soveraign. And therefore whosoever is made Generall of an Army, he that hath the Soveraign Power is alwayes Generallissimo.

10. And of choosing all Counsellours, and Ministers, both of Peace, and Warre

Tenthly, is annexed to the Soveraignty, the choosing of all Counsellours, Ministers, Magistrates, and Officers, both in Peace, and War. For seeing the Soveraign is charged with the End, which is the common Peace and Defence; he is understood to have Power to use such Means, as he shall think most fit for his discharge.

11 And of Rewarding, and Punishing, and that (where no former Law hath

Eleventhly, to the Soveraign is committed the Power of Rewarding with riches, or honour; and of Punishing with corporall, or pecuniary punishment, or with ignominy every Subject according to the Law he hath formerly made; or if there be no Law made, according as he shall judge most to conduce to the encouraging of men to serve the Common-wealth, or deterring of them from doing dis-service to the same.

Lastly, considering what values men are naturally apt to set upon themselves; what respect they look for from others; and how little they value other men; from whence continually arise amongst them, Emulation, Quarrells, Factions, and at last Warre, to the destroying of one another, and diminution of their strength against a Common Enemy; It is necessary that there be Lawes of Honour, and a publique rate of the worth of such men as have deserved, or are able to deserve well of the Common-wealth; and that there be force in the hands of some or other, to put those Lawes in execution. But it hath already been shewn, that not onely the whole *Militia*, or forces of the Common-wealth, but also the Judicature of all Controversies, is annexed to the Soveraignty. To the Soveraign therefore it belongeth also to give titles of Honour; and to appoint what Order of place, and dignity, each man shall hold, and what signes of respect, in publique or private meetings, they shall give to one another.

determined the measure of it) arbitrary

12. And of Honour and Order.

These Rights indivisible.

These are the Rights, which make the Essence of Soveraignty; and which are the markes, whereby a man may discern in what Man, or Assembly of men, the Soveraign Power is placed, and resideth. For these are incommunicable, and inseparable. The Power to coyn Mony; to dispose of the estate and persons of Infant heires, to have præemption in Markets, and all other Statute Prærogatives, may be transferred by the Soveraign; and yet the Power to protect his Subjects be retained. But if he transferre the *Militia*, he retains the Judicature in vain, for want of execution of the [93] Lawes: Or if he grant away the Power of raising Mony; the *Militia* is in vain. or if he give away the government of Doctrines, men will be frighted into rebellion with the feare of Spirits. And so if we consider any one of the said Rights, we shall presently see, that the holding of all the rest, will produce no effect, in the conservation of Peace and Justice, the end for which all Common-wealths are Instituted. And this division is it, whereof it is said, *a Kingdome divided in it selfe cannot stand*: For unlesse this division precede, division into opposite Armies can never happen. If there had not first been an opinion received of the greatest part of *England*, that these Powers were divided between the King, and the Lords, and the House of Commons, the people had never been divided, and fallen into this Civill Warre; first between those that disagreed in Politiques; and after between the Dissenters about the liberty of Religion; which have so instructed men in this point of Soveraign Right, that there be few now (in *England*,) that do not see, that these Rights are inseparable, and will be so generally acknowledged, at the next return of Peace; and so continue, till their miseries are forgotten; and no longer, except the vulgar be better taught than they have hetherto been.

And can by no Grant passe away without direct renouncing of the Soveraign Power.

And because they are essentiall and inseparable Rights, it follows necessarily, that in whatsoever words any of them seem to be granted away, yet if the Soveraign Power it selfe be not in direct termes renounced, and the name of Soveraign no more given by the Grantees to him that Grants them, the Grant is voyd: for when he has granted all he can, if we grant back the Soveraignty, all is restored, as inseparably annexed thereunto.

The Power and Honour of Subjects vanisheth in the presence of the Power Soveraign.

This great Authority being Indivisible, and inseparably annexed to the Soveraignty, there is little ground for the opinion of them, that say of Soveraign Kings, though they be *singulis majores*, of greater Power than every one of their Subjects, yet they be *Universis minores*, of lesse power than them all together. For if by *all together*, they mean not the collective body as one person, then *all together*, and *every one*, signifie the same; and the speech is absurd. But if by *all together*, they understand them as one Person (which person the Soveraign bears,) then the power of all together, is the same with the Soveraigns power; and so again the speech is absurd: which absurdity they see well enough, when the Soveraignty is in an Assembly of the people; but in a Monarch they see it not, and yet the power of Soveraignty is the same in whomsoever it be placed.

And as the Power, so also the Honour of the Soveraign, ought to be greater, than that of any, or all the Subjects. For in the Soveraignty is the fountain of Honour. The dignities of Lord, Earle, Duke, and Prince are his Creatures. As in the presence of the Master, the Servants are equall, and without any honour at all; So are the Subjects, in the presence of the Soveraign. And though they shine some more, some lesse, when they are out of his sight; yet in his presence, they shine no more than the Starres in presence of the Sun.

Soveraigne Power not so hurtfull as the want of it, and the hurt proceeds for the greatest part from not submitting readily, to a lesse.

But a man may here object, that the Condition of [94] Subjects is very miserable; as being obnoxious to the lusts, and other irregular passions of him, or them that have so unlimited a Power in their hands. And commonly they that live under a Monarch, think it the fault of Monarchy; and they that live under the government of Democracy, or other Soveraign Assembly, attribute all the inconvenience to that forme of Common-wealth; whereas the Power in all formes, if they be perfect enough to protect them, is the same; not considering that the estate of Man can never be without some incommodity or other; and that the greatest, that in any forme of Government can possibly happen to the people in generall, is scarce sensible, in respect of the miseries, and horrible calamities, that accompany a Civill Warre, or that dissolute condition of masterlesse men, without subjection to Lawes, and a coërcive Power to tye their hands from rapine, and revenge: nor considering that the greatest pressure of Soveraign Governours, proceedeth not from any delight, or profit they can expect in the dammage, or weakening of their Subjects, in whose vigor, consisteth their own strength and glory; but in the restiveness of themselves, that unwillingly contributing to their own defence, make it necessary for their Governours to draw from them what they can in time of Peace, that they may have means on any emergent occasion, or sudden need, to resist, or take advantage on their Enemies. For all men are by nature provided of notable multiplying glasses, (that is their Passions and Selfe-love,) through which, every little payment appeareth a great grievance; but are destitute of those prospective glasses, (namely Morall and Civill Science,) to see a farre off the miseries that hang over them, and cannot without such payments be avoyded.

CHAP. XIX.

Of the severall Kinds of Common-wealth *by Institution, and of Succession to the Soveraigne Power.*

The different Formes of Common-wealths but three

THE difference of Common-wealths, consisteth in the difference of the Soveraign, or the Person representative of all and every one of the Multitude. And because the Soveraignty is either in one Man, or in an Assembly of more than one; and into that Assembly either Every man hath right to enter, or not every one, but Certain men distinguished from the rest; it is manifest, there can be but Three kinds of Common-wealth. For the Representative must needs be One man, or More: and if more, then it is the Assembly of All, or but of a Part. When the Representative is One man, then is the Common-wealth a MONARCHY: when an Assembly of All that will come together, then it is a DEMOCRACY, or Popular Common-wealth: when an Assembly of a Part onely, then it is called an ARISTOCRACY. Other kind of Common-wealth there can be none: for either One, or More, or All, must have the Soveraign Power (which I have shewn to be indivisible) entire.

Tyranny and Oligarchy, but different names of Monarchy, and Aristocracy.

[95] There be other names of Government, in the Histories, and books of Policy; as *Tyranny*, and *Oligarchy*: But they are not the names of other Formes of Government, but of the same Formes misliked. For they that are discontented under *Monarchy*, call it *Tyranny*; and they that are displeased with *Aristocracy*, called it *Oligarchy*: So also, they which find themselves grieved under a *Democracy*, call it *Anarchy*, (which signifies want of Government;) and yet I think no man believes, that want of Government, is any new kind of Government: nor by the same reason ought they to believe, that the Government is of one kind, when they like it, and another, when they mislike it, or are oppressed by the Governours.

Subordinate Representatives dangerous.

It is manifest, that men who are in absolute liberty, may, if they please, give Authority to One man, to represent them every one; as well as give such Authority to any Assembly of men whatsoever; and consequently may subject themselves, if they think good, to a Monarch, as absolutely, as to any other Representative. Therefore, where there is already erected a Soveraign Power, there can be no other Representative of the same people, but onely to certain particular ends, by the Soveraign limited. For that were to erect two Soveraigns; and every man to have his person represented by two Actors, that by opposing one another, must needs divide that Power, which (if men will live in Peace) is indivisible; and thereby reduce the Multitude into the condition of Warre, contrary to the end for which all Soveraignty is instituted. And therefore as it is absurd, to think that a Soveraign Assembly, inviting the People of their Dominion, to send up their Deputies, with power to make known their Advise, or Desires, should therefore hold such Deputies, rather than themselves, for the absolute Representative of the people: so it is absurd also, to think the same in a Monarchy. And I know not how this so manifest a truth, should of late be so little observed; that in a Monarchy, he that had the Soveraignty from a descent of 600 years, was alone called Soveraign, had the title of Majesty from every one of his Subjects, and was unquestionably taken by them for their King, was notwithstanding never considered as their Representative; that name without contradiction passing for the title of those men, which at his command were sent up by the people to carry their Petitions, and give him (if he permitted it) their advise. Which may serve as an admonition, for those that are the true, and absolute Representative of a People, to instruct men in the nature of that Office, and to take heed how they admit of any other generall Representation upon any occasion whatsoever, if they mean to discharge the trust committed to them.

Compa son of Monar with So raign s sembly

The difference between these three kindes of Common-wealth, consisteth not in the difference of Power; but in the difference of Convenience, or Aptitude to produce the Peace, and Security of the people; for which end they were instituted. And to compare Monarchy with the other two, we may observe; First, that whosoever beareth the Person of the people, or is one of that

Assembly that bears it, beareth also his own naturall [96] Person. And though he be carefull in his politique Person to procure the common interest; yet he is more, or no lesse carefull to procure the private good of himselfe, his family, kindred and friends; and for the most part, if the publique interest chance to crosse the private, he preferrs the private: for the Passions of men, are commonly more potent than their Reason. From whence it follows, that where the publique and private interest are most closely united, there is the publique most advanced. Now in Monarchy, the private interest is the same with the publique. The riches, power, and honour of a Monarch arise onely from the riches, strength and reputation of his Subjects. For no King can be rich, nor glorious, nor secure; whose Subjects are either poore, or contemptible, or too weak through want, or dissention, to maintain a war against their enemies: Whereas in a Democracy, or Aristocracy, the publique prosperity conferres not so much to the private fortune of one that is corrupt, or ambitious, as doth many times a perfidious advice, a treacherous action, or a Civill warre.

Secondly, that a Monarch receiveth counsell of whom, when, and where he pleaseth; and consequently may heare the opinion of men versed in the matter about which he deliberates, of what rank or quality soever, and as long before the time of action, and with as much secrecy, as he will. But when a Soveraigne Assembly has need of Counsell, none are admitted but such as have a Right thereto from the beginning; which for the most part are of those who have beene versed more in the acquisition of Wealth than of Knowledge; and are to give their advice in long discourses, which may, and do commonly excite men to action, but not governe them in it. For the *Understanding* is by the flame of the Passions, never enlightned, but dazled Nor is there any place, or time, wherein an Assemblie can receive Counsell with secrecie, because of their owne Multitude.

Thirdly, that the Resolutions of a Monarch, are subject to no other Inconstancy, than that of Humane Nature; but in Assemblies, besides that of Nature, there ariseth an Inconstancy from the Number. For the absence of a few, that would have the Resolution once taken, continue firme, (which may happen by security, negligence, or private impediments,) or the diligent appearance of a few of the contrary opinion, undoes to day, all that was concluded yesterday.

Fourthly, that a Monarch cannot disagree with himselfe, out of envy, or interest; but an Assembly may; and that to such a height, as may produce a Civill Warre.

Fifthly, that in Monarchy there is this inconvenience; that any Subject, by the power of one man, for the enriching of a favourite or flatterer, may be deprived of all he possesseth; which I confesse is a great and inevitable inconvenience. But the same may as well happen, where the Soveraigne Power is in an Assembly: For their power is the same; and they are as subject to evill Counsell, and to be seduced by Orators, as a Monarch by Flatterers; and becoming one an others Flatterers, serve one anothers Covetousnesse and Ambition by turnes. And whereas the Favorites of Monarchs, are few, and they have none els to advance but their owne Kindred; the Favorites of an Assembly, are many; [97] and the Kindred much more numerous, than of any Monarch. Besides, there is no Favourite of a Monarch, which cannot as well succour his friends, as hurt his enemies: But Orators, that is to say, Favourites of Soveraigne Assemblies, though they have great power to hurt, have little to save. For to accuse, requires lesse Eloquence (such is mans Nature) than to excuse; and condemnation, than absolution more resembles Justice.

Sixtly, that it is an inconvenience in Monarchie, that the Soveraigntie may descend upon an Infant, or one that cannot discerne between Good and Evill: and consisteth in this, that the use of his Power, must be in the hand of another Man, or of some Assembly of men, which are to governe by his right, and in his name; as Curators, and Protectors of his Person, and Authority. But to say there is inconvenience, in putting the use of the Soveraign Power, into the hand of a Man, or an Assembly of men; is to say that all Government is more Inconvenient, than Confusion, and Civill Warre. And therefore all the danger that can be pretended, must arise

from the Contention of those, that for an office of so great honour, and profit, may become Competitors. To make it appear, that this inconvenience, proceedeth not from that forme of Government we call Monarchy, we are to consider, that the precedent Monarch, hath appointed who shall have the Tuition of his Infant Successor, either expressely by Testament, or tacitly, by not controlling the Custome in that case received: And then such inconvenience (if it happen) is to be attributed, not to the Monarchy, but to the Ambition, and Injustice of the Subjects; which in all kinds of Government, where the people are not well instructed in their Duty, and the Rights of Soveraignty, is the same. Or else the precedent Monarch, hath not at all taken order for such Tuition; And then the Law of Nature hath provided this sufficient rule, That the Tuition shall be in him, that hath by Nature most interest in the preservation of the Authority of the Infant, and to whom least benefit can accrue by his death, or diminution. For seeing every man by nature seeketh his own benefit, and promotion; to put an Infant into the power of those, that can promote themselves by his destruction, or dammage, is not Tuition, but Trechery. So that sufficient provision being taken, against all just quarrell, about the Government under a Child, if any contention arise to the disturbance of the publique Peace, it is not to be attributed to the forme of Monarchy, but to the ambition of Subjects, and ignorance of their Duty. On the other side, there is no great Common-wealth, the Soveraignty whereof is in a great Assembly, which is not, as to consultations of Peace, and Warre, and making of Lawes, in the same condition, as if the Government were in a Child. For as a Child wants the judgement to dissent from counsell given him, and is thereby necessitated to take the advise of them, or him, to whom he is committed: So an Assembly wanteth the liberty, to dissent from the counsell of the major part, be it good, or bad. And as a Child has need of a Tutor, or Protector, to preserve his Person, and Authority: So also (in great Common-wealths,) the
[98] Soveraign Assembly, in all great dangers and troubles, have need of *Custodes libertatis*; that is of Dictators, or

Protectors of their Authoritie; which are as much as Temporary Monarchs; to whom for a time, they may commit the entire exercise of their Power; and have (at the end of that time) been oftner deprived thereof, than Infant Kings, by their Protectors, Regents, or any other Tutors.

Though the Kinds of Soveraigntie be, as I have now shewn, but three; that is to say, Monarchie, where One Man has it; or Democracie, where the generall Assembly of Subjects hath it; or Aristocracie, where it is in an Assembly of certain persons nominated, or otherwise distinguished from the rest: Yet he that shall consider the particular Common-wealthes that have been, and are in the world, will not perhaps easily reduce them to three, and may thereby be inclined to think there be other Formes, arising from these mingled together. As for example, Elective Kingdomes; where Kings have the Soveraigne Power put into their hands for a time; or Kingdomes, wherein the King hath a power limited: which Governments, are nevertheles by most Writers called Monarchie. Likewise if a Popular, or Aristocraticall Common-wealth, subdue an Enemies Countrie, and govern the same, by a President, Procurator, or other Magistrate; this may seeme perhaps at first sight, to be a Democraticall, or Aristocraticall Government. But it is not so. For Elective Kings, are not Soveraignes, but Ministers of the Soveraigne; nor limited Kings Soveraignes, but Ministers of them that have the Soveraigne Power: Nor are those Provinces which are in subjection to a Democracie, or Aristocracie of another Common-wealth, Democratically, or Aristocratically governed, but Monarchically.

And first, concerning an Elective King, whose power is limited to his life, as it is in many places of Christendome at this day; or to certaine Yeares or Moneths, as the Dictators power amongst the Romans; If he have Right to appoint his Successor, he is no more Elective but Hereditary. But if he have no Power to elect his Successor, then there is some other Man, or Assembly known, which after his decease may elect a new, or else the Common-wealth dieth, and dissolveth with him, and returneth to the condition of Warre. If it be known who have the power to give the Soveraigntie after his death, it is known also that the Soveraigntie was in them before: For none have right to give that which they have not right to possesse, and keep to themselves, if they think good. But if there be none that can give the Soveraigntie, after the decease of him that was first elected; then has he power, nay he is obliged by the Law of Nature, to provide, by establishing his Successor, to keep those that had trusted him with the Government, from relapsing into the miserable condition of Civill warre. And consequently he was, when elected, a Soveraign absolute.

Secondly, that King whose power is limited, is not superiour to him, or them that have the power to limit it; and he that is not superiour, is not supreme; that is to say not Soveraign. The Soveraignty therefore was
[99] alwaies in that Assembly which had the Right to Limit him; and by consequence the government not Monarchy, but either Democracy, or Aristocracy; as of old time in *Sparta*; where the Kings had a priviledge to lead their Armies; but the Soveraignty was in the *Ephori*.

Thirdly, whereas heretofore the Roman People, governed the land of *Judea* (for example) by a President; yet was not *Judea* therefore a Democracy; because they were not governed by any Assembly, into the which, any of them, had right to enter; nor by an Aristocracy; because they were not governed by any Assembly, into which, any man could enter by their Election: but they were governed by one Person, which though as to the people of *Rome* was an Assembly of the people, or Democracy; yet as to people of *Judea*, which had no right at all of participating in the government, was a Monarch. For though where the people are governed by an Assembly, chosen by themselves out of their own number, the government is called a Democracy, or Aristocracy; yet when they are governed by an Assembly, not of their own choosing, 'tis a Monarchy; not of *One* man, over another man; but of one people, over another people.

Of the Right of Succession.

Of all these Formes of Government, the matter being mortall, so that not onely Monarchs, but also whole Assemblies dy, it is necessary for the conservation of the peace of men, that as there was order taken for an Artificiall Man, so there be order also taken, for an Artificiall Eternity of life; without which, men that are governed by an Assembly, should return into the condition of Warre in every age; and they that are governed by One man, assoon as their Governour dyeth. This Artificiall Eternity, is that which men call the Right of *Succession*.

There is no perfect forme of Government, where the disposing of the Succession is not in the present Soveraign. For if it be in any other particular Man, or private Assembly, it is in a person subject, and may be assumed by the Soveraign at his pleasure; and consequently the Right is in himselfe. And if it be in no particular man, but left to a new choyce; then is the Common-wealth dissolved; and the Right is in him that can get it; contrary to the intention of them that did Institute the Common-wealth, for their perpetuall, and not temporary security.

In a Democracy, the whole Assembly cannot faile, unlesse the Multitude that are to be governed faile. And therefore questions of the right of Succession, have in that forme of Government no place at all.

In an Aristocracy, when any of the Assembly dyeth, the election of another into his room belongeth to the Assembly, as the Soveraign, to whom belongeth the choosing of all Counsellours, and Officers. For that which the Representative doth, as Actor, every one of the Subjects doth, as Author. And though the Soveraign Assembly, may give Power to others, to elect new men, for supply of their court; yet it is still by their Authority, that the Election is made; and by the same it may (when the publique shall require it) be recalled.

[100]

The present Monarch hath Right to

The greatest difficultie about the right of Succession, is in Monarchy: And the difficulty ariseth from this, that at first sight, it is not manifest who is to appoint the Successor; nor many times, who it is whom he hath *dispose of the Succession.*

appointed. For in both these cases, there is required a more exact ratiocination, than every man is accustomed to use. As to the question, who shall appoint the Successor, of a Monarch that hath the Soveraign Authority; that is to say, who shall determine of the right of Inheritance, (for Elective Kings and Princes have not the Soveraign Power in propriety, but in use only,) we are to consider, that either he that is in possession, has right to dispose of the Succession, or else that right is again in the dissolved Multitude For the death of him that hath the Soveraign power in propriety, leaves the Multitude without any Soveraign at all; that is, without any Representative in whom they should be united, and be capable of doing any one action at all: And therefore they are incapable of Election of any new Monarch; every man having equall right to submit himselfe to such as he thinks best able to protect him; or if he can, protect himselfe by his owne sword, which is a returne to Confusion, and to the condition of a War of every man against every man, contrary to the end for which Monarchy had its first Institution. Therfore it is manifest, that by the Institution of Monarchy, the disposing of the Successor, is alwaies left to the Judgment and Will of the present Possessor.

And for the question (which may arise sometimes) who it is that the Monarch in possession, hath designed to the succession and inheritance of his power; it is determined by his expresse Words, and Testament; or by other tacite signes sufficient.

Succession passeth by expresse Words,

By expresse Words, or Testament, when it is declared by him in his life time, *viva voce*, or by Writing; as the first Emperours of *Rome* declared who should be their Heires For the word Heire does not of it selfe imply the Children, or nearest Kindred of a man; but whomsoever a man shall any way declare, he would have to succeed him in his Estate. If therefore a Monarch declare expresly, that such a man shall be his Heire, either by Word or Writing, then is that man immediatly after the decease of his Predecessor, Invested in the right of being Monarch.

But where Testament, and expresse Words are wanting, other naturall signes of the Will are to be followed: whereof the one is Custome. And therefore where the Custome is, that the next of Kindred absolutely succeedeth, there also the next of Kindred hath right to the Succession, for that, if the will of him that was in posession had been otherwise, he might easily have declared the same in his life time. And likewise where the Custome is, that the next of the Male Kindred succeedeth, there also the right of Succession is in the next of the Kindred Male, for the same reason And so it is if the Custome were to advance the Female. For whatsoever Custome a man may by a word controule, and does not, it is a naturall signe he would have that Custome stand.

Or, by not controlling a Custome,

But where neither Custome, nor Testament hath preceded, there it is to be understood, First, that a Monarchs [101] will is, that the government remain Monarchicall, because he hath approved that government in himselfe. Secondly, that a Child of his own, Male, or Female, be preferred before any other, because men are presumed to be more enclined by nature, to advance their own children, than the children of other men, and of their own, rather a Male than a Female, because men, are naturally fitter than women, for actions of labour and danger. Thirdly, where his own Issue faileth, rather a Brother than a stranger, and so still the neerer in bloud, rather than the more remote; because it is alwayes presumed that the neerer of kin, is the neerer in affection; and 'tis evident that a man receives alwayes, by reflexion, the most honour from the greatnesse of his neerest kindred.

Or, by presumption of naturall affection.

But if it be lawfull for a Monarch to dispose of the Succession by words of Contract, or Testament, men may perhaps object a great inconvenience: for he may sell, or give his Right of governing to a stranger, which, because strangers (that is, men not used to live under the same government, nor speaking the same language) do commonly undervalue one another, may turn to the oppression of his Subjects, which is indeed a great inconvenience: but it proceedeth not necessarily from the

To dispose of the Succession, though to a King of another Nation, not unlawfull

subjection to a strangers government, but from the unskilfulnesse of the Governours, ignorant of the true rules of Politiques. And therefore the Romans when they had subdued many Nations, to make their Government digestible, were wont to take away that grievance, as much as they thought necessary, by giving sometimes to whole Nations, and sometimes to Principall men of every Nation they conquered, not onely the Privileges, but also the Name of Romans; and took many of them into the Senate, and Offices of charge, even in the Roman City. And this was it our most wise King, King *James*, aymed at, in endeavouring the Union of his two Realms of *England* and *Scotland*. Which if he could have obtained, had in all likelihood prevented the Civill warres, which make both those Kingdomes, at this present, miserable. It is not therefore any injury to the people, for a Monarch to dispose of the Succession by Will; though by the fault of many Princes, it hath been sometimes found inconvenient. Of the lawfulnesse of it, this also is an argument, that whatsoever inconvenience can arrive by giving a Kingdome to a stranger, may arrive also by so marrying with strangers, as the Right of Succession may descend upon them: yet this by all men is accounted lawfull.

CHAP. XX.

Of Dominion PATERNALL, *and* DESPOTICALL.

A Common-wealth by Acquisition.

A *Common-wealth by Acquisition*, is that, where the Soveraign Power is acquired by Force; And it is acquired by force, when men singly, or many together by plurality of voyces, for fear of death, or bonds, do authorise all [102] the actions of that Man, or Assembly, that hath their lives and liberty in his Power.

Wherein different from a Common-wealth by Institution.

And this kind of Dominion, or Soveraignty, differeth from Soveraignty by Institution, onely in this, That men who choose their Soveraign, do it for fear of one another, and not of him whom they Institute: But in this case, they subject themselves, to him they are afraid of. In both cases they do it for fear: which is to be noted by them, that hold all such Covenants, as proceed from fear of death, or violence, voyd : which if it were true, no man, in any kind of Common-wealth, could be obliged to Obedience. It is true, that in a Commonwealth once Instituted, or acquired, Promises proceeding from fear of death, or violence, are no Covenants, nor obliging, when the thing promised is contrary to the Lawes ; But the reason is not, because it was made upon fear, but because he that promiseth, hath no right in the thing promised. Also, when he may lawfully performe, and doth not, it is not the Invalidity of the Covenant, that absolveth him, but the Sentence of the Soveraign. Otherwise, whensoever a man lawfully promiseth, he unlawfully breaketh : But when the Soveraign, who is the Actor, acquitteth him, then he is acquitted by him that extorted the promise, as by the Author of such absolution.

The Rights of Soveraignty the same in both.

But the Rights, and Consequences of Soveraignty, are the same in both. His Power cannot, without his consent, be Transferred to another : He cannot Forfeit it : He cannot be Accused by any of his Subjects, of Injury : He cannot be Punished by them : He is Judge of what is necessary for Peace ; and Judge of Doctrines : He is Sole Legislator ; and Supreme Judge of Controversies ; and of the Times, and Occasions of Warre, and Peace : to him it belongeth to choose Magistrates, Counsellours, Commanders, and all other Officers, and Ministers ; and to determine of Rewards, and Punishments, Honour, and Order. The reasons whereof, are the same which are alledged in the precedent Chapter, for the same Rights, and Consequences of Soveraignty by Institution

Dominion Paternall how attained.

Dominion is acquired two wayes ; By Generation, and by Conquest. The right of Dominion by Generation, is that, which the Parent hath over his Children ; and is called PATERNALL. And is not so derived from the Generation, as if therefore the Parent had Dominion over his Child because he begat him ; but from the Childs Consent, either expresse, or by other sufficient arguments declared. For as to the Generation, God hath ordained to man a helper , and there be alwayes two that are equally Parents : the Dominion therefore over the Child, should

Not by Generation, but by Contract ;

belong equally to both; and he be equally subject to both, which is impossible; for no man can obey two Masters. And whereas some have attributed the Dominion to the Man onely, as being of the more excellent Sex; they misreckon in it. For there is not alwayes that difference of strength, or prudence between the man and the woman, as that the right can be determined without War. In Common-wealths, this controversie is decided by the Civill Law: and for the most part, (but not alwayes) the sentence is in favour of the Father;
[103] because for the most part Common-wealths have been erected by the Fathers, not by the Mothers of families. But the question lyeth now in the state of meer Nature; where there are supposed no lawes of Matrimony; no lawes for the Education of Children; but the Law of Nature, and the naturall inclination of the Sexes, one to another, and to their children. In this condition of meer Nature, either the Parents between themselves dispose of the dominion over the Child by Contract; or do not dispose thereof at all. If they dispose thereof, the right passeth according to the Contract. We find in History that the *Amazons* Contracted with the Men of the neighbouring Countries, to whom they had recourse for issue, that the issue Male should be sent back, but the Female remain with themselves: so that the dominion of the Females was in the Mother.

Or Education; If there be no Contract, the Dominion is in the Mother. For in the condition of meer Nature, where there are no Matrimoniall lawes, it cannot be known who is the Father, unlesse it be declared by the Mother: and therefore the right of Dominion over the Child dependeth on her will, and is consequently hers. Again, seeing the Infant is first in the power of the Mother, so as she may either nourish, or expose it: if she nourish it, it oweth its life to the Mother; and is therefore obliged to obey her, rather than any other; and by consequence the Dominion over it is hers. But if she expose it, and another find, and nourish it, the Dominion is in him that nourisheth it. For it ought to obey him by whom it is preserved; because preservation of life being the end, for which one man becomes subject to another, every man is supposed to promise obedience, to him, in whose power it is to save, or destroy him.

Or Precedent subjection of one of the Parents to the other.

If the Mother be the Fathers subject, the Child, is in the Fathers power · and if the Father be the Mothers subject, (as when a Soveraign Queen marrieth one of her subjects,) the Child is subject to the Mother , because the Father also is her subject.

If a man and a woman, Monarches of two severall Kingdomes, have a Child, and contract concerning who shall have the Dominion of him, the Right of the Dominion passeth by the Contract. If they contract not, the Dominion followeth the Dominion of the place of his residence For the Soveraign of each Country hath Dominion over all that reside therein.

He that hath the Dominion over the Child, hath Dominion also over the Children of the Child , and over their Childrens Children. For he that hath Dominion over the person of a man, hath Dominion over all that is his ; without which, Dominion were but a Title, without the effect.

The Right of Succession followeth the Rules of the Right of Possession.

The Right of Succession to Paternall Dominion, proceedeth in the same manner, as doth the Right of Succession to Monarchy ; of which I have already sufficiently spoken in the precedent chapter.

Despoticall Dominion how attained.

Dominion acquired by Conquest, or Victory in war, is that which some Writers call DESPOTICALL, from Δεσπότης which signifieth a *Lord*, or *Master* ; and is the Dominion of the Master over his Servant. And this Dominion is then acquired to the Victor, when the Vanquished, to [104]
avoyd the present stroke of death, covenanteth either in expresse words, or by other sufficient signes of the Will, that so long as his life, and the liberty of his body is allowed him, the Victor shall have the use thereof, at his pleasure. And after such Covenant made, the Vanquished is a SERVANT, and not before : for by the word *Servant* (whether it be derived from *Servire*, to Serve, or from *Servare*, to Save, which I leave to Grammarians to dispute) is not meant a Captive, which is kept in prison, or bonds, till the owner of him that took him, or bought him of one that did, shall consider what to do with him : (for such men, (commonly called Slaves,) have no obliga-

tion at all; but may break their bonds, or the prison; and kill, or carry away captive their Master, justly:) but one, that being taken, hath corporall liberty allowed him; and upon promise not to run away, nor to do violence to his Master, is trusted by him.

Not by the Victory, but by the Consent of the Vanquished.

It is not therefore the Victory, that giveth the right of Dominion over the Vanquished, but his own Covenant. Nor is he obliged because he is Conquered; that is to say, beaten, and taken, or put to flight; but because he commeth in, and Submitteth to the Victor; Nor is the Victor obliged by an enemies rendring himselfe, (without promise of life,) to spare him for this his yeelding to discretion; which obliges not the Victor longer, than in his own discretion hee shall think fit.

And that which men do, when they demand (as it is now called) *Quarter*, (which the Greeks called Ζωγρία, *taking alive*,) is to evade the present fury of the Victor, by Submission, and to compound for their life, with Ransome, or Service: and therefore he that hath Quarter hath not his life given, but deferred till farther deliberation; For it is not an yeelding on condition of life, but to discretion. And then onely is his life in security, and his service due, when the Victor hath trusted him with his corporall liberty. For Slaves that work in Prisons, or Fetters, do it not of duty, but to avoyd the cruelty of their task-masters.

The Master of the Servant, is Master also of all he hath; and may exact the use thereof; that is to say, of his goods, of his labour, of his servants, and of his children, as often as he shall think fit. For he holdeth his life of his Master, by the covenant of obedience; that is, of owning, and authorising whatsoever the Master shall do. And in case the Master, if he refuse, kill him, or cast him into bonds, or otherwise punish him for his disobedience, he is himselfe the author of the same, and cannot accuse him of injury.

In summe, the Rights and Consequences of both *Paternall* and *Despoticall* Dominion, are the very same with those of a Soveraign by Institution; and for the same reasons: which reasons are set down in the precedent chapter. So that for a man that is Monarch of divers

Nations, whereof he hath, in one the Soveraignty by Institution of the people assembled, and in another by Conquest, that is by the submission of each particular, to avoyd death or bonds, to demand of one Nation more than of the other, from the title of Conquest, as being a Conquered Nation, is an act of ignorance of the Rights of Soveraignty. For the Soveraign is absolute [105] over both alike; or else there is no Soveraignty at all, and so every man may Lawfully protect himselfe, if he can, with his own sword, which is the condition of war.

Difference between a Family and a Kingdom.

By this it appears, that a great Family if it be not part of some Common-wealth, is of it self, as to the Rights of Soveraignty, a little Monarchy; whether that Family consist of a man and his children; or of a man and his servants; or of a man, and his children, and servants together. wherein the Father or Master is the Soveraign. But yet a Family is not properly a Common-wealth; unlesse it be of that power by its own number, or by other opportunities, as not to be subdued without the hazard of war. For where a number of men are manifestly too weak to defend themselves united, every one may use his own reason in time of danger, to save his own life, either by flight, or by submission to the enemy, as hee shall think best; in the same manner as a very small company of souldiers, surprised by an army, may cast down their armes, and demand quarter, or run away, rather than be put to the sword. And thus much shall suffice; concerning what I find by speculation, and deduction, of Soveraign Rights, from the nature, need, and designes of men, in erecting of Common-wealths, and putting themselves under Monarchs, or Assemblies, entrusted with power enough for their protection.

The Rights of Monarchy from Scripture.

Let us now consider what the Scripture teacheth in the same point. To *Moses*, the children of *Israel* say thus. * *Speak thou to us, and we will heare thee; but let not God speak to us, lest we dye.* This is absolute obedience to *Moses*. Concerning the Right of Kings, God himself by the mouth of *Samuel*, saith, * *This shall be the Right of the King you will have to reigne over you. He shall take your sons, and set them to drive his Chariots,*

* *Exod.* 20. 19.

* 1 *Sam* 8. 11, 12, &c.

and to be his horsemen, and to run before his chariots; and gather in his harvest; and to make his engines of War, and Instruments of his chariots; and shall take your daughters to make perfumes, to be his Cookes, and Bakers. He shall take your fields, your vine-yards, and your olive-yards, and give them to his servants. He shall take the tyth of your corne and wine, and give it to the men of his chamber, and to his other servants. He shall take your man-servants, and your maid-servants, and the choice of your youth, and employ them in his businesse. He shall take the tyth of your flocks; and you shall be his servants. This is absolute power, and summed up in the last words, *you shall be his servants.* Againe, when the people heard what power their King was to have, yet they consented
*Verse. 19, &c. thereto, and say thus, * *We will be as all other nations,*
and our King shall judge our causes, and goe before us, to conduct our wars. Here is confirmed the Right that Soveraigns have, both to the *Militia*, and to all *Judicature*; in which is conteined as absolute power, as one man can possibly transferre to another. Again, the
*1 *Kings* 3 9 prayer of King *Salomon* to God, was this. * *Give to thy*
servant understanding, to judge thy people, and to discerne between Good and Evill. It belongeth therefore to the
[106] Soveraigne to bee *Judge*, and to præscribe the Rules of *discerning Good* and *Evill*: which Rules are Lawes; and therefore in him is the Legislative Power. *Saul* sought the life of *David*; yet when it was in his power to slay *Saul*, and his Servants would have done it, *David* forbad
*1 *Sam.* 24 9. them, saying, * *God forbid I should do such an act against*
my Lord, the anoynted of God. For obedience of servants
**Coll.* 3. 20. St. *Paul* saith, * *Servants obey your masters in All things*;
and, * *Children obey your Parents in All things.* There
**Verse* 22. is simple obedience in those that are subject to Paternall
**Math.*23. 2,3 or Despoticall Dominion. Again, * *The Scribes and*
Pharisees sit in Moses chayre, and therefore All that they shall bid you observe, that observe and do. There again is
**Tit.*3.2. simple obedience. And St *Paul*, * *Warn them that they*
subject themselves to Princes, and to those that are in Authority, & obey them. This obedience is also simple. Lastly, our Saviour himselfe acknowledges, that men ought to pay such taxes as are by Kings imposed, where

he sayes, *Give to Cæsar that which is Cæsars* ; and payed such taxes himselfe. And that the Kings word, is sufficient to take any thing from any Subject, when there is need ; and that the King is Judge of that need : For he himselfe, as King of the Jewes, commanded his Disciples to take the Asse, and Asses Colt to carry him into *Jerusalem*, saying, * *Go into the Village over against you, and you shall find a shee Asse tyed, and her Colt with her, unty them, and bring them to me. And if any man ask you, what you mean by it, Say the Lord hath need of them : And they will let them go.* They will not ask whether his necessity be a sufficient title ; nor whether he be judge of that necessity ; but acquiesce in the will of the Lord.

* *Mat.* 21. 2, 3.

To these places may be added also that of *Genesis*, * *You shall be as Gods, knowing Good and Evill.* And verse 11. *Who told thee that thou wast naked? hast thou eaten of the tree, of which I commanded thee thou shouldest not eat?* For the Cognisance or Judicature of *Good* and *Evill*, being forbidden by the name of the fruit of the tree of Knowledge, as a triall of *Adams* obedience ; The Divel to enflame the Ambition of the woman, to whom that fruit already seemed beautifull, told her that by tasting it, they should be as Gods, knowing *Good* and *Evill.* Whereupon having both eaten, they did indeed take upon them Gods office, which is Judicature of Good and Evill ; but acquired no new ability to distinguish between them aright. And whereas it is sayd, that having eaten, they saw they were naked ; no man hath so interpreted that place, as if they had been formerly blind, and saw not their own skins : the meaning is plain, that it was then they first judged their nakednesse (wherein it was Gods will to create them) to be uncomely ; and by being ashamed, did tacitely censure God himselfe. And thereupon God saith, *Hast thou eaten, &c.* as if he should say, doest thou that owest me obedience, take upon thee to judge of my Commandements? Whereby it is cleerly, (though Allegorically,) signified, that the Commands of them that have the right to command, are not by their Subjects to be censured, nor disputed.

* *Gen.* 3. 5.

So that it appeareth plainly, to my understanding, both from Reason, and Scripture, that the Soveraign
[107] Power, whether placed in One Man, as in Monarchy, or in one Assembly of men, as in Popular, and Aristocraticall Common-wealths, is as great, as possibly men can be imagined to make it. And though of so unlimited a Power, men may fancy many evill consequences, yet the consequences of the want of it, which is perpetuall warre of every man against his neighbour, are much worse The condition of man in this life shall never be without Inconveniences: but there happeneth in no Common-wealth any great Inconvenience, but what proceeds from the Subjects disobedience, and breach of those Covenants, from which the Common-wealth hath its being. And whosoever thinking Soveraign Power too great, will seek to make it lesse; must subject himselfe, to the Power, that can limit it; that is to say, to a greater.

Soveraign Power ought in all Common-wealths to be absolute.

The greatest objection is, that of the Practise; when men ask, where, and when, such Power has by Subjects been acknowledged. But one may ask them again, when, or where has there been a Kingdome long free from Sedition and Civill Warre. In those Nations, whose Common-wealths have been long-lived, and not been destroyed, but by forraign warre, the Subjects never did dispute of the Soveraign Power. But howsoever, an argument from the Practise of men, that have not sifted to the bottom, and with exact reason weighed the causes, and nature of Common-wealths, and suffer daily those miseries, that proceed from the ignorance thereof, is invalid. For though in all places of the world, men should lay the foundation of their houses on the sand, it could not thence be inferred, that so it ought to be. The skill of making, and maintaining Common-wealths, consisteth in certain Rules, as doth Arithmetique and Geometry; not (as Tennis-play) on Practise onely: which Rules, neither poor men have the leisure, nor men that have had the leisure, have hitherto had the curiosity, or the method to find out.

CHAP. XXI.

Of the LIBERTY *of Subjects.*

Liberty what.

LIBERTY, or FREEDOME, signifieth (properly) the absence of Opposition; (by Opposition, I mean externall Impediments of motion;) and may be applyed no lesse to Irrationall, and Inanimate creatures, than to Rationall. For whatsoever is so tyed, or environed, as it cannot move, but within a certain space, which space is determined by the opposition of some externall body, we say it hath not Liberty to go further. And so of all living creatures, whilest they are imprisoned, or restrained, with walls, or chayns; and of the water whilest it is kept in by banks, or vessels, that otherwise would spread it selfe into a larger space, we use to say, they are not at Liberty, to move in such manner, as without those externall impediments they would. But when the impediment of motion, is in the constitution of the thing it selfe, we use not to say, it wants the Liberty; but the Power to move, as when a stone lyeth still, or a man is fastned to his bed by sicknesse.

[108]

What it is to be Free

And according to this proper, and generally received meaning of the word, *A* FREE-MAN, *is he, that in those things, which by his strength and wit he is able to do, is not hindred to doe what he has a will to.* But when the words *Free*, and *Liberty*, are applyed to any thing but *Bodies*, they are abused; for that which is not subject to Motion, is not subject to Impediment: And therefore, when 'tis said (for example) The way is Free, no Liberty of the way is signified, but of those that walk in it without stop. And when we say a Guift is Free, there is not meant any Liberty of the Guift, but of the Giver, that was not bound by any law, or Covenant to give it. So when we *speak Freely*, it is not the Liberty of voice, or pronunciation, but of the man, whom no law hath obliged to speak otherwise then he did. Lastly, from the use of the word *Free-will*, no Liberty can be inferred of the will, desire, or inclination, but the Liberty of the man, which consisteth in this, that he finds no stop, in doing what he has the will, desire, or inclination to doe

Feare and Liberty consistent

Feare, and Liberty are consistent; as when a man throweth his goods into the Sea for *feare* the ship should sink, he doth it neverthelesse very willingly, and may refuse to doe it if he will: It is therefore the action, of one that was *free*: so a man sometimes pays his debt, only for *feare* of Imprisonment, which because no body hindred him from detaining, was the action of a man at *liberty*. And generally all actions which men doe in Common-wealths, for *feare* of the law, are actions, which the doers had *liberty* to omit.

Liberty and Necessity consistent.

Liberty, and *Necessity* are consistent: As in the water, that hath not only *liberty*, but a *necessity* of descending by the Channel; so likewise in the Actions which men voluntarily doe: which, because they proceed from their will, proceed from *liberty*; and yet, because every act of mans will, and every desire, and inclination proceedeth from some cause, and that from another cause, in a continuall chaine, (whose first link is in the hand of God the first of all causes,) they proceed from *necessity*. So that to him that could see the connexion of those causes, the *necessity* of all mens voluntary actions, would appeare manifest. And therefore God, that seeth, and disposeth all things, seeth also that the *liberty* of man in doing what he will, is accompanied with the *necessity* of doing that which God will, & no more, nor lesse. For though men may do many things, which God does not command, nor is therefore Author of them; yet they can have no passion, nor appetite to any thing, of which appetite Gods will is not the cause. And did not his will assure the *necessity* of mans will, and consequently of all that on mans will dependeth, the *liberty* of men would be a contradiction, and impediment to the omnipotence and *liberty* of God. And this shall suffice, (as to the matter in hand) of that naturall *liberty*, which only is properly called *liberty*.

Artificiall Bonds, or Covenants.

But as men, for the atteyning of peace, and conservation of themselves thereby, have made an Artificiall Man, which we call a Common-wealth; so also have they made Artificiall Chains, called *Civill Lawes*, which they
[109] themselves, by mutuall covenants, have fastned at one end, to the lips of that Man, or Assembly, to whom they

have given the Soveraigne Power; and at the other end to their own Ears. These Bonds in their own nature but weak, may neverthelesse be made to hold, by the danger, though not by the difficulty of breaking them.

Liberty of Subjects consisteth in Liberty from covenants

In relation to these Bonds only it is, that I am to speak now, of the *Liberty* of *Subjects*. For seeing there is no Common-wealth in the world, wherein there be Rules enough set down, for the regulating of all the actions, and words of men, (as being a thing impossible:) it followeth necessarily, that in all kinds of actions, by the laws prætermitted, men have the Liberty, of doing what their own reasons shall suggest, for the most profitable to themselves. For if wee take Liberty in the proper sense, for corporall Liberty; that is to say, freedome from chains, and prison, it were very absurd for men to clamor as they doe, for the Liberty they so manifestly enjoy. Againe, if we take Liberty, for an exemption from Lawes, it is no lesse absurd, for men to demand as they doe, that Liberty, by which all other men may be masters of their lives. And yet as absurd as it is, this is it they demand; not knowing that the Lawes are of no power to protect them, without a Sword in the hands of a man, or men, to cause those laws to be put in execution. The Liberty of a Subject, lyeth therefore only in those things, which in regulating their actions, the Soveraign hath prætermitted: such as is the Liberty to buy, and sell, and otherwise contract with one another; to choose their own aboad, their own diet, their own trade of life, and institute their children as they themselves think fit; & the like.

Liberty of the Subject consistent with the unlimited power of the Soveraign.

Neverthelesse we are not to understand, that by such Liberty, the Soveraign Power of life, and death, is either abolished, or limited For it has been already shewn, that nothing the Soveraign Representative can doe to a Subject, on what pretence soever, can properly be called Injustice, or Injury; because every Subject is Author of every act the Soveraign doth; so that he never wanteth Right to any thing, otherwise, than as he himself is the Subject of God, and bound thereby to observe the laws of Nature. And therefore it may, and doth often happen in Common-wealths, that a Subject

may be put to death, by the command of the Soveraign Power; and yet neither doe the other wrong: As when *Jeptha* caused his daughter to be sacrificed: In which, and the like cases, he that so dieth, had Liberty to doe the action, for which he is neverthelesse, without Injury put to death. And the same holdeth also in a Soveraign Prince, that putteth to death an Innocent Subject. For though the action be against the law of Nature, as being contrary to Equitie, (as was the killing of *Uriah*, by *David*;) yet it was not an Injurie to *Uriah*; but to *God*. Not to *Uriah*, because the right to doe what he pleased, was given him by *Uriah* himself: And yet to *God*, because *David* was *Gods* Subject; and prohibited all Iniquitie by the law of Nature. Which distinction, *David* himself, when he repented the fact, evidently confirmed, saying, *To thee only have I sinned*. In the same manner,
[110] the people of *Athens*, when they banished the most potent of their Common-wealth for ten years, thought they committed no Injustice; and yet they never questioned what crime he had done; but what hurt he would doe Nay they commanded the banishment of they knew not whom; and every Citizen bringing his Oystershell into the market place, written with the name of him he desired should be banished, without actuall accusing him, sometimes banished an *Aristides*, for his reputation of Justice; And sometimes a scurrilous Jester. as *Hyperbolus*, to make a Jest of it. And yet a man cannot say, the Soveraign People of *Athens* wanted right to banish them; or an *Athenian* the Libertie to Jest, or to be Just.

The Liberty which writers praise, is the Liberty of Soveraigns; not of Private men.

The Libertie, whereof there is so frequent, and honourable mention, in the Histories, and Philosophy of the Antient Greeks, and Romans, and in the writings, and discourse of those that from them have received all their learning in the Politiques, is not the Libertie of Particular men; but the Libertie of the Common-wealth: which is the same with that, which every man then should have, if there were no Civil Laws, nor Common-wealth at all. And the effects of it also be the same For as amongst masterlesse men, there is perpetuall war, of every man against his neighbour, no inheritance to transmit to the Son, nor to expect from the Father; no propriety of Goods, or Lands; no security; but a full and absolute Libertie in every Particular man: So in States, and Common-wealths not dependent on one another, every Common-wealth, (not every man) has an absolute Libertie, to doe what it shall judge (that is to say, what that Man, or Assemblie that representeth it, shall judge) most conducing to their benefit. But withall, they live in the condition of a perpetuall war, and upon the confines of battel, with their frontiers armed, and canons planted against their neighbours round about. The *Athenians*, and *Romanes* were free; that is, free Common-wealths: not that any particular men had the Libertie to resist their own Representative; but that their Representative had the Libertie to resist, or invade other people. There is written on the Turrets of the city of *Luca* in great characters at this day, the word *LIBERTAS*; yet no man can thence inferre, that a particular man has more Libertie, or Immunitie from the service of the Commonwealth there, than in *Constantinople*. Whether a Common-wealth be Monarchicall, or Popular, the Freedome is still the same.

But it is an easy thing, for men to be deceived, by the specious name of Libertie; and for want of Judgement to distinguish, mistake that for their Private Inheritance, and Birth right, which is the right of the Publique only. And when the same errour is confirmed by the authority of men in reputation for their writings in this subject, it is no wonder if it produce sedition, and change of Government. In these westerne parts of the world, we are made to receive our opinions concerning the Institution, and Rights of Common-wealths, from *Aristotle*, *Cicero*, and other men, Greeks and Romanes, that living under Popular States, derived those Rights, not from the Principles of Nature, but transcribed them into their books, out of the Practise of their own Common-wealths, [111]
which were Popular; as the Grammarians describe the Rules of Language, out of the Practise of the time; or the Rules of Poetry, out of the Poems of *Homer* and *Virgil*. And because the Athenians were taught, (to keep them from desire of changing their Government,)

that they were Freemen, and all that lived under Monarchy were slaves; therefore *Aristotle* puts it down in his *Politiques*, (*lib* 6. *cap.* 2) *In democracy*, Liberty *is to be supposed: for 'tis commonly held, that no man is* Free *in any other Government.* And as *Aristotle*; so *Cicero*, and other Writers have grounded their Civill doctrine, on the opinions of the Romans, who were taught to hate Monarchy, at first, by them that having deposed their Soveraign, shared amongst them the Soveraignty of *Rome*; and afterwards by their Successors. And by reading of these Greek, and Latine Authors, men from their childhood have gotten a habit (under a false shew of Liberty,) of favouring tumults, and of licentious controlling the actions of their Soveraigns; and again of controlling those controllers, with the effusion of so much blood; as I think I may truly say, there was never any thing so deerly bought, as these Western parts have bought the learning of the Greek and Latine tongues

Liberty of Subjects how to be measured

To come now to the particulars of the true Liberty of a Subject; that is to say, what are the things, which though commanded by the Soveraign, he may neverthelesse, without Injustice, refuse to do; we are to consider, what Rights we passe away, when we make a Commonwealth; or (which is all one,) what Liberty we deny our selves, by owning all the Actions (without exception) of the Man, or Assembly we make our Soveraign. For in the act of our *Submission*, consisteth both our *Obligation*, and our *Liberty*; which must therefore be inferred by arguments taken from thence; there being no Obligation on any man, which ariseth not from some Act of his own; for all men equally, are by Nature Free. And because such arguments, must either be drawn from the expresse words, *I Authorise all his Actions*, or from the Intention of him that submitteth himselfe to his Power, (which Intention is to be understood by the End for which he so submitteth;) The Obligation, and Liberty of the Subject, is to be derived, either from those Words, (or others equivalent;) or else from the End of the Institution of Soveraignty; namely, the Peace of the Subjects within themselves, and their Defence against a common Enemy.

Subjects have Liberty to defend their own bodies, even against them that lawfully invade them:

First therefore, seeing Soveraignty by Institution, is by Covenant of every one to every one; and Soveraignty by Acquisition, by Covenants of the Vanquished to the Victor, or Child to the Parent; It is manifest, that every Subject has Liberty in all those things, the right whereof cannot by Covenant be transferred. I have shewn before in the 14. Chapter, that Covenants, not to defend a mans own body, are voyd. Therefore,

If the Soveraign command a man (though justly condemned,) to kill, wound, or mayme himselfe; or not to resist those that assault him; or to abstain from the use of food, ayre, medicine, or any other thing, without which [112] he cannot live; yet hath that man the Liberty to disobey.

Are not bound to hurt themselves;

If a man be interrogated by the Soveraign, or his Authority, concerning a crime done by himselfe, he is not bound (without assurance of Pardon) to confesse it; because no man (as I have shewn in the same Chapter) can be obliged by Covenant to accuse himselfe.

Again, the Consent of a Subject to Soveraign Power, is contained in these words, *I Authorise, or take upon me, all his actions*; in which there is no restriction at all, of his own former naturall Liberty. For by allowing him to *kill me*, I am not bound to kill my selfe when he commands me. 'Tis one thing to say, *Kill me, or my fellow, if you please*; another thing to say, *I will kill my selfe, or my fellow.* It followeth therefore, that

No man is bound by the words themselves, either to kill himselfe, or any other man; And consequently, that the Obligation a man may sometimes have, upon the Command of the Soveraign to execute any dangerous, or dishonourable Office, dependeth not on the Words of our Submission; but on the Intention; which is to be understood by the End thereof. When therefore our refusall to obey, frustrates the End for which the Soveraignty was ordained; then there is no Liberty to refuse: otherwise there is.

Nor to warfare, unlesse they voluntarily undertake it.

Upon this ground, a man that is commanded as a Souldier to fight against the enemy, though his Soveraign have Right enough to punish his refusall with death, may neverthelesse in many cases refuse, without Injustice: as when he substituteth a sufficient Souldier in his place: for in this case he deserteth not the service of the Common-wealth. And there is allowance to be made for naturall timorousnesse, not onely to women, (of whom no such dangerous duty is expected,) but also to men of feminine courage. When Armies fight, there is on one side, or both, a running away; yet when they do it not out of trechery, but fear, they are not esteemed to do it unjustly, but dishonourably. For the same reason, to avoyd battell, is not Injustice, but Cowardise. But he that inrowleth himselfe a Souldier, or taketh imprest mony, taketh away the excuse of a timorous nature; and is obliged, not onely to go to the battell, but also not to run from it, without his Captaines leave. And when the Defence of the Common-wealth, requireth at once the help of all that are able to bear Arms, every one is obliged, because otherwise the Institution of the Common-wealth, which they have not the purpose, or courage to preserve, was in vain.

To resist the Sword of the Common-wealth, in defence of another man, guilty, or innocent, no man hath Liberty; because such Liberty, takes away from the Soveraign, the means of Protecting us. and is therefore destructive of the very essence of Government. But in case a great many men together, have already resisted the Soveraign Power unjustly, or committed some Capitall crime, for which every one of them expecteth death, whether have they not the Liberty then to joyn together, and assist, and defend one another? Certainly they have: For [113] they but defend their lives, which the Guilty man may as well do, as the Innocent There was indeed injustice in the first breach of their duty; Their bearing of Arms subsequent to it, though it be to maintain what they have done, is no new unjust act. And if it be onely to defend their persons, it is not unjust at all But the offer of pardon taketh from them, to whom it is offered, the plea of self-defence, and maketh their perseverance in assisting, or defending the rest, unlawfull.

The Greatest Liberty of Subjects,

As for other Lyberties, they depend on the Silence of the Law. In cases where the Soveraign has prescribed no rule, there the Subject hath the Liberty to do, or forbeare, according to his own discretion. And therefore such Liberty is in some places more, and in some lesse, and in some times more, in other times lesse, according as they that have the Soveraignty shall think most convenient. As for Example, there was a time, when in *England* a man might enter in to his own Land, (and dispossesse such as wrongfully possessed it,) by force. But in after-times, that Liberty of Forcible Entry, was taken away by a Statute made (by the King) in Parliament. And in some places of the world, men have the Liberty of many wives: in other places, such Liberty is not allowed.

dependeth on the Silence of the Law

If a Subject have a controversie with his Soveraigne, of debt, or of right of possession of lands or goods, or concerning any service required at his hands, or concerning any penalty, corporall, or pecuniary, grounded on a precedent Law; he hath the same Liberty to sue for his right, as if it were against a Subject; and before such Judges, as are appointed by the Soveraign. For seeing the Soveraign demandeth by force of a former Law, and not by vertue of his Power, he declareth thereby, that he requireth no more, than shall appear to be due by that Law The sute therefore is not contrary to the will of the Soveraign; and consequently the Subject hath the Liberty to demand the hearing of his Cause; and sentence, according to that Law. But if he demand, or take any thing by pretence of his Power, there lyeth, in that case, no action of Law: for all that is done by him in Vertue of his Power, is done by the Authority of every Subject, and consequently, he that brings an action against the Soveraign, brings it against himselfe.

If a Monarch, or Soveraign Assembly, grant a Liberty to all, or any of his Subjects, which Grant standing, he is disabled to provide for their safety, the Grant is voyd; unlesse he directly renounce, or transferre the Soveraignty to another. For in that he might openly, (if it had been his will,) and in plain termes, have renounced, or transferred it, and did not; it is to be understood it was not his will, but that the Grant proceeded from ignorance of the repugnancy between such a Liberty and the Soveraign Power: and therefore the Soveraignty is still retayned; and consequently all those Powers, which are necessary to the exercising thereof; such as are the Power of Warre, and Peace, of Judicature, of appointing Officers, and Councellours, of levying Mony, and the rest named in the 18th Chapter.

[114] *In what Cases Subjects are absolved of their obedience to their Soveraign.* The Obligation of Subjects to the Soveraign, is understood to last as long, and no longer, than the power lasteth, by which he is able to protect them. For the right men have by Nature to protect themselves, when none else can protect them, can by no Covenant be relinquished. The Soveraignty is the Soule of the Common-wealth; which once departed from the Body, the members doe no more receive their motion from it. The end of Obedience is Protection; which, wheresoever a man seeth it, either in his own, or in anothers sword, Nature applyeth his obedience to it, and his endeavour to maintaine it. And though Soveraignty, in the intention of them that make it, be immortall; yet is it in its own nature, not only subject to violent death, by forreign war; but also through the ignorance, and passions of men, it hath in it, from the very institution, many seeds of a naturall mortality, by Intestine Discord.

In case of Captivity. If a Subject be taken prisoner in war; or his person, or his means of life be within the Guards of the enemy, and hath his life and corporall Libertie given him, on condition to be Subject to the Victor, he hath Libertie to accept the condition; and having accepted it, is the subject of him that took him; because he had no other way to preserve himself. The case is the same, if he be deteined on the same termes, in a forreign country. But if a man be held in prison, or bonds, or is not trusted with the libertie of his bodie, he cannot be understood to be bound by Covenant to subjection; and therefore may, if he can, make his escape by any means whatsoever.

In case the Soveraign cast off the government from himself and his Heyrs. If a Monarch shall relinquish the Soveraignty, both for himself, and his heires; His Subjects returne to the absolute Libertie of Nature; because, though Nature may declare who are his Sons, and who are the nerest of his Kin; yet it dependeth on his own will, (as hath been said in the precedent chapter,) who shall be his Heyr. If therefore he will have no Heyre, there is no

Soveraignty, nor Subjection. The case is the same, if he dye without known Kindred, and without declaration of his Heyre. For then there can no Heire be known, and consequently no Subjection be due.

In case of Banishment

If the Soveraign Banish his Subject; during the Banishment, he is not Subject. But he that is sent on a message, or hath leave to travell, is still Subject; but it is, by Contract between Soveraigns, not by vertue of the covenant of Subjection. For whosoever entreth into anothers dominion, is Subject to all the Laws thereof; unlesse he have a privilege by the amity of the Soveraigns, or by speciall licence.

In case the Soveraign render himself Subject to another.

If a Monarch subdued by war, render himself Subject to the Victor, his Subjects are delivered from their former obligation, and become obliged to the Victor. But if he be held prisoner, or have not the liberty of his own Body, he is not understood to have given away the Right of Soveraigntie; and therefore his Subjects are obliged to yield obedience to the Magistrates formerly placed, governing not in their own name, but in his. For, his Right remaining, the question is only of the Administration; that is to say, of the Magistrates and Officers; [115]
which, if he have not means to name, he is supposed to approve those, which he himself had formerly appointed.

CHAP. XXII.

Of SYSTEMES *Subject, Politicall, and Private.*

The divers sorts of Systemes of People.

HAVING spoken of the Generation, Forme, and Power of a Common-wealth, I am in order to speak next of the parts thereof. And first of Systemes, which resemble the similar parts, or Muscles of a Body naturall By SYSTEMES; I understand any numbers of men joyned in one Interest, or one Businesse. Of which, some are *Regular*, and some *Irregular*. *Regular* are those, where one Man, or Assembly of men, is constituted Representative of the whole number. All other are *Irregular*.

Of Regular, some are *Absolute*, and *Independent*, subject to none but their own Representative: such are only Common-wealths; Of which I have spoken already in the 5. last precedent chapters. Others are Dependent; that is to say, Subordinate to some Soveraign Power, to which every one, as also their Representative is *Subject.*

Of Systemes subordinate, some are *Politicall,* and some *Private. Politicall* (otherwise Called *Bodies Politique,* and *Persons in Law,*) are those, which are made by authority from the Soveraign Power of the Common-wealth. *Private,* are those, which are constituted by Subjects amongst themselves, or by authoritie from a stranger. For no authority derived from forraign power, within the Dominion of another, is Publique there, but Private.

And of Private Systemes, some are *Lawfull*; some *Unlawfull*: *Lawfull,* are those which are allowed by the Common-wealth: all other are *Unlawfull. Irregular* Systemes, are those which having no Representative, consist only in concourse of People; which if not forbidden by the Common-wealth, nor made on evill designe, (such as are conflux of People to markets, or shews, or any other harmelesse end,) are Lawfull. But when the Intention is evill, or (if the number be considerable) unknown, they are Unlawfull.

In all Bodies Politique the power of the Representative is Limited.

In Bodies Politique, the power of the Representative is alwaies Limited: And that which prescribeth the Limits thereof, is the Power Soveraign. For Power Unlimited, is absolute Soveraignty. And the Soveraign, in every Commonwealth, is the absolute Representative of all the subjects; and therefore no other, can be Representative of any part of them, but so far forth, as he shall give leave: And to give leave to a Body Politique of Subjects, to have an absolute Representative to all intents and purposes, were to abandon the government of so much of the Commonwealth, and to divide the Dominion, contrary to their Peace and Defence, which the Soveraign cannot be understood to doe. by
[116] any Grant, that does not plainly, and directly discharge them of their subjection. For consequences of words, are not the signes of his will, when other consequences are signes of the contrary; but rather signes of errour, and misreckonning; to which all mankind is too prone.

The bounds of that Power, which is given to the Representative of a Bodie Politique, are to be taken notice of, from two things. One is their Writt, or Letters from the Soveraign: the other is the Law of the Common-wealth.

By Letters Patents:

For though in the Institution or Acquisition of a Common-wealth, which is independent, there needs no Writing, because the Power of the Representative has there no other bounds, but such as are set out by the unwritten Law of Nature; yet in subordinate bodies, there are such diversities of Limitation necessary, concerning their businesses, times, and places, as can neither be remembred without Letters, nor taken notice of, unlesse such Letters be Patent, that they may be read to them, and withall sealed, or testified, with the Seales, or other permanent signes of the Authority Soveraign.

And the Lawes

And because such Limitation is not alwaies easie, or perhaps possible to be described in writing; the ordinary Lawes, common to all Subjects, must determine, what the Representative may lawfully do, in all Cases, where the Letters themselves are silent. And therefore

When the Representative is one man, his unwarranted Acts are his own onely.

In a Body Politique, if the Representative be one man, whatsoever he does in the Person of the Body, which is not warranted in his Letters, nor by the Lawes, is his own act, and not the act of the Body, nor of any other Member thereof besides himselfe: Because further than his Letters, or the Lawes limit, he representeth no mans person, but his own. But what he does according to these, is the act of every one: For of the Act of the Soveraign every one is Author, because he is their Representative unlimited, and the act of him that recedes not from the Letters of the Soveraign, is the act of the Soveraign, and therefore every member of the Body is Author of it.

When it is an Assembly, it is the act of them that assented onely.

But if the Representative be an Assembly; whatsoever that Assembly shall Decree, not warranted by their Letters, or the Lawes, is the act of the Assembly, or Body Politique, and the act of every one by whose Vote the Decree was made; but not the act of any man that being present Voted to the contrary; nor of any man absent, unlesse he Voted it by procuration.

It is the act of the Assembly, because Voted by the major part; and if it be a crime, the Assembly may be punished, as farre-forth as it is capable, as by dissolution, or forfeiture of their Letters, (which is to such artificiall, and fictitious Bodies, capitall,) or (if the Assembly have a Common stock, wherein none of the Innocent Members have propriety,) by pecuniary Mulct. For from corporall penalties Nature hath exempted all Bodies Politique. But they that gave not their Vote, are therefore Innocent, because the Assembly cannot Represent any man in things unwarranted by their Letters, and consequently are not involved in their Votes.

When the Representative is one man, if he borrow mony, or owe it, by Contract, he is lyable onely, the members not.

If the person of the Body Politique being in one man, borrow mony of a stranger, that is, of one that is not of the same Body, (for no Letters need limit borrowing,
[117] seeing it is left to mens own inclinations to limit lending) the debt is the Representatives. For if he should have Authority from his Letters, to make the members pay what he borroweth, he should have by consequence the Soveraignty of them; and therefore the grant were either voyd, as proceeding from Errour, commonly incident to humane Nature, and an unsufficient signe of the will of the Granter; or if it be avowed by him, then is the Representer Soveraign, and falleth not under the present question, which is onely of Bodies subordinate. No member therefore is obliged to pay the debt so borrowed, but the Representative himselfe: because he that lendeth it, being a stranger to the Letters, and to the qualification of the Body, understandeth those onely for his debtors, that are engaged; and seeing the Representer can ingage himselfe, and none else, has him onely for Debtor; who must therefore pay him, out of the common stock (if there be any), or (if there be none) out of his own estate.

If he come into debt by Contract, or Mulct, the case is the same.

When it is an Assembly, they onely are liable that have assented.

But when the Representative is an Assembly, and the debt to a stranger; all they, and onely they are responsible for the debt, that gave their votes to the borrowing of it, or to the Contract that made it due, or to the fact for which the Mulct was imposed; because every one of those in voting did engage himselfe for the payment: For he that is author of the borrowing, is obliged to the payment, even of the whole debt, though when payd by any one, he be discharged.

If the debt be to one of the Assembly, the Body onely is obliged.

But if the debt be to one of the Assembly, the Assembly onely is obliged to the payment, out of their common stock (if they have any:) For having liberty of Vote, if he Vote the Mony, shall be borrowed, he Votes it shall be payd; If he Vote it shall not be borrowed, or be absent, yet because in lending, he voteth the borrowing, he contradicteth his former Vote, and is obliged by the later, and becomes both borrower and lender, and consequently cannot demand payment from any particular man, but from the common Treasure onely; which fayling he hath no remedy, nor complaint, but against himselfe, that being privy to the acts of the Assembly, and to their means to pay, and not being enforced, did neverthelesse through his own folly lend his mony.

Protestation against the Decrees of Bodies Politique sometimes lawful, but against Soveraign Power never.

It is manifest by this, that in Bodies Politique subordinate and subject to a Soveraign Power, it is sometimes not onely lawfull, but expedient, for a particular man to make open protestation against the decrees of the Representative Assembly, and cause their dissent to be Registred, or to take witnesse of it; because otherwise they may be obliged to pay debts contracted, and be responsible for crimes committed by other men: But in a Soveraign Assembly, that liberty is taken away, both because he that protesteth there, denies their Soveraignty; and also because whatsoever is commanded by the Soveraign Power, is as to the Subject (though not so alwayes in the sight of God) justified by the Command; for of such command every Subject is the Author.

The variety of Bodies Politique, is almost infinite: for they are not onely distinguished by the severall affaires, for which they are constituted, wherein there is an un- [118]
speakable diversitie; but also by the times, places, and numbers, subject to many limitations. And as to their affaires, some are ordained for Government; As first, the Government of a Province may be committed to an Assembly of men, wherein all resolutions shall depend on the Votes of the major part; and then this Assembly

Bodies Politique for Government of a Province, Colony, or Town.

is a Body Politique, and their power limited by Commission. This word Province signifies a charge, or care of businesse, which he whose businesse it is, committeth to another man, to be administred for, and under him; and therefore when in one Common-wealth there be divers Countries, that have their Lawes distinct one from another, or are farre distant in place, the Administration of the Government being committed to divers persons, those Countries where the Soveraign is not resident, but governs by Commission, are called Provinces. But of the government of a Province, by an Assembly residing in the Province it selfe, there be few examples. The Romans who had the Soveraignty of many Provinces; yet governed them alwaies by Presidents, and Prætors; and not by Assemblies, as they governed the City of *Rome*, and Territories adjacent. In like manner, when there were Colonies sent from *England*, to Plant *Virginia*, and *Sommer-Ilands*, though the government of them here, were committed to Assemblies in *London*, yet did those Assemblies never commit the Government under them to any Assembly there; but did to each Plantation send one Governour; For though every man, where he can be present by Nature, desires to participate of government; yet where they cannot be present, they are by Nature also enclined, to commit the Government of their common Interest rather to a Monarchicall, then a Popular form of Government: which is also evident in those men that have great private estates; who when they are unwilling to take the paines of administring the businesse that belongs to them, choose rather to trust one Servant, then an Assembly either of their friends or servants. But howsoever it be in fact, yet we may suppose the Government of a Province, or Colony committed to an Assembly: and when it is, that which in this place I have to say, is this; that whatsoever debt is by that Assembly contracted; or whatsoever unlawfull Act is decreed, is the Act onely of those that assented, and not of any that dissented, or were absent, for the reasons before alledged. Also that an Assembly residing out of the bounds of that Colony whereof they have the government, cannot execute any power over the persons, or goods of any of the Colonie, to seize on them for debt, or other duty, in any place without the Colony it selfe, as having no Jurisdiction, nor Authoritie elsewhere, but are left to the remedie, which the Law of the place alloweth them. And though the Assembly have right, to impose a Mulct upon any of their members, that shall break the Lawes they make; yet out of the Colonie it selfe, they have no right to execute the same. And that which is said here, of the Rights of an Assembly, for the government of a Province, or a Colony, is appliable also to an Assembly for the Government of a Town, an University, or a College, or a Church, or for any other Government over the persons of men.

And generally, in all Bodies Politique, if any parti- [119]
cular member conceive himself Injuried by the Body it self, the Cognisance of his cause belongeth to the Soveraign, and those the Soveraign hath ordained for Judges in such causes, or shall ordaine for that particular cause; and not to the Body it self. For the whole Body is in this case his fellow subject, which in a Soveraign Assembly, is otherwise: for there, if the Soveraign be not Judge, though in his own cause, there can be no Judge at all.

Bodies Politique for ordering of Trade.

In a Bodie Politique, for the well ordering of forraigne Traffique, the most commodious Representative is an Assembly of all the members; that is to say, such a one, as every one that adventureth his mony, may be present at all the Deliberations, and Resolutions of the Body, if they will themselves. For proof whereof, we are to consider the end, for which men that are Merchants, and may buy and sell, export, and import their Merchandise according to their own discretions, doe neverthelesse bind themselves up in one Corporation. It is true, there be few Merchants, that with the Merchandise they buy at home, can fraight a Ship, to export it; or with that they buy abroad, to bring it home; and have therefore need to joyn together in one Society; where every man may either participate of the gaine, according to the proportion of his adventure, or take his own, and sell what he transports, or imports, at such prices as he thinks fit. But this is no Body Politique, there being no Common Representative to oblige them to any other Law, than that which is common to all other subjects. The End of their Incorporating, is to make their gaine the greater; which is done two wayes; by sole buying, and sole selling, both at home, and abroad. So that to grant to a Company of Merchants to be a Corporation, or Body Politique, is to grant them a double Monopoly, whereof one is to be sole buyers; another to be sole sellers. For when there is a Company incorporate for any particular forraign Country, they only export the Commodities vendible in that Country; which is sole buying at home, and sole selling abroad. For at home there is but one buyer, and abroad but one that selleth: both which is gainfull to the Merchant, because thereby they buy at home at lower, and sell abroad at higher rates: And abroad there is but one buyer of forraign Merchandise, and but one that sels them at home; both which againe are gainfull to the adventurers.

Of this double Monopoly one part is disadvantageous to the people at home, the other to forraigners. For at home by their sole exportation they set what price they please on the husbandry, and handy-works of the people; and by the sole importation, what price they please on all forraign commodities the people have need of; both which are ill for the people. On the contrary, by the sole selling of the native commodities abroad, and sole buying the forraign commodities upon the place, they raise the price of those, and abate the price of these, to
[120] the disadvantage of the forraigner: For where but one selleth, the Merchandise is the dearer; and where but one buyeth the cheaper: Such Corporations therefore are no other then Monopolies; though they would be very profitable for a Common-wealth, if being bound up into one body in forraigne Markets they were at liberty at home, every man to buy, and sell at what price he could.

The end then of these Bodies of Merchants, being not a Common benefit to the whole Body, (which have in this case no common stock, but what is deducted out of the particular adventures, for building, buying, victualling and manning of Ships,) but the particular gaine of every adventurer, it is reason that every one be acquainted with the employment of his own; that is, that every one be of the Assembly, that shall have the power to order the same; and be acquainted with their accounts. And therefore the Representative of such a Body must be an Assembly, where every member of the Body may be present at the consultations, if he will.

If a Body Politique of Merchants, contract a debt to a stranger by the act of their Representative Assembly, every Member is lyable by himself for the whole. For a stranger can take no notice of their private Lawes, but considereth them as so many particular men, obliged every one to the whole payment, till payment made by one dischargeth all the rest. But if the debt be to one of the Company, the creditor is debter for the whole to himself, and cannot therefore demand his debt, but only from the common stock, if there be any.

If the Common-wealth impose a Tax upon the Body, it is understood to be layd upon every Member proportionably to his particular adventure in the Company. For there is in this case no other common stock, but what is made of their particular adventures.

If a Mulct be layd upon the Body for some unlawfull act, they only are lyable by whose votes the act was decreed, or by whose assistance it was executed; for in none of the rest is there any other crime but being of the Body, which if a crime, (because the Body was ordeyned by the authority of the Common-wealth,) is not his.

If one of the Members be indebted to the Body, he may be sued by the Body; but his goods cannot be taken, nor his person imprisoned by the authority of the Body; but only by Authority of the Common-wealth: for if they can doe it by their own Authority, they can by their own Authority give judgement that the debt is due; which is as much as to be Judge in their own Cause.

A Bodie Politique for Counsel to be given to the Soveraign.

These Bodies made for the government of Men, or of Traffique, be either perpetuall, or for a time prescribed by writing. But there be Bodies also whose times are limited, and that only by the nature of their businesse. For example, if a Soveraign Monarch, or a Soveraign Assembly, shall think fit to give command to the towns,

and other severall parts of their territory, to send to him their Deputies, to enforme him of the condition, and necessities of the Subjects, or to advise with him for
[121] the making of good Lawes, or for any other cause, as with one Person representing the whole Country, such Deputies, having a place and time of meeting assigned them, are there, and at that time, a Body Politique, representing every Subject of that Dominion; but it is onely for such matters as shall be propounded unto them by that Man, or Assembly, that by the Soveraign Authority sent for them; and when it shall be declared that nothing more shall be propounded, nor debated by them, the Body is dissolved. For if they were the absolute Representative of the people, then were it the Soveraign Assembly; and so there would be two Soveraign Assemblies, or two Soveraigns, over the same people; which cannot consist with their Peace. And therefore where there is once a Soveraignty, there can be no absolute Representation of the people, but by it And for the limits of how farre such a Body shall represent the whole People, they are set forth in the Writing by which they were sent for. For the People cannot choose their Deputies to other intent, than is in the Writing directed to them from their Soveraign expressed.

A Regular Private Body, Lawfull, as a Family.

Private Bodies Regular, and Lawfull, are those that are constituted without Letters, or other written Authority, saving the Lawes common to all other Subjects. And because they be united in one Person Representative, they are held for Regular; such as are all Families, in which the Father, or Master ordereth the whole Family. For he obligeth his Children, and Servants, as farre as the Law permitteth, though not further, because none of them are bound to obedience in those actions, which the Law hath forbidden to be done. In all other actions, during the time they are under domestique government, they are subject to their Fathers, and Masters, as to their immediate Soveraigns. For the Father, and Master being before the Institution of Common-wealth, absolute Soveraigns in their own Families, they lose afterward no more of their Authority, than the Law of the Common-wealth taketh from them.

Private Bodies Regular, but Unlawfull. Private Bodies Regular, but Unlawfull, are those that unite themselves into one person Representative, without any publique Authority at all; such as are the Corporations of Beggars, Theeves and Gipsies, the better to order their trade of begging, and stealing; and the Corporations of men, that by Authority from any forraign Person, unite themselves in anothers Dominion, for the easier propagation of Doctrines, and for making a party, against the Power of the Common-wealth.

Systemes Irregular, such as are Private Leagues. Irregular Systemes, in their nature, but Leagues, or sometimes meer concourse of people, without union to any particular designe, not by obligation of one to another, but proceeding onely from a similitude of wills and inclinations, become Lawfull, or Unlawfull, according to the lawfulnesse, or unlawfulnesse of every particular mans designe therein: And his designe is to be understood by the occasion.

The Leagues of Subjects, (because Leagues are commonly made for mutuall defence,) are in a Common-wealth (which is no more than a League of all the Subjects together) for the most part unnecessary, and savour of unlawfull designe; and are for that cause Unlawfull, [122] and go commonly by the name of Factions, or Conspiracies. For a League being a connexion of men by Covenants, if there be no power given to any one Man, or Assembly (as in the condition of meer Nature) to compell them to performance, is so long onely valid, as there ariseth no just cause of distrust: and therefore Leagues between Common-wealths, over whom there is no humane Power established, to keep them all in awe, are not onely lawfull, but also profitable for the time they last. But Leagues of the Subjects of one and the same Common-wealth, where every one may obtain his right by means of the Soveraign Power, are unnecessary to the maintaining of Peace and Justice, and (in case the designe of them be evill, or Unknown to the Common-wealth) unlawfull. For all uniting of strength by private men, is, if for evill intent, unjust; if for intent unknown, dangerous to the Publique, and unjustly concealed.

Secret Cabals. If the Soveraign Power be in a great Assembly, and a number of men, part of the Assembly, without authority, consult a part, to contrive the guidance of the rest; This is a Faction, or Conspiracy unlawfull, as being a fraudulent seducing of the Assembly for their particular interest. But if he, whose private interest is to be debated, and judged in the Assembly, make as many friends as he can; in him it is no Injustice; because in this case he is no part of the Assembly And though he hire such friends with mony, (unlesse there be an expresse Law against it,) yet it is not Injustice. For sometimes. (as mens manners are,) Justice cannot be had without mony; and every man may think his own cause just, till it be heard, and judged.

Feuds of private Families. In all Common-wealths, if a private man entertain more servants, than the government of his estate, and lawfull employment he has for them requires, it is Faction, and unlawfull. For having the protection of the Common-wealth, he needeth not the defence of private force. And whereas in Nations not throughly civilized, severall numerous Families have lived in continuall hostility, and invaded one another with private force; yet it is evident enough, that they have done unjustly; or else that they had no Common-wealth.

Factions for Government. And as Factions for Kindred, so also Factions for Government of Religion, as of Papists, Protestants, &c. or of State, as Patricians, and Plebeians of old time in *Rome*, and of Aristocraticalls and Democraticalls of old time in *Greece*, are unjust, as being contrary to the peace and safety of the people, and a taking of the Sword out of the hand of the Soveraign.

Concourse of people, is an Irregular Systeme, the lawfulnesse, or unlawfulnesse, whereof dependeth on the occasion, and on the number of them that are assembled. If the occasion be lawfull, and manifest, the Concourse is lawfull; as the usuall meeting of men at Church, or at a publique Shew, in usuall numbers . for if the numbers be extraordinarily great, the occasion is not evident; and consequently he that cannot render a particular and good account of his being amongst them, is to be judged conscious of an unlawfull, and tumultuous designe. It may be lawfull for a thousand men, to joyn in a Peti- [123] tion to be delivered to a Judge, or Magistrate, yet if a thousand men come to present it, it is a tumultuous Assembly; because there needs but one or two for that purpose. But in such cases as these, it is not a set number that makes the Assembly Unlawfull, but such a number, as the present Officers are not able to suppresse, and bring to Justice.

When an unusuall number of men, assemble against a man whom they accuse; the Assembly is an Unlawfull tumult; because they may deliver their accusation to the Magistrate by a few, or by one man.. Such was the case of St. *Paul* at *Ephesus*; where *Demetrius*, and a great number of other men, brought two of *Pauls* companions before the Magistrate, saying with one Voyce, *Great is Diana of the Ephesians*; which was their way of demanding Justice against them for teaching the people such doctrine, as was against their Religion, and Trade. The occasion here, considering the Lawes of that People, was just; yet was their Assembly Judged Unlawfull, and the Magistrate reprehended them for it, in these words, * *If Demetrius and the other work-men can accuse any man, of any thing, there be Pleas, and Deputies, let them accuse one another. And if you have any other thing to demand, your case may be judged in an Assembly Lawfully called For we are in danger to be accused for this dayes sedition, because, there is no cause by which any man can render any reason of this Concourse of People.* Where he calleth an Assembly, whereof men can give no just account, a Sedition, and such as they could not answer for. And this is all I shall say concerning *Systemes*, and Assemblyes of People, which may be compared (as I said,) to the Similar parts of mans Body; such as be Lawfull, to the Muscles, such as are Unlawfull, to Wens, Biles, and Apostemes, engendred by the unnaturall conflux of evill humours.

* *Acts* 19. 40.

CHAP. XXIII.

Of the Publique Ministers *of Soveraign Power.*

In the last Chapter I have spoken of the Similar parts of a Common-wealth: In this I shall speak of the parts Organicall, which are Publique Ministers.

Publique Minister Who.

A Publique Minister, is he, that by the Soveraign, (whether a Monarch, or an Assembly,) is employed in any affaires, with Authority to represent in that employment, the Person of the Common-wealth. And whereas every man, or assembly that hath Soveraignty, representeth two Persons, or (as the more common phrase is) has two Capacities, one Naturall, and another Politique, (as a Monarch, hath the person not onely of the Common-wealth, but also of a man; and a Soveraign Assembly hath the Person not onely of the Common-wealth, but also of the Assembly); they that be servants to them in their naturall Capacity, are not Publique Ministers; but those onely that serve them in the Administration of
[124] the Publique businesse. And therefore neither Ushers, nor Sergeants, nor other Officers that waite on the Assembly, for no other purpose, but for the commodity of the men assembled, in an Aristocracy, or Democracy; nor Stewards, Chamberlains, Cofferers, or any other Officers of the houshold of a Monarch, are Publique Ministers in a Monarchy

Ministers for the generall Administration.

Of Publique Ministers, some have charge committed to them of a generall Administration, either of the whole Dominion, or of a part thereof. Of the whole, as to a Protector, or Regent, may bee committed by the Predecessor of an Infant King, during his minority, the whole Administration of his Kingdome. In which case, every Subject is so far obliged to obedience, as the Ordinances he shall make, and the commands he shall give be in the Kings name, and not inconsistent with his Soveraigne Power. Of a part, or Province; as when either a Monarch, or a Soveraign Assembly, shall give the generall charge thereof to a Governour, Lieutenant, Præfect or Vice-Roy: And in this case also, every one of that Province, is obliged to all he shall doe in the name of the Soveraign, and that not incompatible with the Soveraigns Right. For such Protectors, Vice-Roys, and Governors, have no other right, but what depends on the Soveraigns Will; and no Commission that can be given them, can be interpreted for a Declaration of the will to transferre the Soveraignty, without expresse and perspicuous words to that purpose. And this kind of Publique Ministers resembleth the Nerves, and Tendons that move the severall limbs of a body naturall.

For speciall Administration, as for Oeconomy.

Others have speciall Administration; that is to say, charges of some speciall businesse, either at home, or abroad: As at home; First, for the Oeconomy of a Common-wealth, They that have Authority concerning the *Treasure*, as Tributes, Impositions, Rents, Fines, or whatsoever publique revenue, to collect, receive, issue, or take the Accounts thereof, are Publique Ministers: Ministers, because they serve the Person Representative, and can doe nothing against his Command, nor without his Authority: Publique, because they serve him in his Politicall Capacity.

Secondly, they that have Authority concerning the *Militia*; to have the custody of Armes, Forts, Ports; to Levy, Pay, or Conduct Souldiers; or to provide for any necessary thing for the use of war, either by Land or Sea, are publique Ministers. But a Souldier without Command, though he fight for the Common-wealth, does not therefore represent the Person of it; because there is none to represent it to. For every one that hath command, represents it to them only whom he commandeth.

For instruction of the People.

They also that have authority to teach, or to enable others to teach the people their duty to the Soveraign Power, and instruct them in the knowledge of what is just, and unjust, thereby to render them more apt to live in godlinesse, and in peace amongst themselves, and resist the publique enemy, are Publique Ministers: Ministers, in that they doe it not by their own Authority, but by anothers; and Publique, because they doe it (or should doe it) by no Authority, but that of the Sove- [125]
raign. The Monarch, or the Soveraign Assembly only hath immediate Authority from God, to teach and instruct the people; and no man but the Soveraign,

receiveth his power *Dei gratiâ* simply; that is to say, from the favour of none but God: All other, receive theirs from the favour and providence of God, and their Soveraigns; as in a Monarchy *Dei gratiâ & Regis*; or *Dei providentiâ & voluntate Regis*.

For Judicature. They also to whom Jurisdiction is given, are Publique Ministers. For in their Seats of Justice they represent the person of the Soveraign; and their Sentence, is his Sentence; For (as hath been before declared) all Judicature is essentially annexed to the Soveraignty; and therefore all other Judges are but Ministers of him, or them that have the Soveraign Power. And as Controversies are of two sorts, namely of *Fact* and of *Law*; so are Judgements, some of Fact, some of Law: And consequently in the same controversie, there may be two Judges, one of Fact, another of Law.

And in both these controversies, there may arise a controversie between the party Judged, and the Judge; which because they be both Subjects to the Soveraign, ought in Equity to be Judged by men agreed on by consent of both; for no man can be Judge in his own cause. But the Soveraign is already agreed on for Judge by them both, and is therefore either to heare the Cause, and determine it himself, or appoint for Judge such as they shall both agree on. And this agreement is then understood to be made between them divers wayes, as first, if the Defendant be allowed to except against such of his Judges, whose interest maketh him suspect them, (for as to the Complaynant he hath already chosen his own Judge,) those which he excepteth not against, are Judges he himself agrees on. Secondly, if he appeale to any other Judge, he can appeale no further; for his appeale is his choice. Thirdly, if he appeale to the Soveraign himself, and he by himself, or by Delegates which the parties shall agree on, give Sentence; that Sentence is finall: for the Defendant is Judged by his own Judges, that is to say, by himself.

These properties of just and rationall Judicature considered, I cannot forbeare to observe the excellent constitution of the Courts of Justice, established both for Common, and also for Publique Pleas in *England*. By

Common Pleas, I meane those, where both the Complaynant and Defendant are Subjects: and by Publique, (which are also called Pleas of the Crown) those, where the Complaynant is the Soveraign. For whereas there were two orders of men, whereof one was Lords, the other Commons; The Lords had this Priviledge, to have for Judges in all Capitall crimes, none but Lords; and of them, as many as would be present; which being ever acknowledged as a Priviledge of favour, their Judges were none but such as they had themselves desired. And in all controversies, every Subject (as also in civill controversies the Lords) had for Judges, men of the Country where the matter in controversie lay; against which he might make his exceptions, till at last twelve men with- [126]
out exception being agreed on, they were Judged by those twelve. So that having his own Judges, there could be nothing alledged by the party, why the sentence should not be finall. These publique persons, with Authority from the Soveraign Power, either to Instruct, or Judge the people, are such members of the Common wealth, as may fitly be compared to the organs of Voice in a Body naturall.

For Execution.

Publique Ministers are also all those, that have Authority from the Soveraign, to procure the Execution of Judgements given; to publish the Soveraigns Commands; to suppresse Tumults; to apprehend, and imprison Malefactors; and other acts tending to the conservation of the Peace. For every act they doe by such Authority, is the act of the Common-wealth; and their service, answerable to that of the Hands, in a Bodie naturall.

Publique Ministers abroad, are those that represent the Person of their own Soveraign, to forraign States. Such are Ambassadors, Messengers, Agents, and Heralds, sent by publique Authoritie, and on publique Businesse.

But such as are sent by Authoritie only of some private partie of a troubled State, though they be received, are neither Publique, nor Private Ministers of the Common-wealth; because none of their actions have the Common-wealth for Author. Likewise, an Ambassador sent from a Prince, to congratulate, condole, or to assist at a solemnity, though the Authority be Publique; yet because the businesse is Private, and belonging to him in his naturall capacity; is a Private person. Also if a man be sent into another Country, secretly to explore their counsels, and strength; though both the Authority, and the Businesse be Publique; yet because there is none to take notice of any Person in him, but his own; he is but a Private Minister; but yet a Minister of the Common-wealth; and may be compared to an Eye in the Body naturall. And those that are appointed to receive the Petitions or other informations of the People, and are as it were the publique Eare, are Publique Ministers, and represent their Soveraign in that office

Counsellers without other employment then to Advise are not Publique Ministers.

Neither a Counsellor (nor a Councell of State, if we consider it with no Authority of Judicature or Command, but only of giving Advice to the Soveraign when it is required, or of offering it when it is not required, is a Publique Person. For the Advice is addressed to the Soveraign only, whose person cannot in his own presence, be represented to him, by another. But a Body of Counsellors, are never without some other Authority, either of Judicature, or of immediate Administration: As in a Monarchy, they represent the Monarch, in delivering his Commands to the Publique Ministers: In a Democracy, the Councell, or Senate propounds the Result of their deliberations to the people, as a Councell, but when they appoint Judges, or heare Causes, or give Audience to Ambassadors, it is in the quality of a Minister of the People: And in an Aristocracy the Councell of State is the Soveraign Assembly it self; and gives counsell to none but themselves.

[127]

CHAP. XXIV.

Of the NUTRITION, *and* PROCREATION *of a Common-wealth.*

The Nourishment of a Common-wealth consisteth

THE NUTRITION of a Common-wealth consisteth, in the *Plenty*, and *Distribution* of *Materials* conducing to Life: In *Concoction*, or *Preparation*; and (when concocted) in the *Conveyance* of it, by convenient conduits, to the Publique use.

As for the Plenty of Matter, it is a thing limited by Nature, to those commodities, which from (the two breasts of our common Mother) Land, and Sea, God usually either freely giveth, or for labour selleth to man-kind.

in the Commodities of Sea and Land:

For the Matter of this Nutriment, consisting in Animals, Vegetals, and Minerals, God hath freely layd them before us, in or neer to the face of the Earth; so as there needeth no more but the labour, and industry of receiving them. Insomuch as Plenty dependeth (next to Gods favour) meerly on the labour and industry of men.

This Matter, commonly called Commodities, is partly *Native*, and partly *Forraign*: *Native*, that which is to be had within the Territory of the Common-wealth: *Forraign*, that which is imported from without. And because there is no Territory under the Dominion of one Common-wealth, (except it be of very vast extent,) that produceth all things needfull for the maintenance, and motion of the whole Body; and few that produce not something more than necessary, the superfluous commodities to be had within, become no more superfluous, but supply these wants at home, by importation of that which may be had abroad, either by Exchange, or by just Warre, or by Labour: for a mans Labour also, is a commodity exchangeable for benefit, as well as any other thing: And there have been Common-wealths that having no more Territory, than hath served them for habitation, have neverthelesse, not onely maintained, but also encreased their Power, partly by the labour of trading from one place to another, and partly by selling the Manifactures, whereof the Materials were brought in from other places.

And the right Distribution of them.

The Distribution of the Materials of this Nourishment, is the constitution of *Mine*, and *Thine*, and *His*; that is to say, in one word *Propriety*; and belongeth in all kinds of Common-wealth to the Soveraign Power For where there is no Common-wealth, there is (as hath been already shewn) a perpetuall warre of every man against his neighbour; And therefore every thing is his that getteth it, and keepeth it by force; which is neither

Propriety, nor *Community*; but *Uncertainty*. Which is so evident, that even *Cicero*, (a passionate defender of Liberty,) in a publique pleading, attributeth all Propriety to the Law Civil, *Let the Civill Law*, saith he, *be once abandoned, or but negligently guarded, (not to say*
[128] *oppressed,) and there is nothing, that any man can be sure to receive from his Ancestor, or leave to his Children.* And again; *Take away the Civill Law, and no man knows what is his own, and what another mans.* Seeing therefore the Introduction of *Propriety* is an effect of Common-wealth; which can do nothing but by the Person that Represents it, it is the act onely of the Soveraign; and consisteth in the Lawes, which none can make that have not the Soveraign Power. And this they well knew of old, who called that Νόμος, (that is to say, *Distribution*,) which we call Law; and defined Justice, by *distributing* to every man *his own*.

All private Estates of land proceed originally from the arbitrary Distribution of the Soveraign

In this Distribution, the First Law, is for Division of the Land it selfe: wherein the Soveraign assigneth to every man a portion, according as he, and not according as any Subject, or any number of them, shall judge agreeable to Equity, and the Common Good. The Children of Israel, were a Common-wealth in the Wildernesse; but wanted the commodities of the Earth, till they were masters of the Land of Promise; which afterward was divided amongst them, not by their own discretion, but by the discretion of *Eleazar* the Priest, and *Joshua* their Generall: who when there were twelve Tribes, making them thirteen by subdivision of the Tribe of *Joseph*; made neverthelesse but twelve portions of the Land; and ordained for the Tribe of *Levi* no land; but assigned them the tenth part of the whole fruits; which division was therefore Arbitrary. And though a People comming into possession of a Land by warre, do not alwaies exterminate the antient Inhabitants, (as did the Jewes,) but leave to many, or most, or all of them their estates; yet it is manifest they hold them afterwards, as of the Victors distribution; as the people of *England* held all theirs of *William* the *Conquerour*

Propriety of a Sub-

From whence we may collect, that the propriety which a subject hath in his lands, consisteth in a right to exclude all other subjects from the use of them; and not to exclude their Soveraign, be it an Assembly, or a Monarch. For seeing the Soveraign, that is to say, the Common-wealth (whose Person he representeth,) is understood to do nothing but in order to the common Peace and Security, this Distribution of lands, is to be understod as done in order to the same: And consequently, whatsoever Distribution he shall make in prejudice thereof, is contrary to the will of every subject, that committed his Peace, and safety to his discretion, and conscience; and therefore by the will of every one of them, is to be reputed voyd. It is true, that a Soveraign Monarch, or the greater part of a Soveraign Assembly, may ordain the doing of many things in pursuit of their Passions, contrary to their own consciences, which is a breach of trust, and of the Law of Nature; but this is not enough to authorise any subject, either to make warre upon, or so much as to accuse of Injustice, or any way to speak evill of their Soveraign; because they have authorised all his actions, and in bestowing the Soveraign Power, made them their own. But in what cases the Commands of Soveraigns are contrary to Equity, and the Law of Nature, is to be considered hereafter in another place.

ject excludes not the Dominion of the Soveraign, but onely of another Subject.

In the Distribution of land, the Common-wealth it selfe, may be conceived to have a portion, and possesse, and [129] improve the same by their Representative; and that such portion may be made sufficient, to susteine the whole expence to the common Peace, and defence necessarily required: Which were very true, if there could be any Representative conceived free from humane passions, and infirmities. But the nature of men being as it is, the setting forth of Publique Land, or of any certaine Revenue for the Common-wealth, is in vaine; and tendeth to the dissolution of Government, and to the condition of meere Nature, and War, assoon as ever the Soveraign Power falleth into the hands of a Monarch, or of an Assembly, that are either too negligent of mony, or too hazardous in engaging the publique stock, into a long, or costly war. Common-wealths can endure no Diet: For seeing their expence is not limited by their

The Publique is not to be dieted.

own appetite, but by externall Accidents, and the appetites of their neighbours, the Publique Riches cannot be limited by other limits, than those which the emergent occasions shall require. And whereas in *England*, there were by the Conquerour, divers Lands reserved to his own use, (besides Forrests, and Chases, either for his recreation, or for preservation of Woods,) and divers services reserved on the Land he gave his Subjects; yet it seems they were not reserved for his Maintenance in his Publique, but in his Naturall capacity: For he, and his Successors did for all that, lay Arbitrary Taxes on all Subjects Land, when they judged it necessary. Or if those publique Lands, and Services, were ordained as a sufficient maintenance of the Common-wealth, it was contrary to the scope of the Institution; being (as it appeared by those ensuing Taxes) insufficient, and (as it appeares by the late small Revenue of the Crown) Subject to Alienation, and Diminution. It is therefore in vaine, to assign a portion to the Common-wealth; which may sell, or give it away; and does sell, and give it away when tis done by their Representative.

The Places and matter of Traffique depend, as their Distribution, on the Soveraign.

As the Distribution of Lands at home; so also to assigne in what places, and for what commodities, the Subject shall traffique abroad, belongeth to the Soveraign. For if it did belong to private persons to use their own discretion therein, some of them would bee drawn for gaine, both to furnish the enemy with means to hurt the Common-wealth, and hurt it themselves, by importing such things, as pleasing mens appetites, be neverthelesse noxious, or at least unprofitable to them. And therefore it belongeth to the Common-wealth, (that is, to the Soveraign only,) to approve, or disapprove both of the places, and matter of forraign Traffique.

The Laws of transferring propriety belong also to the Soveraign.

Further, seeing it is not enough to the Sustentation of a Common-wealth, that every man have a propriety in a portion of Land, or in some few commodities, or a naturall property in some usefull art, and there is no art in the world, but is necessary either for the being, or well being almost of every particular man; it is necessary, that men distribute that which they can spare, and transferre their propriety therein, mutually one to another, by exchange, and mutuall contract. And therefore it belongeth to the Common-wealth, (that [130] is to say, to the Soveraign,) to appoint in what manner, all kinds of contract between Subjects, (as buying, selling, exchanging, borrowing, lending, letting, and taking to hire,) are to bee made; and by what words, and signes they shall be understood for valid. And for the Matter, and Distribution of the Nourishment, to the severall Members of the Common-wealth, thus much (considering the modell of the whole worke) is sufficient.

Mony the Bloud of a Common-wealth.

By Concoction, I understand the reducing of all commodities, which are not presently consumed, but reserved for Nourishment in time to come, to some thing of equall value, and withall so portable, as not to hinder the motion of men from place to place; to the end a man may have in what place soever, such Nourishment as the place affordeth. And this is nothing else but Gold, and Silver, and Mony. For Gold and Silver, being (as it happens) almost in all Countries of the world highly valued, is a commodious measure of the value of all things else between Nations; and Mony (of what matter soever coyned by the Soveraign of a Common-wealth,) is a sufficient measure of the value of all things else, between the Subjects of that Common-wealth. By the means of which measures, all commodities, Moveable, and Immoveable, are made to accompany a man, to all places of his resort, within and without the place of his ordinary residence; and the same passeth from Man to Man, within the Common-wealth; and goes round about, Nourishing (as it passeth) every part thereof; In so much as this Concoction, is as it were the Sanguification of the Common-wealth: For naturall Bloud is in like manner made of the fruits of the Earth; and circulating, nourisheth by the way, every Member of the Body of Man.

And because Silver and Gold, have their value from the matter it self; they have first this priviledge, that the value of them cannot be altered by the power of one, nor of a few Common-wealths; as being a common measure of the commodities of all places. But base

Mony, may easily be enhansed, or abased. Secondly. they have the priviledge to make Common-wealths move, and stretch out their armes, when need is, into forraign Countries; and supply, not only private Subjects that travell, but also whole Armies with Provision. But that Coyne, which is not considerable for the Matter, but for the Stamp of the place, being unable to endure change of ayr, hath its effect at home only; where also it is subject to the change of Laws, and thereby to have the value diminished, to the prejudice many times of those that have it.

The Conduits and Way of mony to the Publique use.

The Conduits, and Wayes by which it is conveyed to the Publique use, are of two sorts; One, that Conveyeth it to the Publique Coffers; The other, that Issueth the same out againe for publique payments. Of the first sort, are Collectors, Receivers, and Treasurers; of the second are the Treasurers againe, and the Officers appointed for payment of severall publique or private Ministers. And in this also, the Artificiall Man maintains his resemblance with the Naturall, whose Veins receiv-
[131] ing the Bloud from the severall Parts of the Body, carry it to the Heart; where being made Vitall, the Heart by the Arteries sends it out again, to enliven, and enable for motion all the Members of the same.

The Children of a Common-wealth Colonies.

The Procreation, or Children of a Common-wealth are those we call *Plantations*, or *Colonies*; which are numbers of men sent out from the Common-wealth, under a Conductor, or Governour, to inhabit a Forraign Country, either formerly voyd of Inhabitants, or made voyd then, by warre. And when a Colony is setled, they are either a Common-wealth of themselves, discharged of their subjection to their Soveraign that sent them, (as hath been done by many Common-wealths of antient time,) in which case the Common-wealth from which they went, was called their Metropolis, or Mother, and requires no more of them, then Fathers require of the Children, whom they emancipate, and make free from their domestique government, which is Honour, and Friendship; or else they remain united to their Metropolis, as were the Colonies of the people of *Rome*; and then they are no Common-wealths themselves, but Provinces, and parts of the Common-wealth that sent them. So that the Right of Colonies (saving Honour, and League with their Metropolis,) dependeth wholly on their Licence, or Letters, by which their Soveraign authorised them to Plant.

CHAP. XXV.

Of COUNSELL.

Counsell what.

How fallacious it is to judge of the nature of things, by the ordinary and inconstant use of words, appeareth in nothing more, than in the confusion of Counsels, and Commands, arising from the Imperative manner of speaking in them both, and in many other occasions besides. For the words *Doe this*, are the words not onely of him that Commandeth; but also of him that giveth Counsell; and of him that Exhorteth; and yet there are but few, that see not, that these are very different things; or that cannot distinguish between them, when they perceive who it is that speaketh, and to whom the Speech is directed, and upon what occasion. But finding those phrases in mens writings, and being not able, or not willing to enter into a consideration of the circumstances, they mistake sometimes the Precepts of Counsellours, for the Precepts of them that Command; and sometimes the contrary; according as it best agreeth with the conclusions they would inferre, or the actions they approve. To avoyd which mistakes, and render to those termes of Commanding, Counselling, and Exhorting, their proper and distinct significations. I define them thus.

Differences between command, and Counsell.

COMMAND is where a man saith, *Doe this*, or *Doe not this*, without expecting other reason than the Will of him that sayes it. From this it followeth manifestly, that he that Commandeth, pretendeth thereby his own Benefit: For the reason of his Command is his own | Will onely, and the proper object of every mans Will, is some [132]
Good to himselfe.

COUNSELL, is where a man saith, *Doe*, or *Doe not this*, and deduceth his reasons from the benefit that arriveth by it to him to whom he saith it. And from this it is evident, that he that giveth Counsell, pretendeth onely (whatsoever he intendeth) the good of him, to whom he giveth it.

Therefore between Counsell and Command, one great difference is, that Command is directed to a mans own benefit; and Counsell to the benefit of another man. And from this ariseth another difference, that a man may be obliged to do what he is Commanded; as when he hath covenanted to obey: But he cannot be obliged to do as he is Counselled, because the hurt of not following it, is his own; or if he should covenant to follow it, then is the Counsell turned into the nature of a Command. A third difference between them is, that no man can pretend a right to be of another mans Counsell; because he is not to pretend benefit by it to himselfe: but to demand right to Counsell another, argues a will to know his designes, or to gain some other Good to himselfe; which (as I said before) is of every mans will the proper object.

This also is incident to the nature of Counsell; that whatsoever it be, he that asketh it, cannot in equity accuse, or punish it. For to ask Counsell of another, is to permit him to give such Counsell as he shall think best; And consequently, he that giveth counsell to his Soveraign, (whether a Monarch, or an Assembly) when he asketh it, cannot in equity be punished for it, whether the same be conformable to the opinion of the most, or not, so it be to the Proposition in debate. For if the sense of the Assembly can be taken notice of, before the Debate be ended, they should neither ask, nor take any further Counsell, For the Sense of the Assembly, is the Resolution of the Debate, and End of all Deliberation. And generally he that demandeth Counsell, is Author of it; and therefore cannot punish it; and what the Soveraign cannot, no man else can. But if one Subject giveth Counsell to another, to do any thing contrary to the Lawes, whether that Counsell proceed from evill intention, or from ignorance onely, it is punishable by the Common-wealth; because ignorance of the Law, is no good excuse, where every man is bound to take notice of the Lawes to which he is subject

Exhortation and Dehortation what

EXHORTATION, and DEHORTATION, is Counsell, accompanied with signes in him that giveth it, of vehement desire to have it followed; or to say it more briefly, *Counsell vehemently pressed.* For he that Exhorteth, doth not deduce the consequences of what he adviseth to be done, and tye himselfe therein to the rigour of true reasoning; but encourages him he Counselleth, to Action: As he that Dehorteth, deterreth him from it. And therefore they have in their speeches, a regard to the common Passions, and opinions of men, in deducing their reasons; and make use of Similitudes, Metaphors, Examples, and other tooles of Oratory, to perswade their Hearers of the Utility, Honour, or Justice of following their advise

From whence may be inferred, First, that Exhortation [133] and Dehortation, is directed to the Good of him that giveth the Counsell, not of him that asketh it, which is contrary to the duty of a Counsellour; who (by the definition of Counsell) ought to regard, not his own benefit, but his whom he adviseth. And that he directeth his Counsell to his own benefit, is manifest enough, by the long and vehement urging, or by the artificiall giving thereof; which being not required of him, and consequently proceeding from his own occasions, is directed principally to his own benefit, and but accidentarily to the good of him that is Counselled, or not at all.

Secondly, that the use of Exhortation and Dehortation lyeth onely, where a man is to speak to a Multitude; because when the Speech is addressed to one, he may interrupt him, and examine his reasons more rigorously, than can be done in a Multitude, which are too many to enter into Dispute, and Dialogue with him that speaketh indifferently to them all at once.

Thirdly, that they that Exhort and Dehort, where they are required to give Counsell, are corrupt Counsellours, and as it were bribed by their own interest For though the Counsell they give be never so good; yet he that gives it, is no more a good Counsellour, than he that giveth a Just Sentence for a reward, is a Just Judge. But where a man may lawfully Command, as a Father in his Family, or a Leader in an Army, his Exhortations and Dehortations, are not onely lawfull, but also necessary, and laudable: But then they are no more Counsells, but Commands; which when they are for Execution of soure labour; sometimes necessity, and alwayes humanity requireth to be sweetned in the delivery, by encouragement, and in the tune and phrase of Counsell, rather then in harsher language of Command.

Examples of the difference between Command and Counsell, we may take from the formes of Speech that expresse them in Holy Scripture *Have no other Gods but me; Make to thy selfe no graven Image; Take not Gods name in vain; Sanctifie the Sabbath; Honour thy Parents, Kill not; Steale not,* &c. are Commands; because the reason for which we are to obey them, is drawn from the will of God our King, whom we are obliged to obey. But these words, *Sell all thou hast, give it to the poore; and follow me,* are Counsell; because the reason for which we are to do so, is drawn from our own benefit; which is this, that we shall have *Treasure in heaven.* These words, *Go into the Village over against you, and you shall find an Asse tyed, and her Colt; loose her, and bring her to me,* are a Command: for the reason of their fact is drawn from the will of their Master: but these words, *Repent, and be Baptized in the Name of Jesus,* are Counsell; because the reason why we should so do, tendeth not to any benefit of God Almighty, who shall still be King in what manner soever we rebell, but of our selves, who have no other means of avoyding the punishment hanging over us for our sins.

Differences of fit and unfit Counsellours.

As the difference of Counsell from Command, hath been now deduced from the nature of Counsell, con-
[134] sisting in a deducing of the benefit, or hurt that may arise to him that is to be Counselled, by the necessary or probable consequences of the action he propoundeth; so may also the differences between *apt*, and *inept* Counsellours be derived from the same. For Experience, being but Memory of the consequences of like actions formerly observed, and Counsell but the Speech

whereby that experience is made known to another; the Vertues, and Defects of Counsell, are the same with the Vertues, and Defects Intellectuall: And to the Person of a Common-wealth, his Counsellours serve him in the place of Memory, and Mentall Discourse. But with this resemblance of the Common-wealth, to a naturall man, there is one dissimilitude joyned, of great importance; which is, that a naturall man receiveth his experience, from the naturall objects of sense, which work upon him without passion, or interest of their own; whereas they that give Counsell to the Representative person of a Common-wealth, may have, and have often their particular ends, and passions, that render their Counsells alwayes suspected, and many times unfaithfull. And therefore we may set down for the first condition of a good Counsellour, *That his Ends, and Interest, be not inconsistent with the Ends and Interest of him he Counselleth.*

Secondly, Because the office of a Counsellour, when an action comes into deliberation, is to make manifest the consequences of it, in such manner, as he that is Counselled may be truly and evidently informed, he ought to propound his advise, in such forme of speech, as may make the truth most evidently appear; that is to say, with as firme ratiocination, as significant and proper language, and as briefly, as the evidence will permit. And therefore *rash, and unevident Inferences*; (such as are fetched onely from Examples, or authority of Books, and are not arguments of what is good, or evill, but witnesses of fact, or of opinion,) *obscure, confused, and ambiguous Expressions, also all metaphoricall Speeches, tending to the stirring up of Passion,* (because such reasoning, and such expressions, are usefull onely to deceive, or to lead him we Counsell towards other ends than his own) *are repugnant to the Office of a Counsellour.*

Thirdly, Because the Ability of Counselling proceedeth from Experience, and long study; and no man is presumed to have experience in all those things that to the Administration of a great Common-wealth are necessary to be known, *No man is presumed to be a good Counsellour,*

but in such Businesse, as he hath not onely been much versed in, but hath also much meditated on, and considered. For seeing the businesse of a Common-wealth is this, to preserve the people in Peace at home, and defend them against forraign Invasion, we shall find, it requires great knowledge of the disposition of Man-kind, of the Rights of Government, and of the nature of Equity, Law, Justice, and Honour, not to be attained without study; And of the Strength, Commodities, Places, both of their own Country, and their Neighbours, as also of the inclinations, and designes of all Nations that may any way annoy them. And this is not attained to, without much experience. Of which things, not
[135] onely the whole summe, but every one of the particulars requires the age, and observation of a man in years, and of more than ordinary study. The wit required for Counsel, as I have said before (Chap. 8.) is Judgement. And the differences of men in that point come from different education, of some to one kind of study, or businesse, and of others to another. When for the doing of any thing, there be Infallible rules, (as in Engines, and Edifices, the rules of Geometry,) all the experience of the world cannot equal his Counsell, that has learnt, or found out the Rule. And when there is no such Rule, he that hath most experience in that particular kind of businesse, has therein the best Judgement, and is the best Counsellour.

Fourthly, to be able to give Counsell to a Common-wealth, in a businesse that hath reference to another Common-wealth, *It is necessary to be acquainted with the Intelligences, and Letters* that come from thence, *and with all the records of Treaties, and other transactions of State* between them; which none can doe, but such as the Representative shall think fit. By which we may see, that they who are not called to Counsell, can have no good Counsell in such cases to obtrude.

Fifthly, Supposing the number of Counsellors equall, a man is better Counselled by hearing them apart, then in an Assembly; and that for many causes First, in hearing them apart, you have the advice of every man; but in an Assembly many of them deliver their advise

with *I*, or *No*, or with their hands, or feet, not moved by their own sense, but by the eloquence of another, or for feare of displeasing some that have spoken, or the whole Assembly, by contradiction; or for feare of appearing duller in apprehension, than those that have applauded the contrary opinion. Secondly, in an Assembly of many, there cannot choose but be some whose interests are contrary to that of the Publique; and these their Interests make passionate, and Passion eloquent, and Eloquence drawes others into the same advice. For the Passions of men, which asunder are moderate, as the heat of one brand; in Assembly are like many brands, that enflame one another, (especially when they blow one another with Orations) to the setting of the Common-wealth on fire, under pretence of Counselling it. Thirdly, in hearing every man apart, one may examine (when there is need) the truth, or probability of his reasons, and of the grounds of the advise he gives, by frequent interruptions, and objections, which cannot be done in an Assembly, where (in every difficult question) a man is rather astonied, and dazled with the variety of discourse upon it, than informed of the course he ought to take. Besides, there cannot be an Assembly of many, called together for advice, wherein there be not some, that have the ambition to be thought eloquent, and also learned in the Politiques; and give not their advice with care of the businesse propounded, but of the applause of their motly orations, made of the divers colored threds, or shreds of Authors; which is an Impertinence at least, that takes away the time of serious Consultation, and in the secret way of Counselling apart, is easily avoided. [136]
Fourthly, in Deliberations that ought to be kept secret, (whereof there be many occasions in Publique Businesse,) the Counsells of many, and especially in Assemblies, are dangerous; And therefore great Assemblies are necessitated to commit such affaires to lesser numbers, and of such persons as are most versed, and in whose fidelity they have most confidence.

To conclude, who is there that so far approves the taking of Counsell from a great Assembly of Counsellours, that wisheth for, or would accept of their pains, when there is a question of marrying his Children, disposing of his Lands, governing his Household, or managing his private Estate, especially if there be amongst them such as wish not his prosperity? A man that doth his businesse by the help of many and prudent Counsellours, with every one consulting apart in his proper element, does it best, as he that useth able Seconds at Tennis play, placed in their proper stations. He does next best, that useth his own Judgement only; as he that has no Second at all. But he that is carried up and down to his businesse in a framed Counsell, which cannot move but by the plurality of consenting opinions, the execution whereof is commonly (out of envy, or interest) retarded by the part dissenting, does it worst of all, and like one that is carried to the ball, though by good Players, yet in a Wheele-barrough, or other frame, heavy of it self, and retarded also by the inconcurrent judgements, and endeavours of them that drive it; and so much the more, as they be more that set their hands to it; and most of all, when there is one, or more amongst them, that desire to have him lose. And though it be true, that many eys see more then one; yet it is not to be understood of many Counsellours; but then only, when the finall Resolution is in one man. Otherwise, because many eyes see the same thing in divers lines, and are apt to look asquint towards their private benefit, they that desire not to misse their marke, though they look about with two eyes, yet they never ayme but with one; And therefore no great Popular Common-wealth was ever kept up; but either by a forraign Enemy that united them, or by the reputation of some one eminent Man amongst them; or by the secret Counsell of a few; or by the mutuall feare of equall factions; and not by the open Consultations of the Assembly. And as for very little Common-wealths, be they Popular, or Monarchicall, there is no humane wisdome can uphold them, longer then the Jealousy lasteth of their potent Neighbours.

CHAP XXVI.

Of CIVILL LAWES

Civill Law what.

BY CIVILL LAWES, I understand the Lawes, that men are therefore bound to observe, because they are Members, not of this, or that Common-wealth in particular, but of a Common-wealth. For the knowledge of particular Lawes belongeth to them, that professe the [137] study of the Lawes of their severall Countries ; but the knowledge of Civill Law in generall, to any man. The antient Law of *Rome* was called their *Civil Law*, from the word *Civitas*, which signifies a Common-wealth : And those Countries, which having been under the Roman Empire, and governed by that Law, retaine still such part thereof as they think fit, call that part the Civill Law, to distinguish it from the rest of their own Civill Lawes. But that is not it I intend to speak of here ; my designe being not to shew what is Law here, and there , but what is Law , as *Plato*, *Aristotle*, *Cicero*, and divers others have done, without taking upon them the profession of the study of the Law.

And first it is manifest, that Law in generall, is not Counsell, but Command ; nor a Command of any man to any man ; but only of him, whose Command is addressed to one formerly obliged to obey him. And as for Civill Law, it addeth only the name of the person Commanding, which is *Persona Civitatis*, the Person of the Common-wealth

Which considered, I define Civill Law in this manner. CIVILL LAW, *Is to every Subject, those Rules, which the Common-wealth hath Commanded him, by Word, Writing, or other sufficient Sign of the Will, to make use of, for the Distinction of Right, and Wrong ; that is to say, of what is contrary, and what is not contrary to the Rule.*

In which definition, there is nothing that is not at first sight evident. For every man seeth, that some Lawes are addressed to all the Subjects in generall ; some to particular Provinces ; some to particular Vocations , and some to particular Men ; and are therefore Lawes, to every of those to whom the Command is directed; and to none else. As also, that Lawes are the Rules of Just, and Unjust; nothing being reputed Unjust, that is not contrary to some Law. Likewise, that none can make Lawes but the Common-wealth, because our Subjection is to the Common-wealth only: and that Commands, are to be signified by sufficient Signs; because a man knows not otherwise how to obey them. And therefore, whatsoever can from this definition by necessary consequence be deduced, ought to be acknowledged for truth. Now I deduce from it this that followeth.

The Soveraign is Legislator.

1. The Legislator in all Common-wealths, is only the Soveraign, be he one Man, as in a Monarchy, or one Assembly of men, as in a Democracy, or Aristocracy. For the Legislator, is he that maketh the Law. And the Common-wealth only, præscribes, and commandeth the observation of those rules, which we call Law: Therefore the Common-wealth is the Legislator. But the Common-wealth is no Person, nor has capacity to doe any thing, but by the Representative, (that is, the Soveraign;) and therefore the Soveraign is the sole Legislator. For the same reason, none can abrogate a Law made, but the Soveraign, because a Law is not abrogated, but by another Law, that forbiddeth it to be put in execution.

And not Subject to Civill Law.

2 The Soveraign of a Common-wealth, be it an Assembly, or one Man, is not Subject to the Civill [138] Lawes. For having power to make, and repeale Lawes, he may when he pleaseth, free himselfe from that subjection, by repealing those Lawes that trouble him, and making of new; and consequently he was free before. For he is free, that can be free when he will: Nor is it possible for any person to be bound to himselfe; because he that can bind, can release; and therefore he that is bound to himselfe onely, is not bound

Use, a Law not by vertue of Time, but of the Soveraigns consent

3. When long Use obtaineth the authority of a Law, it is not the Length of Time that maketh the Authority, but the Will of the Soveraign signified by his silence, (for Silence is sometimes an argument of Consent;) and it is no longer Law, then the Soveraign shall be silent therein. And therefore if the Soveraign shall have a question of Right grounded, not upon his present

Will, but upon the Lawes formerly made; the Length of Time shal bring no prejudice to his Right; but the question shal be judged by Equity. For many unjust Actions, and unjust Sentences, go uncontrolled a longer time, than any man can remember. And our Lawyers account no Customes Law, but such as are reasonable, and that evill Customes are to be abolished But the Judgement of what is reasonable, and of what is to be abolished, belongeth to him that maketh the Law, which is the Soveraign Assembly, or Monarch.

The Law of Nature, and the Civill Law contain each other.

4. The Law of Nature, and the Civill Law, contain each other, and are of equall extent. For the Lawes of Nature, which consist in Equity, Justice, Gratitude, and other morall Vertues on these depending, in the condition of meer Nature (as I have said before in the end of the 15th Chapter,) are not properly Lawes, but qualities that dispose men to peace, and to obedience. When a Common-wealth is once settled, then are they actually Lawes, and not before; as being then the commands of the Common-wealth; and therefore also Civill Lawes. For it is the Soveraign Power that obliges men to obey them. For in the differences of private men, to declare, what is Equity, what is Justice, and what is morall Vertue, and to make them binding, there is need of the Ordinances of Soveraign Power, and Punishments to be ordained for such as shall break them; which Ordinances are therefore part of the Civill Law. The Law of Nature therefore is a part of the Civill Law in all Common-wealths of the world. Reciprocally also, the Civill Law is a part of the Dictates of Nature. For Justice, that is to say, Performance of Covenant, and giving to every man his own, is a Dictate of the Law of Nature. But every subject in a Common-wealth, hath covenanted to obey the Civill Law, (either one with another, as when they assemble to make a common Representative, or with the Representative it selfe one by one, when subdued by the Sword they promise obedience, that they may receive life;) And therefore Obedience to the Civill Law is part also of the Law of Nature. Civill, and Naturall Law are not different kinds, but different parts of Law; whereof one part being written, is called Civill, the other un-

written, Naturall. But the Right of Nature, that is, the naturall Liberty of man, may by the Civill Law be abridged, and restrained: nay, the end of making Lawes, is no other, but such Restraint; without the which there cannot possibly be any Peace. And Law was brought [139] into the world for nothing else, but to limit the naturall liberty of particular men, in such manner, as they might not hurt, but assist one another, and joyn together against a common Enemy.

Provinciall Lawes are not made by Custome, but by the Soveraign Power.

5. If the Soveraign of one Common-wealth, subdue a People that have lived under other written Lawes, and afterwards govern them by the same Lawes, by which they were governed before; yet those Lawes are the Civill Lawes of the Victor, and not of the Vanquished Common-wealth. For the Legislator is he, not by whose authority the Lawes were first made, but by whose authority they now continue to be Lawes. And therefore where there be divers Provinces, within the Dominion of a Common-wealth, and in those Provinces diversity of Lawes, which commonly are called the Customes of each severall Province, we are not to understand that such Customes have their force, onely from Length of Time; but that they were antiently Lawes written, or otherwise made known, for the Constitutions, and Statutes of their Soveraigns; and are now Lawes, not by vertue of the Præscription of time, but by the Constitutions of their present Soveraigns. But if an unwritten Law, in all the Provinces of a Dominion, shall be generally observed, and no iniquity appear in the use thereof; that Law can be no other but a Law of Nature, equally obliging all man-kind.

Some foolish opinions of Lawyers concerning the making of Lawes

6. Seeing then all Lawes, written, and unwritten, have their Authority, and force, from the Will of the Common-wealth; that is to say, from the Will of the Representative; which in a Monarchy is the Monarch, and in other Common-wealths the Soveraign Assembly; a man may wonder from whence proceed such opinions, as are found in the Books of Lawyers of eminence in severall Common-wealths, directly, or by consequence making the Legislative Power depend on private men, or subordinate Judges As for example, *That the Common Law,*

hath no Controuler but the Parlament; which is true onely where a Parlament has the Soveraign Power, and cannot be assembled, nor dissolved, but by their own discretion. For if there be a right in any else to dissolve them, there is a right also to controule them, and consequently to controule their controulings. And if there be no such right, then the Controuler of Lawes is not *Parlamentum*, but *Rex in Parlamento*. And where a Parlament is Soveraign, if it should assemble never so many, or so wise men, from the Countries subject to them, for whatsoever cause; yet there is no man will believe, that such an Assembly hath thereby acquired to themselves a Legislative Power. *Item*, that the two arms of a Common-wealth, are *Force, and Justice*; *the first whereof is in the King*; *the other deposited in the hands of the Parlament.* As if a Common-wealth could consist, where the Force were in any hand, which Justice had not the Authority to command and govern

7 That Law can never be against Reason, our Lawyers are agreed, and that not the Letter, (that is, every construction of it,) but that which is according to the Intention of the Legislator, is the Law. And it is true. but the doubt is, of whose Reason it is, that shall be received for Law. It is not meant of any private Reason; for then there would be as much contradiction in the Lawes, [140] as there is in the Schooles; nor yet, (as Sr. *Ed. Coke* makes it,) an *Artificiall perfection of Reason, gotten by long study, observation, and experience*, (as his was.) For it is possible long study may encrease, and confirm erroneous Sentences: and where men build on false grounds, the more they build, the greater is the ruine: and of those that study, and observe with equall time, and diligence, the reasons and resolutions are, and must remain discordant: and therefore it is not that *Juris prudentia*, or wisedome of subordinate Judges, but the Reason of this our Artificiall Man the Common-wealth, and his Command, that maketh Law: And the Common-wealth being in their Representative but one Person, there cannot easily arise any contradiction in the Lawes; and when there doth, the same Reason is able, by interpretation, or alteration, to take it away In all Courts

Sir Edw Coke, *upon* Littleton, *Lib.* 2 *Ch.* 6. *fol.* 97. *b.*

of Justice. the Soveraign (which is the Person of the Common-wealth,) is he that Judgeth : The subordinate Judge, ought to have regard to the reason, which moved his Soveraign to make such Law, that his Sentence may be according thereunto ; which then is his Soveraigns Sentence ; otherwise it is his own, and an unjust one.

Law made, if not also made known, is no Law

8. From this, that the Law is a Command, and a Command consisteth in declaration, or manifestation of the will of him that commandeth, by voyce, writing, or some other sufficient argument of the same, we may understand, that the Command of the Common-wealth, is Law onely to those, that have means to take notice of it. Over naturall fooles, children, or mad-men there is no Law, no more than over brute beasts ; nor are they capable of the title of just, or unjust ; because they had never power to make any covenant, or to understand the consequences thereof ; and consequently never took upon them to authorise the actions of any Soveraign, as they must do that make to themselves a Common-wealth And as those from whom Nature, or Accident hath taken away the notice of all Lawes in generall ; so also every man, from whom any accident, not proceeding from his own default, hath taken away the means to take notice of any particular Law, is excused, if he observe it not , And to speak properly, that Law is no Law to him It is therefore necessary, to consider in this place, what arguments, and signes be sufficient for the knowledge of what is the Law , that is to say, what is the will of the Soveraign, as well in Monarchies, as in other formes of government.

Unwritten Lawes are all of them Lawes of Nature.

And first, if it be a Law that obliges all the Subjects without exception, and is not written. nor otherwise published in such places as they may take notice thereof, it is a Law of Nature. For whatsoever men are to take knowledge of for Law, not upon other mens words, but every one from his own reason, must be such as is agreeable to the reason of all men ; which no Law can be, but the Law of Nature. The Lawes of Nature therefore need not any publishing, nor Proclamation , as being contained in this one Sentence, approved by all the world,

Do not that to another, which thou thinkest unreasonable to be done by another to thy selfe.

Secondly, if it be a Law that obliges only some condition of men, or one particular man, and be not written, nor published by word, then also it is a Law of Nature; and known by the same arguments, and signs, that distinguish those in such a condition, from other Subjects. For whatsoever Law is not written, or some way published by him that makes it Law, can be known no way, but by the reason of him that is to obey it; and is therefore also a Law not only Civill, but Naturall For Example, if the Soveraign employ a Publique Minister, without written Instructions what to doe; he is obliged to take for Instructions the Dictates of Reason; As if he make a Judge, The Judge is to take notice, that his Sentence ought to be according to the reason of his Soveraign, which being alwaies understood to be Equity, he is bound to it by the Law of Nature: Or if an Ambassador, he is (in all things not conteined in his written Instructions) to take for Instruction that which Reason dictates to be most conducing to his Soveraigns interest; and so of all other Ministers of the Soveraignty, publique and private. All which Instructions of naturall Reason may be comprehended under one name of *Fidelity*; which is a branch of naturall Justice [141]

The Law of Nature excepted, it belongeth to the essence of all other Lawes, to be made known, to every man that shall be obliged to obey them, either by word, or writing, or some other act, known to proceed from the Soveraign Authority. For the will of another, cannot be understood, but by his own word, or act, or by conjecture taken from his scope and purpose, which in the person of the Common-wealth, is to be supposed alwaies consonant to Equity and Reason. And in antient time, before letters were in common use, the Lawes were many times put into verse; that the rude people taking pleasure in singing, or reciting them, might the more easily reteine them in memory. And for the same reason *Solomon* adviseth a man, to bind the ten Commandements * upon his ten fingers And for the Law which *Moses* gave to the people of *Israel* at the renewing of the

*Prov. 7 3.

*Deut 11. 19 Covenant, * he biddeth them to teach it their Children, by discoursing of it both at home, and upon the way; at going to bed, and at rising from bed; and to write it upon the posts, and dores of their houses; and * to assemble the people, man, woman, and child, to heare it read.

*Deut 31. 12.

Nothing is Law where the Legislator cannot be known.

Nor is it enough the Law be written, and published; but also that there be manifest signs, that it proceedeth from the will of the Soveraign. For private men, when they have, or think they have force enough to secure their unjust designes, and convoy them safely to their ambitious ends, may publish for Lawes what they please, without, or against the Legislative Authority. There is therefore requisite, not only a Declaration of the Law, but also sufficient signes of the Author, and Authority. The Author, or Legislator is supposed in every Common-wealth to be evident, because he is the Soveraign, who having been Constituted by the consent of every one, is supposed by every one to be sufficiently known. And though the ignorance, and security of men be such, for [142] the most part, as that when the memory of the first Constitution of their Common-wealth is worn out, they doe not consider, by whose power they use to be defended against their enemies, and to have their industry protected, and to be righted when injury is done them; yet because no man that considers, can make question of it, no excuse can be derived from the ignorance of where the Soveraignty is placed. And it is a Dictate of Naturall Reason, and consequently an evident Law of Nature, that no man ought to weaken that power, the protection whereof he hath himself demanded, or wittingly received against others. Therefore of who is Soveraign, no man, but by his own fault, (whatsoever evill men suggest,) can make any doubt. The difficulty consisteth in the evidence of the Authority derived from him; The removing whereof, dependeth on the knowledge of the publique Registers, publique Counsels, publique Ministers, and publique Seales; by which all Lawes are sufficiently verified;

Difference between Verifying and Authorising.

Verifyed, I say, not Authorised: for the Verification, is but the Testimony and Record; not the Authority of the Law; which consisteth in the Command of the Soveraign only.

The Law Verifyed by the subordinate Judge.

If therefore a man have a question of Injury, depending on the Law of Nature; that is to say, on common Equity; the Sentence of the Judge, that by Commission hath Authority to take cognisance of such causes, is a sufficient Verification of the Law of Nature in that individuall case For though the advice of one that professeth the study of the Law, be usefull for the avoyding of contention; yet it is but advice tis the Judge must tell men what is Law, upon the hearing of the Controversy.

By the Publique Registers

But when the question is of injury, or crime, upon a written Law; every man by recourse to the Registers, by himself, or others, may (if he will) be sufficiently enformed, before he doe such injury, or commit the crime, whither it be an injury, or not: Nay he ought to doe so: For when a man doubts whether the act he goeth about, be just, or injust; and may informe himself, if he will, the doing is unlawfull. In like manner, he that supposeth himself injured, in a case determined by the written Law, which he may by himself, or others see and consider; if he complaine before he consults with the Law, he does unjustly, and bewrayeth a disposition rather to vex other men, than to demand his own right.

By Letters Patent, and Publique Seale.

If the question be of Obedience to a publique Officer, To have seen his Commission, with the Publique Seale, and heard it read; or to have had the means to be informed of it, if a man would, is a sufficient Verification of his Authority. For every man is obliged to doe his best endeavour, to informe himself of all written Lawes, that may concerne his own future actions.

The Interpretation of the Law dependeth on the Soveraign Power.

The Legislator known, and the Lawes, either by writing, or by the light of Nature, sufficiently published, there wanteth yet another very materiall circumstance to make them obligatory. For it is not the Letter, but the Intendment, or Meaning; that is to say, the authentique Interpretation of the Law (which is the sense of the Legislator,) in which the nature of the Law consisteth, And therefore the Interpretation of all Lawes [143]
dependeth on the Authority Soveraign, and the Interpreters can be none but those, which the Soveraign, (to

whom only the Subject oweth obedience) shall appoint. For else, by the craft of an Interpreter, the Law may be made to beare a sense, contrary to that of the Soveraign; by which means the Interpreter becomes the Legislator.

All Lawes need Interpretation.

All Laws, written, and unwritten, have need of Interpretation. The unwritten Law of Nature, though it be easy to such, as without partiality, and passion, make use of their naturall reason, and therefore leaves the violaters thereof without excuse; yet considering there be very few, perhaps none, that in some cases are not blinded by self love, or some other passion, it is now become of all Laws the most obscure; and has consequently the greatest need of able Interpreters. The written Laws, if they be short, are easily mis-interpreted, from the divers significations of a word, or two: if long they be more obscure by the diverse significations of many words: in so much as no written Law, delivered in few, or many words, can be well understood, without a perfect understanding of the finall causes, for which the Law was made; the knowledge of which finall causes is in the Legislator. To him therefore there can not be any knot in the Law, insoluble; either by finding out the ends, to undoe it by; or else by making what ends he will, (as *Alexander* did with his sword in the Gordian knot,) by the Legislative power; which no other Interpreter can doe.

The Authenticall Interpretation of Law is not that of writers.

The Interpretation of the Lawes of Nature, in a Common-wealth, dependeth not on the books of Morall Philosophy. The Authority of writers, without the Authority of the Common-wealth, maketh not their opinions Law, be they never so true. That which I have written in this Treatise, concerning the Morall Vertues, and of their necessity, for the procuring, and maintaining peace, though it bee evident Truth, is not therefore presently Law; but because in all Common-wealths in the world, it is part of the Civill Law: For though it be naturally reasonable; yet it is by the Soveraigne Power that it is Law: Otherwise, it were a great errour, to call the Lawes of Nature unwritten Law; whereof wee see so many volumes published, and in them so many contradictions of one another, and of themselves

The Interpreter of the Law is the Judge giving sentence vivâ voce *in every particular case.*

The Interpretation of the Law of Nature, is the Sentence of the Judge constituted by the Soveraign Authority, to heare and determine such controversies, as depend thereon; and consisteth in the application of the Law to the present case. For in the act of Judicature, the Judge doth no more but consider, whither the demand of the party, be consonant to naturall reason, and Equity; and the Sentence he giveth, is therefore the Interpretation of the Law of Nature; which Interpretation is Authentique; not because it is his private Sentence; but because he giveth it by Authority of the Soveraign, whereby it becomes the Soveraigns Sentence; which is Law for that time, to the parties pleading.

[144]

The Sentence of a Judge, does not bind him, or another Judge to give like Sentence in like Cases ever after.

But because there is no Judge Subordinate, nor Soveraign, but may erre in a Judgement of Equity; if afterward in another like case he find it more consonant to Equity to give a contrary Sentence, he is obliged to doe it. No mans error becomes his own Law; nor obliges him to persist in it. Neither (for the same reason) becomes it a Law to other Judges, though sworn to follow it. For though a wrong Sentence given by authority of the Soveraign, if he know and allow it, in such Lawes as are mutable, be a constitution of a new Law, in cases, in which every little circumstance is the same; yet in Lawes immutable, such as are the Lawes of Nature, they are no Lawes to the same, or other Judges, in the like cases for ever after Princes succeed one another; and one Judge passeth, another commeth; nay, Heaven and Earth shall passe; but not one title of the Law of Nature shall passe; for it is the Eternall Law of God. Therefore all the Sentences of precedent Judges that have ever been, cannot all together make a Law contrary to naturall Equity: Nor any Examples of former Judges, can warrant an unreasonable Sentence, or discharge the present Judge of the trouble of studying what is Equity (in the case he is to Judge,) from the principles of his own naturall reason. For example sake, 'Tis against the Law of Nature, *To punish the Innocent*, and Innocent is he that acquitteth himselfe Judicially, and is acknowledged for Innocent by the Judge. Put the case now, that a man is accused of a capitall crime, and seeing the

power and malice of some enemy, and the frequent corruption and partiality of Judges, runneth away for feare of the event, and afterwards is taken, and brought to a legall triall, and maketh it sufficiently appear, he was not guilty of the crime, and being thereof acquitted, is neverthelesse condemned to lose his goods; this is a manifest condemnation of the Innocent. I say therefore, that there is no place in the world, where this can be an interpretation of a Law of Nature, or be made a Law by the Sentences of precedent Judges, that had done the same. For he that judged it first, judged unjustly; and no Injustice can be a pattern of Judgement to succeeding Judges. A written Law may forbid innocent men to fly, and they may be punished for flying: But that flying for feare of injury, should be taken for presumption of guilt, after a man is already absolved of the crime Judicially, is contrary to the nature of a Presumption, which hath no place after Judgement given. Yet this is set down by a great Lawyer for the common Law of *England*. *If a man* (saith he) *that is Innocent, be accused of Felony, and for feare flyeth for the same; albeit he judicially acquitteth himselfe of the Felony; yet if it be found that he fled for the Felony, he shall notwithstanding his Innocency, Forfeit all his goods, chattells, debts, and duties. For as to the Forfeiture of them, the Law will admit no proofe against the Presumption in Law, grounded upon his flight.* Here you see, *An Innocent man, Judicially acquitted, notwithstanding his Innocency*, (when no written Law forbad him to fly) after his acquitall, *upon a Presumption in Law*, condemned to lose all the goods he hath. If the Law ground upon his flight a Presump-
[145] tion of the fact, (which was Capitall,) the Sentence ought to have been Capitall: if the Presumption were not of the Fact, for what then ought he to lose his goods? This therefore is no Law of *England*; nor is the condemnation grounded upon a Presumption of Law, but upon the Presumption of the Judges. It is also against Law, to say that no Proofe shall be admitted against a Presumption of Law. For all Judges, Soveraign and subordinate, if they refuse to heare Proofe, refuse to do Justice: for though the Sentence be Just, yet the Judges

that condemn without hearing the Proofes offered, are Unjust Judges, and their Presumption is but Prejudice; which no man ought to bring with him to the Seat of Justice, whatsoever precedent judgements, or examples he shall pretend to follow. There be other things of this nature, wherein mens Judgements have been perverted, by trusting to Precedents: but this is enough to shew, that though the Sentence of the Judge, be a Law to the party pleading, yet it is no Law to any Judge, that shall succeed him in that Office.

In like manner, when question is of the Meaning of written Lawes, he is not the Interpreter of them, that writeth a Commentary upon them. For Commentaries are commonly more subject to cavill, than the Text; and therefore need other Commentaries; and so there will be no end of such Interpretation. And therefore unlesse there be an Interpreter authorised by the Soveraign, from which the subordinate Judges are not to recede, the Interpreter can be no other than the ordinary Judges, in the same manner, as they are in cases of the unwritten Law; and their Sentences are to be taken by them that plead, for Lawes in that particular case; but not to bind other Judges, in like cases to give like judgements. For a Judge may erre in the Interpretation even of written Lawes; but no errour of a subordinate Judge, can change the Law, which is the generall Sentence of the Soveraigne.

The difference between the Letter and Sentence of the Law.

In written Lawes, men use to make a difference between the Letter, and the Sentence of the Law: And when by the Letter, is meant whatsoever can be gathered from the bare words, 'tis well distinguished. For the significations of almost all words, are either in themselves, or in the metaphoricall use of them, ambiguous; and may be drawn in argument, to make many senses; but there is onely one sense of the Law. But if by the Letter, be meant the literall sense, then the Letter, and the Sentence or intention of the Law, is all one. For the literall sense is that, which the Legislator intended, should by the letter of the Law be signified. Now the Intention of the Legislator is alwayes supposed to be Equity: For it were a great contumely for a Judge to

think otherwise of the Soveraigne. He ought therefore, if the Word of the Law doe not fully authorise a reasonable Sentence, to supply it with the Law of Nature; or if the case be difficult, to respit Judgement till he have received more ample authority. For Example, a written Law ordaineth, that he which is thrust out of his house by force, shall be restored by force: It happens that a man by negligence leaves his house empty, and returning is kept out by force, in which case there is no speciall Law
[146] ordained. It is evident, that this case is contained in the same Law: for else there is no remedy for him at all; which is to be supposed against the Intention of the Legislator. Again, the word of the Law, commandeth to Judge according to the Evidence: A man is accused falsly of a fact, which the Judge saw himself done by another; and not by him that is accused. In this case neither shall the Letter of the Law be followed to the condemnation of the Innocent, nor shall the Judge give Sentence against the evidence of the Witnesses; because the Letter of the Law is to the contrary: but procure of the Soveraign that another be made Judge, and himself Witnesse. So that the incommodity that follows the bare words of a written Law, may lead him to the Intention of the Law, whereby to interpret the same the better; though no Incommodity can warrant a Sentence against the Law. For every Judge of Right, and Wrong, is not Judge of what is Commodious, or Incommodious to the Common-wealth.

The abilities required in a Judge.

The abilities required in a good Interpreter of the Law, that is to say, in a good Judge, are not the same with those of an Advocate; namely the study of the Lawes. For a Judge, as he ought to take notice of the Fact, from none but the Witnesses; so also he ought to take notice of the Law, from nothing but the Statutes, and Constitutions of the Soveraign, alledged in the pleading, or declared to him by some that have authority from the Soveraign Power to declare them; and need not take care before-hand, what hee shall Judge; for it shall bee given him what hee shall say concerning the Fact, by Witnesses; and what hee shall say in point of Law, from those that shall in their pleadings shew it, and by authority interpret it upon the place. The Lords of Parlament in *England* were Judges, and most difficult causes have been heard and determined by them; yet few of them were much versed in the study of the Lawes, and fewer had made profession of them: and though they consulted with Lawyers, that were appointed to be present there for that purpose; yet they alone had the authority of giving Sentence. In like manner, in the ordinary trialls of Right, Twelve men of the common People, are the Judges, and give Sentence, not onely of the Fact, but of the Right; and pronounce simply for the Complaynant, or for the Defendant; that is to say, are Judges not onely of the Fact, but also of the Right: and in a question of crime, not onely determine whether done, or not done; but also whether it be *Murder, Homicide, Felony, Assault*, and the like, which are determinations of Law: but because they are not supposed to know the Law of themselves, there is one that hath Authority to enforme them of it, in the particular case they are to Judge of But yet if they judge not according to that he tells them, they are not subject thereby to any penalty; unlesse it be made appear, they did it against their consciences, or had been corrupted by reward

The things that make a good Judge, or good Interpreter of the Lawes, are, first, *A right understanding* of that principall Law of Nature called *Equity*; which depending not on the reading of other mens Writings, but on the goodnesse of a mans own naturall Reason, [147] and Meditation, is presumed to be in those most, that have had most leisure, and had the most inclination to meditate thereon. Secondly, *Contempt of unnecessary Riches*, and Preferments. Thirdly, *To be able in judgement to devest himselfe of all feare, anger, hatred, love*, and *compassion*. Fourthly, and lastly, *Patience to heare, diligent attention in hearing; and memory to retain, digest and apply what he hath heard.*

Divisions of Law

The difference and division of the Lawes, has been made in divers manners, according to the different methods, of those men that have written of them. For it is a thing that dependeth not on Nature, but on the scope of the Writer; and is subservient to every mans proper method. In the Institutions of *Justinian*, we find seven sorts of Civill Lawes. 1. The *Edicts, Constitutions*, and *Epistles of the Prince*, that is, of the Emperour; because the whole power of the people was in him. Like these, are the Proclamations of the Kings of *England*.

2. *The Decrees of the whole people of Rome* (comprehending the Senate,) when they were put to the Question by the *Senate*. These were Lawes, at first, by the vertue of the Soveraign Power residing in the people; and such of them as by the Emperours were not abrogated, remained Lawes by the Authority Imperiall. For all Lawes that bind, are understood to be Lawes by his authority that has power to repeale them. Somewhat like to these Lawes, are the Acts of Parliament in England.

3. *The Decrees of the Common people* (excluding the Senate,) when they were put to the question by the *Tribune* of the people. For such of them as were not abrogated by the Emperours, remained Lawes by the Authority Imperiall. Like to these, were the Orders of the House of Commons in *England*.

4. *Senatûs consulta*, the *Orders of the Senate*; because when the people of *Rome* grew so numerous, as it was inconvenient to assemble them; it was thought fit by the Emperour, that men should Consult the Senate, in stead of the people: And these have some resemblance with the Acts of Counsell.

5. *The Edicts of Prætors*, and (in some Cases) of the *Ædiles*: such as are the Chiefe Justices in the Courts of *England*.

6. *Responsa Prudentum*; which were the Sentences, and Opinions of those Lawyers, to whom the Emperour gave Authority to interpret the Law, and to give answer to such as in matter of Law demanded their advice; which Answers, the Judges in giving Judgement were obliged by the Constitutions of the Emperour to observe: And should be like the Reports of Cases Judged, if other Judges be by the Law of *England* bound to observe them. For the Judges of the Common Law of *England*, are not properly Judges, but *Juris Consulti*; of whom the Judges, who are either the Lords, or Twelve men of the Country, are in point of Law to ask advice.

7. Also, *Unwritten Customes*, (which in their own nature are an imitation of Law,) by the tacite consent of the Emperour, in case they be not contrary to the Law of Nature, are very Lawes.

Another division of Lawes, is into *Naturall* and *Positive*. *Naturall* are those which have been Lawes from all [148] Eternity; and are called not onely *Naturall*, but also *Morall* Lawes; consisting in the Morall Vertues, as Justice, Equity, and all habits of the mind that conduce to Peace, and Charity; of which I have already spoken in the fourteenth and fifteenth Chapters.

Positive, are those which have not been from Eternity; but have been made Lawes by the Will of those that have had the Soveraign Power over others; and are either written, or made known to men, by some other argument of the Will of their Legislator.

Another Division of Law.

Again, of Positive Lawes, some are *Humane*, some *Divine*: And of Humane positive lawes, some are *Distributive*, some *Penal*. *Distributive* are those that determine the Rights of the Subjects, declaring to every man what it is, by which he acquireth and holdeth a propriety in lands, or goods, and a right or liberty of action: and these speak to all the Subjects. *Penal* are those, which declare, what Penalty shall be inflicted on those that violate the Law; and speak to the Ministers and Officers ordained for execution. For though every one ought to be informed of the Punishments ordained beforehand for their transgression; neverthelesse the Command is not addressed to the Delinquent, (who cannot be supposed will faithfully punish himselfe,) but to publique Ministers appointed to see the Penalty executed. And these Penal Lawes are for the most part written together with the Lawes Distributive, and are sometimes called Judgements. For all Lawes are generall Judgements, or Sentences of the Legislator, as also every particular Judgement, is a Law to him, whose case is Judged.

Divine Positive Law how made known to be Law

Divine Positive Lawes (for Naturall Lawes being Eternall, and Universall, are all Divine,) are those, which being the Commandements of God, (not from all Eternity, nor universally addressed to all men, but onely to a certain people, or to certain persons,) are declared

for such, by those whom God hath authorised to declare them. But this Authority of man to declare what be these Positive Lawes of God, how can it be known? God may command a man by a supernaturall way, to deliver Lawes to other men. But because it is of the essence of Law, that he who is to be obliged, be assured of the Authority of him that declareth it, which we cannot naturally take notice to be from God, *How can a man without supernaturall Revelation be assured of the Revelation received by the declarer?* and *how can he be bound to obey them?* For the first question, how a man can be assured of the Revelation of another, without a Revelation particularly to himselfe, it is evidently impossible: For though a man may be induced to believe such Revelation, from the Miracles they see him doe, or from seeing the Extraordinary sanctity of his life, or from seeing the Extraordinary wisedome, or Extraordinary felicity of his Actions, all which are marks of God[s] extraordinary favour; yet they are not assured evidences of speciall Revelation. Miracles are Marvellous workes: but that which is marvellous to one, may not be so to another. Sanctity may be feigned; and the visible felicities of this world, are most often the work
[149] of God by Naturall, and ordinary causes. And therefore no man can infallibly know by naturall reason, that another has had a supernaturall revelation of Gods will; but only a beliefe; every one (as the signs thereof shall appear greater, or lesser) a firmer, or a weaker belief.

But for the second, how he can be bound to obey them; it is not so hard. For if the Law declared, be not against the Law of Nature (which is undoubtedly Gods Law) and he undertake to obey it, he is bound by his own act; bound I say to obey it, but not bound to believe it: for mens beliefe, and interiour cogitations, are not subject to the commands, but only to the operation of God, ordinary, or extraordinary. Faith of Supernaturall Law, is not a fulfilling, but only an assenting to the same; and not a duty that we exhibite to God, but a gift which God freely giveth to whom he pleaseth; as also Unbelief is not a breach of any of his Lawes; but a rejection of them all, except the Laws Naturall. But this that I say, will be made yet cleerer, by the Examples, and Testimonies concerning this point in holy Scripture. The Covenant God made with *Abraham* (in a Supernaturall manner) was thus, *This is the Covenant which thou shalt observe between Me and Thee and thy Seed after thee.* Gen. 17. 10. *Abrahams* Seed had not this revelation, nor were yet in being; yet they are a party to the Covenant, and bound to obey what *Abraham* should declare to them for Gods Law; which they could not be, but in vertue of the obedience they owed to their Parents; who (if they be Subject to no other earthly power, as here in the case of *Abraham*) have Soveraign power over their children, and servants. Againe, where God saith to *Abraham*, *In thee shall all Nations of the earth be blessed: For I know thou wilt command thy children, and thy house after thee to keep the way of the Lord, and to observe Righteousnesse and Judgement,* it is manifest, the obedience of his Family, who had no Revelation, depended on their former obligation to obey their Soveraign. At Mount *Sinai* *Moses* only went up to God, the people were forbidden to approach on paine of death; yet were they bound to obey all that *Moses* declared to them for Gods Law. Upon what ground, but on this submission of their own, *Speak thou to us, and we will heare thee, but let not God speak to us, lest we dye?* By which two places it sufficiently appeareth, that in a Common-wealth, a subject that has no certain and assured Revelation particularly to himself concerning the Will of God, is to obey for such, the Command of the Common-wealth: for if men were at liberty, to take for Gods Commandements, their own dreams, and fancies, or the dreams and fancies of private men; scarce two men would agree upon what is Gods Commandement, and yet in respect of them, every man would despise the Commandements of the Common-wealth. I conclude therefore, that in all things not contrary to the Morall Law, (that is to say, to the Law of Nature,) all Subjects are bound to obey that for divine Law, which is declared to be so, by the Lawes of the Common-wealth. Which also is evident to any mans reason, for whatsoever is not against the Law of Nature, may be made Law in the name of them that have the [150]

Soveraign power; and there is no reason men should be the lesse obliged by it, when tis propounded in the name of God. Besides, there is no place in the world where men are permitted to pretend other Commandements of God, than are declared for such by the Common-wealth. Christian States punish those that revolt from Christian Religion, and all other States, those that set up any Religion by them forbidden. For in whatsoever is not regulated by the Common-wealth, tis Equity (which is the Law of Nature, and therefore an eternall Law of God) that every man equally enjoy his liberty.

Another division of Lawes

There is also another distinction of Laws, into *Fundamentall*, and *not Fundamentall*: but I could never see in any Author, what a Fundamentall Law signifieth. Neverthelesse one may very reasonably distinguish Laws in that manner.

A Fundamentall Law what

For a Fundamentall Law in every Common-wealth is that, which being taken away, the Common-wealth faileth, and is utterly dissolved, as a building whose Foundation is destroyed. And therefore a Fundamentall Law is that, by which Subjects are bound to uphold whatsoever power is given to the Soveraign, whether a Monarch, or a Soveraign Assembly, without which the Common-wealth cannot stand; such as is the power of War and Peace, of Judicature, of Election of Officers, and of doing whatsoever he shall think necessary for the Publique good. Not Fundamentall is that, the abrogating whereof, draweth not with it the dissolution of the Common-Wealth; such as are the Lawes concerning Controversies between subject and subject. Thus much of the Division of Lawes.

Difference between Law and Right

I find the words *Lex Civilis*, and *Jus Civile*, that is to say, *Law* and *Right Civil*, promiscuously used for the same thing, even in the most learned Authors; which neverthelesse ought not to be so. For *Right* is *Liberty*, namely that Liberty which the Civil Law leaves us But *Civill Law* is an *Obligation*; and takes from us the Liberty which the Law of Nature gave us. Nature gave a Right to every man to secure himselfe by his own strength, and to invade a suspected neighbour, by way of prevention: but the Civill Law takes away that Liberty, in all cases where the protection of the Law may be safely stayd for. Insomuch as *Lex* and *Jus*, are as different as *Obligation* and *Liberty*.

And between a Law and a Charter.

Likewise *Lawes* and *Charters* are taken promiscuously for the same thing. Yet Charters are Donations of the Soveraign, and not Lawes, but exemptions from Law. The phrase of a Law is *Jubeo*, *Injungo*, *I command*, and *Enjoyn*: the phrase of a Charter is *Dedi*, *Concessi*, *I have Given*, *I have Granted*. but what is given or granted, to a man, is not forced upon him, by a Law. A Law may be made to bind All the Subjects of a Common-wealth: a Liberty, or Charter is only to One man, or some One part of the people. For to say all the people of a Common-wealth, have Liberty in any case whatsoever; is to say, that in such case, there hath been no Law made, or else having been made, is now abrogated.

CHAP. XXVII. [151]

Of Crimes, Excuses, *and* Extenuations

Sinne what.

A *Sinne*, is not onely a Transgression of a Law, but also any Contempt of the Legislator. For such Contempt, is a breach of all his Lawes at once. And therefore may consist, not onely in the *Commission* of a Fact, or in the Speaking of Words by the Lawes forbidden, or in the *Omission* of what the Law commandeth, but also in the *Intention*, or purpose to transgresse. For the purpose to breake the Law, is some degree of Contempt of him, to whom it belongeth to see it executed. To be delighted in the Imagination onely, of being possessed of another mans goods, servants, or wife, without any intention to take them from him by force, or fraud, is no breach of the Law, that sayth, *Thou shalt not covet*: nor is the pleasure a man may have in imagining, or dreaming of the death of him, from whose life he expecteth nothing but dammage, and displeasure, a Sinne, but the resolving to put some Act in execution, that tendeth thereto. For to be pleased in the fiction of that, which would please a man if it were reall, is a Passion so adhærent to the Nature both of man, and every other living creature, as to make it a Sinne, were to make Sinne of being a man. The consideration of this, has made me think them too severe, both to themselves, and others, that maintain, that the First motions of the mind, (though checked with the fear of God) be Sinnes. But I confesse it is safer to erre on that hand, than on the other.

A Crime what.

A CRIME, is a sinne, consisting in the Committing (by Deed, or Word) of that which the Law forbiddeth, or the Omission of what it hath commanded. So that every Crime is a sinne; but not every sinne a Crime. To intend to steale, or kill, is a sinne, though it never appeare in Word, or Fact: for God that seeth the thoughts of man, can lay it to his charge: but till it appear by some thing done, or said, by which the intention may be argued by a humane Judge, it hath not the name of Crime: which distinction the Greeks observed, in the word ἁμάρτημα, and ἔγκλημα, or ἀιτία; whereof the former, (which is translated *Sinne*,) signifieth any swarving from the Law whatsoever; but the two later, (which are translated *Crime*,) signifie that sinne onely, whereof one man may accuse another. But of Intentions, which never appear by any outward act, there is no place for humane accusation. In like manner the Latines by *Peccatum*, which is *Sinne*, signifie all manner of deviation from the Law; but by *Crimen*, (which word they derive from *Cerno*, which signifies to perceive,) they mean onely such sinnes, as may be made appear before a Judge; and therfore are not meer Intentions.

From this relation of Sinne to the Law, and of Crime to the Civill Law, may be inferred, First, that where Law
[152] ceaseth, Sinne ceaseth. But because the Law of Nature is eternall, Violation of Covenants, Ingratitude, Arrogance, and all Facts contrary to any Morall vertue, can never cease to be Sinne. Secondly, that the Civill Law ceasing, Crimes cease: for there being no other Law remaining, but that of Nature, there is no place for Accusation; every man being his own Judge, and accused onely by his own Conscience, and cleared by the Uprightnesse of his own Intention. When therefore his Intention is Right, his fact is no Sinne: if otherwise, his

Where no Civill Law is, there is no Crime.

fact is Sinne; but not Crime. Thirdly, That when the Soveraign Power ceaseth, Crime also ceaseth: for where there is no such Power, there is no protection to be had from the Law; and therefore every one may protect himself by his own power: for no man in the Institution of Soveraign Power can be supposed to give away the Right of preserving his own body; for the safety whereof all Soveraignty was ordained. But this is to be understood onely of those, that have not themselves contributed to the taking away of the Power that protected them: for that was a Crime from the beginning.

Ignorance of the Law of Nature excuseth no man.

The source of every Crime, is some defect of the Understanding; or some errour in Reasoning; or some sudden force of the Passions. Defect in the Understanding, is *Ignorance*; in Reasoning, *Erroneous Opinion*. Again, Ignorance is of three sorts; of the *Law*, and of the *Soveraign*, and of the *Penalty*. Ignorance of the Law of Nature Excuseth no man; because every man that hath attained to the use of Reason, is supposed to know, he ought not to do to another, what he would not have done to himselfe. Therefore into what place soever a man shall come, if he do any thing contrary to that Law, it is a Crime. If a man come from the *Indies* hither, and perswade men here to receive a new Religion, or teach them any thing that tendeth to disobedience of the Lawes of this Country, though he be never so well perswaded of the truth of what he teacheth, he commits a Crime, and may be justly punished for the same, not onely because his doctrine is false, but also because he does that which he would not approve in another, namely, that comming from hence, he should endeavour to alter the Religion there. But ignorance of the Civill Law, shall Excuse a man in a strange Country, till it be declared to him; because, till then no Civill Law is binding.

Ignorance of the Civill Law excuseth sometimes

In the like manner, if the Civill Law of a mans own Country, be not so sufficiently declared, as he may know it if he will; nor the Action against the Law of Nature; the Ignorance is a good Excuse: In other cases Ignorance of the Civill Law, Excuseth not.

Ignorance of the Soveraign excuseth not.

Ignorance of the Soveraign Power, in the place of a mans ordinary residence, Excuseth him not; because he ought to take notice of the Power, by which he hath been protected there.

Ignorance of the Penalty excuseth not.

Ignorance of the Penalty, where the Law is declared, Excuseth no man: For in breaking the Law, which without a fear of penalty to follow, were not a Law, but vain words, he undergoeth the penalty, though he know not what it is; because, whosoever voluntarily doth any action, accepteth all the known consequences of it; but Punishment is a known consequence of the viola-
[153] tion of the Lawes, in every Common-wealth; which punishment, if it be determined already by the Law, he is subject to that; if not, then is he subject to Arbitrary punishment. For it is reason, that he which does Injury, without other limitation than that of his own Will, should suffer punishment without other limitation, than that of his Will whose Law is thereby violated.

Punishments declared before the Fact, excuse from greater punishments after it.

But when a penalty, is either annexed to the Crime in the Law it selfe, or hath been usually inflicted in the like cases; there the Delinquent is Excused from a greater penalty. For the punishment foreknown, if not great enough to deterre men from the action, is an invitement to it: because when men compare the benefit of their Injustice, with the harm of their punishment, by necessity of Nature they choose that which appeareth best for themselves: and therefore when they are punished more than the Law had formerly determined, or more than others were punished for the same Crime; it is the Law that tempted, and deceiveth them.

Nothing can be made a Crime by a Law made after the Fact.

No Law, made after a Fact done, can make it a Crime: because if the Fact be against the Law of Nature, the Law was before the Fact; and a Positive Law cannot be taken notice of, before it be made; and therefore cannot be Obligatory. But when the Law that forbiddeth a Fact, is made before the Fact be done: yet he that doth the Fact, is lyable to the Penalty ordained after, in case no lesser Penalty were made known before, neither by Writing, nor by Example, for the reason immediatly before alledged.

From defect in Reasoning, (that is to say, from Errour,) men are prone to violate the Lawes, three wayes. First, by Presumption of false Principles: as when men from having observed how in all places, and in all ages, unjust Actions have been authorised, by the force, and victories of those who have committed them; and that potent men, breaking through the Cob-web Lawes of their Country, the weaker sort, and those that have failed in their Enterprises, have been esteemed the onely Criminals; have thereupon taken for Principles, and grounds of their Reasoning, *That Justice is but a vain word: That whatsoever a man can get by his own Industry, and hazard, is his own: That the Practice of all Nations cannot be unjust: That Examples of former times are good Arguments of doing the like again*; and many more of that kind: Which being granted, no Act in it selfe can be a Crime, but must be made so (not by the Law, but) by the successe of them that commit it; and the same Fact be vertuous, or vicious, as Fortune pleaseth; so that what *Marius* makes a Crime, *Sylla* shall make meritorious, and *Cæsar* (the same Lawes standing) turn again into a Crime, to the perpetuall disturbance of the Peace of the Common-wealth. *False Principles of Right and Wrong causes of Crime*

Secondly, by false Teachers, that either mis-interpret the Law of Nature, making it thereby repugnant to the Law Civill; or by teaching for Lawes, such Doctrines of their own, or Traditions of former times, as are inconsistent with the duty of a Subject. *False Teachers mis-interpreting the Law of Nature,*

Thirdly, by Erroneous Inferences from True Principles; which happens commonly to men that are hasty, and præcipitate in concluding, and resolving what to do; [154] such as are they, that have both a great opinion of their own understanding, and believe that things of this nature require not time and study, but onely common experience, and a good naturall wit; whereof no man thinks himselfe unprovided: whereas the knowledge, of Right and Wrong, which is no lesse difficult, there is no man will pretend to, without great and long study And of those defects in Reasoning, there is none that can Excuse (though some of them may Extenuate) a Crime, in any man, that pretendeth to the administra- *And false Inferences from true Principles, by Teachers.*

tion of his own private businesse; much lesse in them that undertake a publique charge; because they pretend to the Reason, upon the want whereof they would ground their Excuse.

By their Passions; Of the Passions that most frequently are the causes of Crime, one, is Vain-glory, or a foolish over-rating of their own worth; as if difference of worth, were an effect of their wit, or riches, or bloud, or some other naturall quality, not depending on the Will of those that have the Soveraign Authority. From whence proceedeth a Presumption that the punishments ordained by the Lawes, and extended generally to all Subjects, ought not to be inflicted on them, with the same rigour they are inflicted on poore, obscure, and simple men, comprehended under the name of the *Vulgar*.

Presumption of Riches, Therefore it happeneth commonly, that such as value themselves by the greatnesse of their wealth, adventure on Crimes, upon hope of escaping punishment, by corrupting publique Justice, or obtaining Pardon by Mony, or other rewards.

And Friends; And that such as have multitude of Potent Kindred; and popular men, that have gained reputation amongst the Multitude, take courage to violate the Lawes, from a hope of oppressing the Power, to whom it belongeth to put them in execution.

Wisedome. And that such as have a great, and false opinion of their own Wisedome, take upon them to reprehend the actions, and call in question the Authority of them that govern, and so to unsettle the Lawes with their publique discourse, as that nothing shall be a Crime, but what their own designes require should be so. It happeneth also to the same men, to be prone to all such Crimes, as consist in Craft, and in deceiving of their Neighbours; because they think their designes are too subtile to be perceived. These I say are effects of a false presumption of their own Wisdome. For of them that are the first movers in the disturbance of Common-wealth, (which can never happen without a Civill Warre,) very few are left alive long enough, to see their new Designes established: so that the benefit of their Crimes, redoundeth to Posterity, and such as would least have wished it:

which argues they were not so wise, as they thought they were. And those that deceive upon hope of not being observed, do commonly deceive themselves, (the darknesse in which they believe they lye hidden, being nothing else but their own blindnesse ,) and are no wiser than Children, that think all hid, by hiding their own eyes

And generally all vain-glorious men, (unlesse they be withall timorous,) are subject to Anger ; as being more [155] prone than others to interpret for contempt, the ordinary liberty of conversation : And there are few Crimes that may not be produced by Anger.

Hatred, Lust, Ambition, Covetousnesse, causes of Crime

As for the Passions, of Hate, Lust, Ambition, and Covetousnesse, what Crimes they are apt to produce, is so obvious to every mans experience and understanding, as there needeth nothing to be said of them, saving that they are infirmities, so annexed to the nature, both of man, and all other living creatures, as that their effects cannot be hindred, but by extraordinary use of Reason, or a constant severity in punishing them. For in those things men hate, they find a continuall, and unavoydable molestation , whereby either a mans patience must be everlasting, or he must be eased by removing the power of that which molesteth him The former is difficult , the later is many times impossible, without some violation of the Law. Ambition, and Covetousnesse are Passions also that are perpetually incumbent, and pressing ; whereas Reason is not perpetually present, to resist them and therefore whensoever the hope of impunity appears, their effects proceed. And for Lust, what it wants in the lasting, it hath in the vehemence, which sufficeth to weigh down the apprehension of all easie, or uncertain punishments.

Fear sometimes cause of Crime, as when the danger is neither present, nor corporeall.

Of all Passions, that which enclineth men least to break the Lawes, is Fear. Nay, (excepting some generous natures,) it is the onely thing, (when there is apparence of profit, or pleasure by breaking the Lawes,) that makes men keep them. And yet in many cases a Crime may be committed through Feare

For not every Fear justifies the Action it produceth, but the fear onely of corporeall hurt, which we call

Bodily Fear, and from which a man cannot see how to be delivered, but by the action. A man is assaulted, fears present death, from which he sees not how to escape, but by wounding him that assaulteth him; If he wound him to death, this is no Crime; because no man is supposed at the making of a Common-wealth, to have abandoned the defence of his life, or limbes, where the Law cannot arrive time enough to his assistance. But to kill a man, because from his actions, or his threatnings, I may argue he will kill me when he can, (seeing I have time, and means to demand protection, from the Soveraign Power,) is a Crime. Again, a man receives words of disgrace, or some little injuries (for which they that made the Lawes, had assigned no punishment, nor thought it worthy of a man that hath the use of Reason, to take notice of,) and is afraid, unlesse he revenge it, he shall fall into contempt, and consequently be obnoxious to the like injuries from others; and to avoyd this, breaks the Law, and protects himselfe for the future, by the terrour of his private revenge. This is a Crime: For the hurt is not Corporeall, but Phantasticall, and (though in this corner of the world, made sensible by a custome not many years since begun, amongst young and vain men,) so light, as a gallant man, and one that is assured of his own courage, cannot take notice of. Also a man may stand in fear of Spirits, either through his own superstition, or through too much credit given to other men,
[156] that tell him of strange Dreams and Visions; and thereby be made believe they will hurt him, for doing, or omitting divers things, which neverthelesse, to do or omit, is contrary to the Lawes; And that which is so done, or omitted, is not to be Excused by this fear; but is a Crime. For (as I have shewn before in the second Chapter) Dreams be naturally but the fancies remaining in sleep, after the impressions our Senses had formerly received waking; and when men are by any accident unassured they have slept, seem to be reall Visions; and therefore he that presumes to break the Law upon his own, or anothers Dream, or pretended Vision, or upon other Fancy of the power of Invisible

Spirits, than is permitted by the Common-wealth, leaveth the Law of Nature, which is a certain offence, and followeth the imagery of his own, or another private mans brain, which he can never know whether it signifieth any thing, or nothing, nor whether he that tells his Dream, say true, or lye, which if every private man should have leave to do, (as they must by the Law of Nature, if any one have it) there could no Law be made to hold, and so all Common-wealth would be dissolved.

Crimes not equall. From these different sources of Crimes, it appeares already, that all Crimes are not (as the Stoicks of old time maintained) of the same allay. There is place, not only for EXCUSE, by which that which seemed a Crime, is proved to be none at all; but also for EXTENUATION, by which the Crime, that seemed great, is made lesse For though all Crimes doe equally deserve the name of Injustice, as all deviation from a strait line is equally crookednesse, which the Stoicks rightly observed; yet it does not follow that all Crimes are equally unjust, no more than that all crooked lines are equally crooked: which the Stoicks not observing, held it as great a Crime, to kill a Hen, against the Law, as to kill ones Father.

Totall Excuses. That which totally Excuseth a Fact, and takes away from it the nature of a Crime, can be none but that, which at the same time, taketh away the obligation of the Law. For the fact committed once against the Law, if he that committed it be obliged to the Law, can be no other than a Crime.

The want of means to know the Law, totally Excuseth: For the Law whereof a man has no means to enforme himself, is not obligatory But the want of diligence to enquire, shall not be considered as a want of means, Nor shall any man, that pretendeth to reason enough for the Government of his own affairs, be supposed to want means to know the Lawes of Nature; because they are known by the reason he pretends to only Children, and Madmen are Excused from offences against the Law Naturall.

Where a man is captive, or in the power of the enemy, (and he is then in the power of the enemy, when his person, or his means of living, is so,) if it be without his own fault, the Obligation of the Law ceaseth; because he must obey the enemy, or dye, and consequently such obedience is no Crime: for no man is obliged (when the protection of the Law faileth,) not to protect himself, by the best means he can.

[157] If a man by the terrour of present death, be compelled to doe a fact against the Law, he is totally Excused; because no Law can oblige a man to abandon his own preservation. And supposing such a Law were obligatory; yet a man would reason thus, *If I doe it not, I die presently; if I doe it, I die afterwards; therefore by doing it, there is time of life gained*, Nature therefore compells him to the fact.

When a man is destitute of food, or other thing necessary for his life, and cannot preserve himselfe any other way, but by some fact against the Law, as if in a great famine he take the food by force, or stealth, which he cannot obtaine for mony, nor charity; or in defence of his life, snatch away another mans Sword, he is totally Excused, for the reason next before alledged.

Excuses against the Author. Again, Facts done against the Law, by the authority of another, are by that authority Excused against the Author; because no man ought to accuse his own fact in another, that is but his instrument: but it is not Excused against a third person thereby injured; because in the violation of the Law, both the Author, and Actor are Criminalls. From hence it followeth that when that Man, or Assembly, that hath the Soveraign Power, commandeth a man to do that which is contrary to a former Law, the doing of it is totally Excused: For he ought not to condemn it himselfe, because he is the Author; and what cannot justly be condemned by the Soveraign, cannot justly be punished by any other. Besides, when the Soveraign commandeth any thing to be done against his own former Law, the Command, as to that particular fact, is an abrogation of the Law.

If that Man, or Assembly, that hath the Soveraign Power, disclaime any Right essentiall to the Soveraignty, whereby there accrueth to the Subject, any liberty inconsistent with the Soveraign Power, that is to say, with the very being of a Common-wealth, if the Subject shall refuse to obey the Command in any thing, contrary to the liberty granted, this is neverthelesse a Sinne, and contrary to the duty of the Subject: for he ought to take notice of what is inconsistent with the Soveraignty, because it was erected by his own consent, and for his own defence; and that such liberty as is inconsistent with it, was granted through ignorance of the evill consequence thereof. But if he not onely disobey, but also resist a publique Minister in the execution of it, then it is a Crime; because he might have been righted, (without any breach of the Peace,) upon complaint.

The Degrees of Crime are taken on divers Scales, and measured, First, by the malignity of the Source, or Cause: Secondly, by the contagion of the Example: Thirdly, by the mischiefe of the Effect; and Fourthly, by the concurrence of Times, Places, and Persons.

Presumption of Power, aggravateth.

The same Fact done against the Law, if it proceed from Presumption of strength, riches, or friends to resist those that are to execute the Law, is a greater Crime, than if it proceed from hope of not being discovered, or of escape by flight: For Presumption of impunity by force, is a Root, from whence springeth, [158] at all times, and upon all temptations, a contempt of all Lawes; whereas in the later case, the apprehension of danger, that makes a man fly, renders him more obedient for the future. A Crime which we know to be so, is greater than the same Crime proceeding from a false perswasion that it is lawfull: For he that committeth it against his own conscience, presumeth on his force, or other power, which encourages him to commit the same again: but he that doth it by errour, after the errour shewn him, is conformable to the Law.

Evill Teachers, Extenuate

Hee, whose errour proceeds from the authority of a Teacher, or an Interpreter of the Law publiquely authorised, is not so faulty, as he whose errour proceedeth from a peremptory pursute of his own principles, and reasoning: For what is taught by one that teacheth by publique Authority, the Common-wealth teacheth, and hath a resemblance of Law, till the same Authority controuleth it; and in all Crimes that contain not in them a denyall of the Soveraign Power, nor are against an evident Law, Excuseth totally: whereas he that groundeth his actions, on his private Judgement, ought according to the rectitude, or errour thereof, to stand, or fall.

Examples of Impunity, Extenuate.

The same Fact, if it have been constantly punished in other men, is a greater Crime, than if there have been many precedent Examples of impunity. For those Examples, are so many hopes of Impunity, given by the Soveraign himselfe: And because he which furnishes a man with such a hope, and presumption of mercy, as encourageth him to offend, hath his part in the offence; he cannot reasonably charge the offender with the whole.

Præmeditation, Aggravateth.

A Crime arising from a sudden Passion, is not so great, as when the same ariseth from long meditation: For in the former case there is a place for Extenuation, in the common infirmity of humane nature: but he that doth it with præmeditation, has used circumspection, and cast his eye, on the Law, on the punishment, and on the consequence thereof to humane society; all which in committing the Crime, hee hath contemned, and postposed to his own appetite. But there is no suddennesse of Passion sufficient for a totall Excuse: For all the time between the first knowing of the Law, and the Commission of the Fact, shall be taken for a time of deliberation; because he ought by meditation of the Law, to rectifie the irregularity of his Passions.

Where the Law is publiquely, and with assiduity, before all the people read, and interpreted; a fact done against it, is a greater Crime, than where men are left without such instruction, to enquire of it with difficulty, uncertainty, and interruption of their Callings, and be informed by private men: for in this case, part of the fault is discharged upon common infirmity; but in the former, there is apparent negligence, which is not without some contempt of the Soveraign Power.

Those facts which the Law expresly condemneth, but the Law-maker by other manifest signes of his will tacitly approveth, are lesse Crimes, than the same facts, condemned both by the Law, and Law-maker. For seeing the will of the Law-maker is a Law, there appear in this case two contradictory Lawes, which would [159] totally Excuse, if men were bound to take notice of the Soveraigns approbation, by other arguments, than are expressed by his command But because there are punishments consequent, not onely to the transgression of his Law, but also to the observing of it, he is in part a cause of the transgression, and therefore cannot reasonably impute the whole Crime to the Delinquent. For example, the Law condemneth Duells; the punishment is made capitall. On the contrary part, he that refuseth Duell, is subject to contempt and scorne, without remedy, and sometimes by the Soveraign himselfe thought unworthy to have any charge, or preferment in Warre: If thereupon he accept Duell, considering all men lawfully endeavour to obtain the good opinion of them that have the Soveraign Power, he ought not in reason to be rigorously punished; seeing part of the fault may be discharged on the punisher: which I say, not as wishing liberty of private revenges, or any other kind of disobedience, but a care in Governours, not to countenance any thing obliquely, which directly they forbid The examples of Princes, to those that see them, are, and ever have been, more potent to govern their actions, than the Lawes themselves. And though it be our duty to do, not what they do, but what they say, yet will that duty never be performed, till it please God to give men an extraordinary, and supernaturall grace to follow that Precept.

Tacite approbation of the Soveraign, Extenuates.

Again, if we compare Crimes by the mischiefe of their Effects, First, the same fact, when it redounds to the dammage of many, is greater, than when it redounds to the hurt of few And therefore, when a fact hurteth, not onely in the present, but also, (by example) in the future, it is a greater Crime, than if it hurt onely in the present. for the former, is a fertile Crime, and multiplyes to the hurt of many; the later is barren. To

Comparison of Crimes from their Effects

maintain doctrines contrary to the Religion established in the Common-wealth, is a greater fault, in an authorised Preacher, than in a private person: So also is it, to live prophanely, incontinently, or do any irreligious act whatsoever. Likewise in a Professor of the Law, to maintain any point, or do any act, that tendeth to the weakning of the Soveraign Power, is a greater Crime, than in another man. Also in a man that hath such reputation for wisedome, as that his counsells are followed, or his actions imitated by many, his fact against the Law, is a greater Crime, than the same fact in another: For such men not onely commit Crime, but teach it for Law to all other men And generally all Crimes are the greater, by the scandall they give; that is to say, by becomming stumbling-blocks to the weak, that look not so much upon the way they go in, as upon the light that other men carry before them.

Læsæ Majestas. Also Facts of hostility against the present state of the Common-wealth, are greater Crimes, than the same acts done to private men: For the dammage extends it selfe to all Such are the betraying of the strengths, or revealing of the secrets of the Common-wealth to an Enemy; also all attempts upon the Representative of the Common-wealth, be it a Monarch, or an Assembly; [160] and all endeavours by word, or deed to diminish the Authority of the same, either in the present time, or in succession. which Crimes the Latines understand by *Crimina læsæ Majestatis*, and consist in designe, or act, contrary to a Fundamentall Law.

Bribery and False testimony. Likewise those Crimes, which render Judgements of no effect, are greater Crimes, than Injuries done to one. or a few persons; as to receive mony to give False judgement, or testimony, is a greater Crime, than otherwise to deceive a man of the like, or a greater summe; because not onely he has wrong, that falls by such judgements; but all Judgements are rendered uselesse, and occasion ministred to force, and private revenges.

Depeculation. Also Robbery, and Depeculation of the Publique treasure, or Revenues, is a greater Crime, than the robbing, or defrauding of a Private man; because to robbe the publique, is to robbe many at once.

Counterfeiting Authority

Also the Counterfeit usurpation of publique Ministery, the Counterfeiting of publique Seales, or publique Coine, than counterfeiting of a private mans person, or his seale; because the fraud thereof, extendeth to the dammage of many.

Crimes against private men compared.

Of facts against the Law, done to private men, the greater Crime, is that, where the dammage in the common opinion of men, is most sensible And therefore

To kill against the Law, is a greater Crime, than any other injury, life preserved.

And to kill with Torment, greater, than simply to kill.

And Mutilation of a limbe, greater, than the spoyling a man of his goods.

And the spoyling a man of his goods, by Terrour of death, or wounds, than by clandestine surreption.

And by clandestine Surreption, than by consent fraudulently obtained.

And the violation of chastity by Force, greater, than by flattery

And of a woman Married, than of a woman not married.

For all these things are commonly so valued; though some men are more, and some lesse sensible of the same offence But the Law regardeth not the particular, but the generall inclination of mankind.

And therefore the offence men take, from contumely, in words, or gesture, when they produce no other harme, than the present griefe of him that is reproached, hath been neglected in the Lawes of the Greeks, Romans, and other both antient, and moderne Common-wealths; supposing the true cause of such griefe to consist, not in the contumely, (which takes no hold upon men conscious of their own vertue,) but in the Pusillanimity of him that is offended by it.

Also a Crime against a private man, is much aggravated by the person, time, and place. For to kill ones Parent, is a greater Crime, than to kill another · for the Parent ought to have the honour of a Soveraign, (though he have surrendred his Power to the Civill Law,) because he had it originally by Nature And to Robbe a poore

[161] man, is a greater Crime, than to robbe a rich man; because 'tis to the poore a more sensible dammage.

And a Crime committed in the Time, or Place appointed for Devotion, is greater, than if committed at another time or place: for it proceeds from a greater contempt of the Law.

Many other cases of Aggravation, and Extenuation might be added: but by these I have set down, it is obvious to every man, to take the altitude of any other Crime proposed.

Publique Crimes what

Lastly, because in almost all Crimes there is an Injury done, not onely to some Private men, but also to the Common-wealth; the same Crime, when the accusation is in the name of the Common-wealth, is called Publique Crime; and when in the name of a Private man, a Private Crime; And the Pleas according thereunto called Publique, *Judicia Publica*, Pleas of the Crown; or Private Pleas. As in an Accusation of Murder, if the accuser be a Private man, the plea is a Private plea; if the accuser be the Soveraign, the plea is a Publique plea.

CHAP. XXVIII.

Of PUNISHMENTS, *and* REWARDS.

The definition of Punishment

A PUNISHMENT, *is an Evill inflicted by publique Authority, on him that hath done, or omitted that which is Judged by the same Authority to be a Transgression of the Law; to the end that the will of men may thereby the better be disposed to obedience*

Right to Punish whence derived.

Before I inferre any thing from this definition, there is a question to be answered, of much importance; which is, by what door the Right, or Authority of Punishing in any case, came in. For by that which has been said before, no man is supposed bound by Covenant, not to resist violence; and consequently it cannot be intended, that he gave any right to another to lay violent hands upon his person. In the making of a Common-wealth, every man giveth away the right of defending another; but not of defending himselfe. Also he obligeth himselfe, to assist him that hath the Soveraignty, in the Punishing

of another; but of himselfe not. But to covenant to assist the Soveraign, in doing hurt to another, unlesse he that so covenanteth have a right to doe it himselfe, is not to give him a Right to Punish. It is manifest therefore that the Right which the Common-wealth (that is, he, or they that represent it) hath to Punish, is not grounded on any concession, or gift of the Subjects. But I have also shewed formerly, that before the Institution of Common-wealth, every man had a right to every thing, and to do whatsoever he thought necessary to his own preservation; subduing, hurting, or killing any man in order thereunto. And this is the foundation of that right of Punishing, which is exercised in every [162]
Common-wealth. For the Subjects did not give the Soveraign that right; but onely in laying down theirs, strengthned him to use his own, as he should think fit, for the preservation of them all: so that it was not given, but left to him, and to him onely; and (excepting the limits set him by naturall Law) as entire, as in the condition of meer Nature, and of warre of every one against his neighbour.

Private injuries, and revenges no Punishments:

From the definition of Punishment, I inferre, First, that neither private revenges, nor injuries of private men, can properly be stiled Punishment; because they proceed not from publique Authority.

Nor denyall of preferment:

Secondly, that to be neglected, and unpreferred by the publique favour, is not a Punishment; because no new evill is thereby on any man Inflicted; he is onely left in the estate he was in before.

Nor pain inflicted without publique hearing:

Thirdly, that the evill inflicted by publique Authority, without precedent publique condemnation, is not to be stiled by the name of Punishment; but of an hostile act; because the fact for which a man is Punished, ought first to be Judged by publique Authority, to be a transgression of the Law.

Nor pain inflicted by Usurped power:

Fourthly, that the evill inflicted by usurped power, and Judges without Authority from the Soveraign, is not Punishment; but an act of hostility; because the acts of power usurped, have not for Author, the person condemned; and therefore are not acts of publique Authority.

Nor pain inflicted without respect to the future good

Fifthly, that all evill which is inflicted without intention, or possibility of disposing the Delinquent, or (by his example) other men, to obey the Lawes, is not Punishment; but an act of hostility; because without such an end, no hurt done is contained under that name.

Naturall evill consequences, no Punishments.

Sixthly, whereas to certain actions, there be annexed by Nature, divers hurtfull consequences; as when a man in assaulting another, is himselfe slain, or wounded; or when he falleth into sicknesse by the doing of some unlawfull act; such hurt, though in respect of God, who is the author of Nature, it may be said to be inflicted, and therefore a Punishment divine; yet it is not contaned in the name of Punishment in respect of men, because it is not inflicted by the Authority of man.

Hurt inflicted, if lesse than the benefit of transgressing, is not Punishment

Seventhly, If the harm inflicted be lesse than the benefit, or contentment that naturally followeth the crime committed, that harm is not within the definition, and is rather the Price, or Redemption, than the Punishment of a Crime: Because it is of the nature of Punishment, to have for end, the disposing of men to obey the Law; which end (if it be lesse than the benefit of the transgression) it attaineth not, but worketh a contrary effect.

Where the Punishment is annexed to the Law, a greater hurt is not Punishment, but Hostility.

Eighthly, If a Punishment be determined and prescribed in the Law it selfe, and after the crime committed, there be a greater Punishment inflicted, the excesse is not Punishment, but an act of hostility. For seeing the aym of Punishment is not a revenge, but terrour; and the terrour of a great Punishment unknown, is taken away by the declaration of a lesse, the unexpected addition is no part of | the Punishment. [163] But where there is no Punishment at all determined by the Law, there whatsoever is inflicted, hath the nature of Punishment. For he that goes about the violation of a Law, wherein no penalty is determined, expecteth an indeterminate, that is to say, an arbitrary Punishment.

Hurt inflicted for a fact done before the

Ninthly, Harme inflicted for a Fact done before there was a Law that forbad it, is not Punishment, but an act of Hostility. For before the Law, there is no transgression of the Law. But Punishment supposeth a fact judged, to have been a transgression of the Law; Therefore Harme inflicted before the Law made, is not Punishment, but an act of Hostility.

Law, no Punishment

Tenthly, Hurt inflicted on the Representative of the Common-wealth, is not Punishment, but an act of Hostility Because it is of the nature of Punishment, to be inflicted by publique Authority, which is the Authority only of the Representative it self.

The Representative of the Common-wealth Unpunishable.

Lastly, Harme inflicted upon one that is a declared enemy, fals not under the name of Punishment. Because seeing they were either never subject to the Law, and therefore cannot transgresse it, or having been subject to it, and professing to be no longer so, by consequence deny they can transgresse it, all the Harmes that can be done them, must be taken as acts of Hostility. But in declared Hostility, all infliction of evill is lawfull. From whence it followeth, that if a subject shall by fact, or word, wittingly, and deliberatly deny the authority of the Representative of the Common-wealth, (whatsoever penalty hath been formerly ordained for Treason,) he may lawfully be made to suffer whatsoever the Representative will. For in denying subjection, he denyes such Punishment as by the Law hath been ordained; and therefore suffers as an enemy of the Common-wealth; that is, according to the will of the Representative. For the Punishments set down in the Law, are to Subjects, not to Enemies, such as are they, that having been by their own act Subjects, deliberately revolting, deny the Soveraign Power.

Hurt to Revolted Subjects is done by right of War, not by way of Punishment.

The first, and most generall distribution of Punishments, is into *Divine*, and *Humane*. Of the former I shall have occasion, to speak, in a more convenient place hereafter.

Humane, are those Punishments that be inflicted by the Commandement of Man; and are either *Corporall*, or *Pecuniary*, or *Ignominy*, or *Imprisonment*, or *Exile*, or mixt of these.

Corporall Punishment is that, which is inflicted on the body directly, and according to the intention of him that inflicteth it: such as are stripes, or wounds, or

Punishments Corporall.

deprivation of such pleasures of the body, as were before lawfully enjoyed

Capitall. And of these, some be *Capitall*, some *Lesse* than *Capitall* Capitall, is the Infliction of Death, and that either simply, or with torment Lesse than Capitall, are Stripes, Wounds, Chains, and any other corporall Paine, not in its own nature mortall For if upon the Infliction of a Punishment death follow not in the intention of the Inflicter, the Punishment is not to bee esteemed Capitall, though the harme prove mortall by an accident not to [164] be foreseen; in which case death is not inflicted, but hastened

Pecuniary Punishment, is that which consisteth not only in the deprivation of a Summe of Mony, but also of Lands, or any other goods which are usually bought and sold for mony. And in case the Law, that ordaineth such a punishment, be made with design to gather mony, from such as shall transgresse the same, it is not properly a Punishment, but the Price of priviledge, and exemption from the Law, which doth not absolutely forbid the fact, but only to those that are not able to pay the mony except where the Law is Naturall, or part of Religion, for in that case it is not an exemption from the Law, but a transgression of it As where a Law exacteth a Pecuniary mulct, of them that take the name of God in vaine, the payment of the mulct, is not the price of a dispensation to sweare, but the Punishment of the transgression of a Law undispensable In like manner if the Law impose a Summe of Mony to be payd, to him that has been Injured; this is but a satisfaction for the hurt done him and extinguisheth the accusation of the party injured, not the crime of the offender

Ignominy *Ignominy*, is the infliction of such Evill, as is made Dishonorable; or the deprivation of such Good, as is made Honourable by the Common-wealth For there be some things Honorable by Nature; as the effects of Courage, Magna[ni]mity, Strength, Wisdome, and other abilities of body and mind Others made Honorable by the Common-wealth, as Badges, Titles, Offices, or any other singular marke of the Soveraigns favour. The former, (though they may faile by nature, or accident.) cannot be taken away by a Law; and therefore the losse of them is not Punishment. But the later, may be taken away by the publique authority that made them Honorable, and are properly Punishments. Such are degrading men condemned, of their Badges, Titles, and Offices: or declaring them uncapable of the like in time to come.

Imprisonment, is when a man is by publique Authority deprived of liberty; and may happen from two divers ends; whereof one is the safe custody of a man accused, the other is the inflicting of paine on a man condemned. The former is not Punishment; because no man is supposed to be Punisht, before he be Judicially heard, and declared guilty. And therefore whatsoever hurt a man is made to suffer by bonds, or restraint, before his cause be heard, over and above that which is necessary to assure his custody, is against the Law of Nature. But the later is Punishment, because Evill, and inflicted by publique Authority, for somewhat that has by the same Authority been Judged a Transgression of the Law. Under this word Impriso[n]ment, I comprehend all restraint of motion, caused by an externall obstacle, be it a House, which is called by the general name of a Prison; or an Iland, as when men are said to be confined to it; or a place where men are set to worke, as in old time men have been condemned to Quarries, and in these times to Gallies, or be it a Chaine, or any other such impediment. *Imprisonment*

Exile, (Banishment) is when a man is for a crime, condemned to depart out of the dominion of the Common- [165] wealth, or out of a certaine part thereof; and during a prefixed time, or for ever, not to return into it and seemeth not in its own nature, without other circumstances, to be a Punishment, but rather an escape, or a publique commandement to avoid Punishment by flight. And *Cicero* sayes, there was never any such Punishment ordained in the City of *Rome*; but cals it a refuge of men in danger. For if a man banished, be neverthelesse permitted to enjoy his Goods, and the Revenue of his Lands, the meer change of ayr is no Punishment; *Exile.*

nor does it tend to that benefit of the Common-wealth, for which all Punishments are ordained, (that is to say, to the forming of mens wils to the observation of the Law;) but many times to the dammage of the Common-wealth. For a Banished man, is a lawfull enemy of the Common-wealth that banished him; as being no more a Member of the same. But if he be withall deprived of his Lands, or Goods, then the Punishment lyeth not in the Exile, but is to be reckoned amongst Punishments Pecuniary.

The Punishment of Innocent Subjects is contrary to the Law of Nature

All Punishments of Innocent subjects, be they great or little, are against the Law of Nature: For Punishment is only for Transgression of the Law, and therefore there can be no Punishment of the Innocent. It is therefore a violation, First, of that Law of Nature, which forbiddeth all men, in their Revenges, to look at any thing but some future good: For there can arrive no good to the Common-wealth, by Punishing the Innocent. Secondly, of that, which forbiddeth Ingratitude: For seeing all Soveraign Power, is originally given by the consent of every one of the Subjects, to the end they should as long as they are obedient, be protected thereby; the Punishment of the Innocent, is a rendring of Evill for Good. And thirdly, of the Law that commandeth Equity; that is to say, an equall distribution of Justice; which in Punishing the Innocent is not observed.

But the Harme done to Innocents in War, not so.

But the Infliction of what evill soever, on an Innocent man, that is not a Subject, if it be for the benefit of the Common-wealth, and without violation of any former Covenant, is no breach of the Law of Nature. For all men that are not Subjects, are either Enemies, or else they have ceased from being so, by some precedent covenants. But against Enemies, whom the Common-wealth judgeth capable to do them hurt, it is lawfull by the originall Right of Nature to make warre; wherein the Sword Judgeth not, nor doth the Victor make distinction of Nocent, and Innocent, as to the time past; nor has other respect of mercy, than as it conduceth to the good of his own People. And upon this ground it is, that also in Subjects, who deliberatly deny the Authority

Nor that which is done to declared Rebels.

of the Common-wealth established, the vengeance is lawfully extended, not onely to the Fathers, but also to the third and fourth generation not yet in being, and consequently innocent of the fact, for which they are afflicted · because the nature of this offence, consisteth in the renouncing of subjection; which is a relapse into the condition of warre, commonly called Rebellion; and they that so offend, suffer not as Subjects, but as Enemies. For *Rebellion*, is but warre [166] renewed

Reward is either Salary, or Grace.

REWARD, is either of *Gift*, or by *Contract*. When by Contract, it is called *Salary*, and *Wages* , which is benefit due for service performed, or promised. When of Gift, it is benefit proceeding from the *grace* of them that bestow it, to encourage, or enable men to do them service. And therefore when the Soveraign of a Common wealth appointeth a Salary to any publique Office, he that receiveth it, is bound in Justice to performe his office; otherwise, he is bound onely in honour, to acknowledgement, and an endeavour of requitall For though men have no lawfull remedy, when they be commanded to quit their private businesse, to serve the publique, without Reward, or Salary; yet they are not bound thereto, by the Law of Nature, nor by the Institution of the Common-wealth, unlesse the service cannot otherwise be done; because it is supposed the Soveraign may make use of all their means, insomuch as the most common Souldier, may demand the wages of his warrefare, as a debt.

Benefits bestowed for fear, are not Rewards.

The benefits which a Soveraign bestoweth on a Subject, for fear of some power, and ability he hath to do hurt to the Common-wealth, are not properly Rewards; for they are not Salaryes; because there is in this case no contract supposed, every man being obliged already not to do the Common-wealth disservice. nor are they Graces; because they be extorted by fear, which ought not to be incident to the Soveraign Power. but are rather Sacrifices, which the Soveraign (considered in his naturall person, and not in the person of the Common-wealth) makes, for the appeasing the discontent of him he thinks more potent than himselfe, and encourage not to obedience, but on the contrary, to the continuance, and increasing of further extortion

Salaries Certain and Casuall. And whereas some Salaries are certain, and proceed from the publique Treasure, and others uncertain, and casuall, proceeding from the execution of the Office for which the Salary is ordained; the later is in some cases hurtfull to the Common-wealth; as in the case of Judicature. For where the benefit of the Judges, and Ministers of a Court of Justice, ariseth for the multitude of Causes that are brought to their cognisance, there must needs follow two Inconveniences: One, is the nourishing of sutes. for the more sutes, the greater benefit and another that depends on that, which is contention about Jurisdiction: each Court drawing to it selfe, as many Causes as it can. But in offices of Execution there are not those Inconveniences; because their employment cannot be encreased by any endeavour of their own. And thus much shall suffice for the nature of Punishment, and Reward; which are, as it were, the Nerves and Tendons, that move the limbes and joynts of a Common-wealth.

Hitherto I have set forth the nature of Man, (whose Pride and other Passions have compelled him to submit himselfe to Government;) together with the great power of his Governour, whom I compared to *Leviathan*, taking that comparison out of the two last verses of the one and fortieth of *Job*; where God having set forth the great power of *Leviathan*, calleth him King of the Proud.
[167] *There is nothing*, saith he, *on earth, to be compared with him. He is made so as not to be afraid. Hee seeth every high thing below him; and is King of all the children of pride.* But because he is mortall, and subject to decay, as all other Earthly creatures are; and because there is that in heaven, (though not on earth) that he should stand in fear of, and whose Lawes he ought to obey; I shall in the next following Chapters speak of his Diseases, and the causes of his Mortality; and of what Lawes of Nature he is bound to obey.

CHAP. XXIX.

Of those things that Weaken, or tend to the DISSOLUTION *of a Common-wealth*

THOUGH nothing can be immortall, which mortals make; yet, if men had the use of reason they pretend to, their Common-wealths might be secured, at least, from perishing by internall diseases For by the nature of their Institution, they are designed to live, as long as Man-kind, or as the Lawes of Nature, or as Justice it selfe, which gives them life. Therefore when they come to be dissolved, not by externall violence, but intestine disorder, the fault is not in men, as they are the *Matter*; but as they are the *Makers*, and orderers of them. For men, as they become at last weary of irregular justling, and hewing one another, and desire with all their hearts, to conforme themselves into one firme and lasting edifice, so for want, both of the art of making fit Lawes, to square their actions by, and also of humility, and patience, to suffer the rude and combersome points of their present greatnesse to be taken off, they cannot without the help of a very able Architect, be compiled, into any other than a crasie building, such as hardly lasting out their own time, must assuredly fall upon the heads of their posterity

Dissolution of Common-wealths proceedeth from their Imperfect Institution.

Amongst the *Infirmities* therefore of a Common-wealth, I will reckon in the first place, those that arise from an Imperfect Institution, and resemble the diseases of a naturall body, which proceed from a Defectuous Procreation.

Want of Absolute power.

Of which, this is one, *That a man to obtain a Kingdome, is sometimes content with lesse Power, than to the Peace, and defence of the Common-wealth is necessarily required.* From whence it commeth to passe, that when the exercise of the Power layd by, is for the publique safety to be resumed, it hath the resemblance of an unjust act: which disposeth great numbers of men (when occasion is presented) to rebell; In the same manner as the bodies of children, gotten by diseased parents, are subject either to untimely death, or to purge the ill

quality, derived from their vicious conception, by breaking out into biles and scabbs. And when Kings deny themselves some such necessary Power, it is not alwayes (though sometimes) out of ignorance of what is necessary
[168] to the office they undertake; but many times out of a hope to recover the same again at their pleasure: Wherein they reason not well; because such as will hold them to their promises, shall be maintained against them by forraign Common-wealths; who in order to the good of their own Subjects let slip few occasions to *weaken* the estate of their Neighbours. So was *Thomas Becket* Archbishop of *Canterbury*, supported against *Henry* the Second, by the Pope; the subjection of Ecclesiastiques to the Common-wealth, having been dispensed with by *William the Conquerour* at his reception, when he took an Oath, not to infringe the liberty of the Church And so were the *Barons*, whose power was by *William Rufus* (to have their help in transferring the Succession from his Elder brother, to himselfe,) encreased to a degree, inconsistent with the Soveraign Power, maintained in their Rebellion against King *John*, by the French.

Nor does this happen in Monarchy onely. For whereas the stile of the antient Roman Common-wealth, was, *The Senate, and People of Rome*; neither Senate, nor People pretended to the whole Power; which first caused the seditions, of *Tiberius Gracchus*, *Caius Gracchus*, *Lucius Saturninus*, and others; and afterwards the warres between the Senate and the People, under *Marius* and *Sylla*; and again under *Pompey* and *Cæsar*, to the Extinction of their Democraty, and the setting up of Monarchy.

The people of *Athens* bound themselves but from one onely Action; which was, that no man on pain of death should propound the renewing of the warre for the Island of *Salamis*; And yet thereby, if *Solon* had not caused to be given out he was mad, and afterwards in gesture and habit of a mad-man, and in verse, propounded it to the People that flocked about him, they had had an enemy perpetually in readinesse, even at the gates of their Citie; such dammage, or shifts, are all Common-wealths forced to, that have their Power never so little limited.

In the second place, I observe the *Diseases* of a Common-wealth, that proceed from the poyson of seditious doctrines; whereof one is, *That every private man is Judge of Good and Evill actions.* This is true in the condition of meer Nature, where there are no Civill Lawes; and also under Civill Government, in such cases as are not determined by the Law. But otherwise, it is manifest, that the measure of Good and Evill actions, is the Civill Law; and the Judge the Legislator, who is alwayes Representative of the Common-wealth. From this false doctrine, men are disposed to debate with themselves, and dispute the commands of the Common-wealth; and afterwards to obey, or disobey them, as in their private judgements they shall think fit. Whereby the Common-wealth is distracted and *Weakened.* *Private Judgement of Good and Evill.*

Another doctrine repugnant to Civill Society, is, that *whatsoever a man does against his Conscience, is Sinne;* and it dependeth on the presumption of making himself judge of Good and Evill For a mans Conscience, and his Judgement is the same thing; and as the Judgement, so also the Conscience may be erroneous. Therefore, though he that is subject to no Civill Law, sinneth in all [169] he does against his Conscience, because he has no other rule to follow but his own reason; yet it is not so with him that lives in a Common-wealth; because the Law is the publique Conscience, by which he hath already undertaken to be guided. Otherwise in such diversity, as there is of private Consciences, which are but private opinions, the Common-wealth must needs be distracted, and no man dare to obey the Soveraign Power, farther than it shall seem good in his own eyes. *Erroneous Conscience.*

It hath been also commonly taught, *That Faith and Sanctity, are not to be attained by Study and Reason, but by supernaturall Inspiration, or Infusion,* which granted, I see not why any man should render a reason of his Faith; or why every Christian should not be also a Prophet; or why any man should take the Law of his Country, rather than his own Inspiration, for the rule of his action. And thus wee fall again into the fault of taking upon us to Judge of Good and Evill; or to make Judges of it, such private men as pretend to be super- *Pretence of Inspiration.*

naturally Inspired, to the Dissolution of all Civill Government Faith comes by hearing, and hearing by those accidents, which guide us into the presence of them that speak to us; which accidents are all contrived by God Almighty, and yet are not supernaturall, but onely, for the great number of them that concurre to every effect, unobservable. Faith, and Sanctity, are indeed not very frequent; but yet they are not Miracles, but brought to passe by education, discipline, correction, and other naturall wayes, by which God worketh them in his elect, at such time as he thinketh fit. And these three opinions, pernicious to Peace and Government, have in this part of the world, proceeded chiefly from the tongues, and pens of unlearned Divines; who joyning the words of Holy Scripture together, otherwise than is agreeable to reason, do what they can, to make men think, that Sanctity and Naturall Reason, cannot stand together.

Subjecting the Soveraign Power to Civill Lawes.

A fourth opinion, repugnant to the nature of a Common-wealth, is this, *That he that hath the Soveraign Power, is subject to the Civill Lawes.* It is true, that Soveraigns are all subject to the Lawes of Nature; because such lawes be Divine, and cannot by any man, or Common-wealth be abrogated. But to those Lawes which the Soveraign himselfe, that is, which the Common-wealth maketh, he is not subject For to be subject to Lawes, is to be subject to the Common-wealth, that is to the Soveraign Representative, that is to himselfe, which is not subjection, but freedome from the Lawes Which errour, because it setteth the Lawes above the Soveraign, setteth also a Judge above him, and a Power to punish him; which is to make a new Soveraign. and again for the same reason a third, to punish the second, and so continually without end, to the Confusion, and Dissolution of the Common-wealth.

Attributing of absolute Propriety to Subjects.

A Fifth doctrine, that tendeth to the Dissolution of a Common-wealth, is, *That every private man has an absolute Propriety in his Goods; such, as excludeth the Right of the Soveraign* Every man has indeed a Propriety that excludes the Right of every other Subject And he has it onely from the Soveraign Power; without the protection whereof, every other man should have equall [170] Right to the same. But if the Right of the Soveraign also be excluded, he cannot performe the office they have put him into; which is, to defend them both from forraign enemies, and from the injuries of one another, and consequently there is no longer a Common-wealth

And if the Propriety of Subjects, exclude not the Right of the Soveraign Representative to their Goods; much lesse to their offices of Judicature, or Execution, in which they Represent the Soveraign himselfe

Dividing of the Soveraign Power.

There is a Sixth doctrine, plainly, and directly against the essence of a Common-wealth. and 'tis this, *That the Soveraign Power may be divided* For what is it to divide the Power of a Common-wealth, but to Dissolve it; for Powers divided mutually destroy each other And for these doctrines, men are chiefly beholding to some of those, that making profession of the Lawes, endeavour to make them depend upon their own learning, and not upon the Legislative Power

Imitation of Neighbour Nations.

And as False Doctrine, so also often-times the Example of different Government in a neighbouring Nation, disposeth men to alteration of the forme already setled. So the people of the Jewes were stirred up to reject God, and to call upon the Prophet *Samuel*, for a King after the manner of the Nations So also the lesser Cities of *Greece*, were continually disturbed, with seditions of the Aristocraticall, and Democraticall factions; one part of almost every Common-wealth, desiring to imitate the Lacedæmonians; the other, the Athenians. And I doubt not, but many men, have been contented to see the late troubles in *England*, out of an imitation of the Low Countries; supposing there needed no more to grow rich, than to change, as they had done, the forme of their Government. For the constitution of mans nature, is of it selfe subject to desire novelty. When therefore they are provoked to the same, by the neighbourhood also of those that have been enriched by it, it is almost impossible for them, not to be content with those that solicite them to change; and love the first beginnings, though they be grieved with the continuance of disorder; like hot blouds, that having gotten the itch, tear themselves with their own nayles, till they can endure the smart no longer.

Imitation of the Greeks, and Romans

And as to Rebellion in particular against Monarchy; one of the most frequent causes of it, is the Reading of the books of Policy, and Histories of the antient Greeks, and Romans; from which, young men, and all others that are unprovided of the Antidote of solid Reason, receiving a strong, and delightfull impression, of the great exploits of warre, atchieved by the Conductors of their Armies, receive withall a pleasing Idea, of all they have done besides, and imagine their great prosperity, not to have proceeded from the æmulation of particular men, but from the vertue of their popular forme of government. Not considering the frequent Seditions, and Civill warres, produced by the imperfection of their Policy From the reading, I say, of such books, men have undertaken to kill their Kings, because the Greek and [171] Latine writers, in their books, and discourses of Policy, make it lawfull, and laudable, for any man so to do; provided before he do it, he call him Tyrant. For they say not *Regicide*, that is, killing of a King, but *Tyrannicide*, that is, killing of a Tyrant is lawfull From the same books, they that live under a Monarch conceive an opinion, that the Subjects in a Popular Common-wealth enjoy Liberty, but that in a Monarchy they are all Slaves I say, they that live under a Monarchy conceive such an opinion, not they that live under a Popular Government: for they find no such matter. In summe, I cannot imagine, how any thing can be more prejudiciall to a Monarchy, than the allowing of such books to be publikely read, without present applying such correctives of discreet Masters, as are fit to take away their Venime: Which Venime I will not doubt to compare to the biting of a mad Dogge, which is a disease the Physicians call *Hydrophobia*, or *fear of Water*. For as he that is so bitten, has a continuall torment of thirst, and yet abhorreth water; and is in such an estate, as if the poyson endeavoured to convert him into a Dogge So when a Monarchy is once bitten to the quick, by those Democraticall writers, that continually snarle at that estate; it wanteth nothing more than a strong Monarch, which neverthelesse out of a certain *Tyrannophobia*, or feare of being strongly governed, when they have him, they abhorre.

As there have been Doctors, that hold there be three Soules in a man, so there be also that think there may be more Soules, (that is, more Soveraigns,) than one, in a Common-wealth; and set up a *Supremacy* against the *Soveraignty*; *Canons* against *Lawes*; and a *Ghostly Authority* against the *Civill*; working on mens minds, with words and distinctions, that of themselves signifie nothing, but bewray (by their obscurity) that there walketh (as some think invisibly) another Kingdome, as it were a Kingdome of Fayries, in the dark. Now seeing it is manifest, that the Civill Power, and the Power of the Common-wealth is the same thing; and that Supremacy, and the Power of making Canons, and granting Faculties, implyeth a Common-wealth; it followeth, that where one is Soveraign, another Supreme; where one can make Lawes, and another make Canons; there must needs be two Common-wealths, of one & the same Subjects; which is a Kingdome divided in it selfe, and cannot stand. For notwithstanding the insignificant distinction of *Temporall*, and *Ghostly*, they are still two Kingdomes, and every Subject is subject to two Masters. For seeing the *Ghostly* Power challengeth the Right to declare what is Sinne it challengeth by consequence to declare what is Law, (Sinne being nothing but the transgression of the Law,) and again, the Civill Power challenging to declare what is Law, every Subject must obey two Masters, who both will have their Commands be observed as Law; which is impossible. Or, if it be but one Kingdome, either the *Civill*, which is the Power of the Common-wealth, must be subordinate to the *Ghostly*, and then there is no Soveraignty but the *Ghostly*; or the *Ghostly* must be subordinate to the *Temporall*, and then there is no *Supremacy* but the *Temporall*. When therefore these two Powers oppose one another, the Common-wealth cannot but be in great danger of Civill warre, and [172]
Dissolution. For the *Civill* Authority being more visible, and standing in the cleerer light of naturall reason, cannot choose but draw to it in all times a very considerable

part of the people · And the *Spirituall*, though it stand in the darknesse of Schoole distinctions, and hard words; yet because the fear of Darknesse, and Ghosts, is greater than other fears, cannot want a party sufficient to Trouble, and sometimes to Destroy a Common-wealth, And this is a Disease which not unfitly may be compared to the Epilepsie, or Falling-sicknesse (which the Jewes took to be one kind of possession by Spirits) in the Body Naturall. For as in this Disease, there is an unnaturall spirit, or wind in the head that obstructeth the roots of the Nerves, and moving them violently, taketh away the motion which naturally they should have from the power of the Soule in the Brain, and thereby causeth violent, and irregular motions (which men call Convulsions) in the parts; insomuch as he that is seized therewith, falleth down sometimes into the water, and sometimes into the fire, as a man deprived of his senses, so also in the Body Politique, when the spirituall power, moveth the Members of a Common-wealth, by the terrour of punishments, and hope of rewards (which are the Nerves of it,) otherwise than by the Civill Power (which is the Soule of the Common-wealth) they ought to be moved; and by strange, and hard words suffocates their understanding, it must needs thereby Distract the people, and either Overwhelm the Common-wealth with Oppression, or cast it into the Fire of a Civill warre.

Mixt Government.

Sometimes also in the meerly Civill government, there be more than one Soule: As when the Power of levying mony, (which is the Nutritive faculty,) has depended on a generall Assembly; the Power of conduct and command, (which is the Motive faculty,) on one man, and the Power of making Lawes, (which is the Rationall faculty,) on the accidentall consent, not onely of those two, but also of a third, This endangereth the Common-wealth, somtimes for want of consent to good Lawes; but most often for want of such Nourishment, as is necessary to Life, and Motion. For although few perceive, that such government, is not government, but division of the Common-wealth into three Factions, and call it mixt Monarchy; yet the truth is, that it is not one independent Common-wealth, but three independent

Factions; nor one Representative Person, but three In the Kingdome of God, there may be three Persons independent, without breach of unity in God that Reigneth; but where men Reigne, that be subject to diversity of opinions, it cannot be so And therefore if the King bear the person of the People, and the generall Assembly bear also the person of the People, and another Assembly bear the person of a Part of the people, they are not one Person, nor one Soveraign, but three Persons, and three Soveraigns.

To what Disease in the Naturall Body of man I may exactly compare this irregularity of a Common-wealth, I know not. But I have seen a man, that had another man growing out of his side, with an head, armes, breast, and stomach, of his own If he had had another man [173] growing out of his other side, the comparison might then have been exact

Want of Mony

Hitherto I have named such Diseases of a Common-wealth, as are of the greatest, and most present danger There be other, not so great; which neverthelesse are not unfit to be observed At first, the difficulty of raising Mony, for the necessary uses of the Common-wealth, especially in the approach of warre. This difficulty ariseth from the opinion, that every Subject hath of a Propriety in his lands and goods, exclusive of the Soveraigns Right to the use of the same From whence it commeth to passe, that the Soveraign Power, which foreseeth the necessities and dangers of the Common-wealth, (finding the passage of mony to the publique Treasure obstructed, by the tenacity of the people,) whereas it ought to extend it selfe, to encounter, and prevent such dangers in their beginnings, contracteth it selfe as long as it can, and when it cannot longer, struggles with the people by stratagems of Law, to obtain little summes, which not sufficing, he is fain at last violently to open the way for present supply, or Perish, and being put often to these extremities, at last reduceth the people to their due temper; or else the Common-wealth must perish. Insomuch as we may compare this Distemper very aptly to an Ague; wherein, the fleshy parts being congealed, or by venomous matter obstructed; the Veins which by their naturall course empty themselves into the Heart, are not (as they ought to be) supplyed from the Arteries, whereby there succeedeth at first a cold contraction, and trembling of the limbes; and afterwards a hot, and strong endeavour of the Heart, to force a passage for the Bloud; and before it can do that, contenteth it selfe with the small refreshments of such things as coole for a time, till (if Nature be strong enough) it break at last the contumacy of the parts obstructed, and dissipateth the venome into sweat: or (if Nature be too weak) the Patient dyeth.

Monopolies and abuses of Publicans Again, there is sometimes in a Common-wealth, a Disease, which resembleth the Pleurisie; and that is, when the Treasure of the Common-wealth, flowing out of its due course, is gathered together in too much abundance in one, or a few private men, by Monopolies, or by Farmes of the Publique Revenues; in the same manner as the Blood in a Pleurisie, getting into the Membrane of the breast, breedeth there an Inflammation, accompanied with a Fever, and painfull stitches

Popular men. Also, the Popularity of a potent Subject, (unlesse the Commonwealth have very good caution of his fidelity,) is a dangerous Disease, because the people (which should receive their motion from the Authority of the Soveraign,) by the flattery, and by the reputation of an ambitious man, are drawn away from their obedience to the Lawes, to follow a man, of whose vertues, and designes they have no knowledge. And this is commonly of more danger in a Popular Government, than in a Monarchy; because an Army is of so great force, and multitude, as it may easily be made believe, they are the People. By
[174] this means it was, that *Julius Cæsar*, who was set up by the People against the Senate, having won to himselfe the affections of his Army, made himselfe Master, both of Senate and People And this proceeding of popular, and ambitious men, is plain Rebellion, and may be resembled to the effects of Witchcraft

Excessive greatnesse of a Town, multitude of Corporations Another infirmity of a Common-wealth, is the immoderate greatnesse of a Town, when it is able to furnish out of its own Circuit, the number, and expence of a great Army: As also the great number of Corporations; which are as it were many lesser Common-wealths in the bowels of a greater, like wormes in the entrayles of a naturall man. To which may be added, the Liberty of Disputing against absolute Power, by pretenders to Politicall Prudence; which though bred for the most part in the Lees of the people, yet animated by False Doctrines, are perpetually medling with the Fundamentall Lawes, to the molestation of the Common-wealth; like the little Wormes, which Physicians call *Ascarides*.

Liberty of disputing against Soveraign Power.

We may further adde, the insatiable appetite, or *Bulimia*, of enlarging Dominion; with the incurable *Wounds* thereby many times received from the enemy; And the *Wens*, of ununited conquests, which are many times a burthen, and with lesse danger lost, than kept; As also the *Lethargy* of Ease, and *Consumption* of Riot and Vain Expence

Dissolution of the Common-wealth.

Lastly, when in a warre (forraign, or intestine,) the enemies get a finall Victory; so as (the forces of the Common-wealth keeping the field no longer) there is no farther protection of Subjects in their loyalty; then is the Common-wealth DISSOLVED, and every man at liberty to protect himselfe by such courses as his own discretion shall suggest unto him. For the Soveraign, is the publique Soule, giving Life and Motion to the Common-wealth; which expiring, the Members are governed by it no more, than the Carcasse of a man, by his departed (though Immortall) Soule. For though the Right of a Soveraign Monarch cannot be extinguished by the act of another; yet the Obligation of the members may. For he that wants protection, may seek it any where; and when he hath it, is obliged (without fraudulent pretence of having submitted himselfe out of feare,) to protect his Protection as long as he is able. But when the Power of an Assembly is once suppressed, the Right of the same perisheth utterly, because the Assembly it selfe is extinct; and consequently, there is no possibility for the Soveraignty to re-enter.

[175]

CHAP. XXX.

Of the OFFICE *of the Soveraign Representative.*

The Procuration of the Good of the People.

THE OFFICE of the Soveraign, (be it a Monarch, or an Assembly,) consisteth in the end, for which he was trusted with the Soveraign Power, namely the procuration of *the safety of the people*; to which he is obliged by the Law of Nature, and to render an account thereof to God, the Author of that Law, and to none but him. But by Safety here, is not meant a bare Preservation, but also all other Contentments of life, which every man by lawfull Industry, without danger, or hurt to the Common-wealth, shall acquire to himselfe.

By Instruction & Lawes.

And this is intended should be done, not by care applyed to Individualls, further than their protection from injuries, when they shall complain; but by a generall Providence, contained in publique Instruction, both of Doctrine, and Example; and in the making, and executing of good Lawes, to which individuall persons may apply their own cases.

Against the duty of a Soveraign to relinquish any Essentiall Right of Soveraignty:

And because, if the essentiall Rights of Soveraignty (specified before in the eighteenth Chapter) be taken away, the Common-wealth is thereby dissolved, and every man returneth into the condition, and calamity of a warre with every other man, (which is the greatest evill that can happen in this life;) it is the Office of the Soveraign, to maintain those Rights entire; and consequently against his duty, First, to transferre to another, or to lay from himselfe any of them. For he that deserteth the Means, deserteth the Ends; and he deserteth the Means, that being the Soveraign, acknowledgeth himselfe subject to the Civill Lawes; and renounceth the Power of Supreme Judicature; or of making Warre, or Peace by his own Authority; or of Judging of the Necessities of the Common-wealth; or of levying Mony, and Souldiers, when, and as much as in his own conscience he shall judge necessary; or of making Officers, and Ministers both of Warre, and Peace; or of appointing Teachers, and examining what Doctrines are conformable, or contrary to the Defence, Peace, and Good of the people Secondly, it is against his Duty, to let the people be ignorant, or mis-informed of the grounds, and reasons of those his essentiall Rights ; because thereby men are easie to be seduced, and drawn to resist him, when the Common-wealth shall require their use and exercise.

Or not to see the people taught the grounds of them.

And the grounds of these Rights, have the rather need to be diligently, and truly taught ; because they cannot be maintained by any Civill Law, or terrour of legall punishment. For a Civill Law, that shall forbid Rebellion (and such is all resistance to the essentiall Rights of Soveraignty,) is not (as a Civill Law) any obligation, but [176] by vertue onely of the Law of Nature, that forbiddeth the violation of Faith ; which naturall obligation if men know not, they cannot know the Right of any Law the Soveraign maketh And for the Punishment, they take it but for an act of Hostility ; which when they think they have strength enough, they will endeavour by acts of Hostility, to avoyd.

As I have heard some say, that Justice is but a word, without substance , and that whatsoever a man can by force, or art, acquire to himselfe, (not onely in the condition of warre, but also in a Common-wealth,) is his own, which I have already shewed to be false : So there be also that maintain, that there are no grounds, nor Principles of Reason, to sustain those essentiall Rights, which make Soveraignty absolute. For if there were, they would have been found out in some place, or other , whereas we see, there has not hitherto been any Commonwealth, where those Rights have been acknowledged, or challenged Wherein they argue as ill, as if the Savage people of America, should deny there were any grounds, or Principles of Reason, so to build a house, as to last as long as the materials, because they never yet saw any so well built. Time, and Industry, produce every day new knowledge. And as the art of well building, is derived from Principles of Reason, observed by industrious men, that had long studied the nature of materials, and the divers effects of figure, and proportion, long after mankind began (though poorly) to build . So, long time after men have begun to constitute Common-

Objection of those that say there are no Principles of Reason for absolute Soveraignty.

wealths, imperfect, and apt to relapse into disorder, there may, Principles of Reason be found out, by industrious meditation, to make their constitution (excepting by externall violence) everlasting. And such are those which I have in this discourse set forth : Which whether they come not into the sight of those that have Power to make use of them, or be neglected by them, or not, concerneth my particular interest, at this day, very little. But supposing that these of mine are not such Principles of Reason ; yet I am sure they are Principles from Authority of Scripture ; as I shall make it appear, when I shall come to speak of the Kingdome of God, (administred by *Moses*,) over the Jewes, his peculiar people by Covenant.

Objection from the Incapacity of the vulgar.

But they say again, that though the Principles be right, yet Common people are not of capacity enough to be made to understand them. I should be glad, that the Rich, and Potent Subjects of a Kingdome, or those that are accounted the most Learned, were no lesse incapable than they But all men know, that the obstructions to this kind of doctrine, proceed not so much from the difficulty of the matter, as from the interest of them that are to learn Potent men, digest hardly any thing that setteth up a Power to bridle their affections ; and Learned men, any thing that discovereth their errours, and thereby lesseneth their Authority : whereas the Common-peoples minds, unlesse they be tainted with dependance on the Potent, or scribbled over with the opinions of their Doctors, are like clean paper, fit to receive whatsoever by Publique Authority shall be imprinted in them. Shall whole Nations be brought to
[177] *acquiesce* in the great Mysteries of Christian Religion, which are above Reason ; and millions of men be made believe, that the same Body may be in innumerable places, at one and the same time, which is against Reason ; and shall not men be able, by their teaching, and preaching, protected by the Law, to make that received, which is so consonant to Reason, that any unprejudicated man, needs no more to learn it, than to hear it ? I conclude therefore, that in the instruction of the people in the Essentiall Rights (which are the Naturall, and

Fundamentall Lawes) of Soveraignty, there is no difficulty, (whilest a Soveraign has his Power entire,) but what proceeds from his own fault, or the fault of those whom he trusteth in the administration of the Common-wealth; and consequently, it is his Duty, to cause them so to be instructed, and not onely his Duty, but his Benefit also, and Security, against the danger that may arrive to himselfe in his naturall Person, from Rebellion.

Subjects are to be taught, not to affect change of Government.

And (to descend to particulars) the People are to be taught, First, that they ought not to be in love with any forme of Government they see in their neighbour Nations, more than with their own, nor (whatsoever present prosperity they behold in Nations that are otherwise governed than they,) to desire change. For the prosperity of a People ruled by an Aristocraticall, or Democraticall assembly, commeth not from Aristocracy, nor from Democracy, but from the Obedience, and Concord of the Subjects: nor do the people flourish in a Monarchy, because one man has the right to rule them, but because they obey him. Take away in any kind of State, the Obedience, (and consequently the Concord of the People,) and they shall not onely not flourish, but in short time be dissolved. And they that go about by disobedience, to doe no more than reforme the Common-wealth, shall find they do thereby destroy it; like the foolish daughters of *Peleus* (in the fable;) which desiring to renew the youth of their decrepit Father, did by the Counsell of *Medea*, cut him in pieces, and boyle him, together with strange herbs, but made not of him a new man This desire of change, is like the breach of the first of Gods Commandements: For there God sayes, *Non habebis Deos alienos*; Thou shalt not have the Gods of other Nations; and in another place concerning *Kings*, that they are *Gods*.

Nor adhere (against the Soveraign) to Popular men,

Secondly, they are to be taught, that they ought not to be led with admiration of the vertue of any of their fellow Subjects, how high soever he stand, nor how conspicuously soever he shine in the Common-wealth; nor of any Assembly, (except the Soveraign Assembly,) so as to deferre to them any obedience, or honour, appropriate to the Soveraign onely, whom (in their particular stations)

they represent; nor to receive any influence from them, but such as is conveighed by them from the Soveraign Authority. For that Soveraign, cannot be imagined to love his People as he ought, that is not Jealous of them, but suffers them by the flattery of Popular men, to be seduced from their loyalty, as they have often been, not onely secretly, but openly, so as to proclaime Marriage with them *in facie Ecclesiæ* by Preachers; and by pub-
[178] lishing the same in the open streets: which may fitly be compared to the violation of the second of the ten Commandements.

Nor to Dispute the Soveraign Power.

Thirdly, in consequence to this, they ought to be informed, how great a fault it is, to speak evill of the Soveraign Representative, (whether One man, or an Assembly of men,) or to argue and dispute his Power, or any way to use his Name irreverently, whereby he may be brought into Contempt with his People, and their Obedience (in which the safety of the Common-wealth consisteth) slackened. Which doctrine the third Commandement by resemblance pointeth to.

And to have dayes set apart to learn their Duty:

Fourthly, seeing people cannot be taught this, nor when 'tis taught, remember it, nor after one generation past, so much as know in whom the Soveraign Power is placed, without setting a part from their ordinary labour, some certain times, in which they may attend those that are appointed to instruct them; It is necessary that some such times be determined, wherein they may assemble together, and (after prayers and praises given to God, the Soveraign of Soveraigns) hear those their Duties told them, and the Positive Lawes, such as generally concern them all, read and expounded, and be put in mind of the Authority that maketh them Lawes. To this end had the *Jewes* every seventh day, a *Sabbath*, in which the Law was read and expounded, and in the solemnity whereof they were put in mind, that their King was God; that having created the world in six dayes, he rested the seventh day; and by their resting on it from their labour, that that God was their King, which redeemed them from their servile, and painfull labour in *Egypt*, and gave them a time, after they had rejoyced in God, to take joy also in themselves, by lawfull recreation.

So that the first Table of the Commandements, is spent all, in setting down the summe of Gods absolute Power; not onely as God, but as King by pact, (in peculiar) of the Jewes; and may therefore give light, to those that have Soveraign Power conferred on them by the consent of men, to see what doctrine they Ought to teach their Subjects.

And to Honour their Parents.

And because the first instruction of Children, dependeth on the care of their Parents; it is necessary that they should be obedient to them, whilest they are under their tuition; and not onely so, but that also afterwards (as gratitude requireth,) they acknowledge the benefit of their education, by externall signes of honour. To which end they are to be taught, that originally the Father of every man was also his Soveraign Lord, with power over him of life and death; and that the Fathers of families, when by instituting a Common-wealth, they resigned that absolute Power, yet it was never intended, they should lose the honour due unto them for their education. For to relinquish such right, was not necessary to the Institution of Soveraign Power; nor would there be any reason, why any man should desire to have children, or take the care to nourish, and instruct them, if they were afterwards to have no other benefit from them, than from other men. And this accordeth with the fifth Commandement.

And to avoyd doing of Injury:

Again, every Soveraign Ought to cause Justice to be [179]
taught, which (consisting in taking from no man what is his,) is as much as to say, to cause men to be taught not to deprive their Neighbours, by violence, or fraud, of any thing which by the Soveraign Authority is theirs. Of things held in propriety, those that are dearest to a man are his own life, & limbs; and in the next degree (in most men,) those that concern conjugall affection; and after them riches and means of living. Therefore the People are to be taught, to abstain from violence to one anothers person, by private revenges; from violation of conjugall honour; and from forcible rapine, and fraudulent surreption of one anothers goods For which purpose also it is necessary they be shewed the evill consequences of false Judgement, by corruption either of

Judges or Witnesses, whereby the distinction of propriety is taken away, and Justice becomes of no effect: all which things are intimated in the sixth, seventh, eighth, and ninth Commandements.

And to do all this sincerely from the heart.

Lastly, they are to be taught, that not onely the unjust facts, but the designes and intentions to do them, (though by accident hindred,) are Injustice; which consisteth in the pravity of the will, as well as in the irregularity of the act. And this is the intention of the tenth Commandement, and the summe of the second Table; which is reduced all to this one Commandement of mutuall Charity, *Thou shalt love thy neighbour as thy selfe:* as the summe of the first Table is reduced to *the love of God*; whom they had then newly received as their King.

The use of Universities.

As for the Means, and Conduits, by which the people may receive this Instruction, wee are to search, by what means so many Opinions, contrary to the peace of Mankind, upon weak and false Principles, have neverthelesse been so deeply rooted in them. I mean those, which I have in the precedent Chapter specified: as That men shall Judge of what is lawfull and unlawfull, not by the Law it selfe, but by their own Consciences; that is to say, by their own private Judgements: That Subjects sinne in obeying the Commands of the Common-wealth, unlesse they themselves have first judged them to be lawfull: That their Propriety in their riches is such, as to exclude the Dominion, which the Common-wealth hath over the same: That it is lawfull for Subjects to kill such, as they call Tyrants: That the Soveraign Power may be divided, and the like, which come to be instilled into the People by this means. They whom necessity, or covetousnesse keepeth attent on their trades, and labour; and they, on the other side, whom superfluity, or sloth carrieth after their sensuall pleasures, (which two sorts of men take up the greatest part of Man-kind,) being diverted from the deep meditation, which the learning of truth, not onely in the matter of Naturall Justice, but also of all other Sciences necessarily requireth, receive the Notions of their duty, chiefly from Divines in the Pulpit, and partly from such of their Neighbours, or familiar acquaintance, as having the

Faculty of discoursing readily, and plausibly, seem wiser and better learned in cases of Law, and Conscience, than themselves. And the Divines, and such others as make shew of Learning, derive their knowledge from the Universities, and from the Schooles of Law, or from the Books, which by men eminent in those Schooles, and Universities have been published It is therefore manifest, that the Instruction of the people, dependeth wholly, on the right teaching of Youth in the Universities. But are not (may some man say) the Universities of *England* learned enough already to do that ? or is it you will undertake to teach the Universities ? Hard questions Yet to the first, I doubt not to answer ; that till towards the later end of *Henry the eighth*, the Power of the Pope, was alwayes upheld against the Power of the Common-wealth, principally by the Universities ; and that the doctrines maintained by so many Preachers, against the Soveraign Power of the King, and by so many Lawyers, and others, that had their education there, is a sufficient argument, that though the Universities were not authors of those false doctrines, yet they knew not how to plant the true. For in such a contradiction of Opinions, it is most certain, that they have not been sufficiently instructed ; and 'tis no wonder, if they yet retain a relish of that subtile liquor, wherewith they were first seasoned, against the Civill Authority. But to the later question, it is not fit, nor needfull for me to say either I, or No : for any man that sees what I am doing, may easily perceive what I think.

[180]

The safety of the People, requireth further, from him, or them that have the Soveraign Power, that Justice be equally administred to all degrees of People ; that is, that as well the rich, and mighty, as poor and obscure persons, may be righted of the injuries done them , so as the great, may have no greater hope of impunity, when they doe violence, dishonour, or any Injury to the meaner sort, than when one of these, does the like to one of them . For in this consisteth Equity . to which, as being a Precept of the Law of Nature, a Soveraign is as much subject, as any of the meanest of his People All breaches of the Law, are offences against the Common-wealth: but there be some, that are also against private Persons. Those that concern the Common-wealth onely, may without breach of Equity be pardoned; for every man may pardon what is done against himselfe, according to his own discretion. But an offence against a private man, cannot in Equity be pardoned, without the consent of him that is injured; or reasonable satisfaction.

The Inequality of Subjects, proceedeth from the Acts of Soveraign Power; and therefore has no more place in the presence of the Soveraign; that is to say, in a Court of Justice, then the Inequality between Kings, and their Subjects, in the presence of the King of Kings. The honour of great Persons, is to be valued for their beneficence, and the aydes they give to men of inferiour rank, or not at all. And the violences, oppressions, and injuries they do, are not extenuated, but aggravated by the greatnesse of their persons; because they have least need to commit them. The consequences of this partiality towards the great, proceed in this manner. Impunity maketh Insolence; Insolence Hatred; and Hatred, an Endeavour to pull down all oppressing and contumelious greatnesse, though with the ruine of the Common-wealth.

[181] *Equall Taxes* To Equall Justice, appertaineth also the Equall imposition of Taxes; the Equality whereof dependeth not on the Equality of riches, but on the Equality of the debt, that every man oweth to the Common-wealth for his defence. It is not enough, for a man to labour for the maintenance of his life; but also to fight, (if need be,) for the securing of his labour. They must either do as the Jewes did after their return from captivity, in re-edifying the Temple, build with one hand, and hold the Sword in the other; or else they must hire others to fight for them. For the Impositions, that are layd on the People by the Soveraign Power, are nothing else but the Wages, due to them that hold the publique Sword, to defend private men in the exercise of severall Trades, and Callings. Seeing then the benefit that every one receiveth thereby, is the enjoyment of life, which is equally dear to poor, and rich; the debt which a poor

man oweth them that defend his life, is the same which a rich man oweth for the defence of his ; saving that the rich, who have the service of the poor, may be debtors not onely for their own persons, but for many more. Which considered, the Equality of Imposition, consisteth rather in the Equality of that which is consumed, than of the riches of the persons that consume the same. For what reason is there, that he which laboureth much, and sparing the fruits of his labour, consumeth little, should be more charged, then he that living idlely, getteth little, and spendeth all he gets , seeing the one hath no more protection from the Common-wealth, then the other ? But when the Impositions, are layd upon those things which men consume, every man payeth Equally for what he useth : Nor is the Common-wealth defrauded, by the luxurious waste of private men.

Publique Charity.

And whereas many men, by accident unevitable, become unable to maintain themselves by their labour , they ought not to be left to the Charity of private persons ; but to be provided for, (as far-forth as the necessities of Nature require, by the Lawes of the Common-wealth For as it is Uncharitablenesse in any man, to neglect the impotent ; so it is in the Soveraign of a Common-wealth, to expose them to the hazard of such uncertain Charity.

Prevention of Idlenesse.

But for such as have strong bodies, the case is otherwise : they are to be forced to work ; and to avoyd the excuse of not finding employment, there ought to be such Lawes, as may encourage all manner of Arts ; as Navigation, Agriculture, Fishing, and all manner of Manifacture that requires labour. The multitude of poor, and yet strong people still encreasing, they are to be transplanted into Countries not sufficiently inhabited : where neverthelesse, they are not to exterminate those they find there , but constrain them to inhabit closer together, and not range a great deal of ground, to snatch what they find ; but to court each little Plot with art and labour, to give them their sustenance in due season. And when all the world is overcharged with Inhabitants, then the last remedy of all is Warre ; which provideth for every man, by Victory, or Death.

To the care of the Soveraign, belongeth the making of Good Lawes. But what is a good Law? By a Good Law, [182] I mean not a Just Law: for no Law can be Unjust. The Law is made by the Soveraign Power, and all that is done by such Power, is warranted, and owned by every one of the people; and that which every man will have so, no man can say is unjust. It is in the Lawes of a Common-wealth, as in the Lawes of Gaming: whatsoever the Gamesters all agree on, is Injustice to none of them. A good Law is that, which is *Needfull*, for the *Good of the People*, and withall *Perspicuous*.

Good Lawes what.

Such as are Necessary.

For the use of Lawes, (which are but Rules Authorised) is not to bind the People from all Voluntary actions; but to direct and keep them in such a motion, as not to hurt themselves by their own impetuous desires, rashnesse, or indiscretion; as Hedges are set, not to stop Travellers, but to keep them in the way. And therefore a Law that is not Needfull, having not the true End of a Law, is not Good. A Law may be conceived to be Good, when it is for the benefit of the Soveraign; though it be not Necessary for the People; but it is not so. For the good of the Soveraign and People, cannot be separated. It is a weak Soveraign, that has weak Subjects; and a weak People, whose Soveraign wanteth Power to rule them at his will. Unnecessary Lawes are not good Lawes; but trapps for Mony: which where the right of Soveraign Power is acknowledged, are superfluous; and where it is not acknowledged, unsufficient to defend the People.

Such as are Perspicuous.

The Perspicuity, consisteth not so much in the words of the Law it selfe, as in a Declaration of the Causes, and Motives, for which it was made. That is it, that shewes us the meaning of the Legislator; and the meaning of the Legislator known, the Law is more easily understood by few, than many words. For all words, are subject to ambiguity; and therefore multiplication of words in the body of the Law, is multiplication of ambiguity: Besides it seems to imply, (by too much diligence,) that whosoever can evade the words, is without the compasse of the Law. And this is a cause of many unnecessary Processes. For when I consider how short were the

Lawes of antient times; and how they grew by degrees still longer; me thinks I see a contention between the Penners, and Pleaders of the Law; the former seeking to circumscribe the later; and the later to evade their circumscriptions; and that the Pleaders have got the Victory. It belongeth therefore to the Office of a Legislator, (such as is in all Common-wealths the Supreme Representative, be it one Man, or an Assembly,) to make the reason Perspicuous, why the Law was made; and the Body of the Law it selfe, as short, but in as proper, and significant termes, as may be.

Punishments

It belongeth also to the Office of the Soveraign, to make a right application of Punishments, and Rewards. And seeing the end of punishing is not revenge, and discharge of choler; but correction, either of the offender, or of others by his example; the severest Punishments are to be inflicted for those Crimes, that are of most Danger to the Publique; such as are those which proceed from malice to the Government established; those that spring from contempt of Justice; those that provoke Indignation in the Multitude; and those, which unpunished, [183] seem Authorised, as when they are committed by Sonnes, Servants, or Favorites of men in Authority: For Indignation carrieth men, not onely against the Actors, and Authors of Injustice; but against all Power that is likely to protect them; as in the case of *Tarquin*; when for the Insolent act of one of his Sonnes, he was driven out of *Rome*, and the Monarchy it selfe dissolved But Crimes of Infirmity; such as are those which proceed from great provocation, from great fear, great need, or from ignorance whether the Fact be a great Crime, or not, there is place many times for Lenity, without prejudice to the Common-wealth; and Lenity when there is such place for it, is required by the Law of Nature. The Punishment of the Leaders, and teachers in a Commotion; not the poore seduced People, when they are punished, can profit the Common-wealth by their example. To be severe to the People, is to punish that ignorance, which may in great part be imputed to the Soveraign, whose fault it was, they were no better instructed.

Rewards. In like manner it belongeth to the Office, and Duty of the Soveraign, to apply his Rewards alwayes so, as there may arise from them benefit to the Common-wealth: wherein consisteth their Use, and End; and is then done, when they that have well served the Common-wealth, are with as little expence of the Common Treasure, as is possible, so well recompenced, as others thereby may be encouraged, both to serve the same as faithfully as they can, and to study the arts by which they may be enabled to do it better. To buy with Mony, or Preferment, from a Popular ambitious Subject, to be quiet, and desist from making ill impressions in the mindes of the People, has nothing of the nature of Reward; (which is ordained not for disservice, but for service past;) nor a signe of Gratitude, but of Fear: nor does it tend to the Benefit, but to the Dammage of the Publique. It is a contention with Ambition, like that of *Hercules* with the Monster *Hydra*, which having many heads, for every one that was vanquished, there grew up three. For in like manner, when the stubbornnesse of one Popular man, is overcome with Reward, there arise many more (by the Example) that do the same Mischiefe, in hope of like Benefit: and as all sorts of Manifacture, so also Malice encreaseth by being vendible. And though sometimes a Civill warre, may be differred, by such wayes as that, yet the danger growes still the greater, and the Publique ruine more assured. It is therefore against the Duty of the Soveraign, to whom the Publique Safety is committed, to Reward those that aspire to greatnesse by disturbing the Peace of their Country, and not rather to oppose the beginnings of such men, with a little danger, than after a longer time with greater.

Counsellours. Another Businesse of the Soveraign, is to choose good Counsellours; I mean such, whose advice he is to take in the Government of the Common-wealth. For this word Counsell, *Consilium*, corrupted from *Considium*, is of a large signification, and comprehendeth all Assemblies of men that sit together, not onely to deliberate what is to be done hereafter, but also to judge of Facts
[184] past, and of Law for the present. I take it here in the

first sense onely: And in this sense, there is no choyce of Counsell, neither in a Democracy, nor Aristocracy; because the persons Counselling are members of the person Counselled. The choyce of Counsellours therefore is proper to Monarchy; In which, the Soveraign that endeavoureth not to make choyce of those, that in every kind are the most able, dischargeth not his Office as he ought to do. The most able Counsellours, are they that have least hope of benefit by giving evill Counsell, and most knowledge of those things that conduce to the Peace, and Defence of the Common-wealth. It is a hard matter to know who expecteth benefit from publique troubles, but the signes that guide to a just suspicion, is the soothing of the people in their unreasonable, or irremediable grievances, by men whose estates are not sufficient to discharge their accustomed expences, and may easily be observed by any one whom it concerns to know it. But to know, who has most knowledge of the Publique affaires, is yet harder; and they that know them, need them a great deale the lesse. For to know, who knowes the Rules almost of any Art, is a great degree of the knowledge of the same Art; because no man can be assured of the truth of anothers Rules, but he that is first taught to understand them. But the best signes of Knowledge of any Art, are, much conversing in it, and constant good effects of it. Good Counsell comes not by Lot, nor by Inheritance; and therefore there is no more reason to expect good Advice from the rich, or noble, in matter of State, than in delineating the dimensions of a fortresse; unlesse we shall think there needs no method in the study of the Politiques, (as there does in the study of Geometry,) but onely to be lookers on; which is not so For the Politiques is the harder study of the two. Whereas in these parts of *Europe*, it hath been taken for a Right of certain persons, to have place in the highest Councell of State by Inheritance; it is derived from the Conquests of the antient Germans; wherein many absolute Lords joyning together to conquer other Nations, would not enter in to the Confederacy, without such Priviledges, as might be marks of difference in time following, between their Posterity, and the Posterity of their Subjects; which Priviledges being inconsistent with the Soveraign Power, by the favour of the Soveraign, they may seem to keep; but contending for them as their Right, they must needs by degrees let them go, and have at last no further honour, then adhæreth naturally to their abilities.

And how able soever be the Counsellours in any affaire, the benefit of their Counsell is greater, when they give every one his Advice, and the reasons of it apart, than when they do it in an Assembly, by way of Orations, and when they have præmeditated, than when they speak on the sudden; both because they have more time, to survey the consequences of action; and are lesse subject to be carried away to contradiction, through Envy, Emulation, or other Passions arising from the difference of opinion.

The best Counsell, in those things that concern not other Nations, but onely the ease, and benefit the Sub-
[185] jects may enjoy, by Lawes that look onely inward, is to be taken from the generall informations, and complaints of the people of each Province, who are best acquainted with their own wants, and ought therefore, when they demand nothing in derogation of the essentiall Rights of Soveraignty, to be diligently taken notice of. For without those Essentiall Rights, (as I have often before said,) the Common-wealth cannot at all subsist.

Commanders. A Commander of an Army in chiefe, if he be not Popular, shall not be beloved, nor feared as he ought to be by his Army; and consequently cannot performe that office with good successe. He must therefore be Industrious, Valiant, Affable, Liberall and Fortunate, that he may gain an opinion both of sufficiency, and of loving his Souldiers. This is Popularity, and breeds in the Souldiers both desire, and courage, to recommend themselves to his favour; and protects the severity of the Generall, in punishing (when need is) the Mutinous, or negligent Souldiers. But this love of Souldiers, (if caution be not given of the Commanders fidelity,) is a dangerous thing to Soveraign Power; especially when it is in the hands of an Assembly not popular. It belongeth therefore to the safety of the People, both that they be good Conductors, and faithfull Subjects, to whom the Soveraign Commits his Armies.

But when the Soveraign himselfe is Popular; that is, reverenced and beloved of his People, there is no danger at all from the Popularity of a Subject. For Souldiers are never so generally unjust, as to side with their Captain; though they love him, against their Soveraign, when they love not onely his Person, but also his Cause. And therefore those, who by violence have at any time suppressed the Power of their lawfull Soveraign, before they could settle themselves in his place, have been alwayes put to the trouble of contriving their Titles, to save the People from the shame of receiving them. To have a known Right to Soveraign Power, is so popular a quality, as he that has it needs no more, for his own part, to turn the hearts of his Subjects to him, but that they see him able absolutely to govern his own Family: Nor, on the part of his enemies, but a disbanding of their Armies For the greatest and most active part of Mankind, has never hetherto been well contented with the present.

Concerning the Offices of one Soveraign to another, which are comprehended in that Law, which is commonly called the *Law of Nations*, I need not say any thing in this place; because the Law of Nations, and the Law of Nature, is the same thing And every Soveraign hath the same Right, in procuring the safety of his People, that any particular man can have, in procuring the safety of his own Body And the same Law, that dictateth to men that have no Civil Government, what they ought to do, and what to avoyd in regard of one another, dictateth the same to Common-wealths, that is, to the Consciences of Soveraign Princes, and Soveraign Assemblies; there being no Court of Naturall Justice, but in the Conscience onely, where not Man, but God raigneth; whose Lawes, (such of them as oblige all Mankind,) in respect of God, as he is the Author of Nature, are *Naturall*; and in respect of the same God, [186]
as he is King of Kings, are *Lawes* But of the Kingdome of God, as King of Kings, and as King also of a peculiar People, I shall speak in the rest of this discourse.

CHAP. XXXI.

Of the KINGDOME OF GOD BY NATURE.

The scope of the following Chapters.

THAT the condition of meer Nature, that is to say, of absolute Liberty, such as is theirs, that neither are Soveraigns, nor Subjects, is Anarchy, and the condition of Warre: That the Præcepts, by which men are guided to avoyd that condition, are the Lawes of Nature: That a Common-wealth, without Soveraign Power, is but a word, without substance, and cannot stand: That Subjects owe to Soveraigns, simple Obedience, in all things, wherein their obedience is not repugnant to the Lawes of God. I have sufficiently proved, in that which I have already written. There wants onely, for the entire knowledge of Civill duty, to know what are those Lawes of God. For without that, a man knows not, when he is commanded any thing by the Civill Power, whether it be contrary to the Law of God, or not: and so, either by too much civill obedience, offends the Divine Majesty, or through feare of offending God, transgresses the commandements of the Common-wealth. To avoyd both these Rocks, it is necessary to know what are the Lawes Divine. And seeing the knowledge of all Law, dependeth on the knowledge of the Soveraign Power; I shall say something in that which followeth, of the KINGDOME OF GOD

Psal.96 1. *God is King, let the Earth rejoyce,* saith the Psalmist.
Psal 98.1. And again, *God is King though the Nations be angry; and he that sitteth on the Cherubins, though the earth be moved.*

Who are subjects in the kingdome of God.

Whether men will or not, they must be subject alwayes to the Divine Power. By denying the Existence, or Providence of God, men may shake off their Ease, but not their Yoke But to call this Power of God, which extendeth it selfe not onely to Man, but also to Beasts, and Plants, and Bodies inanimate, by the name of Kingdome, is but a metaphoricall use of the word. For he onely is properly said to Raigne, that governs his Subjects, by his Word, and by promise of Rewards to those that obey it, and by threatning them with Punishment that obey it not. Subjects therefore in the Kingdome of God, are not Bodies Inanimate, nor creatures Irrationall, because they understand no Precepts as his: Nor Atheists; nor they that believe not that God has any care of the actions of mankind; because they acknowledge no Word for his, nor have hope of his rewards, or fear of his threatnings. They therefore that believe there is a God that governeth the world, and hath given [187] Præcepts, and propounded Rewards, and Punishments to Mankind, are Gods Subjects; all the rest, are to be understood as Enemies.

A Threefold Word of God, Reason, Revelation, Prophecy.

To rule by Words, requires that such Words be manifestly made known; for else they are no Lawes: For to the nature of Lawes belongeth a sufficient, and clear Promulgation, such as may take away the excuse of Ignorance; which in the Lawes of men is but of one onely kind, and that is, Proclamation, or Promulgation by the voyce of man But God declareth his Lawes three wayes; by the Dictates of *Naturall Reason*, by *Revelation*, and by the *Voyce* of some *man*, to whom by the operation of Miracles, he procureth credit with the rest. From hence there ariseth a triple Word of God, *Rational*, *Sensible*, and *Prophetique:* to which Correspondeth a triple Hearing; *Right Reason*, *Sense Supernaturall*, and *Faith* As for Sense Supernaturall, which consisteth in Revelation, or Inspiration, there have not been any Universall Lawes so given, because God speaketh not in that manner, but to particular persons, and to divers men divers things.

A twofold Kingdome of God, Naturall and Prophetique.

From the difference between the other two kinds of Gods Word, *Rationall*, and *Prophetique*, there may be attributed to God, a two-fold Kingdome, Naturall, and *Prophetique:* Naturall, wherein he governeth as many of Mankind as acknowledge his Providence, by the naturall Dictates of Right Reason; And Prophetique, wherein having chosen out one peculiar Nation (the Jewes) for his Subjects, he governed them, and none but them, not onely by naturall Reason, but by Positive Lawes, which he gave them by the mouths of his holy Prophets Of the Naturall Kingdome of God I intend to speak in this Chapter.

The Right of Gods Soveraignty is derived from his Omnipotence.

The Right of Nature, whereby God reigneth over men, and punisheth those that break his Lawes, is to be derived, not from his Creating them, as if he required obedience, as of Gratitude for his benefits; but from his *Irresistible Power* I have formerly shewn, how the Soveraign Right ariseth from Pact. To shew how the same Right may arise from Nature, requires no more, but to shew in what case it is never taken away. Seeing all men by Nature had Right to All things, they had Right every one to reigne over all the rest. But because this Right could not be obtained by force, it concerned the safety of every one, laying by that Right, to set up men (with Soveraign Authority) by common consent, to rule and defend them. whereas if there had been any man of Power Irresistible; there had been no reason, why he should not by that Power have ruled, and defended both himselfe, and them, according to his own discretion To those therefore whose Power is irresistible, the dominion of all men adhæreth naturally by their excellence of Power; and consequently it is from that Power, that the Kingdome over men, and the Right of afflicting men at his pleasure, belongeth Naturally to God Almighty; not as Creator, and Gracious, but as Omnipotent. And though Punishment be due for Sinne onely, because by that word is understood
[188] Affliction for Sinne; yet the Right of Afflicting, is not alwayes derived from mens Sinne, but from Gods Power.

Sinne not the cause of all Affliction

This question, *Why Evill men often Prosper, and Good men suffer Adversity*, has been much disputed by the Antient, and is the same with this of ours, *by what Right God dispenseth the Prosperities and Adversities of this life*; and is of that difficulty, as it hath shaken the faith not onely of the Vulgar, but of Philosophers, and which is more, of the Saints, concerning the Divine Providence.

Psal 72. ver. 1, 2, 3.

How Good (saith *David*) *is the God of Israel to those that are Upright in Heart; and yet my feet were almost gone, my treadings had well-nigh slipt; for I was grieved at the Wicked, when I saw the Ungodly in such Prosperity.* And *Job*, how earnestly does he expostulate with God, for the many Afflictions he suffered, notwithstanding his

Righteousnesse? This question in the case of *Job*, is decided by God himselfe, not by arguments derived from *Job's* Sinne, but his own Power. For whereas the friends of *Job* drew their arguments from his Affliction to his Sinne, and he defended himselfe by the conscience of his Innocence, God himselfe taketh up the matter, and having justified the Affliction by arguments drawn from his Power, such as this, *Where wast thou when I layd the foundations of the earth*, and the like, both approved *Job's* Innocence, and reproved the Erroneous doctrine of his friends Conformable to this doctrine is the sentence of our Saviour, concerning the man that was born Blind, in these words, *Neither hath this man sinned, nor his fathers; but that the works of God might be made manifest in him.* And though it be said, *That Death entred into the world by sinne*, (by which is meant that if *Adam* had never sinned, he had never dyed, that is, never suffered any separation of his soule from his body,) it follows not thence, that God could not justly have Afflicted him, though he had not Sinned, as well as he afflicteth other living creatures, that cannot sinne.

Job 38. *v.* 4.

Divine Lawes.

Having spoken of the Right of Gods Soveraignty, as grounded onely on Nature; we are to consider next, what are the Divine Lawes, or Dictates of Naturall Reason, which Lawes concern either the naturall Duties of one man to another, or the Honour naturally due to our Divine Soveraign. The first are the same Lawes of Nature, of which I have spoken already in the 14. and 15. Chapters of this Treatise; namely, Equity, Justice, Mercy, Humility, and the rest of the Morall Vertues. It remaineth therefore that we consider, what Præcepts are dictated to men, by their Naturall Reason onely, without other word of God, touching the Honour and Worship of the Divine Majesty.

Honour and Worship what.

Honour consisteth in the inward thought, and opinion of the Power, and Goodnesse of another and therefore to Honour God, is to think as Highly of his Power and Goodnesse, as is possible And of that opinion, the externall signes appearing in the Words, and Actions of men, are called *Worship*; which is one part of that

which the Latines understand by the word *Cultus*: For *Cultus* signifieth properly, and constantly, that labour which a man bestowes on any thing, with a purpose to
[189] make benefit by it. Now those things whereof we make benefit, are either subject to us, and the profit they yeeld, followeth the labour we bestow upon them, as a naturall effect; or they are not subject to us, but answer our labour, according to their own Wills In the first sense the labour bestowed on the Earth, is called *Culture*; and the education of Children a *Culture* of their mindes. In the second sense, where mens wills are to be wrought to our purpose, not by Force, but by Compleasance, it signifieth as much as Courting, that is, a winning of favour by good offices; as by praises, by acknowledging their Power, and by whatsoever is pleasing to them from whom we look for any benefit. And this is properly *Worship*: in which sense *Publicola*, is understood for a Worshipper of the People; and *Cultus Dei*, for the Worship of God.

Severall signes of Honour.

From internall Honour, consisting in the opinion of Power and Goodnesse, arise three Passions; *Love*, which hath reference to Goodnesse; and *Hope*, and *Fear*, that relate to Power. And three parts of externall worship; *Praise*, *Magnifying*, and *Blessing*: The subject of Praise, being Goodnesse; the subject of Magnifying, and Blessing, being Power, and the effect thereof Felicity. Praise, and Magnifying are signified both by Words, and Actions: By Words, when we say a man is Good, or Great By Actions, when we thank him for his Bounty, and obey his Power. The opinion of the Happinesse of another, can onely be expressed by words.

Worship Naturall and Arbitrary.

There be some signes of Honour, (both in Attributes and Actions,) that be Naturally so; as amongst Attributes, *Good*, *Just*, *Liberall*, and the like; and amongst Actions, *Prayers*, *Thanks*, and *Obedience* Others are so by Institution, or Custome of men; and in some times and places are Honourable; in others Dishonourable; in others Indifferent: such as are the Gestures in Salutation, Prayer, and Thanksgiving, in different times and places, differently used. The former is *Naturall*; the later *Arbitrary* Worship.

And of Arbitrary Worship, there bee two differences: For sometimes it is a *Commanded*, sometimes *Voluntary* Worship. Commanded, when it is such as hee requireth, who is Worshipped: Free, when it is such as the Worshipper thinks fit. When it is Commanded, not the words, or gesture, but the obedience is the Worship. But when Free, the Worship consists in the opinion of the beholders: for if to them the words, or actions by which we intend honour, seem ridiculous, and tending to contumely; they are no Worship; because no signes of Honour; and no signes of Honour; because a signe is not a signe to him that giveth it, but to him to whom it is made; that is, to the spectator. *Worship Commanded and Free.*

Again, there is a *Publique*, and a *Private* Worship. Publique, is the Worship that a Common-wealth performeth, as one Person. Private, is that which a Private person exhibiteth. Publique, in respect of the whole Common-wealth, is Free; but in respect of Particular men it is not so. Private, is in secret Free; but in the sight of the multitude, it is never without some Restraint, either from the Lawes, or from the Opinion of men; which is contrary to the nature of Liberty. *Worship Publique and Private.*

The End of Worship amongst men, is Power. For where a man seeth another worshipped, he supposeth him powerfull, and is the readier to obey him; which makes his Power greater. But God has no Ends: the worship we do him, proceeds from our duty, and is directed according to our capacity, by those rules of Honour, that Reason dictateth to be done by the weak to the more potent men, in hope of benefit, for fear of dammage, or in thankfulnesse for good already received from them. *The end of Worship.* [190]

That we may know what worship of God is taught us by the light of Nature, I will begin with his Attributes. Where, First, it is manifest, we ought to attribute to him *Existence*. For no man can have the will to honour that, which he thinks not to have any Beeing. *Attributes of Divine Honour.*

Secondly, that those Philosophers, who sayd the World, or the Soule of the World was God, spake unworthily of him, and denyed his Existence: For by God, is understood the cause of the World; and to say the World is God, is to say there is no cause of it, that is, no God.

Thirdly, to say the World was not Created, but Eternall, (seeing that which is Eternall has no cause,) is to deny there is a God.

Fourthly, that they who attributing (as they think) Ease to God, take from him the care of Man-kind; take from him his Honour: for it takes away mens love, and fear of him, which is the root of Honour.

Fifthly, in those things that signifie Greatnesse, and Power; to say he is *Finite*, is not to Honour him: For it is not a signe of the Will to Honour God, to attribute to him lesse than we can, and Finite, is lesse than we can; because to Finite, it is easie to adde more.

Therefore to attribute *Figure* to him, is not Honour; for all Figure is Finite:

Nor to say we conceive, and imagine, or have an *Idea* of him, in our mind: for whatsoever we conceive is Finite:

Nor to attribute to him *Parts*, or *Totality*; which are the Attributes onely of things Finite:

Nor to say he is in this, or that *Place*: for whatsoever is in Place, is bounded, and Finite.

Nor that he is *Moved*, or *Resteth*: for both these Attributes ascribe to him Place.

Nor that there be more Gods than one, because it implies them all Finite: for there cannot be more than one Infinite

Nor to ascribe to him (unlesse Metaphorically, meaning not the Passion, but the Effect) Passions that partake of Griefe, as *Repentance, Anger, Mercy*: or of Want; as *Appetite, Hope, Desire*, or of any Passive faculty: For Passion, is Power limited by somewhat else.

And therefore when we ascribe to God a *Will*, it is not to be understood, as that of Man, for a *Rationall Appetite*, but as the Power, by which he effecteth every thing

Likewise when we attribute to him *Sight*, and other acts of Sense; as also *Knowledge*, and *Understanding*; which in us is nothing else, but a tumult of the mind, raised by externall things that presse the organicall parts of mans body. For there is no such thing in God; and being things that depend on naturall causes, cannot be attributed to him.

Hee that will attribute to God, nothing but what is warranted by naturall Reason, must either use such Negative Attributes, as *Infinite, Eternall, Incomprehensible*, or Superlatives, as *Most High, most Great*, and the like; or Indefinite, as *Good, Just, Holy, Creator*; and in such sense, as if he meant not to declare what he is, (for that were to circumscribe him within the limits of our Fancy,) but how much wee admire him, and how ready we would be to obey him; which is a signe of Humility, and of a Will to honour him as much as we can. For there is but one Name to signifie our Conception of his Nature, and that is, I AM: and but one Name of his Relation to us, and that is *God*; in which is contained Father, King, and Lord [191]

Actions that are signes of Divine Honour.

Concerning the actions of Divine Worship, it is a most generall Precept of Reason, that they be signes of the Intention to Honour God, such as are, First, *Prayers*: For not the Carvers, when they made Images, were thought to make them Gods, but the People that *Prayed* to them.

Secondly, *Thanksgiving*; which differeth from Prayer in Divine Worship, no otherwise, than that Prayers precede, and Thanks succeed the benefit; the end both of the one, and the other, being to acknowledge God, for Author of all benefits, as well past, as future.

Thirdly, *Gifts*, that is to say, *Sacrifices*, and *Oblations*, (if they be of the best,) are signes of Honour: for they are Thanksgivings.

Fourthly, *Not to swear by any but God*, is naturally a signe of Honour: for it is a confession that God onely knoweth the heart; and that no mans wit, or strength can protect a man against Gods vengeance on the perjured.

Fifthly, it is a part of Rationall Worship, to speak Considerately of God; for it argues a Fear of him, and Fear, is a confession of his Power. Hence followeth, That the name of God is not to be used rashly, and to no purpose; for that is as much, as in Vain. And it is to no purpose unlesse it be by way of Oath, and by order of the Common-wealth. to make Judgements certain; or between Common-wealths, to avoyd Warre And that disputing of Gods nature is contrary to his Honour: For it is supposed, that in this naturall Kingdome of God, there is no other way to know any thing, but by naturall Reason; that is, from the Principles of naturall Science; which are so farre from teaching us any thing of Gods nature, as they cannot teach us our own nature, nor the nature of the smallest creature living. And therefore, when men out of the Principles of naturall Reason, dispute of the Attributes of God, they but dishonour him: For in the Attributes which we give to God, we are not to consider the signification of Philosophicall Truth; but the signification of Pious Intention, to do him the greatest Honour we are able. From the want of which consideration, have proceeded the volumes of disputation about the nature of God, that tend not to his Honour, but to the honour of our own wits, and learning; and are nothing else but inconsiderate, and vain abuses of his Sacred Name

Sixthly, in *Prayers*, *Thanksgiving*, *Offerings* and *Sacrifices*, it is a Dictate of naturall Reason, that they be
[192] every one in his kind the best, and most significant of Honour. As for example, that Prayers, and Thanksgiving, be made in Words and Phrases, not sudden, nor light, nor Plebeian; but beautifull, and well composed; For else we do not God as much honour as we can. And therefore the Heathens did absurdly, to worship Images for Gods: But their doing it in Verse, and with Musick, both of Voyce, and Instruments, was reasonable. Also that the Beasts they offered in sacrifice, and the Gifts they offered, and their actions in Worshipping, were full of submission, and commemorative of benefits received, was according to reason, as proceeding from an intention to honour him.

Seventhly, Reason directeth not onely to worship God in Secret; but also, and especially, in Publique, and in the sight of men: For without that, (that which in honour is most acceptable) the procuring others to honour him, is lost

Lastly, Obedience to his Lawes (that is, in this case to the Lawes of Nature,) is the greatest worship of all. For as Obedience is more acceptable to God than Sacrifice; so also to set light by his Commandements, is the greatest of all contumelies And these are the Lawes of that Divine Worship, which naturall Reason dictateth to private men.

Publique Worship consisteth in Uniformity.

But seeing a Common-wealth is but one Person, it ought also to exhibite to God but one Worship; which then it doth, when it commandeth it to be exhibited by Private men, Publiquely. And this is Publique Worship; the property whereof, is to be *Uniforme*· For those actions that are done differently, by different men, cannot be said to be a Publique Worship. And therefore, where many sorts of Worship be allowed, proceeding from the different Religions of Private men, it cannot be said there is any Publique Worship, nor that the Common-wealth is of any Religion at all.

All Attributes depend on the Lawes Civill.

And because words (and consequently the Attributes of God) have their signification by agreement, and constitution of men; those Attributes are to be held significative of Honour, that men intend shall so be; and whatsoever may be done by the wills of particular men, where there is no Law but Reason, may be done by the will of the Common-wealth, by Lawes Civill. And because a Common-wealth hath no Will, nor makes no Lawes, but those that are made by the Will of him, or them that have the Soveraign Power, it followeth, that those Attributes which the Soveraign ordaineth, in the Worship of God, for signes of Honour, ought to be taken and used for such, by private men in their publique Worship

Not all Actions.

But because not all Actions are signes by Constitution; but some are Naturally signes of Honour, others of Contumely, these later (which are those that men are ashamed to do in the sight of them they reverence) cannot be made by humane power a part of Divine worship; nor the former (such as are decent, modest, humble Behaviour) ever be separated from it. But whereas there be an infinite number of Actions, and Gestures, of an indifferent nature; such of them as the

Common-wealth shall ordain to be Publiquely and Universally in use, as signes of Honour, and part of Gods
[193] Worship, are to be taken and used for such by the Subjects. And that which is said in the Scripture, *It is better to obey God than men*, hath place in the kingdome of God by Pact, and not by Nature.

Naturall Punishments. Having thus briefly spoken of the Naturall Kingdome of God, and his Naturall Lawes, I will adde onely to this Chapter a short declaration of his Naturall Punishments. There is no action of man in this life, that is not the beginning of so long a chayn of Consequences, as no humane Providence, is high enough, to give a man a prospect to the end. And in this Chayn, there are linked together both pleasing and unpleasing events; in such manner, as he that will do any thing for his pleasure, must engage himselfe to suffer all the pains annexed to it; and these pains, are the Naturall Punishments of those actions, which are the beginning of more Harme than Good And hereby it comes to passe, that Intemperance, is naturally punished with Diseases, Rashnesse, with Mischances, Injustice, with the Violence of Enemies; Pride, with Ruine; Cowardise, with Oppression; Negligent government of Princes, with Rebellion; and Rebellion, with Slaughter. For seeing Punishments are consequent to the breach of Lawes; Naturall Punishments must be naturally consequent to the breach of the Lawes of Nature; and therfore follow them as their naturall, not arbitrary effects.

The Conclusion of the Second Part And thus farre concerning the Constitution, Nature, and Right of Soveraigns; and concerning the Duty of Subjects, derived from the Principles of Naturall Reason. And now, considering how different this Doctrine is, from the Practise of the greatest part of the world, especially of these Western parts, that have received their Morall learning from *Rome*, and *Athens*, and how much depth of Morall Philosophy is required, in them that have the Administration of the Soveraign Power; I am at the point of believing this my labour, as uselesse, as the Common-wealth of *Plato*; For he also is of opinion that it is impossible for the disorders of State, and change of Governments by Civill Warre, ever to be taken away, till Soveraigns be Philosophers. But when I consider again, that the Science of Naturall Justice, is the onely Science necessary for Soveraigns, and their principall Ministers; and that they need not be charged with the Sciences Mathematicall, (as by *Plato* they are,) further, than by good Lawes to encourage men to the study of them; and that neither *Plato*, nor any other Philosopher hitherto, hath put into order, and sufficiently or probably proved all the Theoremes of Morall doctrine, that men may learn thereby, both how to govern, and how to obey; I recover some hope, that one time or other, this writing of mine, may fall into the hands of a Soveraign, who will consider it himselfe, (for it is short, and I think clear,) without the help of any interessed, or envious Interpreter; and by the exercise of entire Soveraignty, in protecting the Publique teaching of it, convert this Truth of Speculation, into the Utility of Practice

[195]

OF A CHRISTIAN COMMON-WEALTH.

CHAP. XXXII.

Of the Principles of CHRISTIAN POLITIQUES.

The Word of God delivered by Prophets is the main principle of Christian Politiques.

I HAVE derived the Rights of Soveraigne Power, and the duty of Subjects hitherto, from the Principles of Nature onely; such as Experience has found true, or Consent (concerning the use of words) has made so; that is to say, from the nature of Men, known to us by Experience, and from Definitions (of such words as are Essentiall to all Politicall reasoning) universally agreed on. But in that I am next to handle, which is the Nature and Rights of a CHRISTIAN COMMON-WEALTH, whereof there dependeth much upon Supernaturall Revelations of the Will of God; the ground of my Discourse must be, not only the Naturall Word of God, but also the Propheticall

Yet is not naturall Reason to be renounced.

Neverthelesse, we are not to renounce our Senses, and Experience; nor (that which is the undoubted Word of God) our naturall Reason For they are the talents which he hath put into our hands to negotiate, till the coming again of our blessed Saviour; and therefore not to be folded up in the Napkin of an Implicite Faith, but employed in the purchase of Justice, Peace, and true Religion. For though there be many things in Gods Word above Reason; that is to say, which cannot by naturall reason be either demonstrated, or confuted; yet there is nothing contrary to it, but when it seemeth so, the fault is either in our unskilfull Interpretation, or erroneous Ratiocination.

Therefore, when any thing therein written is too hard for our examination, wee are bidden to captivate our understanding to the Words, and not to labour in sifting out a Philosophicall truth by Logick, of such mysteries as are not comprehensible, nor fall under any rule of naturall science. For it is with the mysteries of our Religion, as with wholsome pills for the sick, which swallowed whole, have the vertue to cure; but chewed, are for the most part cast up again without effect.

What it is to captivate the Understanding.

But by the Captivity of our Understanding, is not [196] meant a Submission of the Intellectuall faculty, to the Opinion of any other man, but of the Will to Obedience, where obedience is due. For Sense, Memory, Understanding, Reason, and Opinion are not in our power to change; but alwaies, and necessarily such, as the things we see, hear, and consider suggest unto us; and therefore are not effects of our Will, but our Will of them. We then Captivate our Understanding and Reason, when we forbear contradiction; when we so speak, as (by lawfull Authority) we are commanded; and when we live accordingly; which in sum, is Trust, and Faith reposed in him that speaketh, though the mind be incapable of any Notion at all from the words spoken.

How God speaketh to men.

When God speaketh to man, it must be either immediately, or by mediation of another man, to whom he had formerly spoken by himself immediately. How God speaketh to a man immediately, may be understood by those well enough, to whom he hath so spoken; but how the same should be understood by another, is hard, if not impossible to know. For if a man pretend to me, that God hath spoken to him supernaturally, and immediately, and I make doubt of it, I cannot easily perceive what argument he can produce, to oblige me to beleeve it. It is true, that if he be my Soveraign, he may oblige me to obedience, so, as not by act or word to declare I beleeve him not; but not to think any otherwise then my reason perswades me. But if one that hath not such authority over me, shall pretend the same, there is nothing that exacteth either beleefe, or obedience.

For to say that God hath spoken to him in the Holy Scripture, is not to say God hath spoken to him immediately, but by mediation of the Prophets, or of the Apostles, or of the Church, in such manner as he speaks to all other Christian men. To say he hath spoken to him in a Dream, is no more then to say he dreamed that God spake to him; which is not of force to win beleef from any man, that knows dreams are for the most part naturall, and may proceed from former thoughts, and such dreams as that, from selfe conceit, and foolish arrogance, and false opinion of a mans own godlinesse, or other vertue, by which he thinks he hath merited the favour of extraordinary Revelation. To say he hath seen a Vision, or heard a Voice, is to say, that he hath dreamed between sleeping and waking: for in such manner a man doth many times naturally take his dream for a vision, as not having well observed his own slumbering. To say he speaks by supernaturall Inspiration, is to say he finds an ardent desire to speak, or some strong opinion of himself, for which hee can alledge no naturall and sufficient reason. So that though God Almighty can speak to a man, by Dreams, Visions, Voice, and Inspiration, yet he obliges no man to beleeve he hath so done to him that pretends it, who (being a man) may erre, and (which is more) may lie.

By what marks Prophets are known. How then can he, to whom God hath never revealed his Wil immediately (saving by the way of natural reason) know when he is to obey, or not to obey his Word, delivered by him, that sayes he is a Prophet? Of 400
1 Kings 22 Prophets, of whom the K of *Israel* asked counsel, con-
[197] cerning the warre he made against *Ramoth Gilead*, only
1 Kings 13. *Micaiah* was a true one. The Prophet that was sent to prophecy against the Altar set up by *Jeroboam*, though a true Prophet, and that by two miracles done in his presence appears to be a Prophet sent from God, was yet deceived by another old Prophet, that perswaded him as from the mouth of God, to eat and drink with him. If one Prophet deceive another, what certainty is there of knowing the will of God, by other way than that of Reason? To which I answer out of the Holy Scripture, that there be two marks, by which together, not asunder, a true Prophet is to be known. One is the doing of miracles; the other is the not teaching any other Religion than that which is already established. Asunder (I say) neither of these is sufficient. *If a Prophet rise amongst*

you, or a Dreamer of dreams, and shall pretend the doing Deut. 13.
of a miracle, and the miracle come to passe ; if he say, Let v. 1, 2, 3,
us follow strange Gods, which thou hast not known, thou 4, 5.
shalt not hearken to him, &c. But that Prophet and Dreamer of dreams shall be put to death, because he hath spoken to you to Revolt from the Lord your God In which words two things are to be observed ; First, that God wil not have miracles alone serve for arguments, to approve the Prophets calling ; but (as it is in the third verse) for an experiment of the constancy of our adherence to himself. For the works of the *Egyptian* Sorcerers, though not so great as those of *Moses*, yet were great miracles. Secondly, that how great soever the miracle be, yet if it tend to stir up revolt against the King, or him that governeth by the Kings authority, he that doth such miracle, is not to be considered otherwise than as sent to make triall of their allegiance. For these words, *revolt from the Lord your God*, are in this place equivalent to *revolt from your King*. For they had made God their King by pact at the foot of Mount *Sinai* ; who ruled them by *Moses* only ; for he only spake with God, and from time to time declared Gods Commandements to the people In like manner, after our Saviour Christ had made his Disciples acknowledge him for the *Messiah*, (that is to say, for Gods anointed, whom the nation of the *Jews* daily expected for their King, but refused when he came,) he omitted not to advertise them of the danger of
miracles *There shall arise* (saith he) *false Christs, and* Mat. 24.
false Prophets, and shall doe great wonders and miracles, 24.
even to the seducing (if it were possible) of the very Elect By which it appears, that false Prophets may have the power of miracles , yet are wee not to take their doctrin
for Gods Word. St. *Paul* says further to the *Galatians*, Gal 1. 8.
that *if himself, or an Angell from heaven preach another Gospel to them, than he had preached, let him be accursed.* That Gospel was, that Christ was King ; so that all preaching against the power of the King received, in consequence to these words, is by St *Paul* accursed. For his speech is addressed to those, who by his preaching had already received *Jesus* for the *Christ*, that is to say, for King of the *Jews*.

The marks of a Prophet in the old law, [198] *Miracles, and Doctrine conformable to the law.*

And as Miracles, without preaching that Doctrine which God hath established; so preaching the true Doctrine, without the doing of Miracles, is an unsufficient argument of immediate Revelation. For if a man that teacheth not false Doctrine, should pretend to bee a Prophet without shewing any Miracle, he is never the more to bee regarded for his pretence, as is evident by *Deut.* 18. *v.* 21, 22 *If thou say in thy heart, How shall we know that the Word* (of the Prophet) *is not that which the Lord hath spoken. When the Prophet shall have spoken in the name of the Lord, that which shall not come to passe, that's the word which the Lord hath not spoken, but the Prophet has spoken it out of the pride of his own heart, fear him not.* But a man may here again ask, When the Prophet hath foretold a thing, how shal we know whether it will come to passe or not? For he may foretel it as a thing to arrive after a certain long time, longer then the time of mans life; or indefinitely, that it will come to passe one time or other: in which case this mark of a Prophet is unusefull; and therefore the miracles that oblige us to beleeve a Prophet, ought to be confirmed by an immediate, or a not long deferr'd event. So that it is manifest, that the teaching of the Religion which God hath established, and the shewing of a present Miracle, joined together, were the only marks whereby the Scripture would have a true Prophet, that is to say, immediate Revelation to be acknowledged; neither of them being singly sufficient to oblige any other man to regard what he saith.

Miracles ceasing, Prophets cease, and the Scripture supplies their place.

Seeing therefore Miracles now cease, we have no sign left, whereby to acknowledge the pretended Revelations, or Inspirations of any private man; nor obligation to give ear to any Doctrine, farther than it is conformable to the Holy Scriptures, which since the time of our Saviour, supply the place, and sufficiently recompense the want of all other Prophecy; and from which, by wise and learned interpretation, and carefull ratiocination, all rules and precepts necessary to the knowledge of our duty both to God and man, without Enthusiasme, or supernaturall Inspiration, may easily be deduced. And this Scripture is it, out of which I am to take the

Principles of my Discourse, concerning the Rights of those that are the Supream Governors on earth, of Christian Common-wealths; and of the duty of Christian Subjects towards their Soveraigns. And to that end, I shall speak in the next Chapter, of the Books, Writers, Scope and Authority of the Bible.

CHAP. XXXIII. [199]

Of the Number, Antiquity, Scope, Authority, and Interpreters of the Books of Holy SCRIPTURE.

Of the Books of Holy Scripture.

BY the Books of Holy SCRIPTURE, are understood those, which ought to be the *Canon*, that is to say, the Rules of Christian life And because all Rules of life, which men are in conscience bound to observe, are Laws, the question of the Scripture, is the question of what is Law throughout all Christendome, both Naturall, and Civill. For though it be not determined in Scripture, what Laws every Christian King shall constitute in his own Dominions; yet it is determined what laws he shall not constitute. Seeing therefore I have already proved, that Soveraigns in their own Dominions are the sole Legislators; those Books only are Canonicall, that is, Law, in every nation, which are established for such by the Soveraign Authority. It is true, that God is the Soveraign of all Soveraigns; and therefore, when he speaks to any Subject, he ought to be obeyed, whatsoever any earthly Potentate command to the contrary. But the question is not of obedience to God, but of *when*, and *what* God hath said; which to Subjects that have no supernaturall revelation, cannot be known, but by that naturall reason, which guided them, for the obtaining of Peace and Justice, to obey the authority of their severall Common-wealths; that is to say, of their lawfull Soveraigns. According to this obligation, I can acknowledge no other Books of the Old Testament, to be Holy Scripture, but those which have been commanded to be acknowledged for such, by the Authority

of the Church of *England*. What Books these are, is sufficiently known, without a Catalogue of them here; and they are the same that are acknowledged by St *Jerome*, who holdeth the rest, namely, the *Wisdome of Solomon*, *Ecclesiasticus*, *Judith*, *Tobias*, the first and the second of *Maccabees*, (though he had seen the first in *Hebrew*) and the third and fourth of *Esdras*, for *Apocrypha*. Of the Canonicall, *Josephus* a learned *Jew*, that wrote in the time of the Emperour *Domitian*, reckoneth *twenty two*, making the number agree with the *Hebrew* Alphabet. St. *Jerome* does the same, though they reckon them in different manner. For *Josephus* numbers *five* Books of *Moses*, *thirteen* of *Prophets*, that writ the History of their own times (which how it agrees with the Prophets writings contained in the Bible wee shall see hereafter), and *four* of *Hymnes* and Morall Precepts But St. *Jerome* reckons *five* Books of *Moses*, *eight* of *Prophets*, and *nine* of other Holy writ, which he calls of *Hagiographa*. The *Septuagint*, who were 70. learned men of the *Jews*, sent for by *Ptolemy* King of *Egypt*, to translate the *Jewish*
[200] law, out of the *Hebrew* into the *Greek*, have left us no other for holy Scripture in the *Greek* tongue, but the same that are received in the Church of *England*.

As for the Books of the New Testament, they are equally acknowledged for Canon by all Christian Churches, and by all Sects of Christians, that admit any Books at all for Canonicall.

Their Antiquity

Who were the originall writers of the severall Books of Holy Scripture, has not been made evident by any sufficient testimony of other History, (which is the only proof of matter of fact): nor can be by any arguments of naturall Reason: for Reason serves only to convince the truth (not of fact, but) of consequence. The light therefore that must guide us in this question, must be that which is held out unto us from the Bookes themselves · And this light, though it shew us not the writer of every book, yet it is not unusefull to give us knowledge of the time, wherein they were written.

And first, for the *Pentateuch*, it is not argument enough that they were written by *Moses*, because they are called the five Books of *Moses*; no more than these titles,

The Book of *Joshua*, the Book of *Judges*, the Book of *Ruth*, and the Books of the *Kings*, are arguments sufficient to prove, that they were written by *Joshua*, by the *Judges*, by *Ruth*, and by the *Kings*. For in titles of Books, the subject is marked, as often as the writer. The *History of Livy*, denotes the Writer; but the *History of Scanderbeg*, is denominated from the subject. We read in the last Chapter of *Deuteronomie, ver.* 6. concerning the sepulcher of *Moses, that no man knoweth of his sepulcher to this day*, that is, to the day wherein those words were written. It is therefore manifest, that those words were written after his interrement. For it were a strange interpretation, to say *Moses* spake of his own sepulcher (though by Prophecy), that it was not found to that day, wherein he was yet living. But it may perhaps be alledged, that the last Chapter only, not the whole *Pentateuch*, was written by some other man, but the rest not: Let us therefore consider that which we find in the Book of *Genesis, chap.* 12. *ver.* 6. *And* Abraham *passed through the land to the place of* Sichem, *unto the plain of* Moreh, *and the* Canaanite *was then in the land*; which must needs bee the words of one that wrote when the *Canaanite* was not in the land; and consequently, not of *Moses*, who dyed before he came into it. Likewise *Numbers* 21. *ver.* 14. the Writer citeth another more ancient Book, Entituled, *The Book of the Warres of the Lord*, wherein were registred the Acts of *Moses*, at the Red-sea, and at the brook of *Arnon*. It is therefore sufficiently evident, that the five Books of *Moses* were written after his time, though how long after it be not so manifest.

The Pentateuch not written by Moses.

But though *Moses* did not compile those Books entirely, and in the form we have them; yet he wrote all that which hee is there said to have written as for example, the Volume of the Law, which is contained, as it seemeth, in the 11 of *Deuteronomie*, and the following Chapters to the 27. which was also commanded to be written on stones, in their entry into the land of *Canaan*. And this did *Moses* himself write, and deliver to the Priests and Elders of *Israel*, to be read every seventh year to all *Israel*, at their assembling in the feast

Deut 31.9.

[201]

of Tabernacles. And this is that Law which God commanded, that their Kings (when they should have established that form of Government) should take a copy
Deut 31. 26. of from the Priests and Levites; and which *Moses* commanded the Priests and Levites to lay in the side of the Arke; and the same which having been lost,
2 *King* 22 8 & 23 1, 2, 3. was long time after found again by *Hilkiah*, and sent to King *Josias*, who causing it to be read to the People, renewed the Covenant between God and them.

The Book of Joshua written after his time.

That the Book of *Joshua* was also written long after the time of *Joshua*, may be gathered out of many places of the Book it self. *Joshua* had set up twelve stones in the middest of *Jordan*, for a monument of their
Josh. 4. 9 passage; of which the Writer saith thus, *They are there unto this day*; for *unto this day*, is a phrase that signifieth
Josh. 5. 9. a time past, beyond the memory of man In like manner, upon the saying of the Lord, that he had rolled off from the people the Reproach of *Egypt*, the Writer saith, *The place is called* Gilgal *unto this day*; which to have said in the time of *Joshua* had been improper. So also the name of the Valley of *Achor*, from the trouble that
Josh 7.26. *Achan* raised in the Camp, the Writer saith, *remaineth unto this day*; which must needs bee therefore long after the time of *Joshua*. Arguments of this kind there be many other; as *Josh*. 8 29 13. 13. 14 14. 15. 63

The Booke of Judges and Ruth written long after the Captivity.

The same is manifest by like arguments of the Book of *Judges*, chap. 1. 21, 26. 6 24 10. 4 15. 19 17. 6. and *Ruth* 1 1. but especially *Judg* 18 30. where it is said, that Jonathan *and his sonnes were Priests to the Tribe of* Dan, *untill the day of the captivity of the land.*

The like of the Bookes of Samuel

That the Books of *Samuel* were also written after his own time, there are the like arguments, 1 *Sam*. 5. 5. 7. 13, 15. 27. 6. & 30. 25. where, after *David* had adjudged equall part of the spoiles, to them that guarded the Ammunition, with them that fought, the Writer saith, *He made it a Statute and an Ordinance to* Israel
2 *Sam*. 6 4. *to this day*. Again, when *David* (displeased, that the Lord had slain *Uzzah*, for putting out his hand to sustain the Ark,) called the place *Perez-Uzzah*. the Writer saith, it is called so *to this day*: the time

therefore of the writing of that Book, must be long after the time of the fact, that is, long after the time of *David*.

The Books of the Kings, and the Chronicles.

As for the two Books of the *Kings*, and the two Books of the *Chronicles*, besides the places which mention such monuments, as the Writer saith, remained till his own days; such as are 1 *Kings* 9.13. 9.21. 10.12. 12.19. 2 *Kings* 2.22. 8.22. 10.27. 14.7. 16.6. 17.23. 17.34. 17 41. 1 *Chron.* 4. 41. 5.26. It is argument sufficient they were written after the captivity in *Babylon*, that the History of them is continued till that time. For the Facts Registred are alwaies more ancient than the Register; and much more ancient than such Books as make mention of, and quote the Register; as these Books doe in divers places, referring the Reader to the Chronicles of the Kings of *Juda*, to the Chronicles of the Kings of *Israel*, to the Books of the Prophet *Samuel*, of the Prophet *Nathan*, of the Prophet *Ahijah*; to the Vision of *Jehdo*, to the Books of the Prophet *Serveiah*, and of the Prophet *Addo*.

[202]

Ezra and Nehemiah.

The Books of *Esdras* and *Nehemiah* were written certainly after their return from captivity; because their return, the re-edification of the walls and houses of *Jerusalem*, the renovation of the Covenant, and ordination of their policy are therein contained.

Esther

The History of Queen *Esther* is of the time of the Captivity; and therefore the Writer must have been of the same time, or after it.

Job.

The Book of *Job* hath no mark in it of the time wherein it was written: and though it appear sufficiently (*Ezekiel* 14 14. and *James* 5. 11) that he was no fained person; yet the Book it self seemeth not to be a History, but a Treatise concerning a question in ancient time much disputed, *why wicked men have often prospered in this world, and good men have been afflicted*: and it is the more probable, because from the beginning, to the third verse of the third chapter, where the complaint of *Job* beginneth, the *Hebrew* is (as St *Jerome* testifies) in prose; and from thence to the sixt verse of the last chapter in Hexameter Verses; and the rest of that chapter again in prose. So that the dispute is all in verse; and the prose is added, but as a Preface in the beginning, and an Epilogue in the end. But Verse is no usuall stile of such, as either are themselves in great pain, as *Job*; or of such as come to comfort them, as his friends; but in Philosophy, especially morall Philosophy, in ancient time frequent.

The Psalter. The *Psalmes* were written the most part by David, for the use of the Quire. To these are added some Songs of *Moses*, and other holy men; and some of them after the return from the Captivity, as the 137. and the 126 whereby it is manifest that the Psalter was compiled, and put into the form it now hath, after the return of the *Jews* from *Babylon*.

The Proverbs. The *Proverbs*, being a Collection of wise and godly Sayings, partly of *Solomon*, partly of *Agur* the son of *Jakeh*, and partly of the Mother of King *Lemuel*, cannot probably be thought to have been collected by *Solomon*, rather then by *Agur*, or the Mother of *Lemuel*; and that, though the sentences be theirs, yet the collection or compiling them into this one Book, was the work of some other godly man, that lived after them all.

Ecclesiastes and the Canticles. The Books of *Ecclesiastes* and the *Canticles* have nothing that was not *Solomons*, except it be the Titles, or Inscriptions. For *The Words of the Preacher, the Son of* David, *King in* Jerusalem; and, *The Song of Songs, which is Solomon's*, seem to have been made for distinctions sake, then, when the Books of Scripture were gathered into one body of the Law; to the end, that not the Doctrine only, but the Authors also might be extant

The Prophets. Of the Prophets, the most ancient, are *Sophoniah*, *Jonas*, *Amos*, *Hosea*, *Isaiah* and *Michaiah*, who lived in the time of *Amaziah*, and *Azariah*, otherwise *Ozias*, Kings of *Judah*. But the Book of *Jonas* is not properly a Register of his Prophecy, (for that is contained in these few words, *Fourty dayes and* Ninivy *shall be destroyed*,) but a History or Narration of his frowardnesse and disputing Gods commandements, so that there is small probability he should be the Author, seeing he is the subject of it. But the Book of *Amos* is his Prophecy.

Jeremiah, Abdias, Nahum, and *Habakkuk* prophecyed [203]
in the time of *Josiah*.

Ezekiel, Daniel, Aggeus, and *Zacharias,* in the Captivity.

When *Joel* and *Malachi* prophecyed, is not evident by their Writings. But considering the Inscriptions, or Titles of their Books, it is manifest enough, that the whole Scripture of the Old Testament, was set forth in the form we have it, after the return of the *Jews* from their Captivity in *Babylon,* and before the time of *Ptolemæus Philadelphus,* that caused it to bee translated into Greek by seventy men, which were sent him out of *Judea* for that purpose And if the Books of *Apocrypha* (which are recommended to us by the Church, though not for Canonicall, yet for profitable Books for our instruction) may in this point be credited, the Scripture was set forth in the form wee have it in, by *Esdras* , as may appear by that which he himself saith, in the second book, chapt. 14. verse 21, 22, &c. where speaking to God, he saith thus. *Thy law is burnt ; therefore no man knoweth the things which thou hast done, or the works that are to begin. But if I have found Grace before thee, send down the holy Spirit into me, and I shall write all that hath been done in the world, since the beginning, which were written in thy Law, that men may find thy path, and that they which will live in the later days, may live.* And verse 45. *And it came to passe when the forty dayes were fulfilled, that the Highest spake, saying, The first that thou hast written, publish openly, that the worthy and unworthy may read it ; but keep the seventy last, that thou mayst deliver them onely to such as be wise among the people.* And thus much concerning the time of the writing of the Bookes of the Old Testament.

The New Testament. The Writers of the New Testament lived all in lesse then an age after Christs Ascension, and had all of them seen our Saviour, or been his Disciples, except St. *Paul,* and St. *Luke* ; and consequently whatsoever was written by them, is as ancient as the time of the Apostles But the time wherein the Books of the New Testament were received, and acknowledged by the Church to be of their writing, is not altogether so ancient. For, as the Bookes of the Old Testament are derived to us, from no higher

time then that of *Esdras*, who by the direction of Gods Spirit retrived them, when they were lost: Those of the New Testament, of which the copies were not many, nor could easily be all in any one private mans hand, cannot bee derived from a higher time, than that wherein the Governours of the Church collected, approved, and recommended them to us, as the writings of those Apostles and Disciples; under whose names they go. The first enumeration of all the Bookes, both of the Old, and New Testament, is in the Canons of the Apostles, supposed to be collected by *Clement* the first (after St. *Peter*) Bishop of *Rome*. But because that is but supposed, and by many questioned, the Councell of *Laodicea* is the first we know, that recommended the Bible to the then Christian Churches, for the Writings of the Prophets and Apostles: and this Councell was held in the 364. yeer after Christ. At which time, though ambition had so far prevailed on the great Doctors of
[204] the Church, as no more to esteem Emperours, though Christian, for the Shepherds of the people, but for Sheep; and Emperours not Christian, for Wolves; and endeavoured to passe their Doctrine, not for Counsell, and Information, as Preachers; but for Laws, as absolute Governours; and thought such frauds as tended to make the people the more obedient to Christian Doctrine, to be pious; yet I am perswaded they did not therefore falsifie the Scriptures, though the copies of the Books of the New Testament, were in the hands only of the Ecclesiasticks; because if they had had an intention so to doe, they would surely have made them more favorable to their power over Christian Princes, and Civill Soveraignty, than they are. I see not therefore any reason to doubt, but that the Old, and New Testament, as we have them now, are the true Registers of those things, which were done and said by the Prophets, and Apostles. And so perhaps are some of those Books which are called Apocrypha, if left out of the Canon, not for inconformity of Doctrine with the rest, but only because they are not found in the Hebrew For after the conquest of Asia by Alexander the Great, there were few learned Jews, that were not perfect in the Greek

tongue. For the seventy Interpreters that converted the Bible into Greek, were all of them Hebrews; and we have extant the works of *Philo* and *Josephus* both Jews, written by them eloquently in Greek. But it is not the Writer, but the authority of the Church, that maketh a Book Canonicall. And although these Books were *Their Scope.* written by divers men, yet it is manifest the Writers were all indued with one and the same Spirit, in that they conspire to one and the same end, which is the setting forth of the Rights of the Kingdome of *God*, the *Father*, *Son*, and *Holy Ghost*. For the Book of *Genesis*, deriveth the Genealogy of Gods people, from the creation of the World, to the going into Egypt: the other four Books of *Moses*, contain the Election of God for their King, and the Laws which hee prescribed for their Government: The Books of *Joshua*, *Judges*, *Ruth*, and *Samuel*, to the time of *Saul*, describe the acts of Gods people, till the time they cast off Gods yoke, and called for a King, after the manner of their neighbour nations: The rest of the History of the Old Testament, derives the succession of the line of *David*, to the Captivity, out of which line was to spring the restorer of the Kingdome of God, even our blessed Saviour *God the Son*, whose coming was foretold in the Bookes of the Prophets, after whom the Evangelists writt his life, and actions, and his claim to the Kingdome, whilst he lived on earth: and lastly, the Acts, and Epistles of the Apostles, declare the coming of God, the *Holy Ghost*, and the Authority he left with them, and their successors, for the direction of the Jews, and for the invitation of the Gentiles. In summe, the Histories and the Prophecies of the old Testament, and the Gospels and Epistles of the New Testament, have had one and the same scope, to convert men to the obedience of God; 1 in *Moses*, and the Priests; 2. in the man *Christ*; and 3. in the *Apostles* and the successors to Apostolicall power. For these three at several times did represent the person of God: *Moses*, and his successors the High Priests, and Kings of Judah, in the Old Testament [205] *Christ* himself, in the time he lived on earth: and the *Apostles*, and their successors, from the day of Pentecost (when the *Holy Ghost* descended on them) to this day.

The question of the Authority of the Scriptures stated.

It is a question much disputed between the divers sects of Christian Religion, *From whence the Scriptures derive their Authority*; which question is also propounded sometimes in other terms, as, *How wee know them to be the Word of God*, or, *Why we beleeve them to be so*: And the difficulty of resolving it, ariseth chiefly from the impropernesse of the words wherein the question it self is couched. For it is beleeved on all hands, that the first and originall *Author* of them is God; and consequently the question disputed, is not that. Again, it is manifest, that none can know they are Gods Word, (though all true Christians beleeve it,) but those to whom God himself hath revealed it supernaturally; and therefore the question is not rightly moved, of our *Knowledge* of it. Lastly, when the question is propounded of our *Beleefe*; because some are moved to beleeve for one, and others for other reasons, there can be rendred no one generall answer for them all. The question truly stated is, *By what Authority they are made Law.*

Their Authority and Interpretation.

As far as they differ not from the Laws of Nature, there is no doubt, but they are the Law of God, and carry their Authority with them, legible to all men that have the use of naturall reason: but this is no other Authority, then that of all other Morall Doctrine consonant to Reason; the Dictates whereof are Laws, not *made*, but *Eternall*.

If they be made Law by God himselfe, they are of the nature of written Law, which are Laws to them only to whom God hath so sufficiently published them, as no man can excuse himself, by saying, he knew not they were his.

He therefore, to whom God hath not supernaturally revealed, that they are his, nor that those that published them, were sent by him, is not obliged to obey them, by any Authority, but his, whose Commands have already the force of Laws; that is to say, by any other Authority, then that of the Common-wealth, residing in the Soveraign, who only has the Legislative power. Again, if it be not the Legislative Authority of the Common-wealth, that giveth them the force of Laws, it must bee some other Authority derived from God, either private, or publique: if private, it obliges onely him, to whom in particular God hath been pleased to reveale it. For if every man should be obliged, to take for Gods Law, what particular men, on pretence of private Inspiration, or Revelation, should obtrude upon him, (in such a number of men, that out of pride, and ignorance, take their own Dreams, and extravagant Fancies, and Madnesse, for testimonies of Gods Spirit; or out of ambition, pretend to such Divine testimonies, falsely, and contrary to their own consciences,) it were impossible that any Divine Law should be acknowledged. If publique, it is the Authority of the *Common-wealth*, or of the *Church*. But the Church, if it be one person, is the same thing with a Common-wealth of Christians, called a *Common-wealth*, because it consisteth of men united in one person, their Soveraign; and a *Church*, because it consisteth in Christian men, united in one Christian Soveraign. But if the Church be not one person, then it hath no authority at all; it can neither command, nor doe any action at all; nor is capable of having any power, or right to any thing; nor has any Will, Reason, nor Voice; for all these qualities are personall. Now if the whole number of Christians be not contained in one Common-wealth, they are not one person; nor is there an Universall Church that hath any authority over them; and therefore the Scriptures are not made Laws, by the Universall Church: or if it bee one Common-wealth, then all Christian Monarchs, and States are private persons, and subject to bee judged, deposed, and punished by an Universall Soveraigne of all Christendome. So that the question of the Authority of the Scriptures, is reduced to this, *Whether Christian Kings, and the Soveraigne Assemblies in Christian Common-wealths, be absolute in their own Territories, immediately under God, or subject to one Vicar of Christ, constituted over the Universall Church; to bee judged, condemned, deposed, and put to death, as hee shall think expedient, or necessary for the common good.* [206]

Which question cannot bee resolved, without a more particular consideration of the Kingdome of God; from whence also, wee are to judge of the Authority of Interpreting the Scripture. For, whosoever hath a lawfull power over any Writing, to make it Law, hath the power also to approve, or disapprove the interpretation of the same.

[207]

CHAP. XXXIV.

Of the Signification of SPIRIT, ANGEL, *and* INSPIRATION *in the Books of Holy Scripture.*

Body and Spirit how taken in the Scripture.

SEEING the foundation of all true Ratiocination, is the constant Signification of words; which in the Doctrine following, dependeth not (as in naturall science) on the Will of the Writer, nor (as in common conversation) on vulgar use, but on the sense they carry in the Scripture, It is necessary, before I proceed any further, to determine, out of the Bible, the meaning of such words, as by their ambiguity, may render what I am to inferre upon them, obscure, or disputable. I will begin with the words BODY, and SPIRIT, which in the language of the Schools are termed, *Substances, Corporeall,* and *Incorporeall.*

The Word *Body,* in the most generall acceptation, signifieth that which filleth, or occupyeth some certain room, or imagined place; and dependeth not on the imagination, but is a reall part of that we call the *Universe.* For the *Universe,* being the Aggregate of all Bodies, there is no reall part thereof that is not also *Body*; nor any thing properly a *Body,* that is not also part of (that Aggregate of all *Bodies*) the *Universe.* The same also, because Bodies are subject to change, that is to say, to variety of apparence to the sense of living creatures, is called *Substance,* that is to say, *Subject,* to various accidents; as sometimes to be Moved, sometimes to stand Still; and to seem to our senses sometimes Hot, sometimes Cold, sometimes of one Colour, Smel, Tast, or Sound, somtimes of another And this diversity of Seeming, (produced by the diversity of the operation of bodies, on the organs of our sense) we attribute to alterations of the Bodies that operate, & call them *Accidents* of those Bodies. And according to this acceptation of the word, *Substance* and *Body*, signifie the same thing, and therefore *Substance incorporeall* are words, which when they are joined together, destroy one another, as if a man should say, an *Incorporeall Body*.

But in the sense of common people, not all the Universe is called Body, but only such parts thereof as they can discern by the sense of Feeling, to resist their force, or by the sense of their Eyes, to hinder them from a farther prospect. Therefore in the common language of men, *Aire*, and *aeriall substances*, use not to be taken for *Bodies*, but (as often as men are sensible of their effects) are called *Wind*, or *Breath*, or (because the same are called in the Latine *Spiritus*) *Spirits*; as when they call that aeriall substance, which in the body of any living creature, gives it life and motion, *Vitall* and *Animall spirits*. But for those Idols of the brain, which represent Bodies to us, where they are not, as in a Looking-glasse, in a Dream, or to a Distempered brain waking, [208] they are (as the Apostle saith generally of all Idols) nothing; Nothing at all, I say, there where they seem to bee; and in the brain it self, nothing but tumult, proceeding either from the action of the objects, or from the disorderly agitation of the Organs of our Sense. And men, that are otherwise imployed, then to search into their causes, know not of themselves, what to call them; and may therefore easily be perswaded, by those whose knowledge they much reverence, some to call them *Bodies*, and think them made of aire compacted by a power supernaturall, because the sight judges them corporeall; and some to call them *Spirits*, because the sense of Touch discerneth nothing in the place where they appear, to resist their fingers: So that the proper signification of *Spirit* in common speech, is either a subtile, fluid, and invisible Body, or a Ghost, or other Idol or Phantasme of the Imagination. But for metaphoricall significations, there be many. for sometimes it is taken for Disposition or Inclination of the mind; as when for the disposition to controwl the sayings of other men, we say, *a spirit of contradiction*, For *a disposition to uncleannesse, an unclean spirit*; for *perversenesse, a froward spirit*; for *sullennesse, a dumb spirit*, and for *inclination to godlinesse, and Gods service, the Spirit of God*: sometimes for any eminent ability, or extraordinary passion, or disease of the mind, as when *great wisdome* is called the *spirit of wisdome*; and *mad men* are said to be *possessed with a spirit.*

Other signification of *Spirit* I find no where any; and where none of these can satisfie the sense of that word in Scripture, the place falleth not under humane Understanding; and our Faith therein consisteth not in our Opinion, but in our Submission; as in all places where God is said to be a *Spirit*; or where by the *Spirit of God*, is meant God himselfe. For the nature of God is incomprehensible; that is to say, we understand nothing of *what he is*, but only *that he is*; and therefore the Attributes we give him, are not to tell one another, *what he is*. nor to signifie our opinion of his Nature, but our desire to honour him with such names as we conceive most honorable amongst our selves.

The Spirit of God taken in the Scripture sometimes for a Wind, or Breath.

Gen 1. 2 *The Spirit of God moved upon the face of the Waters.* Here if by the *Spirit of God* be meant God himself, then is *Motion* attributed to God, and consequently *Place*, which are intelligible only of Bodies, and not of substances incorporeall; and so the place is above our understanding, that can conceive nothing moved that changes not place, or that has not dimension, and whatsoever has dimension, is Body But the meaning of those words is best understood by the like place, *Gen.* 8. 1. Where when the earth was covered with Waters, as in the beginning, God intending to abate them, and again to discover the dry land, useth the like words, *I will bring my Spirit upon the Earth, and the waters shall be diminished* in which place by *Spirit* is understood a Wind, (that is an Aire or *Spirit moved*,) which might be called (as in the former place) the *Spirit of God*, because it was Gods work.

[209]

Secondly, for extraordinary gifts of the Understanding.

Gen. 41. 38. *Pharaoh* calleth the *Wisdome* of *Joseph*, the *Spirit of God* For *Joseph* having advised him to look out a wise and discreet man, and to set him over the land of Egypt, he saith thus, *Can we find such a man as this is, in whom is the Spirit of God*? And Exod. 28. 3. *Thou shalt speak* (saith God) *to all that are wise hearted, whom I have filled with the Spirit of Wisdome, to make Aaron Garments, to consecrate him.* Where extraordinary Understanding, though but in making Garments, as being the *Gift* of God, is called the *Spirit* of God. The same is found again, *Exod.* 31. 3, 4, 5, 6. and 35 31. And *Isaiah* 11. 2, 3 where the Prophet speaking of the Messiah, saith, *The Spirit of the Lord shall abide upon him, the Spirit of wisdome and understanding, the Spirit of counsell, and fortitude; and the Spirit of the fear of the Lord.* Where manifestly is meant, not so many Ghosts, but so many eminent *graces* that God would give him.

Thirdly, for extraordinary Affections.

In the Book of *Judges*, an extraordinary Zeal, and Courage in the defence of Gods people, is called the *Spirit* of God; as when it excited Othoniel, Gideon, Jephtha, and Samson to deliver them from servitude, *Judg.* 3 10 6. 34. 11. 29. 13. 25. 14. 6, 19. And of *Saul*, upon the newes of the insolence of the Ammonites towards the men of Jabesh Gilead, it is said (1 *Sam.* 11. 6) that *The Spirit of God came upon Saul, and his Anger* (or, as it is in the Latine, *his Fury*) *was kindled greatly* Where it is not probable was meant a Ghost, but an extraordinary *Zeal* to punish the cruelty of the Ammonites In like manner by the *Spirit* of God, that came upon Saul, when hee was amongst the Prophets that praised God in Songs, and Musick (1 *Sam.* 19. 20) is to be understood, not a Ghost, but an unexpected and sudden *zeal* to join with them in their devotion

Fourthly, for the gift of Prediction by Dreams and Visions.

The false Prophet *Zedekiah*, saith to *Micaiah* (1 *Kings* 22. 24.) *Which way went the Spirit of the Lord from me to speak to thee?* Which cannot be understood of a Ghost; for *Micaiah* declared before the Kings of Israel and Judah, the event of the battle, as from a *Vision*, and not as from a *Spirit*, speaking in him.

In the same manner it appeareth, in the Books of the Prophets, that though they spake by the *Spirit* of God, that is to say, by a speciall grace of Prediction; yet their knowledge of the future, was not by a Ghost within them, but by some supernaturall *Dream* or *Vision*.

Fiftly, for Life.

Gen 2. 7 It is said, *God made man of the dust of the Earth, and breathed into his nostrills* (spiraculum vitæ) *the breath of life, and man was made a living soul.* There the *breath of life* inspired by God, signifies no more, but that God gave him life; And (*Job* 27. 3) *as long as the Spirit of God is in my nostrils*; is no more then to say, *as long as I live*. So in *Ezek* 1. 20. *the Spirit of life was in the wheels*, is equivalent to, *the wheels were alive*. And (*Ezek*. 2 30.) *the Spirit entred into me, and set me on my feet*, that is, I *recovered my vitall strength*; not that any Ghost, or incorporeall substance entred into; and possessed his body.

Sixtly, for a subordination to authority.

[210] In the 11 chap. of *Numbers*. verse 17. I *will take* (saith God) *of the Spirit, which is upon thee, and will put it upon them, and they shall bear the burthen of the people with thee*; that is, upon the seventy Elders: whereupon two of the seventy are said to prophecy in the campe; of whom some complained, and Joshua desired Moses to forbid them; which Moses would not doe. Whereby it appears; that Joshua knew not they had received authority so to do, and prophecyed according to the mind of Moses, that is to say, by a *Spirit*, or *Authority* subordinate to his own.

In the like sense we read (*Deut* 34 9) that *Joshua was full of the Spirit of wisdome, because Moses had laid his hands upon him*: that is, because he was *ordained* by Moses, to prosecute the work hee had himselfe begun, (namely, the bringing of Gods people into the promised land), but prevented by death, could not finish

In the like sense it is said, (*Rom* 8 9.) *If any man have not the Spirit of Christ, he is none of his*: not meaning thereby the *Ghost* of Christ, but a *submission* to his Doctrine. As also (1 *John* 4. 2.) *Hereby you shall know the Spirit of God; Every Spirit that confesseth that Jesus Christ is come in the flesh, is of God*, by which is meant the Spirit of unfained Christianity, or *submission* to that main Article of Christian faith, that Jesus is the Christ; which cannot be interpreted of a Ghost.

Likewise these words (*Luke* 4. 1.) *And Jesus full of the Holy Ghost* (that is, as it is exprest, *Mat*. 4. 1 and *Mar*. 1. 12. *of the Holy Spirit*,) may be understood, for *Zeal* to doe the work for which hee was sent by God the Father: but to interpret it of a Ghost, is to say, that God himselfe (for so our Saviour was,) was filled with

God; which is very unproper, and unsignificant. How we came to translate *Spirits*, by the word *Ghosts*, which signifieth nothing, neither in heaven, nor earth, but the Imaginary inhabitants of mans brain, I examine not: but this I say, the word *Spirit* in the text signifieth no such thing; but either properly a reall *substance*, or Metaphorically, some extraordinary *ability* or *affection* of the Mind, or of the Body.

Seventhly, for Aeriall Bodies.

The Disciples of Christ, seeing him walking upon the sea, (*Mat* 14 26. and *Marke* 6 49) supposed him to be a *Spirit*, meaning thereby an Aeriall *Body*, and not a Phantasme: for it is said, they all saw him; which cannot be understood of the delusions of the brain, (which are not common to many at once, as visible Bodies are; but singular, because of the differences of Fancies), but of Bodies only. In like manner, where he was taken for a *Spirit*, by the same Apostles (*Luke* 24 3, 7.)· So also (*Acts* 12. 15) when St. *Peter* was delivered out of Prison, it would not be beleeved; but when the Maid said he was at the dore, they said it was his *Angel*; by which must be meant a corporeall substance, or we must say, the Disciples themselves did follow the common opinion of both Jews and Gentiles, that some such apparitions were not Imaginary, but Reall; and such as needed not the fancy of man for their Existence. These the Jews called *Spirits*, and *Angels*, Good or Bad; as the Greeks called the same by the name of *Dæmons*. And some such apparitions may be reall, and sub- [211] stantiall; that is to say, subtile Bodies, which God can form by the same power, by which he formed all things, and make use of, as of Ministers, and Messengers (that is to say, Angels) to declare his will, and execute the same when he pleaseth, in extraordinary and supernaturall manner. But when hee hath so formed them they are Substances, endued with dimensions, and take up roome, and can be moved from place to place, which is peculiar to Bodies; and therefore are not Ghosts *incorporeall*, that is to say, Ghosts that are in *no place*; that is to say, that are *no where*; that is to say, that seeming to be *somewhat*, are *nothing*. But if Corporeall be taken in the most vulgar manner, for such Substances as are perceptible by our externall Senses; then is Substance Incorporeall, a thing not Imaginary, but Reall; namely, a thin Substance, Invisible, but that hath the same dimensions that are in grosser Bodies.

Angel what. By the name of ANGEL, is signified generally, a *Messenger*; and most often, a *Messenger of God*: And by a Messenger of God, is signified, any thing that makes known his extraordinary Presence, that is to say, the extraordinary manifestation of his power, especially by a Dream, or Vision.

Concerning the creation of *Angels*, there is nothing delivered in the Scriptures. That they are Spirits, is often repeated: but by the name of Spirit, is signified both in Scripture, and vulgarly, both amongst Jews, and Gentiles, sometimes thin Bodies; as the Aire, the Wind, the Spirits Vitall, and Animall, of living creatures; and sometimes the Images that rise in the fancy in Dreams, and Visions; which are not reall Substances, nor last any longer then the Dream, or Vision they appear in; which Apparitions, though no reall Substances, but Accidents of the brain; yet when God raiseth them supernaturally, to signifie his Will, they are not unproperly termed Gods Messengers, that is to say, his *Angels*.

And as the Gentiles did vulgarly conceive the Imagery of the brain, for things really subsistent without them, and not dependent on the fancy; and out of them framed their opinions of *Dæmons*, Good and Evill; which because they seemed to subsist really, they called *Substances*; and because they could not feel them with their hands, *Incorporeall*: so also the Jews upon the same ground, without any thing in the Old Testament that constrained them thereunto, had generally an opinion, (except the sect of the *Sadduces*,) that those apparitions (which it pleased God sometimes to produce in the fancie of men, for his own service, and therefore called them his *Angels*) were substances, not dependent on the fancy, but permanent creatures of God; whereof those which they thought were good to them, they esteemed the *Angels of God*, and those they thought would hurt them, they called *Evill Angels*, or Evill Spirits; such as was the Spirit of Python. and the Spirits of Mad-men, of Lunatiques, and Epileptiques: For they esteemed such as were troubled with such diseases, *Dæmoniaques*

But if we consider the places of the Old Testament where Angels are mentioned, we shall find, that in most of them, there can nothing else be understood by the [212] word *Angel*, but some image raised (supernaturally) in the fancy, to signifie the presence of God in the execution of some supernaturall work; and therefore in the rest, where their nature is not exprest, it may be understood in the same manner.

For we read *Gen.* 16. that the same apparition is called, not onely an *Angel*, but *God*; where that which (verse 7) is called the *Angel* of the Lord, in the tenth verse, saith to Agar, *I will multiply thy seed exceedingly*; that is, speaketh in the person of God. Neither was this apparition a Fancy figured, but a Voice. By which it is manifest, that *Angel* signifieth there, nothing but *God* himself, that caused Agar supernaturally to apprehend a voice from heaven; or rather, nothing else but a Voice supernaturall, testifying Gods speciall presence there. Why therefore may not the Angels that appeared to Lot, and are called *Gen.* 19. 13. *Men*, and to whom, though they were two, Lot speaketh (ver. 18.) as but to one, and that one, as God, (for the words are, *Lot said unto them, Oh not so my Lord*) be understood of images of men, supernaturally formed in the Fancy; as well as before by Angel was understood a fancyed Voice? When the Angel called to Abraham out of heaven, to stay his hand (*Gen.* 22. 11) from slaying Isaac, there was no Apparition, but a Voice; which neverthelesse was called properly enough a Messenger, or *Angel* of God, because it declared Gods will supernaturally, and saves the labour of supposing any permanent Ghosts. The Angels which Jacob saw on the Ladder of Heaven (*Gen* 28. 12) were a Vision of his sleep; therefore onely Fancy, and a Dream; yet being supernaturall, and signs of Gods speciall presence, those apparitions are not improperly called *Angels.* The same is to be understood (*Gen* 31. 11.) where Jacob saith thus, *The Angel of the*

Lord appeared to mee in my sleep. For an apparition made to a man in his sleep, is that which all men call a Dreame, whether such Dreame be naturall, or supernaturall: and that which there Jacob calleth an *Angel*, was God himselfe; for the same Angel saith (verse 13) *I am the God of Bethel.*

Also (*Exod.* 14 9) the Angel that went before the Army of Israel to the Red Sea, and then came behind it, is (verse 19) the Lord himself; and he appeared not in the form of a beautifull man, but in form (by day) of a *pillar of cloud*, and (by night) in form of a *pillar of fire*, and yet this Pillar was all the apparition, and *Angel* promised to Moses (*Exod.* 14. 9) for the Armies guide For this cloudy pillar, is said, to have descended, and stood at the dore of the Tabernacle, and to have talked with Moses.

There you see Motion, and Speech, which are commonly attributed to Angels, attributed to a Cloud, because the Cloud served as a sign of Gods presence; and was no lesse an Angel, then if it had had the form of a Man, or Child of never so great beauty; or Wings, as usually they are painted, for the false instruction of common people. For it is not the shape, but their use, that makes them Angels. But their use is to be signi-
[213] fications of Gods presence in supernaturall operations; As when Moses (*Exod.* 33. 14.) had desired God to goe along with the Campe, (as he had done alwaies before the making of the Golden Calfe,) God did not answer, *I will goe*, nor *I will send an Angell in my stead*; but thus, *my presence shall goe with thee.*

To mention all the places of the Old Testament where the name of Angel is found, would be too long. Therefore to comprehend them all at once, I say, there is no text in that part of the Old Testament, which the Church of England holdeth for Canonicall, from which we can conclude, there is, or hath been created, any permanent thing (understood by the name of *Spirit* or *Angel*,) that hath not quantity; and that may not be, by the understanding divided, that is to say, considered by parts; so as one part may bee in one place, and the next part in the next place to it; and, in summe, which is not (taking Body for that, which is some what, or some where) Corporeall; but in every place, the sense will bear the interpretation of Angel, for Messenger; as John Baptist is called an Angel, and Christ the Angel of the Covenant; and as (according to the same Analogy) the Dove, and the Fiery Tongues, in that they were signes of Gods speciall presence, might also be called Angels. Though we find in Daniel two names of Angels, *Gabriel*, and *Michael*; yet it is cleer out of the text it selfe, (*Dan.* 12. 1.) that by *Michael* is meant *Christ*, not as an Angel, but as a Prince: and that *Gabriel* (as the like apparitions made to other holy men in their sleep) was nothing but a supernaturall phantasme, by which it seemed to *Daniel*, in his dream, that two Saints being in talke, one of them said to the other, *Gabriel, let us make this man understand his Vision*: For God needeth not, to distinguish his Celestiall servants by names, which are usefull onely to the short memories of Mortalls. Nor in the New Testament is there any place, out of which it can be proved, that Angels (except when they are put for such men, as God hath made the Messengers, and Ministers of his word, or works) are things permanent, and withall incorporeall. That they are permanent, may bee gathered from the words of our Saviour himselfe, (*Mat.* 25. 41.) where he saith, it shall be said to the wicked in the last day, *Go ye cursed into everlasting fire prepared for the Devil and his Angels*: which place is manifest for the permanence of Evill Angels, (unlesse wee might think the name of Devill and his Angels may be understood of the Churches Adversaries and their Ministers;) but then it is repugnant to their Immateriality; because Everlasting fire is no punishment to impatible substances, such as are all things Incorporeall. Angels therefore are not thence proved to be Incorporeall. In like manner where St. Paul sayes (1 *Cor.* 6. 3.) *Know ye not that wee shall judge the Angels?* And (2 *Pet.* 2. 4.) *For if God spared not the Angels that sinned, but cast them down into hell.* And (*Jude* 1, 6.) *And the Angels that kept not their first estate, but left their owne habitation, hee hath reserved in everlasting chaines under darknesse unto the Judgment of the last*

day; though it prove the Permanence of Angelicall nature, it confirmeth also their Materiality. And
[214] (*Mat.* 22. 30.) *In the resurrection men doe neither marry, nor give in marriage, but are as the Angels of God in heaven*: but in the resurrection men shall be Permanent, and not Incorporeall; so therefore also are the Angels.

There be divers other places out of which may be drawn the like conclusion. To men that understand the signification of these words, *Substance*, and *Incorporeall*; as *Incorporeall* is taken not for subtile body but for *not Body*, they imply a contradiction: insomuch as to say, an Angel, or Spirit is (in that sense) an Incorporeall Substance, is to say in effect, there is no Angel nor Spirit at all. Considering therefore the signification of the word Angel in the Old Testament, and the nature of Dreams and Visions that happen to men by the ordinary way of Nature; I was enclined to this opinion, that Angels were nothing but supernaturall apparitions of the Fancy, raised by the speciall and extraordinary operation of God, thereby to make his presence and commandements known to mankind, and chiefly to his own people. But the many places of the New Testament, and our Saviours own words, and in such texts, wherein is no suspicion of corruption of the Scripture, have extorted from my feeble Reason, an acknowledgment, and beleef, that there be also Angels substantiall, and permanent. But to beleeve they be in no place, that is to say, no where, that is to say, nothing, as they (though indirectly) say, that will have them Incorporeall, cannot by Scripture bee evinced.

Inspiration what. On the signification of the word *Spirit*, dependeth that of the word INSPIRATION; which must either be taken properly; and then it is nothing but the blowing into a man some thin and subtile aire, or wind, in such manner as a man filleth a bladder with his breath; or if Spirits be not corporeall, but have their existence only in the fancy, it is nothing but the blowing in of a Phantasme; which is improper to say, and impossible; for Phantasmes are not, but only seem to be

somewhat. That word therefore is used in the Scripture metaphorically onely: As (*Gen.* 2 7.) where it is said, that God *inspired* into man the breath of life, no more is meant, then that God gave unto him vitall motion. For we are not to think that God made first a living breath, and then blew it into Adam after he was made, whether that breath were reall, or seeming; but only as it is (*Acts* 17. 25) *that he gave him life, and breath*; that is, made him a living creature. And where it is said (2 *Tim.* 3. 16.) *all Scripture is given by Inspiration from God,* speaking there of the Scripture of the Old Testament, it is an easie metaphor, to signifie, that God enclined the spirit or mind of those Writers, to write that which should be usefull, in teaching, reproving, correcting, and instructing men in the way of righteous living. But where St. Peter (2 *Pet* 1. 21.) saith, that *Prophecy came not in old time by the will of man, but the holy men of God spake as they were moved by the Holy Spirit,* by the Holy Spirit, is meant the voice of God in a Dream, or Vision supernaturall, which is not *Inspiration*. Nor when our Saviour breathing on his Disciples, said, *Receive the Holy Spirit,* was that Breath the Spirit, but a sign of the spirituall graces he gave unto them. And though it be said of many, and of our Saviour himself, [215]
that he was full of the Holy *Spirit*; yet that Fulnesse is not to be understood for *Infusion* of the substance of God, but for accumulation of his gifts, such as are the gift of sanctity of life, of tongues, and the like, whether attained supernaturally, or by study and industry; for in all cases they are the gifts of God. So likewise where God sayes (*Joel* 2. 28.) *I will powre out my Spirit upon all flesh, and your Sons and your Daughters shall prophecy, your Old men shall dream Dreams, and your Young men shall see Visions,* wee are not to understand it in the proper sense, as if his *Spirit* were like water, subject to effusion, or infusion; but as if God had promised to give them Propheticall Dreams, and Visions For the proper use of the word *infused,* in speaking of the graces of God, is an abuse of it; for those graces are Vertues, not Bodies to be

carryed hither and thither, and to be powred into men, as into barrels.

In the same manner, to take *Inspiration* in the proper sense, or to say that Good *Spirits* entred into men to make them prophecy, or Evill *Spirits* into those that became Phrenetique, Lunatique, or Epileptique, is not to take the word in the sense of the Scripture; for the Spirit there is taken for the power of God, working by causes to us unknown. As also (*Acts* 2. 2) the wind, that is there said to fill the house wherein the Apostles were assembled on the day of Pentecost, is not to be understood for the Holy *Spirit*, which is the Deity it self; but for an Externall sign of Gods speciall working on their hearts, to effect in them the internall graces, and holy vertues hee thought requisite for the performance of their Apostleship.

[216

CHAP XXXV.

Of the Signification in Scripture of KINGDOME OF GOD, *of* HOLY, SACRED, *and* SACRAMENT.

The Kingdom of God taken by Divines Metaphorically, but in the Scriptures properly.

THE *Kingdome of God* in the Writings of Divines, and specially in Sermons, and Treatises of Devotion, is taken most commonly for Eternall Felicity, after this life, in the Highest Heaven, which they also call the Kingdome of Glory; and sometimes for (the earnest of that felicity) Sanctification, which they terme the Kingdome of Grace, but never for the Monarchy, that is to say, the Soveraign Power of God over any Subjects acquired by their own consent, which is the proper signification of Kingdome.

To the contrary, I find the KINGDOME OF GOD, to signifie in most places of Scripture, a *Kingdome properly so named*, constituted by the Votes of the People of Israel in peculiar manner; wherein they chose God for their King by Covenant made with him, upon Gods promising them the possession of the land of Canaan; and but seldom metaphorically; and then it is taken for *Dominion over sinne*; (and only in the New Testament;) because such a Dominion as that, every Subject shall have in the Kingdome of God, and without prejudice to the Soveraign.

From the very Creation, God not only reigned over all men *naturally* by his might; but also had *peculiar* Subjects, whom he commanded by a Voice, as one man speaketh to another. In which manner he *reigned* over Adam, and gave him commandement to abstaine from the tree of cognizance of Good and Evill, which when he obeyed not, but tasting thereof, took upon him to be as God, judging between Good and Evill, not by his Creators commandement, but by his own sense, his punishment was a privation of the estate of Eternall life, wherein God had at first created him: And afterwards God punished his posterity, for their vices, all but eight persons, with an universall deluge; And in these eight did consist the then *Kingdom of God*.

The originall of the Kingdome of God.

After this, it pleased God to speak to Abraham, and (*Gen.* 17. 7, 8.) to make a Covenant with him in these words, *I will establish my Covenant between me, and thee, and thy seed after thee in their generations, for an everlasting Covenant, to be a God to thee, and to thy seed after thee; And I will give unto thee, and to thy seed after thee, the land wherein thou art a stranger, all the land of Canaan for an everlasting possession.* In this Covenant *Abraham promiseth for himselfe and his posterity to obey as God, the Lord that spake to him: and God on his part promiseth to Abraham the land of Canaan for an everlasting possession.* And for a memoriall, and a token of this Covenant, he ordaineth [217] (verse 11) the *Sacrament of Circumcision.* This is it which is called the *Old Covenant*, or *Testament*, and containeth a Contract between God and Abraham; by which Abraham obligeth himself, and his posterity, in a peculiar manner to be subject to Gods positive Law; for to the Law Morall he was obliged before, as by an Oath of Allegiance. And though the name of *King* be not yet given to God, nor of *Kingdome* to Abraham and his seed; yet the thing is the same;

namely, an Institution by pact, of Gods peculiar Soveraignty over the seed of Abraham; which in the renewing of the same Covenant by Moses, at Mount Sinai, is expressely called a peculiar *Kingdome of God* over the Jews: and it is of Abraham (not of Moses) St. Paul saith (*Rom.* 4. 11.) that he is the *Father of the Faithfull*; that is, of those that are loyall, and doe not violate their Allegiance sworn to God, then by Circumcision, and afterwards in the *New Covenant* by Baptisme.

That the Kingdome of God is properly his Civill Soveraignty over a peculiar people by pact.

This Covenant, at the Foot of Mount Sinai, was renewed by Moses (*Exod* 19. 5.) where the Lord commandeth Moses to speak to the people in this manner, *If you will obey my voice indeed, and keep my Covenant, then yee shall be a peculiar people to me, for all the Earth is mine, And yee shall be unto me a Sacerdotall Kingdome, and an holy Nation.* For a *Peculiar people*, the vulgar Latine hath, *Peculium de cunctis populis*: the English Translation made in the beginning of the Reign of King James, hath, a *Peculiar treasure unto me above all Nations*; and the Geneva French, *the most precious Jewel of all Nations.* But the truest Translation is the first, because it is confirmed by St. Paul himself (*Tit.* 2. 14.) where he saith, alluding to that place, that our blessed Saviour *gave himself for us, that he might purifie us to himself, a peculiar* (that is, an extraordinary) *people:* for the word is in the Greek περιούσιος, which is opposed commonly to the word ἐπιούσιος: and as this signifieth *ordinary, quotidian*, or (as in the Lords Prayer) *of daily use*; so the other signifieth that which is *overplus*, and *stored up*, and *enjoyed in a speciall manner*; which the Latines call *Peculium*: and this meaning of the place is confirmed by the reason God rendereth of it, which followeth immediately, in that he addeth, *For all the Earth is mine*, as if he should say, *All the Nations of the world are mine*; but it is not so that you are mine, but in a *speciall manner*: For they are all mine, by reason of my Power; but you shall be mine, by your own Consent, and Covenant; which is an addition to his ordinary title, to all nations.

The same is again confirmed in expresse words in the same text, *Yee shall be to me a Sacerdotall Kingdome, and an holy Nation.* The Vulgar Latine hath it, *Regnum Sacerdotale*, to which agreeth the Translation of that place (1 *Pet.* 2. 9.) *Sacerdotium Regale, a Regal Priesthood*; as also the Institution it self, by which no man might enter into the *Sanctum Sanctorum*, that is to say, no man might enquire Gods will immediately of God himselfe, but onely the High Priest. The English Translation before mentioned, following that of Geneva, has, *a Kingdom of Priests*; which is either meant of the succession of one High Priest after [218] another, or else it accordeth not with St. Peter, nor with the exercise of the High priesthood: For there was never any but the High priest onely, that was to informe the People of Gods Will; nor any Convocation of Priests ever allowed to enter into the *Sanctum Sanctorum.*

Again, the title of a *Holy Nation* confirmes the same · for *Holy* signifies, that which is Gods by speciall, not by generall Right. All the Earth (as is said in the text) is Gods; but all the Earth is not called *Holy*, but that onely which is set apart for his especiall service, as was the Nation of the Jews. It is therefore manifest enough by this one place, that by the *Kingdome of God*, is properly meant a Common-wealth, instituted (by the consent of those which were to be subject thereto) for their Civill Government, and the regulating of their behaviour, not onely towards God their King, but also towards one another in point of justice, and towards other Nations both in peace and warre; which properly was a Kingdome, wherein God was King, and the High priest was to be (after the death of Moses) his sole Viceroy, or Lieutenant.

But there be many other places that clearly prove the same. As first (1 *Sam.* 8. 7.) when the Elders of Israel (grieved with the corruption of the Sons of Samuel) demanded a King, Samuel displeased therewith, prayed unto the Lord; and the Lord answering said unto him, *Hearken unto the voice of the People, for they have not rejected thee, but they have rejected me, that I should not reign over them* Out of which it is evident, that God himself was then their King: and Samuel did not command the people, but only delivered to them that which God from time to time appointed him.

Again, (1 *Sam.* 12. 12.) where Samuel saith to the People, *When yee saw that Nahash King of the Children of Ammon came against you, ye said unto me, Nay, but a King shall reign over us, when the Lord your God was your King:* It is manifest that God was their King, and governed the Civill State of their Common-wealth

And after the Israelites had rejected God, the Prophets did foretell his restitution; as (*Isaiah* 24. 23) *Then the Moon shall be confounded, and the Sun ashamed, when the Lord of Hosts shall reign in Mount Zion, and in Jerusalem*; where he speaketh expressely of his Reign in Zion, and Jerusalem; that is, on Earth. And (*Micah* 4. 7.) *And the Lord shall reign over them in Mount Zion*: This Mount Zion is in Jerusalem upon the Earth. And (*Ezek.* 20 33.) *As I live, saith the Lord God, surely with a mighty hand, and a stretched out arme, and with fury powred out, I wil rule over you; and* (verse 37.) *I will cause you to passe under the rod, and I will bring you into the bond of the Covenant*; that is, I will reign over you, and make you to stand to that Covenant which you made with me by Moses, and brake in your rebellion against me in the days of Samuel, and in your election of another King.

And in the New Testament, the Angel Gabriel saith of our Saviour (*Luke* 1. 32, 33.) *He shall be great, and be called the Son of the most High, and the Lord shall*
[219] *give him the throne of his Father David; and he shall reign over the house of Jacob for ever, and of his Kingdome there shall be no end.* This is also a Kingdome upon Earth; for the claim whereof, as an enemy to Cæsar, he was put to death; the title of his crosse, was, *Jesus of Nazareth, King of the Jews*; hee was crowned in scorn with a crown of Thornes; and for the proclaiming of him, it is said of the Disciples (*Acts* 17. 7.) *That they did all of them contrary to the decrees of Cæsar, saying there was another King, one*

Jesus. The Kingdome therefore of God, is a reall, not a metaphoricall Kingdome; and so taken, not onely in the Old Testament, but the New; when we say, *For thine is the Kingdome, the Power, and Glory,* it is to be understood of Gods Kingdome, by force of our Covenant, not by the Right of Gods Power; for such a Kingdome God alwaies hath; so that it were superfluous to say in our prayer, *Thy Kingdome come,* unlesse it be meant of the Restauration of that Kingdome of God by Christ, which by revolt of the Israelites had been interrupted in the election of Saul. Nor had it been proper to say, *The Kingdome of Heaven is at hand*; or to pray, *Thy Kingdome come,* if it had still continued.

There be so many other places that confirm this interpretation, that it were a wonder there is no greater notice taken of it, but that it gives too much light to Christian Kings to see their right of Ecclesiasticall Government. This they have observed, that in stead of a *Sacerdotall Kingdome,* translate, *a Kingdome of Priests*: for they may as well translate a *Royall Priesthood,* (as it is in St. Peter) into a *Priesthood of Kings.* And whereas, for a *peculiar people,* they put a *pretious jewel,* or *treasure,* a man might as well call the speciall Regiment, or Company of a Generall, the Generalls pretious Jewel, or his Treasure.

In short, the Kingdome of God is a Civill Kingdome; which consisted, first in the obligation of the people of Israel to those Laws, which Moses should bring unto them from Mount Sinai, and which afterwards the High Priest for the time being, should deliver to them from before the *Cherubins* in the *Sanctum Sanctorum*; and which Kingdome having been cast off, in the election of Saul, the Prophets foretold, should be restored by Christ; and the Restauration whereof we daily pray for, when we say in the Lords Prayer, *Thy Kingdome come*; and the Right whereof we acknowledge, when we adde, *For thine is the Kingdome, the Power, and Glory, for ever and ever, Amen*; and the Proclaiming whereof, was the Preaching of the Apostles; and to which men are prepared, by the Teachers of the

Gospel; to embrace which Gospel, (that is to say, to promise obedience to Gods government) is, to bee in the *Kingdome of Grace*, because God hath *gratis* given to such the power to bee the Subjects (that is, Children of God hereafter, when Christ shall come in Majesty to judge the world, and actually to govern his owne people, which is called *the Kingdome of Glory*. If the Kingdome of God (called also the Kingdome of Heaven, from the gloriousnesse, and admirable height of that throne) were not a Kingdome which God by his Lieu-
[220] tenants, or Vicars, who deliver his Commandements to the people, did exercise on Earth; there would not have been so much contention, and warre, about who it is, by whom God speaketh to us; neither would many Priests have troubled themselves with Spirituall Jurisdiction, nor any King have denied it them.

Holy what.

Out of this literall interpretation of the *Kingdome of God*, ariseth also the true interpretation of the word HOLY. For it is a word, which in Gods Kingdome answereth to that, which men in their Kingdomes use to call *Publique*, or the *Kings*.

The King of any Countrey is the *Publique* Person, or Representative of all his own Subjects. And God the King of Israel was the *Holy one* of Israel. The Nation which is subject to one earthly Soveraign, is the Nation of that Soveraign, that is, of the Publique Person. So the Jews, who were Gods Nation. were called (*Exod.* 19. 6.) *a Holy Nation*. For by *Holy*, is alwaies understood, either God himselfe, or that which is Gods in propriety; as by Publique, is alwaies meant either the Person of the Common-wealth it self, or something that is so the Common-wealths, as no private person can claim any propriety therein.

Therefore the Sabbath (Gods day) is a *Holy day*; the Temple, (Gods house) *a Holy house*; Sacrifices, Tithes, and Offerings (Gods tribute) *Holy duties*; Priests, Prophets, and anointed Kings, under Christ (Gods Ministers) *Holy men*; the Cœlestiall ministring Spirits (Gods Messengers) *Holy Angels*; and the like: and wheresoever the word Holy is taken properly, there is still something signified of Propriety, gotten by consent In saying *Hallowed be thy name*, we do but pray to God for grace to keep the first Commandement, of *having no other Gods but him*. Mankind is Gods Nation in propriety: but the Jews only were a *Holy Nation*. Why, but because they became his Propriety by covenant?

And the word *Profane*, is usually taken in the Scripture for the same with *Common*, and consequently their contraries, *Holy*, and *Proper*, in the Kingdome of God must be the same also. But figuratively, those men also are called *Holy*, that led such godly lives, as if they had forsaken all worldly designs, and wholly devoted, and given themselves to God. In the proper sense, that which is made *Holy* by Gods appropriating or separating it to his own use, is said to be *sanctified* by God, as the Seventh day in the fourth Commandement; and as the Elect in the New Testament were said to bee *sanctified*, when they were endued with the Spirit of godlinesse. And that which is made *Holy* by the dedication of men, and given to God, so as to be used onely in his publique service, is called also SACRED, and said to be consecrated, as Temples, and other Houses of Publique Prayer, and their Utensils, Priests, and Ministers, Victimes, Offerings, and the externall matter of Sacraments *Sacred what.*

Of *Holinesse* there be degrees: for of those things that are set apart for the service of God, there may bee some set apart again, for a neerer and more especial service The whole Nation of the Israelites were a people Holy to God, yet the tribe of Levi was amongst the Israelites a Holy tribe; and amongst [221] the Levites, the Priests were yet more Holy; and amongst the Priests, the High Priest was the most Holy. So the Land of Judea was the Holy Land, but the Holy City wherein God was to be worshipped, was more Holy, and again, the Temple more Holy than the City; and the *Sanctum Sanctorum* more Holy than the rest of the Temple *Degrees of Sanctity*

A SACRAMENT, is a separation of some visible thing from common use; and a consecration of it to Gods service, for a sign, either of our admission into the *Sacrament.*

Kingdome of God, to be of the number of his peculiar people, or for a Commemoration of the same. In the Old Testament, the sign of Admission was *Circumcision*; in the New Testament, *Baptisme*. The Commemoration of it in the Old Testament, was the *Eating* (at a certaine time, which was Anniversary) of the *Paschall Lamb*; by which they were put in mind of the night wherein they were delivered out of their bondage in Egypt; and in the New Testament, the celebrating of the *Lords Supper*; by which, we are put in mind, of our deliverance from the bondage of sin, by our Blessed Saviours death upon the crosse. The Sacraments of *Admission*, are but once to be used, because there needs but one *Admission*; but because we have need of being often put in mind of our deliverance, and of our Alleagance, the Sacraments of *Commemoration* have need to be reiterated And these are the principall Sacraments, and as it were the solemne oathes we make of our Alleageance. There be also other Consecrations, that may be called Sacraments, as the word implyeth onely Consecration to Gods service; but as it implies an oath, or promise of Alleageance to God, there were no other in the Old Testament, but *Circumcision*, and the *Passeover*; nor are there any other in the New Testament, but *Baptisme*, and the *Lords Supper*.

[222]

CHAP. XXXVI.

Of the WORD OF GOD, *and of* PROPHETS

Word what.

WHEN there is mention of the *Word of God*, or of *Man*, it doth not signifie a part of Speech, such as Grammarians call a Nown, or a Verb, or any simple voice, without a contexture with other words to make it significative; but a perfect Speech or Discourse, whereby the speaker *affirmeth*, *denieth*, *commandeth*, *promiseth*, *threatneth*, *wisheth*, or *interrogateth* In which sense it is not *Vocabulum*, that signifies a *Word*; but *Sermo*, (in Greek λόγος) that is, some *Speech*, *Discourse*, or *Saying*

The words spoken by God, and concerning God, both are called Gods Word in Scripture.

Again, if we say the *Word* of *God*, or of *Man*, it may bee understood sometimes of the Speaker, (as the words that God hath spoken, or that a Man hath spoken: In which sense, when we say, the Gospel of St. Matthew, we understand St. Matthew to be the Writer of it: and sometimes of the Subject: In which sense, when we read in the Bible, *The words of the days of the Kings of Israel, or Judah*, 'tis meant, that the acts that were done in those days, were the Subject of those Words; And in the Greek, which (in the Scripture) retaineth many Hebraismes, by the Word of God is oftentimes meant, not that which is spoken by God, but concerning God, and his government; that is to say, the Doctrine of Religion: Insomuch, as it is all one, to say λόγος θεοῦ, and *Theologia*; which is, that Doctrine which wee usually call *Divinity*, as is manifest by the places following [*Acts* 13. 46.] *Then Paul and Barnabas waxed bold*, and *said, It was necessary that the Word of God should first have been spoken to you, but seeing you put it from you, and judge your selves unworthy of everlasting life, loe, we turn to the Gentiles.* That which is here called the Word of God, was the Doctrine of Christian Religion; as it appears evidently by that which goes before. And [*Acts* 5. 20.] where it is said to the Apostles by an Angel, *Go stand and speak in the Temple, all the Words of this life*; by the Words of this life, is meant, the Doctrine of the Gospel; as is evident by what they did in the Temple, and is expressed in the last verse of the same Chap. *Daily in the Temple, and in every house they ceased not to teach and preach Christ Jesus*: In which place it is manifest, that Jesus Christ was the subject of this *Word of life*; or (which is all one) the subject of the *Words of this life eternall*, that our Saviour offered them. So [*Acts* 15. 7.] the Word of God, is called *the Word of the Gospel*, because it containeth the Doctrine of the Kingdome of Christ; and the same Word [*Rom.* 10. 8, 9.] is called *the Word of Faith*; that is, as is there expressed, the Doctrine of Christ come, and raised from the dead. Also [223] [*Mat.* 13. 19.] *When any one heareth the Word of the*

Kingdome; that is, the Doctrine of the Kingdome taught by Christ. Again, the same Word, is said [*Acts* 12 24] *to grow and to be multiplyed*; which to understand of the Evangelicall Doctrine is easie, but of the Voice, or Speech of God, hard and strange. In the same sense the *Doctrine of Devils*, signifieth not the Words of any Devill, but the Doctrine of Heathen men concerning *Dæmons*, and those Phantasms which they worshipped as Gods.

1 Tim. 4 1.

Considering these two significations of the WORD OF GOD, as it is taken in Scripture, it is manifest in this later sense (where it is taken for the Doctrine of Christian Religion,) that the whole Scripture is the Word of God: but in the former sense not so. For example, though these words, *I am the Lord thy God, &c.* to the end of the Ten Commandements, were spoken by God to Moses; yet the Preface, *God spake these words and said*, is to be understood for the Words of him that wrote the holy History. The *Word of God*, as it is taken for that which he hath spoken, is understood sometimes *Properly*, sometimes *Metaphorically*. *Properly*, as the words, he hath spoken to his Prophets. *Metaphorically*, for his Wisdome, Power, and eternall Decree, in making the world. in which sense, those *Fiats, Let their be light, Let there be a firmament, Let us make man, &c.* [*Gen.* 1.] are the Word of God. And in the same sense it is said [*John* 1. 3.] *All things were made by it, and without it was nothing made that was made*: And [*Heb.* 1. 3.] *He upholdeth all things by the Word of his Power*, that is, by the Power of his Word; that is, by his Power. and [*Heb* 11 3] *The worlds were framed by the Word of God*; and many other places to the same sense: As also amongst the Latines, the name of *Fate*, which signifieth properly *The word spoken*, is taken in the same sense.

The Word of God metaphorically used, first, for the Decrees and Power of God

Secondly, for the effect of his Word.

Secondly, for the effect of his Word; that is to say, for the thing it self, which by his Word is Affirmed, Commanded, Threatned, or Promised, as [*Psalm* 105 19.] where Joseph is said to have been kept in prison, *till his Word was come*, that is, till that was come to passe which he had [*Gen.* 40 13] foretold to

Pharaohs Butler, concerning his being restored to his office: for there by *his word was come*, is meant, the thing it self was come to passe. So also [1 *King*. 18. 36.] Elijah saith to God, *I have done all these thy Words*, in stead of *I have done all these things at thy Word*, or commandement: and [*Jer*. 17. 15.] *Where is the Word of the Lord*, is put for, *Where is the Evill he threatned*: And [*Ezek* 12. 28.] *There shall none of my Words be prolonged any more*: by *words* are understood those *things*, which God promised to his people. And in the New Testament [*Mat*. 24. 35.] *heaven and earth shal pass away, but my Words shal not pass away*; that is, there is nothing that I have promised or foretold, that shall not come to passe. And in this sense it is, that St John the Evangelist, and, I think, St John onely calleth our Saviour himself as in the flesh *the Word of God* [as *Joh*. 1. 14.] *the Word was made Flesh*; that is to say, the Word, or Promise that Christ should come into the world; *who in the beginning was with God*; that is to say, it was in the purpose of God [224]
the Father, to send God the Son into the world, to enlighten men in the way of Eternall life, but it was not till then put in execution, and actually incarnate; So that our Saviour is there called *the Word*, not because he was the promise, but the thing promised. They that taking occasion from this place, doe commonly call him the Verbe of God, do but render the text more obscure. They might as well term him the Nown of God: for as by *Nown*, so also by *Verbe*, men understand nothing but a part of speech, a voice, a sound, that neither affirms, nor denies, nor commands, nor promiseth, nor is any substance corporeall, or spirituall; and therefore it cannot be said to bee either God, or Man: whereas our Saviour is both. And this *Word* which St. *John* in his Gospel saith was with God, is [in his 1 Epistle, verse 1.] called the *Word of life*; and [verse 2.] *the Eternall life, which was with the Father*. so that he can be in no other sense called the *Word*, then in that, wherein he is called Eternall life; that is, *he that hath procured us Eternall life*, by his comming in the flesh. So also [*Apocalypse* 19. 13.] the Apostle speaking of

Christ, clothed in a garment dipt in bloud, faith; his name is *the Word of God*; which is to be understood, as if he had said his name had been, *He that was come according to the purpose of God from the beginning, and according to his Word and promises delivered by the Prophets.* So that there is nothing here of the Incarnation of a Word, but of the Incarnation of God the Son, therefore called *the Word*, because his Incarnation was the Performance of the Promise; In like manner as the Holy Ghost is called *the Promise.*

Acts 1. 4. *Luke* 24. 49.

Thirdly, for the words of reason and equity

There are also places of the Scripture, where, by the *Word of God*, is signified such Words as are consonant to reason, and equity, though spoken sometimes neither by Prophet, nor by a holy man For Pharaoh Necho was an Idolater; yet his Words to the good King Josiah, in which he advised him by Messengers, not to oppose him in his march against *Carchemish*, are said to have proceeded from the mouth of God; and that Josiah not hearkning to them, was slain in the battle; as is to be read 2 *Chron* 35. vers. 21, 22, 23. It is true, that as the same History is related in the first Book of Esdras, not Pharaoh, but Jeremiah spake these words to Josiah, from the mouth of the Lord. But wee are to give credit to the Canonicall Scripture, whatsoever be written in the Apocrypha.

The *Word* of *God*, is then also to be taken for the Dictates of reason, and equity, when the same is said in the Scriptures to bee written in mans heart; as *Psalm* 36 31. *Jerem.* 31. 33. *Deut.* 30. 11, 14. and many other like places.

Divers acceptions of the word Prophet

The name of PROPHET, signifieth in Scripture sometimes *Prolocutor*, that is, he that speaketh from God to Man, or from man to God: And sometimes *Prædictor*, or a foreteller of things to come · And sometimes one that speaketh incoherently, as men that are distracted It is most frequently used in the sense of speaking from God to the People. So *Moses, Samuel, Elijah, Isaiah, Jeremiah*, and others were *Prophets* And in this sense the High Priest was a *Prophet*, for he only went into the *Sanctum Sanctorum*, to enquire of God; and was to
[225] declare his answer to the people. And therefore when

Caiphas said, it was expedient that one man should die for the people, St. John saith [chap. 11. 51.] that *He spake not this of himselfe, but being High Priest that year, he prophesied that one man should dye for the nation.* Also they that in Christian Congregations taught the people [1 *Cor.* 14 3.] are said to Prophecy. In the like sense it is, that God saith to *Moses* [*Exod.* 4 16] concerning *Aaron, He shall be thy Spokes-man to the People* ; *and he shall be to thee a mouth, and thou shalt be to him instead of God* : that which here is *Spokes-man,* is [chap. 7. 1.] interpreted Prophet ; *See* (saith God) *I have made thee a God to Pharaoh, and Aaron thy Brother shall be thy Prophet.* In the sense of speaking from man to God, Abraham is called a Prophet [*Genes.* 20. 7.] where God in a Dream speaketh to Abimelech in this manner, *Now therefore restore the man his wife, for he is a Prophet, and shall pray for thee* ; whereby may be also gathered, that the name of Prophet may be given, not unproperly to them that in Christian Churches, have a Calling to say publique prayers for the Congregation. In the same sense, the Prophets that came down from the High place (or Hill of God) with a Psaltery, and a Tabret, and a Pipe, and a Harp [1 *Sam.* 10. 5, 6.] and [vers 10] Saul amongst them, are said to Prophecy, in that they praised God, in that manner publiquely. In the like sense, is Miriam [*Exod* 15. 20] called a Prophetesse. So is it also to be taken [1 *Cor.* 11. 4, 5] where St. Paul saith, *Every man that prayeth or prophecyeth with his head covered, &c. and every woman that prayeth or prophecyeth with her head uncovered* : For Prophecy in that place, signifieth no more, but praising God in Psalmes, and Holy Songs ; which women might doe in the Church, though it were not lawfull for them to speak to the Congregation And in this signification it is, that the Poets of the Heathen, that composed Hymnes and other sorts of Poems in the honor of their Gods, were called *Vates* (Prophets) as is well enough known by all that are versed in the Books of the Gentiles, and as is evident [*Tit.* 1. 12.] where St. Paul saith of the Cretians, that a Prophet of their owne said, they were Liars ; not that St. Paul held their Poets for Prophets, but acknowledgeth that the word Prophet was commonly used to signifie them that celebrated the honour of God in Verse

Prædiction of future contingents, not alwaies Prophecy.

When by Prophecy is meant Prædiction, or foretelling of future Contigents; not only they were Prophets, who were Gods Spokes-men, and foretold those things to others, which God had foretold to them; but also all those Impostors, that pretend by the helpe of familiar spirits, or by superstitious divination of events past, from false causes, to foretell the like events in time to come: of which (as I have declared already in the 12. chapter of this Discourse) there be many kinds, who gain in the opinion of the common sort of men, a greater reputation of Prophecy, by one casuall event that may bee but wrested to their purpose, than can be lost again by never so many failings Prophecy is not an Art, nor (when it is taken for Prædiction) a constant Vocation; but an extraordinary, and temporary Employment from
[226] God, most often of Good men, but sometimes also of the Wicked. The woman of Endor, who is said to have had a familiar spirit, and thereby to have raised a Phantasme of Samuel, and foretold Saul his death, was not therefore a Prophetesse; for neither had she any science, whereby she could raise such a Phantasme; nor does it appear that God commanded the raising of it, but onely guided that Imposture to be a means of Sauls terror and discouragement; and by consequent, of the discomfiture, by which he fell. And for Incoherent Speech, it was amongst the Gentiles taken for one sort of Prophecy, because the Prophets of their Oracles, intoxicated with a spirit, or vapor from the cave of the Pythian Oracle at Delphi, were for the time really mad, and spake like madmen; of whose loose words a sense might be made to fit any event, in such sort, as all bodies are said to be made of *Materia prima*. In the Scripture I find it also so taken [1 *Sam*. 18. 10.] in these words, *And the Evill spirit came upon Saul, and he Prophecyed in the midst of the house.*

The manner how God hath spoken to the Prophets.

And although there be so many significations in Scripture of the word *Prophet*; yet is that the most frequent, in which it is taken for him, to whom God speaketh immediately, that which the Prophet is to say from him, to some other man, or to the people. And hereupon a question may be asked, in what manner God speaketh to such a Prophet. Can it (may some say) be properly said, that God hath voice and language, when it cannot be properly said, he hath a tongue, or other organs, as a man? The Prophet David argueth thus, *Shall he that made the eye, not see? or he that made the ear, not hear?* But this may be spoken, not (as usually) to signifie Gods nature, but to signifie our intention to honor him. For to *see*, and *hear*, are Honorable Attributes, and may be given to God, to declare (as far as our capacity can conceive) his Almighty power. But if it were to be taken in the strict, and proper sense, one might argue from his making of all other parts of mans body, that he had also the same use of them which we have; which would be many of them so uncomely, as it would be the greatest contumely in the world to ascribe them to him. Therefore we are to interpret Gods speaking to men immediately, for that way (whatsoever it be), by which God makes them understand his will: And the wayes whereby he doth this, are many, and to be sought onely in the Holy Scripture: where though many times it be said, that God spake to this, and that person, without declaring in what manner; yet there be again many places, that deliver also the signes by which they were to acknowledge his presence, and commandement; and by these may be understood, how he spake to many of the rest.

To the Extraordinary Prophets of the Old Testament hespakeby Dreams, or Visions.

In what manner God spake to *Adam*, and *Eve*, and *Cain*, and *Noah*, is not expressed, nor how he spake to *Abraham*, till such time as he came out of his own countrey to *Sichem* in the land of *Canaan*, and then [*Gen.* 12. 7] God is said to have *appeared* to him So there is one way, whereby God made his presence manifest, that is, by an *Apparition*, or *Vision*. And again, [*Gen.* 15. 1.] The Word of the Lord came to Abraham in a Vision; that is to say, somewhat, as a sign of Gods presence, appeared as Gods Messenger, to speak to him. Again, [227]
the Lord appeared to Abraham [*Gen.* 18. 1.] by an apparition of three Angels; and to Abimelech [*Gen* 20. 3] in a dream To Lot [*Gen* 19 1] by an apparition of two Angels: And to Hagar [*Gen.* 21. 17.] by the apparition of one Angel. And to Abraham again [*Gen.* 22. 11.] by

the apparition of a voice from heaven: And [*Gen* 26 24] to Isaac in the night; (that is, in his sleep, or by dream): And to Jacob [*Gen.* 18. 12.] in a dream; that is to say (as are the words of the text) *Jacob dreamed that he saw a ladder, &c.* And [*Gen.* 32 1] in a Vision of Angels: And to Moses [*Exod.* 3. 2] in the apparition of a flame of fire out of the midst of a bush: And after the time of Moses, (where the manner how God spake immediately to man in the Old Testament, is expressed) hee spake alwaies by a Vision, or by a Dream; as to *Gideon, Samuel, Eliah, Elisha, Isaiah, Ezekiel,* and the rest of the Prophets; and often in the New Testament, as to *Joseph,* to St. *Peter,* to St. *Paul,* and to St. *John* the Evangelist in the Apocalypse.

Onely to Moses hee spake in a more extraordinary manner in Mount *Sinai,* and in the *Tabernacle*; and to the High Priest in the *Tabernacle,* and in the *Sanctum Sanctorum* of the Temple. But Moses, and after him the High Priests were Prophets of a more eminent place, and degree in Gods favour; And God himself in express words declareth, that to other Prophets hee spake in Dreams and Visions, but to his servant Moses, in such manner as a man speaketh to his friend. The words are these [*Numb* 12 6, 7, 8] *If there be a Prophet among you, I the Lord will make my self known to him in a Vision, and will speak unto him in a Dream. My servant Moses is not so, who is faithfull in all my house; with him I will speak mouth to mouth, even apparently, not in dark speeches; and the similitude of the Lord shall he behold.* And [*Exod.* 33. 11.] *The Lord spake to Moses face to face, as a man speaketh to his friend.* And yet this speaking of God to Moses, was by mediation of an Angel, or Angels, as appears expressely, *Acts* 7. ver. 35. and 53. and *Gal.* 3. 19. and was therefore a Vision, though a more cleer Vision than was given to other Prophets, And conformable hereunto, where God saith (*Deut.* 13. 1.) *If there arise amongst you a Prophet, or Dreamer of Dreams,* the later word is but the interpretation of the former. And [*Joel* 2 28] *Your sons and your daughters shall Prophecy; your old men shall dream Dreams, and your young men shall see Visions.* where again, the word

Prophecy is expounded by *Dream*, and *Vision*. And in the same manner it was, that God spake to Solomon, promising him Wisdome, Riches, and Honor; for the text saith, [1 *Kings* 3. 15.] *And Solomon awoak, and behold it was a Dream*: So that generally the Prophets extraordinary in the Old Testament took notice of the Word of God no otherwise, than from their Dreams, or Visions; that is to say, from the imaginations which they had in their sleep, or in an Extasie which imaginations in every true Prophet were supernaturall, but in false Prophets were either naturall, or feigned.

The same Prophets were neverthelesse said to speak by the Spirit; as [*Zach.* 7. 12] where the Prophet [228] speaking of the Jewes, saith, *They made their hearts hard as Adamant, lest they should hear the law, and the words which the Lord of Hosts hath sent in his Spirit by the former Prophets* By which it is manifest, that speaking by the *Spirit*, or *Inspiration*, was not a particular manner of Gods speaking, different from Vision, when they that were said to speak by the Spirit, were extraordinary Prophets, such as for every new message, were to have a particular Commission, or (which is all one) a new Dream, or Vision.

To Prophets of perpetuall Calling, and Supreme, God spake in the Old Testament from the Mercy Seat, in a manner not expressed in the Scripture.

Of Prophets, that were so by a perpetuall Calling in the Old Testament, some were *supreme*, and some *subordinate*: Supreme were first Moses; and after him the High Priests, every one for his time, as long as the Priesthood was Royall; and after the people of the Jews, had rejected God, that he should no more reign over them, those Kings which submitted themselves to Gods government, were also his chief Prophets, and the High Priests office became Ministeriall. And when God was to be consulted, they put on the holy vestments, and enquired of the Lord, as the King commanded them, and were deprived of their office, when the King thought fit. For King Saul [1 *Sam.* 13 9.] commanded the burnt offering to be brought, and [1 *Sam.* 14. 18.] he commands the Priest to bring the Ark neer him; and [ver. 19] again to let it alone, because he saw an advantage upon his enemies. And in the same chapter Saul asketh counsell of God. In like manner King David, after his being anointed, though before he had possession of the Kingdome, is said to *enquire of the Lord* [1 *Sam*. 23. 2] whether he should fight against the Philistines at *Keilah*; and [verse 10] David commandeth the Priest to bring him the Ephod, to enquire whether he should stay in *Keilah*, or not. And King Solomon [1 *Kings* 2 27.] took the Priesthood from *Abiathar*, and gave it [verse 35.] to *Zadoc* Therefore Moses, and the High Priests, and the pious Kings, who enquired of God on all extraordinary occasions, how they were to carry themselves, or what event they were to have, were all Soveraign Prophets. But in what manner God spake unto them, is not manifest. To say that when Moses went up to God in Mount *Sinai*, it was a Dream, or Vision, such as other Prophets had, is contrary to that distinction which God made between Moses, and other Prophets, *Numb*. 12. 6, 7, 8. To say God spake or appeared as he is in his own nature, is to deny his Infinitenesse, Invisibility, Incomprehensibility. To say he spake by Inspiration, or Infusion of the Holy Spirit, as the Holy Spirit signifieth the Deity, is to make Moses equall with Christ, in whom onely the Godhead [as St Paul speaketh *Col* 2 9.] dwelleth bodily And lastly, to say he spake by the Holy Spirit, as it signifieth the graces, or gifts of the Holy Spirit, is to attribute nothing to him supernaturall For God disposeth men to Piety, Justice, Mercy, Truth, Faith, and all manner of Vertue, both Morall, and Intellectuall, by doctrine, example, and by severall occasions, naturall, and ordinary.

And as these ways cannot be applyed to God, in his speaking to Moses, at Mount *Sinai*, so also, they cannot [229] be applyed to him, in his speaking to the High Priests, from the Mercy-Seat. Therefore in what manner God spake to those Soveraign Prophets of the Old Testament, whose office it was to enquire of him, is not intelligible. In the time of the New Testament, there was no Soveraign Prophet, but our Saviour; who was both God that spake, and the Prophet to whom he spake.

To Prophets of perpetuall Calling, but sub-

To subordinate Prophets of perpetuall Calling, I find not any place that proveth God spake to them supernaturally; but onely in such manner, as naturally he inclineth men to Piety, to Beleef, to Righteousnesse, and to other vertues all other Christian men Which way, though it consist in Constitution, Instruction, Education, and the occasions and invitements men have to Christian vertues; yet it is truly attributed to the operation of the Spirit of God, or Holy Spirit, (which we in our language call the Holy Ghost). For there is no good inclination, that is not of the operation of God. But these operations are not alwaies supernaturall When therefore a Prophet is said to speak in the Spirit, or by the Spirit of God, we are to understand no more, but that he speaks according to Gods will, declared by the supreme Prophet For the most common acceptation of the word Spirit, is in the signification of a mans intention, mind, or disposition

ordinate,

God spake by the Spirit.

In the time of Moses, there were seventy men besides himself, that *Prophecyed* in the Campe of the Israelites. In what manner God spake to them, is declared in the 11 of *Numbers*, verse 25 *The Lord came down in a cloud, and spake unto Moses, and took of the Spirit that was upon him, and gave it to the seventy Elders. And it came to passe, when the Spirit rested upon them, they Prophecyed, and did not cease.* By which it is manifest, first, that their Prophecying to the people, was subservient, and subordinate to the Prophecying of Moses; for that God took of the Spirit of Moses, to put upon them; so that they Prophecyed as Moses would have them: otherwise they had not been suffered to Prophecy at all. For there was [verse 27.] a complaint made against them to Moses; and Joshua would have Moses to have forbidden them: which he did not, but said to Joshua, Bee not jealous in my behalf. Secondly, that the Spirit of God in that place, signifieth nothing but the Mind and Disposition to obey, and assist Moses in the administration of the Government. For if it were meant they had the substantiall Spirit of God; that is, the Divine nature, inspired into them, then they had it in no lesse manner then Christ himself, in whom onely the Spirit of God dwelt bodily It is meant therefore of the Gift and Grace of God, that guided them to co-operate with Moses; from whom their Spirit was derived And it appeareth [verse 16.] that, they were such as Moses himself should appoint for Elders and Officers of the People: For the words are, *Gather unto me seventy men, whom thou knowest to be Elders and Officers of the people* where, *thou knowest,* is the same with *thou appointest,* or *hast appointed to be such.* For we are told before [*Exod.* 18] that Moses following the counsell of Jethro his Father-in-law, did appoint Judges, and Officers over [230] the people, such as feared God; and of these, were those Seventy, whom God by putting upon them Moses spirit, inclined to aid Moses in the Administration of the Kingdome: and in this sense the Spirit of God is said [1 *Sam.* 16. 13, 14] presently upon the anointing of David, to have come upon David, and left Saul; God giving his graces to him he chose to govern his people, and taking them away from him, he rejected. So that by the Spirit is meant Inclination to Gods service; and not any supernaturall Revelation.

God sometimes also spake by Lots.

God spake also many times by the event of Lots; which were ordered by such as he had put in Authority over his people. So wee read that God manifested by the Lots which Saul caused to be drawn [1 *Sam* 14. 43] the fault that Jonathan had committed, in eating a honey-comb, contrary to the oath taken by the people. And [*Josh.* 18 10] God divided the land of Canaan amongst the Israelite, by the *lots that Joshua did cast before the Lord in Shiloh.* In the same manner it seemeth to be, that God discovered [*Joshua* 7. 16, *&c.*] the crime of Achan. And these are the wayes whereby God declared his Will in the Old Testament.

All which ways he used also in the New Testament. To the *Virgin Mary,* by a Vision of an Angel: To *Joseph* in a Dream: again to *Paul* in the way to Damascus in a Vision of our Saviour: and to *Peter* in the Vision of a sheet let down from heaven, with divers sorts of flesh, of clean, and unclean beasts; and in prison, by Vision of an Angel: And to all the Apostles, and Writers of the New Testament, by the graces of his Spirit; and to the Apostles again (at the choosing of Matthias in the place of Judas Iscariot) by lot.

Every man ought

Seeing then all Prophecy supposeth Vision, or Dream, (which two, when they be naturall, are the same,) or some especiall gift of God, so rarely observed in mankind, as to be admired where observed; And seeing as well such gifts, as the most extraordinary Dreams, and Visions, may proceed from God, not onely by his supernaturall, and immediate, but also by his naturall operation, and by mediation of second causes; there is need of Reason and Judgment to discern between naturall, and supernaturall Gifts, and between naturall, and supernaturall Visions, or Dreams And consequently men had need to be very circumspect, and wary, in obeying the voice of man, that pretending himself to be a Prophet, requires us to obey God in that way, which he in Gods name telleth us to be the way to happinesse. For he that pretends to teach men the way of so great felicity, pretends to govern them; that is to say, to rule, and reign over them; which is a thing, that all men naturally desire, and is therefore worthy to be suspected of Ambition and Imposture; and consequently, ought to be examined, and tryed by every man, before hee yeeld them obedience, unlesse he have yeelded it them already, in the institution of a Common-wealth; as when the Prophet is the Civill Soveraign, or by the Civil Soveraign Authorized. And if this examination of Prophets, and Spirits, were not allowed to every one of the people, it had been to no purpose, to set out the marks, by which every man might be able, to distinguish between those, whom they ought, and those whom they ought not to follow Seeing therefore such [231] marks are set out [*Deut.* 13. 1, &c] to know a Prophet by, and [1 *John* 4. 1. &c.] to know a Spirit by: and seeing there is so much Prophecying in the Old Testament, and so much Preaching in the New Testament against Prophets; and so much greater a number ordinarily of false Prophets, then of true; every one is to beware of obeying their directions, at their own perill. And first, that there were many more false then true Prophets, appears by this, that when Ahab [1 *Kings* 12.] consulted four hundred Prophets, they were all false Impostors, but onely one Michaiah And a little before the time of the Captivity, the Prophets were generally lyars. *The Prophets* (saith the Lord by *Jeremy*, cha. 14,

to examine the probability of a pretended Prophets Calling.

verse 14) *prophecy Lies in my name I sent them not. neither have I commanded them, nor spake unto them, they prophecy to you a false Vision, a thing of naught; and the deceit of their heart.* In so much as God commanded the People by the mouth of the Prophet *Jeremiah* [chap 23. 16.] not to obey them. *Thus saith the Lord of Hosts, hearken not unto the words of the Prophets, that prophecy to you. They make you vain, they speak a Vision of their own heart, and not out of the mouth of the Lord*

All prophecy but of the Soveraign Prophet is to be examined by every Subject.

Seeing then there was in the time of the Old Testament, such quarrells amongst the Visionary Prophets, one contesting with another, and asking, When departed the Spirit from me, to go to thee? as between Michaiah, and the rest of the four hundred; and such giving of the Lye to one another, (as in *Jerem* 14 14) and such controversies in the New Testament at this day, amongst the Spirituall Prophets: Every man then was, and now is bound to make use of his Naturall Reason, to apply to all Prophecy those Rules which God hath given us, to discern the true from the false. Of which Rules, in the Old Testament, one was, conformable doctrine to that which Moses the Soveraign Prophet had taught them; and the other the miraculous power of foretelling what God would bring to passe, as I have already shewn out of *Deut.* 13 1 *&c.* And in the New Testament there was but one onely mark; and that was the preaching of this Doctrine, *That Jesus is the Christ*, that is, the King of the Jews, promised in the Old Testament. Whosoever denyed that Article, he was a false Prophet, whatsoever miracles he might seem to work, and he that taught it was a true Prophet. For St. *John* [1 Epist 4. 2, &c.] speaking expressely of the means to examine Spirits, whether they be of God, or not; after he had told them that there would arise false Prophets, saith thus, *Hereby know ye the Spirit of God Every Spirit that confesseth that Jesus Christ is come in the flesh, is of God*; that is, is approved and allowed as a Prophet of God: not that he is a godly man, or one of the Elect, for this, that he confesseth, professeth, or preacheth Jesus to be the Christ; but for that he is a Prophet avowed For God sometimes speaketh by Prophets, whose persons he hath

not accepted; as he did by Baalam; and as he foretold Saul of his death, by the Witch of Endor. Again in the next verse, *Every Spirit that confesseth not that Jesus Christ is come in the flesh, is not of Christ. And this is the Spirit of Antichrist.* So that the Rule is perfect on both sides; that he is a true Prophet, which preacheth [232]
the Messiah already come, in the person of Jesus; and he a false one that denyeth him come, and looketh for him in some future Impostor, that shall take upon him that honour falsely, whom the Apostle there properly calleth Antichrist. Every man therefore ought to consider who is the Soveraign Prophet; that is to say, who it is, that is Gods Vicegerent on Earth; and hath next under God, the Authority of Governing Christian men, and to observe for a Rule, that Doctrine, which in the name of God, hee hath commanded to bee taught; and thereby to examine and try out the truth of those Doctrines, which pretended Prophets with miracle, or without, shall at any time advance: and if they find it contrary to that Rule, to doe as they did, that came to Moses, and complained that there were some that Prop[h]ecyed in the Campe, whose Authority so to doe they doubted of; and leave to the Soveraign, as they did to Moses to uphold, or to forbid them, as hee should see cause; and if hee disavow them, then no more to obey their voice; or if he approve them, then to obey them, as men to whom God hath given a part of the Spirit of their Soveraigne. For when Christian men, take not their Christian Soveraign, for Gods Prophet; they must either take their owne Dreames, for the Prophecy they mean to bee governed by, and the tumour of their own hearts for the Spirit of God; or they must suffer themselves to bee lead by some strange Prince; or by some of their fellow subjects, that can bewitch them, by slaunder of the government, into rebellion, without other miracle to confirm their calling, then sometimes an extraordinary successe, and Impunity; and by this means destroying all laws, both divine, and humane, reduce all Order, Government, and Society, to the first Chaos of Violence, and Civill warre.

[233]

CHAP. XXXVII.

Of Miracles, and their Use.

A Miracle is a work that causeth Admiration.

By *Miracles* are signified the Admirable works of God: & therefore they are also called *Wonders*. And because they are for the most part, done, for a signification of his commandement, in such occasions, as without them, men are apt to doubt, (following their private naturall reasoning,) what he hath commanded, and what not, they are commonly in Holy Scripture, called *Signes*, in the same sense, as they are called by the Latines, *Ostenta*, and *Portenta*, from shewing, and foresignifying that, which the Almighty is about to bring to passe.

And must therefore be rare, and whereof there is no naturall cause known.

To understand therefore what is a Miracle, we must first understand what works they are, which men wonder at, and call Admirable. And there be but two things, which make men wonder at any event. The one is, if it be strange, that is to say, such, as the like of it hath never, or very rarely been produced: The other is, if when it is produced, we cannot imagine it to have been done by naturall means, but onely by the immediate hand of God. But when wee see some possible, naturall cause of it, how rarely soever the like has been done; or if the like have been often done, how impossible soever it be to imagine a naturall means thereof, we no more wonder, nor esteem it for a Miracle.

Therefore, if a Horse, or Cow should speak, it were a Miracle; because both the thing is strange, & the naturall cause difficult to imagin: So also were it, to see a strange deviation of nature, in the production of some new shape of a living creature But when a man, or other Animal, engenders his like, though we know no more how this is done, than the other; yet because 'tis usuall, it is no Miracle In like manner, if a man be metamorphosed into a stone, or into a pillar, it is a Miracle; because strange: but if a peece of wood be so changed; because we see it often, it is no Miracle and yet we know no more, by what operation of God, the one is brought to passe, than the other.

The first Rainbow that was seen in the world, was a Miracle, because the first; and consequently strange; and served for a sign from God, placed in heaven, to assure his people, there should be no more an universall destruction of the world by Water. But at this day, because they are frequent, they are not Miracles, neither to them that know their naturall causes, nor to them who know them not. Again, there be many rare works produced by the Art of man: yet when we know they are done; because thereby wee know also the means how they are done, we count them not for Miracles, because not wrought by the immediate hand of God, but by [234] mediation of humane Industry.

That which seemeth a Miracle to one man, may seem otherwise to another.

Furthermore, seeing Admiration and Wonder, is consequent to the knowledge and experience, wherewith men are endued, some more, some lesse; it followeth, that the same thing, may be a Miracle to one, and not to another. And thence it is, that ignorant, and superstitious men make great Wonders of those works, which other men, knowing to proceed from Nature, (which is not the immediate, but the ordinary work of God,) admire not at all: As when Ecclipses of the Sun and Moon have been taken for supernaturall works, by the common people; when neverthelesse, there were others, could from their naturall causes, have foretold the very hour they should arrive. Or, as when a man, by confederacy, and secret intelligence, getting knowledge of the private actions of an ignorant, unwary man, thereby tells him, what he has done in former time, it seems to him a Miraculous thing; but amongst wise, and cautelous men, such Miracles as those, cannot easily be done.

The End of Miracles.

Again, it belongeth to the nature of a Miracle, that it be wrought for the procuring of credit to Gods Messengers, Ministers, and Prophets, that thereby men may know, they are called, sent, and employed by God, and thereby be the better inclined to obey them. And therefore, though the creation of the world, and after that the destruction of all living creatures in the universall deluge, were admirable works; yet because they were not done to procure credit to any Prophet, or other Minister of God, they use not to be called Miracles.

For how admirable soever any work be, the Admiration
consisteth not in that it could be done, because men
naturally beleeve the Almighty can doe all things, but
because he does it at the Prayer, or Word of a man.
But the works of God in Egypt, by the hand of Moses,
were properly Miracles: because they were done with
intention to make the people of Israel beleeve, that
Moses came unto them, not out of any design of his owne
interest, but as sent from God. Therefore after God had
commanded him to deliver the Israelites from the
Egyptian bondage, when he said *They will not beleeve me,*
but will say, the Lord hath not appeared unto me, God gave
him power, to turn the Rod he had in his hand into
a Serpent, and again to return it into a Rod; and by
putting his hand into his bosome, to make it leprous;
and again by pulling it out to make it whole, to make
the Children of Israel beleeve (as it is verse 5.) that the
God of their Fathers had appeared unto him: And if
that were not enough, he gave him power to turn their
waters into bloud. And when hee had done these
Exo. 4. 1, *&c.* Miracles before the people, it is said (verse 41.) that *they*
beleeved him. Neverthelesse, for fear of Pharaoh, they
durst not yet obey him. Therefore the other works
which were done to plague Pharaoh, and the Egyptians,
tended all to make the Israelites beleeve in Moses, and
were properly Miracles. In like manner if we consider
all the Miracles done by the hand of Moses, and all the
rest of the Prophets, till the Captivity; and those of
our Saviour, and his Apostles afterward; we shall find,
[235] their end was alwaies to beget, or confirm beleefe, that
they came not of their own motion, but were sent by
God. Wee may further observe in Scripture, that the
end of Miracles, was to beget beleef, not universally in
all men, elect, and reprobate; but in the elect only;
that is to say, in such as God had determined should
become his Subjects. For those miraculous plagues of
Egypt, had not for end, the conversion of Pharaoh; For
God had told Moses before, that he would harden the
heart of Pharaoh, that he should not let the people goe:
And when he let them goe at last, not the Miracles
perswaded him, but the plagues forced him to it So

also of our Saviour, it is written, (*Mat.* 13. 58.) that he wrought not many Miracles in his own countrey, because of their unbeleef; and (in *Marke* 6 5.) in stead of, *he wrought not many*, it is, *he could work none.* It was not because he wanted power; which to say, were blasphemy against God; nor that the end of Miracles was not to convert incredulous men to Christ; for the end of all the Miracles of Moses, of the Prophets, of our Saviour, and of his Apostles was to adde men to the Church; but it was, because the end of their Miracles, was to adde to the Church (not all men, but) such as should be saved; that is to say, such as God had elected. Seeing therefore our Saviour was sent from his Father, hee could not use his power in the conversion of those, whom his Father had rejected They that expounding this place of St. *Marke*, say, that this word, *Hee could not*, is put for, *He would not*, do it without example in the Greek tongue, (where *Would not*, is put sometimes for *Could not*, in things inanimate, that have no will; but *Could not*, for *Would not*, never,) and thereby lay a stumbling block before weak Christians; as if Christ could doe no Miracles, but amongst the credulous.

From that which I have here set down, of the nature, and use of a Miracle, we may define it thus, *A* MIRACLE, *is a work of God, (besides his operation by the way of Nature, ordained in the Creation,) done, for the making manifest to his elect, the mission of an extraordinary Minister for their salvation.*

The definition of a Miracle

And from this definition, we may inferre; First, that in all Miracles, the work done, is not the effect of any vertue in the Prophet; because it is the effect of the immediate hand of God; that is to say, God hath done it, without using the Prophet therein, as a subordinate cause.

Secondly, that no Devil, Angel, or other created Spirit, can do a Miracle. For it must either be by vertue of some naturall science, or by Incantation, that is, vertue of words. For if the Inchanters do it by their own power independent, there is some power that proceedeth not from God; which all men deny: and if they doe it by power given them, then is the work not from the immediate hand of God, but naturall, and consequently no Miracle.

There be some texts of Scripture, that seem to attribute the power of working wonders (equall to some of those immediate Miracles, wrought by God himself,) to certain Arts of Magick, and Incantation. As for example, when
[236] we read that after the Rod of Moses being cast on the
Exod. 7. 11. ground became a Serpent, *the Magicians of Egypt did the like by their Enchantments*, and that after Moses had turned the waters of the Egyptian Streams, Rivers, Ponds,
Exod. 7. 22. and Pooles of water into blood, *the Magicians of Egypt did so likewise, with their Enchantments*; and that after Moses had by the power of God brought frogs upon the
Exod. 8. 7. land, *the Magicians also did so with their Enchantments, and brought up frogs upon the land of Egypt*, will not a man be apt to attribute Miracles to Enchantments; that is to say, to the efficacy of the sound of Words; and think the same very well proved out of this, and other such places? and yet there is no place of Scripture that telleth us what an Enchantment is. If therefore Enchantment be not, as many think it, a working of strange effects by spells, and words; but Imposture, and delusion, wrought by ordinary means; and so far from supernaturall, as the Impostors need not the study so much as of naturall causes, but the ordinary ignorance, stupidity, and superstition of mankind, to doe them; those texts that seem to countenance the power of Magick, Witchcraft, and Enchantment, must needs have another sense, than at first sight they seem to bear.

That men are apt to be deceived by false Miracles.

For it is evident enough, that Words have no effect, but on those that understand them; and then they have no other, but to signifie the intentions, or passions of them that speak; and thereby produce, hope, fear, or other passions, or conceptions in the hearer. Therefore when a Rod seemeth a Serpent, or the Waters Bloud, or any other Miracle seemeth done by Enchantment; if it be not to the edification of Gods people, not the Rod, nor the Water, nor any other thing is enchanted; that is to say, wrought upon by the Words, but the Spectator. So that all the Miracle consisteth in this, that the Enchanter has deceived a man; which is no Miracle, but a very easie matter to doe.

For such is the ignorance, and aptitude to error generally of all men, but especially of them that have not much knowledge of naturall causes, and of the nature, and interests of men; as by innumerable and easie tricks to be abused. What opinion of miraculous power, before it was known there was a Science of the course of the Stars, might a man have gained, that should have told the people, This hour, or day the Sun should be darkned? A Juggler by the handling of his goblets, and other trinkets, if it were not now ordinarily practised, would be thought to do his wonders by the power at least of the Devil. A man that hath practised to speak by drawing in of his breath, (which kind of men in antient time were called *Ventriloqui*,) and so make the weaknesse of his voice seem to proceed, not from the weak impulsion of the organs of Speech, but from distance of place, is able to make very many men beleeve it is a voice from Heaven, whatsoever he please to tell them. And for a crafty man, that hath enquired into the secrets, and familiar confessions that one man ordinarily maketh to another of his actions and adventures past, to tell them him again is no hard matter; and yet there be many, that by such means as that, obtain the reputation of being Conjurers. But it is too long a businesse, to [237] reckon up the severall sorts of those men, which the Greeks called *Thaumaturgi*, that is to say, workers of things wonderfull; and yet these do all they do, by their own single dexterity. But if we looke upon the Impostures wrought by Confederacy, there is nothing how impossible soever to be done, that is impossible to bee beleeved. For two men conspiring, one to seem lame, the other to cure him with a charme, will deceive many: but many conspiring, one to seem lame, another so to cure him, and all the rest to bear witnesse; will deceive many more.

Cautions against the Imposture of Miracles.

In this aptitude of mankind, to give too hasty beleefe to pretended Miracles, there can be no better, nor I think any other caution, then that which God hath prescribed, first by Moses, (as I have said before in the precedent chapter,) in the beginning of the 13. and end of the 18. of *Deuteronomy*; That wee take not any for Prophets, that teach any other Religion, then that which Gods Lieutenant, (which at that time was Moses,) hath established; nor any, (though he teach the same Religion,) whose Prædiction we doe not see come to passe. Moses therefore in his time, and Aaron, and his successors in their times, and the Soveraign Governour of Gods people, next under God himself, that is to say, the Head of the Church in all times, are to be consulted, what doctrine he hath established, before wee give credit to a pretended Miracle, or Prophet. And when that is done, the thing they pretend to be a Miracle, we must both see it done, and use all means possible to consider, whether it be really done; and not onely so, but whether it be such, as no man can do the like by his naturall power, but that it requires the immediate hand of God And in this also we must have recourse to Gods Lieutenant; to whom in all doubtfull cases, wee have submitted our private judgments. For example; if a man pretend, that after certain words spoken over a peece of bread, that presently God hath made it not bread, but a God, or a man, or both, and neverthelesse it looketh still as like bread as ever it did; there is no reason for any man to think it really done, nor consequently to fear him, till he enquire of God, by his Vicar, or Lieutenant, whether it be done, or not. If he say not, then followeth that which Moses saith, (*Deut.* 18. 22) *he hath spoken it presumptuously, thou shalt not fear him.* If he say 'tis done, then he is not to contradict it. So also if wee see not, but onely hear tell of a Miracle, we are to consult the Lawful Church; that is to say, the lawful Head thereof, how far we are to give credit to the relators of it. And this is chiefly the case of men, that in these days live under Christian Soveraigns. For in these times, I do not know one man, that ever saw any such wondrous work, done by the charm, or at the word, or prayer of a man, that a man endued but with a mediocrity of reason, would think supernaturall: and the question is no more, whether what wee see done, be a Miracle, whether the Miracle we hear, or read of, were a reall work, and not the Act of a tongue, or pen; but in plain terms, whether the report be true, or a lye. In which question we are not every one. to make our own private Reason, or Conscience, but the Publique Reason, that is, the reason of Gods Supreme Lieutenant, Judge; and indeed we have made him Judge already, if wee have given him a Soveraign power, to [238] doe all that is necessary for our peace and defence. A private man has alwaies the liberty, (because thought is free,) to beleeve, or not beleeve in his heart, those acts that have been given out for Miracles, according as he shall see, what benefit can accrew by mens belief, to those that pretend, or countenance them, and thereby conjecture, whether they be Miracles, or Lies But when it comes to confession of that faith, the Private Reason must submit to the Publique; that is to say, to Gods Lieutenant But who is this Lieutenant of God, and Head of the Church, shall be considered in its proper place hereafter.

CHAP. XXXVIII.

Of the Signification in Scripture of ETERNALL LIFE, HELL, SALVATION, THE WORLD TO COME, *and* REDEMPTION

THE maintenance of Civill Society, depending on Justice, and Justice on the power of Life and Death, and other lesse Rewards and Punishments, residing in them that have the Soveraignty of the Common-wealth; It is impossible a Common-wealth should stand. where any other than the Soveraign, hath a power of giving greater rewards than Life; and of inflicting greater punishments, than Death Now seeing *Eternall life* is a greater reward, than the *life present*; and *Eternall torment* a greater punishment than the *death of Nature*; It is a thing worthy to be well considered, of all men that desire (by obeying Authority) to avoid the calamities of Confusion, and Civill war, what is meant in holy Scripture, by *Life Eternall*, and *Torment Eternall*; and for what offences, and against whom committed, men are to be *Eternally tormented*, and for what actions, they are to obtain *Eternall life*

The place of Adams Eternity if he had not sinned, had been the terrestiall Paradise

And first we find, that Adam was created in such a condition of life, as had he not broken the commandement of God, he had enjoyed it in the Paradise of Eden Everlastingly. For there was the *Tree of life*, whereof he was so long allowed to eat, as he should forbear to eat of the tree of Knowledge of Good and Evill; which was not allowed him. And therefore as soon as he had eaten of it, God thrust him out of Paradise, *lest he should put forth his hand, and take also of the tree of life, and live for ever.* (*Gen.* 3 22) By which it seemeth to me, (with submission neverthelesse both in this, and in all questions, whereof the determination dependeth on the Scriptures, to the interpretation of the Bible authorized by the Common-wealth, whose Subject I am,) that Adam if he had not sinned, had had an Eternall Life on Earth: and that Mortality entred upon himself, and his posterity, by his first Sin. Not that actuall Death then entred; for Adam then could never have had children; whereas he lived long after, and saw a numerous posterity ere he dyed. But where it is said, *In the day that thou eatest thereof, thou shalt surely die*, it must needs bee meant of his Mortality, and certitude of death. Seeing then Eternall life was lost by Adams forfeiture, in committing sin, he that should cancell that forfeiture was to recover [239] thereby, that Life again Now Jesus Christ hath satisfied for the sins of all that beleeve in him; and therefore recovered to all beleevers, that ETERNALL LIFE, which was lost by the sin of Adam. And in this sense it is, that the comparison of St. Paul holdeth (*Rom.* 5. 18, 19.) *As by the offence of one, Judgment came upon all men to condemnation, even so by the righteousnesse of one, the free gift came upon all men to Justification of Life.* Which is again (1 *Cor.* 15 21, 22) more perspicuously delivered in these words, *For since by man came death, by man came also the resurrection of the dead. For as in Adam all die, even so in Christ shall all be made alive.*

Texts concerning the place of Life Eternall, for Beleevers.

Concerning the place wherein men shall enjoy that Eternall Life, which Christ hath obtained for them, the texts next before alledged seem to make it on Earth. For if as in Adam, all die, that is, have forfeited Paradise, and Eternall Life on Earth, even so in Christ all shall bee made alive ; then all men shall be made to live on Earth ; for else the comparison were not proper. Hereunto seemeth to agree that of the Psalmist, (*Psal.* 133. 3.) *Upon Zion God commanded the blessing, even Life for evermore*· for Zion, is in Jerusalem, upon Earth · as also that of S. Joh. (*Rev.* 2. 7.) *To him that overcommeth I will give to eat of the tree of life, which is in the midst of the Paradise of God.* This was the tree of Adams Eternall life ; but his life was to have been on Earth. The same seemeth to be confirmed again by St. Joh (*Rev.* 21. 2.) where he saith, *I John saw the Holy City, New Jerusalem, coming down from God out of heaven, prepared as a Bride adorned for her husband* · and again v. 10. to the same effect As if he should say, the new Jerusalem, the Paradise of God, at the coming again of Christ, should come down to Gods people from Heaven, and not they goe up to it from Earth. And this differs nothing from that, which the two men in white clothing (that is, the two Angels) said to the Apostles, that were looking upon Christ ascending (*Acts* 1. 11.) *This same Jesus, who is taken up from you into Heaven, shall so come, as you have seen him go up into Heaven.* Which soundeth as if they had said, he should come down to govern them under his Father, Eternally here , and not take them up to govern them in Heaven ; and is conformable to the Restauration of the Kingdom of God, instituted under Moses ; which was a Political government of the Jews on Earth. Again, that saying of our Saviour (*Mat.* 22. 30.) *that in the Resurrection they neither marry, nor are given in marriage, but are as the Angels of God in heaven,* is a description of an Eternall Life, resembling that which we lost in Adam in the point of Marriage. For seeing Adam, and Eve, if they had not sinned, had lived on Earth Eternally, in their individuall persons ; it is manifest, they should not continually have procreated their kind. For if Immortals should have generated, as Mankind doth now ; the Earth in a small time, would not have been able to afford them place to stand on The Jews that asked our Saviour the question, whose wife the woman that had married many brothers, should be, in the resurrection, knew not what were the consequences of Life Eternall: and therefore our Saviour puts them in mind of this consequence of Immortality; that there shal be no Generation, and consequently no marriage, no more than there is Marriage, or generation among the Angels. The comparison between that Eternall life which Adam lost, and our Saviour by his Victory [240] over death hath recovered, holdeth also in this, that as Adam lost Eternall Life by his sin, and yet lived after it for a time; so the faithful Christian hath recovered Eternal Life by Christs passion, though he die a natural death, and remaine dead for a time; namely, till the Resurrection For as Death is reckoned from the Condemnation of Adam, not from the Execution; so Life is reckoned from the Absolution, not from the Resurrection of them that are elected in Christ.

Ascension into heaven.

That the place wherein men are to live Eternally, after the Resurrection, is the Heavens, meaning by Heaven, those parts of the world, which are the most remote from Earth, as where the stars are, or above the stars, in another Higher Heaven, called *Cœlum Empyreum*, (whereof there is no mention in Scripture, nor ground in Reason) is not easily to be drawn from any text that I can find By the Kingdome of Heaven, is meant the Kingdom of the King that dwelleth in Heaven; and his Kingdome was the people of Israel, whom he ruled by the Prophets his Lieutenants, first Moses, and after him Eleazar, and the Soveraign Priests, till in the days of Samuel they rebelled, and would have a mortall man for their King, after the manner of other Nations. And when our Saviour Christ, by the preaching of his Ministers, shall have perswaded the Jews to return, and called the Gentiles to his obedience, then shall there be a new Kingdom of Heaven; because our King shall then be God, whose *throne* is Heaven, without any necessity evident in the Scripture, that man shall ascend to his happinesse any higher than Gods *footstool*, the Earth. On the contrary, we find written (*Joh.* 3 13) that *no man hath ascended into Heaven, but he that came down from Heaven, even the Son of man, that is in Heaven.* Where I observe by the way, that these words are not, as those which go immediately before, the words of our

Saviour, but of St. John himself; for Christ was then not in Heaven, but upon the Earth. The like is said of David (*Acts* 2. 34.) where St Peter, to prove the Ascension of Christ, using the words of the Psalmist, (*Psal.* 16. 10.) *Thou wilt not leave my soule in Hell, nor suffer thine Holy one to see corruption*, saith, they were spoken (not of David, but) of Christ; and to prove it, addeth this Reason, *For David is not ascended into Heaven.* But to this a man may easily answer, and say, that though their bodies were not to ascend till the generall day of Judgment, yet their souls were in Heaven as soon as they were departed from their bodies, which also seemeth to be confirmed by the words of our Saviour (*Luke* 20 37, 38.) who proving the Resurrection out of the words of Moses, saith thus, *That the dead are raised, even Moses shewed, at the bush, when he calleth the Lord, the God of Abraham, and the God of Isaac, and the God of Jacob For he is not a God of the Dead, but of the Living; for they all live to him.* But if these words be to be understood only of the Immortality of the Soul, they prove not at all that which our Saviour intended to prove, which was the Resurrection of the Body, that is to say, the Immortality of the Man. Therefore our Saviour meaneth, that those Patriarchs were Immortall; not by a property consequent to the essence, and nature of mankind; but by the will of God, that was pleased of his mere grace, to bestow *Eternall life* upon the faithfull. And though at that time the Patriarchs and many other [241] faithfull men were *dead*, yet as it is in the text, they *lived to God*; that is, they were written in the Book of Life with them that were absolved of their sinnes, and ordained to Life eternall at the Resurrection That the Soul of man is in its own nature Eternall, and a living Creature independent on the body; or that any meer man is Immortall, otherwise than by the Resurrection in the last day, (except *Enos* and *Elias*,) is a doctrine not apparent in Scripture. The whole 14. Chapter of *Job*, which is the speech not of his friends, but of himselfe, is a complaint of this Mortality of Nature; and yet no contradiction of the Immortality at the Resurrection. *There is hope of a tree* (saith hee verse 7.) *if it be cast down, Though the root thereof wax old, and the stock thereof die in the ground, yet when it senteth the water it will bud, and bring forth boughes like a Plant. But man dyeth, and wasteth away, yea, man giveth up the Ghost, and where is he?* and (verse 12.) *man lyeth down, and riseth not, till the heavens be no more* But when is it, that the heavens shall be no more? St. Peter tells us, that it is at the generall Resurrection For in his 2. Epistle, 3 Chapter, and 7 verse, he saith, that *the Heavens and the Earth that are now, are reserved unto fire against the day of Judgment, and perdition of ungodly men*, and (verse 12.) *looking for, and hasting to the comming of God, wherein the Heavens shall be on fire, and shall be dissolved, and the Elements shall melt with fervent heat Neverthelesse, we according to the promise look for new Heavens, and a new Earth, wherein dwelleth righteousnesse.* Therefore where Job saith, man riseth not till the Heavens be no more; it is all one, as if he had said, the Immortall Life (and Soule and Life in the Scripture, do usually signifie the same thing) beginneth not in man, till the Resurrection, and day of Judgement, and hath for cause, not his specificall nature, and generation; but the Promise For St. Peter saies not, *Wee look for new heavens, and a new earth,* (*from Nature,*) but *from Promise.*

Lastly, seeing it hath been already proved out of divers evident places of Scripture, in the 35. chapter of this book, that the Kingdom of God is a Civil Commonwealth, where God himself is Soveraign, by vertue first of the *Old*, and since of the *New* Covenant, wherein he reigneth by his Vicar, or Lieutenant, the same places do therefore also prove, that after the comming again of our Saviour in his Majesty, and glory, to reign actually, and Eternally; the Kingdom of God is to be on Earth. But because this doctrine (though proved out of places of Scripture not few, nor obscure) will appear to most men a novelty; I doe but propound it, maintaining nothing in this, or any other paradox of Religion; but attending the end of that dispute of the sword, concerning the Authority, (not yet amongst my Countreymen decided,) by which all sorts of doctrine are to bee approved, or rejected; and whose commands, both in speech, and writing, (whatsoever be the opinions of private men) must by all men, that mean to be protected by their Laws, be obeyed. For the points of doctrine concerning the Kingdome [of] God, have so great influence on the Kingdome of Man, as not to be determined, but [242] by them, that under God have the Soveraign Power.

The place after Judgment, of those who were never in the Kingdome of God, or having been in, are cast out.

As the Kingdome of God, and Eternal Life, so also Gods Enemies, and their Torments after Judgment, appear by the Scripture, to have their place on Earth. The name of the place, where all men remain till the Resurrection, that were either buryed, or swallowed up of the Earth, is usually called in Scripture, by words that signifie *under ground*; which the Latines read generally *Infernus*, and *Inferi*, and the Greeks ᾅδης; that is to say, a place where men cannot see; and containeth as well the Grave, as any other deeper place But for the place of the damned after the Resurrection, it is not determined, neither in the Old, nor New Testament, by any note of situation; but onely by the company as that it shall bee, where such wicked men were, as God in former times in extraordinary, and miraculous manner, had destroyed from off the face of the Earth: As for example, that they are *in Inferno*, in *Tartarus*, or in the bottomelesse pit, because *Corah*, *Dathan*, and *Abirom*, were swallowed up alive into the earth. Not that the Writers of the Scripture would have us beleeve, there could be in the globe of the Earth, which is not only finite, but also (compared to the height of the Stars) of no considerable magnitude, a pit without a bottome, that is, a hole of infinite depth, such as the Greeks in their *Dæmonologie* (that is to say, in their doctrine concerning *Dæmons*,) and after them the Romans called *Tartarus*; of which Virgill sayes,

Tartarus.

Bis patet in præceps, tantum tenditque sub umbras,
Quantus ad æthereum cœli suspectus Olympum:

for that is a thing the proportion of Earth to Heaven cannot bear: but that wee should beleeve them there, indefinitely, where those men are, on whom God inflicted that Exemplary punnishment.

The congregation of Giants.

Again, because those mighty men of the Earth, that lived in the time of Noah, before the floud, (which the Greeks called *Heroes*, and the Scripture *Giants*, and both say, were begotten, by copulation of the children of God, with the children of men,) were for their wicked life destroyed by the generall deluge: the place of the Damned, is therefore also sometimes marked out, by the company of those deceased Giants; as *Proverbs* 21. 16. *The man that wandreth out of the way of understanding, shall remain in the congregation of the Giants*, and Job 26. 5. *Behold the Giants groan under water, and they that dwell with them.* Here the place of the Damned, is under the water. And *Isaiah* 14 9 *Hell is troubled how to meet thee*, (that is, the King of Babylon) *and will displace the Giants for thee*: and here again the place of the Damned, (if the sense be literall,) is to be under water.

Lake of Fire

Thirdly, because the Cities of Sodom, and Gomorrah, by the extraordinary wrath of God, were consumed for their wickednesse with Fire and Brimstone, and together with them the countrey about made a stinking bituminous Lake· the place of the Damned is sometimes expressed by Fire, and a Fiery Lake· as in the *Apocalypse* ch. 21 8. *But the timorous, incredulous, and abominable, and Mur-*
[243] *derers, and Whoremongers, and Sorcerers, and Idolaters, and all Lyars, shall have their part in the Lake that burneth with Fire, and Brimstone; which is the second Death.* So that it is manifest, that Hell Fire, which is here expressed by Metaphor, from the reall Fire of Sodome, signifieth not any certain kind, or place of Torment; but is to be taken indefinitely, for Destruction, as it is in the 20. Chapter, at the 14 verse; where it is said, that *Death and Hell were cast into the Lake of Fire*; that is to say, were abolished, and destroyed; as if after the day of Judgment, there shall be no more Dying, nor no more going into Hell; that is, no more going to *Hades* (from which word perhaps our word Hell is derived,) which is the same with no more Dying

Utter Darknesse.

Fourthly, from the Plague of Darknesse inflicted on the Egyptians, of which it is written (*Exod.* 10. 23) *They saw not one another, neither rose any man from his place for three days, but all the Children of Israel had light in their dwellings*; the place of the wicked after Judgment, is called *Utter Darknesse*, or (as it is in the originall) *Darknesse without*. And so it is expressed (*Mat.* 22. 13.) where the King commandeth his Servants, *to bind hand and foot the man that had not on his Wedding garment, and to cast him out*, εἰς τὸ σκότος τὸ ἐξώτερον, *Externall darknesse*, or *Darknesse without*: which though translated *Utter darknesse*, does not signifie *how great*, but *where* that darknesse is to be; namely, *without the habitation* of Gods Elect.

Gehenna, and Tophet.

Lastly, whereas there was a place neer Jerusalem, called the *Valley of the Children of Hinnon*; in a part whereof, called *Tophet*, the Jews had committed most grievous Idolatry, sacrificing their children to the Idol Moloch; and wherein also God had afflicted his enemies with most grievous punishments; and wherein Josias had burnt the Priests of Moloch upon their own Altars, as appeareth at large in the 2 of *Kings* chap. 23 the place served afterwards, to receive the filth, and garbage which was carried thither, out of the City; and there used to be fires made, from time to time, to purifie the aire, and take away the stench of Carrion From this abominable place, the Jews used ever after to call the place of the Damned, by the name of *Gehenna*, or *Valley of Hinnon*. And this *Gehenna*, is that word, which is usually now translated HELL, and from the fires from time to time there burning, we have the notion of *Everlasting*, and *Unquenchable Fire*.

Of the literall sense of the Scripture concerning Hell.

Seeing now there is none, that so interprets the Scripture, as that after the day of Judgment, the wicked are all Eternally to be punished in the Valley of Hinnon; or that they shall so rise again, as to be ever after under ground, or under water, or that after the Resurrection, they shall no more see one another, nor stir from one place to another, it followeth, me thinks, very necessarily, that that which is thus said concerning Hell Fire, is spoken metaphorically; and that therefore there is a proper sense to bee enquired after, (for of all Metaphors there is some reall ground, that may be expressed in proper words) both of the *Place* of *Hell*, and the nature of *Hellish Torments*, and *Tormentors*.

[244] And first for the Tormenters, wee have their nature, and properties, exactly and properly delivered by the names of, *The Enemy*, or *Satan*; *The Accuser*, or *Diabolus*; *The Destroyer*, or *Abaddon*. Which significant names, *Satan*, *Devill*, *Abaddon*, set not forth to us any Individuall person, as proper names use to doe; but onely an office, or quality; and are therefore Appellatives; which ought not to have been left untranslated, as they are, in the Latine, and Modern Bibles; because thereby they seem to be the proper names of *Dæmons*; and men are the more easily seduced to beleeve the doctrine of Devills; which at that time was the Religion of the Gentiles, and contrary to that of Moses, and of Christ.

Satan, Devill, not Proper names, but Appellatives.

And because by the *Enemy*, the *Accuser*, and *Destroyer*, is meant, the Enemy of them that shall be in the Kingdome of God; therefore if the Kingdome of God after the Resurrection, bee upon the Earth, (as in the former Chapter I have shewn by Scripture it seems to be,) The Enemy, and his Kingdome must be on Earth also For so also was it, in the time before the Jews had deposed God. For Gods Kingdome was in Palestine; and the Nations round about, were the Kingdomes of the Enemy; and consequently by *Satan*, is meant any Earthly Enemy of the Church.

Torments of Hell.

The Torments of Hell, are expressed sometimes, by *weeping, and gnashing of teeth*, as *Mat* 8 12. Sometimes, by *the worm of Conscience*; as *Isa*. 66 24. and *Mark* 9. 44, 46, 48: sometimes, by *Fire*, as in the place now quoted, *where the worm dyeth not, and the fire is not quenched*, and many places beside: sometimes by *shame, and contempt*, as *Dan*. 12 2. *And many of them that sleep in the dust of the Earth, shall awake; some to Everlasting life, and some to shame, and everlasting contempt* All which places design metaphorically a grief, and discontent of mind, from the sight of that Eternal felicity in others, which they themselves through their own incredulity, and disobedience have lost. And because such felicity in others, is not sensible but by comparison with their own actuall miseries. it followeth that they are to suffer such bodily paines, and calamities, as are incident to those, who not onely live under evill and cruell Governours, but have also for Enemy, the Eternall King of the Saints, God Almighty. And amongst these bodily paines, is to be reckoned also to every one of the wicked a second Death. For though the Scripture bee clear for an universall Resurrection ; yet wee do not read, that to any of the Reprobate is promised an Eternall life. For whereas St. *Paul* (1 *Cor.* 15. 42, 43.) to the question concerning what bodies men shall rise with again, saith, that *the body is sown in corruption, and is raised in incorruption ; It is sown in dishonour, it is raised in glory ; it is sown in weaknesse, it is raised in power* ; Glory and Power cannot be applyed to the bodies of the wicked : Nor can the name of *Second Death*, bee applyed to those that can never die but once : And although in Metaphoricall speech, a Calamitous life Everlasting, may bee called an Everlasting Death yet it cannot well be understood of a *Second Death.* The fire prepared for the wicked, is an Everlasting [245] Fire : that is to say, the estate wherein no man can be without torture, both of body and mind, after the Resurrection, shall endure for ever ; and in that sense the Fire shall be unquenchable, and the torments Everlasting · but it cannot thence be inferred, that hee who shall be cast into that fire, or be tormented with those torments, shall endure, and resist them so, as to be eternally burnt, and tortured, and yet never be destroyed, nor die. And though there be many places that affirm Everlasting Fire, and Torments (into which men may be cast successively one after another for ever ; yet I find none that affirm there shall bee an Eternall Life therein of any individuall person ; but to the contrary, an Everlasting Death, which is the Second Death *For after Death, and the Grave shall have delivered* *Apoc.* 20 *up the dead which were in them, and every man be judged* 13, 14. *according to his works ; Death and the Grave shall also be cast into the Lake of Fire. This is the Second Death.* Whereby it is evident, that there is to bee a Second Death of every one that shall bee condemned at the day of Judgement, after which hee shall die no more.

The Joyes of Life Eternall, and Salvation the same thing.

The joyes of Life Eternall, are in Scripture comprehended all under the name of SALVATION, or *being saved*. To be saved, is to be secured, either respectively, against speciall Evills, or absolutely, against all Evill, comprehending Want, Sicknesse, and Death it self. And because man was created in a condition Immortall, not subject to corruption, and consequently to nothing that tendeth to the dissolution of his nature, and fell from that happinesse by the sin of Adam; it followeth, that to be *saved* from Sin, is to be saved from all the Evill, and Calamities that Sinne hath brought upon us. And therefore in the Holy Scripture, Remission of Sinne, and Salvation from Death and Misery, is the same thing, as it appears by the words of our Saviour, who having cured a man sick of the Palsey, by saying, (*Mat.* 9. 2.) *Son be of good cheer, thy Sins be forgiven thee*; and knowing that the Scribes took for blasphemy, that a man should pretend to forgive Sins, asked them (v. 5) *whether it were easier to say, Thy Sinnes be forgiven thee, or, Arise and walk*; signifying thereby, that it was all one, as to the saving of the sick, to say, *Thy Sins are forgiven*, and *Arise and walk*; and that he used that form of speech, onely to shew he had power to forgive Sins. And it is besides evident in reason, that since Death and Misery, were the punishments of Sin, the discharge of Sinne, must also be a discharge of Death and Misery; that is to say, Salvation absolute, such as the faithfull are to enjoy after the day of Judgment, by the power, and favour of Jesus Christ, who for that cause is called our SAVIOUR.

Salvation from Sin, and from Misery, all one.

Concerning Particular Salvations, such as are understood, 1 *Sam.* 14 39. *as the Lord liveth that saveth Israel*, that is, from their temporary enemies, and 2 *Sam.* 22 4. *Thou art my Saviour, thou savest me from violence*; and 2 *Kings* 13 5 *God gave the Israelites a Saviour, and so they were delivered from the hand of the Assyrians*, and the
[246] like, I need say nothing, there being neither difficulty, nor interest, to corrupt the interpretation of texts of that kind.

The Place of Eternall Salvation.

But concerning the Generall Salvation, because it must be in the Kingdome of Heaven, there is great difficulty concerning the Place On one side, by *Kingdome* (which is an estate ordained by men for their perpetuall security against enemies, and want) it seemeth that this Salvation should be on Earth. For by Salvation is set forth unto us, a glorious Reign of our King, by Conquest; not a safety by Escape: and therefore there where we look for Salvation, we must look also for Triumph; and before Triumph, for Victory, and before Victory, for Battell; which cannot well be supposed, shall be in Heaven. But how good soever this reason may be, I will not trust to it, without very evident places of Scripture. The state of Salvation is described at large, *Isaiah* 33. ver. 20, 21, 22, 23, 24.

Look upon Zion, the City of our solemnities; thine eyes shall see Jerusalem a quiet habitation, a tabernacle that shall not be taken down; not one of the stakes thereof shall ever be removed, neither shall any of the cords thereof be broken.

But there the glorious Lord will be unto us a place of broad rivers, and streams; wherein shall goe no Gally with oares; neither shall gallant ship passe thereby.

For the Lord is our Judge, the Lord is our Lawgiver, the Lord is our King, he will save us

Thy tacklings are loosed; they could not well strengthen their mast; they could not spread the sail: then is the prey of a great spoil divided; the lame take the prey.

And the Inhabitant shall not say, I am sicke; the people that shall dwell therein shall be forgiven their Iniquity.

In which words wee have the place from whence Salvation is to proceed, *Jerusalem, a quiet habitation*; the Eternity of it, *a tabernacle that shall not be taken down, &c.* The Saviour of it, *the Lord, their Judge, their Lawgiver, their King, he will save us*; the Salvation, *the Lord shall be to them as a broad mote of swift waters, &c.* the condition of their Enemies, *their tacklings are loose, their masts weak, the lame shal take the spoil of them.* The condition of the Saved, *The Inhabitant shal not say, I am sick*: And lastly, all this is comprehended in Forgivenesse of sin, *The people that dwell therein shall be forgiven their iniquity.* By which it is evident, that Salvation shall be on Earth, then, when God shall reign, (at the coming again of Christ) in Jerusalem; and from Jerusalem shall proceed the Salvation of the Gentiles

that shall be received into Gods Kingdome as is also more expressely declared by the same Prophet, Chap 65. 20, 21. *And they* (that is, the Gentiles who had any Jew in bondage) *shall bring all your brethren, for an offering to the Lord, out of all nations, upon horses, and in charets, and in litters, and upon mules, and upon swift beasts, to my holy mountain, Jerusalem, saith the Lord, as the Children of Israel bring an offering in a clean vessell into the House of the Lord. And I will also take of them for Priests and for Levites, saith the Lord.* Whereby it is manifest, that the chief seat of Gods Kingdome (which
[247] is the Place, from whence the Salvation of us that were Gentiles, shall proceed) shall be Jerusalem: And the same is also confirmed by our Saviour, in his discourse with the woman of Samaria, concerning the place of Gods worship; to whom he saith, *John* 4. 22. that the Samaritans worshipped they knew not what, but the Jews worship what they knew, *For Salvation is of the Jews* (*ex Judæis,* that is, begins at the Jews): as if he should say, you worship God, but know not by whom he wil save you, as we doe, that know it shall be by one of the tribe of Judah, a Jew, not a Samaritan. And therefore also the woman not impertinently answered him again, *We know the Messias shall come.* So that which our Saviour saith, *Salvation is from the Jews,* is the same that Paul sayes (*Rom.* 1 16, 17.) *The Gospel is the power of God to Salvation to every one that beleeveth: To the Jew first, and also to the Greek For therein is the righteousnesse of God revealed from faith to faith*; from the faith of the Jew, to the faith of the Gentile. In the like sense the Prophet *Joel* describing the day of Judgment, (chap 2 30, 31) that God would *shew wonders in heaven, and in earth, bloud, and fire, and pillars of smoak. The Sun should be turned to darknesse, and the Moon into bloud, before the great and terrible day of the Lord come,* he addeth verse 32. *and it shall come to passe, that whosoever shall call upon the name of the Lord, shall be saved. For in Mount Zion, and in Jerusalem shall be Salvation.* And *Obadiah* verse 17. saith the same, *Upon Mount Zion shall be Deliverance; and there shall be holinesse, and the house of Jacob shall possesse their possessions,* that is, the

possessions of the *Heathen*, which *possessions* he expresseth more particularly in the following verses, by the *mount of Esau*, the *Land of the Philistines*, the *fields of Ephraim*, of *Samaria*, *Gilead*, and the *Cities of the South*, and concludes with these words, *the Kingdom shall be the Lords*. All these places are for Salvation, and the Kingdome of God (after the day of Judgement) upon Earth. On the other side, I have not found any text that can probably be drawn, to prove any Ascension of the Saints into Heaven : that is to say, into any *Cœlum Empyreum*, or other ætheriall Region ; saving that it is called the Kingdome of Heaven · which name it may have, because God, that was King of the Jews, governed them by his commands, sent to Moses by Angels from Heaven ; and after their revolt, sent his Son from Heaven, to reduce them to their obedience ; and shall send him thence again, to rule both them, and all other faithfull men, from the day of Judgment, Everlastingly : or from that, that the Throne of this our Great King is in Heaven ; whereas the Earth is but his Footstoole But that the Subjects of God should have any place as high as his Throne, or higher than his Footstoole, it seemeth not sutable to the dignity of a King, nor can I find any evident text for it in holy Scripture

From this that hath been said of the Kingdom of God, and of Salvation, it is not hard to interpret what is meant by the WORLD TO COME There are three worlds mentioned in Scripture, the *Old World*, the *Present World*, and the *World to come*. Of the first, St. Peter speaks, *2 Pet* 2 5.
If God spared not the Old World, but saved Noah the eighth person, a Preacher of righteousnesse, bringing the flood upon the world of the ungodly, &c. So the *first World*, [248]
was from Adam to the generall Flood Of the present World, our Saviour speaks (*John* 18. 36) My *Kingdome is not of this World*. For he came onely to teach men the way of Salvation, and to renew the Kingdome of his Father, by his doctrine. Of the World to come, St Peter *2 Pet*. 3. 13.
speaks, *Neverthelesse we according to his promise look for new Heavens, and a new Earth.* This is that WORLD, wherein Christ coming down from Heaven, in the clouds, with great power, and glory, shall send his Angels, and

shall gather together his elect, from the four winds, and from the uttermost parts of the Earth, and thence forth reign over them, (under his Father) Everlastingly.

Redemption.

Salvation of a sinner, supposeth a precedent REDEMPTION; for he that is once guilty of Sin, is obnoxious to the Penalty of the same; and must pay (or some other for him) such Ransome, as he that is offended, and has him in his power, shall require. And seeing the person offended, is Almighty God, in whose power are all things; such Ransome is to be paid before Salvation can be acquired, as God hath been pleased to require. By this Ransome, is not intended a satisfaction for Sin, equivalent to the Offence, which no sinner for himselfe, nor righteous man can ever be able to make for another: The dammage a man does to another, he may make amends for by restitution, or recompence, but sin cannot be taken away by recompence; for that were to make the liberty to sin, a thing vendible. But sins may bee pardoned to the repentant, either *gratis*, or upon such penalty, as God is pleased to accept. That which God usually accepted in the Old Testament, was some Sacrifice, or Oblation. To forgive sin is not an act of Injustice, though the punishment have been threatned. Even amongst men, though the promise of Good, bind the promiser; yet threats, that is to say, promises of Evill, bind them not; much lesse shall they bind God, who is infinitely more mercifull then men. Our Saviour Christ therefore to *Redeem* us, did not in that sense satisfie for the Sins of men, as that his Death, of its own vertue, could make it unjust in God to punish sinners with Eternall death; but did make that Sacrifice, and Oblation of himself, at his first coming, which God was pleased to require, for the Salvation at his second coming, of such as in the mean time should repent, and beleeve in him. And though this act of our *Redemption*, be not alwaies in Scripture called a *Sacrifice*, and *Oblation*, but sometimes a *Price*; yet by *Price* we are not to understand any thing, by the value whereof, he could claim right to a pardon for us, from his offended Father; but that Price which God the Father was pleased in mercy to demand.

CHAP. XXXIX. [247]

Of the signification in Scripture of the word CHURCH.

THE word *Church, (Ecclesia)* signifieth in the Books of Holy Scripture divers things Sometimes (though not often) it is taken for *Gods House,* that is to say, for a Temple, wherein Christians assemble to perform holy duties publiquely; as, 1 *Cor.* 14. ver. 34 *Let your women keep silence in the Churches* · but this is Metaphorically put, for the Congregation there assembled; and hath been since used for the Edifice it self, to distinguish between the Temples of Christians, and Idolaters. The Temple of Jerusalem was *Gods house,* and the House of Prayer; and so is any Edifice dedicated by Christians to the worship of Christ, *Christs house* · and therefore the Greek Fathers call it Κυριακὴ, *The Lords house*; and thence, in our language it came to be called *Kyrke,* and *Church.* *Church the Lords house*

Church (when not taken for a House) signifieth the same that *Ecclesia* signified in the Grecian Common-wealths; that is to say, a Congregation, or an Assembly of Citizens, called forth, to hear the Magistrate speak unto them; and which in the Common-wealth of Rome was called *Concio,* as he that spake was called *Ecclesiastes,* and *Concionator* And when they were called forth by lawfull Authority, it was *Ecclesia legitima,* a *Lawfull Church,* ἔννομος Εκκλησία. But when they were excited by tumultuous, and seditious clamor, then it was a confused Church, Εκκλησία συγκεχυμένη *Ecclesia properly what.* *Acts* 19. 39

It is taken also sometimes for the men that have right to be of the Congregation, though not actually assembled; that is to say, for the whole multitude of Christian men, how far soever they be dispersed: as (*Act* 8. 3.) where it is said, that *Saul made havock of the Church*: And in this sense is *Christ* said to be Head of the Church. And sometimes for a certain part of Christians, as (*Col.* 4. 15.) *Salute the Church that is in his house* Sometimes also for the Elect onely; as (*Ephes* 5. 27) *A Glorious Church, without spot, or wrinkle, holy, and without blemish*; which is meant of the *Church triumphant,* or, *Church to come.* Sometimes, for a Congregation assembled, of professors of Christianity, whether their profession be true, or counterfeit, as it is understood, *Mat* 18. 17. where it is said, *Tell it to the Church, and if hee neglect to hear the Church, let him be to thee as a Gentile, or Publican.*

In what sense the Church is one Person. And in this last sense only it is that the *Church* can be taken for one Person; that is to say, that it can be said to have power to will, to pronounce, to command, to be obeyed, to make laws, or to doe any other action whatsoever; For without authority from a lawfull Congregation, whatsoever act be done in a concourse of people, [248] it is the particular act of every one of those that were present, and gave their aid to the performance of it; and not the act of them all in grosse, as of one body; much lesse the act of them that were absent, or that being present, were not willing it should be done According to this sense, I define a CHURCH to be, *A company of men professing Christian Religion, united in the person of one Soveraign; at whose command they ought to assemble, and without whose authority they ought not to assemble.* And because in all Common-wealths, that Assembly, which is without warrant from the Civil Soveraign, is unlawful; that Church also, which is assembled in any Common-wealth, that hath forbidden them to assemble, is an unlawfull Assembly.

Church defined.

A Christian Common-wealth, and a Church all one. It followeth also, that there is on Earth, no such universall Church, as all Christians are bound to obey; because there is no power on Earth, to which all other Common-wealths are subject: There are Christians, in the Dominions of severall Princes and States; but every one of them is subject to that Common-wealth, whereof he is himself a member; and consequently, cannot be subject to the commands of any other Person. And therefore a Church, such a one as is capable to Command, to Judge, Absolve, Condemn, or do any other act, is the same thing with a Civil Common-wealth, consisting of Christian men; and is called a *Civill State*, for that the subjects of it are *Men*; and a *Church*, for that the subjects thereof are *Christians*. *Temporall* and *Spirituall* Government, are but two words brought into the world, to make men see double, and mistake their *Lawfull Soveraign*. It is true, that the bodies of the faithfull, after the Resurrection, shall be not onely Spirituall, but Eternall: but in this life they are grosse, and corruptible. There is therefore no other Government in this life, neither of State, nor Religion, but Temporall; nor teaching of any doctrine, lawfull to any Subject, which the Governour both of the State, and of the Religion, forbiddeth to be taught: And that Governor must be one; or else there must needs follow Faction, and Civil war in the Common-wealth, between the *Church* and *State*; between *Spiritualists*, and *Temporalists*, between the *Sword of Justice*, and the *Shield of Faith*; and (which is more) in every Christian mans own brest, between the *Christian*, and the *Man*. The Doctors of the Church, are called Pastors; so also are Civill Soveraignes: But if Pastors be not subordinate one to another, so as that there may bee one chief Pastor, men will be taught contrary Doctrines, whereof both may be, and one must be false. Who that one chief Pastor is, according to the law of Nature, hath been already shewn; namely, that it is the Civill Soveraign And to whom the Scripture hath assigned that Office, we shall see in the Chapters following.

CHAP. XL. [249]

Of the RIGHTS *of the Kingdome of God, in* Abraham, Moses, *the* High Priests, *and the* Kings of Judah.

The Soveraign Rights of Abraham.

THE Father of the Faithfull, and first in the Kingdome of God by Covenant, was *Abraham*. For with him was the Covenant first made; wherein he obliged himself, and his seed after him, to acknowledge and obey the commands of God; not onely such, as he could take notice of, (as Morall Laws,) by the light of Nature; but also such, as God should in speciall manner deliver to him by Dreams, and Visions. For as to the Morall law, they were already obliged, and needed not have been contracted withall, by promise of the Land of Canaan. Nor was there any Contract, that could adde to, or strengthen the Obligation, by which both they, and all men else were bound naturally to obey God Almighty:

And therefore the Covenant which Abraham made with God, was to take for the Commandement of God, that which in the name of God was commanded him, in a Dream, or Vision; and to deliver it to his family, and cause them to observe the same.

In this Contract of God with Abraham, wee may observe three points of important consequence in the government of Gods people First, that at the making of this Covenant, God spake onely to Abraham, and therefore contracted not with any of his family, or seed, otherwise then as their wills (which make the essence of all Covenants) were before the Contract involved in the will of Abraham; who was therefore supposed to have had a lawfull power, to make them perform all that he covenanted for them. According whereunto (*Gen.* 18. 18, 19) God saith, *All the Nations of the Earth shall be blessed in him, For I know him that he will command his children and his houshold after him, and they shall keep the way of the Lord.* From whence may be concluded this first point, that they to whom God hath not spoken immediately, are to receive the positive commandements of God, from their Soveraign; as the family and seed of Abraham did from Abraham their Father, and Lord, and Civill Soveraign. And consequently in every Common-wealth, they who have no supernaturall Revelation to the contrary, ought to obey the laws of their own Soveraign, in the externall acts and profession of Religion. As for the inward *thought*, and *beleef* of men, which humane Governours can take no notice of, (for God onely knoweth the heart) they are not voluntary, nor [250] the effect of the laws, but of the unrevealed will, and of the power of God; and consequently fall not under obligation.

Abraham had the sole power of ordering the Religion of his own people.

No pretence of Private Spirit against the Religion of Abraham.

From whence proceedeth another point, that it was not unlawfull for Abraham, when any of his Subjects should pretend Private Vision, or Spirit, or other Revelation from God, for the countenancing of any doctrine which Abraham should forbid, or when they followed, or adhered to any such pretender, to punish them; and consequently that it is lawfull now for the Soveraign to punish any man that shall oppose his Private Spirit against the

Laws: For hee hath the same place in the Common-wealth, that Abraham had in his own Family.

Abraham sole Judge, and Interpreter of what God spake.

There ariseth also from the same, a third point; that as none but Abraham in his family, so none but the Soveraign in a Christian Common-wealth, can take notice what is, or what is not the Word of God. For God spake onely to Abraham, and it was he onely, that was able to know what God said, and to interpret the same to his family: And therefore also, they that have the place of Abraham in a Common-wealth, are the onely Interpreters of what God hath spoken.

The authority of Moses whereon grounded.

The same Covenant was renewed with Isaac; and afterwards with Jacob, but afterwards no more, till the Israelites were freed from the Egyptians, and arrived at the Foot of Mount Sinai. and then it was renewed by Moses (as I have said before, chap 35.) in such manner, as they became from that time forward the Peculiar Kingdome of God; whose Lieutenant was Moses, for his owne time. and the succession to that office was setled upon Aaron, and his heirs after him, to bee to God a Sacerdotall Kingdome for ever.

By this constitution, a Kingdome is acquired to God. But seeing Moses had no authority to govern the Israelites, as a successor to the right of Abraham, because he could not claim it by inheritance, it appeareth not as yet, that the people were obliged to take him for Gods Lieutenant, longer than they beleeved that God spake unto him And therefore his authority (notwithstanding the Covenant they made with God) depended yet merely upon the opinion they had of his Sanctity, and of the reality of his Conferences with God, and the verity of his Miracles; which opinion coming to change, they were no more obliged to take any thing for the law of God, which he propounded to them in Gods name We are therefore to consider, what other ground there was, of their obligation to obey him. For it could not be the commandement of God that could oblige them; because God spake not to them immediately, but by the mediation of Moses himself· And our Saviour saith of himself, *If I bear witnesse of my self, my witnesse is not true*: much lesse if Moses bear witnesse of himselfe, (especially in a claim *John* 5.31.

of Kingly power over Gods people) ought his testimony to be received. His authority therefore, as the authority of all other Princes, must be grounded on the Consent of the People, and their Promise to obey him. And so it was: For *the people* (*Exod* 20. 18) *when they saw the*
[251] *Thunderings, and the Lightnings, and the noyse of the Trumpet, and the mountaine smoaking, removed, and stood a far off. And they said unto Moses, speak thou with us, and we will hear, but let not God speak with us lest we die.* Here was their promise of obedience; and by this it was they obliged themselves to obey whatsoever he should deliver unto them for the Commandement of God.

Moses was (under God) Soveraign of the Jews, all his own time, though Aaron had the Priesthood.

And notwithstanding the Covenant constituteth a Sacerdotall Kingdome, that is to say, a Kingdome hereditary to Aaron; yet that is to be understood of the succession, after Moses should bee dead. For whosoever ordereth, and establisheth the Policy, as first founder of a Common-wealth (be it Monarchy, Aristocracy, or Democracy) must needs have Soveraign Power over the people all the while he is doing of it. And that Moses had that power all his own time, is evidently affirmed in the Scripture. First, in the text last before cited, because the people promised obedience, not to Aaron but to him. Secondly, (*Exod.* 24. 1, 2.) *And God said unto Moses, Come up unto the Lord, thou, and Aaron, Nadab and Abihu, and seventy of the Elders of Israel. And Moses alone shall come neer the Lord, but they shall not come nigh, neither shall the people goe up with him* By which it is plain, that Moses who was alone called up to God, (and not Aaron, nor the other Priests, nor the Seventy Elders, nor the People who were forbidden to come up) was alone he, that represented to the Israelites the Person of God; that is to say, was their sole Soveraign under God. And though afterwards it be said (verse 9) *Then went up Moses, and Aaron, Nadab, and Abihu, and seventy of the Elders of Israel, and they saw the God of Israel, and there was under his feet, as it were a paved work of a saphire stone, &c.* yet this was not till after Moses had been with God before, and had brought to the people the words which God had said to him.

He onely went for the businesse of the people; the others, as the Nobles of his retinue, were admitted for honour to that speciall grace, which was not allowed to the people; which was, (as in the verse after appeareth) to see God and live. *God laid not his hand upon them, they saw God, and did eat and drink* (that is, did live), but did not carry any commandement from him to the people. Again, it is every where said, *The Lord spake unto Moses*, as in all other occasions of Government; so also in the ordering of the Ceremonies of Religion, contained in the 25, 26, 27, 28, 29, 30, and 31 Chapters of *Exodus*, and throughout *Leviticus*: to Aaron seldome The Calfe that Aaron made, Moses threw into the fire. Lastly, the question of the Authority of Aaron, by occasion of his and Miriams mutiny against Moses, was (*Numbers* 12) judged by God himself for Moses. So also in the question between Moses, and the People, who had the Right of Governing the People, when Corah, Dathan, and Abiram, and two hundred and fifty Princes of the Assembly *gathered themselves together* (Numb. 16. 3) *against Moses, and against Aaron, and said unto them, Ye take too much upon you, seeing all the congregation are Holy, every one of them, and the Lord is amongst them, why lift up your selves above the congregation of the Lord?* God caused the Earth to swallow Corah, Dathan, and Abiram with their wives and children alive, and consumed those two [252] hundred and fifty Princes with fire Therefore neither Aaron, nor the People, nor any Aristocracy of the chief Princes of the People, but Moses alone had next under God the Soveraignty over the Israelites And that not onely in causes of Civill Policy, but also of Religion · For Moses onely spake with God, and therefore onely could tell the People, what it was that God required at their hands. No man upon pain of death might be so presumptuous as to approach the Mountain where God talked with Moses. *Thou shalt set bounds* (saith the Lord, *Exod.* 19. 12.) *to the people round about, and say, Take heed to your selves that you goe not up into the Mount, or touch the border of it; whosoever toucheth the Mount shall surely be put to death* And again (verse 21.) *Goe down, charge the people, lest they break through unto the Lord to gaze.* Out of which we may conclude, that whosoever in a Christian Common-wealth holdeth the place of Moses, is the sole Messenger of God, and Interpreter of his Commandements. And according hereunto, no man ought in the interpretation of the Scripture to proceed further then the bounds which are set by their severall Soveraigns. For the Scriptures since God now speaketh in them, are the Mount Sinai; the bounds whereof are the Laws of them that represent Gods Person on Earth. To look upon them, and therein to behold the wondrous works of God, and learn to fear him is allowed, but to interpret them; that is, to pry into what God saith to him whom he appointeth to govern under him, and make themselves Judges whether he govern as God commandeth him, or not, is to transgresse the bounds God hath set us, and to gaze upon God irreverently.

All spirits were subordinate to the spirit of Moses.

There was no Prophet in the time of Moses, nor pretender to the Spirit of God, but such as Moses had approved, and Authorized. For there were in his time but Seventy men, that are said to Prophecy by the Spirit of God, and these were of all Moses his election; concerning whom God said to Moses (*Numb.* 11. 16.) *Gather to mee Seventy of the Elders of Israel, whom thou knowest to be the Elders of the People.* To these God imparted his Spirit, but it was not a different Spirit from that of Moses; for it is said (verse 25) *God came down in a cloud, and took of the Spirit that was upon Moses, and gave it to the Seventy Elders* But as I have shewn before (chap. 36.) by *Spirit*, is understood the *Mind*, so that the sense of the place is no other than this, that God endued them with a mind conformable, and subordinate to that of Moses, that they might Prophecy, that is to say, speak to the people in Gods name, in such manner, as to set forward (as Ministers of Moses, and by his authority) such doctrine as was agreeable to Moses his doctrine. For they were but Ministers; and when two of them Prophecyed in the Camp, it was thought a new and unlawfull thing; and as it is in the 27 and 28 verses of the same Chapter, they were accused of it, and Joshua advised Moses to forbid them, as not knowing that it was by Moses his Spirit that they Prophecyed. By which it is manifest, that no Subject ought to pretend to Prophecy, or to the Spirit, in opposition to the doctrine established by him, whom God hath set in the place of [253] Moses.

After Moses the Soveraignty was in the High Priest.

Aaron being dead, and after him also Moses, the Kingdome, as being a Sacerdotall Kingdome, descended by vertue of the Covenant, to Aarons Son, Eleazar the High Priest: And God declared him (next under himself) for Soveraign, at the same time that he appointed Joshua for the Generall of their Army. For thus God saith expressely (*Numb.* 27. 21.) concerning Joshua; *He shall stand before Eleazar the Priest, who shall ask counsell for him, before the Lord, at his word shall they goe out, and at his word they shall come in, both he, and all the Children of Israel with him*: Therefore the Supreme Power of making War and Peace, was in the Priest. The Supreme Power of Judicature belonged also to the High Priest: For the Book of the Law was in their keeping; and the Priests and Levites onely, were the subordinate Judges in causes Civill, as appears in *Deut.* 17. 8, 9, 10. And for the manner of Gods worship, there was never doubt made, but that the High Priest till the time of Saul, had the Supreme Authority. Therefore the Civill and Ecclesiasticall Power were both joined together in one and the same person, the High Priest; and ought to bee so, in whosoever governeth by Divine Right; that is, by Authority immediate from God.

Of the Soveraign power between the time of Joshua and of Saul.

After the death of Joshua, till the time of Saul, the time between is noted frequently in the Book of Judges, *that there was in those dayes no King in Israel*; and sometimes with this addition, that *every man did that which was right in his own eyes.* By which is to bee understood, that where it is said, *there was no King*, is meant, *there was no Soveraign Power* in Israel And so it was, if we consider the Act, and Exercise of such power. For after the death of Joshua, & Eleazar, *there arose another generation* (Judges 2. 10) *that knew not the Lord, nor the works which he had done for Israel, but did evill in the sight of the Lord, and served Baalim.* And the Jews had that quality which St. Paul noteth, *to look for a sign*, not onely before they would submit themselves to the government of Moses, but also after they had obliged themselves by their submission. Whereas Signs, and Miracles had for End to procure Faith, not to keep men from violating it, when they have once given it; for to that men are obliged by the law of Nature. But if we consider not the Exercise, but the Right of Governing, the Soveraign power was still in the High Priest There-fore whatsoever obedience was yeelded to any of the Judges (who were men chosen by God extraordinarily, to save his rebellious subjects out of the hands of the enemy,) it cannot bee drawn into argument against the Right the High Priest had to the Soveraign Power, in all matters, both of Policy and Religion. And neither the Judges, nor Samuel himselfe had an ordinary, but extraordinary calling to the Government; and were obeyed by the Israelites, not out of duty, but out of reverence to their favour with God, appearing in their wisdome, courage, or felicity. Hitherto therefore the Right of Regulating both the Policy, and the Religion, were inseparable.

[254] *Of the Rights of the Kings of Israel.* To the Judges, succeeded Kings: And whereas before, all authority, both in Religion, and Policy, was in the High Priest; so now it was all in the King. For the Soveraignty over the people, which was before, not onely by vertue of the Divine Power, but also by a particular pact of the Israelites in God, and next under him, in the High Priest, as his Vicegerent on earth, was cast off by the People, with the consent of God himselfe For when they said to Samuel (1 *Sam.* 8. 5.) *make us a King to judge us, like all the Nations*, they signified that they would no more bee governed by the commands that should bee laid upon them by the Priest, in the name of God; but by one that should command them in the same manner that all other nations were commanded; and consequently in deposing the High Priest of Royall authority, they deposed that peculiar Government of God. And yet God consented to it, saying to Samuel (verse 7) *Hearken unto the voice of the People, in all that they shall say unto thee; for they have not rejected thee, but they have rejected mee, that I should not reign over them.* Having therefore rejected God, in whose Right the Priests

governed, there was no authority left to the Priests, but such as the King was pleased to allow them; which was more, or lesse, according as the Kings were good, or evill And for the Government of Civill affaires, it is manifest, it was all in the hands of the King. For in the same Chapter, verse 20. They say they will be like all the Nations; that their King shall be their Judge, and goe before them, and fight their battells; that is, he shall have the whole authority, both in Peace and War. In which is contained also the ordering of Religion: for there was no other Word of God in that time, by which to regulate Religion, but the Law of Moses, which was their Civill Law Besides, we read (1 *Kings* 2. 27.) that Solomon *thrust out Abiathar from being Priest before the Lord*: He had therefore authority over the High Priest, as over any other Subject; which is a great mark of Supremacy in Religion. And we read also (1 *Kings* 8.) that hee dedicated the Temple; that he blessed the People; and that he himselfe in person made that excellent prayer, used in the Consecrations of all Churches, and houses of Prayer; which is another great mark of Supremacy in Religion. Again, we read (2 *Kings* 22) that when there was question concerning the Book of the Law found in the Temple, the same was not decided by the High Priest, but Josiah sent both him, and others to enquire concerning it, of Hulda, the Prophetesse; which is another mark of the Supremacy in Religion. Lastly, wee read (1 *Chron.* 26. 30) that David made Hashabiah and his brethren, Hebronites, Officers of Israel among them Westward, *in all businesse of the Lord, and in the service of the King*. Likewise (verse 32) that hee made other Hebronites, *rulers over the Reubenites, the Gadites, and the halfe tribe of Manasseh* (these were the rest of Israel that dwelt beyond Jordan) *for every matter pertaining to God, and affairs of the King*. Is not this full Power, both *temporall* and *spirituall*, as they call it, that would divide it? To conclude; from the first institution of Gods Kingdome, to the Captivity, the Supremacy of [255]
Religion, was in the same hand with that of the Civill Soveraignty; and the Priests office after the election of Saul, was not Magisteriall, but Ministeriall.

The practice of Suprem-acy in Religion, was not in the time of the Kings, according to the Right thereof

Notwithstanding the government both in Policy and Religion, were joined, first in the High Priests, and afterwards in the Kings, so far forth as concerned the Right; yet it appeareth by the same Holy History, that the people understood it not; but there being amongst them a great part, and probably the greatest part, that no longer than they saw great miracles, or (which is equivalent to a miracle) great abilities, or great felicity in the enterprises of their Governours, gave sufficient credit, either to the fame of Moses, or to the Colloquies between God and the Priests; they took occasion as oft as their Governours displeased them, by blaming sometimes the Policy, sometimes the Religion, to change the Government, or revolt from their Obedience at their pleasure: And from thence proceeded from time to time the civill troubles, divisions, and calamities of the Nation. As for example, after the death of Eleazar and Joshua, the next generation which had not seen the wonders of God, but were left to their own weak reason, not knowing themselves obliged by the Covenant of a Sacerdotall Kingdome, regarded no more the Commandement of the Priest, nor any law of Moses, but did every man that which was right in his own eyes; and obeyed in Civill affairs, such men, as from time to time they thought able to deliver them from the neighbour Nations that oppressed them; and consulted not with God (as they ought to doe,) but with such men, or women, as they guessed to bee Prophets by their Prædictions of things to come; and though they had an Idol in their Chappel, yet if they had a Levite for their Chaplain, they made account they worshipped the God of Israel.

And afterwards when they demanded a King, after the manner of the nations; yet it was not with a design to depart from the worship of God their King; but despairing of the justice of the sons of Samuel, they would have a King to judg them in Civill actions; but not that they would allow their King to change the Religion which they thought was recommended to them by Moses So that they alwaies kept in store a pretext, either of Justice, or Religion, to discharge them selves of their obedience, whensoever they had hope to prevaile.

Samuel was displeased with the people, for that they desired a King, (for God was their King already, and Samuel had but an authority under him); yet did Samuel, when Saul observed not his counsell, in destroying Agag as God had commanded, anoint another King, namely, David, to take the succession from his heirs. Rehoboam was no Idolater; but when the people thought him an Oppressor; that Civil pretence carried from him ten Tribes to Jeroboam an Idolater. And generally through the whole History of the Kings, as well of Judah, as of Israel, there were Prophets that alwaies controlled the Kings, for transgressing the Religion; and sometimes also for Errours of State; as *2 Chro.* 19. 2. Jehosaphat was reproved by the Prophet Jehu, for aiding the King of Israel against the Syrians; and Hezekiah, by [256] Isaiah, for shewing his treasures to the Ambassadors of Babylon. By all which it appeareth, that though the power both of State and Religion were in the Kings; yet none of them were uncontrolled in the use of it, but such as were gracious for their own naturall abilities, or felicities. So that from the practise of those times, there can no argument be drawn, that the Right of Supremacy in Religion was not in the Kings, unlesse we place it in the Prophets; and conclude, that because Hezekiah praying to the Lord before the Cherubins, was not answered from thence, nor then, but afterwards by the Prophet Isaiah, therefore Isaiah was supreme Head of the Church; or because Josiah consulted Hulda the Prophetesse, concerning the Book of the Law, that therefore neither he, nor the High Priest, but Hulda the Prophetesse had the Supreme authority in matter of Religion; which I thinke is not the opinion of any Doctor

After the Captivity the Jews had no setled Common-wealth.

During the Captivity, the Jews had no Common-wealth at all: And after their return, though they renewed their Covenant with God, yet there was no promise made of obedience, neither to Esdras, nor to any other · And presently after they became subjects to the Greeks (from whose Customes, and Dæmonology, and from the doctrine of the Cabalists, their Religion became much corrupted): In such sort as nothing can be gathered from their confusion, both in State and Religion, concerning the Supremacy in either. And therefore so far forth as concerneth the Old Testament, we may conclude, that whosoever had the Soveraignty of the Common-wealth amongst the Jews, the same had also the Supreme Authority in matter of Gods externall worship; and represented Gods Person; that is the person of God The Father; though he were not called by the name of Father, till such time as he sent into the world his Son Jesus Christ, to redeem mankind from their sins, and bring them into his Everlasting Kingdome, to be saved for evermore. Of which we are to speak in the Chapter following.

[261]

CHAP. XLI.

Of the Office *of our BLESSED SAVIOUR.*

Three parts of the Office of Christ

We find in Holy Scripture three parts of the *Office* of the *Messiah*. The first of a *Redeemer*, or *Saviour*: The second of a *Pastor*, *Counsellor*, or *Teacher*, that is, of a Prophet sent from God, to convert such as God hath elected to Salvation: The third of a *King*, an *eternall King*, but under his Father, as Moses and the High Priests were in their severall times. And to these three parts are correspondent three times. For our Redemption he wrought at his first coming, by the Sacrifice, wherein he offered up himself for our sinnes upon the Crosse: our Conversion he wrought partly then in his own Person; and partly worketh now by his Ministers; and will continue to work till his coming again. And after his coming again, shall begin that his glorious Reign over his elect, which is to last eternally.

His Office as a Redeemer.

To the *Office* of a *Redeemer*, that is, of one that payeth the Ransome of Sin, (which Ransome is Death,) it appertaineth, that he was Sacrificed, and thereby bare upon his own head, and carryed away from us our iniquities, in such sort as God had required. Not that the death of one man, though without sinne, can satisfie for the offences of all men, in the rigour of Justice, but in the Mercy of God, that ordained such Sacrifices for sin, as he was pleased in his mercy to accept. In the

Old Law (as we may read, *Leviticus* the 16.) the Lord required, that there should every year once, bee made an Atonement for the Sins of all Israel, both Priests, and others; for the doing whereof, Aaron alone was to sacrifice for himself and the Priests a young Bullock; and for the rest of the people, he was to receive from them two young Goates, of which he was to *sacrifice* one, but as for the other, which was the *Scape Goat,* he was to lay his hands on the head thereof, and by a confession of the iniquities of the people, to lay them all on that head, and then by some opportune man, to cause the Goat to be led into the wildernesse, and there to *escape,* and carry away with him the iniquities of the people As the Sacrifice of the one Goat was a sufficient (because an acceptable) price for the Ransome of all Israel; so the death of the Messiah, is a sufficient price, for the Sins of all mankind, because there was no more required. Our Saviour Christs sufferings seem to be here figured, as cleerly, as in the oblation of Isaac, or in any other type of him in the Old Testament · He was both the sacrificed Goat, and the Scape Goat; *Hee was oppressed, and he was afflicted* (Esay 53. 7.); *he opened not his mouth; he is brought as a lamb to the slaughter, and as a sheep is dumbe before the shearer, so opened he not his* [262] *mouth.* Here he is the *sacrificed Goat. He hath born our Griefs,* (ver 4.) *and carried our sorrows.* And again, (ver. 6.) *the Lord hath laid upon him the iniquities of us all* And so he is the *Scape Goat. He was cut off from the land of the living* (ver 8.) *for the transgression of my People:* There again he is the *sacrificed Goat.* And again, (ver. 11.) *he shall bear their sins* Hee is the *Scape Goat* Thus is the Lamb of God equivalent to both those Goates; sacrificed, in that he dyed; and escaping, in his Resurrection; being raised opportunely by his Father, and removed from the habitation of men in his Ascension.

Christs Kingdome not of this world.

For as much therefore, as he that *redeemeth,* hath no title to the *thing redeemed,* before *the Redemption,* and Ransome paid; and this Ransome was the Death of the Redeemer, it is manifest, that our Saviour (as man) was not King of those that he Redeemed, before hee suffered death; that is, during that time hee conversed

bodily on the Earth. I say, he was not then King in present, by vertue of the Pact, which the faithfull make with him in Baptisme: Neverthelesse, by the renewing of their Pact with God in Baptisme, they were obliged to obey him for King, (under his Father) whensoever he should be pleased to take the Kingdome upon him. According whereunto, our Saviour himself expressely saith, (*John* 18. 36) *My Kingdome is not of this world.* Now seeing the Scripture maketh mention but of two worlds; this that is now, and shall remain to the day of Judgment, (which is therefore also called, *the last day*,) and that which shall bee after the day of Judgement, when there shall bee a new Heaven, and a new Earth; the Kingdome of Christ is not to begin till the generall Resurrection And that is it which our Saviour saith, (*Mat.* 16. 27.) *The Son of man shall come in the glory of his Father, with his Angels; and then he shall reward every man according to his works.* To reward every man according to his works, is to execute the Office of a King; and this is not to be till he come in the glory of his Father, with his Angells. When our Saviour saith, (*Mat.* 23. 2.) *The Scribes and Pharisees sit in Moses seat; All therefore whatsoever they bid you doe, that observe and doe*; hee declareth plainly, that hee ascribeth Kingly Power, for that time, not to himselfe, but to them. And so hee doth also, where he saith, (*Luke* 12. 14) *Who made mee a Judge, or Divider over you?* And (*John* 12. 47) *I came not to judge the world, but to save the world* And yet our Saviour came into this world that hee might bee a King, and a Judge in the world to come: For hee was the Messiah, that is, the Christ, that is, the Anointed Priest, and the Soveraign Prophet of God; that is to say, he was to have all the power that was in Moses the Prophet, in the High Priests that succeeded Moses, and in the Kings that succeeded the Priests. And St. *John* saies expressely (chap 5 ver. 22) *The Father judgeth no man, but hath committed all judgment to the Son.* And this is not repugnant to that other place, *I came not to*
[263] *judge the world*: for this is spoken of the world present, the other of the world to come, as also where it is said, that at the second coming of Christ, (*Mat.* 19. 28) *Yee*

that have followed me in the Regeneration, when the Son of man shall sit in the throne of his Glory, yee shall also sit on twelve thrones, judging the twelve tribes of Israel.

The End of Christs coming was to renew the Covenant of the Kingdome of God, and to perswade the Elect to imbrace it, which was the second part of his Office.

If then Christ whilest hee was on Earth, had no Kingdome in this world, to what end was his first coming? It was to restore unto God, by a new Covenant, the Kingdom, which being his by the Old Covenant, had been cut off by the rebellion of the Israelites in the election of Saul. Which to doe, he was to preach unto them, that he was the *Messiah*, that is, the King promised to them by the Prophets; and to offer himselfe in sacrifice for the sinnes of them that should by faith submit themselves thereto; and in case the nation generally should refuse him, to call to his obedience such as should beleeve in him amongst the Gentiles. So that there are two parts of our Saviours Office during his aboad upon the Earth. One to Proclaim himself the Christ; and another by Teaching, and by working of Miracles, to perswade, and prepare men to live so, as to be worthy of the Immortality Beleevers were to enjoy, at such time as he should come in majesty, to take possession of his Fathers Kingdome. And therefore it is, that the time of his preaching, is often by himself called the *Regeneration*; which is not properly a Kingdome, and thereby a warrant to deny obedience to the Magistrates that then were, (for hee commanded to obey those that sate then in Moses chaire, and to pay tribute to Cæsar; but onely an earnest of the Kingdome of God that was to come, to those to whom God had given the grace to be his disciples, and to beleeve in him; For which cause the Godly are said to bee already in the *Kingdome of Grace*, as naturalized in that heavenly Kingdome.

The preaching of Christ not contrary to the then law of the Jews, nor of Cæsar.

Hitherto therefore there is nothing done, or taught by Christ, that tendeth to the diminution of the Civill Right of the Jewes, or of Cæsar. For as touching the Common-wealth which then was amongst the Jews, both they that bare rule amongst them, and they that were governed, did all expect the Messiah, and Kingdome of God; which they could not have done if their Laws had forbidden him (when he came) to manifest, and declare himself. Seeing therefore he did nothing, but by Preach-

ing, and Miracles go about to prove himselfe to be that Messiah, hee did therein nothing against their laws. The Kingdome hee claimed was to bee in another world: He taught all men to obey in the mean time them that sate in Moses seat: He allowed them to give Cæsar his tribute, and refused to take upon himselfe to be a Judg. How then could his words, or actions bee seditious, or tend to the overthrow of their then Civill Government? But God having determined his sacrifice, for the reduction of his elect to their former covenanted obedience, for the means, whereby he would bring the same to effect,
[264] made use of their malice, and ingratitude Nor was it contrary to the laws of Cæsar. For though Pilate himself (to gratifie the Jews) delivered him to be crucified; yet before he did so, he pronounced openly, that he found no fault in him. And put for title of his condemnation, not as the Jews required, *that he pretended to bee, King*; but simply, *That hee was King of the Jews*; and notwithstanding their clamour, refused to alter it; saying, *What I have written, I have written*

The third part of his Office was to be King (under his Father) of the Elect.

As for the third part of his Office, which was to be *King*, I have already shewn that his Kingdome was not to begin till the Resurrection. But then he shall be King, not onely as God, in which sense he is King already, and ever shall be, of all the Earth, in vertue of his omnipotence; but also peculiarly of his own Elect, by vertue of the pact they make with him in their Baptisme. And therefore it is, that our Saviour saith (*Mat.* 19. 28.) that his Apostles should sit upon twelve thrones, judging the twelve tribes of Israel, *When the Son of man shall sit in the throne of his glory*: whereby he signified that he should reign then in his humane nature; and (*Mat.* 16 27) *The Son of man shall come in the glory of his Father, with his Angels, and then he shall reward every man according to his works.* The same we may read, *Marke* 13 26. and 14. 62. and more expressely for the time, *Luke* 22. 29, 30 *I appoint unto you a Kingdome, as my Father hath appointed to mee, that you may eat and drink at my table in my Kingdome, and sit on thrones judging the twelve tribes of Israel.* By which it is manifest, that the Kingdome of Christ appointed to him by his

Father, is not to be before the Son of Man shall come in Glory, and make his Apostles Judges of the twelve tribes of Israel. But a man may here ask, seeing there is no marriage in the Kingdome of Heaven, whether men shall then eat, and drink; what eating therefore is meant in this place? This is expounded by our Saviour (*John* 6 27) where he saith, *Labour not for the meat which perisheth, but for that meat which endureth unto everlasting life, which the Son of man shall give you.* So that by eating at Christs table, is meant the eating of the Tree of Life; that is to say, the enjoying of Immortality, in the Kingdome of the Son of Man By which places, and many more, it is evident, that our Saviours Kingdome is to bee exercised by him in his humane nature.

Christs authority in the Kingdome of God subordinate to that of his Father.

Again, he is to be King then, no otherwise than as subordinate, or Vicegerent of God the Father, as Moses was in the wildernesse, and as the High Priests were before the reign of Saul: and as the Kings were after it. For it is one of the Prophecies concerning Christ, that he should be like (in Office) to Moses: *I will raise them up a Prophet* (saith the Lord, *Deut* 18. 18) *from amongst their Brethren like unto thee, and will put my words into his mouth*, and this similitude with Moses, is also apparent in the actions of our Saviour himself, whilest he was conversant on Earth. For as Moses chose twelve Princes of the tribes, to govern under him; so did our Saviour choose twelve Apostles, who shall sit on twelve thrones, [265] and judge the twelve tribes of Israel: And as Moses authorized Seventy Elders, to receive the Spirit of God, and to Prophecy to the people, that is, (as I have said before,) to speak unto them in the name of God; so our Saviour also ordained seventy Disciples, to preach his Kingdome, and Salvation to all Nations. And as when a complaint was made to Moses, against those of the Seventy that prophecyed in the camp of Israel, he justified them in it, as being subservient therein to his government; so also our Saviour, when St. John complained to him of a certain man that cast out Devills in his name, justified him therein, saying, (*Luke* 9. 50) *Forbid him not, for hee that is not against us, is on our part.*

Again, our Saviour resembled Moses in the institution of *Sacraments*, both of *Admission* into the Kingdome of God, and of *Commemoration* of his deliverance of his Elect from their miserable condition. As the Children of Israel had for Sacrament of their Reception into the Kingdome of God, before the time of Moses, the rite of *Circumcision*, which rite having been omitted in the Wildernesse, was again restored as soon as they came into the land of Promise; so also the Jews, before the coming of our Saviour, had a rite of *Baptizing*, that is, of washing with water all those that being Gentiles, embraced the God of Israel. This rite St. John the Baptist used in the reception of all them that gave their names to the Christ, whom hee preached to bee already come into the world; and our Saviour instituted the same for a Sacrament to be taken by all that beleeved in him From what cause the rite of Baptisme first proceeded, is not expressed formally in the Scripture; but it may be probably thought to be an imitation of the law of Moses, concerning Leprousie; wherein the Leprous man was commanded to be kept out of the campe of Israel for a certain time; after which time being judged by the Priest to be clean, hee was admitted into the campe after a solemne Washing. And this may therefore bee a type of the Washing in Baptisme, wherein such men as are cleansed of the Leprousie of Sin by Faith, are received into the Church with the solemnity of Baptisme There is another conjecture drawn from the Ceremonies of the Gentiles, in a certain case that rarely happens; and that is, when a man that was thought dead, chanced to recover, other men made scruple to converse with him, as they would doe to converse with a Ghost, unlesse hee were received again into the number of men, by Washing, as Children new born were washed from the uncleannesse of their nativity, which was a kind of new birth. This ceremony of the Greeks, in the time that Judæa was under the Dominion of Alexander, and the Greeks his successors, may probably enough have crept into the Religion of the Jews. But seeing it is not likely our Saviour would countenance a Heathen rite, it is most likely it proceeded from the

Legall Ceremony of Washing after Leprosie. And for the other Sacrament, of eating the *Paschall Lambe*, it is [266] manifestly imitated in the Sacrament of the *Lords Supper*, in which the Breaking of the Bread, and the pouring out of the Wine, do keep in memory our deliverance from the Misery of Sin, by Christs Passion, as the eating of the Paschall Lambe, kept in memory the deliverance of the Jewes out of the Bondage of Egypt. Seeing therefore the authority of Moses was but subordinate, and hee but a Lieutenant to God: it followeth, that Christ, whose authority, as man, was to bee like that of Moses, was no more but subordinate to the authority of his Father. The same is more expressely signified, by that that hee teacheth us to pray, *Our Father, Let thy Kingdome come*; and, *For thine is the Kingdome, the Power, and the Glory*; and by that it is said, that *Hee shall come in the Glory of his Father*; and by that which St. Paul saith, (1 *Cor.* 15. 24.) *then cometh the end, when hee shall have delivered up the Kingdome to God, even the Father*; and by many other most expresse places.

One and the same God is the Person represented by Moses, and by Christ.

Our Saviour therefore, both in Teaching, and Reigning, representeth (as Moses did) the Person of God; which God from that time forward, but not before, is called the Father; and being still one and the same substance, is one Person as represented by Moses, and another Person as represented by his Sonne the Christ. For *Person* being a relative to a *Representer*, it is consequent to plurality of Representers, that there bee a plurality of Persons, though of one and the same Substance.

CHAP. XLII. [267]

Of Power Ecclesiasticall.

For the understanding of Power Ecclesiasticall, what, and in whom it is, we are to distinguish the time from the Ascension of our Saviour, into two parts; one before the Conversion of Kings, and men endued with Soveraign Civill Power; the other after their Conversion. For it was long after the Ascension, before any King, or Civill Soveraign embraced, and publiquely allowed the teaching of Christian Religion.

Of the Holy Spirit that fel on the Apostles.

And for the time between, it is manifest, that the *Power Ecclesiasticall*, was in the Apostles; and after them in such as were by them ordained to Preach the Gospell, and to convert men to Christianity, and to direct them that were converted in the way of Salvation; and after these the Power was delivered again to others by these ordained, and this was done by Imposition of hands upon such as were ordained; by which was signified the giving of the Holy Spirit, or Spirit of God, to those whom they ordained Ministers of God, to advance his Kingdome. So that Imposition of hands, was nothing else but the Seal of their Commission to Preach Christ, and teach his Doctrine; and the giving of the Holy Ghost by that ceremony of Imposition of hands, was an imitation of that which Moses did. For Moses used the same ceremony to his Minister Joshua, as wee read *Deuteronomy* 34. ver. 9. *And Joshua the Son of Nun was full of the Spirit of Wisdome; for Moses had laid his hands upon him.* Our Saviour therefore between his Resurrection, and Ascension, gave his Spirit to the Apostles; first, by *Breathing on them, and saying,* (*John* 20. 22.) *Receive yee the Holy Spirit*; and after his Ascension (*Acts* 2. 2, 3.) by sending down upon them, a *mighty wind, and Cloven tongues of fire*; and not by Imposition of hands; as neither did God lay his hands on Moses: and his Apostles afterward, transmitted the same Spirit by Imposition of hands, as Moses did to Joshua. So that it is manifest hereby, in whom the Power Ecclesiasticall continually remained, in those first times, where there was not any Christian Common-wealth; namely, in them that received the same from the Apostles, by successive laying on of hands.

Of the Trinity

Here wee have the Person of God born now the third time. For as Moses, and the High Priests, were Gods Representative in the Old Testament; and our Saviour himselfe as Man, during his abode on earth So the Holy Ghost, that is to say, the Apostles, and their successors, [268] in the Office of Preaching, and Teaching, that had received the Holy Spirit, have Represented him ever since. But a Person, (as I have shewn before, chapt. 13.) is he that is Represented, as often as hee is Represented;

and therefore God, who has been Represented (that is, Personated) thrice, may properly enough be said to be three Persons; though neither the word *Person*, nor *Trinity* be ascribed to him in the Bible. St. *John* indeed (1 Epist. 5. 7) saith, *There be three that bear witnesse in heaven, the Father, the Word, and the Holy Spirit; and these Three are One*: But this disagreeth not, but accordeth fitly with three Persons in the proper signification of Persons; which is, that which is Represented by another. For so God the Father, as Represented by Moses, is one Person; and as Represented by his Sonne, another Person; and as Represented by the Apostles, and by the Doctors that taught by authority from them derived, is a third Person; and yet every Person here, is the Person of one and the same God. But a man may here ask, what it was whereof these three bare witnesse. St. *John* therefore tells us (verse 11.) that they bear witnesse, that *God hath given us eternall life in his Son*. Again, if it should bee asked, wherein that testimony appeareth, the Answer is easie; for he hath testified the same by the miracles he wrought, first by Moses, secondly, by his Son himself; and lastly by his Apostles, that had received the Holy Spirit, all which in their times Represented the Person of God; and either prophecyed, or preached Jesus Christ. And as for the Apostles, it was the character of the Apostleship, in the twelve first and great Apostles, to bear Witnesse of his Resurrection; as appeareth expressely (*Acts* 1. ver. 21, 22) where St. Peter, when a new Apostle was to be chosen in the place of Judas Iscariot, useth these words, *Of these men which have companied with us all the time that the Lord Jesus went in and out amongst us, beginning at the Baptisme of John, unto that same day that hee was taken up from us, must one bee ordained to be a Witnesse with us of his Resurrection* · which words interpret the *bearing of Witnesse*, mentioned by St. John There is in the same place mentioned another Trinity of Witnesses in Earth. For (ver 8.) he saith, *there are three that bear Witnesse in Earth, the Spirit, and the Water, and the Bloud, and these three agree in one*: that is to say, the graces of Gods Spirit, and the two Sacraments, Baptisme, and the Lords

Supper, which all agree in one Testimony, to assure the consciences of beleevers, of eternall life; of which Testimony he saith (verse 10.) *He that beleeveth on the Son of man hath the Witnesse in himself.* In this Trinity on Earth, the Unity is not of the thing; for the Spirit, the Water, and the Bloud, are not the same substance, though they give the same testimony: But in the Trinity of Heaven, the Persons are the persons of one and the same God, though Represented in three different times and occasions. To conclude, the doctrine of the Trinity, as far as can be gathered directly from the Scripture, is in substance this; that God who is alwaies One and the [269] same, was the Person Represented by Moses; the Person Represented by his Son Incarnate; and the Person Represented by the Apostles. As Represented by the Apostles, the Holy Spirit by which they spake, is God; As Represented by his Son (that was God and Man), the Son is that God; As represented by Moses, and the High Priests, the Father, that is to say, the Father of our Lord Jesus Christ, is that God. From whence we may gather the reason why those names *Father, Son,* and *Holy Spirit* in the signification of the Godhead, are never used in the Old Testament. For they are Persons, that is, they have their names from Representing; which could not be, till divers men had Represented Gods Person in ruling, or in directing under him.

Thus wee see how the Power Ecclesiasticall was left by our Saviour to the Apostles; and how they were (to the end they might the better exercise that Power,) endued with the Holy Spirit, which is therefore called sometime in the New Testament *Paracletus* which signifieth an *Assister,* or one called to for helpe, though it bee commonly translated a *Comforter.* Let us now consider the Power it selfe, what it was, and over whom.

The Power Ecclesiasticall is but the power to teach.

Cardinall Bellarmine in his third generall Controversie, hath handled a great many questions concerning the Ecclesiasticall Power of the Pope of Rome; and begins with this, Whether it ought to be Monarchicall, Aristocraticall, or Democraticall All which sorts of Power, are Soveraign, and Coercive. If now it should appear, that there is no Coercive Power left them by our Saviour; but onely a Power to proclaim the Kingdom of Christ, and to perswade men to submit themselves thereunto, and by precepts and good counsell, to teach them that have submitted, what they are to do, that they may be received into the Kingdom of God when it comes; and that the Apostles, and other Ministers of the Gospel, are our Schoolemasters, and not our Commanders, and their Precepts not Laws, but wholesome Counsells; then were all that dispute in vain.

An argument thereof, the Power of Christ himself.

I have shewn already (in the last Chapter,) that the Kingdome of Christ is not of this world: therefore neither can his Ministers (unlesse they be Kings,) require obedience in his name. For if the Supreme King, have not his Regall Power in this world; by what authority can obedience be required to his Officers? As my Father sent me, (so saith our Saviour) I send you. But our Saviour was sent to perswade the Jews to return to, and to invite the Gentiles, to receive the Kingdome of his Father, and not to reign in Majesty, no not, as his Fathers Lieutenant, till the day of Judgment.

From the name of Regeneration:

The time between the Ascension, and the generall Resurrection, is called, not a Reigning, but a Regeneration; that is, a Preparation of men for the second and glorious coming of Christ, at the day of Judgment: as appeareth by the words of our Saviour, *Mat.* 19. 28. *You that have followed me in the Regeneration, when the Son of man shall sit in the throne of his glory, you shall* [270]
also sit upon twelve Thrones, And of St. Paul (*Ephes* 6. 15.) *Having your feet shod with the Preparation of the Gospell of Peace.*

From the comparison of it, with Fishing, Leaven, Seed.

And is compared by our Saviour, to Fishing, that is, to winning men to obedience, not by Coercion, and Punishing, but by Perswasion: and therefore he said not to his Apostles, hee would make them so many Nimrods, *Hunters of men; but Fishers of men* It is compared also to Leaven; to Sowing of Seed, and to the Multiplication of a grain of Mustard-seed, by all which Compulsion is excluded; and consequently there can in that time be no actual Reigning The work of Christs Ministers, is Evangelization; that is, a Proclamation of

Christ, and a preparation for his second comming; as the Evangelization of John Baptist, was a preparation to his first coming.

From the nature of Faith: Again, the Office of Christs Ministers in this world, is to make men Beleeve, and have Faith in Christ: But Faith hath no relation to, nor dependence at all upon Compulsion, or Commandement; but onely upon certainty, or probability of Arguments drawn from Reason, or from something men beleeve already. Therefore the Ministers of Christ in this world, have no Power by that title, to Punish any man for not Beleeving, or for Contradicting what they say; they have I say no Power by that title of Christs Ministers, to Punish such: but if they have Soveraign Civill Power, by politick institution, then they may indeed lawfully Punish any Contradiction to their laws whatsoever: And St. Paul, of himselfe and
2Cor.1.24. other the then Preachers of the Gospell, saith in expresse words, *Wee have no Dominion over your Faith, but are Helpers of your Joy.*

From the Authority Christ hath left to Civill Princes. Another Argument, that the Ministers of Christ in this present world have no right of Commanding, may be drawn from the lawfull Authority which Christ hath left to all Princes, as well Christians, as Infidels. St. Paul saith (*Col.* 3 20) *Children obey your Parents in all things; for this is well pleasing to the Lord.* And ver. 22 *Servants obey in all things your Masters according to the flesh, not with eye-service, as men-pleasers, but in singlenesse of heart, as fearing the Lord*: This is spoken to them whose Masters were Infidells; and yet they are bidden to obey them *in all things* And again, concerning obedience to Princes (*Rom.* 13 the first 6 verses) exhorting *to be subject to the Higher Powers,* he saith, *that all Power is ordained of God*; and *that we ought to be subject to them, not onely for* fear of incurring their *wrath, but also for conscience sake.* And St. *Peter,* (1 Epist. chap. 2 ver. 13, 14, 15) *Submit your selves to every Ordinance of Man, for the Lords sake, whether it bee to the King, as Supreme, or unto Governours, as to them that be sent by him for the punishment of evill doers, and for the praise of them that doe well; for so is the will of God.* And again St. Paul (*Tit* 3. 1.) *Put men in mind to be subject to*

Principalities, and Powers, and to obey Magistrates. These Princes, and Powers, whereof St. Peter, and St. Paul here speak, were all Infidels; much more therefore we are [271] to obey those Christians, whom God hath ordained to have Soveraign Power over us. How then can wee be obliged to obey any Minister of Christ, if he should command us to doe any thing contrary to the Command of the King, or other Soveraign Representant of the Common-wealth, whereof we are members, and by whom we look to be protected? It is therefore manifest, that Christ hath not left to his Ministers in this world, unlesse they be also endued with Civill Authority, any authority to Command other men.

What Christians may do to avoid persecution.

But what (may some object) if a King, or a Senate, or other Soveraign Person forbid us to beleeve in Christ? To this I answer, that such forbidding is of no effect; because Beleef, and Unbeleef never follow mens Commands. Faith is a gift of God, which Man can neither give, nor take away by promise of rewards, or menaces of torture. And if it be further asked, What if wee bee commanded by our lawfull Prince, to say with our tongue, wee beleeve not; must we obey such command? Profession with the tongue is but an externall thing, and no more then any other gesture whereby we signifie our obedience; and wherein a Christian, holding firmely in his heart the Faith of Christ, hath the same liberty which the Prophet Elisha allowed to Naaman the Syrian. Naaman was converted in his heart to the God of Israel; For hee saith (2 *Kings* 5. 17.) *Thy servant will henceforth offer neither burnt offering, nor sacrifice unto other Gods but unto the Lord. In this thing the Lord pardon thy servant, that when my Master goeth into the house of Rimmon to worship there, and he leaneth on my hand, and I bow my selfe in the house of Rimmon; when I bow my selfe in the house of Rimmon, the Lord pardon thy servant in this thing.* This the Prophet approved, and bid him *Goe in peace.* Here Naaman beleeved in his heart; but by bowing before the Idol Rimmon, he denyed the true God in effect, as much as if he had done it with his lips. But then what shall we answer to our Saviours saying, *Whosoever denyeth me before men, I will deny him before*

my Father which is in Heaven? This we may say, that whatsoever a subject, as Naaman was, is compelled to in obedience to his Soveraign, and doth it not in order to his own mind, but in order to the laws of his country, that action is not his, but his Soveraigns; nor is it he that in this case denyeth Christ before men, but his Governour, and the law of his countrey. If any man shall accuse this doctrine, as repugnant to true, and unfeigned Christianity; I ask him, in case there should be a subject in any Christian Common-wealth, that should be inwardly in his heart of the Mahometan Religion, whether if his Soveraign command him to bee present at the divine service of the Christian Church, and that on pain of death, he think that Mahometan obliged in conscience to suffer death for that cause, rather than to obey that command of his lawfull Prince. If he say, he ought rather to suffer death, then he authorizeth all private men, to disobey their Princes, in maintenance of their Religion, true, or false: if he say,
[272] he ought to bee obedient, then he alloweth to himself, that which hee denyeth to another, contrary to the words of our Saviour, *Whatsoever you would that men should doe unto you, that doe yee unto them*; and contrary to the Law of Nature, (which is the indubitable everlasting Law of God) *Do not to another, that which thou wouldest not he should doe unto thee*

Of Martyrs. But what then shall we say of all those Martyrs we read of in the History of the Church, that they have needlessely cast away their lives? For answer hereunto, we are to distinguish the persons that have been for that cause put to death; whereof some have received a Calling to preach, and professe the Kingdome of Christ openly; others have had no such Calling, nor more has been required of them than their owne faith. The former sort, if they have been put to death, for bearing witnesse to this point, that Jesus Christ is risen from the dead, were true Martyrs; For a *Martyr* is, (to give the true definition of the word) a Witnesse of the Resurrection of Jesus the Messiah; which none can be but those that conversed with him on earth, and saw him after he was risen: For a Witnesse must have seen what he testifieth, or else his testimony is not good. And that none but such, can properly be called Martyrs of Christ, is manifest out of the words of St. Peter, *Act* 1. 21, 22. *Wherefore of these men which have companyed with us all the time that the Lord Jesus went in and out amongst us, beginning from the Baptisme of John unto that same day hee was taken up from us, must one be ordained to be a Martyr* (that is a Witnesse) *with us of his Resurrection* : Where we may observe, that he which is to bee a Witnesse of the truth of the Resurrection of Christ, that is to say, of the truth of this fundamentall article of Christian Religion, that Jesus was the Christ, must be some Disciple that conversed with him, and saw him before, and after his Resurrection; and consequently must be one of his originall Disciples: whereas they which were not so, can Witnesse no more, but that their antecessors said it, and are therefore but Witnesses of other mens testimony; and are but second Martyrs, or Martyrs of Christs Witnesses

He, that to maintain every doctrine which he himself draweth out of the History of our Saviours life, and of the Acts, or Epistles of the Apostles; or which he beleeveth upon the authority of a private man, wil oppose the Laws and Authority of the Civill State, is very far from being a Martyr of Christ, or a Martyr of his Martyrs. 'Tis one Article onely, which to die for, meriteth so honorable a name, and that Article is this, that *Jesus is the Christ*, that is to say, He that hath redeemed us, and shall come again to give us salvation, and eternall life in his glorious Kingdome. To die for every tenet that serveth the ambition, or profit of the Clergy, is not required; nor is it the Death of the Witnesse, but the Testimony it self that makes the Martyr: for the word signifieth nothing else, but the man that beareth Witnesse, whether he be put to death for his testimony, or not.

Also he that is not sent to preach this fundamentall article, but taketh it upon him of his private authority, [273] though he be a Witnesse, and consequently a Martyr, either primary of Christ, or secundary of his Apostles, Disciples, or their Successors; yet is he not obliged to suffer death for that cause; because being not called thereto, tis not required at his hands; nor ought hee to complain, if he loseth the reward he expecteth from those that never set him on work. None therefore can be a Martyr, neither of the first, nor second degree, that have not a warrant to preach Christ come in the flesh; that is to say, none, but such as are sent to the conversion of Infidels For no man is a Witnesse to him that already beleeveth, and therefore needs no Witnesse, but to them that deny, or doubt, or have not heard it. Christ sent his Apostles, and his Seventy Disciples, with authority to preach; he sent not all that beleeved: And he sent them to unbeleevers; *I send you* (saith he) *as sheep amongst wolves*; not as sheep to other sheep.

Argument from the points of their Commission. Lastly, the points of their Commission, as they are expressely set down in the Gospel, contain none of them any authority over the Congregation.

ToPreach We have first (*Mat.* 10) that the twelve Apostles were sent *to the lost sheep of the house of Israel*, and commanded to Preach, *that the Kingdome of God was at hand.* Now Preaching in the originall, is that act, which a Crier, Herald, or other Officer useth to doe publiquely in Proclaiming of a King. But a Crier hath not right to Command any man. And (*Luke* 10. 2.) the seventy Disciples are sent out, as *Labourers, not as Lords of the Harvest*; and are bidden (verse 9) to say, *The Kingdome of God is come nigh unto you*; and by Kingdom here is meant, not the Kingdome of Grace, but the Kingdome of Glory; for they are bidden to denounce it (ver. 11.) to those Cities which shall not receive them, as a threatning, that it shall be more tolerable in that day for *Sodome*, than for such a City. And (*Mat.* 20. 28) our Saviour telleth his Disciples, that sought Priority of place, their Office was to minister, even as the Son of man came, not to be ministred unto, but to minister. Preachers therefore have not Magisteriall, but Ministeriall power: *Bee not called Masters*, (saith our Saviour, *Mat.* 23. 10.) *for one is your Master, even Christ.*

And Teach. Another point of their Commission, is, to *Teach all nations*; as it is in *Mat.* 28. 19. or as in St. *Mark* 16. 15. *Goe into all the world, and Preach the Gospel to every creature.* Teaching therefore, and Preaching is the same thing. For they that Proclaim the comming of a King, must withall make known by what right he commeth, if they mean men shall submit themselves unto him: As St. Paul did to the Jews of Thessalonica, when *three Sabbath dayes he reasoned with them out of the Scriptures, opening, and alledging that Christ must needs have suffered, and risen again from the dead, and that this Jesus is Christ.* But to teach out of the Old Testament that Jesus was Christ, (that is to say, King,) and risen from the dead, is not to say, that men are bound after they beleeve it, to obey those that tell them so, against the laws, and commands of their Soveraigns; but that they shall doe wisely, to expect the coming of Christ hereafter, in [274] Patience, and Faith, with Obedience to their present Magistrates

To Baptize;

Another point of their Commission, is to *Baptize, in the name of the Father, and of the Son, and of the Holy Ghost.* What is Baptisme? Dipping into water But what is it to Dip a man into the water in the name of any thing? The meaning of these words of Baptisme is this. He that is Baptized, is Dipped or Washed, as a sign of becomming a new man, and a loyall subject to that God, whose Person was represented in old time by Moses, and the High Priests, when he reigned over the Jews; and to Jesus Christ, his Sonne, God, and Man, that hath redeemed us, and shall in his humane nature Represent his Fathers Person in his eternall Kingdome after the Resurrection; and to acknowledge the Doctrine of the Apostles, who assisted by the Spirit of the Father, and of the Son, were left for guides to bring us into that Kingdome, to be the onely, and assured way thereunto. This, being our promise in Baptisme; and the Authority of Earthly Soveraigns being not to be put down till the day of Judgment, (for that is expressely affirmed by S Paul 1 *Cor.* 15 22, 23, 24, where he saith, *As in Adam all die, so in Christ all shall be made alive. But every man in his owne order, Christ the first fruits, afterward they that are Christs, at his comming; Then commeth the end, when he shall have delivered up the Kingdom to God, even the Father, when he shall have put down all Rule, and all*

Authority and Power) it is manifest, that we do not in Baptisme constitute over us another authority, by which our externall actions are to bee governed in this life; but promise to take the doctrine of the Apostles for our direction in the way to life eternall.

And to Forgive, and Retain Sinnes.

The Power of *Remission, and Retention of Sinnes,* called also the Power of *Loosing,* and *Binding,* and sometimes the *Keyes of the Kingdome of Heaven,* is a consequence of the Authority to Baptize, or refuse to Baptize. For Baptisme is the Sacrament of Allegeance, of them that are to be received into the Kingdome of God, that is to say, into Eternall life; that is to say, to Remission of Sin For as Eternall life was lost by the Committing, so it is recovered by the Remitting of mens Sins. The end of Baptisme is Remission of Sins: and therefore St. Peter, when they that were converted by his Sermon on the day of Pentecost, asked what they were to doe, advised them to *repent, and be Baptized in the name of Jesus, for the Remission of Sins.* And therefore seeing to Baptize is to declare the Reception of men into Gods Kingdome; and to refuse to Baptize is to declare their Exclusion; it followeth, that the Power to declare them Cast out, or Retained in it, was given to the same Apostles, and their Substitutes, and Successors And therefore after our Saviour had breathed upon them, saying, (*John* 20 22) *Receive the Holy Ghost,* hee addeth in the next verse, *Whose soever Sins ye Remit, they are Remitted unto them, and whose soever Sins ye Retain, they are Retained* By which words, is not granted an Authority to Forgive, or Retain Sins, simply and absolutely, as God Forgiveth or Retaineth them, who
[275] knoweth the Heart of man, and truth of his Penitence and Conversion; but conditionally, to the Penitent: And this Forgivenesse, or Absolution, in case the absolved have but a feigned Repentance, is thereby without other act, or sentence of the Absolvent, made void, and hath no effect at all to Salvation, but on the contrary, to the Aggravation of his Sin. Therefore the Apostles, and their Successors, are to follow but the outward marks of Repentance; which appearing, they have no Authority to deny Absolution: and if they appeare not, they have

no authority to Absolve The same also is to be observed in Baptisme for to a converted Jew, or Gentile, the Apostles had not the Power to deny Baptisme; nor to grant it to the Un-penitent. But seeing no man is able to discern the truth of another mans Repentance, further than by externall marks, taken from his words, and actions, which are subject to hypocrisie; another question will arise, Who it is that is constituted Judge of those marks. And this question is decided by our Saviour himself; *If thy Brother* (saith he) *shal trespasse against thee, go and tell him his fault between thee, and him alone, if he shall hear thee, thou hast gained thy Brother. But if he will not hear thee, then take with thee one, or two more. And if he shall neglect to hear them, tell it unto the Church; but if he neglect to hear the Church, let him be unto thee as an Heathen man, and a Publican.* By which it is manifest, that the Judgment concerning the truth of Repentance, belonged not to any one Man, but to the Church, that is, to the Assembly of the Faithfull, or to them that have authority to bee their Representant. But besides the Judgment, there is necessary also the pronouncing of Sentence And this belonged alwaies to the Apostle, or some Pastor of the Church, as Prolocutor, and of this our Saviour speaketh in the 18 verse, *Whatsoever ye shall bind on earth, shall be bound in heaven; and whatsoever ye shall loose on earth, shall be loosed in heaven* And conformable hereunto was the practise of St. Paul (1 *Cor.* 5 3, 4, & 5.) where he saith, *For I verily, as absent in body, but present in spirit, have determined already, as though I were present, concerning him that hath so done this deed; In the name of our Lord Jesus Christ when ye are gathered together, and my spirit, with the power of our Lord Jesus Christ, To deliver such a one to Satan*: that is to say, to cast him out of the Church, as a man whose Sins are not Forgiven. Paul here pronounceth the Sentence; but the Assembly was first to hear the Cause, (for St. Paul was absent;) and by consequence to condemn him. But in the same chapter (ver 11, 12) the Judgment in such a case is more expressely attributed to the Assembly. *But now I have written unto you, not to keep company, if any man that is called a Brother be*

Mat. 18. 15, 16, 17.

a Fornicator, &c with such a one no not to eat. For what have I to do to judg them that are without? Do not ye judg them that are within? The Sentence therefore by which a man was put out of the Church, was pronounced by the Apostle, or Pastor; but the Judgment concerning the merit of the cause, was in the Church, that is to say, (as the times were before the conversion of Kings, and men that had Soveraign Authority in the Common-wealth,) the Assembly of the Christians dwelling in
[276] the same City; as in Corinth, in the Assembly of the Christians of Corinth.

Of Excommunication.

This part of the Power of the Keyes, by which men were thrust out from the Kingdom of God, is that which is called *Excommunication*: and to *excommunicate*, is in the Originall, ἀποσυνάγωγον ποιεῖν, *to cast out of the Synagogue*; that is, out of the place of Divine service, a word drawn from the custome of the Jews, to cast out of their Synagogues, such as they thought in manners, or doctrine, contagious, as Lepers were by the Law of Moses separated from the congregation of Israel, till such time as they should be by the Priest pronounced clean.

The use of Excommunication without Civill Power,

The Use and Effect of Excommunication, whilest it was not yet strengthened with the Civill Power, was no more, than that they, who were not Excommunicate, were to avoid the company of them that were. It was not enough to repute them as Heathen, that never had been Christians, for with such they might eate, and drink; which with Excommunicate persons they might not do; as appeareth by the words of St. Paul, (1 *Cor.* 5. ver 9. 10, *&c*) where he telleth them, he had formerly forbidden them to *company with Fornicators*; but (because that could not bee without going out of the world,) he restrained it to such Fornicators, and otherwise vicious persons, as were of the brethren; *with such a one* (he saith) they ought not to keep company, *no not to eat* And this is no more than our Saviour saith (*Mat.* 18 17.) *Let him be to thee as a Heathen, and as a Publican.* For Publicans (which signifieth Farmers, and Receivers of the revenue of the Common-wealth) were so hated, and detested by the Jews that were to pay it, as that

Publican and *Sinner* were taken amongst them for the same thing: Insomuch, as when our Saviour accepted the invitation of *Zacchæus* a Publican; though it were to Convert him, yet it was objected to him as a Crime. And therefore, when our Saviour, to *Heathen*, added *Publican*, he did forbid them to eat with a man Excommunicate.

As for keeping them out of their Synagogues, or places of Assembly, they had no Power to do it, but that of the owner of the place, whether he were Christian, or Heathen. And because all places are by right, in the Dominion of the Common-wealth; as well hee that was Excommunicated, as hee that never was Baptized, might enter into them by Commission from the Civill Magistrate; as Paul *Acts* 9. 2.
before his conversion entred into their Synagogues at Damascus, to apprehend Christians, men and women, and to carry them bound to Jerusalem, by Commission from the High Priest.

Of no effect upon an Apostate.

By which it appears, that upon a Christian, that should become an Apostate, in a place where the Civill Power did persecute, or not assist the Church, the effect of Excommunication had nothing in it, neither of dammage in this world, nor of terrour: Not of terrour, because of their unbeleef; nor of dammage, because they returned thereby into the favour of the world; and in the world to come, were to be in no worse estate, then they which never had beleeved. The dammage redounded rather to the Church, by provocation of them [277]
they cast out, to a freer execution of their malice.

But upon the faithfull only.

Excommunication therefore had its effect onely upon those, that beleeved that Jesus Christ was to come again in Glory, to reign over, and to judge both the quick, and the dead, and should therefore refuse entrance into his Kingdom, to those whose Sins were Retained; that is, to those that were Excommunicated by the Church. And thence it is that St. Paul calleth Excommunication, a delivery of the Excommunicate person to Satan. For without the Kingdom of Christ, all other Kingdomes after Judgment, are comprehended in the Kingdome of Satan. This is it that the faithfull stood in fear of, as long as they stood Excommunicate, that is to say, in an estate wherein their sins were not Forgiven. Whereby wee may understand, that Excommunication in the time that Christian Religion was not authorized by the Civill Power, was used onely for a correction of manners, not of errours in opinion for it is a punishment, whereof none could be sensible but such as beleeved, and expected the coming again of our Saviour to judge the world; and they who so beleeved, needed no other opinion. but onely uprightnesse of life, to be saved.

For what fault lyeth Excommunication.

There lyeth Excommunication for Injustice, as (*Mat.* 18) If thy Brother offend thee, tell it him privately; then with Witnesses; lastly, tell the Church; and then if he obey not, *Let him be to thee as an Heathen man, and a Publican.* And there lieth Excommunication for a Scandalous Life, as (1 *Cor.* 5. 11.) *If any man that is called a Brother, be a Fornicator, or Covetous, or an Idolater, or a Drunkard, or an Extortioner, with such a one yee are not to eat.* But to Excommunicate a man that held this foundation, that *Jesus was the Christ,* for difference of opinion in other points, by which that Foundation was not destroyed, there appeareth no authority in the Scripture, nor example in the Apostles. There is indeed in St Paul (*Titus* 3. 10.) a text that seemeth to be to the contrary. *A man that is an Hæretique, after the first and second admonition, reject.* For an *Hæretique,* is he, that being a member of the Church, teacheth neverthelesse some private opinion, which the Church has forbidden and such a one, S. Paul adviseth *Titus,* after the first, and second admonition, to *Reject.* But to *Reject* (in this place) is not to Excommunicate the Man; But to *give over admonishing him, to let him alone, to set by disputing with him,* as one that is to be convinced onely by himselfe. The same Apostle saith (2 *Tim.* 2 23) *Foolish and unlearned questions avoid* The word *Avoid* in this place, and *Reject* in the former, is the same in the Originall, παραιτοῦ: but Foolish questions may bee set by without Excommunication. And again, (*Tit.* 3. 9) *Avoid Foolish questions,* where the Originall περιΐστασο, (*set them by*) is equivalent to the former word *Reject.* There is no other place that can so much as colourably be drawn, to countenance the Casting out of the Church faithfull men, such as beleeved the foundation, onely for a singular superstructure of their own, proceeding perhaps from a good & pious conscience. But on the contrary, all such places as command avoiding such [278] disputes, are written for a Lesson to Pastors, (such as Timothy and Titus were) not to make new Articles of Faith, by determining every small controversie, which oblige men to a needlesse burthen of Conscience, or provoke them to break the union of the Church. Which Lesson the Apostles themselves observed well. S. Peter, and S. Paul, though their controversie were great, (as we may read in *Gal.* 2 11.) yet they did not cast one another out of the Church. Neverthelesse, during the Apostles times, there were other Pastors that observed it not; As Diotrephes (3 *John* 9 *&c.*) who cast out of the Church, such as S. John himself thought fit to be received into it, out of a pride he took in Præeminence; so early it was, that Vain-glory, and Ambition had found entrance into the Church of Christ.

Of persons liable to Excommunication.

That a man be liable to Excommunication, there be many conditions requisite, as First, that he be a member of some Commonalty, that is to say, of some lawfull Assembly, that is to say, of some Christian Church, that hath power to judge of the cause for which hee is to bee Excommunicated. For where there is no Community, there can bee no Excommunication, nor where there is no power to Judge, can there bee any power to give Sentence.

From hence it followeth, that one Church cannot be Excommunicated by another: For either they have equall power to Excommunicate each other, in which case Excommunication is not Discipline, nor an act of Authority, but Schisme, and Dissolution of charity, or one is so subordinate to the other, as that they both have but one voice, and then they be but one Church; and the part Excommunicated, is no more a Church, but a dissolute number of individuall persons.

And because the sentence of Excommunication, importeth an advice, not to keep company, nor so much as to eat with him that is Excommunicate, if a Soveraign Prince, or Assembly bee Excommunicate, the sentence is of no effect For all Subjects are bound to be in the company and presence of their own Soveraign (when he requireth it) by the law of Nature; nor can they lawfully either expell him from any place of his own Dominion, whether profane or holy; nor go out of his Dominion, without his leave; much lesse (if he call them to that honour,) refuse to eat with him. And as to other Princes and States, because they are not parts of one and the same congregation, they need not any other sentence to keep them from keeping company with the State Excommunicate. for the very Institution, as it uniteth many men into one Community, so it dissociateth one Community from another: so that Excommunication is not needfull for keeping Kings and States asunder; nor has any further effect then is in the nature of Policy it selfe; unlesse it be to instigate Princes to warre upon one another.

Nor is the Excommunication of a Christian Subject, that obeyeth the laws of his own Soveraign, whether Christian, or Heathen, of any effect. For if he beleeve [279] that *Jesus is the Christ, he hath the Spirit of God*, (1 Joh. 4 1.) *and God dwelleth in him, and he in God*, (1 Joh 4. 15.) But hee that hath the Spirit of God; hee that dwelleth in God; hee in whom God dwelleth, can receive no harm by the Excommunication of men. Therefore, he that beleeveth Jesus to be the Christ, is free from all the dangers threatned to persons Excommunicate. He that beleeveth it not, is no Christian. Therefore a true and unfeigned Christian is not liable to Excommunication: Nor he also that is a professed Christian, till his Hypocrisy appear in his Manners, that is, till his behaviour bee contrary to the law of his Soveraign, which is the rule of Manners, and which Christ and his Apostles have commanded us to be subject to For the Church cannot judge of Manners but by externall Actions, which Actions can never bee unlawfull, but when they are against the Law of the Common-wealth

If a mans Father, or Mother, or Master bee Excommunicate, yet are not the Children forbidden to keep them Company, nor to Eat with them; for that were (for the most part) to oblige them not to eat at all, for want of means to get food; and to authorise them to disobey their Parents, and Masters, contrary to the Precept of the Apostles.

In summe, the Power of Excommunication cannot be extended further than to the end for which the Apostles and Pastors of the Church have their Commission from our Saviour; which is not to rule by Command and Coaction, but by Teaching and Direction of men in the way of Salvation in the world to come. And as a Master in any Science, may abandon his Scholar, when hee obstinately neglecteth the practise of his rules; but not accuse him of Injustice, because he was never bound to obey him: so a Teacher of Christian doctrine may abandon his Disciples that obstinately continue in an unchristian life; but he cannot say, they doe him wrong, because they are not obliged to obey him For to a Teacher that shall so complain, may be applyed the Answer of God to Samuel in the like place, *They have* *not rejected thee, but mee.* Excommunication therefore when it wanteth the assistance of the Civill Power, as it doth, when a Christian State, or Prince is Excommunicate by a forain Authority, is without effect, and consequently ought to be without terrour. The name of *Fulmen Excommunicationis* (that is, *the Thunderbolt of Excommunication*) proceeded from an imagination of the Bishop of Rome, which first used it, that he was King of Kings, as the Heathen made Jupiter King of the Gods, and assigned him in their Poems, and Pictures, a Thunderbolt, wherewith to subdue, and punish the Giants, that should dare to deny his power: Which imagination was grounded on two errours, one, that the Kingdome of Christ is of this world, contrary to our Saviours owne words, *My Kingdome is not of this world*, the other, that hee is Christs Vicar, not onely over his owne Subjects, but over all the Christians of the World; whereof there is no ground in Scripture, and the contrary shall bee [280] proved in its due place

1 Sam. 8.

Of the Interpreter of the Scriptures before Civil Sove-

St Paul coming to *Thessalonica*, where was a Synagogue of the Jews, (*Acts* 17 2, 3.) *As his manner was, went in unto them, and three Sabbath dayes reasoned with them out of the Scriptures, Opening and alledging, that Christ must needs have suffered and risen again from the*

raigns became Christians.

dead; and that this Jesus whom he preached was the Christ. The Scriptures here mentioned were the Scriptures of the Jews, that is, the Old Testament. The men, to whom he was to prove that Jesus was the Christ, and risen again from the dead, were also Jews, and did beleeve already, that they were the Word of God. Hereupon (as it is verse 4.) some of them beleeved, and (as it is in the 5. ver.) some beleeved not What was the reason, when they all beleeved the Scripture, that they did not all beleeve alike; but that some approved, others disapproved the Interpretation of St. Paul that cited them; and every one Interpreted them to himself? It was this; S. Paul came to them without any Legall Commission, and in the manner of one that would not Command, but Perswade; which he must needs do, either by Miracles, as Moses did to the Israelites in Egypt, that they might see his Authority in Gods works; or by Reasoning from the already received Scripture, that they might see the truth of his doctrine in Gods Word But whosoever perswadeth by reasoning from principles written, maketh him to whom hee speaketh Judge, both of the meaning of those principles, and also of the force of his inferences upon them If these Jews of Thessalonica were not, who else was the Judge of what S Paul alledged out of Scripture? If S. Paul, what needed he to quote any places to prove his doctrine? It had been enough to have said, I find it so in Scripture, that is to say, in your Laws, of which I am Interpreter, as sent by Christ. The Interpreter therefore of the Scripture, to whose Interpretation the Jews of Thessalonica were bound to stand, could be none every one might beleeve, or not beleeve, according as the Allegations seemed to himselfe to be agreeable, or not agreeable to the meaning of the places alledged. And generally in all cases of the world, hee that pretendeth any proofe, maketh Judge of his proofe him to whom he addresseth his speech And as to the case of the Jews in particular, they were bound by expresse words (*Deut.* 17.) to receive the determination of all hard questions, from the Priests and Judges of Israel for the time being. But this is to bee understood of the Jews that were yet unconverted.

For the conversion of the Gentiles, there was no use of alledging the Scriptures, which they beleeved not The Apostles therefore laboured by Reason to confute their Idolatry; and that done, to perswade them to the faith of Christ, by their testimony of his Life, and Resurrection. So that there could not yet bee any controversie concerning the authority to Interpret Scripture; seeing no man was obliged during his infidelity, to follow any mans Interpretation of any Scripture, except his Soveraigns Interpretation of the Law of his countrey.

Let us now consider the Conversion it self, and see [281] what there was therein, that could be cause of such an obligation. Men were converted to no other thing then to the Beleef of that which the Apostles preached: And the Apostles preached nothing, but that Jesus was the Christ, that is to say, the King that was to save them, and reign over them eternally in the world to come; and consequently that hee was not dead, but risen again from the dead, and gone up into Heaven, and should come again one day to judg the world, (which also should rise again to be judged,) and reward every man according to his works None of them preached that himselfe, or any other Apostle was such an Interpreter of the Scripture, as all that became Christians, ought to take their Interpretation for Law. For to Interpret the Laws, is part of the Administration of a present Kingdome; which the Apostles had not They prayed then, and all other Pastors ever since, *Let thy Kingdome come*, and exhorted their Converts to obey their then Ethnique Princes. The New Testament was not yet published in one Body. Every of the Evangelists was Interpreter of his own Gospel; and every Apostle of his own Epistle, And of the Old Testament, our Saviour himselfe saith to the Jews (*John* 5 39) *Search the Scriptures; for in them yee thinke to have eternall life, and they are they that testifie of me* If hee had not meant they should Interpret them, hee would not have bidden them take thence the proof of his being the Christ he would either have Interpreted them himselfe, or referred them to the Interpretation of the Priests.

When a difficulty arose, the Apostles and Elders of the Church assembled themselves together, and determined what should bee preached, and taught, and how they should Interpret the Scriptures to the People; but took not from the People the liberty to read, and Interpret them to themselves. The Apostles sent divers Letters to the Churches, and other Writings for their instruction; which had been in vain, if they had not allowed them to Interpret, that is, to consider the meaning of them. And as it was in the Apostles time, it must be till such time as there should be Pastors, that could authorise an Interpreter, whose Interpretation should generally be stood to: But that could not be till Kings were Pastors, or Pastors Kings.

Of the Power to make Scripture Law

There be two senses, wherein a Writing may be said to be *Canonicall*; for *Canon*, signifieth a *Rule*, and a Rule is a Precept, by which a man is guided, and directed in any action whatsoever. Such Precepts, though given by a Teacher to his Disciple, or a Counsellor to his friend, without power to Compell him to observe them, are neverthelesse Canons; because they are Rules: But when they are given by one, whom he that receiveth them is bound to obey, then are those Canons, not onely Rules, but Laws. The question therefore here, is of the Power to make the Scriptures (which are the Rules of Christian Faith) Laws

Of the Ten Commandements

That part of the Scripture, which was first Law, was the Ten Commandements, written in two Tables of Stone, and delivered by | God himselfe to Moses; and
[282] by Moses made known to the people. Before that time there was no written Law of God, who as yet having not chosen any people to bee his peculiar Kingdome, had given no Law to men, but the Law of Nature, that is to say, the Precepts of Naturall Reason, written in every mans own heart. Of these two Tables, the first containeth the law of Soveraignty; 1 That they should not obey, nor honour the Gods of other Nations, in these words, *Non habebis Deos alienos coram me*, that is, *Thou shalt not have for Gods, the Gods that other Nations worship: but onely me*. whereby they were forbidden to obey, or honor, as their King and Governour, any other God,

than him that spake unto them then by Moses, and afterwards by the High Priest. 2 That they *should not make any Image to represent him*; that is to say, they were not to choose to themselves, neither in heaven, nor in earth, any Representative of their own fancying, but obey Moses and Aaron, whom he had appointed to that office. 3 That *they should not take the Name of God in vain*; that is, they should not speak rashly of their King, nor dispute his Right, nor the commissions of Moses and Aaron, his Lieutenants 4. That *they should every Seventh day abstain from their ordinary labour*, and employ that time in doing him Publique Honor. The second Table containeth the Duty of one man towards another, as *To honor Parents; Not to kill; Not to Commit Adultery; Not to steale; Not to corrupt Judgment by false witnesse*; and finally, *Not so much as to designe in their heart the doing of any injury one to another.* The question now is, Who it was that gave to these written Tables the obligatory force of Lawes. There is no doubt but they were made Laws by God himselfe But because a Law obliges not, nor is Law to any, but to them that acknowledge it to be the act of the Soveraign; how could the people of Israel that were forbidden to approach the Mountain to hear what God said to Moses, be obliged to obedience to all those laws which Moses propounded to them? Some of them were indeed the Laws of Nature, as all the Second Table; and therefore to be acknowledged for Gods Laws; not to the Israelites alone, but to all people · But of those that were peculiar to the Israelites, as those of the first Table, the question remains; saving that they had obliged themselves, presently after the propounding of them, to obey Moses, in these words (*Exod* 20 19) *Speak thou to us, and we will hear thee; but let not God speak to us, lest we dye.* It was therefore onely Moses then, and after him the High Priest, whom (by Moses) God declared should administer this his peculiar Kingdome, that had on Earth, the power to make this short Scripture of the Decalogue to bee Law in the Common-wealth of Israel. But Moses, and Aaron, and the succeeding High Priests were the Civill Soveraigns. Therefore hitherto, the Canonizing, or making of the Scripture Law, belonged to the Civill Soveraigne.

Of the Judiciall, and Leviticall Law. The Judiciall Law, that is to say, the Laws that God prescribed to the Magistrates of Israel, for the rule of their administration of | Justice, and of the Sentences, or [283] Judgments they should pronounce, in Pleas between man and man; and the Leviticall Law, that is to say, the rule that God prescribed touching the Rites and Ceremonies of the Priests and Levites, were all delivered to them by Moses onely, and therefore also became Lawes, by vertue of the same promise of obedience to Moses. Whether these laws were then written, or not written, but dictated to the People by Moses (after his forty dayes being with God in the Mount) by word of mouth, is not expressed in the Text; but they were all positive Laws, and equivalent to holy Scripture, and made Canonicall by Moses the Civill Soveraign.

The Second Law. After the Israelites were come into the Plains of Moab over against Jericho, and ready to enter into the land of Promise, Moses to the former Laws added divers others; which therefore are called *Deuteronomy*; that is, *Second Laws.* And are (as it is written, *Deut.* 29. 1) *The words of a Covenant which the Lord commanded Moses to make with the Children of Israel, besides the Covenant which he made with them in Horeb.* For having explained those former Laws, in the beginning of the Book of *Deuteronomy,* he addeth others, that begin at the 12 Cha. and continue to the end of the 26 of the same Book This Law (*Deut.* 27. 1.) they were commanded to write upon great stones playstered over, at their passing over Jordan: This Law also was written by Moses himself in a Book; and delivered into the hands of the *Priests, and to the Elders of Israel.* (*Deut.* 31. 9.) and commanded (ve. 26.) *to be put in the side of the Arke*; for in the Ark it selfe was nothing but the *Ten Commandements.* This was the Law, which Moses (*Deuteronomy* 17. 18) commanded the Kings of Israel should keep a copie of. And this is the Law, which having been long time lost, was found again in the Temple in the time of Josiah, and by his authority received for the Law of God. But both Moses at the writing, and Josiah at the recovery thereof, had both of them the Civill Soveraignty. Hitherto therefore the Power of making Scripture Canonicall, was in the Civill Soveraign.

Besides this Book of the Law, there was no other Book, from the time of Moses, till after the Captivity, received amongst the Jews for the Law of God. For the Prophets (except a few) lived in the time of the Captivity it selfe; and the rest lived but a little before it; and were so far from having their Prophecies generally received for Laws, as that their persons were persecuted, partly by false Prophets, and partly by the Kings which were seduced by them. And this Book it self, which was confirmed by Josiah for the Law of God, and with it all the History of the Works of God, was lost in the Captivity and sack of the City of Jerusalem, as appears by that of 2 *Esdras* 14. 21 *Thy Law is burnt; therefore no man knoweth the things that are done of thee, or the works that shall begin.* And before the Captivity, between the time when the Law was lost, (which is not mentioned in the Scripture, but may probably be thought to be the time of Rehoboam, when * Shishak King of Egypt took the spoile of the Temple,) and the time of Josiah, when it was found againe, they had no written Word of God, [284] but ruled according to their own discretion, or by the direction of such, as each of them esteemed Prophets.

* 1 *Kings* 14. 26.

The Old Testament when made Canonicall.

From hence we may inferre, that the Scriptures of the Old Testament, which we have at this day, were not Canonicall, nor a Law unto the Jews, till the renovation of their Covenant with God at their return from the Captivity, and restauration of their Common-wealth under *Esdras*. But from that time forward they were accounted the Law of the Jews, and for such translated into Greek by Seventy Elders of Judæa, and put into the Library of Ptolemy at Alexandria, and approved for the Word of God. Now seeing Esdras was the High Priest, and the High Priest was their Civill Soveraigne, it is manifest, that the Scriptures were never made Laws, but by the Soveraign Civill Power.

The New Testament began to be Canonicall under Christian Soveraigns.

By the Writings of the Fathers that lived in the time before the Christian Religion was received, and authorized by Constantine the Emperour, we may find, that the Books wee now have of the New Testament, were held by the Christians of that time (except a few, in respect of whose paucity the rest were called the Catholique Church, and others Hæretiques) for the dictates of the Holy Ghost; and consequently for the Canon, or Rule of Faith: such was the reverence and opinion they had of their Teachers, as generally the reverence that the Disciples bear to their first Masters, in all manner of doctrine they receive from them, is not small. Therefore there is no doubt, but when S. Paul wrote to the Churches he had converted; or any other Apostle, or Disciple of Christ, to those which had then embraced Christ, they received those their Writings for the true Christian Doctrine. But in that time, when not the Power and Authority of the Teacher, but the Faith of the Hearer caused them to receive it, it was not the Apostles that made their own Writings Canonicall, but every Convert made them so to himself.

But the question here, is not what any Christian made a Law, or Canon to himself, (which he might again reject, by the same right he received it;) but what was so made a Canon to them, as without injustice they could not doe any thing contrary thereunto. That the New Testament should in this sense be Canonicall, that is to say, a Law in any place where the Law of the Commonwealth had not made it so, is contrary to the nature of a Law. For a Law, (as hath been already shewn) is the Commandement of that Man, or Assembly, to whom we have given Soveraign Authority, to make such Rules for the direction of our actions, as hee shall think fit; and to punish us, when we doe any thing contrary to the same. When therefore any other man shall offer unto us any other Rules, which the Soveraign Ruler hath not prescribed, they are but Counsell, and Advice; which, whether good, or bad, hee that is counselled, may
[285] without injustice refuse to observe, and when contrary to the Laws already established, without injustice cannot observe, how good soever he conceiveth it to be. I say,

he cannot in this case observe the same in his actions, nor in his discourse with other men; though he may without blame beleeve his private Teachers, and wish he had the liberty to practise their advice; and that it were publiquely received for Law. For internall Faith is in its own nature invisible, and consequently exempted from all humane jurisdiction; whereas the words, and actions that proceed from it, as breaches of our Civill obedience, are injustice both before God and Man. Seeing then our Saviour hath denyed his Kingdome to be in this world, seeing he hath said, he came not to judge, but to save the world, he hath not subjected us to other Laws than those of the Common-wealth; that is, the Jews to the Law of Moses, (which he saith (*Mat.* 5.) he came not to destroy, but to fulfill,) and other Nations to the Laws of their severall Soveraigns, and all men to the Laws of Nature, the observing whereof, both he himselfe, and his Apostles have in their teaching recommended to us, as a necessary condition of being admitted by him in the last day into his eternall Kingdome, wherein shall be Protection, and Life everlasting Seeing then our Saviour, and his Apostles, left not new Laws to oblige us in this world, but new Doctrine to prepare us for the next; the Books of the New Testament, which containe that Doctrine, untill obedience to them was commanded, by them that God had given power to on earth to be Legislators, were not obligatory Canons, that is, Laws, but onely good, and safe advice, for the direction of sinners in the way to salvation, which every man might take, and refuse at his owne perill, without injustice.

Again, our Saviour Christs Commission to his Apostles, and Disciples, was to Proclaim his Kingdome (not present, but) to come, and to Teach all Nations; and to Baptize them that should beleeve; and to enter into the houses of them that should receive them; and where they were not received, to shake off the dust of their feet against them; but not to call for fire from heaven to destroy them, nor to compell them to obedience by the Sword. In all which there is nothing of Power, but of Perswasion He sent them out as Sheep unto

Wolves, not as Kings to their Subjects They had not in Commission to make Laws; but to obey, and teach obedience to Laws made, and consequently they could not make their Writings obligatory Canons, without the help of the Soveraign Civill Power. And therefore the Scripture of the New Testament is there only Law, where the lawfull Civill Power hath made it so. And there also the King, or Soveraign, maketh it a Law to himself; by which he subjecteth himselfe, not to the Doctor, or Apostle that converted him, but to God himself, and his Son Jesus Christ, as immediately as did the Apostles themselves

Of the Power of Councells to make the Scriptures Law.

That which may seem to give the New Testament, in respect of those that have embraced Christian Doctrine, the force of Laws, in the times, and places of persecution, is the decrees they made amongst themselves in their Synods For we read (*Acts* 15. 28.) the stile of the Councell of the Apostles, the Elders, and the whole
[286] Church, in this manner, *It seemed good to the Holy Ghost, and to us, to lay upon you no greater burthen than these necessary things, &c.* which is a stile that signifieth a Power to lay a burthen on them that had received their Doctrine. Now *to lay a burden on another*, seemeth the same that *to oblige*, and therefore the Acts of that Councell were Laws to the then Christians Neverthelesse, they were no more Laws than are these other Precepts, *Repent*: *Be Baptized*; *Keep the Commandements*; *Beleeve the Gospel*: *Come unto me*; *Sell all that thou hast*; *Give it to the poor*, and, *Follow me*, which are not Commands, but Invitations, and Callings of men to Christianity, like that of *Esay* 55. 1. *Ho, every man that thirsteth, come yee to the waters, come, and buy wine and milke without money.* For first, the Apostles power was no other than that of our Saviour, to invite men to embrace the Kingdome of God, which they themselves acknowledged for a Kingdome (not present, but) to come, and they that have no Kingdome, can make no Laws And secondly, if their Acts of Councell, were Laws, they could not without sin be disobeyed. But we read not any where, that they who received not the Doctrine of Christ, did therein sin; but that they

died in their sins; that is, that their sins against the Laws to which they owed obedience, were not pardoned And those Laws were the Laws of Nature, and the Civill Laws of the State, whereto every Christian man had by pact submitted himself. And therefore by the Burthen, which the Apostles might lay on such as they had converted, are not to be understood Laws, but Conditions, proposed to those that sought Salvation; which they might accept, or refuse at their own perill, without a new sin, though not without the hazard of being condemned, and excluded out of the Kingdome of God for their sins past. And therefore of Infidels, S John saith not, the wrath of God shall *come* upon them, but *the wrath of God remaineth upon them*; and *John* 3.36.
not that they shall be condemned; but that *they are* *John* 3.18.
condemned already Nor can it be conceived, that the benefit of Faith, *is Remission of sins*, unlesse we conceive withall, that the dammage of Infidelity, is *the Retention of the same sins.*

But to what end is it (may some man aske), that the Apostles, and other Pastors of the Church, after their time, should meet together, to agree upon what Doctrine should be taught, both for Faith and Manners, if no man were obliged to observe their Decrees? To this may be answered, that the Apostles, and Elders of that Councell, were obliged even by their entrance into it, to teach the Doctrine therein concluded, and decreed to be taught, so far forth, as no precedent Law, to which they were obliged to yeeld obedience, was to the contrary; but not that all other Christians should be obliged to observe, what they taught. For though they might deliberate what each of them should teach, yet they could not deliberate what others should do, unless their Assembly had had a Legislative Power; which none could have but Civil Soveraigns For though God be the Soveraign of all the world, we are not bound to take for his Law, whatsoever is propounded by every man in his name, nor any thing contrary to the Civill [287]
Law, which God hath expressely commanded us to obey.

Seeing then the Acts of Councell of the Apostles, were then no Laws, but Counsells, much lesse are Laws the Acts of any other Doctors, or Councells since, if assembled without the Authority of the Civil Soveraign And consequently, the Books of the New Testament, though most perfect Rules of Christian Doctrine, could not be made Laws by any other authority then that of Kings, or Soveraign Assemblies

The first Councell, that made the Scriptures we now have, Canon, is not extant · For that Collection of the Canons of the Apostles, attributed to *Clemens*, the first Bishop of Rome after S. Peter, is subject to question For though the Canonicall books bee there reckoned up; yet these words, *Sint vobis omnibus Clericis & Laicis Libri venerandi, &c.* containe a distinction of Clergy, and Laity, that was not in use so neer St. Peters time. The first Councell for setling the Canonicall Scripture, that is extant, is that of Laodicea, *Can.* 59. which forbids the reading of other Books then those in the Churches; which is a Mandate that is not addressed to every Christian, but to those onely that had authority to read any thing publiquely in the Church; that is, to Ecclesiastiques onely.

Of the Right of constituting Ecclesiasticall Officers in the time of the Apostles.

Of Ecclesiasticall Officers in the time of the Apostles, some were Magisteriall, some Ministeriall. Magisteriall were the Offices of preaching of the Gospel of the Kingdom of God to Infidels; of administring the Sacraments, and Divine Service; and of teaching the Rules of Faith and Manners to those that were converted. Ministeriall was the Office of Deacons, that is, of them that were appointed to the administration of the secular necessities of the Church, at such time as they lived upon a common stock of mony, raised out of the voluntary contributions of the faithfull.

Amongst the Officers Magisteriall, the first, and principall were the Apostles; whereof there were at first but twelve; and these were chosen and constituted by our Saviour himselfe; and their Office was not onely to Preach, Teach, and Baptize, but also to be Martyrs, (Witnesses of our Saviours Resurrection.) This Testimony, was the specificall, and essentiall mark; whereby the Apostleship was distinguished from other Magistracy Ecclesiasticall, as being necessary for an Apostle, either to have seen our Saviour after his Resurrection, or to have conversed with him before, and seen his works, and other arguments of his Divinity, whereby they might be taken for sufficient Witnesses. And therefore at the election of a new Apostle in the place of Judas Iscariot, S. Peter saith (*Acts* 1. 21, 22.) *Of these men that have companyed with us, all the time that the Lord Jesus went in and out among us, beginning from the Baptisme of John unto that same day that he was taken up from us,* must *one be ordained to be a* Witnesse *with us of his Resurrection*. where, by this word *must*, is implyed a necessary property of an Apostle, to have [288] companyed with the first and prime Apostles in the time that our Saviour manifested himself in the flesh.

Matthias made Apostle by the Congregation.

The first Apostle, of those which were not constituted by Christ in the time he was upon the Earth, was *Matthias*, chosen in this manner: There were assembled together in Jerusalem about 120 Christians (*Acts* 1. 15) These appointed two, *Joseph* the *Just*, and *Matthias* (ver. 23.) and caused lots to be drawn; *and* (ver. 26) *the Lot fell on Matthias, and he was numbred with the Apostles* So that here we see the ordination of this Apostle, was the act of the Congregation, and not of St. Peter, nor of the eleven, otherwise then as Members of the Assembly

Paul and Barnabas made Apostles by the Church of Antioch.

After him there was never any other Apostle ordained, but Paul and Barnabas; which was done (as we read *Acts* 13. 1, 2, 3.) in this manner *There were in the Church that was at Antioch, certaine Prophets, and Teachers: as Barnabas, and Simeon that was called Niger, and Lucius of Cyrene, and Manaen; which had been brought up with Herod the Tetrarch, and Saul. As they ministred unto the Lord, and fasted, the Holy Ghost said, Separate mee Barnabas, and Saul for the worke whereunto I have called them. And when they had fasted, and prayed, and laid their hands on them, they sent them away.*

By which it is manifest, that though they were called by the Holy Ghost, their Calling was declared unto them, and their Mission authorized by the particular Church of Antioch. And that this their calling was to the Apostleship, is apparent by that, that they are both called (*Acts* 14. 14.) Apostles: And that it was by vertue of this act of the Church of Antioch, that they were Apostles, S Paul declareth plainly (*Rom.* 1 1) in that hee useth the word, which the Holy Ghost used at his calling: For hee stileth himself, *An Apostle separated unto the Gospel of God*; alluding to the words of the Holy Ghost, *Separate me Barnabas and Saul, &c* But seeing the work of an Apostle, was to be a Witnesse of the Resurrection of Christ, a man may here aske, how S. Paul, that conversed not with our Saviour before his passion, could know he was risen To which is easily answered, that our Saviour himself appeared to him in the way to Damascus, from Heaven, after his Ascension; *and chose him for a vessell to bear his name before the Gentiles, and Kings, and Children of Israel*, and consequently (having seen the Lord after his passion) was a competent Witnesse of his Resurrection: And as for Barnabas, he was a Disciple before the Passion. It is therefore evident that Paul, and Barnabas were Apostles; and yet chosen, and authorized (not by the first Apostles alone, but) by the Church of Antioch as Matthias was chosen, and authorized by the Church of Jerusalem.

What Offices in the Church are Magisteriall.

Bishop, a word formed in our language, out of the Greek *Episcopus*, signifieth an Overseer, or Superintendent of any businesse, and particularly a Pastor, or Shepherd, and thence by metaphor was taken, not only amongst the Jews that were originally Shepherds,
[289] but also amongst the Heathen, to signifie the Office of a King, or any other Ruler, or Guide of People, whether he ruled by Laws, or Doctrine And so the Apostles were the first Christian Bishops, instituted by Christ himselfe. in which sense the Apostleship of Judas is called (*Acts* 1. 20.) *his Bishoprick.* And afterwards, when there were constituted Elders in the Christian Churches, with charge to guide Christs flock by their doctrine, and advice; these Elders were also called Bishops. Timothy was an Elder (which word *Elder*, in the New Testament is a name of Office, as well as of Age.) yet he was also a Bishop. And Bishops were

then content with the Title of Elders. Nay S John himselfe, the Apostle beloved of our Lord, beginneth his Second Epistle with these words, *The Elder to the Elect Lady* By which it is evident, that *Bishop*, *Pastor*, *Elder*, *Doctor*, that is to say, *Teacher*, were but so many divers names of the same Office in the time of the Apostles. For there was then no government by Coercion, but only by Doctrine, and Perswading. The Kingdome of God was yet to come, in a new world; so that there could be no authority to compell in any Church, till the Common-wealth had embraced the Christian Faith, and consequently no diversity of Authority, though there were diversity of Employments.

Besides these Magisteriall employments in the Church; namely, Apostles, Bishops, Elders, Pastors, and Doctors, whose calling was to proclaim Christ to the Jews, and Infidels, and to direct, and teach those that beleeved we read in the New Testament of no other. For by the names of *Evangelists* and *Prophets*, is not signified any Office, but severall Gifts, by which severall men were profitable to the Church as Evangelists, by writing the life and acts of our Saviour, such as were S. *Matthew* and S *John* Apostles, and S. *Marke* and S. *Luke* Disciples, and whosoever else wrote of that subject, (as S. *Thomas*, and S *Barnabas* are said to have done, though the Church have not received the Books that have gone under their names :) and as Prophets, by the gift of interpreting the Old Testament, and sometimes by declaring their speciall Revelations to the Church. For neither these gifts, nor the gifts of Languages, nor the gift of Casting out Devils, or of Curing other diseases, nor any thing else did make an Officer in the Church, save onely the due calling and election to the charge of Teaching.

Ordination of Teachers.

As the Apostles, Matthias, Paul, and Barnabas, were not made by our Saviour himself, but were elected by the Church, that is, by the Assembly of Christians, namely, Matthias by the Church of Jerusalem, and Paul, and Barnabas by the Church of Antioch, so were also the *Presbyters*, and *Pastors* in other Cities, elected by the Churches of those Cities. For proof whereof, let us consider, first, how S. Paul proceeded in the Ordination of Presbyters, in the Cities where he had converted men to the Christian Faith, immediately after he and Barnabas had received their Apostleship. We read (*Acts* 14. 23) that *they ordained Elders in every Church*: which at [290] first sight may be taken for an Argument, that they themselves chose, and gave them their authority: But if we consider the Originall text, it will be manifest, that they were authorized, and chosen by the Assembly of the Christians of each City. For the words there are, χειροτονήσαντες αὐτοῖς πρεσβυτέρους κατ' ἐκκλησίαν, that is, *When they had Ordained them Elders by the Holding up of Hands in every Congregation* Now it is well enough known, that in all those Cities, the manner of choosing Magistrates, and Officers, was by plurality of suffrages, and (because the ordinary way of distinguishing the Affirmative Votes from the Negatives, was by Holding up of Hands) to ordain an Officer in any of the Cities, was no more but to bring the people together, to elect them by plurality of Votes, whether it were by plurality of elevated hands, or by plurality of voices, or plurality of balls, or beans, or small stones, of which every man cast in one, into a vessell marked for the Affirmative, or Negative; for divers Cities had divers customes in that point. It was therefore the Assembly that elected their own Elders. the Apostles were onely Presidents of the Assembly to call them together for such Election, and to pronounce them Elected, and to give them the benediction, which now is called Consecration And for this cause they that were Presidents of the Assemblies, as (in the absence of the Apostles) the Elders were, were called προεστῶτες, and in Latin *Antistites*; which words signifie the Principall Person of the Assembly, whose office was to number the Votes, and to declare thereby who was chosen; and where the Votes were equall, to decide the matter in question, by adding his own; which is the Office of a President in Councell. And (because all the Churches had their Presbyters ordained in the same manner,) where the word is *Constitute*, (as *Titus* 1. 5.) ἵνα καταστήσῃς κατὰ πόλιν πρεσβυτέρους, *For this cause left I thee in Crete, that thou shouldest constitute Elders in every City,* we are to understand the same thing; namely, that hee should call the faithfull together, and ordain them Presbyters by plurality of suffrages. It had been a strange thing, if in a Town, where men perhaps had never seen any Magistrate otherwise chosen then by an Assembly, those of the Town becomming Christians, should so much as have thought on any other way of Election of their Teachers, and Guides, that is to say, of their Presbyters, (otherwise called Bishops,) then this of plurality of suffrages, intimated by S. Paul (*Acts* 14. 23.) in the word χειροτονήσαντες· Nor was there ever any choosing of Bishops, (before the Emperors found it necessary to regulate them in order to the keeping of the peace amongst them,) but by the Assemblies of the Christians in every severall Town.

The same is also confirmed by the continuall practise even to this day, in the Election of the Bishops of Rome. For if the Bishop of any place, had the right of choosing another, to the succession of the Pastorall Office, in any City, at such time as he went from thence, to plant the same in another place; much more had he had the Right, to appoint his successour in that place, in which he last
resided and dyed. And we find not, that ever any Bishop [291]
of Rome appointed his successor. For they were a long time chosen by the People, as we may see by the sedition raised about the Election, between *Damasus,* and *Ursicinus*; which Ammianus Marcellinus saith was so great, that *Juventius* the Præfect, unable to keep the peace between them, was forced to goe out of the City, and that there were above an hundred men found dead upon that occasion in the Church it self. And though they afterwards were chosen, first, by the whole Clergy of Rome, and afterwards by the Cardinalls; yet never any was appointed to the succession by his predecessor. If therefore they pretended no right to appoint their own successors, I think I may reasonably conclude, they had no right to appoint the successors of other Bishops, without receiving some new power; which none could take from the Church to bestow on them, but such as had a lawfull authority, not onely to Teach,

but to Command the Church, which none could doe, but the Civill Soveraign.

Ministers of the Church what: The word *Minister* in the Originall Διάκονος, signifieth one that voluntarily doth the businesse of another man, and differeth from a Servant onely in this, that Servants are obliged by their condition, to what is commanded them; whereas Ministers are obliged onely by their undertaking, and bound therefore to no more than that they have undertaken: So that both they that teach the Word of God, and they that administer the secular affairs of the Church, are both Ministers, but they are Ministers of different Persons. For the Pastors of the Church, called (*Acts* 6. 4.) *The Ministers of the Word*, are Ministers of Christ, whose Word it is: But the Ministery of a *Deacon*, which is called (verse 2 of the same Chapter) *Serving of Tables*, is a service done to the Church, or Congregation: So that neither any one man, nor the whole Church, could ever of their Pastor say, he was their Minister; but of a Deacon, whether the charge he undertook were to serve tables, or distribute maintenance to the Christians, when they lived in each City on a common stock, or upon collections, as in the first times, or to take a care of the House of Prayer, or of the Revenue, or other worldly businesse of the Church, the whole Congregation might properly call him their Minister.

For their employment, as Deacons, was to serve the Congregation; though upon occasion they omitted not to Preach the Gospel, and maintain the Doctrine of Christ, every one according to his gifts, as S. Steven did; and both to Preach, and Baptize, as Philip did: For that Philip, which (*Act.* 8. 5.) Preached the Gospell at Samaria, and (verse 38.) Baptized the Eunuch, was Philip the Deacon, not Philip the Apostle. For it is manifest (verse 1.) that when Philip preached in Samaria, the Apostles were at Jerusalem, and (verse 14.) *when they heard that Samaria had received the Word of God, sent Peter and John to them*; by imposition of whose hands, they that were Baptized, (verse 15) received (which before by the Baptisme of Philip they had not
[292] received) the Holy Ghost. For it was necessary for the conferring of the Holy Ghost, that their Baptisme

should be administred, or confirmed by a Minister of the Word, not by a Minister of the Church. And therefore to confirm the Baptisme of those that Philip the Deacon had Baptized, the Apostles sent out of their own number from Jerusalem to Samaria, Peter, and John; who conferred on them that before were but Baptized, those graces that were signs of the Holy Spirit, which at that time did accompany all true Beleevers; which what they were may be understood by that which S. *Marke* saith (chap. 16. 17.) *These signes follow them that beleeve in my Name, they shall cast out Devills; they shall speak with new tongues; They shall take up Serpents, and if they drink any deadly thing, it shall not hurt them; They shall lay hands on the sick, and they shall recover* This to doe, was it that Philip could not give; but the Apostles could, and (as appears by this place) effectually did to every man that truly beleeved; and was by a Minister of Christ himself Baptized: which power either Christs Ministers in this age cannot conferre, or else there are very few true Beleevers, or Christ hath very few Ministers.

And how chosen.

That the first Deacons were chosen, not by the Apostles, but by a Congregation of the Disciples; that is, of Christian men of all sorts, is manifest out of *Acts* 6 where we read that the *Twelve*, after the number of Disciples was multiplyed, called them together, and having told them, that it was not fit that the Apostles should leave the Word of God, and serve tables, said unto them (verse 3) *Brethren looke you out among you seven men of honest report, full of the Holy Ghost, and of Wisdome, whom we may appoint over this businesse* Here it is manifest, that though the Apostles declared them elected; yet the Congregation chose them; which also, (verse the fift) is more expressely said, where it is written, that *the saying pleased the multitude, and they chose seven, &c.*

Of Ecclesiasticall Revenue, under the Law of Moses.

Under the Old Testament, the Tribe of Levi were onely capable of the Priesthood, and other inferiour Offices of the Church. The land was divided amongst the other Tribes (Levi excepted,) which by the subdivision of the Tribe of Joseph, into Ephraim and Manasses, were still twelve. To the Tribe of Levi were assigned certain Cities for their habitation, with the

suburbs for their cattell: but for their portion, they were to have the tenth of the fruits of the land of their Brethren. Again, the Priests for their maintenance had the tenth of that tenth, together with part of the oblations, and sacrifices. For God had said to Aaron (*Numb.* 18 20) *Thou shalt have no inheritance in their land, neither shalt thou have any part amongst them, I am thy part, and thine inheritance amongst the Children of Israel.* For God being then King, and having constituted the Tribe of Levi to be his Publique Ministers, he allowed them for their maintenance, the Publique revenue, that is to say, the part that God had reserved to himself; which were Tythes, and Offerings. and that is it which is meant, where God saith, I am thine inheritance And therefore
[293] to the Levites might not unfitly be attributed the name of *Clergy* from Κλῆρος, which signifieth Lot, or Inheritance, not that they were heirs of the Kingdome of God, more than other; but that Gods inheritance, was their maintenance. Now seeing in this time God himself was their King, and Moses, Aaron, and the succeeding High Priests were his Lieutenants; it is manifest, that the Right of Tythes, and Offerings was constituted by the Civill Power.

After their rejection of God in the demanding of a King, they enjoyed still the same revenue; but the Right thereof was derived from that, that the Kings did never take it from them for the Publique Revenue was at the disposing of him that was the Publique Person; and that (till the Captivity) was the King. And again, after the return from the Captivity, they paid their Tythes as before to the Priest. Hitherto therefore Church Livings were determined by the Civill Soveraign.

In our Saviours time, and after.

Of the maintenance of our Saviour, and his Apostles, we read onely they had a Purse, (which was carried by Judas Iscariot,) and, that of the Apostles, such as were Fisher-men, did sometimes use their trade, and that when our Saviour sent the Twelve Apostles to Preach,
Mat 10.9, 10 he forbad them *to carry Gold, and Silver, and Brasse in their purses, for that the workman is worthy of his hire*: By which it is probable, their ordinary maintenance was not unsuitable to their employment; for their employ-

ment was (ver. 8.) *freely to give, because they had freely received*, and their maintenance was the *free gift* of those that beleeved the good tyding they carryed about of the coming of the Messiah their Saviour. To which we may adde, that which was contributed out of gratitude; by such as our Saviour had healed of diseases; of which are mentioned *Certain women* (Luke 8. 2, 3.) *which had been healed of evill spirits and infirmities; Mary Magdalen, out of whom went seven Devills; and Joanna the wife of Chuza, Herods Steward; and Susanna, and many others, which ministred unto him of their substance.*

After our Saviours Ascension, the Christians of every City lived in Common,* upon the mony which was made of the sale of their lands and possessions, and laid down at the feet of the Apostles, of good will, not of duty; for *whilest the Land remained* (saith S. Peter to Ananias *Acts* 5. 4.) *was it not thine? and after it was sold, was it not in thy power?* which sheweth he needed not have saved his land, nor his money by lying, as not being bound to contribute any thing at all, unlesse he had pleased. And as in the time of the Apostles, so also all the time downward, till after Constantine the Great, we shall find, that the maintenance of the Bishops, and Pastors of the Christian Church, was nothing but the voluntary contribution of them that had embraced their Doctrine. There was yet no mention of Tythes: but such was in the time of Constantine, and his Sons, the affection of Christians to their Pastors, as Ammianus Marcellinus saith (describing the sedition of *Damasus* and *Ursicinus* about the Bishopricke,) that it was worth their contention, in that the Bishops of those times by the liberality of their flock, and especially of Matrons, [294] lived splendidly, were carryed in Coaches, and were sumptuous in their fare and apparell.

**Acts, 4. 34.*

The Ministers of the Gospel lived on the Benevolence of their flocks

But here may some ask, whether the Pastor were then bound to live upon voluntary contribution, as upon almes, *For who* (saith S. Paul 1 *Cor.* 9. 7.) *goeth to war at his own charges? or who feedeth a flock, and eateth not of the milke of the flock?* And again, *Doe ye not know that they which minister about holy things, live of the things of the Temple, and they which wait at the Altar, partake*

1Cor.9.13.

with the Altar; that is to say, have part of that which is offered at the Altar for their maintenance? And then he concludeth, *Even so hath the Lord appointed, that they which preach the Gospel should live of the Gospel.* From which place may be inferred indeed, that the Pastors of the Church ought to be maintained by their flocks; but not that the Pastors were to determine, either the quantity, or the kind of their own allowance, and be (as it were) their own Carvers. Their allowance must needs therefore be determined, either by the gratitude, and liberality of every particular man of their flock, or by the whole Congregation. By the whole Congregation it could not be, because their Acts were then no Laws: Therefore the maintenance of Pastors, before Emperours and Civill Soveraigns had made Laws to settle it, was nothing but Benevolence. They that served at the Altar lived on what was offered So may the Pastors also take what is offered them by their flock; but not exact what is not offered. In what Court should they sue for it, who had no Tribunalls? Or if they had Arbitrators amongst themselves, who should execute their Judgments, when they had no power to arme their Officers? It remaineth therefore, that there could be no certaine maintenance assigned to any Pastors of the Church, but by the whole Congregation; and then onely, when their Decrees should have the force (not onely of *Canons*, but also) of *Laws*; which Laws could not be made, but by Emperours, Kings, or other Civill Soveraignes. The Right of Tythes in Moses Law, could not be applyed to the then Ministers of the Gospell: because Moses and the High Priests were the Civill Soveraigns of the people under God, whose Kingdom amongst the Jews was present; whereas the Kingdome of God by Christ is yet to come.

Hitherto hath been shewn what the Pastors of the Church are; what are the points of their Commission (as that they were to Preach, to Teach, to Baptize, to be Presidents in their severall Congregations;) what is Ecclesiasticall Censure, *viz.* Excommunication, that is to say, in those places where Christianity was forbidden by the Civill Laws, a putting of themselves out of the company of the Excommunicate, and where Christianity was by the Civill Law commanded, a putting the Excommunicate out of the Congregations of Christians; who elected the Pastors and Ministers of the Church, (that it was, the Congregation); who consecrated and blessed them, (that it was the Pastor); what was their due revenue, (that it was none but their own possessions, and their own labour, and the voluntary contributions of devout and gratefull Christians). We are to consider [295] now, what Office in the Church those persons have, who being Civill Soveraignes, have embraced also the Christian Faith.

That the Civill Soveraign being a Christian hath the Right of appointing Pastors.

And first, we are to remember, that the Right of Judging what Doctrines are fit for Peace, and to be taught the Subjects, is in all Common-wealths inseparably annexed (as hath been already proved cha. 18.) to the Soveraign Power Civill, whether it be in one Man, or in one Assembly of men. For it is evident to the meanest capacity, that mens actions are derived from the opinions they have of the Good, or Evill, which from those actions redound unto themselves, and consequently, men that are once possessed of an opinion, that their obedience to the Soveraign Power, will bee more hurtfull to them, than their disobedience, will disobey the Laws, and thereby overthrow the Common-wealth, and introduce confusion, and Civill war; for the avoiding whereof, all Civill Government was ordained. And therefore in all Common-wealths of the Heathen, the Soveraigns have had the name of Pastors of the People, because there was no Subject that could lawfully Teach the people, but by their permission and authority.

This Right of the Heathen Kings, cannot bee thought taken from them by their conversion to the Faith of Christ; who never ordained, that Kings for beleeving in him, should be deposed, that is, subjected to any but himself, or (which is all one) be deprived of the power necessary for the conservation of Peace amongst their Subjects, and for their defence against foraign Enemies. And therefore Christian Kings are still the Supreme Pastors of their people, and have power to ordain what Pastors they please, to teach the Church, that is, to teach the People committed to their charge.

Again, let the right of choosing them be (as before the conversion of Kings) in the Church, for so it was in the time of the Apostles themselves (as hath been shewn already in this chapter); even so also the Right will be in the Civill Soveraign, Christian. For in that he is a Christian, he allowes the Teaching; and in that he is the Soveraign (which is as much as to say, the Church by Representation,) the Teachers hee elects, are elected by the Church. And when an Assembly of Christians choose their Pastor in a Christian Common-wealth, it is the Soveraign that electeth him, because tis done by his Authority; In the same manner, as when a Town choose their Maior, it is the act of him that hath the Soveraign Power: For every act done, is the act of him, without whose consent it is invalid. And therefore whatsoever examples may be drawn out of History, concerning the Election of Pastors, by the People, or by the Clergy, they are no arguments against the Right of any Civill Soveraign, because they that elected them did it by his Authority.

Seeing then in every Christian Common-wealth, the Civill Soveraign is the Supreme Pastor, to whose charge [296] the whole flock of his Subjects is committed, and consequently that it is by his authority, that all other Pastors are made, and have power to teach, and performe all other Pastorall offices; it followeth also, that it is from the Civill Soveraign, that all other Pastors derive their right of Teaching, Preaching, and other functions pertaining to that Office; and that they are but his Ministers; in the same manner as the Magistrates of Towns, Judges in Courts of Justice, and Commanders of Armies, are all but Ministers of him that is the Magistrate of the whole Common-wealth, Judge of all Causes, and Commander of the whole Militia, which is alwaies the Civill Soveraign. And the reason hereof, is not because they that Teach, but because they that are to Learn, are his Subjects. For let it be supposed, that a Christian King commit the Authority of Ordaining Pastors in his Dominions to another King, (as divers Christian Kings allow that power to the Pope;) he doth not thereby constitute a Pastor over himself, nor a Soveraign Pastor over his

People; for that were to deprive himself of the Civill Power; which depending on the opinion men have of their Duty to him, and the fear they have of Punishment in another world, would depend also on the skill, and loyalty of Doctors, who are no lesse subject, not only to Ambition, but also to Ignorance, than any other sort of men. So that where a stranger hath authority to appoint Teachers, it is given him by the Soveraign in whose Dominions he teacheth. Christian Doctors are our Schoolmasters to Christianity; But Kings are Fathers of Families, and may receive Schoolmasters for their Subjects from the recommendation of a stranger, but not from the command; especially when the ill teaching them shall redound to the great and manifest profit of him that recommends them: nor can they be obliged to retain them, longer than it is for the Publique good; the care of which they stand so long charged withall, as they retain any other essentiall Right of the Soveraignty.

The Pastorall Authority of Soveraigns only is de Jure Divino, *that of other Pastors is* Jure Civili.

If a man therefore should ask a Pastor, in the execution of his Office, as the chief Priests and Elders of the people (*Mat* 21. 23.) asked our Saviour, *By what authority dost thou these things, and who gave thee this authority*: he can make no other just Answer, but that he doth it by the Authority of the Common-wealth, given him by the King, or Assembly that representeth it. All Pastors, except the Supreme, execute their charges in the Right, that is by the Authority of the Civill Soveraign, that is, *Jure Civili*. But the King, and every other Soveraign, executeth his Office of Supreme Pastor, by immediate Authority from God, that is to say, *in Gods Right*, or *Jure Divino*. And therefore none but Kings can put into their Titles (a mark of their submission to God onely) *Dei gratiâ Rex, &c.* Bishops ought to say in the beginning of their Mandates, *By the favour of the Kings Majesty, Bishop of such a Diocesse*; or as Civill Ministers, *In his Majesties Name*. For in saying, *Divinâ providentiâ*, which is the same with *Dei gratiâ*, though disguised, they deny to have received their authority from the Civill State; and sliely slip off the Collar of their Civill Sub- [297]
jection, contrary to the unity and defence of the Common-wealth.

Christian Kings have Power to execute all manner of Pastoral function

But if every Christian Soveraign be the Supreme Pastor of his own Subjects, it seemeth that he hath also the Authority, not only to Preach (which perhaps no man will deny;) but also to Baptize, and to Administer the Sacrament of the Lords Supper; and to Consecrate both Temples, and Pastors to Gods service; which most men deny; partly because they use not to do it; and partly because the Administration of Sacraments, and Consecration of Persons, and Places to holy uses, requireth the Imposition of such mens hands, as by the like Imposition successively from the time of the Apostles have been ordained to the like Ministery. For proof therefore that Christian Kings have power to Baptize, and to Consecrate, I am to render a reason, both why they use not to doe it, and how, without the ordinary ceremony of Imposition of hands, they are made capable of doing it, when they will.

There is no doubt but any King, in case he were skilfull in the Sciences, might by the same Right of his Office, read Lectures of them himself, by which he authorizeth others to read them in the Universities. Neverthelesse, because the care of the summe of the businesse of the Common-wealth taketh up his whole time, it were not convenient for him to apply himself in Person to that particular. A King may also if he please, sit in Judgment, to hear and determine all manner of Causes, as well as give others authority to doe it in his name, but that the charge that lyeth upon him of Command and Government, constrain him to bee continually at the Helm, and to commit the Ministeriall Offices to others under him. In the like manner our Saviour (who surely had power to Baptize) Baptized none * himselfe, but sent his Apostles and Disciples to Baptize. So also S. Paul, by the necessity of Preaching in divers and far distant places, Baptized few: Amongst all the Corinthians he Baptized only * *Crispus*, *Cajus*, and *Stephanus*, and the reason was, because his principall *Charge was to Preach. Whereby it is manifest, that the greater Charge, (such as is the Government of the Church,) is a dispensation for the lesse. The reason therefore why Christian Kings use not to Baptize, is evi-

* *John* 4. 2.

* 1 *Cor* 1. 14, 16.

* 1 *Cor.* 1. 17.

dent, and the same, for which at this day there are few Baptized by Bishops, and by the Pope fewer.

And as concerning Imposition of Hands, whether it be needfull, for the authorizing of a King to Baptize, and Consecrate, we may consider thus.

Imposition of Hands, was a most ancient publique ceremony amongst the Jews, by which was designed, and made certain, the person, or other thing intended in a mans prayer, blessing, sacrifice, consecration, condemnation, or other speech. So Jacob in blessing the children of Joseph (*Gen.* 48 14) *Laid his right Hand on Ephraim the younger, and his left Hand on Manasseh the first born*; and this he did *wittingly* (though they were [298]
so presented to him by Joseph, as he was forced in doing it to stretch out his arms acrosse) to design to whom he intended the greater blessing So also in the sacrificing of the Burnt offering, Aaron is commanded [*Exod.* 29. 10] *to Lay his Hands on the head of the bullock*; and [ver. 15.] *to Lay his Hand on the head of the ramme.* The same is also said again, *Levit.* 1 4 & 8 14. Likewise Moses when he ordained Joshua to be Captain of the Israelites, that is, consecrated him to Gods service, [*Numb.* 27. 23] *Laid his Hands upon him, and gave him his Charge,* designing, and rendring certain, who it was they were to obey in war. And in the consecration of the Levites [*Numb.* 8. 10.] God commanded that *the Children of Israel should Put their Hands upon the Levites* And in the condemnation of him that had blasphemed the Lord [*Levit.* 24. 14] God commanded that *all that heard him should Lay their Hands on his head, and that all the Congregation should stone him.* And why should they only that heard him, Lay their Hands upon him, and not rather a Priest, Levite, or other Minister of Justice, but that none else were able to design, and demonstrate to the eyes of the Congregation, who it was that had blasphemed, and ought to die? And to design a man, or any other thing, by the Hand to the Eye, is lesse subject to mistake, than when it is done to the Eare by a Name.

And so much was this ceremony observed, that in blessing the whole Congregation at once, which cannot be done by Laying on of Hands, yet *Aaron* [*Levit* 9 22.]

did lift up his Hand towards the people when he blessed them And we read also of the like ceremony of Consecration of Temples amongst the Heathen, as that the Priest laid his Hands on some post of the Temple, all the while he was uttering the words of Consecration. So naturall it is to design any individuall thing, rather by the Hand, to assure the Eyes, than by Words to inform the Eare in matters of Gods Publique service.

This ceremony was not therefore new in our Saviours time. For Jairus [*Mark* 5. 23.] whose daughter was sick, besought our Saviour (not to heal her, but) *to Lay his Hands upon her, that shee might bee healed.* And [*Matth* 19 13.] *they brought unto him little children, that hee should Put his Hands on them, and Pray*

According to this ancient Rite, the Apostles, and Presbyters, and the Presbytery it self, Laid Hands on them whom they ordained Pastors, and withall prayed for them that they might receive the Holy Ghost, and that not only once, but sometimes oftner, when a new occasion was presented. but the end was still the same, namely a punctuall, and religious designation of the person, ordained either to the Pastorall Charge in general, or to a particular Mission so [*Act.* 6 6] *The Apostles Prayed, and Laid their Hands* on the seven Deacons, which was done, not to give them the Holy Ghost, (for they were full of the Holy Ghost before they
[299] were chosen, as appeareth immediately before, verse 3) but to design them to that Office. And after Philip the Deacon had converted certain persons in Samaria, Peter and John went down [*Act* 8. 17] *and Laid their Hands on them, and they received the Holy Ghost.* And not only an Apostle, but a Presbyter had this power. For S Paul adviseth Timothy [1 *Tim.* 5 22.] *Lay Hands suddenly on no man*; that is, designe no man rashly to the Office of a Pastor. The whole Presbytery Laid their Hands on Timothy, as we read 1 *Tim* 4 14. but this is to be understood, as that some did it by the appointment of the Presbytery, and most likely their προεστὼς, or Prolocutor, which it may be was St. Paul himself For in his 2 Epist to *Tim.* ver 6. he saith to him, *Stirre up the gift of God which is in thee, by the*

Laying on of my Hands· where note by the way, that by the Holy Ghost, is not meant the third Person in the Trinity, but the Gifts necessary to the Pastorall Office We read also, that St Paul had Imposition of Hands twice; once from Ananias at Damascus [*Acts* 9. 17, 18] at the time of his Baptisme; and again [*Acts* 13. 3] at Antioch, when he was first sent out to Preach The use then of this ceremony considered in the Ordination of Pastors, was to design the Person to whom they gave such Power. But if there had been then any Christian, that had had the Power of Teaching before; the Baptizing of him, that is, the making him a Christian, had given him no new Power, but had onely caused him to preach true Doctrine, that is, to use his Power aright, and therefore the Imposition of Hands had been unnecessary; Baptisme it selfe had been sufficient. But every Soveraign, before Christianity, had the power of Teaching, and Ordaining Teachers; and therefore Christianity gave them no new Right, but only directed them in the way of teaching Truth; and consequently they needed no Imposition of Hands (besides that which is done in Baptisme) to authorize them to exercise any part of the Pastorall Function, as namely, to Baptize, and Consecrate. And in the Old Testament, though the Priest only had right to Consecrate, during the time that the Soveraignty was in the High Priest; yet it was not so when the Soveraignty was in the King: For we read [1 *Kings* 8] That Solomon Blessed the People, Consecrated the Temple, and pronounced that Publique Prayer, which is the pattern now for Consecration of all Christian Churches, and Chappels whereby it appears, he had not only the right of Ecclesiasticall Government; but also of exercising Ecclesiasticall Functions.

The Civill Soveraigne if a Christian, is head of the Church in his own Dominions.

From this consolidation of the Right Politique, and Ecclesiastique in Christian Soveraigns, it is evident, they have all manner of Power over their Subjects, that can be given to man, for the government of mens externall actions, both in Policy, and Religion; and may make such Laws, as themselves shall judge fittest, for the government of their own Subjects, both as they are the

Common-wealth, and as they are the Church: for both State, and Church are the same men.

[300] If they please therefore, they may (as many Christian Kings now doe) commit the government of their Subjects in matters of Religion to the Pope; but then the Pope is in that point Subordinate to them, and exerciseth that Charge in anothers Dominion *Jure Civili*, in the Right of the Civill Soveraign, not *Jure Divino*, in Gods Right; and may therefore be discharged of that Office, when the Soveraign for the good of his Subjects shall think it necessary. They may also if they please, commit the care of Religion to one Supreme Pastor, or to an Assembly of Pastors; and give them what power over the Church, or one over another, they think most convenient; and what titles of honor, as of Bishops, Archbishops, Priests, or Presbyters, they will, and make such Laws for their maintenance, either by Tithes, or otherwise, as they please, so they doe it out of a sincere conscience, of which God onely is the Judge. It is the Civill Soveraign, that is to appoint Judges, and Interpreters of the Canonicall Scriptures, for it is he that maketh them Laws It is he also that giveth strength to Excommunications; which but for such Laws and Punishments, as may humble obstinate Libertines, and reduce them to union with the rest of the Church, would bee contemned In summe, he hath the Supreme Power in all causes, as well Ecclesiasticall, as Civill, as far as concerneth actions, and words, for those onely are known, and may be accused, and of that which cannot be accused, there is no Judg at all, but God, that knoweth the heart And these Rights are incident to all Soveraigns, whether Monarchs, or Assemblies: for they that are the Representants of a Christian People, are Representants of the Church: for a Church, and a Common-wealth of Christian People, are the same thing.

Cardinal Bellarmines Books De *Summo Pontifice considered.*

Though this that I have here said, and in other places of this Book, seem cleer enough for the asserting of the Supreme Ecclesiasticall Power to Christian Soveraigns; yet because the Pope of Romes challenge to that Power universally, hath been maintained chiefly, and I think as strongly as is possible, by Cardinall Bellarmine, in his

Controversie *De Summo Pontifice* ; I have thought it necessary, as briefly as I can, to examine the grounds, and strength of his Discourse.

The first book Of five Books he hath written of this subject, the first containeth three Questions : One, Which is simply the best government, *Monarchy*, *Aristocracy*, or *Democracy* ; and concludeth for neither, but for a government mixt of all three . Another, which of these is the best Government of the Church ; and concludeth for the mixt, but which should most participate of Monarchy: The third, whether in this mixt Monarchy, St. Peter had the place of Monarch. Concerning his first Conclusion, I have already sufficiently proved (chapt. 18) that all Governments, which men are bound to obey, are Simple, and Absolute. In Monarchy there is but One Man Supreme ; and all other men that have any kind of Power in the State, have it by his Commission, during his pleasure ; and execute it in his name · And in Aristocracy, and Democracy, but One Supreme Assembly, with the same [301] Power that in Monarchy belongeth to the Monarch, which is not a Mixt, but an Absolute Soveraignty. And of the three sorts, which is the best, is not to be disputed, where any one of them is already established ; but the present ought alwaies to be preferred, maintained, and accounted best ; because it is against both the Law of Nature, and the Divine positive Law, to doe any thing tending to the subversion thereof. Besides, it maketh nothing to the Power of any Pastor, (unlesse he have the Civill Soveraignty,) what kind of Government is the best ; because their Calling is not to govern men by Commandement, but to teach them, and perswade them by Arguments, and leave it to them to consider, whether they shall embrace, or reject the Doctrine taught. For Monarchy, Aristocracy, and Democracy, do mark out unto us three sorts of Soveraigns, not of Pastors ; or, as we may say, three sorts of Masters of Families, not three sorts of Schoolmasters for their children.

And therefore the second Conclusion, concerning the best form of Government of the Church, is nothing to the question of the Popes Power without his own

Dominions: For in all other Common-wealths his Power (if hee have any at all) is that of the Schoolmaster onely, and not of the Master of the Family.

For the third Conclusion, which is, that St. Peter was Monarch of the Church, he bringeth for his chiefe argument the place of S. *Matth* (chap 16 18, 19) *Thou art Peter, And upon this rock I will build my Church, &c And I will give thee the keyes of Heaven; whatsoever thou shalt bind on Earth, shall be bound in Heaven, and whatsoever thou shalt loose on Earth, shall be loosed in Heaven.* Which place well considered, proveth no more, but that the Church of Christ hath for foundation one onely Article, namely, that which Peter in the name of all the Apostles professing, gave occasion to our Saviour to speak the words here cited; which that wee may cleerly understand, we are to consider, that our Saviour preached by himself, by John Baptist, and by his Apostles, nothing but this Article of Faith, *that he was the Christ*, all other Articles requiring faith no otherwise, than as founded on that. John began first, (*Mat* 3. 2) preaching only this, *The Kingdome of God is at hand* Then our Saviour himself (*Mat* 4 17) preached the same. And to his Twelve Apostles, when he gave them their Commission (*Mat.* 10. 7.) there is no mention of preaching any other Article but that. This was the fundamentall Article, that is the Foundation of the Churches Faith. Afterwards the Apostles being returned to him, he asketh them all, (*Mat* 16 13) not Peter onely, *Who men said he was*; and they answered, that *some said he was John the Baptist, some Elias, and others Jeremias, or one of the Prophets*: Then (ver. 15.) he asked them all again, (not Peter onely) *Whom say yee that I am?* Therefore S Peter answered (for them all) *Thou art Christ, the Son of the Living God*; which I said is the Foundation of the Faith of the whole
[302] Church, from which our Saviour takes the occasion of saying, *Upon this stone I will build my Church*: By which it is manifest, that by the Foundation-Stone of the Church, was meant the Fundamentall Article of the Churches Faith. But why then (will some object) doth our Saviour interpose these words, *Thou art Peter*?

If the originall of this text had been rigidly translated, the reason would easily have appeared. We are therefore to consider, that the Apostle Simon, was surnamed *Stone*, (which is the signification of the Syriacke word *Cephas*, and of the Greek word *Petrus*). Our Saviour therefore after the confession of that Fundamentall Article, alluding to his name, said (as if it were in English) thus, Thou art *Stone*, and upon this Stone I will build my Church: which is as much as to say, this Article, that *I am the Christ*, is the Foundation of all the Faith I require in those that are to bee members of my Church: Neither is this allusion to a name, an unusuall thing in common speech · But it had been a strange, and obscure speech, if our Saviour intending to build his Church on the Person of S. Peter, had said, *thou art a Stone, and upon this Stone I will build my Church*, when it was so obvious without ambiguity to have said, *I will build my Church on thee*; and yet there had been still the same allusion to his name.

And for the following words, *I will give thee the Keyes of Heaven, &c.* it is no more than what our Saviour gave also to all the rest of his Disciples [*Matth* 18. 18.] *Whatsoever yee shall bind on Earth, shall be bound in Heaven. And whatsoever ye shall loose on Earth, shall be loosed in Heaven* But howsoever this be interpreted, there is no doubt but the Power here granted belongs to all Supreme Pastors; such as are all Christian Civill Soveraignes in their own Dominions In so much, as if St. Peter, or our Saviour himself had converted any of them to beleeve him, and to acknowledge his Kingdome, yet because his Kingdome is not of this world, he had left the supreme care of converting his subjects to none but him; or else hee must have deprived him of the Soveraignty, to which the Right of Teaching is inseparably annexed And thus much in refutation of his first Book, wherein hee would prove St Peter to have been the Monarch Universall of the Church, that is to say, of all the Christians in the world

The second Book.

The second Book hath two Conclusions: One, that S Peter was Bishop of Rome, and there dyed The other, that the Popes of Rome are his Successors. Both which have been disputed by others. But supposing them true; yet if by Bishop of Rome, bee understood either the Monarch of the Church, or the Supreme Pastor of it; not Silvester, but Constantine (who was the first Christian Emperour) was that Bishop; and as Constantine, so all other Christian Emperors were of Right supreme Bishops of the Roman Empire; I say of the Roman Empire, not of all Christendome: For other Christian Soveraigns had the same Right in their severall Territories, as to an Office essentially adhærent to their Soveraignty. Which shall serve for answer to his second Book

[303] *The third Book.* In the third Book, he handleth the question whether the Pope be Antichrist. For my part, I see no argument that proves he is so, in that sense the Scripture useth the name: nor will I take any argument from the quality of Antichrist, to contradict the Authority he exerciseth, or hath heretofore exercised in the Dominions of any other Prince, or State.

It is evident that the Prophets of the Old Testament foretold, and the Jews expected a Messiah, that is, a Christ, that should re-establish amongst them the kingdom of God, which had been rejected by them in the time of Samuel, when they required a King after the manner of other Nations. This expectation of theirs, made them obnoxious to the Imposture of all such, as had both the ambition to attempt the attaining of the Kingdome, and the art to deceive the People by counterfeit miracles, by hypocriticall life, or by orations and doctrine plausible Our Saviour therefore, and his Apostles forewarned men of False Prophets, and of False Christs. False Christs, are such as pretend to be the *Christ*, but are not, and are called properly *Antichrists*, in such sense, as when there happeneth a Schisme in the Church by the election of two Popes, the one calleth the other *Antipapa*, or the false Pope. And therefore Antichrist in the proper signification hath two essentiall marks; One, that he denyeth Jesus to be Christ, and another that he professeth himselfe to bee Christ The first Mark is set down by *S. John* in his 1 Epist. 4. ch. 3. ver. *Every Spirit that confesseth not*

that Jesus Christ is come in the flesh, is not of God; And this is the Spirit of Antichrist The other Mark is expressed in the words of our Saviour, (*Mat.* 24. 5.) *Many shall come in my name, saying, I am Christ;* and again, *If any man shall say unto you, Loe, here is Christ, there is Christ, beleeve it not.* And therefore Antichrist must be a False Christ, that is, some one of them that shall pretend themselves to be Christ. And out of these two Marks, *to deny Jesus to be the Christ*, and to *affirm himselfe to be the Christ*, it followeth, that he must also be an *Adversary of Jesus the true Christ*, which is another usuall signification of the word Antichrist. But of these many Antichrists, there is one speciall one, ὁ Ἀντίχριστος, *The Antichrist*, or *Antichrist* definitely, as one certaine person; not indefinitely *an Antichrist*. Now seeing the Pope of Rome, neither pretendeth himself, nor denyeth Jesus to bee the Christ, I perceive not how he can be called Antichrist; by which word is not meant, one that falsely pretendeth to be *His* Lieutenant, or Vicar generall, but to be *Hee*. There is also some Mark of the time of this speciall Antichrist, as (*Mat.* 24, 15) when that abominable Destroyer, spoken of
by Daniel,* shall stand in the Holy place, and such * *Dar.* 9
tribulation as was not since the beginning of the world, 27.
nor ever shall be again, insomuch as if it were to last long, (ver. 22) *no flesh could be saved; but for the elects sake those days shall be shortened* (made fewer). But that tribulation is not yet come; for it is to be followed immediately (ver. 29.) by a darkening of the Sun and Moon, a falling of the Stars, a concussion of the Heavens, and the glorious coming again of our Saviour in the
cloudes. And therefore *The Antichrist* is not yet come; [304]
whereas, many Popes are both come and gone. It is true, the Pope in taking upon him to give Laws to all Christian Kings, and Nations, usurpeth a Kingdome in this world, which Christ took not on him · but he doth it not *as Christ*, but as *for Christ*, wherein there is nothing of *The Antichrist*.

In the fourth Book, to prove the Pope to be the *The fourth*
supreme Judg in all questions of Faith and Manners, *Book.*
(*which is as much as to be the absolute Monarch of all*

Christians in the world,) he bringeth three Propositions: The first, that his Judgments are Infallible: The second, that he can make very Laws, and punish those that observe them not The third, that our Saviour conferred all Jurisdiction Ecclesiasticall on the Pope of Rome.

Texts for the Infallibility of the Popes Judgement in points of Faith.

For the Infallibility of his Judgments, he alledgeth the Scriptures · and first, that of *Luke* 22. 31. *Simon, Simon, Satan hath desired you that hee may sift you as wheat; but I have prayed for thee, that thy faith faile not; and when thou art converted, strengthen thy Brethren.* This, according to Bellarmines exposition, is, that Christ gave here to Simon Peter two priviledges: one, that neither his Faith should fail, nor the Faith of any of his successors: the other, that neither he, nor any of his successors should ever define any point concerning Faith, or Manners erroneously, or contrary to the definition of a former Pope: Which is a strange, and very much strained interpretation. But he that with attention readeth that chapter, shall find there is no place in the whole Scripture, that maketh more against the Popes Authority, than this very place The Priests and Scribes seeking to kill our Saviour at the Passeover, and Judas possessed with a resolution to betray him, and the day of killing the Passeover being come, our Saviour celebrated the same with his Apostles, which he said, till the Kingdome of God was come hee would doe no more; and withall told them, that one of them was to betray him: Hereupon they questioned, which of them it should be. and withall (seeing the next Passeover their Master would celebrate should be when he was King) entred into a contention, who should then be the greatest man. Our Saviour therefore told them, that the Kings of the Nations had Dominion over their Subjects, and are called by a name (in Hebrew) that signifies Bountifull; but I cannot be so to you, you must endeavour to serve one another; I ordain you a Kingdome, but it is such as my Father hath ordained mee; a Kingdome that I am now to purchase with my blood, and not to possesse till my second coming; then yee shall eat and drink at my Table, and sit on

Thrones, judging the twelve Tribes of Israel: And then addressing himself to St. Peter, he saith, *Simon, Simon*, Satan seeks by suggesting a present domination, to weaken your faith of the future; but I have prayed for thee, that thy faith shall not fail; Thou therefore (Note this,) being converted, and understanding my Kingdome as of another world, confirm the same faith in thy Brethren: To which S. Peter answered (as one that no more expected any authority in this world) *Lord I am ready to goe with thee, not onely to Prison, but* [305]
to Death. Whereby it is manifest, S. Peter had not onely no jurisdiction given him in this world, but a charge to teach all the other Apostles, that they also should have none. And for the Infallibility of St. Peters sentence definitive in matter of Faith, there is no more to be attributed to it out of this Text, than that Peter should continue in the beleef of this point, namely, that Christ should come again, and possesse the Kingdome at the day of Judgement; which was not given by this Text to all his Successors; for wee see they claime it in the World that now is.

The second place is that of *Matth* 16 *Thou art Peter, and upon this rocke I will build my Church, and the gates of Hell shall not prevail against it* By which (as I have already shewn in this chapter) is proved no more, than that the gates of Hell shall not prevail against the confession of Peter, which gave occasion to that speech; namely this, that *Jesus is Christ the Sonne of God*.

The third Text is *John* 21. ver. 16, 17. *Feed my sheep*; which contains no more but a Commission of Teaching: And if we grant the rest of the Apostles to be contained in that name of *Sheep*; then it is the supreme Power of Teaching: but it was onely for the time that there were no Christian Soveraigns already possessed of that Supremacy. But I have already proved, that Christian Soveraignes are in their owne Dominions the supreme Pastors, and instituted thereto, by vertue of their being Baptized, though without other Imposition of Hands. For such Imposition being a Ceremony of designing the person, is needlesse, when hee is already designed to the Power of Teaching what Doctrine he will, by his institution to an Absolute Power over his Subjects. For as I have proved before, Soveraigns are supreme Teachers (in generall) by their Office; and therefore oblige themselves (by their Baptisme) to teach the Doctrine of Christ. And when they suffer others to teach their people, they doe it at the perill of their own souls, for it is at the hands of the Heads of Families that God will require the account of the instruction of his Children and Servants. It is of Abraham himself, not of a hireling, that God saith (*Gen.* 18. 19.) *I know him that he will command his Children, and his houshold after him, that they keep the way of the Lord, and do justice and judgement.*

The fourth place is that of *Exod.* 28. 30. *Thou shalt put in the Breastplate of Judgment, the Urim and the Thummin* which hee saith is interpreted by the Septuagint δήλωσιν καὶ ἀλήθειαν, that is, *Evidence* and *Truth*: And thence concludeth, God had given Evidence, and Truth, (which is almost Infallibility,) to the High Priest. But be it Evidence and Truth it selfe that was given; or be it but Admonition to the Priest to endeavour to inform himself cleerly, and give judgment uprightly; yet in that it was given to the High Priest, it was given to the Civill Soveraign: For such next under God was the High Priest in the Common-wealth of Israel; and
[306] is an argument for Evidence and Truth, that is, for the Ecclesiasticall Supremacy of Civill Soveraigns over their own Subjects, against the pretended Power of the Pope. These are all the Texts hee bringeth for the Infallibility of the Judgement of the Pope, in point of Faith.

Texts for the same in point of Manners.

For the Infallibility of his Judgment concerning Manners, hee bringeth one Text, which is that of *John* 16. 13. *When the Spirit of truth is come, hee will lead you into all truth*. where (saith he) by *all truth*, is meant, at least, *all truth necessary to salvation.* But with this mitigation, he attributeth no more Infallibility to the Pope, than to any man that professeth Christianity, and is not to be damned: For if any man erre in any point, wherein not to erre is necessary to Salvation, it is impossible he should be saved ; for that onely is necessary to Salvation, without which to be saved is impossible. What points these are, I shall declare out of the Scripture in the Chapter following. In this place I say no more, but that though it were granted, the Pope could not possibly teach any error at all, yet doth not this entitle him to any Jurisdiction in the Dominions of another Prince, unlesse we shall also say, a man is obliged in conscience to set on work upon all occasions the best workman, even then also when he hath formerly promised his work to another.

Besides the Text, he argueth from Reason, thus If the Pope could erre in necessaries, then Christ hath not sufficiently provided for the Churches Salvation ; because he hath commanded her to follow the Popes directions But this Reason is invalid, unlesse he shew when, and where Christ commanded that, or took at all any notice of a Pope : Nay granting whatsoever was given to S. Peter, was given to the Pope ; yet seeing there is in the Scripture no command to any man to obey St. Peter, no man can bee just, that obeyeth him, when his commands are contrary to those of his lawfull Soveraign.

Lastly, it hath not been declared by the Church, nor by the Pope himselfe, that he is the Civill Soveraign of all the Christians in the world ; and therefore all Christians are not bound to acknowledge his Jurisdiction in point of Manners. For the Civill Soveraignty, and supreme Judicature in controversies of Manners, are the same thing : And the Makers of Civill Laws, are not onely Declarers, but also Makers of the justice, and injustice of actions ; there being nothing in mens Manners that makes them righteous, or unrighteous, but their conformity with the Law of the Soveraign. And therefore when the Pope challengeth Supremacy in controversies of Manners, hee teacheth men to disobey the Civill Soveraign ; which is an erroneous Doctrine, contrary to the many precepts of our Saviour and his Apostles, delivered to us in the Scripture.

To prove the Pope has Power to make Laws, he alledgeth many places ; as first, *Deut* 17. 12. *The man*

that will doe presumptuously, and will not hearken unto the Priest, (that standeth to Minister there before the
[307] *Lord thy God, or unto the Judge,) even that man shall die. and thou shalt put away the evill from Israel.* For answer whereunto, we are to remember that the High Priest (next and immediately under God) was the Civill Soveraign; and all Judges were to be constituted by him. The words alledged sound therefore thus *The man that will presume to disobey the Civill Soveraign for the time being, or any of his Officers in the execution of their places. that man shall die, &c.* which is cleerly for the Civill Soveraignty, against the Universall power of the Pope.

Secondly, he alledgeth that of *Matth.* 16 *Whatsoever yee shall bind, &c.* and interpreteth it for such *binding* as is attributed (*Matth.* 23. 4.) to the Scribes and Pharisees, *They bind heavy burthens, and grievous to be born, and lay them on mens shoulders*; by which is meant (he sayes) Making of Laws; and concludes thence, that the Pope can make Laws. But this also maketh onely for the Legislative power of Civill Soveraigns: For the Scribes, and Pharisees sat in Moses Chaire, but Moses next under God was Soveraign of the People of Israel: and therefore our Saviour commanded them to doe all that they should say, but not all that they should do. That is, to obey their Laws, but not follow their Example.

The third place, is *John* 21. 16. *Feed my sheep*; which is not a Power to make Laws, but a command to Teach. Making Laws belongs to the Lord of the Family; who by his owne discretion chooseth his Chaplain, as also a Schoolmaster to Teach his children

The fourth place *John* 20. 21 is against him The words are, *As my Father sent me, so send I you.* But our Saviour was sent to Redeem (by his Death) such as should Beleeve; and by his own, and his Apostles preaching to prepare them for their entrance into his Kingdome, which he himself saith, is not of this world, and hath taught us to pray for the coming of it hereafter, though hee refused (*Acts* 1. 6, 7.) to tell his Apostles when it should come; and in which, when it comes, the twelve Apostles shall sit on twelve Thrones (every one perhaps as high as that of St. Peter) to judge the twelve tribes of Israel. Seeing then God the Father sent not our Saviour to make Laws in this present world, wee may conclude from the Text, that neither did our Saviour send S. Peter to make Laws here, but to perswade men to expect his second comming with a stedfast faith; and in the mean time, if Subjects, to obey their Princes; and if Princes, both to beleeve it themselves, and to do their best to make their Subjects doe the same; which is the Office of a Bishop. Therefore this place maketh most strongly for the joining of the Ecclesiasticall Supremacy to the Civill Soveraignty, contrary to that which Cardinall Bellarmine alledgeth it for.

The fift place is *Acts* 15. 28. *It hath seemed good to the Holy Spirit, and to us, to lay upon you no greater burden, than these necessary things, that yee abstaine from meats offered to Idols, and from bloud, and from things strangled, and from fornication.* Here hee notes the word *Laying of burdens* for the Legislative Power But [308] who is there, that reading this Text, can say, this stile of the Apostles may not as properly be used in giving Counsell, as in making Laws? The stile of a Law is, *We command*: But, *We think good*, is the ordinary stile of them, that but give Advice, and they lay a Burthen that give Advice, though it bee conditionall, that is, if they to whom they give it, will attain their ends: And such is the Burthen, of abstaining from things strangled, and from bloud; not absolute, but in case they will not erre. I have shewn before (chap. 25.) that Law, is distinguished from Counsell, in this, that the reason of a Law, is taken from the designe, and benefit of him that prescribeth it; but the reason of a Counsell, from the designe, and benefit of him, to whom the Counsell is given. But here, the Apostles aime onely at the benefit of the converted Gentiles, namely their Salvation; not at their own benefit; for having done their endeavour, they shall have their reward, whether they be obeyed, or not And therefore the Acts of this Councell, were not Laws, but Counsells.

The sixt place is that of *Rom.* 13. *Let every Soul be subject to the Higher Powers, for there is no Power but of God*; which is meant, he saith not onely of Secular, but also of Ecclesiasticall Princes. To which I answer, first, that there are no Ecclesiasticall Princes but those that are also Civill Soveraignes; and their Principalities exceed not the compasse of their Civill Soveraignty; without those bounds though they may be received for Doctors, they cannot be acknowledged for Princes. For if the Apostle had meant, we should be subject both to our own Princes, and also to the Pope, he had taught us a doctrine, which Christ himself hath told us is impossible, namely, *to serve two Masters* And though the Apostle say in another place, I *write these things being absent, lest being present I should use sharpnesse, according to the Power which the Lord hath given me*, it is not, that he challenged a Power either to put to death, imprison, banish, whip, or fine any of them, which are Punishments; but onely to Excommunicate, which (without the Civill Power) is no more but a leaving of their company, and having no more to doe with them, than with a Heathen man, or a Publican, which in many occasions might be a greater pain to the Excommunicant, than to the Excommunicate.

The seventh place is 1 *Cor.* 4 21 *Shall I come unto you with a Rod, or in love, and the spirit of lenity?* But here again, it is not the Power of a Magistrate to punish offenders, that is meant by a Rod; but onely the Power of Excommunication, which is not in its owne nature a Punishment, but onely a Denouncing of punishment, that Christ shall inflict, when he shall be in possession of his Kingdome, at the day of Judgment Nor then also shall it bee properly a Punishment, as upon a Subject that hath broken the Law, but a Revenge, as upon an Enemy, or Revolter, that denyeth the Right of our Saviour to the Kingdome: And therefore this proveth not the Legislative Power of any Bishop, that has not also the Civill Power.

[309] The eighth place is, *Timothy* 3. 2. *A Bishop must be the husband but of one wife, vigilant, sober, &c.* which he saith was a Law. I thought that none could make a Law in the Church, but the Monarch of the Church, St Peter. But suppose this Precept made by the authority of

St. Peter ; yet I see no reason why to call it a Law, rather than an Advice, seeing Timothy was not a Subject, but a Disciple of S Paul ; nor the flock under the charge of Timothy, his Subjects in the Kingdome, but his Scholars in the Schoole of Christ: If all the Precepts he giveth Timothy, be Laws, why is not this also a Law, *Drink no longer water, but use a little wine for thy healths sake?* And why are not also the Precepts of good Physitians, so many Laws? but that it is not the Imperative manner of speaking, but an absolute Subjection to a Person, that maketh his Precepts Laws

In like manner, the ninth place, 1 *Tim.* 5. 19 *Against an Elder receive not an accusation, but before two or three Witnesses*, is a wise Precept, but not a Law.

The tenth place is, *Luke* 10. 16. *He that heareth you, heareth mee; and he that despiseth you, despiseth me.* And there is no doubt, but he that despiseth the Counsell of those that are sent by Christ, despiseth the Counsell of Christ himself. But who are those now that are sent by Christ, but such as are ordained Pastors by lawfull Authority? and who are lawfully ordained, that are not ordained by the Soveraign Pastor? and who is ordained by the Soveraign Pastor in a Christian Common-wealth, that is not ordained by the authority of the Soveraign thereof? Out of this place therefore it followeth, that he which heareth his Soveraign being a Christian, heareth Christ; and hee that despiseth the Doctrine which his King being a Christian, authorizeth, despiseth the Doctrine of Christ (which is not that which Bellarmine intendeth here to prove, but the contrary). But all this is nothing to a Law. Nay more, a Christian King, as a Pastor, and Teacher of his Subjects, makes not thereby his Doctrines Laws. He cannot oblige men to beleeve; though as a Civill Soveraign he may make Laws suitable to his Doctrine, which may oblige men to certain actions, and sometimes to such as they would not otherwise do, and which he ought not to command; and yet when they are commanded, they are Laws; and the externall actions done in obedience to them, without the inward approbation, are the actions of the Soveraign, and not of the Subject, which is in that case but as an instrument, without any motion of his owne at all, because God hath commanded to obey them.

The eleventh, is every place, where the Apostle for Counsell, putteth some word, by which men use to signifie Command; or calleth the following of his Counsell, by the name of Obedience. And therefore they are alledged out of 1 *Cor.* 11. 2. *I commend you for keeping my Precepts as I delivered them to you.* The Greek is, *I commend you for keeping those things I delivered to you, as I delivered them.* Which is far from signifying that
[310] they were Laws, or any thing else, but good Counsell. And that of 1 *Thess* 4 2 *You know what commandements we gave you*: where the Greek word is παραγγελίας ἐδώκαμεν, equivalent to παρεδώκαμεν, *what wee delivered to you,* as in the place next before alledged, which does not prove the Traditions of the Apostles, to be any more than Counsells, though as is said in the 8 verse, *he that despiseth them, despiseth not man, but God* For our Saviour himself came not to Judge, that is, to be King in this world; but to Sacrifice himself for Sinners, and leave Doctors in his Church, to lead, not to drive men to Christ, who never accepteth forced actions, (which is all the Law produceth,) but the inward conversion of the heart; which is not the work of Laws, but of Counsell, and Doctrine.

And that of 2 *Thess.* 3. 14. *If any man Obey not our word by this Epistle, note that man, and have no company with him, that he may bee ashamed.* where from the word *Obey,* he would inferre, that this Epistle was a Law to the Thessalonians The Epistles of the Emperours were indeed Laws. If therefore the Epistle of S Paul were also a Law, they were to obey two Masters. But the word *Obey,* as it is in the Greek ὑπακούει, signifieth *hearkning to,* or *putting in practice,* not onley that which is Commanded by him that has right to punish, but also that which is delivered in a way of Counsell for our good; and therefore St Paul does not bid kill him that disobeys, nor beat, nor imprison, nor amerce him, which Legislators may all do; but avoid his company, that he may bee ashamed: whereby it is evident, it was not the Empire of an Apostle, but his Reputation amongst the Faithfull, which the Christians stood in awe of.

The last place is that of *Heb.* 13. 17. *Obey your Leaders, and submit your selves to them, for they watch for your souls, as they that must give account*: And here also is intended by Obedience, a following of their Counsell: For the reason of our Obedience, is not drawn from the will and command of our Pastors, but from our own benefit, as being the Salvation of our Souls they watch for, and not for the Exaltation of their own Power, and Authority. If it were meant here, that all they teach were Laws, then not onely the Pope, but every Pastor in his Parish should have Legislative Power. Again, they that are bound to obey, their Pastors, have no power to examine their commands. What then shall wee say to St. *John* who bids us (1 Epist. chap. 4. ver. 1.) *Not to beleeve every Spirit, but to try the Spirits whether they are of God, because many false Prophets are gone out into the world*? It is therefore manifest, that wee may dispute the Doctrine of our Pastors; but no man can dispute a Law. The Commands of Civill Soveraigns are on all sides granted to be Laws if any else can make a Law besides himselfe, all Common-wealth, and consequently all Peace, and Justice must cease; which is contrary to all Laws, both Divine and Humane Nothing therefore can be drawn from these, or any other places of Scripture, to prove the Decrees of the Pope, where he has not also the Civill Soveraignty, to be Laws.

The question of Superiority between the Pope and other Bishops.

The last point hee would prove, is this, *That our Saviour Christ has committed Ecclesiasticall Jurisdiction immediately to none but the Pope* [311] Wherein he handleth not the Question of Supremacy between the Pope and Christian Kings, but between the Pope and other Bishops. And first, he sayes it is agreed, that the Jurisdiction of Bishops, is at least in the generall *de Jure Divino*, that is, in the Right of God; for which he alledges S. Paul, *Ephes.* 4. 11. where hee sayes, that Christ after his Ascension into heaven, *gave gifts to men, some Apostles, some Prophets, and some Evangelists, and some Pastors, and some Teachers* And thence inferres, they have indeed their Jurisdiction in Gods Right; but will not grant they have it immediately from God, but derived through the Pope. But if a man may be said to have his Jurisdiction *de Jure Divino,* and yet not immediately; what lawfull Jurisdiction, though but Civill, is there in a Christian Common-wealth, that is not also *de Jure Divino*? For Christian Kings have their Civill Power from God immediately; and the Magistrates under him exercise their severall charges in vertue of his Commission; wherein that which they doe, is no lesse *de Jure Divino mediato,* than that which the Bishops doe, in vertue of the Popes Ordination. All lawfull Power is of God, immediately in the Supreme Governour, and mediately in those that have Authority under him. So that either hee must grant every Constable in the State to hold his Office in the Right of God: or he must not hold that any Bishop holds his so, besides the Pope himselfe.

But this whole Dispute, whether Christ left the Jurisdiction to the Pope onely, or to other Bishops also, if considered out of those places where the Pope has the Civill Soveraignty, is a contention *de lana Caprina*: For none of them (where they are not Soveraigns) has any Jurisdiction at all. For Jurisdiction is the Power of hearing and determining Causes between man and man, and can belong to none, but him that hath the Power to prescribe the Rules of Right and Wrong, that is, to make Laws, and with the Sword of Justice to compell men to obey his Decisions, pronounced either by himself, or by the Judges he ordaineth thereunto; which none can lawfully do, but the Civill Soveraign

Therefore when he alledgeth out of the 6 of *Luke,* that our Saviour called his Disciples together, and chose twelve of them which he named Apostles, he proveth that he Elected them (all, except Matthias, Paul and Barnabas,) and gave them Power and Command to Preach, but not to Judge of Causes between man and man: for that is a Power which he refused to take upon himselfe, saying, *Who made me a Judge, or a Divider, amongst you?* and in another place, *My Kingdome is not of this world* But hee that hath not the Power to hear, and determine Causes between man and man, cannot be said to have any Jurisdiction at all.

And yet this hinders not, but that our Saviour gave them Power to Preach and Baptize in all parts of the world, supposing they were not by their own lawfull Soveraign forbidden.: For to our own Soveraigns Christ himself, and his Apostles, have in sundry places expressely [312] commanded us in all things to be obedient.

The arguments by which he would prove, that Bishops receive their Jurisdiction from the Pope (seeing the Pope in the Dominions of other Princes hath no Jurisdiction himself,) are all in vain Yet because they prove, on the contrary, that all Bishops receive Jurisdiction when they have it from their Civill Soveraigns, I will not omit the recitall of them.

The first, is from *Numbers* 11. where Moses not being able alone to undergoe the whole burthen of administring the affairs of the People of Israel, God commanded him to choose Seventy Elders, and took part of the spirit of Moses, to put it upon those Seventy Elders: by which is understood, not that God weakned the spirit of Moses, for that had not eased him at all; but that they had all of them their authority from him; wherein he doth truly, and ingenuously interpret that place But seeing Moses had the entire Soveraignty in the Common-wealth of the Jews, it is manifest, that it is thereby signified, that they had their Authority from the Civill Soveraign· and therefore that place proveth, that Bishops in every Christian Common-wealth have their Authority from the Civill Soveraign; and from the Pope in his own Territories only, and not in the Territories of any other State.

The second argument, is from the nature of Monarchy; wherein all Authority is in one Man, and in others by derivation from him: But the Government of the Church, he says, is Monarchicall. This also makes for Christian Monarchs For they are really Monarchs of their own people; that is, of their own Church (for the Church is the same thing with a Christian people;) whereas the Power of the Pope, though hee were S. Peter, is neither Monarchy, nor hath any thing of *Archicall*, nor *Craticall*, but onely of *Didacticall*, For God accepteth not a forced, but a willing obedience.

The third, is, from that the *Sea* of S Peter is called by S. Cyprian, the *Head*, the *Source*, the *Roote*, the *Sun*, from whence the Authority of Bishops is derived. But by the Law of Nature (which is a better Principle of Right and Wrong, than the word of any Doctor that is but a man) the Civill Soveraign in every Common-wealth, is the *Head*, the *Source*, the *Root*, and the *Sun*, from which all Jurisdiction is derived. And therefore the Jurisdiction of Bishops, is derived from the Civill Soveraign.

The fourth, is taken from the Inequality of their Jurisdictions: For if God (saith he) had given it them immediately, he had given aswell Equality of Jurisdiction, as of Order · But wee see, some are Bishops but of [one] Town, some of a hundred Towns, and some of many whole Provinces; which differences were not determined by the command of God; their Jurisdiction therefore is not of God, but of Man; and one has a greater, another a lesse, as it pleaseth the Prince of the Church. Which argument, if he had proved before, that the Pope had had an Universall Jurisdiction over all Chris-
[313] tians, had been for his purpose. But seeing that hath not been proved, and that it is notoriously known, the large Jurisdiction of the Pope was given him by those that had it, that is, by the Emperours of Rome, (for the Patriarch of Constantinople, upon the same title, namely, of being Bishop of the Capitall City of the Empire, and Seat of the Emperour, claimed to be equall to him,) it followeth, that all other Bishops have their Jurisdiction from the Soveraigns of the place wherein they exercise the same: And as for that cause they have not their Authority *de Jure Divino*; so neither hath the Pope his *de Jure Divino*, except onely where hee is also the Civill Soveraign

His fift argument is this, *If Bishops have their Jurisdiction immediately from God, the Pope could not take it from them, for he can doe nothing contrary to Gods ordination*; And this consequence is good, and well proved. *But* (saith he) *the Pope can do this, and has done it.* This also is granted, so he doe it in his own Dominions, or in the Dominions of any other Prince that hath given him that Power; but not universally, in Right of the Popedome. For that power belongeth to every Christian Soveraign, within the bounds of his owne Empire, and is inseparable from the Soveraignty. Before the People of Israel had (by the commandment of God to Samuel) set over themselves a King, after the manner of other Nations, the High Priest had the Civill Government; and none but he could make, nor depose an inferiour Priest: But that Power was afterwards in the King, as may be proved by this same argument of Bellarmine; For if the Priest (be he the High Priest or any other) had his Jurisdiction immediately from God, then the King could not take it from him; *for he could doe nothing contrary to Gods ordinance*: But it is certain, that King Solomon (1 *Kings* 2. 26.) deprived Abiathar the High Priest of his Office, and placed Zadok (verse 35) in his room. Kings therefore may in the like manner Ordaine, and Deprive Bishops, as they shall thinke fit, for the well governing of their Subjects.

His sixth argument is this, If Bishops have their Jurisdiction *de Jure Divino* (that is, *immediately from God*,) they that maintaine it, should bring some Word of God to prove it: But they can bring none. The argument is good; I have therefore nothing to say against it. But it is an argument no lesse good, to prove the Pope himself to have no Jurisdiction in the Dominion of any other Prince.

Lastly, hee bringeth for argument, the testimony of two Popes, *Innocent*, and *Leo*, and I doubt not but hee might have alledged, with as good reason, the testimonies of all the Popes almost since S. Peter: For considering the love of Power naturally implanted in mankind, whosoever were made Pope, he would be tempted to uphold the same opinion. Neverthelesse, they should therein but doe, as *Innocent*, and *Leo* did, bear witnesse of themselves, and therefore their witnesse should not be good.

In the fift Book he hath four Conclusions. The [314]
first is, *That the Pope is not Lord of all the world*: *Of the*
The second, *That the Pope is not Lord of all the* *Popes*
Christian world: The third, *That the Pope* (without his *Temporall Power.*

owne Territory) *has not any Temporall Jurisdiction DIRECTLY*: These three Conclusions are easily granted The fourth is, *That the Pope has* (in the Dominions of other Princes) the Supreme *Temporall Power INDIRECTLY* which is denyed; unlesse hee mean by *Indirectly*, that he has gotten it by Indirect means; then is that also granted. But I understand, that when he saith he hath it *Indirectly*, he means, that such Temporall Jurisdiction belongeth to him of Right, but that this Right is but a Consequence of his Pastorall Authority, the which he could not exercise, unlesse he have the other with it: And therefore to the Pastorall Power (which he calls Spirituall) the Supreme Power Civill is necessarily annexed, and that thereby hee hath a Right to change Kingdomes, giving them to one, and taking them from another, when he shall think it conduces to the Salvation of Souls.

Before I come to consider the Arguments by which hee would prove this Doctrine, it will not bee amisse to lay open the Consequences of it; that Princes, and States, that have the Civill Soveraignty in their severall Common-wealths, may bethink themselves, whether it bee convenient for them, and conducing to the good of their Subjects, of whom they are to give an account at the day of Judgment, to admit the same.

When it is said, the Pope hath not (in the Territories of other States) the Supreme Civill Power *Directly*; we are to understand, he doth not challenge it, as other Civill Soveraigns doe, from the originall submission thereto of those that are to be governed For it is evident, and has already been sufficiently in this Treatise demonstrated, that the Right of all Soveraigns, is derived originally from the consent of every one of those that are to bee governed; whether they that choose him, doe it for their common defence against an Enemy, as when they agree amongst themselves to appoint a Man, or an Assembly of men to protect them; or whether they doe it, to save their lives, by submission to a conquering Enemy. The Pope therefore, when he disclaimeth the Supreme Civill Power over other States *Directly*, denyeth no more, but that his Right

cometh to him by that way; He ceaseth not for all that, to claime it another way, and that is, (without the consent of them that are to be governed) by a Right given him by God, (which hee calleth *Indirectly*,) in his Assumption to the Papacy. But by what way soever he pretend, the Power is the same; and he may (if it bee granted to be his Right) depose Princes and States, as often as it is for the Salvation of Soules, that is, as often as he will; for he claimeth also the Sole Power to Judge, whether it be to the Salvation of mens Souls, or not. And this is the Doctrine, not onely that Bellarmine here, and many other Doctors teach in their Sermons and Books, but also that some Councells have decreed, and the Popes have accordingly, when the occasion hath [315]
served them, put in practise. For the fourth Councell of Lateran held under Pope *Innocent* the third, (in the third Chap. *De Hæreticis*,) hath this Canon *If a King at the Popes admonition, doe not purge his Kingdome of Hæretiques, and being Excommunicate for the same, make not satisfaction within a yeer, his Subjects are absolved of their Obedience.* And the practise hereof hath been seen on divers occasions; as in the Deposing of *Chilperique*, King of France, in the Translation of the Roman Empire to *Charlemaine*; in the Oppression of *John* King of England; in Transferring the Kingdome of *Navarre*, and of late years, in the League against *Henry* the third of France, and in many more occurrences. I think there be few Princes that consider not this as Injust, and Inconvenient, but I wish they would all resolve to be Kings, or Subjects. Men cannot serve two Masters They ought therefore to ease them, either by holding the Reins of Government wholly in their own hands; or by wholly delivering them into the hands of the Pope; that such men as are willing to be obedient, may be protected in their obedience For this distinction of Temporall, and Spirituall Power is but words. Power is as really divided, and as dangerously to all purposes, by sharing with another *Indirect* Power, as with a *Direct* one But to come now to his Arguments

The first is this, *The Civill Power is subject to the Spirituall: Therefore he that hath the Supreme Power*

Spirituall, hath right to command Temporall Princes, and dispose of their Temporalls in order to the Spirituall. As for the distinction of Temporall, and Spirituall, let us consider in what sense it may be said intelligibly, that the Temporall, or Civill Power is subject to the Spirituall. There be but two ways that those words can be made sense. For when wee say, one Power is subject to another Power, the meaning either is, that he which hath the one, is subject to him that hath the other; or that the one Power is to the other, as the means to the end. For wee cannot understand, that one Power hath Power over another Power, or that one Power can have Right or Command over another: For Subjection, Command, Right, and Power are accidents, not of Powers, but of Persons: One Power may be subordinate to another, as the art of a Sadler, to the art of a Rider. If then it bee granted, that the Civill Government be ordained as a means to bring us to a Spirituall felicity; yet it does not follow, that if a King have the Civill Power, and the Pope the Spirituall, that therefore the King is bound to obey the Pope, more then every Sadler is bound to obey every Rider. Therefore as from Subordination of an Art, cannot be inferred the Subjection of the Professor, so from the Subordination of a Government, cannot be inferred the Subjection of the Governor. When therefore he saith, the Civill Power is Subject to the Spirituall, his meaning is, that the Civill Soveraign, is Subject to the Spirituall Soveraign. And the Argument stands thus, *The Civil Soveraign, is subject to the Spirituall; Therefore the Spirituall Prince may command*
[316] *Temporall Princes.* Where the Conclusion is the same, with the Antecedent he should have proved. But to prove it, he alledgeth first, this reason, *Kings and Popes, Clergy and Laity make but one Common-wealth; that is to say, but one Church: And in all Bodies the Members depend one upon another: But things Spirituall depend not of things Temporall: Therefore Temporall depend on Spirituall. And therefore are Subject to them.* In which Argumentation there be two grosse errours: one is, that all Christian Kings, Popes, Clergy, and all other Christian men, make but one Common-wealth: For it is evident

that France is one Common-wealth, Spain another, and Venice a third, &c. And these consist of Christians; and therefore also are severall Bodies of Christians, that is to say, severall Churches: And their severall Soveraigns Represent them, whereby they are capable of commanding and obeying, of doing and suffering, as a naturall man; which no Generall or Universall Church is, till it have a Representant; which it hath not on Earth: for if it had, there is no doubt but that all Christendome were one Common-wealth, whose Soveraign were that Representant, both in things Spirituall and Temporall: And the Pope, to make himself this Representant, wanteth three things that our Saviour hath not given him, to *Command*, and to *Judge*, and to *Punish*, otherwise than (by Excommunication) to run from those that will not Learn of him: For though the Pope were Christs onely Vicar, yet he cannot exercise his government, till our Saviours second coming: And then also it is not the Pope, but St Peter himselfe, with the other Apostles, that are to be Judges of the world.

The other errour in this his first Argument is, that he sayes, the Members of every Common-wealth, as of a naturall Body, depend one of another. It is true, they cohære together; but they depend onely on the Soveraign, which is the Soul of the Common-wealth; which failing, the Common-wealth is dissolved into a Civill war, no one man so much as cohæring to another, for want of a common Dependance on a known Soveraign; Just as the Members of the naturall Body dissolve into Earth, for want of a Soul to hold them together. Therefore there is nothing in this similitude, from whence to inferre a dependance of the Laity on the Clergy, or of the Temporall Officers on the Spirituall; but of both on the Civill Soveraign; which ought indeed to direct his Civill commands to the Salvation of Souls; but is not therefore subject to any but God himselfe. And thus you see the laboured fallacy of the first Argument, to deceive such men as distinguish not between the Subordination of Actions in the way to the End; and the Subjection of Persons one to another in the administration of the Means For to every End, the Means are determined by Nature, or by God himselfe supernaturally: but the Power to make men use the Means, is in every nation resigned (by the Law of Nature, which forbiddeth men to violate their Faith given) to the Civill Soveraign

[317] His second Argument is this, *Every Common-wealth, (because it is supposed to be perfect and sufficient in it self,) may command any other Common-wealth, not subject to it, and force it to change the administration of the Government; nay depose the Prince, and set another in his room, if it cannot otherwise defend it selfe against the injuries he goes about to doe them: much more may a Spirituall Common-wealth command a Temporall one to change the administration of their Government, and may depose Princes, and institute others, when they cannot otherwise defend the Spirituall Good*

That a Common-wealth, to defend it selfe against injuries, may lawfully doe all that he hath here said, is very true; and hath already in that which hath gone before been sufficiently demonstrated And if it were also true, that there is now in this world a Spirituall Common-wealth, distinct from a Civill Common-wealth, then might the Prince thereof, upon injury done him, or upon want of caution that injury be not done him in time to come, repaire, and secure himself by Warre, which is in summe, deposing, killing, or subduing, or doing any act of Hostility. But by the same reason, it would be no lesse lawfull for a Civill Soveraign, upon the like injuries done, or feared, to make warre upon the Spirituall Soveraign, which I beleeve is more than Cardinall Bellarmine would have inferred from his own proposition.

But Spirituall Common-wealth there is none in this world. for it is the same thing with the Kingdome of Christ, which he himselfe saith, is not of this world; but shall be in the next world, at the Resurrection, when they that have lived justly, and beleeved that he was the Christ, shall (though they died *Naturall* bodies) rise *Spirituall* bodies; and then it is, that our Saviour shall judge the world, and conquer his Adversaries, and make a Spirituall Common-wealth. In the mean time, seeing there are no men on earth, whose bodies are Spirituall; there can be no Spirituall Common-wealth amongst men that are yet in the flesh ; unlesse wee call Preachers, that have Commission to Teach, and prepare men for their reception into the Kingdome of Christ at the Resurrection, a Common-wealth ; which I have proved already to bee none.

The third Argument is this ; *It is not lawfull for Christians to tolerate an Infidel, or Hæreticall King, in case he endeavour to draw them to his Hæresie, or Infidelity. But to judge whether a King draw his subjects to Hæresie, or not, belongeth to the Pope Therefore hath the Pope Right, to determine whether the Prince be to be deposed, or not deposed*

To this I answer, that both these assertions are false. For Christians, (or men of what Religion soever,) if they tolerate not their King, whatsoever law hee maketh, though it bee concerning Religion, doe violate their faith, contrary to the Divine Law, both *Naturall* and *Positive* Nor is there any Judge of Hæresie amongst Subjects, but their owne Civill Soveraign : For *Hæresie is nothing else, but a private opinion, obstinately maintained, contrary to the opinion which the Publique Person* (that is to say, [318] the Representant of the Common-wealth) *hath commanded to bee taught* By which it is manifest, that an opinion publiquely appointed to bee taught, cannot be Hæresie ; nor the Soveraign Princes that authorize them, Hæretiques For Hæretiques are none but private men, that stubbornly defend some Doctrine, prohibited by their lawfull Soveraigns.

But to prove that Christians are not to tolerate Infidell, or Hæreticall Kings, he alledgeth a place in *Deut* 17. where God forbiddeth the Jews, when they shall set a King over themselves, to choose a stranger : And from thence inferreth, that it is unlawfull for a Christian, to choose a King, that is not a Christian And 'tis true, that he that is a Christian, that is, hee that hath already obliged himself to receive our Saviour when he shall come, for his King, shal tempt God too much in choosing for King in this world, one that hee knoweth will endeavour, both by terrour, and perswasion to make him violate his faith. But, it is (saith hee) the same danger, to choose one that is not a Christian, for King, and not

to depose him, when hee is chosen. To this I say, the question is not of the danger of not deposing; but of the Justice of deposing him. To choose him, may in some cases bee unjust; but to depose him, when he is chosen, is in no case Just. For it is alwaies violation of faith, and consequently against the Law of Nature, which is the eternall Law of God. Nor doe wee read, that any such Doctrine was accounted Christian in the time of the Apostles; nor in the time of the Romane Emperours, till the Popes had the Civill Soveraignty of Rome. But to this he hath replyed, that the Christians of old, deposed not *Nero*, nor *Dioclesian*, nor *Julian*, nor *Valens* an Arrian, for this cause onely, that they wanted Temporall forces. Perhaps so. But did our Saviour, who for calling for, might have had twelve Legions of immortall, invulnerable Angels to assist him, want forces to depose *Cæsar*, or at least *Pilate*, that unjustly, without finding fault in him, delivered him to the Jews to bee crucified? Or if the Apostles wanted Temporall forces to depose *Nero*, was it therefore necessary for them in their Epistles to the new made Christians, to teach them (as they did) to obey the Powers constituted over them, (whereof *Nero* in that time was one,) and that they ought to obey them, not for fear of their wrath, but for conscience sake? Shall we say they did not onely obey, but also teach what they meant not, for want of strength? It is not therefore for want of strength, but for conscience sake, that Christians are to tolerate their Heathen Princes, or Princes (for I cannot call any one whose Doctrine is the Publique Doctrine, an Hæretique) that authorize the teaching of an Errour. And whereas for the Temporall Power of the Pope, he alledgeth further, that St. Paul (1 *Cor.* 6.) appointed Judges under the Heathen Princes of those times, such as were not ordained by those Princes; it is not true. For St. Paul does but advise them, to take some of their Brethren to compound
[319] their differences, as Arbitrators, rather than to goe to law one with another before the Heathen Judges; which is a wholsome Precept, and full of Charity, fit to be practised also in the best Christian Common-wealths. And for the danger that may arise to Religion, by the

Subjects tolerating of an Heathen, or an Erring Prince, it is a point, of which a Subject is no competent Judge; or if hee bee, the Popes Temporall Subjects may judge also of the Popes Doctrine. For every Christian Prince, as I have formerly proved, is no lesse Supreme Pastor of his own Subjects, than the Pope of his

The fourth Argument, is taken from the Baptisme of Kings, wherein, that they may be made Christians they submit their Scepters to Christ; and promise to keep, and defend the Christian Faith This is true; for Christian Kings are no more but Christs Subjects. but they may, for all that, bee the Popes Fellowes; for they are Supreme Pastors of their own Subjects; and the Pope is no more but King, and Pastor, even in Rome it selfe

The fifth Argument, is drawn from the words spoken by our Saviour, *Feed my sheep*; by which was given all Power necessary for a Pastor, as the Power to chase away Wolves, such as are Hæretiques, the Power to shut up Rammes, if they be mad, or push at the other Sheep with their Hornes, such as are Evill (though Christian) Kings; and Power to give the Flock convenient food: From whence hee inferreth, that St. Peter had these three Powers given him by Christ To which I answer, that the last of these Powers, is no more than the Power, or rather Command to Teach. For the first, which is to chase away Wolves, that is, Hæretiques, the place hee quoteth is (*Matth* 7 15) *Beware of false Prophets which come to you in Sheeps clothing, but inwardly are ravening Wolves.* But neither are Hæretiques false Prophets, or at all Prophets nor (admitting Hæretiques for the Wolves there meant,) were the Apostles commanded to kill them, or if they were Kings, to depose them; but to beware of, fly, and avoid them. nor was it to St Peter, nor to any of the Apostles, but to the multitude of the Jews that followed him into the mountain, men for the most part not yet converted, that hee gave this Counsell, to Beware of false Prophets. which therefore if it conferre a Power of chasing away Kings, was given, not onely to private men, but to men that were not at all Christians. And as to the Power of Separating, and Shutting up of furious Rammes, (by

which hee meaneth Christian Kings that refuse to submit themselves to the Roman Pastor,) our Saviour refused to take upon him that Power in this world himself, but advised to let the Corn and Tares grow up together till the day of Judgment. much lesse did hee give it to St Peter, or can S Peter give it to the Popes St. Peter, and all other Pastors, are bidden to esteem those Christians that disobey the Church, that is, (that disobey the
[320] Christian Soveraigne) as Heathen men, and as Publicans. Seeing then men challenge to the Pope no authority over Heathen Princes, they ought to challenge none over those that are to bee esteemed as Heathen.

But from the Power to Teach onely, hee inferreth also a Coercive Power in the Pope, over Kings. The Pastor (saith he) must give his flock convenient food: Therefore the Pope may, and ought to compell Kings to doe their duty. Out of which it followeth, that the Pope, as Pastor of Christian men, is King of Kings which all Christian Kings ought indeed either to Confesse, or else they ought to take upon themselves the Supreme Pastorall Charge, every one in his own Dominion.

His sixth, and last Argument, is from Examples To which I answer, first, that Examples prove nothing: Secondly, that the Examples he alledgeth make not so much as a probability of Right The fact of Jehoiada, in Killing Athaliah (2 *Kings* 11.) was either by the Authority of King Joash, or it was a horrible Crime in the High Priest, which (ever after the election of King Saul) was a mere Subject The fact of St. Ambrose, in Excommunicating Theodosius the Emperour, (if it were true hee did so,) was a Capitall Crime And for the Popes, Gregory 1 Greg. 2. Zachary, and Leo 3 their Judgments are void, as given in their own Cause; and the Acts done by them conformably to this Doctrine, are the greatest Crimes (especially that of Zachary) that are incident to Humane Nature And thus much of *Power Ecclesiasticall*; wherein I had been more briefe, forbearing to examine these Arguments of Bellarmine, if they had been his, as a Private man, and not as the Champion of the Papacy, against all other Christian Princes, and States.

CHAP. XLIII. [321]

Of what is NECESSARY for a Mans Reception into the Kingdome of Heaven

The difficulty of obeying God and Man both at once,

THE most frequent prætext of Sedition, and Civill Warre, in Christian Common-wealths hath a long time proceeded from a difficulty, not yet sufficiently resolved, of obeying at once, both God, and Man, then when their Commandements are one contrary to the other It is manifest enough, that when a man receiveth two contrary Commands, and knows that one of them is Gods, he ought to obey that, and not the other, though it be the command even of his lawfull Soveraign (whether a Monarch, or a soveraign Assembly,) or the command of his Father. The difficulty therefore consisteth in this; that men when they are commanded in the name of God, know not in divers Cases, whether the command be from God, or whether he that commandeth, doe but abuse Gods name for some private ends of his own. For as there were in the Church of the Jews, many false Prophets, that sought reputation with the people, by feigned Dreams, and Visions; so there have been in all times in the Church of Christ, false Teachers, that seek reputation with the people, by phantasticall and false Doctrines, and by such reputation (as is the nature of Ambition,) to govern them for their private benefit

Is none to them that distinguish between what is, and what is not Necessary to Salvation.

But this difficulty of obeying both God, and the Civill Soveraign on earth, to those that can distinguish between what is *Necessary*, and what is not *Necessary* for their *Reception* into the *Kingdome of God*, is of no moment. For if the command of the Civill Soveraign bee such, as that it may be obeyed, without the forfeiture of life Eternall, not to obey it is unjust, and the precept of the Apostle takes place, *Servants obey your Masters in all things*, and, *Children obey your Parents in all things*; and the precept of our Saviour, *The Scribes and Pharisees sit in Moses Chaire, All therefore they shall say, that observe, and doe.* But if the command be such, as cannot be obeyed, without being damned to Eternall Death, then it were madnesse to obey it, and the Counsell of our Saviour takes place, (*Mat.* 10. 28.) *Fear not those that kill the body, but cannot kill the soule.* All men therefore that would avoid, both the punishments that are to be in this world inflicted, for disobedience to their earthly Soveraign, and those that shall be inflicted in the world to come for disobedience to God, have need be taught to distinguish well between what is, and what is not Necessary to Eternall Salvation

All that is Necessary to Salvation is contained in Faith and Obedience.

[322] All that is NECESSARY *to Salvatian,* is contained in two Vertues, *Faith in Christ,* and *Obedience to Laws.* The latter of these, if it were perfect, were enough to us. But because wee are all guilty of disobedience to Gods Law, not onely originally in Adam, but also actually by our own transgressions, there is required at our hands now, not onely *Obedience* for the rest of our time, but also a *Remission* of sins for the time past; which Remission is the reward of our Faith in Christ That nothing else is Necessarily required to Salvation, is manifest from this, that the Kingdome of Heaven is shut to none but to Sinners; that is to say, to the disobedient, or transgressors of the Law, nor to them, in case they Repent, and Beleeve all the Articles of Christian Faith, Necessary to Salvation.

What Obedience is Necessary;

The Obedience required at our hands by God, that accepteth in all our actions the Will for the Deed, is a serious Endeavour to Obey him; and is called also by all such names as signifie that Endeavour. And therefore Obedience, is sometimes called by the names of *Charity,* and *Love,* because they imply a Will to Obey; and our Saviour himself maketh our Love to God, and to one another, a Fulfilling of the whole Law: and sometimes by the name of *Righteousnesse*; for Righteousnesse is but the will to give to every one his owne, that is to say, the will to obey the Laws: and sometimes by the name of *Repentance*; because to Repent, implyeth a turning away from sinne, which is the same, with the return of the will to Obedience Whosoever therefore unfeignedly desireth to fulfill the Commandements of God, or repenteth him truely of his transgressions, or that loveth God with all his heart, and his neighbor as himself, hath all the Obedience Necessary to his Reception into the Kingdom of God: For if God should require perfect Innocence, there could no flesh be saved.

And to what Laws. But what Commandements are those that God hath given us? Are all those Laws which were given to the Jews by the hand of Moses, the Commandements of God? If they bee, why are not Christians taught to Obey them? If they be not, what others are so, besides the Law of Nature? For our Saviour Christ hath not given us new Laws, but Counsell to observe those wee are subject to, that is to say, the Laws of Nature, and the Laws of our severall Soveraigns: Nor did he make any new Law to the Jews in his Sermon on the Mount, but onely expounded the Laws of Moses, to which they were subject before. The Laws of God therefore are none but the Laws of Nature, whereof the principall is, that we should not violate our Faith, that is, a commandement to obey our Civill Soveraigns, which wee constituted over us, by mutuall pact one with another. And this Law of God, that commandeth Obedience to the Law Civill, commandeth by consequence Obedience to all the Precepts of the Bible; which (as I have proved in the precedent Chapter) is there onely Law, where the Civill Soveraign hath made it so, and in other places but Counsell; which a man at his own perill, may without injustice refuse to obey

[323]

In the Faith of a Christian, who is the Person beleeved. Knowing now what is the Obedience Necessary to Salvation, and to whom it is due, we are to consider next concerning Faith, whom, and why we beleeve; and what are the Articles, or Points necessarily to be beleeved by them that shall be saved And first, for the Person whom we beleeve, because it is impossible to beleeve any Person, before we know what he saith, it is necessary he be one that wee have heard speak The Person therefore, whom Abraham, Isaac, Jacob, Moses and the Prophets beleeved, was God himself, that spake unto them supernaturally. And the Person, whom the Apostles and Disciples that conversed with Christ beleeved, was our Saviour himself But of them, to whom neither God the Father, nor our Saviour ever spake, it cannot be said, that the Person whom they beleeved, was God. They beleeved the Apostles, and after them the Pastors and Doctors of the Church, that recommended to their faith the History of the Old and New Testament: so that the Faith of Christians ever since our Saviours time, hath had for foundation, first, the reputation of their Pastors, and afterward, the authority of those that made the Old and New Testament to be received for the Rule of Faith; which none could do but Christian Soveraignes; who are therefore the Supreme Pastors, and the onely Persons, whom Christians now hear speak from God; except such as God speaketh to, in these days supernaturally But because there be many false Prophets *gone out into the world*, other men are to examine such Spirits (as St *John* adviseth us, 1 Epistle, Chap 4 ver. 1) *whether they be of God, or not.* And therefore, seeing the Examination of Doctrines belongeth to the Supreme Pastor, the Person which all they that have no speciall revelation are to beleeve, is (in every Common-wealth) the Supreme Pastor, that is to say, the Civill Soveraigne.

The causes of Christian Faith.

The causes why men beleeve any Christian Doctrine, are various: For Faith is the gift of God, and he worketh it in each severall man, by such wayes, as it seemeth good unto himself The most ordinary immediate cause of our beleef, concerning any point of Christian Faith, is, that wee beleeve the Bible to be the Word of God. But why wee beleeve the Bible to be the Word of God, is much disputed, as all questions must needs bee, that are not well stated. For they make not the question to be, *Why we Beleeve it*, but, *How wee Know it*; as if *Beleeving* and *Knowing* were all one. And thence while one side ground their Knowledge upon the Infallibility of the Church, and the other side, on the Testimony of the Private Spirit, neither side concludeth what it pretends. For how shall a man know the Infallibility of the Church, but by knowing first the Infallibility of the Scripture? Or how shall a man know his own Private spirit to be other than a beleef, grounded upon the Authority, and Arguments of his Teachers; or upon a Presumption of his own Gifts? Besides, there is nothing in the Scripture, from which can be inferred the Infallibility of the Church, much lesse, of any particular Church; and least of all, the Infallibility of any particular man

It is manifest therefore, that Christian men doe not know, but onely beleeve the Scripture to be the Word of God; and that the means of making them beleeve which God is pleased to afford men ordinarily, is according to the way of Nature, that is to say, from their Teachers. It is the Doctrine of St. Paul concerning Christian Faith in generall, (*Rom* 10 17) *Faith cometh by Hearing*, that is, by Hearing our lawfull Pastors. He saith also (ver. 14, 15. of the same Chapter) *How shall they beleeve in him of whom they have not heard? and how shall they hear without a Preacher? and how shall they Preach, except they be sent?* Whereby it is evident, that the ordinary cause of beleeving that the Scriptures are the Word of God, is the same with the cause of the beleeving of all other Articles of our Faith, namely, the Hearing of those that are by the Law allowed and appointed to Teach us, as our Parents in their Houses, and our Pastors in the Churches: Which also is made more manifest by experience. For what other cause can there bee assigned, why in Christian Common-wealths all men either beleeve, or at least professe the Scripture to bee the Word of God, and in other Common-wealths scarce any; but that in Christian Common-wealths they are taught it from their infancy; and in other places they are taught otherwise? [324]

Faith comes by Hearing.

But if Teaching be the cause of Faith, why doe not all beleeve? It is certain therefore that Faith is the gift of God, and hee giveth it to whom he will. Neverthelesse, because to them to whom he giveth it, he giveth it by the means of Teachers, the immediate cause of Faith is Hearing. In a School, where many are taught, and some profit, others profit not, the cause of learning in them that profit, is the Master, yet it cannot be thence inferred, that learning is not the gift of God All good things proceed from God; yet cannot all that have them, say they are Inspired, for that implies a gift supernaturall, and the immediate hand of God; which he that pretends to, pretends to be a Prophet, and is subject to the examination of the Church.

But whether men *Know*, or *Beleeve*, or *Grant* the Scriptures to be the Word of God, if out of such places of them, as are without obscurity, I shall shew what Articles of Faith are necessary, and onely necessary for Salvation, those men must needs *Know, Beleeve*, or *Grant* the same.

The onely Necessary Article of Christian Faith,

The (*Unum Necessarium*) Onely Article of Faith, which the Scripture maketh simply Necessary to Salvation, is this, that JESUS IS THE CHRIST. By the name of *Christ*, is understood the King, which God had before promised by the Prophets of the Old Testament, to send into the world, to reign (over the Jews, and over such of other nations as should beleeve in him) under himself eternally; and to give them that eternall life, which was lost by the sin of Adam. Which when I have proved out of Scripture, I will further shew when, and in what sense some other Articles may bee also called *Necessary*.

[325]

Proved from the Scope of the Evangelists.

For Proof that the Beleef of this Article, *Jesus is the Christ*, is all the Faith required to Salvation, my first Argument shall bee from the Scope of the Evangelists; which was by the description of the life of our Saviour, to establish that one Article, *Jesus is the Christ.* The summe of St Matthews Gospell is this, That Jesus was of the stock of David, Born of a Virgin; which are the Marks of the true Christ. That the *Magi* came to worship him as King of the Jews. That Herod for the same cause sought to kill him: That John Baptist proclaimed him. That he preached by himselfe, and his Apostles that he was that King. That he taught the Law, not as a Scribe, but as a man of Authority. That he cured diseases by his Word onely, and did many other Miracles, which were foretold the Christ should doe: That he was saluted King when hee entred into Jerusalem: That he fore-warned them to beware of all others that should pretend to be Christ: That he was taken, accused, and put to death, for saying, hee was King. That the cause of his condemnation written on the Crosse, was JESUS OF NAZARETH, THE KING OF THE JEWES. All which tend to no other end than this, that men should beleeve, that *Jesus is the Christ.* Such therefore was the Scope of St Matthews Gospel. But the

Scope of all the Evangelists (as may appear by reading them) was the same. Therefore the Scope of the whole Gospell, was the establishing of that onely Article And St. John expressely makes it his conclusion, *John* 20 31 *These things are written, that you may know that Jesus is the Christ, the Son of the living God.*

From the Sermons of the Apostles.

My second Argument is taken from the Subject of the Sermons of the Apostles, both whilest our Saviour lived on earth, and after his Ascension. The Apostles in our Saviours time were sent, *Luke* 9. 2 to Preach the Kingdome of God · For neither there, nor *Mat.* 10. 7. giveth he any Commission to them, other than this, *As ye go, Preach, saying, the Kingdome of Heaven is at hand*; that is, that *Jesus* is the *Messiah*, the *Christ*, the *King* which was to come. That their Preaching also after his ascension was the same, is manifest out of *Acts* 17. 6. *They drew* (saith St Luke) *Jason and certain Brethren unto the Rulers of the City, crying, These that have turned the world upside down are come hither also, whom Jason hath received. And these all do contrary to the Decrees of Cæsar, saying, that there is another King, one Jesus* · And out of the 2 & 3 verses of the same Chapter, where it is said, that St *Paul as his manner was, went in unto them, and three Sabbath dayes reasoned with them out of the Scriptures; opening and alledging, that Christ must needs have suffered, and risen againe from the dead, and that this Jesus (whom hee preached) is Christ*

From the easinesse of the Doctrine

The third Argument is, from those places of Scripture, by which all the Faith required to Salvation is declared to be Easie For if an inward assent of the mind to all the Doctrines concerning Christian Faith now taught, (whereof the greatest part are disputed,) were necessary to Salvation, there would be nothing in the world so hard, as to be a Christian The Thief upon the Crosse though repenting, could not have been saved for saying, [326] *Lord remember me when thou commest into thy Kingdome*; by which he testified no beleefe of any other Article, but this, That *Jesus was the King*. Nor could it bee said (as it is *Mat* 11 30) that *Christs yoke is Easy, and his burthen Light* Nor that *Little Children beleeve in him*, as it is *Matth.* 18 6. Nor could St. Paul have said (1 *Cor.*

1. 21.) *It pleased God by the Foolishnesse of preaching, to save them that beleeve*: Nor could St. Paul himself have been saved, much lesse have been so great a Doctor of the Church so suddenly, that never perhaps thought of Transubstantiation, nor Purgatory, nor many other Articles now obtruded.

From formall and cleer texts.

The fourth Argument is taken from places expresse, and such as receive no controversie of Interpretation, as first, *John* 5. 39. *Search the Scriptures, for in them yee thinke yee have eternall life; and they are they that testifie of mee* Our Saviour here speaketh of the Scriptures onely of the Old Testament; for the Jews at that time could not search the Scriptures of the New Testament, which were not written. But the Old Testament hath nothing of Christ, but the Markes by which men might know him when hee came, as that he should descend from David, be born at Bethlem, and of a Virgin; doe great Miracles, and the like. Therefore to beleeve that this Jesus was He, was sufficient to eternall life: but more than sufficient is not Necessary; and consequently no other Article is required. Again, (*John* 11 26) *Whosoever liveth and beleeveth in mee, shall not die eternally*, Therefore to beleeve in Christ, is faith sufficient to eternall life, and consequently no more faith than that is Necessary, But to beleeve in Jesus, and to beleeve that Jesus is the Christ, is all one, as appeareth in the verses immediately following For when our Saviour (verse 26) had said to Martha, *Beleevest thou this?* she answereth (verse 27.) *Yea Lord, I beleeve that thou art the Christ, the Son of God, which should come into the world*· Therefore this Article alone is faith sufficient to life eternall; and more than sufficient is not Necessary. Thirdly, *John* 20. 31. *These things are written that yee might beleeve, That Jesus is the Christ, the Son of God, and that beleeving yee might have life through his name.* There, to beleeve that *Jesus is the Christ*, is faith sufficient to the obtaining of life; and therefore no other Article is Necessary. Fourthly, 1 *John* 4 2 *Every spirit that confesseth that Jesus Christ is come in the flesh, is of God.* And 1 *Joh* 5 1. *Whosoever beleeveth that Jesus is the Christ, is born of God.* And verse 5 *Who is hee that overcommeth the world, but he that beleeveth that Jesus is the Son of God?* Fiftly, *Act* 8 ver. 36, 37. *See* (saith the Eunuch) *here is water, what doth hinder me to be baptized? And Philip said, If thou beleevest with all thy heart thou mayst. And hee answered and said, I beleeve that Jesus Christ is the Son of God.* Therefore this Article beleeved, *Jesus is the Christ,* is sufficient to Baptisme, that is to say, to our Reception into the Kingdome of God, and by consequence, onely Necessary. And generally in all places where our Saviour saith to any man, *Thy faith hath saved thee,* the [327] cause he saith it, is some Confession, which directly, or by consequence, implyeth a beleef, that *Jesus is the Christ.*

From that it is the Foundation of all other Articles.

The last Argument is from the places, where this Article is made the Foundation of Faith For he that holdeth the Foundation shall bee saved Which places are first, *Mat* 24 23 *If any man shall say unto you, Loe, here is Christ, or there, beleeve it not, for there shall arise false Christs, and false Prophets, and shall shew great signes and wonders, &c.* Here wee see, this Article *Jesus is the Christ,* must bee held, though hee that shall teach the contrary should doe great miracles The second place is, *Gal.* 1. 8 *Though we, or an Angell from Heaven preach any other Gospell unto you, than that wee have preached unto you, let him bee accursed.* But the Gospell which Paul, and the other Apostles, preached, was onely this Article, that *Jesus is the Christ*: Therefore for the Beleef of this Article, we are to reject the Authority of an Angell from heaven, much more of any mortall man, if he teach the contrary This is therefore the Fundamentall Article of Christian Faith. A third place is, 1 *Joh.* 4. 1. *Beloved, beleeve not every spirit. Hereby yee shall know the Spirit of God, every spirit that confesseth that Jesus Christ is come in the flesh, is of God.* By which it is evident, that this Article, is the measure, and rule, by which to estimate, and examine all other Articles; and is therefore onely Fundamentall A fourth is, *Matt* 16 18. where after St Peter had professed this Article, saying to our Saviour, *Thou art Christ the Son of the living God,* Our Saviour answered, *Thou art Peter, and upon this Rock I will build my Church*: from whence

I inferre, that this Article is that, on which all other Doctrines of the Church are built, as on their Foundation. A fift is (1 *Cor.* 3 ver. 11, 12, &c.) *Other Foundation can no man lay, than that which is laid, Jesus is the Christ. Now if any man build upon this Foundation, Gold, Silver, pretious Stones, Wood, Hay, Stubble; Every mans work shall be made manifest; For the Day shall declare it, because it shall be revealed by fire, and the fire shall try every mans work, of what sort it is. If any mans work abide, which he hath built thereupon, he shall receive a reward: If any mans work shall bee burnt, he shall suffer losse; but he himself shall be saved, yet so as by fire.* Which words, being partly plain and easie to understand, and partly allegoricall and difficult, out of that which is plain, may be inferred, that Pastors that teach this Foundation, that *Jesus is the Christ*, though they draw from it false consequences, (which all men are sometimes subject to,) they may neverthelesse bee saved; much more that they may bee saved, who being no Pastors, but Hearers, beleeve that which is by their lawfull Pastors taught them. Therefore the beleef of this Article is sufficient; and by consequence, there is no other Article of Faith Necessarily required to Salvation.

[328] Now for the part which is Allegoricall, as *That the fire shall try every mans work*, and that *They shall be saved, but so as by fire*, or *through fire*, (for the originall is διὰ πυρὸς,) it maketh nothing against this conclusion which I have drawn from the other words, that are plain. Neverthelesse, because upon this place there hath been an argument taken, to prove the fire of Purgatory, I will also here offer you my conjecture concerning the meaning of this triall of Doctrines, and saving of men as by Fire. The Apostle here seemeth to allude to the words of the Prophet Zachary, Ch. 13. 8, 9. who speaking of the Restauration of the Kingdome of God, saith thus, *Two parts therein shall be cut off, and die, but the third shall be left therein; And I will bring the third part through the Fire, and will refine them as Silver is refined, and will try them as Gold is tryed; they shall call on the name of the Lord, and I will hear them.* The day of Judgment, is the day of the Restauration of the Kingdome of God; and

2 Pet 3. *v* 7, 10, 12.

at that day it is, that St. Peter tells us * shall be the Conflagration of the world, wherein the wicked shall perish, but the remnant which God will save, shall passe through that Fire, unhurt, and be therein (as Silver and Gold are refined by the fire from their drosse) tryed, and refined from their Idolatry, and be made to call upon the name of the true God Alluding whereto St. Paul here saith, That *the Day* (that is, the Day of Judgment, the Great Day of our Saviours comming to restore the Kingdome of God in Israel) shall try every mans doctrine, by Judging, which are Gold, Silver, Pretious Stones, Wood, Hay, Stubble, And then they that have built false Consequences on the true Foundation, shall see their Doctrines condemned; neverthelesse they themselves shall be saved, and passe unhurt through this universall Fire, and live eternally, to call upon the name of the true and onely God. In which sense there is nothing that accordeth not with the rest of Holy Scripture, or any glimpse of the fire of Purgatory.

In what sense other Articles may be called Necessary.

But a man may here aske, whether it bee not as necessary to Salvation, to beleeve, that God is Omnipotent; Creator of the world; that Jesus Christ is risen, and that all men else shall rise again from the dead at the last day, as to beleeve, that *Jesus is the Christ.* To which I answer, they are, and so are many more Articles but they are such, as are contained in this one, and may be deduced from it, with more, or lesse difficulty. For who is there that does not see, that they who beleeve Jesus to be the Son of the God of Israel, and that the Israelites had for God the Omnipotent Creator of all things, doe therein also beleeve, that God is the Omnipotent Creator of all things? Or how can a man beleeve, that Jesus is the King that shall reign eternally, unlesse hee beleeve him also risen again from the dead? For a dead man cannot exercise the Office of a King. In summe, he that holdeth this Foundation, *Jesus is the Christ*, holdeth Expressely all that hee seeth rightly deduced from it, and Implicitely all that is consequent thereunto, though he have not skill enough to discern the consequence. And therefore it holdeth still good, [329]
that the beleef of this one Article is sufficient faith to

obtaine remission of sinnes to the *Penitent*, and consequently to bring them into the Kingdome of Heaven

That Faith, and Obedience are both of them Necessary to Salvation.

Now that I have shewn, that all the Obedience required to Salvation, consisteth in the will to obey the Law of God, that is to say, in Repentance; and all the Faith required to the same, is comprehended in the beleef of this Article *Jesus is the Christ*; I will further alledge those places of the Gospell, that prove, that all that is Necessary to Salvation is contained in both these joined together. The men to whom St. Peter preached on the day of Pentecost, next after the Ascension of our Saviour, asked him, and the rest of the Apostles, saying, (*Act*. 2. 37.) *Men and Brethren what shall we doe?* To whom St. Peter answered (in the next verse) *Repent, and be Baptized every one of you, for the remission of sins, and ye shall receive the gift of the Holy Ghost.* Therefore Repentance, and Baptisme, that is, beleeving that *Jesus is the Christ*, is all that is Necessary to Salvation. Again, our Saviour being asked by a certain Ruler, (*Luke* 18. 18.) *What shall I doe to inherite eternall life?* Answered (verse 20.) *Thou knowest the Commandements, Doe not commit Adultery, Doe not Kill, Doe not Steal, Doe not bear false witnesse, Honor thy Father, and thy Mother*: which when he said he had observed, our Saviour added, *Sell all thou hast, give it to the Poor, and come and follow me*: which was as much as to say, Relye on me that am the King: Therefore to fulfill the Law, and to beleeve that Jesus is the King, is all that is required to bring a man to eternall life. Thirdly, St. Paul saith (*Rom*. 1. 17.) *The Just shall live by Faith*; not every one, but the *Just*; therefore *Faith* and *Justice* (that is, the *will to be Just*, or *Repentance*) are all that is Necessary to life eternall. And (*Mark* 1. 15.) our Saviour preached, saying, *The time is fulfilled, and the Kingdom of God is at hand, Repent and Beleeve the Evangile*, that is, the Good news that the Christ was come. Therefore to Repent, and to Beleeve that Jesus is the Christ, is all that is required to Salvation.

What each of them contributes thereunto.

Seeing then it is Necessary that Faith, and Obedience (implyed in the word Repentance) do both concurre to our Salvation; the question by which of the two we are Justified, is impertinently disputed. Neverthelesse,

it will not be impertinent, to make manifest in what manner each of them contributes thereunto, and in what sense it is said, that we are to be Justified by the one, and by the other. And first, if by Righteousnesse be understood the Justice of the Works themselves, there is no man that can be saved, for there is none that hath not transgressed the Law of God. And therefore when wee are said to be Justified by Works, it is to be understood of the Will, which God doth alwaies accept for the Work it selfe, as well in good, as in evill men. And in this sense onely it is, that a man is called *Just*, or *Unjust*; and that his Justice Justifies him, that is, gives him the title, in Gods acceptation, of *Just*; and renders him capable of *living by his Faith*, which before he was not
So that Justice Justifies in that sense, in which to [330]
Justifie, is the same that to *Denominate a man Just*; and not in the signification of discharging the Law; whereby the punishment of his sins should be unjust.

But a man is then also said to be Justified, when his Plea, though in it selfe unsufficient, is accepted; as when we Plead our Will, our Endeavour to fulfill the Law, and Repent us of our failings, and God accepteth it for the Performance it selfe: And because God accepteth not the Will for the Deed, but onely in the Faithfull; it is therefore Faith that makes good our Plea, and in this sense it is, that Faith onely Justifies: So that *Faith* and *Obedience* are both Necessary to Salvation; yet in severall senses each of them is said to Justifie

Obedience to God and to the Civill Soveraign not inconsistent, whether Christian,

Having thus shewn what is Necessary to Salvation; it is not hard to reconcile our Obedience to God, with our Obedience to the Civill Soveraign, who is either Christian, or Infidel. If he bee a Christian, he alloweth the beleefe of this Article, that *Jesus is the Christ*; and of all the Articles that are contained in, or are by evident consequence deduced from it: which is all the Faith Necessary to Salvation. And because he is a Soveraign, he requireth Obedience to all his owne, that is, to all the Civill Laws; in which also are contained all the Laws of Nature, that is, all the Laws of God for besides the Laws of Nature, and the Laws of the Church, which are part of the Civill Law, (for the Church that can make Laws is the Common-wealth,) there bee no other Laws Divine. Whosoever therefore obeyeth his Christian Soveraign, is not thereby hindred, neither from beleeving, nor from obeying God. But suppose that a Christian King should from this Foundation *Jesus is the Christ*, draw some false consequences, that is to say, make some superstructions of Hay, or Stubble, and command the teaching of the same; yet seeing St. Paul says, he shal be saved; much more shall he be saved, that teacheth them by his command; and much more yet, he that teaches not, but onely beleeves his lawfull Teacher And in case a Subject be forbidden by the Civill Soveraign to professe some of those his opinions, upon what just ground can he disobey? Christian Kings may erre in deducing a Consequence, but who shall Judge? Shall a private man Judge, when the question is of his own obedience? or shall any man Judg but he that is appointed thereto by the Church, that is, by the Civill Soveraign that representeth it? or if the Pope, or an Apostle Judge, may he not erre in deducing of a consequence? did not one of the two, St. Peter, or St. Paul erre in a superstructure, when St. Paul withstood St. Peter to his face? There can therefore be no contradiction between the Laws of God, and the Laws of a Christian Common-wealth.

Or Infidel. And when the Civill Soveraign is an Infidel, every one of his own Subjects that resisteth him, sinneth against the Laws of God (for such as are the Laws of Nature,) and rejecteth the counsell of the Apostles, that admonisheth all Christians to obey their Princes, and all Children and Servants to obey their Parents, and Masters, [331] in all things And for their *Faith*, it is internall, and invisible; They have the licence that Naaman had, and need not put themselves into danger for it. But if they do, they ought to expect their reward in Heaven, and not complain of their Lawfull Soveraign, much lesse make warre upon him. For he that is not glad of any just occasion of Martyrdome, has not the faith he professeth, but pretends it onely, to set some colour upon his own contumacy. But what Infidel King is so unreasonable, as knowing he has a Subject, that waiteth for the second comming of Christ, after the present world shall bee burnt, and intendeth then to obey him (which is the intent of beleeving that Jesus is the Christ,) and in the mean time thinketh himself bound to obey the Laws of that Infidel King, (which all Christians are obliged in conscience to doe,) to put to death, or to persecute such a Subject ?

And thus much shall suffice, concerning the Kingdome of God, and Policy Ecclesiasticall Wherein I pretend not to advance any Position of my own, but onely to shew what are the Consequences that seem to me deducible from the Principles of Christian Politiques, (which are the holy Scriptures,) in confirmation of the Power of Civill Soveraigns, and the Duty of their Subjects And in the allegation of Scripture, I have endeavoured to avoid such texts as are of obscure, or controverted Interpretation , and to alledge none, but in such sense as is most plain, and agreeable to the harmony and scope of the whole Bible ; which was written for the re-establishment of the Kingdome of God in Christ For it is not the bare Words, but the Scope of the writer that giveth the true light, by which any writing is to bee interpreted , and they that insist upon single Texts, without considering the main Designe, can derive no thing from them cleerly , but rather by casting atomes of Scripture, as dust before mens eyes, make every thing more obscure than it is , an ordinary artifice of those that seek not the truth, but their own advantage.

[333]

OF THE KINGDOME OF DARKNESSE.

CHAP. XLIV.

Of Spirituall Darknesse from MISINTERPRETATION *of Scripture.*

The Kingdom of Darknesse what BESIDES these Soveraign Powers, *Divine*, and *Humane*, of which I have hitherto discoursed, there is mention in Scripture of another Power, namely, * that of *the Rulers of the Darknesse of this world*, * *the Kingdome of Satan*, and * *the Principality of Beelzebub over Dæmons*, that is to say, over Phantasmes that appear in the Air: For which cause Satan is also called * *the Prince of the Power of the Air*; and (because he ruleth in the darknesse of this world) * *The Prince of this world* And in consequence hereunto, they who are under his Dominion, in opposition to the faithfull (who are the *Children of the Light*) are called the *Children of Darknesse*. For seeing Beelzebub is Prince of Phantasmes, Inhabitants of his Dominion of Air and Darknesse, the Children of Darknesse, and these Dæmons, Phantasmes, or Spirits of Illusion, signifie allegorically the same thing This considered, the Kingdome of Darknesse, as it is set forth in these, and other places of the Scripture, is nothing else but a *Confederacy of Deceivers, that to obtain dominion over men in this present world, endeavour by dark, and erroneous Doctrines, to extinguish in them the Light, both of Nature, and of the Gospell; and so to dis-prepare them for the Kingdome of God to come.*

* *Eph* 6. 12
* *Mat* 12. 26
* *Mat* 9. 34
* *Eph.* 2 2
* *Joh.* 16. 11.

[334] As men that are utterly deprived from their Nativity, of the light of the bodily Eye, have no Idea at all, of any

such light; and no man conceives in his imagination any greater light, than he hath at some time, or other, perceived by his outward Senses. so also is it of the light of the Gospel, and of the light of the Understanding, that no man can conceive there is any greater degree of it, than that which he hath already attained unto. And from hence it comes to passe, that men have no other means to acknowledge their owne Darknesse, but onely by reasoning from the un-foreseen mischances, that befall them in their ways; The Darkest part of the Kingdom of Satan, is that which is without the Church of God; that is to say, amongst them that beleeve not in Jesus Christ. But we cannot say, that therefore the Church enjoyeth (as the land of Goshen) all the light, which to the performance of the work enjoined us by God, is necessary Whence comes it, that in Christendome there has been, almost from the time of the Apostles, such justling of one another out of their places, both by forraign, and Civill war? such stumbling at every little asperity of their own fortune, and every little eminence of that of other men? and such diversity of ways in running to the same mark, *Felicity*, if it be not Night amongst us, or at least a Mist? wee are therefore yet in the Dark

The Church not yet fully freed of Darknesse.

The Enemy has been here in the Night of our naturall Ignorance, and sown the tares of Spirituall Errors; and that, First, by abusing, and putting out the light of the Scriptures: For we erre, not knowing the Scriptures. Secondly, by introducing the Dæmonology of the Heathen Poets, that is to say, their fabulous Doctrine concerning Dæmons, which are but Idols, or Phantasms of the braine, without any reall nature of their own, distinct from humane fancy, such as are dead mens Ghosts, and Fairies, and other matter of old Wives tales Thirdly, by mixing with the Scripture divers reliques of the Religion, and much of the vain and erroneous Philosophy of the Greeks, especially of Aristotle Fourthly, by mingling with both these, false, or uncertain Traditions, and fained, or uncertain History. And so we come to erre, by *giving heed to seducing Spirits*, and the Dæmonology of such *as speak lies in Hypocrisie*, (or as it is in the

Four Causes of Spirituall Darknesse.

Originall, 1 *Tim* 4. 1, 2. *of those that play the part of lyars*) *with a seared conscience*, that is, contrary to their own knowledge. Concerning the first of these, which is the Seducing of men by abuse of Scripture, I intend to speak briefly in this Chapter

Errors from mis-interpreting the Scriptures, concerning the Kingdome of God

The greatest, and main abuse of Scripture, and to which almost all the rest are either consequent, or subservient, is the wresting of it, to prove that the Kingdome of God, mentioned so often in the Scripture, is the present Church, or multitude of Christian men now living, or that being dead, are to rise again at the last day: whereas the Kingdome of God was first instituted by the Ministery of Moses, over the Jews onely, who were therefore called his Peculiar People; and ceased afterward, in the election of Saul, when they refused to be governed by God any
[335] more, and demanded a King after the manner of the nations; which God himself consented unto, as I have more at large proved before, in the 35 Chapter. After that time, there was no other Kingdome of God in the world, by any Pact, or otherwise, than he ever was, is, and shall be King, of all men, and of all creatures, as governing according to his Will, by his infinite Power Neverthelesse, he promised by his Prophets to restore this his Government to them again, when the time he hath in his secret counsell appointed for it shall bee fully come, and when they shall turn unto him by repentance, and amendment of life. and not onely so, but he invited also the Gentiles to come in, and enjoy the happinesse of his Reign, on the same conditions of conversion and repentance, and hee promised also to send his Son into the world, to expiate the sins of them all by his death, and to prepare them by his Doctrine, to receive him at his second coming Which second coming not yet being, the Kingdome of God is not yet come, and wee are not now under any other Kings by Pact, but our Civill Soveraigns, saving onely, that Christian men are already in the Kingdome of Grace, in as much as they have already the Promise of being received at his comming againe.

As that the Kingdome

Consequent to this Errour, that the present Church is Christs Kingdome, there ought to be some one Man, or Assembly, by whose mouth our Saviour (now in heaven) speaketh, giveth law, and which representeth his Person to all Christians, or divers Men, or divers Assemblies that doe the same to divers parts of Christendome This power Regal under Christ, being challenged, universally by the Pope, and in particular Commonwealths by Assemblies of the Pastors of the place, (when the Scripture gives it to none but to Civill Soveraigns,) comes to be so passionately disputed, that it putteth out the Light of Nature, and causeth so great a Darknesse in mens understanding, that they see not who it is to whom they have engaged their obedience

of God is the present Church:

Consequent to this claim of the Pope to Vicar Generall of Christ in the present Church, (supposed to be that Kingdom of his, to which we are addressed in the Gospel,) is the Doctrine, that it is necessary for a Christian King, to receive his Crown by a Bishop; as if it were from that Ceremony, that he derives the clause of *Dei gratiâ* in his title, and that then onely he is made King by the favour of God, when he is crowned by the authority of Gods universall Vicegerent on earth; and that every Bishop whosoever be his Soveraign, taketh at his Consecration an oath of absolute Obedience to the Pope. Consequent to the same, is the Doctrine of the fourth Councell of Lateran, held under Pope *Innocent* the third, (Chap 3 *de Hæreticis.*) *That if a King at the Popes admonition, doe not purge his Kingdome of Hæresies, and being excommunicate for the same, doe not give satisfaction within a year, his Subjects are absolved of the bond of their obedience* Where, by Hæresies are understood all opinions which the Church of Rome hath forbidden to be maintained And by this means, as often as there [336] is any repugnancy between the Politicall designes of the Pope, and other Christian Princes, as there is very often, there ariseth such a Mist amongst their Subjects, that they know not a stranger that thrusteth himself into the throne of their lawfull Prince, from him whom they had themselves placed there, and in this Darknesse of mind, are made to fight one against another, without discerning their enemies from their friends, under the conduct of another mans ambition.

And that the Pope is his Vicar generall

And that the Pastors are the Clergy.

From the same opinion, that the present Church is the Kingdome of God, it proceeds that Pastours, Deacons, and all other Ministers of the Church, take the name to themselves of the *Clergy*, giving to other Christians the name of *Laity*, that is, simply *People*. For Clergy signifies those, whose maintenance is that Revenue, which God having reserved to himselfe during his Reign over the Israelites, assigned to the tribe of Levi (who were to be his publique Ministers, and had no portion of land set them out to live on, as their brethren) to be their inheritance. The Pope therefore, (pretending the present Church to be, as the Realme of Israel, the Kingdome of God) challenging to himselfe and his subordinate Ministers, the like revenue, as the Inheritance of God, the name of Clergy was sutable to that claime And thence it is, that Tithes, and other tributes paid to the Levites, as Gods Right, amongst the Israelites, have a long time been demanded, and taken of Christians, by Ecclesiastiques, *Jure divino*, that is, in Gods Right. By which meanes, the people every where were obliged to a double tribute ; one to the State, another to the Clergy ; whereof, that to the Clergy, being the tenth of their revenue, is double to that which a King of Athens (and esteemed a Tyrant) exacted of his subjects for the defraying of all publique charges For he demanded no more but the twentieth part ; and yet abundantly maintained therewith the Commonwealth. And in the Kingdome of the Jewes, during the Sacerdotall Reigne of God, the Tithes and Offerings were the whole Publique Revenue.

From the same mistaking of the present Church for the Kingdom of God, came in the distinction betweene the *Civill* and the *Canon* Laws The Civil Law being the Acts of *Soveraigns* in their own Dominions, and the Canon Law being the Acts of the *Pope* in the same Dominions Which Canons, though they were but Canons, that is, *Rules Propounded,* and but voluntarily received by Christian Princes, till the translation of the Empire to *Charlemain* ; yet afterwards, as the power of the Pope encreased, became *Rules Commanded,* and the Emperours themselves (to avoyd greater mischiefes, which the people blinded might be led into) were forced to let them passe for Laws

From hence it is, that in all Dominions, where the Popes Ecclesiasticall power is entirely received, Jewes, Turkes, and Gentiles, are in the Roman Church tolerated in their Religion, as farre forth, as in the exercise and profession thereof they offend not against the civill power. whereas in a Christian, though a stranger, not to be of the Roman Religion, is Capitall; because the Pope pretendeth that all Christians are his Subjects. [337]
For otherwise it were as much against the law of Nations, to persecute a Christian stranger, for professing the Religion of his owne country, as an Infidell; or rather more, in as much as they that are not against Christ, are with him.

From the same it is, that in every Christian State there are certaine men, that are exempt, by Ecclesiasticall liberty, from the tributes, and from the tribunals of the Civil State, for so are the secular Clergy, besides Monks and Friars, which in many places, bear so great a proportion to the common people, as if need were, there might be raised out of them alone, an Army, sufficient for any warre the Church militant should imploy them in, against their owne, or other Princes.

Error from mistaking Consecration for Conjuration.

A second generall abuse of Scripture, is the turning of Consecration into Conjuration, or Enchantment. To *Consecrate*, is in Scripture, to Offer, Give, or Dedicate, in pious and decent language and gesture, a man, or any other thing to God, by separating of it from common use, that is to say, to Sanctifie, or make it Gods, and to be used only by those, whom God hath appointed to be his Publike Ministers, (as I have already proved at large in the 35 Chapter,) and thereby to change, not the thing Consecrated, but onely the use of it, from being Profane and common, to be Holy, and peculiar to Gods service But when by such words, the nature or qualitie of the thing it selfe, is pretended to be changed, it is not Consecration, but either an extraordinary worke of God, or a vaine and impious Conjuration. But seeing (for the frequency of pretending the change of Nature in their Consecrations,) it cannot be esteemed a work extra-

ordinary, it is no other than a *Conjuration* or *Incantation*, whereby they would have men to beleeve an alteration of Nature that is not, contrary to the testimony of mans Sight, and of all the rest of his Senses. As for example, when the Priest, in stead of Consecrating Bread and Wine to Gods peculiar service in the Sacrament of the Lords Supper, (which is but a separation of it from the common use, to signifie, that is, to put men in mind of their Redemption, by the Passion of Christ, whose body was broken, and blood shed upon the Crosse for our transgressions,) pretends, that by saying of the words of our Saviour, *This is my Body*, and *This is my Blood*, the nature of Bread is no more there, but his very Body; notwithstanding there appeareth not to the Sight, or other Sense of the Receiver, any thing that appeared not before the Consecration. The Egyptian Conjurers, that are said to have turned their Rods to Serpents, and the Water into Bloud, are thought but to have deluded the senses of the Spectators by a false shew of things, yet are esteemed Enchanters: But what should wee have thought of them, if there had appeared in their Rods nothing like a Serpent, and in the Water enchanted, nothing like Bloud, nor like any thing else but Water, but that they had faced down the King, that they were Serpents that looked like Rods, and that it was Bloud that seemed Water? That had been both Enchantment, and Lying. And yet in this daily act of the Priest, they
[338] doe the very same, by turning the holy words into the manner of a Charme, which produceth nothing new to the Sense; but they face us down, that it hath turned the Bread into a Man; nay more, into a God, and require men to worship it, as if it were our Saviour himself present God and Man, and thereby to commit most grosse Idolatry. For if it bee enough to excuse it of Idolatry, to say it is no more Bread, but God; why should not the same excuse serve the Egyptians, in case they had the faces to say, the Leeks, and Onyons they worshipped, were not very Leeks, and Onyons, but a Divinity under their *species*, or likenesse The words, *This is my Body*, are æquivalent to these, *This signifies, or represents my Body*, and it is an ordinary figure of

Speech . but to take it literally, is an abuse ; nor though so taken, can it extend any further, than to the Bread which Christ himself with his own hands Consecrated. For hee never said, that of what Bread soever, any Priest whatsoever, should say, *This is my body*, or, *This is Christs Body*, the same should presently be transubstantiated. Nor did the Church of Rome ever establish this Transubstantiation, till the time of *Innocent* the third ; which was not above 500 years agoe, when the Power of Popes was at the Highest, and the Darknesse of the time grown so great, as men discerned not the Bread that was given them to eat, especially when it was stamped with the figure of Christ upon the Crosse, as if they would have men beleeve it were Transubstantiated, not onely into the Body of Christ, but also into the Wood of his Crosse, and that they did eat both together in the Sacrament.

Incantation in the Ceremonies of Baptisme.

The like Incantation, in stead of Consecration, is used also in the Sacrament of Baptisme Where the abuse of Gods name in each severall Person, and in the whole Trinity, with the sign of the Crosse at each name, maketh up the Charm · As first, when they make the Holy water, the Priest saith, *I Conjure thee, thou Creature of Water, in the name of God the Father Almighty, and in the name of Jesus Christ his onely Son our Lord, and in vertue of the Holy Ghost, that thou become Conjured water, to drive away all the Powers of the Enemy; and to eradicate, and supplant the Enemy, &c.* And the same in the Benediction of the Salt to be mingled with it , *That thou become Conjured Salt, that all Phantasmes, and Knavery of the Devills fraud may fly and depart from the place wherein thou art sprinkled ; and every unclean Spirit bee Conjured by Him that shall come to judg the quicke and the dead.* The same in the Benediction of the Oyle, *That all the Power of the Enemy, all the Host of the Devill, all Assaults and Phantasmes of Satan, may be driven away by this Creature of Oyle.* And for the Infant that is to be Baptized, he is subject to many Charms First, at the Church dore the Priest blows thrice in the Childs face, and sayes, *Goe out of him unclean Spirit, and give place to the Holy Ghost the Comforter.* As if all Children, till blown on by the Priest were

Dæmoniaques Again, before his entrance into the Church, he saith as before, *I Conjure thee, &c. to goe out,*
[339] *and depart from this Servant of God* And again the same Exorcisme is repeated once more before he be Baptized. These, and some other Incantations, are those that are used in stead of Benedictions, and Consecrations, in administration of the Sacraments of Baptisme, and the Lords Supper ; wherein every thing that serveth to those holy uses (except the unhallowed Spittle of the Priest) hath some set form of Exorcisme.

And in Marriage, in Visitation of the Sick, and in Consecration of Places.

Nor are the other rites, as of Marriage, of Extreme Unction, of Visitation of the Sick, of Consecrating Churches, and Church-yards, and the like, exempt from Charms , in as much as there is in them the use of Enchanted Oyle, and Water, with the abuse of the Crosse, and of the holy word of David, *Asperges me Domine Hyssopo,* as things of efficacy to drive away Phantasmes, and Imaginary Spirits.

Errors from mistaking Eternall Life, and Everlasting Death:

Another generall Error, is from the Misinterpretation of the words *Eternall Life, Everlasting Death,* and the *Second Death.* For though we read plainly in holy Scripture, that God created Adam in an estate of Living for Ever, which was conditionall, that is to say, if he disobeyed not his Commandement ; which was not essentiall to Humane Nature, but consequent to the vertue of the Tree of Life ; whereof hee had liberty to eat, as long as hee had not sinned , and that hee was thrust out of Paradise after he had sinned, lest hee should eate thereof, and live for ever ; and that Christs Passion is a Discharge of sin to all that beleeve on him ; and by consequence, a restitution of Eternall Life, to all the Faithfull, and to them onely . yet the Doctrine is now, and hath been a long time far otherwise ; namely, that every man hath Eternity of Life by Nature, in as much as his Soul is Immortall · So that the flaming Sword at the entrance of Paradise, though it hinder a man from coming to the Tree of Life, hinders him not from the Immortality which God took from him for his Sin , nor makes him to need the sacrificing of Christ, for the recovering of the same ; and consequently, not onely the faithfull and righteous, but also the wicked, and the Heathen, shall enjoy Eternall Life, without any Death at all; much lesse a Second, and Everlasting Death. To salve this, it is said, that by *Second*, and *Everlasting Death*, is meant a Second, and Everlasting Life, but in Torments; a Figure never used, but in this very Case.

All which Doctrine is founded onely on some of the obscurer places of the New Testament; which neverthelesse, the whole scope of the Scripture considered, are cleer enough in a different sense, and unnecessary to the Christian Faith. For supposing that when a man dies, there remaineth nothing of him but his carkasse; cannot God that raised inanimated dust and clay into a living creature by his Word, as easily raise a dead carkasse to life again, and continue him alive for Ever, or make him die again, by another Word? The *Soule* in Scripture, signifieth alwaies, either the Life, or the Living Creature; and the Body and Soule jointly, the *Body alive*. In the fift day of the Creation, God said, Let the [340]
waters produce *Reptile animæ viventis*, the creeping thing that hath in it a Living Soule; the English translate it, *that hath Life*. And again, God created Whales, & *omnem animam viventem*; which in the English is, *every Living Creature*: And likewise of Man, God made him of the dust of the earth, and breathed in his face the breath of Life, & *factus est Homo in animam viventem*, that is, *and Man was made a Living Creature*. And after *Noah* came out of the Arke, God saith, hee will no more smite *omnem animam viventem*, that is, *every Living Creature*: And Deut. 12. 23. *Eate not the Bloud, for the Bloud is the Soule*; that is, *the Life*. From which places, if by *Soule* were meant a *Substance Incorporeall*, with an existence separated from the Body, it might as well be inferred of any other living Creature, as of Man. But that the Souls of the Faithfull, are not of their own Nature, but by Gods speciall Grace, to remaine in their Bodies, from the Resurrection to all Eternity, I have already I think sufficiently proved out of the Scriptures, in the 38. Chapter. And for the places of the New Testament, where it is said that any man shall be cast Body and Soul into Hell fire, it is no more than Body and Life; that is to say, they shall be cast alive into the perpetuall fire of Gehenna.

As the Doctrine of Purgatory, and Exorcismes, and Invocation of Saints

This window it is, that gives entrance to the Dark Doctrine, first, of Eternall Torments; and afterwards of Purgatory, and consequently of the walking abroad, especially in places Consecrated, Solitary, or Dark, of the Ghosts of men deceased; and thereby to the pretences of Exorcisme and Conjuration of Phantasmes; as also of Invocation of men dead; and to the Doctrine of Indulgences; that is to say, of exemption for a time, or for ever, from the fire of Purgatory, wherein these Incorporeall Substances are pretended by burning to be cleansed, and made fit for Heaven. For men being generally possessed before the time of our Saviour, by contagion of the Dæmonology of the Greeks, of an opinion, that the Souls of men were substances distinct from their Bodies, and therefore that when the Body was dead, the Soule of every man, whether godly, or wicked, must subsist somewhere by vertue of its own nature, without acknowledging therein any supernaturall gift of Gods; the Doctors of the Church doubted a long time, what was the place, which they were to abide in, till they should be re-united to their Bodies in the Resurrection, supposing for a while, they lay under the Altars: but afterward the Church of Rome found it more profitable, to build for them this place of Purgatory; which by some other Churches in this later age, has been demolished.

The Texts alledged for the Doctrines aforementioned have been answered before.

Let us now consider, what texts of Scripture seem most to confirm these three generall Errors, I have here touched. As for those which Cardinall Bellarmine hath alledged, for the present Kingdome of God administred by the Pope, (than which there are none that make [341] a better shew of proof,) I have already answered them; and made it evident, that the Kingdome of God, instituted by Moses, ended in the election of Saul: After which time the Priest of his own authority never deposed any King. That which the High Priest did to Athaliah, was not done in his owne right, but in the right of the young King Joash her Son: But Solomon in his own right deposed the High Priest Abiathar, and set up another in his place. The most difficult place to answer, of all those that can be brought, to prove the Kingdome of God by Christ is already in this world, is alledged, not by Bellarmine, nor any other of the Church of Rome; but by Beza; that will have it to begin from the Resurrection of Christ. But whether hee intend thereby, to entitle the Presbytery to the Supreme Power Ecclesiasticall in the Common-wealth of Geneva, (and consequently to every Presbytery in every other Common-wealth,) or to Princes, and other Civill Soveraigns, I doe not know. For the Presbytery hath challenged the power to Excommunicate their owne Kings, and to bee the Supreme Moderators in Religion, in the places where they have that form of Church government, no lesse then the Pope challengeth it universally.

Answer to the text on which Beza inferreth that the Kingdome of Christ began at the Resurrection.

The words are (Marke 9. 1.) *Verily I say unto you, that there be some of them that stand here, which shall not tast of death, till they have seene the Kingdome of God come with power* Which words, if taken grammatically, make it certaine, that either some of those men that stood by Christ at that time, are yet alive; or else, that the Kingdome of God must be now in this present world. And then there is another place more difficult. For when the Apostles after our Saviours Resurrection, and immediately before his Ascension, asked our Saviour, saying, (Acts 1. 6.) *Wilt thou at this time restore again the Kingdome to Israel,* he answered them, *It is not for you to know the times and the seasons, which the Father hath put in his own power; But ye shall receive power by the comming of the Holy Ghost upon you, and yee shall be my (Martyrs) witnesses both in Jerusalem, & in all Judæa, and in Samaria, and unto the uttermost part of the Earth:* Which is as much as to say, My Kingdome is not yet come, nor shall you foreknow when it shall come; for it shall come as a theefe in the night, But I will send you the Holy Ghost, and by him you shall have power to beare witnesse to all the world (by your preaching) of my Resurrection, and the workes I have done, and the doctrine I have taught, that they may beleeve in me, and expect eternall life, at my comming againe. How does this agree with the comming of Christs Kingdome at the Resurrection? And that which St. *Paul* saies (1 *Thessal.* 1. 9, 10) *That they turned*

from Idols, to serve the living and true God, and to waite for his Sonne from Heaven; Where to waite for his Sonne from Heaven, is to wait for his comming to be King in power; which were not necessary, if his Kingdome had beene then present. Againe, if the Kingdome of God began (as *Beza* on that place (*Mark* 9 1) would have it) at the Resurrection, what reason is there for Christians ever since the Resurrection to say in their prayers, *Let thy Kingdom Come*? It is therefore manifest,
[342] that the words of St. *Mark* are not so to be interpreted. There be some of them that stand here (saith our Saviour) that shall not tast of death till they have seen the Kingdome of God come in power If then this Kingdome were to come at the Resurrection of Christ, why is it said, *some of them*, rather than *all*? For they all lived till after Christ was risen.

Explication of the Place in Mark 9.

But they that require an exact interpretation of this text, let them interpret first the like words of our Saviour to St *Peter* concerning St John, (chap. 21. 22.) *If I will that he tarry till I come, what is that to thee?* upon which was grounded a report that hee should not dye: Neverthelesse the truth of that report was neither confirmed, as well grounded; nor refuted, as ill grounded on those words; but left as a saying not understood The same difficulty is also in the place of St. Marke. And if it be lawfull to conjecture at their meaning, by that which immediately followes, both here, and in St Luke, where the same is againe repeated, it is not unprobable, to say they have relation to the Transfiguration, which is described in the verses immediately following; where it is said, that *After six dayes Jesus taketh with him Peter, and James, and John* (not all, but some of his Disciples) *and leadeth them up into an high mountaine apart by themselves, and was transfigured before them And his rayment became shining, exceeding white as snow, so as no Fuller on earth can white them. And there appeared unto them Elias with Moses, and they were talking with Jesus, &c.* So that they saw Christ in Glory and Majestie, as he is to come; insomuch as *They were sore afraid* And thus the promise of our Saviour was accomplished by way of *Vision*: For it was a Vision, as may probably bee inferred out of St. Luke, that reciteth the same story (ch. 9 ve 28.) and saith, that Peter and they that were with him, were heavy with sleep: But most certainly out of Matth. 17. 9. (where the same is again related,) for our Saviour charged them, saying, *Tell no man the Vision untill the Son of man be Risen from the dead.* Howsoever it be, yet there can from thence be taken no argument, to prove that the Kingdome of God taketh beginning till the day of Judgement.

Abuse of some other texts in defence of the Power of the Pope.

As for some other texts, to prove the Popes Power over civill Soveraignes (besides those of *Bellarmine*,) as that the two Swords that Christ and his Apostles had amongst them, were the Spirituall and the Temporall Sword, which they say St. Peter had given him by Christ: And, that of the two Luminaries, the greater signifies the Pope, and the lesser the King; One might as well inferre out of the first verse of the Bible, that by Heaven is meant the Pope, and by Earth the King: Which is not arguing from Scripture, but a wanton insulting over Princes, that came in fashion after the time the Popes were growne so secure of their greatnesse, as to contemne all Christian Kings; and Treading on the necks of Emperours, to mocke both them, and the Scripture, in the words of the 91. Psalm, *Thou shalt Tread upon the Lion and the Adder, the young Lion and the Dragon thou shalt Trample under thy feet.*

The manner of Consecrations in the Scripture, was without Exorcisms.

As for the rites of Consecration, though they depend for the most part upon the discretion and judgement of the governors of the Church, and not upon the Scriptures, yet those governors are obliged to such direction, [343]
as the nature of the action it selfe requireth, as that the ceremonies, words, and gestures, be both decent, and significant, or at least conformable to the action. When Moses consecrated the Tabernacle, the Altar, and the Vessels belonging to them, (*Exod* 40.) he anointed them with the Oyle which God had commanded to bee made for that purpose; and they were holy: There was nothing Exorcized, to drive away Phantasmes. The same Moses (the civill Soveraigne of Israel) when he consecrated Aaron (the High Priest,) and his Sons, did wash them with Water, (not Exorcized water,) put their

Garments upon them, and anointed them with Oyle; and they were sanctified, to minister unto the Lord in the Priests office; which was a simple and decent cleansing, and adorning them, before hee presented them to God, to be his servants. When King *Solomon*, (the civill Soveraigne of Israel) consecrated the Temple hee had built, (2 *Kings* 8) he stood before all the Congregation of Israel; and having blessed them, he gave thankes to God, for putting into the heart of his father, to build it, and for giving to himselfe the grace to accomplish the same; and then prayed unto him, first, to accept that House, though it were not sutable to his infinite Greatnesse; and to hear the prayers of his Servants that should pray therein, or (if they were absent,) towards it, and lastly, he offered a sacrifice of Peace-offering, and the House was dedicated Here was no Procession, the King stood still in his first place; no Exorcised Water, no *Asperges me*, nor other impertinent application of words spoken upon another occasion; but a decent, and rationall speech, and such as in making to God a present of his new built House, was most conformable to the occasion.

We read not that St. John did Exorcize the Water of Jordan; nor Philip the Water of the river wherein he baptized the Eunuch; nor that any Pastor in the time of the Apostles, did take his spittle, and put it to the nose of the person to be Baptized, and say, *In odorem suavitatis*, that is, *for a sweet savour unto the Lord*; wherein neither the Ceremony of Spittle, for the uncleannesse, nor the application of that Scripture for the levity, can by any authority of man be justified

The immortality of mans Soule, not proved by Scripture to be of Nature, but of Grace.

To prove that the Soule separated from the Body, liveth eternally, not onely the Soules of the Elect, by especiall grace, and restauration of the Eternall Life which Adam lost by Sinne, and our Saviour restored by the Sacrifice of himself, to the Faithfull; but also the Soules of Reprobates, as a property naturally consequent to the essence of mankind, without other grace of God, but that which is universally given to all mankind; there are divers places, which at the first sight seem sufficiently to serve the turn: but such, as when I compare them with that which I have before (Chapter 38) alledged out of the 14 of *Job*, seem to mee much more subject to a divers interpretation, than the words of *Job*.

And first there are the words of Solomon (*Ecclesiastes*
12 7) *Then shall the Dust return to Dust, as it was, and* [344]
the Spirit shall return to God that gave it. Which may bear well enough (if there be no other text directly against it) this interpretation, that God onely knows, (but Man not,) what becomes of a mans spirit, when he expireth; and the same Solomon, in the same Book, (Chap 3. ver. 20, 21.) delivereth the same sentence in the sense I have given it. His words are, *All goe* (man and beast) *to the same place; all are of the dust, and all turn to dust again; who knoweth that the spirit of Man goeth upward, and that the spirit of the Beast goeth downward to the earth?* That is, none knows but God; Nor is it an unusuall phrase to say of things we understand not, *God Knows what*, and *God Knows where*. That of *Gen*. 5. 24 *Enoch walked with God, and he was not; for God took him*; which is expounded Heb 13 5. *He was translated, that he should not die; and was not found, because God had translated him. For before his Translation, he had this testimony, that he pleased God*, making as much for the Immortality of the Body, as of the Soule, proveth, that this his translation was peculiar to them that please God; not common to them with the wicked, and depending on Grace, not on Nature. But on the contrary, what interpretation shall we give, besides the literall sense of the words of Solomon (*Eccles*. 3 19) *That which befalleth the Sons of Men, befalleth Beasts, even one thing befalleth them, as the one dyeth, so doth the other, yea, they have all one breath* (one spirit;) *so that a Man hath no præeminence above a Beast, for all is vanity* By the literall sense, here is no Naturall Immortality of the Soule; nor yet any repugnancy with the Life Eternall, which the Elect shall enjoy by Grace. And (chap 4. ver. 3.) *Better is he that hath not yet been, than both they*; that is, than they that live, or have lived; which, if the Soule of all them that have lived, were Immortall, were a hard saying; for then to have an Immortall Soule, were worse than to have no Soule at all And againe, (Chapt. 9. 5.)

The living know they shall die, but the dead know not any thing; that is, Naturally, and before the resurrection of the body.

Another place which seems to make for a Naturall Immortality of the Soule, is that, where our Saviour saith, that Abraham, Isaac, and Jacob are living: but this is spoken of the promise of God, and of their certitude to rise again, not of a Life then actuall, and in the same sense that God said to Adam, that on the day hee should eate of the forbidden fruit, he should certainly die; from that time forward he was a dead man by sentence, but not by execution, till almost a thousand years after. So Abraham, Isaac, and Jacob were alive by promise, then, when Christ spake, but are not actually till the Resurrection. And the History of Dives and Lazarus, make nothing against this, if wee take it (as it is) for a Parable.

But there be other places of the New Testament, where an Immortality seemeth to be directly attributed to the wicked For it is evident, that they shall all rise to Judgement And it is said besides in many places, that
[345] they shall goe into *Everlasting fire, Everlasting torments, Everlasting punishments; and that the worm of conscience never dyeth*, and all this is comprehended in the word *Everlasting Death*, which is ordinarily interpreted *Everlasting Life in torments*: And yet I can find no where that any man shall live in torments Everlastingly. Also, it seemeth hard, to say, that God who is the Father of Mercies, that doth in Heaven and Earth all that hee will; that hath the hearts of all men in his disposing; that worketh in men both to doe, and to will; and without whose free gift a man hath neither inclination to good, nor repentance of evill, should punish mens transgressions without any end of time, and with all the extremity of torture, that men can imagine, and more. We are therefore to consider, what the meaning is, of *Everlasting Fire*, and other the like phrases of Scripture.

I have shewed already, that the Kingdome of God by Christ beginneth at the day of Judgment. That in that day, the Faithfull shall rise again, with glorious, and spirituall Bodies, and bee his Subjects in that his Kingdome, which shall be Eternall That they shall neither marry, nor be given in marriage, nor eate and drink, as they did in their naturall bodies; but live for ever in their individuall persons, without the specificall eternity of generation: And that the Reprobates also shall rise again, to receive punishments for their sins: As also, that those of the Elect, which shall be alive in their earthly bodies at that day, shall have their bodies suddenly changed, and made spirituall, and Immortall. But that the bodies of the Reprobate, who make the Kingdome of Satan, shall also be glorious, or spirituall bodies, or that they shall bee as the Angels of God, neither eating, nor drinking, nor engendring, or that their life shall be Eternall in their individuall persons, as the life of every faithfull man is, or as the life of Adam had been if hee had not sinned, there is no place of Scripture to prove it; save onely these places concerning Eternall Torments; which may otherwise be interpreted.

From whence may be inferred, that as the Elect after the Resurrection shall be restored to the estate, wherein Adam was before he had sinned, so the Reprobate shall be in the estate, that Adam, and his posterity were in after the sin committed; saving that God promised a Redeemer to Adam, and such of his seed as should trust in him, and repent; but not to them that should die in their sins, as do the Reprobate

Eternall Torments what.

These things considered, the texts that mention *Eternall Fire, Eternall Torments, or the Worm that never dieth*, contradict not the Doctrine of a Second, and Everlasting Death, in the proper and naturall sense of the word *Death* The Fire, or Torments prepared for the wicked in *Gehenna, Tophet*, or in what place soever, may continue for ever, and there may never want wicked men to be tormented in them; though not every, nor any one Eternally. For the wicked being left in the estate they were in after Adams sin, may at the Resurrection live as they did, marry, and give in marriage, and have grosse and corruptible bodies, as all mankind now have; and consequently may engender perpetually, [346] after the Resurrection, as they did before: For there is no place of Scripture to the contrary. For St. Paul, speaking of the Resurrection (1 *Cor.* 15) understandeth it onely of the Resurrection to Life Eternall; and not the Resurrection to Punishment And of the first, he saith that the Body is *Sown in Corruption, raised in Incorruption; sown in Dishonour, raised in Honour; sown in Weaknesse, raised in Power, sown a Naturall body, raised a Spirituall body*. There is no such thing can be said of the bodies of them that rise to Punishment. So also our Saviour, when hee speaketh of the Nature of Man after the Resurrection, meaneth, the Resurrection to Life Eternall, not to Punishment The text is *Luke* 20. verses 34. 35, 36. a fertile text *The Children of this world marry, and are given in marriage, but they that shall be counted worthy to obtaine that world, and the Resurrection from the dead, neither marry, nor are given in marriage: Neither can they die any more; for they are equall to the Angells, and are the Children of God, being the Children of the Resurrection*· The Children of this world, that are in the estate which Adam left them in, shall marry, and be given in marriage; that is, corrupt, and generate successively; which is an Immortality of the Kind, but not of the Persons of men: They are not worthy to be counted amongst them that shall obtain the next world, and an absolute Resurrection from the dead, but onely a short time, as inmates of that world; and to the end onely to receive condign punishment for their contumacy. The Elect are the onely children of the Resurrection; that is to say, the sole heirs of Eternall Life: they only can die no more. it is they that are equall to the Angels, and that are the children of God, and not the Reprobate To the Reprobate there remaineth after the Resurrection, a *Second*, and *Eternall* Death: between which Resurrection, and their Second, and Eternall death, is but a time of Punishment and Torment; and to last by succession of sinners thereunto, as long as the kind of Man by propagation shall endure; which is Eternally.

Answer of the Texts alledged for Purgatory.

Upon this Doctrine of the Naturall Eternity of separated Soules, is founded (as I said) the Doctrine of Purgatory For supposing Eternall Life by Grace onely, there is no Life, but the Life of the Body; and no

Immortality till the Resurrection The texts for Purgatory alledged by Bellarmine out of the Canonicall Scripture of the old Testament, are first, the Fasting of *David* for *Saul* and *Jonathan*, mentioned (2 *Kings*, 1 12); and againe, (2 *Sam.* 3 35) for the death of *Abner*. This Fasting of *David*, he saith, was for the obtaining of something for them at Gods hands, after their death; because after he had Fasted to procure the recovery of his owne child, assoone as he knew it was dead, he called for meate Seeing then the Soule hath an existence separate from the Body, and nothing can be obtained by mens Fasting for the Soules that are already either in Heaven, or Hell, it followeth that there be some Soules of dead men, that are neither in Heaven, nor in Hell; and therefore they must bee in some third place, which must be Purgatory. And thus with hard straining, hee has wrested those places [347] to the proofe of a Purgatory: whereas it is manifest, that the ceremonies of Mourning, and Fasting, when they are used for the death of men, whose life was not profitable to the Mourners, they are used for honours sake to their persons; and when tis done for the death of them by whose life the Mourners had benefit, it proceeds from their particular dammage: And so *David* honoured *Saul*, and *Abner*, with his Fasting; and in the death of his owne child, recomforted himselfe, by receiving his ordinary food.

In the other places, which he alledgeth out of the old Testament, there is not so much as any shew, or colour of proofe. He brings in every text wherein there is the word *Anger*, or *Fire*, or *Burning*, or *Purging*, or *Clensing*, in case any of the Fathers have but in a Sermon rhetorically applied it to the Doctrine of Purgatory, already beleeved. The first verse of *Psalme*, 37. *O Lord rebuke me not in thy wrath, nor chasten me in thy hot displeasure*: What were this to Purgatory, if Augustine had not applied the *Wrath* to the fire of Hell, and the *Displeasure* to that of Purgatory? And what is it to Purgatory, that of *Psalme*, 66 12 *Wee went through fire and water, and thou broughtest us to a moist place*, and other the like texts, (with which the Doctors of those times entended to adorne, or extend their Sermons, or Commentaries) haled to their purposes by force of wit?

Places of the New Testament for Purgatory answered.

But he alledgeth other places of the New Testament, that are not so easie to be answered: And first that of Matth. 12. 32. *Whosoever speaketh a word against the Sonne of man, it shall be forgiven him, but whosoever speaketh against the Holy Ghost, it shall not bee forgiven him neither in this world, nor in the world to come*: Where he will have Purgatory to be the World to come, wherein some sinnes may be forgiven, which in this World were not forgiven notwithstanding that it is manifest, there are but three Worlds, one from the Creation to the Flood, which was destroyed by Water, and is called in Scripture *the Old World*, another from the Flood, to the day of Judgement, which is *the Present World*, and shall bee destroyed by Fire, and the third, which shall bee from the day of Judgement forward, everlasting, which is called *the World to come*; and in which it is agreed by all, there shall be no Purgatory: And therefore the World to come, and Purgatory, are inconsistent. But what then can bee the meaning of those our Saviours words? I confesse they are very hardly to bee reconciled with all the Doctrines now unanimously received Nor is it any shame, to confesse the profoundnesse of the Scripture, to bee too great to be sounded by the shortnesse of humane understanding. Neverthelesse, I may propound such things to the consideration of more learned Divines, as the text it selfe suggesteth. And first, seeing to speake against the Holy Ghost, as being the third Person of the Trinity, is to speake against the Church, in which the Holy Ghost resideth; it seemeth the comparison is made, betweene the Easinesse of our Saviour, in bearing with offences done to him while hee himselfe taught the world, that is, when he was on earth, and the Severity of the Pastors after him, against those which should deny their authority, which was from the Holy
[348] Ghost: As if he should say, You that deny my Power; nay you that shall crucifie me, shall be pardoned by mee, as often as you turne unto mee by Repentance: But if you deny the Power of them that teach you hereafter, by vertue of the Holy Ghost, they shall be inexorable,

and shall not forgive you, but persecute you in this World, and leave you without absolution, (though you turn to me, unlesse you turn also to them,) to the punishments (as much as lies in them) of the World to come: And so the words may be taken as a Prophecy, or Prædiction concerning the times, as they have along been in the Christian Church: Or if this be not the meaning, (for I am not peremptory in such difficult places,) perhaps there may be place left after the Resurrection for the Repentance of some sinners: And there is also another place, that seemeth to agree therewith. For considering the words of St Paul (1 *Cor*. 15 29) *What shall they doe which are Baptized for the dead, if the dead rise not at all? why also are they Baptized for the dead?* a man may probably inferre, as some have done, that in St. Pauls time, there was a custome by receiving Baptisme for the dead, (as men that now beleeve, are Sureties and Undertakers for the Faith of Infants, that are not capable of beleeving,) to undertake for the persons of their deceased friends, that they should be ready to obey, and receive our Saviour for their King, at his coming again; and then the forgivenesse of sins in the world to come, has no need of a Purgatory. But in both these interpretations, there is so much of paradox, that I trust not to them; but propound them to those that are throughly versed in the Scripture, to inquire if there be no clearer place that contradicts them Onely of thus much, I see evident Scripture, to perswade me, that there is neither the word, nor the thing of Purgatory, neither in this, nor any other text; nor any thing that can prove a necessity of a place for the Soule without the Body, neither for the Soule of Lazarus during the four days he was dead; nor for the Soules of them which the Romane Church pretend to be tormented now in Purgatory. For God, that could give a life to a peece of clay, hath the same power to give life again to a dead man, and renew his inanimate, and rotten Carkasse, into a glorious, spirituall, and immortall Body.

Another place is that of 1 *Cor* 3 where it is said, that they which built Stubble, Hay, &c on the true Foundation, their work shall perish, but *they themselves shall*

be saved ; but as through Fire : This Fire, he will have to be the Fire of Purgatory. The words, as I have said before, are an allusion to those of *Zach* 13 9 where he saith, *I will bring the third part through the Fire, and refine them as Silver is refined, and will try them as Gold is tryed* : Which is spoken of the comming of the Messiah in Power and Glory ; that is, at the day of Judgment, and Conflagration of the present world ; wherein the Elect shall not be consumed, but be refined ; that is, depose their erroneous Doctrines, and Traditions, and have them as it were sindged of ; and shall afterwards call upon the name of the true God. In like manner, the Apostle saith of them, that holding this Foundation
[349] *Jesus is the Christ*, shall build thereon some other Doctrines that be erroneous, that they shall not be consumed in that fire which reneweth the world, but shall passe through it to Salvation ; but so, as to see, and relinquish their former Errours. The Builders, are the *Pastors* ; the Foundation, that *Jesus is the Christ* ; the Stubble and Hay, *False Consequences drawn from it through Ignorance, or Frailty* , the Gold, Silver, and pretious Stones, are their *True Doctrines* ; and their Refining or Purging, the *Relinquishing of their Errors* In all which there is no colour at all for the burning of Incorporeall, that is to say, Impatible Souls.

Baptisme for the Dead, how understood

A third place is that of 1 *Cor*. 15. before mentioned, concerning Baptisme for the Dead . out of which he concludeth, first, that Prayers for the Dead are not unprofitable , and out of that, that there is a Fire of Purgatory : But neither of them rightly. For of many interpretations of the word Baptisme, he approveth this in the first place, that by Baptisme is meant (metaphorically) a Baptisme of Penance, and that men are in this sense Baptized, when they Fast, and Pray, and give Almes : And so Baptisme for the Dead, and Prayer for the Dead, is the same thing. But this is a Metaphor, of which there is no example, neither in the Scripture, nor in any other use of language ; and which is also discordant to the harmony, and scope of the Scripture. The word Baptisme is used (*Mar* 10. 38. & *Luk*. 12. 50.) for being Dipped in ones own bloud, as Christ was upon the Cross, and as most of the Apostles were, for giving testimony of him. But it is hard to say, that Prayer, Fasting, and Almes, have any similitude with Dipping The same is used also *Mat* 3. 11. (which seemeth to make somewhat for Purgatory) for a Purging with Fire. But it is evident the Fire and Purging here mentioned, is the same whereof the Prophet *Zachary* speaketh (chap. 13. v. 9) *I will bring the third part through the Fire, and will Refine them, &c.* And St. Peter after him (1 Epist. 1. 7.) *That the triall of your Faith, which is much more precious than of Gold that perisheth, though it be tryed with Fire, might be found unto praise, and honour, and glory at the Appearing of Jesus Christ*; and St. Paul (1 *Cor.* 3. 13) *The Fire shall trie every mans work of what sort it is.* But St. Peter, and St. Paul speak of the Fire that shall be at the Second Appearing of Christ; and the Prophet Zachary of the Day of Judgment. And therefore this place of S. Mat. may be interpreted of the same; and then there will be no necessity of the Fire of Purgatory.

Another interpretation of Baptisme for the Dead, is that which I have before mentioned, which he preferreth to the second place of probability. And thence also he inferreth the utility of Prayer for the Dead. For if after the Resurrection, such as have not heard of Christ, or not beleeved in him, may be received into Christs Kingdome; it is not in vain, after their death, that their friends should pray for them, till they should be risen. But granting that God, at the prayers of the faithfull, may convert unto him some of those that have not heard Christ preached, and consequently cannot have rejected Christ, and that the charity of men in that point, cannot be blamed; yet this concludeth nothing for Purgatory, because to rise from Death to Life, is one thing; to rise [350] from Purgatory to Life is another, as being a rising from Life to Life, from a Life in torments to a Life in joy

A fourth place is that of *Mat* 5 25. *Agree with thine Adversary quickly, whilest thou art in the way with him, lest at any time the Adversary deliver thee to the Judge, and the Judge deliver thee to the Officer, and thou be cast into prison Verily I say unto thee, thou shalt by no means come out thence, till thou hast paid the uttermost farthing.*

In which Allegory, the Offender is the *Sinner*; both the Adversary and the Judge is *God*; the Way is this *Life*; the Prison is the *Grave*, the Officer, *Death*; from which, the sinner shall not rise again to life eternall, but to a second Death, till he have paid the utmost farthing, or Christ pay it for him by his Passion, which is a full Ransome for all manner of sin, as well lesser sins, as greater crimes; both being made by the passion of Christ equally veniall.

The fift place, is that of *Matth.* 5. 22. *Whosoever is angry with his Brother without a cause, shall be guilty in Judgment. And whosoever shall say to his Brother, RACHA, shall be guilty in the Councel. But whosoever shall say, Thou Foole, shall be guilty to hell fire.* From which words he inferreth three sorts of Sins, and three sorts of Punishments, and that none of those sins, but the last, shall be punished with hell fire; and consequently, that after this life, there is punishment of lesser sins in Purgatory Of which inference, there is no colour in any interpretation that hath yet been given of them: Shall there be a distinction after this life of Courts of Justice, as there was amongst the Jews in our Saviours time, to hear, and determine divers sorts of Crimes; as the Judges, and the Councell? Shall not all Judicature appertain to Christ, and his Apostles? To understand therefore this text, we are not to consider it solitarily, but jointly with the words precedent, and subsequent Our Saviour in this Chapter interpreteth the Law of Moses; which the Jews thought was then fulfilled, when they had not transgressed the Grammaticall sense thereof, however they had transgressed against the sentence, or meaning of the Legislator. Therefore whereas they thought the Sixth Commandement was not broken, but by Killing a man; nor the Seventh, but when a man lay with a woman, not his wife; our Saviour tells them, the inward Anger of a man against his brother, if it be without just cause, is Homicide: You have heard (saith hee) the Law of Moses, *Thou shalt not Kill*, and that *Whosoever shall Kill, shall bee condemned before the Judges*, or before the Session of the Seventy: But I say unto you, to be Angry with ones Brother without cause; or to say

unto him *Racha*, or *Foole*, is Homicide, and shall be punished at the day of Judgment, and Session of Christ, and his Apostles, with Hell fire. so that those words were not used to distinguish between divers Crimes, and divers Courts of Justice, and divers Punishments; but to taxe the distinction between sin, and sin, which the Jews drew not from the difference of the Will in Obeying God, but from the difference of their Temporall [351]
Courts of Justice; and to shew them that he that had the Will to hurt his Brother, though the effect appear but in Reviling, or not at all, shall be cast into hell fire, by the Judges, and by the Session, which shall be the same, not different Courts at the day of Judgment. This considered, what can be drawn from this text, to maintain Purgatory, I cannot imagine

The sixth place is *Luke* 16. 9 *Make yee friends of the unrighteous Mammon, that when yee faile, they may receive you into Everlasting Tabernacles* This he alledges to prove Invocation of Saints departed. But the sense is plain, That we should make friends with our Riches, of the Poore, and thereby obtain their Prayers whilest they live *He that giveth to the Poore, lendeth to the Lord.*

The seventh is *Luke* 23 42 *Lord remember me when thou commest into thy Kingdome* Therefore, saith hee, there is Remission of sins after this life. But the consequence is not good. Our Saviour then forgave him; and at his comming againe in Glory, will remember to raise him againe to Life Eternall

The Eight is *Acts* 2. 24 where St Peter saith of Christ, *that God had raised him up, and loosed the Paines of Death, because it was not possible he should be holden of it*: Which hee interprets to bee a descent of Christ into Purgatory, to loose some Soules there from their torments: whereas it is manifest, that it was Christ that was loosed, it was hee that could not bee holden of Death, or the Grave; and not the Souls in Purgatory. But if that which Beza sayes in his notes on this place be well observed, there is none that will not see, that in stead of *Paynes*, it should be *Bands*, and then there is no further cause to seek for Purgatory in this Text.

[352]

CHAP. XLV.

Of DÆMONOLOGY, *and other Reliques of the Religion of the Gentiles.*

The Originall of Dæmonology.

THE impression made on the organs of Sight, by lucide Bodies, either in one direct line, or in many lines, reflected from Opaque, or refracted in the passage through Diaphanous Bodies, produceth in living Creatures, in whom God hath placed such Organs, an Imagination of the Object, from whence the Impression proceedeth; which Imagination is called *Sight*; and seemeth not to bee a meer Imagination, but the Body it selfe without us; in the same manner, as when a man violently presseth his eye, there appears to him a light without, and before him, which no man perceiveth but himselfe; because there is indeed no such thing without him, but onely a motion in the interiour organs, pressing by resistance outward, that makes him think so. And the motion made by this pressure, continuing after the object which caused it is removed, is that we call *Imagination*, and *Memory*, and (in sleep, and sometimes in great distemper of the organs by Sicknesse, or Violence) a *Dream*: of which things I have already spoken briefly, in the second and third Chapters.

This nature of Sight having never been discovered by the ancient pretenders to Naturall Knowledge; much lesse by those that consider not things so remote (as that Knowledge is) from their present use; it was hard for men to conceive of those Images in the Fancy, and in the Sense, otherwise, than of things really without us: Which some (because they vanish away, they know not whither, nor how,) will have to be absolutely Incorporeall, that is to say Immateriall, or Formes without Matter; Colour and Figure, without any coloured or figured Body; and that they can put on Aiery bodies (as a garment) to make them Visible when they will to our bodily Eyes; and others say, are Bodies, and living Creatures, but made of Air, or other more subtile and æthereall Matter, which is, then, when they will be seen, condensed.

But Both of them agree on one generall appellation of them, DÆMONS. As if the Dead of whom they Dreamed, were not Inhabitants of their own Brain, but of the Air, or of Heaven, or Hell; not Phantasmes, but Ghosts; with just as much reason, as if one should say, he saw his own Ghost in a Looking-Glasse, or the Ghosts of the Stars in a River; or call the ordinary apparition of the Sun, of the quantity of about a foot, the *Dæmon*, or Ghost of that great Sun that enlighteneth the whole visible world. And by that means have feared them, as things of an unknown, that is, of an unlimited power to doe them good, or harme; and consequently, [353] given occasion to the Governours of the Heathen Common-wealths to regulate this their fear, by establishing that DÆMONOLOGY (in which the Poets, as Principall Priests of the Heathen Religion, were specially employed, or reverenced) to the Publique Peace, and to the Obedience of Subjects necessary thereunto; and to make some of them Good *Dæmons*, and others Evill, the one as a Spurre to the Observance, the other, as Reines to withhold them from Violation of the Laws.

What were the Dæmons of the Ancients

What kind of things they were, to whom they attributed the name of *Dæmons*, appeareth partly in the Genealogie of their Gods, written by *Hesiod*, one of the most ancient Poets of the Græcians; and partly in other Histories, of which I have observed some few before, in the 12. Chapter of this discourse.

How that Doctrine was spread.

The Græcians, by their Colonies and Conquests, communicated their Language and Writings into Asia, Egypt, and Italy; and therein, by necessary consequence their *Dæmonology*, or (as St. *Paul* calles it) *their Doctrines of Devils*. And by that meanes, the contagion was derived also to the Jewes, both of *Judæa*, and *Alexandria*, and other parts, whereinto they were dispersed.

How far received by the Jews.

But the name of *Dæmon* they did not (as the Græcians) attribute to Spirits both Good, and Evill; but to the Evill onely: And to the Good *Dæmons* they gave the name of the Spirit of God; and esteemed those into whose bodies they entred to be Prophets. In summe, all singularity if Good, they attributed to the Spirit of God; and if Evill, to some *Dæmon*, but a κακοδάιμων, an Evill *Dæmon*, that is, a *Devill*. And therefore, they called *Dæmoniaques*, that is, *possessed by the Devill*, such as we call Madmen or Lunatiques; or such as had the Falling Sicknesse; or that spoke any thing, which they for want of understanding, thought absurd: As also of an Unclean person in a notorious degree, they used to say he had an Unclean Spirit; of a Dumbe man, that he had a Dumbe Devill; and of *John Baptist* (*Math.* 11. 18) for the singularity of his fasting, that he had a Devill, and of our Saviour, because he said, hee that keepeth

John 8. 52 his sayings should not see Death *in æternum*, *Now we know thou hast a Devill*; *Abraham is dead, and the Prophets are dead* And again, because he said (*John* 7. 20) *They went about to kill him*, the people answered, *Thou hast a Devill, who goeth about to kill thee?* Whereby it is manifest, that the Jewes had the same opinions concerning Phantasmes, namely, that they were not Phantasmes, that is, Idols of the braine, but things reall, and independent on the Fancy.

Why our Saviour controlled it not.

Which doctrine if it be not true, why (may some say) did not our Saviour contradict it, and teach the contrary? nay why does he use on diverse occasions, such forms of speech as seem to confirm it? To this I answer, that first, where Christ saith, *A spirit hath not flesh and bone*, though hee shew that there be Spirits, yet hee denies not that they are Bodies: And where St. *Paul* saies, *We shall rise spirituall Bodies*, he acknowledgeth the nature of Spirits, but that they are Bodily Spirits, which is not difficult to understand. For Air and many other things are Bodies, though not Flesh and Bone, or

[354] any other grosse body, to bee discerned by the eye. But when our Saviour speaketh to the Devill, and commandeth him to go out of a man, if by the Devill, be meant a Disease, as Phrenesy, or Lunacy, or a corporeal Spirit, is not the speech improper? can Diseases heare? or can there be a corporeall Spirit in a Body of Flesh and Bone, full already of vitall and animall Spirits? Are there not therefore Spirits, that neither have Bodies, nor are meer Imaginations? To the first I answer, that the addressing of our Saviours command to the Madnesse, or Lunacy he cureth, is no more improper, then was his rebuking of

the Fever, or of the Wind, and Sea; for neither do these hear: Or than was the command of God, to the Light, to the Firmament, to the Sunne, and Starres, when he commanded them to bee. for they could not heare before they had a beeing. But those speeches are not improper, because they signifie the power of Gods Word: no more therefore is it improper, to command Madnesse, or Lunacy (under the appellation of Devils, by which they were then commonly understood,) to depart out of a mans body. To the second, concerning their being Incorporeall, I have not yet observed any place of Scripture, from whence it can be gathered, that any man was ever possessed with any other Corporeall Spirit, but that of his owne, by which his body is naturally moved.

The Scriptures doe not teach that Spirits are Incorporeall

Our Saviour, immediately after the Holy Ghost descended upon him in the form of a Dove, is said by St *Matthew* (Chapt. 4. 1.) to have been *led up by the Spirit into the Wildernesse*; and the same is recited (*Luke* 4. 1.) in these words, *Jesus being full of the Holy Ghost, was led in the Spirit into the Wildernesse*: Whereby it is evident, that by *Spirit* there, is meant the Holy Ghost. This cannot be interpreted for a Possession · For Christ, and the Holy Ghost, are but one and the same substance; which is no possession of one substance, or body, by another. And whereas in the verses following, he is said *to have been taken up by the Devill into the Holy City, and set upon a pinnacle of the Temple*, shall we conclude thence that hee was possessed of the Devill, or carryed thither by violence? And again, *carryed thence by the Devill into an exceeding high mountain, who shewed him them thence all the Kingdomes of the world* Wherein, wee are not to beleeve he was either possessed, or forced by the Devill; nor that any Mountaine is high enough, (according to the literall sense,) to shew him one whole Hemisphere. What then can be the meaning of this place, other than that he went of himself into the Wildernesse; and that this carrying of him up and down, from the Wildernesse to the City, and from thence into a Mountain, was a Vision? Conformable whereunto, is also the phrase of St Luke, that hee was led into the Wildernesse, not *by*, but *in* the Spirit: whereas concerning His being

Taken up into the Mountaine, and unto the Pinnacle of the Temple, hee speaketh as St. Matthew doth. Which suiteth with the nature of a Vision.

Again, where St Luke sayes of Judas Iscariot, that *Satan entred into him, and thereupon that he went and communed with the Chief Priests, and Captaines, how he*
[355] *might betray Christ unto them*: it may be answered, that by the Entring of *Satan* (that is the *Enemy*) into him, is meant, the hostile and traiterous intention of selling his Lord and Master. For as by the Holy Ghost, is frequently in Scripture understood, the Graces and good Inclinations given by the Holy Ghost, so by the Entring of Satan, may bee understood the wicked Cogitations, and Designs of the Adversaries of Christ, and his Disciples. For as it is hard to say, that the Devill was entred into Judas, before he had any such hostile designe, so it is impertinent to say, he was first Christs Enemy in his heart, and that the Devill entred into him afterwards Therefore the Entring of Satan, and his Wicked Purpose, was one and the same thing.

But if there be no Immateriall Spirit, nor any Possession of mens bodies by any Spirit Corporeall, it may again be asked, why our Saviour and his Apostles did not teach the People so, and in such cleer words, as they might no more doubt thereof. But such questions as these, are more curious, than necessary for a Christian mans Salvation Men may as well aske, why Christ that could have given to all men Faith, Piety, and all manner of morall Vertues, gave it to some onely, and not to all: and why he left the search of naturall Causes, and Sciences, to the naturall Reason and Industry of men, and did not reveal it to all, or any man supernaturally; and many other such questions: Of which neverthelesse there may be alledged probable and pious reasons. For as God, when he brought the Israelites into the Land of Promise, did not secure them therein, by subduing all the Nations round about them, but left many of them, as thornes in their sides, to awaken from time to time their Piety and Industry so our Saviour, in conducting us toward his heavenly Kingdome, did not destroy all the difficulties of Naturall Questions; but left them to exercise our Industry, and Reason; the Scope of his preaching, being onely to shew us this plain and direct way to Salvation, namely, the beleef of this Article, *that he was the Christ, the Son of the living God, sent into the world to sacrifice himselfe for our Sins, and at his comming again, gloriously to reign over his Elect, and to save them from their Enemies eternally*. To which, the opinion of Possession by Spirits, or Phantasmes, are no impediment in the way; though it be to some an occasion of going out of the way, and to follow their own Inventions. If wee require of the Scripture an account of all questions, which may be raised to trouble us in the performance of Gods commands; we may as well complaine of Moses for not having set downe the time of the creation of such Spirits, as well as of the Creation of the Earth, and Sea, and of Men, and Beasts. To conclude, I find in Scripture that there be Angels, and Spirits, good and evill; but not that they are Incorporeall, as are the Apparitions men see in the Dark, or in a Dream, or Vision; which the Latines call *Spectra*, and took for *Dæmons*. And I find that there are Spirits Corporeall, (though subtile and Invisible,) but not that any mans body was possessed, or inhabited by them; And that the Bodies of the Saints shall be such, namely, Spirituall Bodies, as [356] St Paul calls them.

The Power of Casting out Devills, not the same it was in the Primitive Church

Neverthelesse, the contrary Doctrine, namely, that there be Incorporeall Spirits, hath hitherto so prevailed in the Church, that the use of Exorcisme, (that is to say, of ejection of Devills by Conjuration) is thereupon built; and (though rarely and faintly practised) is not yet totally given over. That there were many Dæmoniaques in the Primitive Church, and few Mad-men, and other such singular diseases; whereas in these times we hear of, and see many Mad-men, and few Dæmoniaques, proceeds not from the change of Nature; but of Names. But how it comes to passe, that whereas heretofore the Apostles, and after them for a time, the Pastors of the Church, did cure those singular Diseases, which now they are not seen to doe; as likewise, why it is not in the power of every true Beleever now, to doe all that the Faithfull did then, that is to say, as we read (*Mark*

16 17) *In Christs name to cast out Devills, to speak with new Tongues, to take up Serpents, to drink deadly Poison without harm taking, and to cure the Sick by the laying on of their hands*, and all this without other words, but *in the Name of Jesus*, is another question And it is probable, that those extraordinary gifts were given to the Church, for no longer a time, than men trusted wholly to Christ, and looked for their felicity onely in his Kingdome to come; and consequently, that when they sought Authority, and Riches, and trusted to their own Subtilty for a Kingdome of this world, these supernaturall gifts of God were again taken from them.

Another relique of Gentilisme, Worshipping of Images, left in the Church, not brought into it.

Another relique of Gentilisme, is the *Worship of Images*, neither instituted by Moses in the Old, nor by Christ in the New Testament; nor yet brought in from the Gentiles; but left amongst them, after they had given their names to Christ. Before our Saviour preached, it was the generall Religion of the Gentiles, to worship for Gods, those Apparences that remain in the Brain from the impression of externall Bodies upon the organs of their Senses, which are commonly called *Ideas, Idols, Phantasmes, Conceits*, as being Representations of those externall Bodies, which cause them, and have nothing in them of reality, no more than there is in the things that seem to stand before us in a Dream And this is the reason why St. Paul says, *Wee know that an Idol is Nothing* Not that he thought that an Image of Metall, Stone, or Wood, was nothing, but that the thing which they honored, or feared in the Image, and held for a God, was a meer Figment, without place, habitation, motion, or existence, but in the motions of the Brain. And the worship of these with Divine Honour, is that which is in the Scripture called Idolatry, and Rebellion against God. For God being King of the Jews, and his Lieutenant being first Moses, and afterward the High Priest; if the people had been permitted to worship, and pray to Images, (which are Representations of their own Fancies,) they had had no farther dependence on the true God, of
[357] whom their can be no similitude; nor on his prime Ministers, Moses, and the High Priests, but every man had governed himself according to his own appetite, to

the utter eversion of the Common-wealth, and their own destruction for want of Union. And therefore the first Law of God was, *They should not take for Gods,* ALIENOS DEOS, that is, *the Gods of other nations, but that onely true God, who vouchsafed to commune with Moses, and by him to give them laws and directions, for their peace, and for their salvation from their enemies.* And the second was, that *they should not make to themselves any Image to Worship, of their own Invention.* For it is the same deposing of a King, to submit to another King, whether he be set up by a neighbour nation, or by our selves.

Answer to certain seeming texts for Images

The places of Scripture pretended to countenance the setting up of Images, to worship them; or to set them up at all in the places where God is worshipped, are First, two Examples; one of the Cherubins over the Ark of God; the other of the Brazen Serpent Secondly, some texts whereby we are commanded to worship certain Creatures for their relation to God; as to worship his Footstool. And lastly, some other texts, by which is authorized, a religious honoring of Holy things. But before I examine the force of those places, to prove that which is pretended, I must first explain what is to be understood by *Worshipping*, and what by *Images*, and *Idols*.

What is Worship.

I have already shewn in the 20 Chapter of this Discourse, that to Honor, is to value highly the Power of any person and that such value is measured, by our comparing him with others. But because there is nothing to be compared with God in Power, we Honor him not but Dishonour him by any Value lesse than Infinite And thus Honor is properly of its own nature, secret, and internall in the heart. But the inward thoughts of men, which appeare outwardly in their words and actions, are the signes of our Honoring, and these goe by the name of WORSHIP, in Latine CULTUS. Therefore, to Pray to, to Swear by, to Obey, to bee Diligent, and Officious in Serving. in summe, all words and actions that betoken Fear to Offend, or Desire to Please, is *Worship*, whether those words and actions be sincere, or feigned: and because they appear as signes of Honoring, are ordinarily also called *Honor*.

Distinction between Divine and Civill Worship. The Worship we exhibite to those we esteem to be but men, as to Kings, and men in Authority, is *Civill Worship*: But the worship we exhibite to that which we think to bee God, whatsoever the words, ceremonies, gestures, or other actions be, is *Divine Worship*. To fall prostrate before a King, in him that thinks him but a Man, is but Civill Worship. And he that but putteth off his hat in the Church, for this cause, that he thinketh it the House of God, worshippeth with Divine Worship They that seek the distinction of Divine and Civill Worship, not in the intention of the Worshipper, but in the Words δουλεία, and λατρεία, deceive themselves For whereas there be two sorts of Servants; that sort, which is of
[358] those that are absolutely in the power of their Masters, as Slaves taken in war, and their Issue, whose bodies are not in their own power, (their lives depending on the Will of their Masters, in such manner as to forfeit them upon the least disobedience,) and that are bought and sold as Beasts, were called Δοῦλοι, that is properly, Slaves, and their Service Δουλεία The other, which is of those that serve (for hire, or in hope of benefit from their Masters) voluntarily, are called Θῆτες; that is, Domestique Servants; to whose service the Masters have no further right, than is contained in the Covenants made betwixt them. These two kinds of Servants have thus much common to them both, that their labour is appointed them by another And the word Λάτεις, is the generall name of both, signifying him that worketh for another, whether, as a Slave, or a voluntary Servant: So that Λατρεία signifieth generally all Service; but Δουλεία the service of Bondmen onely, and the condition of Slavery And both are used in Scripture (to signifie our Service of God) promiscuously. Δουλεία, because we are Gods Slaves, Λατρεία, because wee Serve him. and in all kinds of Service is contained, not onely Obedience, but also Worship; that is, such actions, gestures, and words, as signifie Honor.

An Image what. Phantasmes. An IMAGE (in the most strict signification of the word) is the Resemblance of some thing visible. In which sense the Phantasticall Formes, Apparitions, or Seemings of visible Bodies to the Sight, are onely *Images*; such as are the Shew of a man, or other thing in the Water, by Reflexion, or Refraction; or of the Sun, or Stars by Direct Vision in the Air; which are nothing reall in the things seen, nor in the place where they seem to bee; nor are their magnitudes and figures the same with that of the object; but changeable, by the variation of the organs of Sight, or by glasses; and are present oftentimes in our Imagination, and in our Dreams, when the object is absent; or changed into other colours, and shapes, as things that depend onely upon the Fancy. And these are the Images which are originally and most properly called *Ideas*, and IDOLS, and derived from the language of the Græcians, with whom the word Εἴδω signifieth to *See*. They are also called PHANTASMES, which is in the same language, *Apparitions*. And from these Images it is that one of the faculties of mans Nature, is called the *Imagination*. And from hence it is manifest, that there neither is, nor can bee any Image made of a thing Invisible

It is also evident, that there can be no Image of a thing Infinite for all the Images, and Phantasmes that are made by the Impression of things visible, are figured · but Figure is a quantity every way determined: And therefore there can bee no Image of God; nor of the Soule of Man, nor of Spirits; but onely of Bodies Visible, that is, Bodies that have light in themselves, or are by such enlightened.

Fictions. And whereas a man can fancy Shapes he never saw; making up a Figure out of the parts of divers creatures; as the Poets make their Centaures, Chimæras, and other [359] Monsters never seen · So can he also give Matter to those Shapes, and make them in Wood, Clay or Metall. And *Materiall Images.* these are also called Images, not for the resemblance of any corporeall thing, but for the resemblance of some Phantasticall Inhabitants of the Brain of the Maker. But in these Idols, as they are originally in the Brain, and as they are painted, carved, moulded, or moulten in matter, there is a similitude of the one to the other, for which the Materiall Body made by Art, may be said to be the Image of the Phantasticall Idoll made by Nature.

But in a larger use of the word Image, is contained also, any Representation of one thing by another. So an earthly Soveraign may be called the Image of God And an inferiour Magistrate the Image of an earthly Soveraign. And many times in the Idolatry of the Gentiles there was little regard to the similitude of their Materiall Idol to the Idol in their fancy, and yet it was called the Image of it. For a Stone unhewn has been set up for Neptune, and divers other shapes far different from the shapes they conceived of their Gods. And at this day we see many Images of the Virgin Mary, and other Saints, unlike one another, and without correspondence to any one mans Fancy; and yet serve well enough for the purpose they were erected for; which was no more but by the Names onely, to represent the Persons mentioned in the History; to which every man applyeth a Mentall Image of his owne making, or none at all. And thus an Image in the largest sense, is either the Resemblance, or the Representation of some thing Visible; or both together, as it happeneth for the most part.

But the name of Idoll is extended yet further in Scripture, to signifie also the Sunne, or a Starre, or any other Creature, visible or invisible, when they are worshipped for Gods

Idolatry what.

Having shewn what is *Worship*, and what an *Image*; I will now put them together, and examine what that IDOLATRY is, which is forbidden in the Second Commandement, and other places of the Scripture.

To worship an Image, is voluntarily to doe those externall acts, which are signes of honoring either the matter of the Image, which is Wood, Stone, Metall, or some other visible creature; or the Phantasme of the brain, for the resemblance, or representation whereof, the matter was formed and figured, or both together, as one animate Body, composed of the Matter and the Phantasme, as of a Body and Soule.

To be uncovered, before a man of Power and Authority, or before the Throne of a Prince, or in such other places as hee ordaineth to that purpose in his absence, is to Worship that man, or Prince with Civill Worship; as being a signe, not of honoring the stoole, or place, but the Person, and is not Idolatry. But if hee that doth it, should suppose the Soule of the Prince to be in the Stool, or should present a Petition to the Stool, it were Divine Worship, and Idolatry.

To pray to a King for such things, as hee is able to [360] doe for us, though we prostrate our selves before him, is but Civill Worship; because we acknowledge no other power in him, but humane: But voluntarily to pray unto him for fair weather, or for any thing which God onely can doe for us, is Divine Worship, and Idolatry. On the other side, if a King compell a man to it by the terrour of Death, or other great corporall punishment, it is not Idolatry: For the Worship which the Soveraign commandeth to bee done unto himself by the terrour of his Laws, is not a sign that he that obeyeth him, does inwardly honour him as a God, but that he is desirous to save himselfe from death, or from a miserable life; and that which is not a sign of internall honor, is no Worship; and therefore no Idolatry. Neither can it bee said, that hee that does it, scandalizeth, or layeth any stumbling block before his Brother; because how wise, or learned soever he be that worshippeth in that manner, another man cannot from thence argue, that he approveth it; but that he doth it for fear; and that it is not his act, but the act of his Soveraign

To worship God, in some peculiar Place, or turning a mans face towards an Image, or determinate Place, is not to worship, or honor the Place, or Image, but to acknowledge it Holy, that is to say, to acknowledge the Image, or the Place to be set apart from common use: for that is the meaning of the word *Holy*; which implies no new quality in the Place, or Image, but onely a new Relation by Appropriation to God; and therefore is not Idolatry, no more than it was Idolatry to worship God before the Brazen Serpent, or for the Jews when they were out of their owne countrey, to turn their faces (when they prayed) toward the Temple of Jerusalem; or for Moses to put off his Shoes when he was before the Flaming Bush, the ground appertaining to Mount Sinai; which place God had chosen to appear in, and to give

his Laws to the People of Israel, and was therefore Holy ground, not by inhærent sanctity, but by separation to Gods use, or for Christians to worship in the Churches, which are once solemnly dedicated to God for that purpose, by the Authority of the King, or other true Representant of the Church. But to worship God, as inanimating, or inhabiting, such Image, or place, that is to say, an infinite substance in a finite place, is Idolatry for such finite Gods, are but Idols of the brain, nothing reall; and are commonly called in the Scripture by the names of *Vanity*, and *Lyes*, and *Nothing*. Also to worship God, not as inanimating, or present in the place, or Image, but to the end to be put in mind of him, or of some works of his, in case the Place, or Image be dedicated, or set up by private authority, and not by the authority of them that are our Soveraign Pastors, is Idolatry. For the Commandement is, *Thou shalt not make to thy selfe any graven Image* God commanded Moses to set up the Brazen Serpent, hee did not make it to himselfe, it was not therefore against the Commandement. But the making of the Golden Calfe by
[361] Aaron, and the People, as being done without authority from God, was Idolatry; not onely because they held it for God, but also because they made it for a Religious use, without warrant either from God their Soveraign, or from Moses, that was his Lieutenant.

The Gentiles worshipped for Gods, Jupiter, and others; that living, were men perhaps that had done great and glorious Acts; and for the Children of God, divers men and women, supposing them gotten between an Immortall Deity, and a mortall man. This was Idolatry, because they made them so to themselves, having no authority from God, neither in his eternall Law of Reason, nor in his positive and revealed Will. But though our Saviour was a man, whom wee also beleeve to bee God Immortall, and the Son of God, yet this is no Idolatry; because wee build not that beleef upon our own fancy, or judgment, but upon the Word of God revealed in the Scriptures And for the adoration of the Eucharist, if the words of Christ, *This is my Body*, signifie, *that he himselfe, and the seeming bread in his hand; and not onely so, but that all the seeming morsells of bread that have ever since been, and any time hereafter shall bee consecrated by Priests, bee so many Christs bodies, and yet all of them but one body*, then is that no Idolatry, because it is authorized by our Saviour: but if that text doe not signifie that, (for there is no other that can be alledged for it,) then, because it is a worship of humane institution, it is Idolatry. For it is not enough to say, God can transubstantiate the Bread into Christs Body For the Gentiles also held God to be Omnipotent; and might upon that ground no lesse excuse their Idolatry, by pretending, as well as others, a transubstantiation of their Wood, and Stone into God Almighty.

Whereas there be, that pretend Divine Inspiration, to be a supernaturall entring of the Holy Ghost into a man, and not an acquisition of Gods graces, by doctrine, and study; I think they are in a very dangerous Dilemma. For if they worship not the men whom they beleeve to be so inspired, they fall into Impiety; as not adoring Gods supernaturall Presence. And again, if they worship them, they commit Idolatry; for the Apostles would never permit themselves to be so worshipped. Therefore the safest way is to beleeve, that by the Descending of the Dove upon the Apostles; and by Christs Breathing on them, when hee gave them the Holy Ghost; and by the giving of it by Imposition of Hands, are understood the signes which God hath been pleased to use, or ordain to bee used, of his promise to assist those persons in their study to Preach his Kingdome, and in their Conversation, that it might not be Scandalous, but Edifying to others.

Scandalous worship of Images.

Besides the Idolatrous Worship of Images, there is also a Scandalous Worship of them; which is also a sin; but not Idolatry For *Idolatry* is to worship by signes of an internall, and reall honour. but *Scandalous Worship*, is but Seeming Worship; and may sometimes bee joined with an inward, and hearty detestation, both of the Image, and of the Phantasticall *Dæmon*, or Idol, to [362] which it is dedicated; and proceed onely from the fear of death, or other grievous punishment; and is neverthelesse a sin in them that so worship, in case they be men whose actions are looked at by others, as lights to guide them by; because following their ways, they cannot but stumble, and fall in the way of Religion. Whereas the example of those we regard not, works not on us at all, but leaves us to our own diligence and caution; and consequently are no causes of our falling.

If therefore a Pastor lawfully called to teach and direct others, or any other, of whose knowledge there is a great opinion, doe externall honor to an Idol for fear; unlesse he make his feare, and unwillingnesse to it, as evident as the worship; he Scandalizeth his Brother, by seeming to approve Idolatry. For his Brother arguing from the action of his teacher, or of him whose knowledge he esteemeth great, concludes it to bee lawfull in it selfe. And this Scandall, is Sin, and a *Scandall given* But if one being no Pastor, nor of eminent reputation for knowledge in Christian Doctrine, doe the same; and another follow him, this is no Scandall given; for he had no cause to follow such example: but is a pretence of Scandall which hee taketh of himselfe for an excuse before men: For an unlearned man, that is in the power of an Idolatrous King, or State, if commanded on pain of death to worship before an Idoll, hee detesteth the Idoll in his heart, hee doth well; though if he had the fortitude to suffer death, rather than worship it, he should doe better But if a Pastor, who as Christs Messenger, has undertaken to teach Christs Doctrine to all nations, should doe the same, it were not onely a sinfull Scandall, in respect of other Christian mens consciences, but a perfidious forsaking of his charge.

The summe of that which I have said hitherto, concerning the Worship of Images, is this, that he that worshippeth in an Image, or any Creature, either the Matter thereof, or any Fancy of his own, which he thinketh to dwell in it; or both together; or beleeveth that such things hear his Prayers, or see his Devotions, without Ears, or Eyes, committeth Idolatry: and he that counterfeiteth such Worship for fear of punishment, if he bee a man whose example hath power amongst his Brethren, committeth a sin. But he that worshippeth the Creator of the world before such an Image, or in such a place as he hath not made, or chosen of himselfe, but taken from the commandement of Gods Word, as the Jewes did in worshipping God before the Cherubins, and before the Brazen Serpent for a time, and in, or towards the Temple of Jerusalem, which was also but for a time, committeth not Idolatry.

Now for the Worship of Saints, and Images, and Reliques, and other things at this day practised in the Church of Rome, I say they are not allowed by the Word of God, nor brought into the Church of Rome, from the Doctrine there taught; but partly left in it at [363] the first conversion of the Gentiles, and afterwards countenanced, and confirmed, and augmented by the Bishops of Rome.

Answer to the Argument from the Cherubins, and Brazen Serpent.

As for the proofs alledged out of Scripture, namely, those examples of Images appointed by God to bee set up; They were not set up for the people, or any man to worship; but that they should worship God himselfe before them, as before the Cherubins over the Ark, and the Brazen Serpent. For we read not, that the Priest, or any other did worship the Cherubins; but contrarily wee read (2 *Kings* 18. 4) that Hezekiah brake in pieces the Brazen Serpent which Moses had set up, because the People burnt incense to it. Besides, those examples are not put for our Imitation, that we also should set up Images, under pretence of worshipping God before them; because the words of the second Commandement, *Thou shalt not make to thy selfe any graven Image, &c.* distinguish between the Images that God commanded to be set up, and those which wee set up to our selves. And therefore from the Cherubins, or Brazen Serpent, to the Images of mans devising; and from the Worship commanded by God, to the Will-Worship of men, the argument is not good. This also is to bee considered, that as Hezekiah brake in pieces the Brazen Serpent, because the Jews did worship it, to the end they should doe so no more; so also Christian Soveraigns ought to break down the Images which their Subjects have been accustomed to worship, that there be no more occasion of such Idolatry. For at this day, the ignorant People, where Images are worshipped, doe really beleeve there is a Divine Power in the Images; and are told by their Pastors, that some of them have spoken, and have bled, and that miracles have been done by them, which they apprehend as done by the Saint, which they think either is the Image it self, or in it. The Israelites, when they worshipped the Calfe, did think they worshipped the God that brought them out of Egypt; and yet it was Idolatry, because they thought the Calfe either was that God, or had him in his belly. And though some man may think it impossible for people to be so stupid, as to think the Image to be God, or a Saint, or to worship it in that notion; yet it is manifest in Scripture to the contrary; where when the Golden Calfe was made, the people said, * *These are thy Gods O Israel;* and where the Images of Laban * are called his Gods. And wee see daily by experience in all sorts of People, that such men as study nothing but their food and ease, are content to beleeve any absurdity, rather than to trouble themselves to examine it; holding their faith as it were by entaile unalienable, except by an expresse and new Law.

** Exod. 32 2*
** Gen. 31 30.*

Painting of Fancies no Idolatry: but abusing them to Religious Worship is. [364]

But they inferre from some other places, that it is lawfull to paint Angels, and also God himselfe. as from Gods walking in the Garden; from Jacobs seeing God at the top of the ladder; and from other Visions, and Dreams. But Visions, and Dreams, whether naturall, or supernaturall, are but Phantasmes: and he that painteth an Image of any of them, maketh not an Image of God, but of his own Phantasm, which is, making of an Idol. I say not, that to draw a Picture after a fancy, is a Sin; but when it is drawn, to hold it for a Representation of God, is against the second Commandement, and can be of no use, but to worship. And the same may be said of the Images of Angels, and of men dead; unlesse as Monuments of friends, or of men worthy remembrance: For such use of an Image, is not Worship of the Image; but a civill honoring of the Person, not that is, but that was. But when it is done to the Image which we make of a Saint, for no other reason, but that we think he heareth our prayers, and is pleased with the honour wee doe him when dead, and without sense, wee attribute to him more than humane power, and therefore it is Idolatry.

Seeing therefore there is no authority, neither in the Law of Moses, nor in the Gospel, for the religious Worship of Images, or other Representations of God, which men set up to themselves; or for the Worship of the Image of any Creature in Heaven, or Earth, or under the Earth And whereas Christian Kings, who are living Representants of God, are not to be worshipped by their Subjects, by any act, that signifieth a greater esteem of his power, than the nature of mortall man is capable of; It cannot be imagined, that the Religious Worship now in use, was brought into the Church, by misunderstanding of the Scripture. It resteth therefore, that it was left in it, by not destroying the Images themselves, in the conversion of the Gentiles that worshipped them.

How Idolatry was left in the Church.

The cause whereof, was the immoderate esteem, and prices set upon the workmanship of them, which made the owners (though converted, from worshipping them as they had done Religiously for Dæmons) to retain them still in their houses, upon pretence of doing it in the honor of *Christ*, of the *Virgin Mary*, and of the *Apostles*, and other the Pastors of the Primitive Church; as being easie, by giving them new names, to make that an Image of the *Virgin Mary*, and of her *Sonne* our Saviour, which before perhaps was called the Image of *Venus*, and *Cupid*; and so of a *Jupiter* to make a *Barnabas*, and of *Mercury* a *Paul*, and the like. And as worldly ambition creeping by degrees into the Pastors, drew them to an endeavour of pleasing the new made Christians; and also to a liking of this kind of honour, which they also might hope for after their decease, as well as those that had already gained it: so the worshipping of the Images of Christ and his Apostles, grew more and more Idolatrous, save that somewhat after the time of Constantine, divers Emperors, and Bishops, and generall Councells observed, and opposed the unlawfulnesse thereof; but too late, or too weakly.

Canonizing of Saints.

The *Canonizing of Saints*, is another Relique of Gentilisme. It is neither a misunderstanding of Scripture, nor a new invention of the Roman Church, but a custome as ancient as the Common-wealth of *Rome* it self The first that ever was canonized at Rome, was *Romulus*, and that upon the narration of *Julius Proculus*, that swore

before the Senate, he spake with him after his death,
[365] and was assured by him, he dwelt in Heaven, and was there called *Quirinus*, and would be propitious to the State of their new City: And thereupon the Senate gave *publique testimony* of his Sanctity *Julius Cæsar*, and other Emperors after him, had the like *testimony*; that is, were Canonized for Saints; for by such testimony is CANONIZATION, now defined; and is the same with the Ἀποθέωσις of the Heathen.

The name of Pontifex. It is also from the Roman Heathen, that the Popes have received the name, and power of PONTIFEX MAXIMUS This was the name of him that in the ancient Common-wealth of Rome, had the Supreme Authority under the Senate and People, of regulating all Ceremonies, and Doctrines concerning their Religion: And when *Augustus Cæsar* changed the State into a Monarchy, he took to himselfe no more but this office, and that of Tribune of the People, (that is to say, the Supreme Power both in State, and Religion,) and the succeeding Emperors enjoyed the same But when the Emperour Constantine lived, who was the first that professed and authorized Christian Religion, it was consonant to his profession, to cause Religion to be regulated (under his authority) by the Bishop of Rome: Though it doe not appear they had so soon the name of *Pontifex*; but rather, that the succeeding Bishops took it of themselves, to countenance the power they exercised over the Bishops of the Roman Provinces. For it is not any Priviledge of St. Peter, but the Priviledge of the City of Rome, which the Emperors were alwaies willing to uphold, that gave them such authority over other Bishops; as may be evidently seen by that, that the Bishop of Constantinople, when the Emperour made that City the Seat of the Empire, pretended to bee equall to the Bishop of Rome; though at last, not without contention, the Pope carryed it, and became the *Pontifex Maximus*; but in right onely of the Emperour, and not without the bounds of the Empire; nor any where, after the Emperour had lost his power in Rome; though it were the Pope himself that took his power from him From whence wee may by the way observe that there is no place for the superiority of the Pope over other Bishops, except in the territories whereof he is himself the Civill Soveraign; and where the Emperour having Soveraign Power Civill, hath expressely chosen the Pope for the chief Pastor under himselfe, of his Christian Subjects.

Procession of Images.

The carrying about of Images in *Procession*; is another Relique of the Religion of the Greeks, and Romans. For they also carried their Idols from place to place, in a kind of Chariot, which was peculiarly dedicated to that use, which the Latines called *Thensa*, and *Vehiculum Deorum*; and the Image was placed in a frame, or Shrine, which they called *Ferculum*: And that which they called *Pompa*, is the same that now is named *Procession* According whereunto, amongst the Divine Honors which were given to *Julius Cæsar* by the Senate, this was one, that in the Pompe (or Procession) at the Circæan games, he should have *Thensam & Ferculum*, a sacred Chariot, and a Shrine; which was as much, as to be carried up and down as a God: Just as at this day the Popes are carried by Switzers under a Canopie.

Wax Candles, and Torches lighted.

To these Processions also belonged the bearing of [366]
burning Torches, and Candles, before the Images of the Gods, both amongst the Greeks, and Romans. For afterwards the Emperors of Rome received the same honor; as we read of *Caligula*, that at his reception to the Empire, he was carried from *Misenum* to *Rome*, in the midst of a throng of People, the wayes beset with Altars, and Beasts for Sacrifice, and burning *Torches*: And of *Caracalla* that was received into *Alexandria* with Incense, and with casting of Flowers, and δαδουχίαις, that is, with Torches; for Δαδοῦχοι were they that amongst the Greeks carried Torches lighted in the Processions of their Gods And in processe of time, the devout, but ignorant People, did many times honor their Bishops with the like pompe of Wax Candles, and the Images of our Saviour, and the Saints, constantly, in the Church it self And thus came in the use of Wax Candles; and was also established by some of the ancient Councells.

The Heathens had also their *Aqua Lustralis*, that is to say, *Holy Water*. The Church of Rome imitates them also in their *Holy Dayes* They had their *Bacchanalia*; and we have our *Wakes*, answering to them: They their *Saturnalia*, and we our *Carnevalls*, and Shrove-tuesdays liberty of Servants. They their Procession of *Priapus*, wee our fetching in, erection, and dancing about *May-poles*; and Dancing is one kind of Worship: They had their Procession called *Ambarvalia*; and we our Procession about the fields in the *Rogation week*. Nor do I think that these are all the Ceremonies that have been left in the Church, from the first conversion of the Gentiles: but they are all that I can for the present call to mind; and if a man would wel observe that which is delivered in the Histories, concerning the Religious Rites of the Greeks and Romanes, I doubt not but he might find many more of these old empty Bottles of Gentilisme, which the Doctors of the Romane Church, either by Negligence, or Ambition, have filled up again with the new Wine of Christianity, that will not faile in time to break them.

[367]

CHAP. XLVI.

Of DARKNESSE *from* VAIN PHILOSOPHY, *and* FABULOUS TRADITIONS

What Philosophy is.

BY PHILOSOPHY, is understood *the Knowledge acquired by Reasoning, from the Manner of the Generation of any thing, to the Properties, or from the Properties, to some possible Way of Generation of the same, to the end to bee able to produce, as far as matter, and humane force permit, such Effects, as humane life requireth* So the Geometrician, from the Construction of Figures, findeth out many Properties thereof, and from the Properties, new Ways of their Construction, by Reasoning, to the end to be able to measure Land, and Water, and for infinite other uses So the Astronomer, from the Rising, Setting, and Moving of the Sun, and Starres, in divers parts of the Heavens, findeth out the Causes of Day, and Night, and of the different Seasons of the Year, whereby he keepeth an account of Time: And the like of other Sciences.

Prudence no part of Philosophy.

By which Definition it is evident, that we are not to account as any part thereof, that originall knowledge called Experience, in which consisteth Prudence: Because it is not attained by Reasoning, but found as well in Brute Beasts, as in Man; and is but a Memory of successions of events in times past, wherein the omission of every little circumstance altering the effect, frustrateth the expectation of the most Prudent. whereas nothing is produced by Reasoning aright, but generall, eternall, and immutable Truth.

No false Doctrine is part of Philosophy:

Nor are we therefore to give that name to any false Conclusions· For he that Reasoneth aright in words he understandeth, can never conclude an Error:

No more is Revelation supernaturall.

Nor to that which any man knows by supernaturall Revelation, because it is not acquired by Reasoning·

Nor learning taken upon credit of Authors

Nor that which is gotten by Reasoning from the Authority of Books, because it is not by Reasoning from the Cause to the Effect, nor from the Effect to the Cause, and is not Knowledg, but Faith

Of the Beginnings and Progresse of Philosophy.

The faculty of Reasoning being consequent to the use of Speech, it was not possible, but that there should have been some generall Truthes found out by Reasoning, as ancient almost as Language it selfe The Savages of America, are not without some good Morall Sentences, also they have a little Arithmetick, to adde, and divide in Numbers not too great· but they are not therefore Philosophers. For as there were Plants of Corn and Wine in small quantity dispersed in the Fields and [368] Woods, before men knew their vertue, or made use of them for their nourishment, or planted them apart in Fields, and Vineyards, in which time they fed on Akorns, and drank Water: so also there have been divers true, generall, and profitable Speculations from the beginning; as being the naturall plants of humane Reason: But they were at first but few in number, men lived upon grosse Experience, there was no Method, that is to say, no Sowing, nor Planting of Knowledge by it self, apart from the Weeds, and common Plants of Errour and Conjecture And the cause of it being the want of leasure from procuring the necessities of life, and defending themselves against their neighbors, it was impossible, till the erecting of great Common-wealths, it should be otherwise. *Leasure* is the mother of *Philosophy*; and *Common-wealth*, the mother of *Peace*, and *Leasure*: Where first were great and flourishing *Cities*, there was first the study of *Philosophy*. The *Gymnosophists* of *India*, the *Magi* of *Persia*, and the *Priests* of *Chaldæa* and *Egypt*, are counted the most ancient Philosophers; and those Countreys were the most ancient of Kingdomes *Philosophy* was not risen to the *Græcians*, and other people of the West, whose *Common-wealths* (no greater perhaps then *Lucca*, or *Geneva*) had never *Peace*, but when their fears of one another were equall; nor the *Leasure* to observe any thing but one another. At length, when Warre had united many of these *Græcian* lesser Cities, into fewer, and greater; then began *Seven men*, of severall parts of *Greece*, to get the reputation of being *Wise*; some of them for *Morall* and *Politique* Sentences; and others for the learning of the *Chaldæans* and *Egyptians*, which was *Astronomy*, and *Geometry*. But we hear not yet of any *Schools* of *Philosophy*.

Of the Schools of Philosophy amongst the Athenians.

After the *Athenians* by the overthrow of the *Persian* Armies, had gotten the Dominion of the Sea; and thereby, of all the Islands, and Maritime Cities of the *Archipelago*, as well of *Asia* as *Europe*; and were grown wealthy, they that had no employment, neither at home, nor abroad, had little else to employ themselves in, but either (as St *Luke* says, *Acts* 17 21 *in telling and hearing news*, or in discoursing of *Philosophy* publiquely to the youth of the City. Every Master took some place for that purpose *Plato* in certain publique Walks called *Academia*, from one *Academus* *Aristotle* in the Walk of the Temple of *Pan*, called *Lycæum*· others in the *Stoa*, or covered Walk, wherein the Merchants Goods were brought to land· others in other places; where they spent the time of their Leasure, in teaching or in disputing of their Opinions. and some in any place, where they could get the youth of the City together to hear them talk. And this was it which *Carneades* also did at *Rome*, when he was Ambassadour: which caused *Cato* to advise the Senate to dispatch him quickly, for feare of corrupting the manners of the young men that delighted to hear him speak (as they thought) fine things.

From this it was, that the place where any of them taught, and disputed, was called *Schola*, which in their Tongue signifieth *Leasure*; and their Disputations, *Diatribæ*, that is to say, *Passing of the time*. Also the [369] Philosophers themselves had the name of their Sects, some of them from these their Schools: For they that followed *Plato*'s Doctrine, were called *Academiques*; The followers of *Aristotle*, *Peripatetiques*, from the Walk hee taught in, and those that *Zeno* taught, *Stoiques*, from the *Stoa* as if we should denominate men from *More-fields*, from *Pauls-Church*, and from the *Exchange*, because they meet there often, to prate and loyter.

Neverthelesse, men were so much taken with this custome, that in time it spread it selfe over all Europe, and the best part of Afrique; so as there were Schools publiquely erected, and maintained for Lectures, and Disputations, almost in every Common-wealth.

Of the Schools of the Jews.

There were also Schools, anciently, both before, and after the time of our Saviour, amongst the *Jews*: but they were Schools of their Law. For though they were called *Synagogues*, that is to say, Congregations of the People; yet in as much as the Law was every Sabbath day read, expounded, and disputed in them, they differed not in nature, but in name onely from Publique Schools; and were not onely in Jerusalem, but in every City of the Gentiles, where the Jews inhabited. There was such a Schoole at *Damascus*, whereinto *Paul* entred, to persecute. There were others at *Antioch*, *Iconium* and *Thessalonica*, whereinto he entred, to dispute. And such was the Synagogue of the *Libertines*, *Cyrenians*, *Alexandrians*, *Cilicians*, and those of *Asia*; that is to say, the Schoole of *Libertines*, and of *Jewes*, that were strangers in *Jerusalem*: And of this Schoole they were that disputed (*Act*. 6. 9) with *Saint Steven*.

The Schoole of the Græcians unprofitable.

But what has been the Utility of those Schools? what Science is there at this day acquired by their Readings and Disputings? That wee have of Geometry, which is the Mother of all Naturall Science, wee are not indebted for it to the Schools. *Plato* that was the best Philosopher

of the Greeks, forbad entrance into his Schoole, to all that were not already in some measure Geometricians. There were many that studied that Science to the great advantage of mankind. but there is no mention of their Schools; nor was there any Sect of Geometricians, nor did they then passe under the name of Philosophers. The naturall Philosophy of those Schools, was rather a Dream than Science, and set forth in senselesse and insignificant Language; which cannot be avoided by those that will teach Philosophy, without having first attained great knowledge in Geometry: For Nature worketh by Motion; the Wayes, and Degrees whereof cannot be known, without the knowledge of the Proportions and Properties of Lines, and Figures. Their Morall Philosophy is but a description of their own Passions For the rule of Manners, without Civill Government, is the Law of Nature, and in it, the Law Civill; that determineth what is *Honest*, and *Dishonest*; what is *Just*, and *Unjust*; and generally what is *Good*, and *Evill*: whereas they make the Rules of *Good*, and *Bad*, by their own *Liking*, and *Disliking*: By which
[370] means, in so great diversity of taste, there is nothing generally agreed on; but every one doth (as far as he dares) whatsoever seemeth good in his owne eyes, to the subversion of Common-wealth. Their *Logique* which should bee the Method of Reasoning, is nothing else but Captions of Words, and Inventions how to puzzle such as should goe about to pose them. To conclude, there is nothing so absurd, that the old Philosophers (as *Cicero* saith, who was one of them) have not some of them maintained And I beleeve that scarce any thing can be more absurdly said in naturall Philosophy, than that which now is called *Aristotles Metaphysiques*; nor more repugnant to Government, than much of that hee hath said in his *Politiques*; nor more ignorantly, than a great part of his *Ethiques*

The Schools of the Jews unprofitable.

The Schoole of the Jews, was originally a Schoole of the Law of *Moses*; who commanded (*Deut*. 31 10) that at the end of every seventh year at the Feast of the Tabernacles, it should be read to all the people, that they might hear, and learn it. Therefore the reading of the Law (which was in use after the Captivity) every Sabbath day, ought to have had no other end, but the acquainting of the people with the Commandements which they were to obey, and to expound unto them the writings of the Prophets. But it is manifest, by the many reprehensions of them by our Saviour, that they corrupted the Text of the Law with their false Commentaries, and vain Traditions; and so little understood the Prophets, that they did neither acknowledge Christ, nor the works he did; of which the Prophets prophecyed. So that by their Lectures and Disputations in their Synagogues, they turned the Doctrine of their Law into a Phantasticall kind of Philosophy, concerning the incomprehensible nature of God, and of Spirits; which they compounded of the Vain Philosophy and Theology of the Græcians, mingled with their own fancies, drawn from the obscurer places of the Scripture, and which might most easily bee wrested to their purpose; and from the Fabulous Traditions of their Ancestors

University what it is. That which is now called an *University*, is a Joyning together, and an Incorporation under one Government of many Publique Schools, in one and the same Town or City In which, the principall Schools were ordained for the three Professions, that is to say, of the Romane Religion, of the Romane Law, and of the Art of Medicine. And for the study of Philosophy it hath no otherwise place, then as a handmaid to the Romane Religion: And since the Authority of Aristotle is onely current there, that study is not properly Philosophy, (the nature whereof dependeth not on Authors,) but Aristotelity. And for Geometry, till of very late times it had no place at all; as being subservient to nothing but rigide Truth. And if any man by the ingenuity of his owne nature, had attained to any degree of perfection therein, hee was commonly thought a Magician, and his Art Diabolicall.

[371] *Errors brought into Religion from Aristotles Metaphysiques.* Now to descend to the particular Tenets of Vain Philosophy, derived to the Universities, and thence into the Church, partly from Aristotle, partly from Blindnesse of understanding; I shall first consider their Principles. There is a certain *Philosophia prima*, on which all other Philosophy ought to depend, and consisteth principally,

in right limiting of the significations of such Appellations, or Names, as are of all others the most Universall Which Limitations serve to avoid ambiguity, and æquivocation in Reasoning; and are commonly called Definitions; such as are the Definitions of Body, Time, Place, Matter, Forme, Essence, Subject, Substance, Accident, Power, Act, Finite, Infinite, Quantity, Quality, Motion, Action, Passion, and divers others, necessary to the explaining of a mans Conceptions concerning the Nature and Generation of Bodies The Explication (that is, the setling of the meaning) of which, and the like Terms, is commonly in the Schools called *Metaphysiques*; as being a part of the Philosophy of Aristotle, which hath that for title. but it is in another sense; for there it signifieth as much, as *Books written, or placed after his naturall Philosophy*: But the Schools take them for *Books of supernaturall Philosophy*: for the word *Metaphysiques* will bear both these senses. And indeed that which is there written, is for the most part so far from the possibility of being understood, and so repugnant to naturall Reason, that whosoever thinketh there is any thing to bee understood by it, must needs think it supernaturall.

Errors concerning Abstract Essences

From these Metaphysiques, which are mingled with the Scripture to make Schoole Divinity, wee are told, there be in the world certain Essences separated from Bodies, which they call *Abstract Essences, and Substantiall Formes*. For the Interpreting of which *Jargon*, there is need of somewhat more than ordinary attention in this place Also I ask pardon of those that are not used to this kind of Discourse, for applying my selfe to those that are. The World, (I mean not the Earth onely, that denominates the Lovers of it *Worldly men*, but the *Universe*, that is, the whole masse of all things that are) is Corporeall, that is to say, Body; and hath the dimensions of Magnitude, namely, Length, Bredth, and Depth: also every part of Body, is likewise Body, and hath the like dimensions, and consequently every part of the Universe, is Body, and that which is not Body, is no part of the Universe And because the Universe is All, that which is no part of it, is *Nothing*; and consequently *no where*. Nor does it follow from hence, that Spirits are *nothing*: for they have dimensions, and are therefore really *Bodies*; though that name in common Speech be given to such Bodies onely, as are visible, or palpable; that is, that have some degree of Opacity· But for Spirits, they call them Incorporeall, which is a name of more honour, and may therefore with more piety bee attributed to God himselfe, in whom wee consider not what Attribute expresseth best his Nature, which is Incomprehensible, but what best expresseth our desire to honour Him.

To know now upon what grounds they say there be [372] *Essences Abstract*, or *Substantiall Formes*, wee are to consider what those words do properly signifie. The use of Words, is to register to our selves, and make manifest to others the Thoughts and Conceptions of our Minds Of which Words, some are the names of the Things conceived; as the names of all sorts of Bodies, that work upon the Senses, and leave an Impression in the Imagination Others are the names of the Imaginations themselves; that is to say, of those Ideas, or mentall Images we have of all things wee see, or remember. And others againe are names of Names, or of different sorts of Speech· As *Universall, Plurall, Singular*, are the names of Names; and *Definition, Affirmation, Negation, True, False, Syllogisme, Interrogation, Promise, Covenant*, are the names of certain Forms of Speech. Others serve to shew the Consequence, or Repugnance of one name to another; as when one saith, *A Man is a Body*, hee intendeth that the name of *Body* is necessarily consequent to the name of *Man*; as being but severall names of the same thing, *Man*, which Consequence is signified by coupling them together with the word *Is*. And as wee use the Verbe *Is*, so the Latines use their Verbe *Est*, and the Greeks their Ἔστι through all its Declinations. Whether all other Nations of the world have in their severall languages a word that answereth to it, or not, I cannot tell; but I am sure they have not need of it: For the placing of two names in order may serve to signifie their Consequence, if it were the custome, (for Custome is it, that give words their force,) as well as the words *Is*, or *Bee*, or *Are*, and the like.

And if it were so, that there were a Language without any Verb answerable to *Est*, or *Is*, or *Bee*, yet the men that used it would bee not a jot the lesse capable of Inferring, Concluding, and of all kind of Reasoning, than were the Greeks, and Latines But what then would become of these Terms, of *Entity*, *Essence*, *Essentiall*, *Essentiality*, that are derived from it, and of many more that depend on these, applyed as most commonly they are? They are therefore no Names of Things, but Signes, by which wee make known, that wee conceive the Consequence of one name or Attribute to another. as when we say, *a Man, is, a living Body*, wee mean not that the *Man* is one thing, the *Living Body* another, and the *Is*, or *Beeing* a third· but that the *Man*, and the *Living Body*, is the same thing, because the Consequence, *If hee bee a Man, hee is a living Body*, is a true Consequence, signified by that word Is Therefore, *to bee a Body, to Walke, to bee Speaking, to Live, to See*, and the like Infinitives; also *Corporeity, Walking, Speaking, Life, Sight*, and the like, that signifie just the same, are the names of *Nothing*; as I have elsewhere more amply expressed.

But to what purpose (may some man say) is such subtilty in a work of this nature, where I pretend to nothing but what is necessary to the doctrine of Government and Obedience? It is to this purpose, that men
[373] may no longer suffer themselves to be abused, by them, that by this doctrine of *Separated Essences*, built on the Vain Philosophy of Aristotle, would fright them from Obeying the Laws of their Countrey, with empty names, as men fright Birds from the Corn with an empty doublet, a hat, and a crooked stick For it is upon this ground, that when a Man is dead and buried, they say his Soule (that is his Life) can walk separated from his Body, and is seen by night amongst the graves. Upon the same ground they say, that the Figure, and Colour, and Tast of a peece of Bread, has a being, there, where they say there is no Bread· And upon the same ground they say, that Faith, and Wisdome, and other Vertues are sometimes *powred* into a man, sometimes *blown* into him from Heaven; as if the Vertuous, and their Vertues could be

asunder; and a great many other things that serve to lessen the dependance of Subjects on the Soveraign Power of their Countrey. For who will endeavour to obey the Laws, if he expect Obedience to be Powred or Blown into him? Or who will not obey a Priest, that can make God, rather than his Soveraign, nay than God himselfe? Or who, that is in fear of Ghosts, will not bear great respect to those that can make the Holy Water, that drives them from him? And this shall suffice for an example of the Errors, which are brought into the Church, from the *Entities*, and *Essences* of Aristotle: which it may be he knew to be false Philosophy; but writ it as a thing consonant to, and corroborative of their Religion; and fearing the fate of Socrates.

Being once fallen into this Error of *Separated Essences*, they are thereby necessarily involved in many other absurdities that follow it. For seeing they will have these Forms to be reall, they are obliged to assign them *some place*. But because they hold them Incorporeall, without all dimension of Quantity, and all men know that Place is Dimension, and not to be filled, but by that which is Corporeall; they are driven to uphold their credit with a distinction, that they are not indeed any where *Circumscriptive*, but *Definitive*: Which Terms being meer Words, and in this occasion insignificant, passe onely in Latine, that the vanity of them may bee concealed. For the Circumscription of a thing, is nothing else but the Determination, or Defining of its Place; and so both the Terms of the Distinction are the same. And in particular, of the Essence of a Man, which (they say) is his Soule, they affirm it, to be All of it in his little Finger, and All of it in every other Part (how small soever) of his Body; and yet no more Soule in the Whole Body, than in any one of those Parts. Can any man think that God is served with such absurdities? And yet all this is necessary to beleeve, to those that will beleeve the Existence of an Incorporeall Soule, Separated from the Body.

And when they come to give account, how an Incorporeall Substance can be capable of Pain, and be tormented in the fire of Hell, or Purgatory, they have nothing at all to answer, but that it cannot be known how fire can burn Soules.

[374] Again, whereas Motion is change of Place, and Incorporeall Substances are not capable of Place, they are troubled to make it seem possible, how a Soule can goe hence, without the Body to Heaven, Hell, or Purgatory; and how the Ghosts of men (and I may adde of their clothes which they appear in) can walk by night in Churches, Church-yards, and other places of Sepulture. To which I know not what they can answer, unlesse they will say, they walke, *definitivè*, not *circumscriptivè*, or *spiritually*, not *temporally*: for such egregious distinctions are equally applicable to any difficulty whatsoever.

Nunc-stans. For the meaning of *Eternity*, they will not have it to be an Endlesse Succession of Time; for then they should not be able to render a reason how Gods Will, and Præordaining of things to come, should not be before his Præscience of the same, as the Efficient Cause before the Effect, or Agent before the Action; nor of many other their bold opinions concerning the Incomprehensible Nature of God. But they will teach us, that Eternity is the Standing still of the Present Time, a *Nunc-stans* (as the Schools call it;) which neither they, nor any else understand, no more than they would a *Hic-stans* for an Infinite greatnesse of Place.

One Body in many places, and many Bodies in one place at once. And whereas men divide a Body in their thought, by numbring parts of it, and in numbring those parts, number also the parts of the Place it filled; it cannot be, but in making many parts, wee make also many places of those parts; whereby there cannot bee conceived in the mind of any man, more, or fewer parts, than there are places for: yet they will have us beleeve, that by the Almighty power of God, one body may be at one and the same time in many places; and many bodies at one and the same time in one place: As if it were an acknowledgment of the Divine Power, to say, that which is, is not; or that which has been, has not been. And these are but a small part of the Incongruities they are forced to, from their disputing Philosophically, in stead of admiring, and adoring of the Divine and Incomprehensible Nature; whose Attributes cannot signifie what he is, but ought to signifie our desire to honour him, with the best Appellations we can think on. But they that venture to reason of his Nature, from these Attributes of Honour, losing their understanding in the very first attempt, fall from one Inconvenience into another, without end, and without number ; in the same manner, as when a man ignorant of the Ceremonies of Court, comming into the presence of a greater Person than he is used to speak to, and stumbling at his entrance, to save himselfe from falling, lets slip his Cloake ; to recover his Cloake, lets fall his Hat , and with one disorder after another, discovers his astonishment and rusticity.

Absurdities in naturall Philosophy, as Gravity the Cause of Heavinesse.

Then for *Physiques*, that is, the knowledge of the subordinate, and secundary causes of naturall events ; they render none at all, but empty words. If you desire to know why some kind of bodies sink naturally downwards toward the Earth, and others goe naturally from it , The Schools will tell you out of Aristotle, that the bodies | that sink downwards, are *Heavy* ; and that this Heavinesse is it that causes them to descend But if [375] you ask what they mean by *Heavinesse*, they will define it to bee an endeavour to goe to the center of the Earth : so that the cause why things sink downward, is an Endeavour to be below : which is as much as to say, that bodies descend, or ascend, because they doe. Or they will tell you the center of the Earth is the place of Rest, and Conservation for Heavy things , and therefore they endeavour to be there : As if Stones, and Metalls had a desire, or could discern the place they would bee at, as Man does , or loved Rest, as Man does not ; or that a peece of Glasse were lesse safe in the Window, than falling into the Street.

Quantity put into Body already made.

If we would know why the same Body seems greater (without adding to it) one time, than another ; they say, when it seems lesse, it is *Condensed* , when greater, *Rarefied*. What is that *Condensed*, and *Rarefied* ? Condensed, is when there is in the very same Matter, lesse Quantity than before ; and Rarefied, when more. As if there could be Matter, that had not some determined Quantity ; when Quantity is nothing else but the

Determination of Matter; that is to say of Body, by which we say one Body is greater, or lesser than another, by thus, or thus much. Or as if a Body were made without any Quantity at all, and that afterwards more, or lesse were put into it, according as it is intended the Body should be more, or lesse Dense.

Powring in of Soules.

For the cause of the Soule of Man, they say, *Creatur Infundendo,* and *Creando Infunditur*: that is, *It is Created by Powring it in,* and *Powred in by Creation.*

Ubiquity of Apparition.

For the Cause of Sense, an ubiquity of *Species*, that is, of the *Shews* or *Apparitions* of objects; which when they be Apparitions to the Eye, is *Sight*; when to the Eare, *Hearing*, to the Palate, *Tast*, to the Nostrill, *Smelling*, and to the rest of the Body, *Feeling*.

Will, the Cause of Willing.

For cause of the Will, to doe any particular action, which is called *Volitio,* they assign the Faculty, that is to say, the Capacity in generall, that men have, to will sometimes one thing, sometimes another, which is called *Voluntas*, making the *Power* the cause of the *Act*. As if one should assign for cause of the good or evill Acts of men, their Ability to doe them.

Ignorance an occult Cause.

And in many occasions they put for cause of Naturall events, their own Ignorance, but disguised in other words. As when they say, Fortune is the cause of things contingent, that is, of things whereof they know no cause. And as when they attribute many Effects to *occult qualities*; that is, qualities not known to them, and therefore also (as they thinke) to no Man else. And to *Sympathy, Antipathy, Antiperistasis, Specificall Qualities,* and other like Termes, which signifie neither the Agent that produceth them, nor the Operation by which they are produced.

[376] If such *Metaphysiques,* and *Physiques* as this, be not *Vain Philosophy,* there was never any; nor needed St Paul to give us warning to avoid it.

One makes the things incongruent, another the Incongruity.

And for their Morall, and Civill Philosophy, it hath the same, or greater absurdities. If a man doe an action of Injustice, that is to say, an action contrary to the Law, God they say is the prime cause of the Law, and also the prime cause of that, and all other Actions; but no cause at all of the Injustice; which is the Inconformity of the Action to the Law. This is Vain Philosophy A man might as well say, that one man maketh both a streight line, and a crooked, and another maketh their Incongruity. And such is the Philosophy of all men that resolve of their Conclusions, before they know their Premises; pretending to comprehend, that which is Incomprehensible; and of Attributes of Honour to make Attributes of Nature, as this distinction was made to maintain the Doctrine of Free-Will, that is, of a Will of man, not subject to the Will of God.

Private Appetite the rule of Publique good:

Aristotle, and other Heathen Philosophers define Good, and Evill, by the Appetite of men; and well enough, as long as we consider them governed every one by his own Law For in the condition of men that have no other Law but their own Appetites, there can be no generall Rule of Good, and Evill Actions. But in a Common-wealth this measure is false Not the Appetite of Private men, but the Law, which is the Will and Appetite of the State is the measure And yet is this Doctrine still practised; and men judge the Goodnesse, or Wickednesse of their own, and of other mens actions, and of the actions of the Common-wealth it selfe, by their own Passions, and no man calleth Good or Evill, but that which is so in his own eyes, without any regard at all to the Publique Laws; except onely Monks, and Friers, that are bound by Vow to that simple obedience to their Superiour, to which every Subject ought to think himself bound by the Law of Nature to the Civill Soveraign. And this private measure of Good, is a Doctrine, not onely Vain, but also Pernicious to the Publique State.

And that lawfull Marriage is Unchastity.

It is also Vain and false Philosophy, to say the work of Marriage is repugnant to Chastity, or Continence, and by consequence to make them Morall Vices, as they doe, that pretend Chastity, and Continence, for the ground of denying Marriage to the Clergy. For they confesse it is no more, but a Constitution of the Church, that requireth in those holy Orders that continually attend the Altar, and administration of the Eucharist, a continuall Abstinence from women, under the name of continuall Chastity, Continence, and Purity. Therefore they call the lawfull use of Wives, want of Chastity, and Continence; and so make Marriage a Sin, or at least a thing so impure, and unclean, as to render a man unfit for the Altar. If the Law were made because the use of Wives is Incontinence, and contrary to Chastity, then all Marriage is vice: If because it is a thing too impure, and unclean for a man consecrated to God, much more should other naturall, necessary, and daily works which [377] all men doe, render men unworthy to bee Priests, because they are more unclean.

But the secret foundation of this prohibition of Marriage of Priests, is not likely to have been laid so slightly, as upon such errours in Morall Philosophy; nor yet upon the preference of single life, to the estate of Matrimony, which proceeded from the wisdome of St. Paul, who perceived how inconvenient a thing it was, for those that in those times of persecution were Preachers of the Gospel, and forced to fly from one countrey to another, to be clogged with the care of wife and children; but upon the designe of the Popes, and Priests of after times, to make themselves the Clergy, that is to say, sole Heirs of the Kingdome of God in this world; to which it was necessary to take from them the use of Marriage, because our Saviour saith, that at the coming of his Kingdome the Children of God *shall neither Marry, nor bee given in Marriage, but shall bee as the Angels in heaven*, that is to say, Spirituall. Seeing then they had taken on them the name of Spirituall, to have allowed themselves (when there was no need) the propriety of Wives, had been an Incongruity.

And that all Government but Popular, is Tyranny:

From Aristotles Civill Philosophy, they have learned, to call all manner of Common-wealths but the Popular, (such as was at that time the state of Athens,) *Tyranny*. All Kings they called Tyrants; and the Aristocracy of the thirty Governours set up there by the Lacedemonians that subdued them, the thirty Tyrants. As also to call the condition of the people under the Democracy, *Liberty*. A *Tyrant* originally signified no more simply, but a *Monarch*. But when afterwards in most parts of Greece that kind of government was abolished, the name began to signifie, not onely the thing it did before, but with it, the hatred which the Popular States bare towards it: As also the name of King became odious after the deposing of the Kings in Rome, as being a thing naturall to all men, to conceive some great Fault to be signified in any Attribute, that is given in despight, and to a great Enemy. And when the same men shall be displeased with those that have the administration of the Democracy, or Aristocracy, they are not to seek for disgracefull names to expresse their anger in, but call readily the one *Anarchy*, and the other, *Oligarchy*, or the *Tyranny of a Few*. And that which offendeth the People, is no other thing, but that they are governed, not as every one of them would himselfe, but as the Publique Representant, be it one Man, or an Assembly of men thinks fit, that is, by an Arbitrary government: for which they give evill names to their Superiors, never knowing (till perhaps a little after a Civill warre) that without such Arbitrary government, such Warre must be perpetuall, and that it is Men, and Arms, not Words, and Promises, that make the Force and Power of the Laws.

That not Men, but Law governs. [378]

And therefore this is another Errour of Aristotles Politiques, that in a wel ordered Common-wealth, not Men should govern, but the Laws What man, that has his naturall Senses, though he can neither write nor read, does not find himself governed by them he fears, and beleeves can kill or hurt him when he obeyeth not? or that beleeves the Law can hurt him; that is, Words, and Paper, without the Hands, and Swords of men? And this is of the number of pernicious Errors. for they induce men, as oft as they like not their Governours, to adhære to those that call them Tyrants, and to think it lawfull to raise warre against them: And yet they are many times cherished from the Pulpit, by the Clergy.

Laws over the Conscience.

There is another Errour in their Civill Philosophy (which they never learned of Aristotle, nor Cicero, nor any other of the Heathen,) to extend the power of the Law, which is the Rule of Actions onely, to the very Thoughts, and Consciences of men, by Examination, and *Inquisition* of what they Hold, notwithstanding the Conformity of their Speech and Actions: By which, men are either punished for answering the truth of their thoughts, or constrained to answer an untruth for fear of punishment. It is true, that the Civill Magistrate intending to employ a Minister in the charge of Teaching may enquire of him, if hee bee content to Preach such, and such Doctrines; and in case of refusall, may deny him the employment But to force him to accuse himselfe of Opinions, when his Actions are not by Law forbidden, is against the Law of Nature, and especially in them, who teach, that a man shall bee damned to Eternall and extream torments, if he die in a false opinion concerning an Article of the Christian Faith For who is there, that knowing there is so great danger in an error, whom the naturall care of himself, compelleth not to hazard his Soule upon his own judgement, rather than that of any other man that is unconcerned in his damnation?

Private Interpretation of Law

For a Private man, without the Authority of the Common-wealth, that is to say, without permission from the Representant thereof, to Interpret the Law by his own Spirit, is another Error in the Politiques, but not drawn from Aristotle, nor from any other of the Heathen Philosophers. For none of them deny, but that in the Power of making Laws, is comprehended also the Power of Explaining them when there is need And are not the Scriptures, in all places where they are Law, made Law by the Authority of the Common-wealth, and consequently, a part of the Civill Law?

Of the same kind it is also, when any but the Soveraign restraineth in any man that power which the Common-wealth hath not restrained, as they do, that impropriate the Preaching of the Gospell to one certain Order of men, where the Laws have left it free. If the State give me leave to preach, or teach; that is, if it forbid me not, no man can forbid me. If I find my selfe amongst the Idolaters of America, shall I that am a Christian, though not in Orders, think it a sin to preach Jesus Christ, till I have received Orders from Rome? or when I have preached, shall not I answer their doubts, and expound the Scriptures to them, that is, shall I not Teach? But for this may some say, as also for administring to them the Sacraments, the necessity shall be [379] esteemed for a sufficient Mission, which is true But this is true also, that for whatsoever, a dispensation is due for the necessity, for the same there needs no dispensation, when there is no Law that forbids it. Therefore to deny these Functions to those, to whom the Civill Soveraigne hath not denyed them, is a taking away of a lawfull Liberty, which is contrary to the Doctrine of Civill Government

Language of Schoole-Divines.

More examples of Vain Philosophy, brought into Religion by the Doctors of Schoole-Divinity, might be produced, but other men may if they please observe them of themselves I shall onely adde this, that the Writings of Schoole-Divines, are nothing else for the most part, but insignificant Traines of strange and barbarous words, or words otherwise used, then in the common use of the Latine tongue; such as would pose Cicero, and Varro, and all the Grammarians of ancient Rome. Which if any man would see proved, let him (as I have said once before) see whether he can translate any Schoole-Divine into any of the Modern tongues, as French, English, or any other copious language. for that which cannot in most of these be made Intelligible, is not Intelligible in the Latine. Which Insignificancy of language, though I cannot note it for false Philosophy; yet it hath a quality, not onely to hide the Truth, but also to make men think they have it, and desist from further search

Errors from Tradition.

Lastly, for the Errors brought in from false, or uncertain History, what is all the Legend of fictitious Miracles, in the lives of the Saints, and all the Histories of Apparitions, and Ghosts, alledged by the Doctors of the Romane Church, to make good their Doctrines of Hell, and Purgatory, the power of Exorcisme, and other Doctrines which have no warrant, neither in Reason, nor Scripture; as also all those Traditions which they call the unwritten Word of God, but old Wives Fables? Whereof, though they find dispersed somewhat in the Writings of the ancient Fathers; yet those Fathers were men, that might too easily beleeve false reports; and the producing of their opinions for testimony of the truth of what they beleeved, hath no other force with them that (according to the Counsell of St. *John* 1 Epist. chap. 4. verse 1) examine Spirits, than in all things that concern the power of the Romane Church, (the abuse whereof either they suspected not, or had benefit by it,) to discredit their testimony, in respect of too rash beleef of reports; which the most sincere men, without great knowledge of naturall causes, (such as the Fathers were) are commonly the most subject to For naturally, the best men are the least suspicious of fraudulent purposes. Gregory the Pope, and S. Bernard have somewhat of Apparitions of Ghosts, that said they were in Purgatory, and so has our Beda: but no where, I beleeve, but by report from others But if they, or any other, relate any such stories of their own knowledge, they shall not thereby confirm the more such vain reports; but discover their own Infirmity, or Fraud.

[380] *Suppression of Reason.* With the Introduction of False, we may joyn also the suppression of True Philosophy, by such men, as neither by lawfull authority, nor sufficient study, are competent Judges of the truth. Our own Navigations make manifest, and all men learned in humane Sciences, now acknowledge there are Antipodes · And every day it appeareth more and more, that Years, and Dayes are determined by Motions of the Earth. Neverthelesse, men that have in their Writings but supposed such Doctrine, as an occasion to lay open the reasons for, and against it, have been punished for it by Authority Ecclesiasticall. But what reason is there for it? Is it because such opinions are contrary to true Religion? that cannot be, if they be true Let therefore the truth be first examined by competent Judges, or confuted by them that pretend to know the contrary Is it because they be contrary to the Religion established? Let them be silenced by the Laws of those, to whom the Teachers of them are subject, that is, by the Laws Civill · For disobedience may lawfully be punished in them, that against the Laws teach even true Philosophy. Is it because they tend to disorder in Government, as countenancing Rebellion, or Sedition? then let them be silenced, and the Teachers punished by vertue of his Power to whom the care of the

Publique quiet is committed; which is the Authority Civill For whatsoever Power Ecclesiastiques take upon themselves (in any place where they are subject to the State) in their own Right, though they call it Gods Right, is but Usurpation.

CHAP. XLVII. [381]

Of the BENEFIT *that proceedeth from such Darknesse, and to whom it accreweth.*

He that receiveth Benefit by a Fact, is presumed to be the Author.

Cicero maketh honorable mention of one of the *Cassii*, a severe Judge amongst the Romans, for a custome he had, in Criminall causes, (when the testimony of the witnesses was not sufficient,) to ask the Accusers, *Cui bono*, that is to say, what Profit, Honor, or other Contentment, the accused obtained, or expected by the Fact For amongst Præsumptions, there is none that so evidently declareth the Author, as doth the BENEFIT of the Action. By the same rule I intend in this place to examine, who they may be, that have possessed the People so long in this part of Christendome, with these Doctrines, contrary to the Peaceable Societies of Mankind.

That the Church Militant is the Kingdome of God, was first taught by the Church of Rome.

And first, to this Error, *that the present Church now Militant on Earth, is the Kingdome of God*, (that is, the Kingdome of Glory, or the Land of Promise; not the Kingdome of Grace, which is but a Promise of the Land,) are annexed these worldly Benefits, First, that the Pastors, and Teachers of the Church, are entitled thereby, as Gods Publique Ministers, to a Right of Governing the Church; and consequently (because the Church, and Common-wealth are the same Persons) to be Rectors, and Governours of the Common-wealth. By this title it is, that the Pope prevailed with the subjects of all Christian Princes, to beleeve, that to disobey him, was to disobey Christ himselfe; and in all differences between him and other Princes, (charmed with the word *Power Spirituall*,) to abandon their lawfull Soveraigns; which is in effect an universall Monarchy over all Christendome. For though they were first invested in the right of being

Supreme Teachers of Christian Doctrine, by, and under Christian Emperors, within the limits of the Romane Empire (as is acknowledged by themselves) by the title of *Pontifex Maximus*, who was an Officer subject to the Civill State, yet after the Empire was divided, and dissolved, it was not hard to obtrude upon the people already subject to them, another Title, namely, the Right of St Peter; not onely to save entire their pretended Power; but also to extend the same over the same Christian Provinces, though no more united in the Empire of Rome This Benefit of an Universall Monarchy, (considering the desire of men to bear Rule) is a sufficient Presumption, that the Popes that pretended to it, and for a long time enjoyed it, were the Authors of the Doctrine, by which it was obtained, namely, that the Church now on Earth, is the Kingdome of Christ. For that granted, it must be understood, that Christ hath some Lieutenant amongst us, by whom we are to be told what are his Commandements.

[382] After that certain Churches had renounced this universall Power of the Pope, one would expect in reason, that the Civill Soveraigns in all those Churches, should have recovered so much of it, as (before they had unadvisedly let it goe) was their own Right, and in their own hands. And in England it was so in effect, saving that they, by whom the Kings administred the Government of Religion, by maintaining their imployment to be in Gods Right, seemed to usurp, if not a Supremacy, yet an Independency on the Civill Power and they but seemed to usurpe it, in as much as they acknowledged a Right in the King, to deprive them of the Exercise of their Functions at his pleasure.

And maintained also by the Presbytery.

But in those places where the Presbytery took that Office, though many other Doctrines of the Church of Rome were forbidden to be taught; yet this Doctrine, that the Kingdome of Christ is already come, and that it began at the Resurrection of our Saviour, was still retained But *cui bono*? What Profit did they expect from it? The same which the Popes expected: to have a Soveraign Power over the People For what is it for men to excommunicate their lawful King, but to keep him from all places of Gods publique Service in his own Kingdom? and with force to resist him, when he with force endeavoureth to correct them? Or what is it, without Authority from the Civill Soveraign, to excommunicate any person, but to take from him his Lawfull Liberty, that is, to usurpe an unlawfull Power over their Brethren? The Authors therefore of this Darknesse in Religion, are the Romane, and the Presbyterian Clergy

Infallibility. To this head, I referre also all those Doctrines, that serve them to keep the possession of this spirituall Soveraignty after it is gotten. As first, that the *Pope in his publique capacity cannot erre.* For who is there, that beleeving this to be true, will not readily obey him in whatsoever he commands?

Subjection of Bishops Secondly, that all other Bishops, in what Common-wealth soever, have not their Right, neither immediately from God, nor mediately from their Civill Soveraigns, but from the Pope, is a Doctrine, by which there comes to be in every Christian Common-wealth many potent men, (for so are Bishops,) that have their dependance on the Pope, and owe obedience to him, though he be a forraign Prince; by which means he is able, (as he hath done many times) to raise a Civill War against the State that submits not it self to be governed according to his pleasure and Interest.

Exemptions of the Clergy. Thirdly, the exemption of these, and of all other Priests, and of all Monkes, and Fryers, from the Power of the Civill Laws For by this means, there is a great part of every Common-wealth, that enjoy the benefit of the Laws, and are protected by the Power of the Civill State, which neverthelesse pay no part of the Publique expence; nor are lyable to the penalties, as other Subjects, due to their crimes, and consequently, stand not in fear of any man, but the Pope, and adhere to him onely, to uphold his universall Monarchy.

The names of Sacerdotes *and Sacrifices.* Fourthly, the giving to their Priests (which is no more in the New Testament but Presbyters, that is, Elders) the name of *Sacerdotes*, | that is, Sacrificers, which was [383] the title of the Civill Soveraign, and his publique Ministers, amongst the Jews, whilest God was their King. Also, the making the Lords Supper a Sacrifice, serveth to make the People beleeve the Pope hath the same power over all Christians, that Moses and Aaron had over the Jews, that is to say, all Power, both Civill and Ecclesiasticall, as the High Priest then had.

The Sacramentation of Marriage Fiftly, the teaching that Matrimony is a Sacrament, giveth to the Clergy the Judging of the lawfulnesse of Marriages, and thereby, of what Children are Legitimate, and consequently, of the Right of Succession to hæreditary Kingdomes.

The single life of Priests Sixtly, the Deniall of Marriage to Priests, serveth to assure this Power of the Pope over Kings. For if a King be a Priest, he cannot Marry, and transmit his Kingdome to his Posterity; If he be not a Priest, then the Pope pretendeth this Authority Ecclesiasticall over him, and over his people.

Auricular Confession. Seventhly, from Auricular Confession, they obtain, for the assurance of their Power, better intelligence of the designs of Princes, and great persons in the Civill State, than these can have of the designs of the State Ecclesiasticall.

Canonization of Saints, and declaring of Martyrs. Eighthly, by the Canonization of Saints, and declaring who are Martyrs, they assure their Power, in that they induce simple men into an obstinacy against the Laws and Commands of their Civill Soveraigns even to death, if by the Popes excommunication, they be declared Heretiques or Enemies to the Church; that is, (as they interpret it,) to the Pope.

Transubstantiation, Pennance, Absolution. Ninthly, they assure the same, by the Power they ascribe to every Priest, of making Christ; and by the Power of ordaining Pennance; and of Remitting, and Retaining of sins.

Purgatory, Indulgences, Externall works. Tenthly, by the Doctrine of Purgatory, of Justification by externall works, and of Indulgences, the Clergy is enriched.

Dæmonology and Exorcism. Eleventhly, by their Dæmonology, and the use of Exorcisme, and other things appertaining thereto, they keep (or thinke they keep) the People more in awe of their Power.

School-Divinity. Lastly, the Metaphysiques, Ethiques, and Politiques of Aristotle, the frivolous Distinctions, barbarous Terms, and obscure Language of the Schoolmen, taught in the Universities, (which have been all erected and regulated by the Popes Authority,) serve them to keep these Errors from being detected, and to make men mistake the *Ignis fatuus* of Vain Philosophy, for the Light of the Gospell.

The Authors of spirituall Darknesse, who they be.

To these, if they sufficed not, might be added other of their dark Doctrines, the profit whereof redoundeth manifestly, to the setting up of an unlawfull Power over the lawfull Soveraigns of Christian People; or for the sustaining of the same, when it is set up; or to the worldly Riches, Honour, and Authority of those that sustain it. And therefore by the aforesaid rule, of *Cui bono,* we may justly pronounce for the Authors of all this Spirituall Darknesse, the Pope, and Roman Clergy, and all those besides that endeavour to settle in the mindes of men this erroneous Doctrine, that the Church now on Earth, is that Kingdome of God mentioned in the Old and New Testament.

But the Emperours, and other Christian Soveraigns, [384]
under whose Government these Errours, and the like encroachments of Ecclesiastiques upon their Office, at first crept in, to the disturbance of their possessions, and of the tranquillity of their Subjects, though they suffered the same for want of foresight of the Sequel, and of insight into the designs of their Teachers, may neverthelesse bee esteemed accessaries to their own, and the Publique dammage: For without their Authority there could at first no seditious Doctrine have been publiquely preached. I say they might have hindred the same in the beginning: But when the people were once possessed by those spirituall men, there was no humane remedy to be applyed, that any man could invent. And for the remedies that God should provide, who never faileth in his good time to destroy all the Machinations of men against the Truth, wee are to attend his good pleasure, that suffereth many times the prosperity of his enemies, together with their ambition, to grow to such a height, as the violence thereof openeth the eyes, which the warinesse of their predecessours had before sealed up, and makes men by too much grasping

let goe all, as Peters net was broken, by the struggling of too great a multitude of Fishes; whereas the Impatience of those, that strive to resist such encroachment, before their Subjects eyes were opened, did but encrease the power they resisted. I doe not therefore blame the Emperour Frederick for holding the stirrop to our countryman Pope Adrian, for such was the disposition of his subjects then, as if hee had not done it, hee was not likely to have succeeded in the Empire But I blame those, that in the beginning, when their power was entire, by suffering such Doctrines to be forged in the Universities of their own Dominions, have holden the Stirrop to all the succeeding Popes, whilest they mounted into the Thrones of all Christian Soveraigns, to ride, and tire, both them, and their people, at their pleasure.

But as the Inventions of men are woven, so also are they ravelled out; the way is the same, but the order is inverted. The web begins at the first Elements of Power, which are Wisdom, Humility, Sincerity, and other vertues of the Apostles, whom the people converted, obeyed, out of Reverence, not by Obligation: Their Consciences were free, and their Words and Actions subject to none but the Civill Power. Afterwards the Presbyters (as the Flocks of Christ encreased) assembling to consider what they should teach, and thereby obliging themselves to teach nothing against the Decrees of their Assemblies, made it to be thought the people were thereby obliged to follow their Doctrine, and when they refused, refused to keep them company, (that was then called Excommunication,) not as being Infidels, but as being disobedient. And this was the first knot upon their Liberty And the number of Presbyters encreasing, the Presbyters of the chief City or Province, got themselves an authority over the Parochiall Presbyters, and appropriated to themselves the names of Bishops: And this
[385] was a second knot on Christian Liberty. Lastly, the Bishop of Rome, in regard of the Imperiall City, took upon him an Authority (partly by the wills of the Emperours themselves, and by the title of *Pontifex Maximus*, and at last when the Emperours were grown weak,

by the priviledges of St Peter) over all other Bishops of the Empire · Which was the third and last knot, and the whole *Synthesis* and *Construction* of the Pontificall Power

And therefore the *Analysis*, or *Resolution* is by the same way; but beginneth with the knot that was last tyed, as wee may see in the dissolution of the præter-politicall Church Government in England. First, the Power of the Popes was dissolved totally by Queen Elizabeth; and the Bishops, who before exercised their Functions in Right of the Pope, did afterwards exercise the same in Right of the Queen and her Successours; though by retaining the phrase of *Jure Divino*, they were thought to demand it by immediate Right from God · And so was untyed the first knot After this, the Presbyterians lately in England obtained the putting down of Episcopacy: And so was the second knot dissolved · And almost at the same time, the Power was taken also from the Presbyterians And so we are reduced to the Independency of the Primitive Christians to follow Paul, or Cephas, or Apollos, every man as he liketh best: Which, if it be without contention, and without measuring the Doctrine of Christ, by our affection to the Person of his Minister, (the fault which the Apostle reprehended in the Corinthians,) is perhaps the best: First, because there ought to be no Power over the Consciences of men, but of the Word it selfe, working Faith in every one, not alwayes according to the purpose of them that Plant and Water, but of God himself, that giveth the Increase and secondly, because it is unreasonable in them, who teach there is such danger in every little Errour, to require of a man endued with Reason of his own, to follow the Reason of any other man, or of the most voices of many other men; Which is little better, then to venture his Salvation at crosse and pile Nor ought those Teachers to be displeased with this losse of their antient Authority · For there is none should know better then they, that power is preserved by the same Vertues by which it is acquired; that is to say, by Wisdome, Humility, Clearnesse of Doctrine, and sincerity of Conversation; and not by suppression of the Naturall Sciences, and of the Morality of Naturall Reason; nor by obscure Language; nor by Arrogating to themselves more Knowledge than they make appear, nor by Pious Frauds; nor by such other faults, as in the Pastors of Gods Church are not only Faults, but also scandalls, apt to make men stumble one time or other upon the suppression of their Authority.

Comparison of the Papacy with the Kingdome of Fayries

But after this Doctrine, *that the Church now Militant, is the Kingdome of God spoken of in the Old and New Testament*, was received in the World; the ambition, and canvasing for the Offices that belong thereunto, and especially for that great Office of being | Christs [386] Lieutenant, and the Pompe of them that obtained therein the principall Publique Charges, became by degrees so evident, that they lost the inward Reverence due to the Pastorall Function: in so much as the Wisest men, of them that had any power in the Civill State needed nothing but the authority of their Princes, to deny them any further Obedience For, from the time that the Bishop of Rome had gotten to be acknowledged for Bishop Universall, by pretence of Succession to St. Peter, their whole Hierarchy, or Kingdome of Darknesse, may be compared not unfitly to the *Kingdome of Fairies*; that is, to the old wives *Fables* in England, concerning *Ghosts* and *Spirits*, and the feats they play in the night. And if a man consider the originall of this great Ecclesiasticall Dominion, he will easily perceive, that the *Papacy*, is no other, than the *Ghost* of the deceased *Romane Empire*, sitting crowned upon the grave thereof: For so did the Papacy start up on a Sudden out of the Ruines of that Heathen Power.

The *Language* also, which they use, both in the Churches, and in their Publique Acts, being *Latine*, which is not commonly used by any Nation now in the world, what is it but the *Ghost* of the Old *Romane Language*?

The *Fairies* in what Nation soever they converse, have but one Universall King, which some Poets of ours call King *Oberon*; but the Scripture calls *Beelzebub*, Prince of *Dæmons*. The *Ecclesiastiques* likewise, in whose Dominions soever they be found, acknowledge but one Universall King, the *Pope*.

The *Ecclesiastiques* are *Spirituall* men, and *Ghostly* Fathers. The Fairies are *Spirits*, and *Ghosts*. *Fairies* and *Ghosts* inhabite Darknesse, Solitudes, and Graves. The *Ecclesiastiques* walke in Obscurity of Doctrine, in Monasteries, Churches, and Church-yards.

The *Ecclesiastiques* have their Cathedrall Churches; which, in what Towne soever they be erected, by vertue of Holy Water, and certain Charmes called Exorcismes, have the power to make those Townes, Cities, that is to say, Seats of Empire. The *Fairies* also have their enchanted Castles, and certain Gigantique Ghosts, that domineer over the Regions round about them.

The *Fairies* are not to be seized on; and brought to answer for the hurt they do. So also the *Ecclesiastiques* vanish away from the Tribunals of Civill Justice.

The *Ecclesiastiques* take from young men, the use of Reason, by certain Charms compounded of Metaphysiques, and Miracles, and Traditions, and Abused Scripture, whereby they are good for nothing else, but to execute what they command them. The *Fairies* likewise are said to take young Children out of their Cradles, and to change them into Naturall Fools, which Common people do therefore call *Elves*, and are apt to mischief.

In what Shop, or Operatory the Fairies make their Enchantment, the old Wives have not determined. But the Operatories of the *Clergy*, are well enough known to be the Universities, that received their Discipline from Authority Pontificiall

When the *Fairies* are displeased with any body, they [387] are said to send their Elves, to pinch them. The *Ecclesiastiques*, when they are displeased with any Civill State, make also their Elves, that is, Superstitious, Enchanted Subjects, to pinch their Princes, by preaching Sedition; or one Prince enchanted with promises, to pinch another

The *Fairies* marry not; but there be amongst them *Incubi*, that have copulation with flesh and bloud The *Priests* also marry not.

The *Ecclesiastiques* take the Cream of the Land, by Donations of ignorant men, that stand in aw of them, and by Tythes So also it is in the Fable of *Fairies*, that they enter into the Dairies, and Feast upon the Cream, which they skim from the Milk.

What kind of Money is currant in the Kingdome of *Fairies*, is not recorded in the Story. But the *Ecclesiastiques* in their Receipts accept of the same Money that we doe; though when they are to make any Payment, it is in Canonizations, Indulgences, and Masses.

To this, and such like resemblances between the *Papacy*, and the Kingdome of *Fairies*, may be added this, that as the *Fairies* have no existence, but in the Fancies of ignorant people, rising from the Traditions of old Wives, or old Poets: so the Spirituall Power of the *Pope* (without the bounds of his own Civill Dominion) consisteth onely in the Fear that Seduced people stand in, of their Excommunications; upon hearing of false Miracles, false Traditions, and false Interpretations of the Scripture.

It was not therefore a very difficult matter, for Henry 8. by his Exorcisme, nor for Qu Elizabeth by hers, to cast them out. But who knows that this Spirit of Rome, now gone out, and walking by Missions through the dry places of China, Japan, and the Indies, that yeeld him little fruit, may not return, or rather an Assembly of Spirits worse than he, enter, and inhabite this clean swept house, and make the End thereof worse than the Beginning? For it is not the Romane Clergy onely, that pretends the Kingdome of God to be of this World, and thereby to have a Power therein, distinct from that of the Civill State. And this is all I had a designe to say, concerning the Doctrine of the POLITIQUES Which when I have reviewed, I shall willingly expose it to the censure of my Countrey.

A *REVIEW*, and *CONCLUSION*. [389]

FROM the contrariety of some of the Naturall Faculties of the Mind, one to another, as also of one Passion to another, and from their reference to Conversation, there has been an argument taken, to inferre an impossibility that any one man should be sufficiently disposed to all sorts of Civill duty. The Severity of Judgment, they say, makes men Censorious, and unapt to pardon the Errours and Infirmities of other men : and on the other side, Celerity of Fancy, makes the thoughts lesse steddy than is necessary, to discern exactly between Right and Wrong. Again, in all Deliberations, and in all Pleadings, the faculty of solid Reasoning, is necessary : for without it, the Resolutions of men are rash, and their Sentences unjust : and yet if there be not powerfull Eloquence, which procureth attention and Consent, the effect of Reason will be little. But these are contrary Faculties ; the former being grounded upon principles of Truth ; the other upon Opinions already received, true, or false ; and upon the Passions and Interests of men, which are different, and mutable

And amongst the Passions, *Courage*, (by which I mean the Contempt of Wounds, and violent Death) enclineth men to private Revenges, and sometimes to endeavour the unsetling of the Publique Peace : And *Timorousnesse*, many times disposeth to the desertion of the Publique Defence. Both these they say cannot stand together in the same person.

And to consider the contrariety of mens Opinions, and Manners in generall, It is they say, impossible to entertain a constant Civill Amity with all those, with whom the Businesse of the world constrains us to converse : Which Businesse, consisteth almost in nothing else but a perpetuall contention for Honor, Riches, and Authority.

To which I answer, that these are indeed great difficulties, but not Impossibilities : For by Education, and

Discipline, they may bee, and are sometimes reconciled. Judgment, and Fancy may have place in the same man; but by turnes; as the end which he aimeth at requireth. As the Israelites in Egypt, were sometimes fastened to their labour of making Bricks, and other times were ranging abroad to gather Straw: So also may the Judgement sometimes be fixed upon one certain Consideration, and the Fancy at another time wandring about the world So also Reason, and Eloquence, (though not perhaps in the Naturall Sciences, yet in the Morall) may
[390] stand very well together. For wheresoever there is place for adorning and preferring of Errour, there is much more place for adorning and preferring of Truth, if they have it to adorn. Nor is there any repugnancy between fearing the Laws, and not fearing a publique Enemy; nor between abstaining from Injury, and pardoning it in others. There is therefore no such Inconsistence of Humane Nature, with Civill Duties, as some think. I have known cleernesse of Judgment, and largenesse of Fancy, strength of Reason, and gracefull Elocution; a Courage for the Warre, and a Fear for the Laws, and all eminently in one man; and that was my most noble and honored friend Mr. *Sidney Godolphin*; who hating no man, nor hated of any, was unfortunately slain in the beginning of the late Civill warre, in the Publique quarrell, by an undiscerned, and an undiscerning hand.

To the Laws of Nature, declared in the 15. Chapter, I would have this added, *That every man is bound by Nature, as much as in him lieth, to protect in Warre, the Authority, by which he is himself protected in time of Peace.* For he that pretendeth a Right of Nature to preserve his owne body, cannot pretend a Right of Nature to destroy him, by whose strength he is preserved: It is a manifest contradiction of himselfe. And though this Law may bee drawn by consequence, from some of those that are there already mentioned; yet the Times require to have it inculcated, and remembred.

And because I find by divers English Books lately printed, that the Civill warres have not yet sufficiently taught men, in what point of time it is, that a Subject becomes obliged to the Conquerour; nor what is Conquest; nor how it comes about, that it obliges men to obey his Laws: Therefore for farther satisfaction of men therein, I say, the point of time, wherein a man becomes subject to a Conquerour, is that point, wherein having liberty to submit to him, he consenteth, either by expresse words, or by other sufficient sign, to be his Subject. When it is that a man hath the liberty to submit, I have shewed before in the end of the 21. Chapter; namely, that for him that hath no obligation to his former Soveraign but that of an ordinary Subject, it is then, when the means of his life is within the Guards and Garrisons of the Enemy; for it is then, that he hath no longer Protection from him, but is protected by the adverse party for his Contribution. Seeing therefore such contribution is every where, as a thing inevitable, (notwithstanding it be an assistance to the Enemy,) esteemed lawfull; a totall Submission, which is but an assistance to the Enemy, cannot be esteemed unlawful. Besides, if a man consider that they who submit, assist the Enemy but with part of their estates, whereas they that refuse, assist him with the whole, there is no reason to call their Submission, or Composition an Assistance; but rather a Detriment to the Enemy. But if a man, besides the obligation of a Subject, hath taken upon him a new obligation of a Souldier, then he hath not the liberty to submit to a new Power, as long as the old one keeps the field, and giveth him means of subsistence, either in his Armies, or Garrisons: for in this case, he cannot complain of want of Protection, and means to live as a [391] Souldier: But when that also failes, a Souldier also may seek his Protection wheresoever he has most hope to have it; and may lawfully submit himself to his new Master. And so much for the Time when he may do it lawfully, if hee will. If therefore he doe it, he is undoubtedly bound to be a true Subject. For a Contract lawfully made, cannot lawfully be broken.

By this also a man may understand, when it is, that men may be said to be Conquered; and in what the nature of Conquest, and the Right of a Conquerour consisteth: For this Submission is it implyeth them all. Conquest, is not the Victory it self; but the Acquisition by Victory, of a Right, over the persons of men. He therefore that is slain, is Overcome, but not Conquered: He that is taken, and put into prison, or chaines, is not Conquered, though Overcome; for he is still an Enemy, and may save himself if hee can: But he that upon promise of Obedience, hath his Life and Liberty allowed him, is then Conquered, and a Subject; and not before. The Romanes used to say, that their Generall had *Pacified* such a *Province*, that is to say, in English, *Conquered* it; and that the Countrey was *Pacified* by Victory, when the people of it had promised *Imperata facere*, that is, *To doe what the Romane People commanded them*. this was to be Conquered. But this promise may be either expresse, or tacite: Expresse, by Promise: Tacite, by other signes. As for example, a man that hath not been called to make such an expresse Promise, (because he is one whose power perhaps is not considerable,) yet if he live under their Protection openly, hee is understood to submit himselfe to the Government But if he live there secretly, he is lyable to any thing that may bee done to a Spie, and Enemy of the State I say not, hee does any Injustice, (for acts of open Hostility bear not that name); but that he may be justly put to death. Likewise, if a man, when his Country is conquered, be out of it, he is not Conquered, nor Subject: but if at his return, he submit to the Government, he is bound to obey it. So that *Conquest* (to define it) is the Acquiring of the Right of Soveraignty by Victory. Which Right, is acquired, in the peoples Submission, by which they contract with the Victor, promising Obedience, for Life and Liberty.

In the 29. Chapter I have set down for one of the causes of the Dissolutions of Common-wealths, their Imperfect Generation, consisting in the want of an Absolute and Arbitrary Legislative Power; for want whereof, the Civill Soveraign is fain to handle the Sword of Justice unconstantly, and as if it were too hot for him to hold. One reason whereof (which I have not there mentioned) is this, That they will all of them justifie the War, by which their Power was at first gotten, and whereon (as they think) their Right dependeth, and not on the Possession. As if, for example, the Right of the Kings of England did depend on the goodnesse of the cause of *William* the Conquerour, and upon their lineall, and directest Descent from him; by which means, there would perhaps be no tie of the Subjects obedience to their Soveraign at this day in all the world: wherein whilest they needlessely think to justifie them- [392] selves, they justifie all the successefull Rebellions that Ambition shall at any time raise against them, and their Successors. Therefore I put down for one of the most effectuall seeds of the Death of any State, that the Conquerors require not onely a Submission of mens actions to them for the future, but also an Approbation of all their actions past; when there is scarce a Common-wealth in the world, whose beginnings can in conscience be justified.

And because the name of Tyranny, signifieth nothing more, nor lesse, than the name of Soveraignty, be it in one, or many men, saving that they that use the former word, are understood to bee angry with them they call Tyrants; I think the toleration of a professed hatred of Tyranny, is a Toleration of hatred to Common-wealth in generall, and another evill seed, not differing much from the former. For to the Justification of the Cause of a Conqueror, the Reproach of the Cause of the Conquered, is for the most part necessary: but neither of them necessary for the Obligation of the Conquered. And thus much I have thought fit to say upon the Review of the first and second part of this Discourse.

In the 35. Chapter, I have sufficiently declared out of the Scripture, that in the Common-wealth of the Jewes, God himselfe was made the Soveraign, by Pact with the People; who were therefore called his *Peculiar People*, to distinguish them from the rest of the world, over whom God reigned not by their Consent, but by his own Power. And that in this Kingdome Moses was Gods Lieutenant on Earth; and that it was he that told them what Laws God appointed them to be ruled by. But I have omitted to set down who were the Officers appointed to doe Execution; especially in Capitall Punishments; not then thinking it a matter of so

necessary consideration, as I find it since Wee know that generally in all Common-wealths, the Execution of Corporeall Punishments, was either put upon the Guards, or other Souldiers of the Soveraign Power; or given to those, in whom want of means, contempt of honour, and hardnesse of heart, concurred, to make them sue for such an Office. But amongst the Israelites it was a Positive Law of God their Soveraign, that he that was convicted of a capitall Crime, should be stoned to death by the People; and that the Witnesses should cast the first Stone, and after the Witnesses, then the rest of the People. This was a Law that designed who were to be the Executioners; but not that any one should throw a Stone at him before Conviction and Sentence, where the Congregation was Judge. The Witnesses were neverthelesse to be heard before they proceeded to Execution, unlesse the Fact were committed in the presence of the Congregation it self, or in sight of the lawfull Judges; for then there needed no other Witnesses but the Judges themselves. Neverthelesse, this manner of proceeding being not throughly understood, hath given occasion to a dangerous opinion, that any man may kill another, in some cases, by a Right of Zeal; as if the Executions done upon Offenders in the Kingdome of God in old
[393] time, proceeded not from the Soveraign Command, but from the Authority of Private Zeal: which, if we consider the texts that seem to favour it, is quite contrary.

First, where the Levites fell upon the People, that had made and worshipped the Golden Calfe, and slew three thousand of them; it was by the Commandement of Moses, from the mouth of God; as is manifest, *Exod.* 32. 27. And when the Son of a woman of Israel had blasphemed God, they that heard it, did not kill him, but brought him before Moses, who put him under custody, till God should give Sentence against him, as appears, *Levit.* 25. 11, 12. Again, (*Numbers* 25 6, 7.) when Phinehas killed Zimri and Cosbi, it was not by right of Private Zeale: Their Crime was committed in the sight of the Assembly; there needed no Witnesse; the Law was known, and he the heir apparent to the Soveraignty;

and which is the principall point, the Lawfulnesse of his Act depended wholly upon a subsequent Ratification by Moses, whereof he had no cause to doubt. And this Presumption of a future Ratification, is sometimes necessary to the safety [of] a Common-wealth ; as in a sudden Rebellion, any man that can suppresse it by his own Power in the Countrey where it begins, without expresse Law or Commission, may lawfully doe it, and provide to have it Ratified, or Pardoned, whilest it is in doing, or after it is done. Also *Numb.* 35. 30. it is expressely said, *Whosoever shall kill the Murtherer, shall kill him upon the word of Witnesses*: but Witnesses suppose a formall Judicature, and consequently condemn that pretence of *Jus Zelotarum*. The Law of Moses concerning him that enticeth to Idolatry, (that is to say, in the Kingdome of God to a renouncing of his Allegiance (*Deut.* 13. 8) forbids to conceal him, and commands the Accuser to cause him to be put to death, and to cast the first stone at him ; but not to kill him before he be Condemned. And (*Deut.* 17. ver. 4, 5, 6.) the Processe against Idolatry is exactly set down : For God there speaketh to the People, as Judge, and commandeth them, when a man is Accused of Idolatry, to Enquire diligently of the Fact, and finding it true, then to Stone him ; but still the hand of the Witnesse throweth the first stone. This is not Private Zeale, but Publique Condemnation. In like manner when a Father hath a rebellious Son, the Law is (*Deut.* 21. 18) that he shall bring him before the Judges of the Town, and all the people of the Town shall Stone him. Lastly, by pretence of these Laws it was, that St. Steven was Stoned, and not by pretence of Private Zeal: for before hee was carried away to Execution, he had Pleaded his Cause before the High Priest. There is nothing in all this, nor in any other part of the Bible, to countenance Executions by Private Zeal; which being oftentimes but a conjunction of Ignorance and Passion, is against both the Justice and Peace of a Common-wealth.

In the 36. Chapter I have said, that it is not declared in what manner God spake supernaturally to Moses: Not that he spake not to him sometimes by Dreams and

Visions, and by a supernaturall Voice, as to other Prophets · For the manner how he spake unto him from the Mercy-Seat, is expressely set down *Numbers* 7. 89 in
[394] these words, *From that time forward, when Moses entred into the Tabernacle of the Congregation to speak with God, he heard a Voice which spake unto him from over the Mercy-Seate, which is over the Arke of the Testimony, from between the Cherubins he spake unto him.* But it is not declared in what consisted the præeminence of the manner of Gods speaking to Moses, above that of his speaking to other Prophets, as to Samuel, and to Abraham, to whom he also spake by a Voice, (that is, by Vision) Unlesse the difference consist in the cleernesse of the Vision For *Face to Face*, and *Mouth to Mouth*, cannot be literally understood of the Infinitenesse, and Incomprehensibility of the Divine Nature.

And as to the whole Doctrine, I see not yet, but the Principles of it are true and proper ; and the Ratiocination solid. For I ground the Civill Right of Soveraigns, and both the Duty and Liberty of Subjects, upon the known naturall Inclinations of Mankind, and upon the Articles of the Law of Nature ; of which no man, that pretends but reason enough to govern his private family, ought to be ignorant. And for the Power Ecclesiasticall of the same Soveraigns, I ground it on such Texts, as are both evident in themselves, and consonant to the Scope of the whole Scripture And therefore am perswaded, that he that shall read it with a purpose onely to be informed, shall be informed by it But for those that by Writing, or Publique Discourse, or by their eminent actions, have already engaged themselves to the maintaining of contrary opinions, they will not bee so easily satisfied. For in such cases, it is naturall for men, at one and the same time, both to proceed in reading, and to lose their attention, in the search of objections to that they had read before Of which, in a time wherein the interests of men are changed (seeing much of that Doctrine, which serveth to the establishing of a new Government, must needs be contrary to that which conduced to the dissolution of the old,) there cannot choose but be very many.

In that part which treateth of a Christian Common-wealth, there are some new Doctrines, which, it may be, in a State where the contrary were already fully determined, were a fault for a Subject without leave to divulge, as being an usurpation of the place of a Teacher. But in this time, that men call not onely for Peace, but also for Truth, to offer such Doctrines as I think True, and that manifestly tend to Peace and Loyalty, to the consideration of those that are yet in deliberation, is no more, but to offer New Wine, to bee put into New Cask, that both may be preserved together. And I suppose, that then, when Novelty can breed no trouble, nor disorder in a State, men are not generally so much inclined to the reverence of Antiquity, as to preferre Ancient Errors, before New and well proved Truth.

There is nothing I distrust more than my Elocution; which neverthelesse I am confident (excepting the Mischances of the Presse) is not obscure. That I have neglected the Ornament of quoting ancient Poets, Orators, and Philosophers, contrary to the custome of late time, (whether I have done well or ill in it,) proceedeth from my judgment, grounded on many reasons. [395]
For first, all Truth of Doctrine dependeth either upon *Reason*, or upon *Scripture*; both which give credit to many, but never receive it from any Writer. Secondly, the matters in question are not of *Fact*, but of *Right*, wherein there is no place for *Witnesses*. There is scarce any of those old Writers, that contradicteth not sometimes both himself, and others; which makes their Testimonies insufficient. Fourthly, such Opinions as are taken onely upon Credit of Antiquity, are not intrinsecally the Judgment of those that cite them, but Words that passe (like gaping) from mouth to mouth. Fiftly, it is many times with a fraudulent Designe that men stick their corrupt Doctrine with the Cloves of other mens Wit. Sixtly, I find not that the Ancients they cite, took it for an Ornament, to doe the like with those that wrote before them. Seventhly, it is an argument of Indigestion; when Greek and Latine Sentences unchewed come up again, as they use to doe, unchanged. Lastly, though I reverence those men of

Ancient time, that either have written Truth perspicuously, or set us in a better way to find it out our selves; yet to the Antiquity it self I think nothing due For if we will reverence the Age, the Present is the Oldest If the Antiquity of the Writer, I am not sure, that generally they to whom such honor is given, were more Ancient when they wrote, than I am that am Writing: But if it bee well considered, the praise of Ancient Authors, proceeds not from the reverence of the Dead, but from the competition, and mutuall envy of the Living.

To conclude, there is nothing in this whole Discourse, nor in that I writ before of the same Subject in Latine, as far as I can perceive, contrary either to the Word of God, or to good Manners, or to the disturbance of the Publique Tranquillity. Therefore I think it may be profitably printed, and more profitably taught in the Universities, in case they also think so, to whom the judgment of the same belongeth. For seeing the Universities are the Fountains of Civill, and Morall Doctrine, from whence the Preachers, and the Gentry, drawing such water as they find, use to sprinkle the same (both from the Pulpit, and in their Conversation) upon the People, there ought certainly to be great care taken, to have it pure, both from the Venime of Heathen Politicians, and from the Incantation of Deceiving Spirits. And by that means the most men, knowing their Duties, will be the less subject to serve the Ambition of a few discontented persons, in their purposes against the State; and be the lesse grieved with the Contributions necessary for their Peace, and Defence; and the Governours themselves have the lesse cause, to maintain at the Common charge any greater Army, than is necessary to make good the Publique Liberty, against the Invasions and Encroachments of forraign Enemies.

And thus I have brought to an end my Discourse of Civill and Ecclesiasticall Government, occasioned by the disorders of the present time, without partiality, without application, and without other designe, than to
[396] set before mens eyes the mutuall Relation between Protection and Obedience; of which the condition of

Humane Nature, and the Laws Divine, (both Naturall and Positive) require an inviolable observation. And though in the revolution of States, there can be no very good Constellation for Truths of this nature to be born under, (as having an angry aspect from the dissolvers of an old Government, and seeing but the backs of them that erect a new,) yet I cannot think it will be condemned at this time, either by the Publique Judge of Doctrine, or by any that desires the continuance of Publique Peace. And in this hope I return to my interrupted Speculation of Bodies Naturall, wherein, (if God give me health to finish it,) I hope the Novelty will as much please, as in the Doctrine of this Artificiall Body it useth to offend. For such Truth, as opposeth no mans profit, nor pleasure, is to all men welcome.

PRINTED IN GREAT BRITAIN AT THE UNIVERSITY PRESS, OXFORD
BY JOHN JOHNSON, PRINTER TO THE UNIVERSITY

CPSIA information can be obtained at www.ICGtesting.com
Printed in the USA
LVOW052035130312

272919LV00012B/160/P

9 781177 696135